The Spiritual
TREASURE TROVE

A Collection of Bible Topics for Meditation and Study

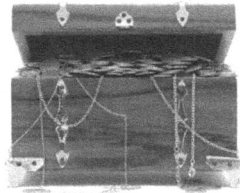

CHARLES RAY SMITH

The Spiritual Treasure Trove
A Collection of Bible Topics for Meditation and Study

ISBNs:
978-1-7375285-1-7 (paperback)
978-1-7375285-0-0 (hardcover)

Published by:
Charles R. Smith
P.O. Box 451065
Houston, TX 77245
torrentsoftruthllc@gmail.com

Contents

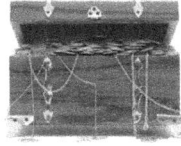

The Spiritual Treasure Trove

A Unique Topical Study Book with a Literary Flow

*W*riting this book has indeed been a labor of love. It has been an ardent compilation of Scriptural text over a period of four years, in order to facilitate the study and enhancement of both the knowledge and the understanding of the Word of God. Many people ponder effective ways to read their Bibles. Reading the Bible topically provides an excellent way. After over thirty-five years of teaching, researching, reading, studying, meditating, and praying in order to give students insight into God's Book Divine, I have drawn the conclusion that the best and most ideal way to gain an understanding of the Bible is to search the Scriptures by topics. Therefore, over the past four years, I have amassed a preponderance of truly beneficial and desirable topics that are useful to enhance spiritual growth. It must be noted that each topic is segmented by number into a daily reading that is conducive to sending out daily texts, so that friends, family members, co-workers, and acquaintances may be involved in the reading and participate in discussion in study groups. The King James Version of the Bible is used throughout this book. May God bless you tremendously as you draw nearer to Him in the study and application of His Word.

Charles R. Smith

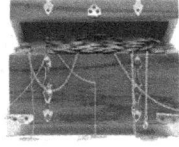

Introduction

I recall when I was about twelve years old, while I was flying a kite in a meadow behind my house. The kite flew so high that it became a small dot in the sky. I remember that, as I was looking upward at the sky, I talked to God. I said, "God, are you up there? God, what is life supposed to be about?"

This was a response to things I had seen, experienced, and pondered. The first six years were somewhat sketchy. I didn't know what life with a mom and dad was truly about. Mom had been sick during my early years, and Dad was in military service overseas. I spent most of that period being raised by my aunt. As time elapsed, finally, we came together as a family and moved to a new town as a family. Yet, I found that, even in family life, there were challenges.

Reflecting upon a time spent in high school, I remember being in the twelfth grade. We had to do an essay for the final exam for Ms. Baker's English class. I chose to write about God as the topic of my essay. I got an A+ and praise for that paper. Mostly, it was contemplations I had within my heart.

Seems like, from my early existence (and even to now), I've always had questions about God and life and His expectations. This has been the quest that has most preoccupied me on my life's journey.

This book entails not only the thoughts I have pondered and the questions I've asked and longed to know the answers for, but also the answers I've found through many hours of research, prayer, and meditation. I now have the peace, knowledge, and wisdom. God provides for those who diligently seek him through the study of His Word. And I know that, if I have been blessed by His Word, I can be a blessing to others by sharing His Word to the many people who also have questions about life and living and God's Will for their lives. If His Word has strengthened, helped, and healed me, I truly believe and know that others can find the solace and encouragement they're longing for, especially during these troublesome and trying times.

May God Bless,

Charles R Smith
Author

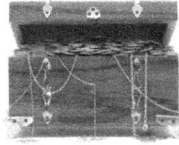

Acknowledgments

I give thanks to God for placing on my mind and heart the desire to write a book that I believe will inspire and encourage others in the most holy faith. I truly believe that, in order to be spiritually led, we must be spiritually fed. There should be a constant diet of the Word of God. God's desire is that we read, study, and meditate on His Word, that we may grow and be in tune with His holy and divine will.

> "And they said one to another, did not our heart burn within us, while he talked with us by the way, and while he opened to us the scriptures? Then opened he their understanding, that they might understand the scriptures" (Luke 24:32, 45).

> "Seek ye out of the book of the Lord and read: No one of these fail, none shall want her mate: for my mouth hath commanded, and his spirit it hath gathered them" (Isaiah 34:16).

> "O earth, earth, earth, hear the word of Lord" (Jeremiah 22:29).

> "Study to shew thyself approved unto God, a workman that needeth not to be ashamed, rightly dividing the word of truth" (2 Timothy 2:15).

> "Jesus answered and said unto them, ye do err, not knowing the scriptures, nor the power of God" (Matthew 22:29).

I would also like to give thanks to my wife, Dolores, for her seemingly tireless resolve and dedication in assisting me to bring this book to fruition. She did an excellent job in typing and proofreading, along with my son, Charles O. Smith, and daughter, Angela Smith. It was a team and family effort. Not only did they share in the dream, but they also believed in the dream and what could be accomplished through it. And, for that, I am both grateful and give thanks to a host of friends, Bible study participants, and fellow Christians who rendered prayers, support, and encouragement. I am truly blessed by all.

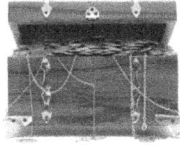

Don't Forget to Remember

Don't Forget to Remember (1)

"Remember now thy Creator in the days of thy youth, while the evil days come not, nor the years draw nigh, when thy shalt say, I have no pleasure in them;" (Ecclesiastes 12:1)

Don't Forget to Remember (2)

"But if a man live many years, and rejoice in them all: yet let him remember the days of darkness; for they shall be many. All that cometh is vanity." (Ecclesiastes 11:8)

Don't Forget to Remember (3)

"Remember the word that I said unto you, The servant is not greater than his lord. If they have persecuted me, they will also persecute you; if they have kept my saying, they will keep yours also.

Discussion Questions

1. What exhortation was given in Deuteronomy 9:7?
2. What observations were made in Psalms 78:34-42?
3. What observations are to be made in 2 Peter 1:2-15?
4. Explain John 12:16.
5. Explain John 14:26. 657

Fill in the Blanks

1. "I_____ thy_____ of old, O Lord; and have comforted myself."
2. "_____ that thou His work, which men behold."
3. "therefore_____ from whence thou art fallen, and_____."
4. "And the Lord turned, and looked upon Peter. And Peter_____ the_____ of the_____, how He had said unto him..."
5. "Then _____I the_____ of the_____, how that he said, John indeed_____ with____; but ye shall be baptized with the_____ _____."

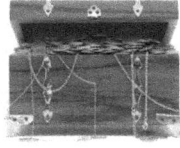

Don't Forget to Remember

"But he that lacketh these things is blind, and cannot see afar off, and hath forgotten that he was purged from his old sins" (2 Peter 1:9).

*F*or a child of God not to remember what our Lord and Savior Jesus hath done on his behalf at Calvary is a truly sad condition. May it never be said that we have forgotten the price paid and the One who paid the price for the purging of the sins of our soul. Because of His sacrifice, we now enjoy peace with God through His atoning blood. Forever a sense of gratitude, indebtedness, adoration, and thankfulness should be reflected in our daily lives. Don't forget to remember.

Don't Forget to Remember (1)

Old Testament – Deuteronomy-5:15, 7:17-18 8:2, 11-20, 9:7, 24- 27 Psalms 119:49-55, 106:21-27, 43-45, 105:5-8, 89:46-50, 77:9-12, 63:1-7, 44:20-21, 42:1-6, 9:17 Job 8:11-13 Jeremiah 2:10-13, 31-32 Ecclesiastes 12:1, 11;8

New Testament – Luke 22:61-62, 24:1-8 John 15:20-21, 16:1-4, 2 Peter 3:1-2, 16-17

Don't Forget to Remember (2)

Old Testament – Genesis 8:1-3, 9:9-16 Exodus 12:12-14, 24-28, 13:3, 8-9 Joshua 4:1-9, 1:13 Numbers 15:37-41 Judges 2:6-10, 3:5-7, 8:32-34 Nehemiah 9:21-33 Psalms 106:6-7, 13-15, 78:34-42

New Testament – John 2:16-22, 12:12-16, 14:25-26, 16:20-21 Acts 11:15-16, 20:35

Don't Forget to Remember (3)

Old Testament – Numbers 10:9 Psalms 9:11-12, 16-20, 42:3-6, 9-11, 74:1-4, 10, 18-22, 79:8-10, 106:4-5, 119:16, 49-50, 61, 136:1-4, 23-24, 137:1-6 Habakkuk 3:2 Nehemiah 13:7-14, 22, 29-31 Isaiah 38:1-6, 49:14-16

New Testament – Luke 1:53-54, 68-72, 2 Peter 1:2-9, 12-15, 2 Timothy 2:11-14

Don't Forget to Remember (4)

Old Testament – Deuteronomy 32:5-7 Isaiah 46:8-11, 57:11-12, 64:5-9 Jeremiah 2:31-32, 13:23-25 Hosea 13:4-8, 9:9, 8:8-14, 7:1-2, 5:3-6, 15, 4:6, 2:13 Psalms 50:22-23

New Testament – 2 Timothy 2:11-14, 2 Corinthians 7:13-15 Jude 1:5-8, 17-18 Revelation 2:5, 3:3

Don't Forget to Remember (5)

Old Testament – Leviticus 26:40-45 Isaiah 26:7-8 Jonah 2:3-7 Jb 7:7, 10:9, 36:22-24 Psalms 20:7, 22:27-31, 25:6-7, 30:4, 97:12, 102:6-12, 103:13-18

New Testament – Luke 22:14-20, 1 Corinthians 11:23-25 Ephesians 2:11-13 Hebrews 8:6-12, 10:16-17

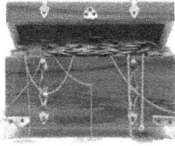

Life Within Boundaries

Life Within Boundaries (1)

"And hath made of one blood, all nations of men for to dwell on all the face of the earth, and hath determined the times appointed, and the bounds of their habitation;" (Acts 17:26)

Life Within Boundaries (2)

"... If Balak would give me his house full of silver and gold, I cannot go beyond the word of the LORD my God, to do less or more." (Numbers 22:18)

Life Within Boundaries (3)

"...but if any man draw back, my soul shall have no pleasure in him. But we are not of them who draw back unto perdition; but of them that believe to the saving of the soul." (Heb 10:38-39)

Discussion Questions

1. What restriction or limitation did God place on Adam in the Garden of Eden? 27 Life Within Boundaries
2. What are the consequences of going beyond established boundaries given by God?
3. Are there boundaries for human conduct we must learn in order to be pleasing unto Him? Explain.
4. What does vile affection mean?

5. Explain how every transgression and disobedience will receive a just recompense.

Fill in the Blanks

1. "And Moses said unto the Lord, The people____ come up to Mount_____ ; for thou ____us, saying, Set____ about the____ , and_____ it."
2. "Fear ye_____ me? saith the Lord: will ye not_____ at my ____ , which have placed the sand for the_____ of the sea by a _____ _____, that it____ ____ pass it."
3. "____ in_____ , and_____ in you. As the branch_____ bear fruit of_____ , except it abide in the vine; no more can ye, except ye _____ in me."
4. "Whosoever_____ , and _____not in the_____ of Christ, hath not_____ ."
5. "And hath made of____ blood all ____of men for to dwell on all the_____ of the earth, and hath_____ the times before appointed, and the_____ of their habitation."

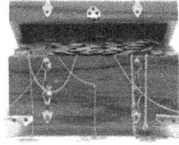

Life Within Boundaries

G od has boundaries or limits on all of His creation. The Psalmist writes in Psalms 74:17, "Thou hast set all the borders of the earth: thou hast made summer and winter."

Life Within Boundaries (1)

Old Testament – Genesis 2:16-17, 3:9-17, 22-24, 6:3 Job 11:10, 14:5, 23:13-14, 26:8-10, 38:4-11, 33-37 Deuteronomy 32:8, 27:17, 11:22-24 Joshua 22:25-28 Psalms 16:5-6, 33:6-9, 104:5-9 Jeremiah 5:22-24 Proverbs 8:25-30

New Testament – Acts 17:26-27 Jude 1:6-7, 1 Thessalonians 4:1, 6, 2 John 1:9-11 Hebrews 6:4-6

Life Within Boundaries (2)

Old Testament – Exodus 19:12, 23, 23:31-33, 34:24 Proverbs 22:28, 23:10-11, 30:6 Deuteronomy 4:1-2, 12:32, 18:20 Numbers 22:17-18, 37-38, 24:13 Job 24:2-4 Hosea 5:10 Psalms 19:1-4, 2:1-5 Amos 1:13 Habakkuk 2:9-10

New Testament – Jn 8:31, 51, 15:1-10, 1 Timothy 4:16, 2 Timothy 2:16-19 Revelation 22:18-19

Life Within Boundaries (3)

Old Testament – Leviticus 18:1-5, 20:22-25, 26:3-6, 14-19 Deuteronomy 5:32, 12:8, 30-31, 28:14-15 Joshua 23:6-13 Ezekiel 20:1-8, 11-13 Jeremiah 5:3-6, 12 Psalms 119:21, 32, 35, 101, 118, 147:11-14 Proverbs 4:25-27, 15:25

New Testament – John 17:6-8, 8:47, 1 Corinthians 4:6 Revelation 22:7, 14

Life Within Boundaries (4)

Old Testament – 2 Samuel 22:22-23, 8:2, 2 Kings 21:13 Malachi 1:4-5 Zephaniah 2:8-10 Isaiah 28:16-17, 34:8-11, 54:12, 60:18 Jeremiah 31:39-40 Ezekiel 40:3, 43:10-12, 44:5-9 Zechariah 1:16, 2:1-5 Psalms 74:17, 78:54-55

New Testament – Romans 11:22-23 Jude 1:21-23, 2 Peter 2:20-22 Revelation 11:1, 21:15, 27, 22:15

Life Within Boundaries (5)

Old Testament – Deuteronomy 19:14 Numbers 35:10-11, 26-27 Leviticus 10:9-10 Ezekiel 45:6-7, 44:23, 22:26 Amos 6:1-3 Proverbs 4:14-15, 12:28, 21:16 Psalms 18:21, 44:18, 119:51, 53, 157, 158

New Testament – 1 John 2:3-6, 24, 2 John 9-11 Colossians 2:6-8, 19, 2 Corinthians 6:14-17 Hebrews 2:1-3, 6:4-8, 10:38-39, 12:12-13

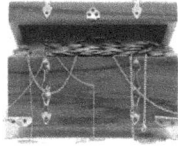

Servants Serve

Servants Serve (1)

"For do I now persuade men, or God? or do I seek to please men? for if I yet pleased men, I should not be a servant of Christ." (Galatians 1:10)

Servants Serve (2)

"The same followed Paul and us, and cried, saying, These men are the servants of the most high God, which shew unto us the way of salvation." (Acts 16:17)

Servants Serve (3)

"And the servant of the Lord must not strive; but be gentle to all men, apt to teach, patient, In meekness instructing those that oppose themselves; if God will give them repentance...that they may recover themselves out of the snare of the devil.. (2 Tim 2:24-26)

Discussion Questions

1. What are the attributes of a servant?
2. If we prove to be good and faithful servants, what will be our reward?
3. If we seek to please man, can we be a servant of Christ?
4. According to 1 Corinthians 9:19, did Paul consider himself a servant of all men? Explain.

5. What is a bond servant?

Fill in the Blanks

1. "And the servant of the Lord must____ ____ ; but be____ unto all men, apt to_____ , _____ ."
2. "But he that is_____ among you shall be your_____ ."
3. "Therefore, thus saith the Lord GOD, Behold, my _____shall eat, but ye shall be hungry: behold, my_____ shall_____ , but ye shall be_____ : behold, my shall_____ , but ye shall be_____ ."
4. "For do I now_____ men, or God? or do I seek to_____ men? for if I yet pleased men, I should be the_____ of Christ."
5. "His Lord said unto him, Well done, good and faithful servant; thou hast been over a____ things, I will make thee_____ over many things: enter thou into the joy of thy Lord.

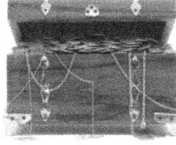

Servants Serve

*I*n Matthew 20:28, Jesus states that He did not come to be served, but to serve. Jesus is our example. We are to follow in His footsteps. My prayer is that we all develop a servant's heart and willingness to serve.

Servants Serve (1)

Old Testament – Exodus 3:11-12, 4:22-23, 10:3, 7-11, 24-29 Deuteronomy 6:13-14, 11:13-17 Joshua 22:1-6, 24:13-16, 19-24 Job 36:11-12 Ezekiel 20:40-42 Psalms 2:11, 22:30, 34:22, 69: 36, 102:18-22, 123:1-2

New Testament – Matthew 4:8-10, 20:25-27 Luke 16:13, 22:24-27 John 12:26 Colossians 3:23-24

Servants Serve (2)

Old Testament – Deuteronomy 10:20, 13:4, 28:47-48, 1 Samuel 12:14-15, 24 Daniel 6:19-23, 3:16-18, 28, 1 Kings 8:22-23 Isaiah 54:17, 65:13-16 Malachi 3:14-18 Psalms 86:2, 4, 116:16-17

New Testament – Philippians 2:5-8 John 13:3-8, 12-16 Matthew 24:45-51, 25:21-30 Luke 12:37-48, 17:7-10 Hebrews 12:28 Ephesians 6:5-7

Servants Serve (3)

Old Testament – Leviticus 25:55 Numbers 18:20-22, 2 Chronicles 29:11-15, 30:8, 33:1-2, 11-16, 1 Chronicles 16:13-22 Daniel 7:13-14, 27 Zechariah 3:8-10 Ezra 5:9-11 Ps 119:17, 38, 65, 134:1-2, 135:1-2, 143:12

New Testament – John 8:34-35 Acts 16:17, 2 Corinthians 4:5, 1 Corinthians 9:19 Romans 6:17-22, 14:4, 2 Timothy 2:24-26

Servants Serve (4)

Old Testament – 1 Samuel 7:3-4, 12:7-11 Nehemiah 9:30-36 Isaiah 60:12, 56:3-7, 43:22-24, 41:8-13 Jeremiah 30:4-9 Psalms 89:1-2, 20-29, 100:1-2, 101:6, 119:74-76, 121-125, 140

New Testament – Luke 2:36-38 Romans 12:1, 11, 14:17-18 Acts 20:16-19 Galatians 5:13-14, 1:10 Hebrews 9:11-14, 13:10

Servants Serve (5)

Old Testament – 1 Kings 3:5-10, 1 Chronicles 28:9, 2 Chronicles 34:1-3, 35:1-2 Proverbs 14:35 Isaiah 42:1-4, 49:1-7, 52:13-15, 53:10-11 Ezekiel 34:22-24 Jeremiah 33:15-26 Psalms 109:28, 102:27-28

New Testament – Acts 4:29-30 Mark 9:35 Romans 1:1-5, 1 Peter 2:15-16 Revelation 19:1-2, 5, 10, 22:9

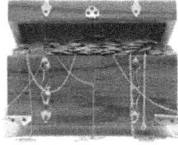

The Test

The Test (1)

"Because thou hast kept the word of My patience, I also will keep thee from the hour of temptation, which shall come upon all the world, to try them that dwell upon the earth." (Revelation 3:10)

The Test (2)

"...behold, the devil shall cast some of you into prison, that ye may be tried:...be thou faithful unto death, and I will give thee a crown of life." (Revelation 2:10)

The Test (3)

"The LORD is in His holy temple, ...His eyes behold, His eyelids try, the children of men. The LORD trieth the righteous: but the wicked and him that loveth violence His soul hateth." (Psalm 11:4-5)

Discussion Questions

1. What request was made in Psalms 139:23-24?
2. Explain 1 Thessalonians 2:4.
3. Are we tested for integrity according to Job 31:6?
4. Explain Jeremiah 17:10
5. Explain Luke 22:31-32.

Fill in the Blanks

1. "Talk no more so exceedingly_____ ; let not_____ come out of your_____ : for the Lord is a God of_____ , and by him____ are_____ ."

2. "And the Lord said, Simon, Simon, behold, _____ hath_____ to have you, that he may_____ you as_____ ."

3. "But he knoweth the ____that I take: when he hath____ me, I shall come forth as____ ."

4. "Fear none of those things which thou shalt_____ : behold, the_____ shall cast some of you into_____ , that ye may be_____ ."

5. "But as we were allowed of God to be put in trust with the_____ , even so we speak; not as_____ men, but_____ , which_____ our_____ ."

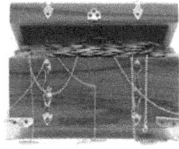

The Test

The psalmist writes in Psalm 11:5, "The Lord trieth the righteous: but the wicked and him that loveth violence His soul hateth." We are tested for the genuineness of our faith. Without true faith, it is impossible to please God. And, over the course of time, all of us will demonstrate what we treasure and cling to the most.

The Test (1)

Old Testament – Genesis 22:1-17 Deuteronomy 8:1-2, 10-19, 13:1-4 Exodus 15:23-26, 16:4, 20:18-20 Daniel 1:8-16, 6:4-24 Job 1:6-12, 2:1-6 Psalms 7:9

New Testament – Matthew 4:1-11 Hebrews 11:17-19, 1 Corinthians 10:13 John 6:5-6, 8:47, 10:25-28, 14:21-24 Revelation 3:10

The Test (2)

Old Testament – Daniel 12:9-10, 11:32-35 Hosea 14:1-2, 9, 1 Chronicles 29:17-18, 1 Samuel 2:3 Proverbs 16:2, 27:21-22 Jeremiah 11:19-20, 17:9-10 Psalms 139:1-5, 23-24, 105:17-19, 66:10-12, 31:7 Isaiah 1:22-25, 30:20-21, 43:2, 48:10- 11

New Testament – Matthew 20:22 Luke 22:28, 1 Peter 1:5-7, 5:8-9, 1 John 4:1 Revelation 2:1-2, 10

The Test (3)

Old Testament – Job 7:17-20, 13:9-10, 25-28, 23:10-12, 30:15-31, 31:6-8, 34:35-36 Jeremiah 6:27-30, 9:6-7, 12:1-3, 20:10-12 Proverbs 24:10-12, 17:3

New Testament – Matthew 13:19-23, 1 Thessalonians 2:1-4, 1 Corinthians 2:1-4, 4:9-13, 2 Corinthians 11:24-30, 13:3-6

The Test (4)

Old Testament – Numbers 16:1-5, 28-33 Daniel 3:1-6, 12-28, 1 Kings 17:8-16, 20:22-23, 28-30 Ezekiel 9:1-11, 21:12-13 Zechariah 3:1-8, 5:1-6 Psalms 11:4-5, 17:1-3, 26:1-3, 44:20-21 Lamentations 3:40

New Testament – Luke 22:28-32 James 1:2-4, 12-15, 1 Peter 4:12-14 Hebrews 11:36-40, 2 Corinthians 2:4-9, 12:15-16 Galatians 6:4

The Test (5)

Old Testament – Numbers 20:1-13, 14:1-5, 26-30, 11:1-15 Psalms 78:37-41, 95:8-9 Judges 2:20-22, 3:1-2, 7:4-7, 2 Kings 13:14-20, 2 Chronicles 32:27-31 Malachi 3:1-3, 10 Zechariah 13:8-9 Ezekiel 22:18-22

New Testament – Mark 9:49, 1 Corinthians 3:12-15, 10:1-9, 11:18-19, 1 Timothy 3:8-10, 1 Thessalonians 3:1-7 Hebrews 4:14-15

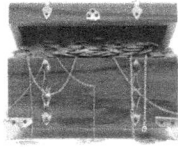

In God We Trust

In God We Trust (1)

"Trust in the LORD with all thine heart: and lean not unto thine own understanding." (Pr 3:5)

In God We Trust (2)

"For therefore we both labour and suffer reproach, because we trust in the living God, who is the Saviour of all men, especially of those that believe." (1 Tim 4:10)

In God We Trust (3)

"The LORD is good, a strong hold in the day of trouble; and he knoweth them that trust in Him." (Nahum 1:7)

Discussion Questions

1. Explain Daniel 3:14-18.
2. Are we to trust in God more than in ourselves? Explain.
3. Does a person whose trust is anchored in God live noticeably different from a person whose trust is not in God? Explain.
4. Explain Hebrews 2:13.
5. Explain Mark 10:23-24.

Fill in the Blanks

1. "He that_____ in his____ shall fall: but the_____ shall flourish as a____ ."
2. "Trust ye in the_____ for ever: for in the____ _____ is everlasting strength."
3. "Now she that is a widow indeed, and desolate, _____in , and in supplications and____ night and____ ."
4. "For therefore we both_____ and_____ reproach, because we_____ in the____ ____ , who is the_____ of all men, specially of those that_____ ."
5. "He that____ in his own____ is a_____ : but whoso walketh wisely, he shall be____ ."

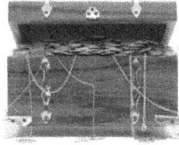

In God We Trust

*T*rusting God means placing all your confidence in God. It is to be fully persuaded that God will do what He says He will do. This trust is imperative in deciding how we live our lives.

In God We Trust (1)

Old Testament – Daniel 3:14-20, 25-28, 2 Kings 18:1-5, 2 Chronicles 32:10-16, 20-22 Isaiah 26:3-4, 31:1-5 Psalms 2:1-5, 9-12, 5:10-11, 7:1, 20:7, 33:16-21, 44:5-7, 52:7-8 Proverbs 11:28 Job 35:13-14

New Testament – Luke 16:10-11 Matthew 27:42-43, 49-54 Hebrews 2:9-13, 2 Timothy 1:12

In God We Trust (2)

Old Testament – Proverbs 16:20 Psalms 9:9-10, 11:1, 3, 13:3, 5, 34:7-8, 40:1-4, 56:3-4, 11, 57:1-7, 84: 11-12, 115:2-12, 146:3-4 Jeremiah 49:4-5, 48:7-8, 17:5-8, 13:23-25

New Testament – 1 Timothy 6:17, 5:5-6, 4:10 Romans 15:8-12

In God We Trust (3)

Old Testament – Ruth 2:12, 2 Samuel 22:3, 29-31 Isaiah 57:11-13, 50:5-10, 30:1-3, 12-13, 12:2-3 Psalms 22:4-8, 26:1, 31:1-6, 13-14, 18-19, 118:8-9, 143:6-8 Job 15:27-31, 1 Chronicles 5:18-20 Nahum 1:7, 2 Chronicles 16:7-9, 13:18

New Testament – 2 Corinthians 1:8-10, 3:1-4 Romans 4:19-21 Ephesians 1:11-12

In God We Trust (4)

Old Testament – Job 13:15, 12:13-20, 8:11-14, 4:12-19 Zephaniah 3:12 Psalms 16:1-3, 28:7, 32:10, 49:6-9, 62:8-10, 73:19-22, 91:1-4, 112:5-7 Proverbs 29:25

New Testament – Mark 10:23-24 Matthew 12:18-21, 1 Thessalonians 2:1-4, 1 Peter 3:1-5

In God We Trust (5)

Old Testament – Job 39:9-11, 15:11-15 Isaiah 57:11-13, 47:6-10 Hosea 10:12-13 Proverbs 30:5, 28:25-26, 22:17-19, 3:5-6 Psalms 4:4-5, 17:4-7, 25:2, 37:3-5, 119:1-2, 125:1-2 Jeremiah 39:15-18

New Testament – John 5:42-45 Luke 11:21-22, 2 Corinthians 10:7

A Purposed Life

A Purposed Life (1)

"And to make all men see what is the fellowship of the mystery.. According to the eternal purpose which He purposed in Christ Jesus our Lord:" (Eph 3:9, 11)

A Purposed Life (2)

"I am crucified with Christ: nevertheless I live; yet not I, but Christ liveth in me: and the life which I now live in the flesh I live by the faith of the Son of God, who loved me, and gave himself for me." (GaL2:20)

A Purposed Life (3)

"Because thy lovingkindness is better than life, my lips shall praise thee. Thus will I bless thee while I live: I will lift up my hands in thy name." (Ps 63:3-4)

Discussion Questions

1. What did Hannah purpose to do with her son in 1 Samuel 1:9-17?
2. What did Jacob purpose to do in Genesis 28:20-22?
3. What did the apostle Paul purpose to do with his life in Acts 20:19-24?
4. What did Ruth purpose to do with her life in Ruth 1:16-17?

5. What did the prophet Jonah purpose to do with his life in Jonah 2:2-9,

Fill in the Blanks

1. "And Ruth said, Intreat me not to leave thee, or to return from____ after thee: for whither thou goest, I__ __ ; and when thou lodgest, I will____ : thy people shall be__ __ , and thy____ my__ ."
2. "Till I die I will not remove____ ____ from me."
3. "For to me to live is____ , and to____ is gain."
4. "And that he died for all, that they____ ____ should not henceforth____ ____ ____ , but unto him which __ __ ___, and rose again."
5. "In holiness and____ before him, all the of our____ ."

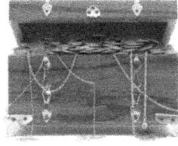

A Purposed Life

*L*iving a purposed life is to dream dreams, then pursue aspirations and goals, and then to stretch and to reach out on faith in order to ascertain measured success in goals and accomplishments.

A Purposed Life (1)

Old Testament – 1 Samuel 1:9-17, 26-28, 7:15 Genesis 28:20-22, 31:13, 35:3 Exodus 3:1-12 Deuteronomy 34:10 Esther 4:14 Isaiah 14:24-27, 46:9-11, 49:1-5 Haggai 2:23 Jeremiah 1:5, 10 Psalms 71:5-8

New Testament – Luke 1:13-17, 76-80 Ephesians 1:11, 3:9, 11 Galatians 1:15-16 Acts 9:15, 20:19-24, 1 Corinthians 9:16 Romans 8:28- 29, 36-39

A Purposed Life (2)

Old Testament – Genesis 17:1-9, 37:5-28, 45:1-8, 50:20 Job 23:13-14 Numbers 23:19-21 Isaiah 41:8-14, 44:24-28, 45:1-4, 13 Ezra 1:1-3 Jeremiah 23:5-6 Zc 6:12-15 Psalms 105:17-22

New Testament – Acts 26:13-16 Galatians 1:15-17, 2:20, 1 Peter 2:5, 9, 4:1-2, 1 Corinthians 6:20, 2 Timothy 2:4 Colossians 2:20-23

A Purposed Life (3)

Old Testament – Deuteronomy 31:14, 23 Joshua 4:14 Daniel 1:3-5, 8-15, 3:10-29, 6:7-26 Job 1:13-22, 13:14-15, 19:25-27, 23:8-12, 27:3-6 Psalms 16:8, 17:3, 27:1-4, 44:15-22

New Testament – Romans 1:13-16, 12:1-2, 2 Timothy 2:11-12 Colossians 3:3-4, 2 Corinthians 4:8-12, 5:4, 9 Philippians 1:21

A Purposed Life (4)

Old Testament – Deuteronomy 7:6, 28:9-10 Ex 19:6 Leviticus 20:7 Isaiah 62:12, 61:6 Numbers 6:1-8 Judges 13:2-7, 16:16-17, 30 Job 33:14, 17 Ecclesiastes 3:1, 17 Proverbs 20:18

New Testament – Romans 14:7-8, 6:6-8, 11-13, 2 Corinthians 5:14-15, 1 John 3:1-3, 1 Peter 1:15-16 Revelation 1:5-6, 5:10

A Purposed Life (5)

Old Testament – Genesis 49:8, 13, 16, 19-24, 27 Ruth 1:16-17, 4:9-15 Jonah 2:7-9 Ecclesiastes 8:5-6 Proverbs 15:22 Job 17:9-12 Isaiah 1:11-13, 16-17 Jeremiah 6:20-21, 26:2-3, 36:1-3 Psalms 119:175, 66:8-9, 13-16, 63:3-4

New Testament – Romans 9:11, 17, 1 Corinthians 1:17-20, 2 Timothy 1:8-9, 3:10-11, 1 John 3:8

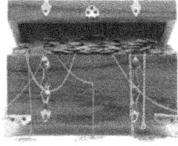

Call on His Name

Call on His Name (1)

"And to Seth, to him also there was born a son; and he called his name Enos: then began men to call upon the name of the LORD." (Genesis 4:26)

Call on His Name (2)

"For thou shalt be his witness unto all men of what thou hast seen and heard. And now why tarriest thou? arise, and be baptized, and wash away thy sins, calling on the name of the Lord. (Acts 22:15-16)

Call on His Name (3)

"Because he hath set his love on Me, therefore will I deliver him: I will set him on high because he hath known My name. He shall call upon Me, and I will answer him:.." (Psalm 91:14-15)

Discussion Questions

1. Explain Genesis 4:26.
2. Explain Romans 10:6-15.
3. What conditions were given for calling on the name of God in Isaiah 58:9?
4. What command was given to the apostle Paul in Acts 22:16?
5. Explain 2 Timothy 2:19.

Fill in the Blanks

1. "Neither is there____ in any other____: for there is none other____ under____ given among men, whereby we must be____ ."

2. "Seek ye the Lord while he may be found, ____ ye upon____ while he is____ ."

3. "And if ye____ on the____ , who without respect of persons judgeth according to every man's work, pass the____ of your____ here in____ ."

4. "And the seventy returned again with joy, saying, ____ , even the devils are____ unto us through____ ____ ."

5. "Even every one that is called by my____ : for I have____ him for my____ ."

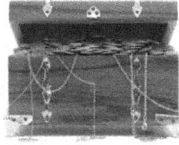

Call on His Name

The expression "call on His name" is more than an enunciation; it also involves a willingness to submit to God's authority with the intent of doing His will.

Call on His Name (1)

Old Testament – Genesis 4:26, 12:7-8, 13:1-4, 21:33 Exodus 23:20-22, 20:24 Proverbs 30:4, 1 Kings 8:52, 18:22-39, 1 Chronicles 4:10, 16:8-10 Isaiah 62:2, 58:9, 55:6 Job 27:8-10 Psalms 79:6, 145:18-20

New Testament – Acts 22:16, 8:12, 4:12, 3:16 Romans 10:6-15, 2 Timothy 2:19, 22

Call on His Name (2)

Old Testament – Genesis 26:24-25, 2 Samuel 22:4 Deuteronomy 4:7-8, 10:8, 18:5 Zephaniah 7:9 Hosea 7:14, 16, 11:7 Psalms 14:4, 17:1, 6-7, 31:16-17, 50:16-17, 55:16-18 Proverbs 18:10

New Testament – Matthew 18:20, 7:22-23 Acts 9:20-21, 21:13, 1 Corinthians 1:2, 10, 1 Peter 1:17 Colossians 3:17 Revelation 19:9-13

Call on His Name (3)

Old Testament – 2 Kings g 5:1, 9-11, 14 Jonah 1:4-6, 9, 2:1-2, 7 Psalms 20:6-9, 18:3, 6-19, 10:17 Isaiah 43:3-7 Jeremiah 3:19, 29:11-12, 33:1-3 Zechariah 10:8-10, 13:9 JoeL 2:28-32

New Testament – Acts 2:14-21, 36-38, 11:26, 15:11-17, 1 Peter 4:14 Philippians 2:9-11

Call on His Name (4)

Old Testament – Exodus 23:13 Joshua 23:7 Isaiah 36:6-7, 13-20, 37:6-7, 23-38, 64:6-7, 65:24 Hosea 2:16-17 Micah 4:5 Psalms 16:4, 54:1-2, 6, 66:5-17, 80:17-19, 86:1-7, 91:14-16, 99:5-9, 118:5-6

New Testament – Luke 9:49-50, 10:17 Acts 4:6-10, 17-20, 16:16-18, 19:1-5, 23-41

Call on His Name (5)

Old Testament – Exodus 20:7, 22:22-24 Isaiah 12:4-6, 26:8, 13 Lamentations 3:54-58 Jeremiah 10:6-7 Psalms 44:5-8, 20-21, 53:4-6, 72:17-19, 105:1-3, 116:1-6, 13-17, 124:6-8

New Testament – John 14:13-14, 15:16, 16:23-24 James 2:7, 1 John 3:22

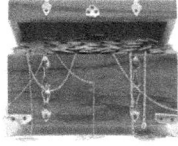

Vengeance

Vengeance (1)

"Say not thou, I will recompense evil; but wait on the LORD, and He shall save thee." (Proverbs 20:22)

Vengeance (2)

"God is jealous, and the LORD revengeth; the LORD revengeth, and is furious; the LORD will take vengeance on His adversaries, and reserveth wrath for His enemies." (Nahum 1:2)

Vengeance (3)

"...when the Lord Jesus shall be revealed from heaven with his mighty angels, In flaming fire taking vengeance on them that know not God, and obey not the gospel of our Lord Jesus Christ: Who will be punished with everlasting destruction ... (2 Thessalonians 1:6-9)

Discussion Questions

1. What instructions are given in Romans 12:17-21?
2. Discuss Colossians 3:25.
3. Discuss Hebrews 2:1-3
4. What observations are made in Job 34:21-33?
5. What comments are made by the prophet Isaiah in Isaiah 50:6-11?

Fill in the Blanks

1. "Say not thou, I will____ evil; but____ on the Lord, and he shall____ thee."

2. "But I say unto you, That ye_____ not____ : but whosoever shall smite thee on thy right____ , turn to him the other also_____."

3. "Who, when he was_____ , _____not again; when he suffered, he_____ not; but committed himself to him that judgeth_____ ."

4. "O Lord God, to whom_____ belongeth; shew thyself."

5. "Say to them that are of a fearful heart, Be strong, fear not: behold, your God will come with_____ , even God with a____ ; he will come and ____you."

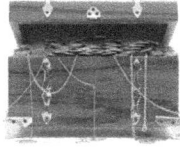

Vengeance

*I*n life, we may encounter various hurtful and painful experiences. These experiences oftentime leave their mark or perhaps a scar on us. They trouble us, vex us, and rob us of the inner peace, joy, and happiness we desire. Feelings of rage, and the urge for retaliation, revenge, and getting even now become fixations with many. All those feelings, all those thoughts, and all those compulsions are released when we turn them over to God. Because God has said, "Dearly beloved, avenge not yourselves, but rather give place unto wrath: for it is written, Vengeance is mine; I will repay, saith the Lord" (Romans 12:19).

Vengeance (1)

Old Testament – Genesis 4:15, 24 Deuteronomy 32:35, 41-43, 7:9-10 Leviticus 19:17-18 Joshua 10:24-25 Isaiah 35:3-4, 49:23-26, 50:6-11, 51:20-23 Lamentations 3:57-65 Psalms 11:2-6, 28:4-5, 59:3-11 Proverbs 20:22, 24:19-22 Micah 7:8-10

New Testament – Luke 17:1-2 Matthew 5:39-45 Romans 12:17-21 Hebrews 10:30-31, 2 Thessalonians 1:4-9, 2 Peter 2:9

Vengeance (2)

Old Testament – Exodus 23:20-22, 32:31-34 Obadiah 10-15, 2 Chronicles 6:22-23, 1 Samuel 24:12-13, 26:7-10 Nahum 1:2 Ps 37:12-13, 7:11-16 Esther 7:1-10, 9:22-25, 2 Samuel 16:5-13, 1 Kings 2:8-10, 36-44 Isaiah 1:21-25 Job 4:7-9, 20:11-29, 34:20-33

New Testament – Luke 18:3-8, 2 Timothy 4:14-15 Colossians 3:25

Vengeance (3)

Old Testament – Judges 1:5-7 Habakkuk 2:4-10 Job 13:7-10, 19:22, 28-29, 21:28-31 Psalms 94:1-2, 20-23, 99:8 Jeremiah 5:28-29, 46:10, 50:28-31, 51:56 Isaiah 65:6, 14, 66:6 Hosea 9:7-9, 12:2 Micah 5:15

New Testament – Hebrews 2:1-3, 1 Peter 2:19-23, 1 Thessalonians 4:3-6 Revelation 18:4-6, 6:10

Vengeance (4)

Old Testament – Hosea 7:1-4, 11-16, 8:11-13, 9:9 Ezekiel 25:11, 14, 17, 23:48-49, 17:19-20, 16:43, 62-63 Jeremiah 51:11-12, 35-36, 50:14-15, 20:12, 11:20-23 Psalms 10:14-15, 79:9-12 Proverbs 24:12, 29 Isaiah 59:17-20, 63:3-4

New Testament – Romans 1:21-27, 3:5-6, 13:1-4, 1 Thessalonians 5:15

Vengeance (5)

Old Testament – Isaiah 10:12-19, 33-34, 13:11, 34:8-10, 47:3-5 Jeremiah 2513-17, 21:14, 16:18, 8:12-14, Amos 1:3-15, 2:1-8, 2 Samuel 3:39, Ezra 9:5-14 Psalms 59:12-17, 140:8-12, 149:6-7 Proverbs 11:21, 31

New Testament – Luke 21:22, 34-36, Jude 1:7, 15-19, Revelation 11:18-20, 19:2

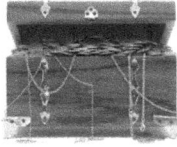

Unless/Except/Lest

Unless/Except/Lest (1)

"Unless thy law had been my delights, I should then have perished in mine affliction." (Psalm 119:92)

Unless/Except/Lest (2)

"And Jesus called a little child unto him, and set him in the midst of them, And said, Verily I say unto you, Except ye be converted, and become as little children, ye shall not enter into the kingdom of heaven." (Matt 18:2-3)

Unless/Except/Lest (3)

"No man can come to me, except the Father which hath sent me draw him:...Verily, verily, I say unto you, Except ye eat the flesh of the Son of man, and drink his blood, ye have no life in you." (Jn 6:44, 53)

Discussion Question

1. Discuss Genesis 32:26-30.
2. Explain Proverbs 30:5-6.
3. Discuss Amos 3:3.
4. Discuss James 5:9.
5. Discuss 2 Corinthians 2:9-11

Fill in the Blanks

1. "O Lord, correct me, but with_____ ; not in thine_____ , lest thou bring me to_____ ."
2. "Now consider this, ye that_____ God, _____ I tear you in pieces, and there be_____ to_____ ."
3. "For I say unto you, That _____your_____ shall exceed the_____ of the scribes and Pharisees, ye shall in no case_____ into the_____ of_____ ."
4. "And said, Verily I say unto you, _____ye be_____ , and become as little_____ , ye shall not_____ into the_____ of_____ ."
5. "Jesus answered and said unto him, Verily, verily, I say unto thee, _____a man be_____ again, he_____ see the_____ of_____ ."

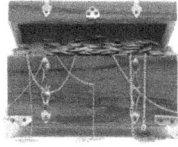

Unless/Except/Lest

*U*nless is a conjunction that establishes conditions and circumstances to be done or to be true. *Except* is a synonym for *unless*. It is also used to specify a category or group that is not to be included. *Lest* is also a synonym for *unless*, and it could be defined as something done in order to avoid dire circumstances or consequences. There are many passages in the Bible that utilizes or emphasizes these conjunctions.

Unless/Except/Lest (1)

Old Testament – Genesis 3:1-4, 22-23, 19:15-17, 26 Deuteronomy 4:7-9, 8:10-14, 32:15, 27-30 Jeremiah 6:8, 10:24 Psalms 2:11-12, 27:13, 28:1, 38:12-16, 94:17, 119:92, 143:7 Pr 30:5-6, 31:4-5

New Testament – Matthew 7:6, 13:15, 24-29 John 3:2-5, 20-21, 27, 8:23-24, 19:7-11

Unless/Except/Lest (2)

Old Testament – Genesis 14:21-23, 26:7-10 Exodus 20:18-19, 34:12, 15 Judges 7:2 Deuteronomy 20:5-8, 24:14-15 Amos 5:6 Zechariah 7:12 Isaiah 6:10 Jeremiah 1:17 , 4:4 Job 36:18 Psalms 50:22-23, 106:21-23, 125:3, 140:8

New Testament – Luke 13:3-5, 21:34, 22:46 Romans 7:7-8, 1 Thessalonians 3:5

Unless/Except/Lest (3)

Old Testament – Genesis 31:42 Deuteronomy 29:16-20 Joshua 7:12, 1 Samuel 25:32-34 Daniel 6:5 Amos 3:3 Isaiah 1:9, 28:22 Psalms 127:1 Malachi 4:6

New Testament – Matthew 5:20, 18:2-3, 19:9, 26:42 John 20: 25-29, 15:4, 6:44, 53, 65 Acts 8:30-31 Romans 10:15, 9:29 Hebrews 2:1-3, 3:12-13, 4:1, 12:14-16

Unless/Except/Lest (4)

Old Testament – Exodus 5:3, 23:29, 33, 33:2-3 Numbers 4:20, 22:22-33 Jeremiah 21:12, 51:45-46

New Testament – John 5:14, 12:24 Romans 11:21-25, 1 Corinthians 8:9, 13, 9:12, 27, 10:12, 15:1-2, 2 Corinthians 2:9-11, 4:3-4, 11:2-3 Galatians 2:2, 4:11, 6:1, 12 James 5:9, 12, 2 Peter 3:17

Unless/Except/Lest (5)

Old Testament – Genesis 32:26-29 Leviticus 10:6-9 Exodus 13:17-18 Job 34:29-30, 36:18, 42:8 Proverbs 9:8, 24:17-18, 26:4-5, 30:10 Ecclesiastes 7:21

New Testament – Matthew 25:8-9 John 12:35 Luke 8:12, 14:12-14, 18:3-5, 1 Timothy 3:6-7 Colossians 2:4-8, 3:21 Revelation 16:15

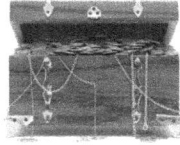

Hand of God

Hand of God (1)

"Who knoweth not in all these that the hand of the LORD hath wrought this? In whose hand is the soul of every living thing, and the breath of all mankind." Job 12:9-10

Hand of God (2)

"Behold, I have graven thee upon the palms of My hands; thy walls are continually before Me." (Isaiah 49:16)

Hand of God (3)

"These wait all upon thee; that thou mayest givest them meat in due season. That thou givest them they gather: thou openest thine hand, they are filled with good.""Thou openest thine hand, and satisfiest the desire of every living thing." Ps 104:27-28, 145:16

Discussion Question

1. Discuss Psalms 18:35.
2. How much power or control does man have over the universe?
3. Explain Luke 1:66.
4. Explain Jeremiah 1:9-10.
5. Discuss Ecclesiastes 9:1.

Fill in the Blanks

1. "And the ____ of the ____ was with them: and a great number believed; and turned unto the ____, "
2. "It is a ____ thing to fall into the ____ of the ____ ____."
3. "Who knoweth not in all these that the ____ of the ____ hath wrought this?"
4. "And when Jesus had cried with a loud voice, he said, Father, into ____ ____ I commend my spirit."
5. "Humble yourselves therefore under the mighty ____ of ____, that He may exalt you in due ____.

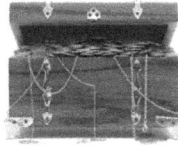

Hand of God

"Both riches and honour come of thee, and thou reignest over all; and in thine hand is power and might; and in thine hand it is to make great and to give strength unto all" (1 Chronicles 29:12).

What an amazing topic that puts all things in its proper perspective.

Hand of God (1)

Old Testament – Deuteronomy 32:39-41 Daniel 4:30-35, 5:1-6, 22-31, 1 Chronicles 29:12-13, 21:13, 17, 4:10 Job 12:9-10, 26:12-14 Psalms 8:3-6, 18:35, 31:1-5, 13-15, 75:7-8, 92:4, 104:24-28, 143:5, 145:16

New Testament – John 10:27-29 Luke 23:46 Acts 2:32-36, 5:30-31, 13:9-11

Hand of God (2)

Old Testament – Deuteronomy 3:24, 4:32-34, 5:15, 11:1-2, 33:1-2 Joshua 4:23-24, 2 Chronicles 30:5-6, 30:12, 2 Samuel 24:14 Isaiah 14:26-27, 26:11, 40:10-12, 41:10, 48:13, 49:16, 62:3, 64:8 Ecclesiastes 9:1 Psalms 95:4-5

New Testament – Luke 1:66 Acts 4:29-30, 11:21, 1 Peter 5:6

Hand of God (3)

Old Testament – Exodus 3:19-20, 6:1, 7:4-5, 13:3, 9, 14, 15:6, 12 Habakkuk 3:3-4 Jeremiah 32:17, 21 Ezekiel 14:13-14, 20:15-16, 33, -34, 42, 21:17, 39:21-22 Psalms 74:10-12, 89:13-21, 98:1, 138:7, 144:7 Proverbs 21:1

New Testament – Matthew 19:13-15 Luke 4:40, 24:50 Acts 7:48-50, 13:6-11 Colossians 3:11 Ephesians 1:19-20

Hand of God (4)

Old Testament – Jeremiah 1:9-10, 15:17 Ezekiel 1:3, 2:6-9, 3:8-14, 21-22, 37:1, 1 Kings 18:46, 1 Chronicles 28:19 Nehemiah 2:8 Ezra 7:6, 9, 28, 8:18, 22 Job 27:11 Isaiah 51:16-17, 49:2, 22 Psalms 10:12, 60:4-5

New Testament – Mark 6:2, 8:23-25, 10:16 John 13:3 Luke 20:42, 22:69 Hebrews 8:1

Hand of God (5)

Old Testament – 1 Samuel 5:1-9, 7:13, 12:15 Judges 2:11, 15 Numbers 11:23 Isaiah 50:2-3, 59:1-2, 65:2 Jeremiah 15:6, 25:15-17, 28, 51:7, 25 Lamentations 1:14, 2:3-4, 8 Job 19:21 Ruth 1:13 Psalms 28:4-5, 32:3-5, 38:1-2

New Testament – Romans 10:21 Hebrews 10:31 Revelation 14:14-19 Matthew 3:11-12

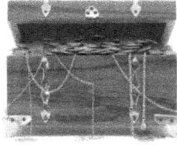

Be Ye Thankful

Be Ye Thankful (1)

"Enter into His gates with thanksgiving, and into His courts with praise: be thankful unto Him, and bless His name. (Psalm 100:4)

Be Ye Thankful (2)

"In every thing give thanks; for this is the will of God in Christ Jesus concerning you. (1 Thessalonians 5:18)

Be Ye Thankful (3)

"By him therefore let us offer the sacrifice of praise to God continually, that is, the fruit of our lips giving thanks to his name." (Hebrews 13:15)

Discussion Questions

1. List some of the reasons we ought to be thankful.
2. Is being thankful a part of our worship to God?
3. What problem did Paul observe in Romans 1:21 that became the detriment of many? 471 Be Ye Thankful
4. Is Hebrews 13:15-16 a commandment or a suggestion?
5. When we are thankful, will that change our outlook on many things?

Fill in the Blanks

1. "O give____ unto the____ ____ ; for he is____ ; for his____
    endureth forever."
2. "By Him therefore let us offer the____ ____ of____ ____ to
    God continually, that is, the fruit of our____ giving____ to
    his name."
3. "At midnight I will____ to give____ unto thee because of
    thy____ ____ ."
4. "Because that, when they knew God, they glorified him not as
    God, neither were____ ."
5. "Giving____ always for____ ____ ____ unto God and the____ in
    the name of our____ ____ ____ ."

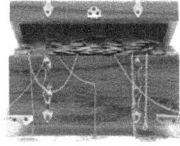

Be Ye Thankful

*I*n the passage of Scripture, in Job 37:14, Job was urged to "Stand still, and consider the wondrous works of God." What a wonderful thought! In the midst of sorrow, in the midst of trials, in the midst of life's difficulties, we should turn our minds and thoughts toward God and how He has always been a good God, and how He has always showered us with an abundance of blessings in spite of our current situation. If we reflect upon the wondrous works of God, that should conjure up feelings and sentiments of thankfulness in our hearts. No matter what we go through on the time side of life, God will bless us over and over and over again if we remain true, faithful, and thankful to Him.

Be Ye Thankful (1)

Old Testament – Leviticus 22:29 Psalms 30:4, 35:18, 69:30, 92:1, 95:2, 107:21-22, 118:28-29, 1 Chronicles 16:28-36, 29:11-13

New Testament – Luke 6:32-36 Romans 1:20-21, 14:6 Colossians 2:6-7, 3:15, 4:2 Philippians 4:4-7, 2 Thessalonians 2:13

Be Ye Thankful (2)

Old Testament – Daniel 2:23, 6:10 Ezra 3:10-11 Jonah 2:7-9 Psalms 6:3-5, 26:6-7, 30:8-12, 79:11-13, 106:47, 107:21-32, 119:62-63

New Testament – Luke 2:36-38, 10:21-24 Matthew 15:36-37, 1 Timothy 4:1-4, 1:12-14, 2 Timothy 1:3-4, 1 Thessalonians 5:16-18 Revelation 7:9-12

Be Ye Thankful (3)

Old Testament – 2 Samuel 22:47-50, 2 Chronicles 5:13-14 Psalms 147:7, 140:12-13, 136:1-3, 26, 107:1-2, 97:9-12, 50:14

New Testament – Luke 17:11-18, 22:17-20, 1 Corinthians 11:23-26, 2 Corinthians 9:6-12, 15 Hebrews 13:12-15 Ephesians 1:15-16, 5:1-4, 19-20 Colossians 1:3-6, 9-12, 1 Thessalonianss 3:7-9

Be Ye Thankful (4)

Old Testament – 1 Chronicles 23:27-30, 25:3, 2 Chronicles 31:2 Nehemiah 12:23-24, 27, 31, 38, 40, 43, 46 Isaiah 51:3 Jeremiah 30:17-19 Psalms 68:28-29, 118:1, 122:1-4

New Testament – Philemon 1:4-5 Romans 1:8-9, 16:17 Acts 27:33-35, 28:14-15, 2 Corinthians 4:13-15 Revelation 4:1-9

Be Ye Thankful (5)

Old Testament – 1 Chronicles 16:8, 34-36, 39-41 Amos 4:4-5 Psalms 75:1-2, 100:4, 105:1-2, 106:1-3, 116:17-19

New Testament – Romans 7:24-25, 16:3-4, 1 Timothy 2:1, 1 C1:4-6, 15:57-58, 2 Corinthians 1:8-11, 2:12-14, 8:15-16, 1 Thessalonians 2:11-13

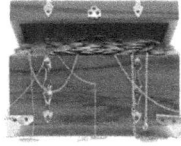

The Empty Chair

The Empty Chair (1)

"...there is but one step between me and death.""And it came to pass on the morrow...that David's place was empty...For as long as the son of Jesse liveth...thou shalt not be established...fetch him unto me, for he shall surely die." (1 Sam 20:3, 27, 31)

The Empty Chair (2)

"...Blessed are the dead which die in the Lord from henceforth: Yea, saith the Spirit, and they may rest from their labours; and their works do follow them." (Revelation 14:13)

The Empty Chair (3)

"O death, where is thy sting? O grave, where is thy victory?...The sting of death is sin...But thanks be to God, which giveth us victory through our Lord Jesus Christ." (1 Corinthians 15:55-57)

Discussion Questions

1. What does the empty chair represent in 1 Samuel 20:25-27?
2. What observations are made in Psalm 90:3-12?
3. How are our lives characterized in James 4:14?
4. Explain John 8:51.
5. What message is conveyed in Hebrews 11:13-16?

Fill in the Blanks

1. "These all died in_____, not having received the promises, but having seen them afar off, and were _____of them."
2. "Death is swallowed up in_____ ."
3. "For all flesh is as____ , and all the glory of man as the____ of____. The grass____, and the flower thereof_____ away."
4. "There is no man that hath power over the spirit to retain the_____ ; neither hath he_____ in the day of_____ ."
5. "So teach us to ___our days, that we may apply our____ unto_____."

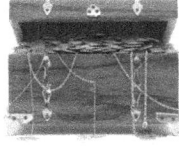

The Empty Chair

*A*t certain times in our lives, we reflect upon those we deeply love and miss who have gone on to their eternal home. We hold on to treasured memories of the joy and tender moments we once shared with them. We acknowledge and appreciate that God brought them into our lives. God used them to encourage us, help us, and even bless us. This is noted in this week's topic: the empty chair.

TheEmptyChair (1)

Old Testament – 1 Samuel 20:1-3, 25-27, 31, 2 Samuel 12:22-23, 1 Chronicles 29:14-15, 1 Kings 2:1-2, 10 Job 30:22-23, 14:1-2, 5-22, 9:25-26, 4:18-20 Psalms 90:3-12, 89:47-48 Proverbs 27:1

New Testament – Hebrews 9:27, 2 Corinthians 5:1-4, 1 Corinthians 15:19-26, 51-57 John 14:1-4, 11:50-51, 8:51 James 4:14

TheEmptyChair (2)

Old Testament – 2 Samuel 14:14 Joshua 23:14 Ecclesiastes 12:3-7, 11:5, 8, 8:8, 12-13, 7:1-4, 4:1-3 Psalms 104:29-31 Job 16:18-22, 7:6-7 Isaiah 25:8-9, 26:19

New Testament – Romans 14:7-9, 8:1-13, 38-39 John 11:25-27 Revelation 14:12-13, 1 Thessalonians 4:14-17, 1 John 5:11-12, 1 Peter 1:21-25

TheEmptyChair (3)

Old Testament – Genesis 3:19 Job 34:14-15, 10:20-22, 8:8-9 Isaiah 40:6-8, 38:1-5, 12 Psalms 146:3-4, 144:3-4, 139:15-16, 102:3, 11-12, 22:14-15

New Testament – John 3:15-18, 4:14, 5:24-27, 6:50-51, 54, 58, 63-68 Hebrews 2:9-15, 5:5-9

TheEmptyChair (4)

Old Testament – Ecclesiastes 9:3-6, 9-10, 6:3-6, 12, 3:1-2, 19-22 Job 1:20-21, 3:17-19, 17:11-16, 19:25-27, 21:17-26 Psalms 103:13-16, 92:7, 49:8-20, 39:4-7, 23:4-6, 17:13-15 Proverbs 10:7

New Testament – Matthew 4:16-17 Acts 24:14-15, 20:22-24, 2 Corinthians 5:15, 1:8-9, 2 Timothy 1:8-10, 1 Timothy 6:7

TheEmptyChair (5)

Old Testament – 1 Samuel 2:6 Job 7:8-10, 8:11-19, 20:4-9, 21:17-26, 24:17-24, 36:20 Proverbs 2:21-22 Psalms 37:34-38, 116:3-9, 15, 141:7-10 Ezekiel 18:26-32, 33:7-11 Hosea 13:14-15

New Testament – John 8:24 Romans 5:17-21, 2 Corinthians 15:12-21, 2 Corinthians 4:10-14, 1 Thessalonians 5:9-10, 2 Timothy 4:6-8, 2 Peter 1:13-14

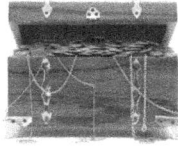

The Heart of the Matter

The Heart of the Matter (1)

"Keep thy heart with all diligence; for out of it are the issues of life."
(Proverbs 4:23)

The Heart of the Matter (2)

"The LORD our God be with us... That He may incline our hearts unto
Him, to walk in all His ways, and to keep His commandments and
His statutes and His judgements, which He commanded our fathers.
(1 K8:57-58)

The Heart of the Matter (3)

"...He raised up unto them David to be their king; to whom also He
gave their testimony, and said, I have found David the son of Jesse, a
man after mine own Heart, which shall fulfil all My will." (Acts 13:22}

Discussion Questions

1. What does it mean to keep our heart?
2. What is hardness of the heart, and why is it so detrimental?
3. Ezra prepared his heart to seek the Lord. Why was that
   important?
4. What did Jesus say defiles a man?
5. What attribute should we have in order to see God?

Fill in the Blanks

1.   "But I know you, that you have not the____ of____ in you."
2.   "I have found_____ the son of_____ , a man after mine own____ , which shall fulfill____ my____ ."
3.   "If any man among you seem to be____ , and bridleth not his_____ , but deceiveth his own____ , this man's religion is____ ."
4.   "Draw nigh to God, and he will ____nigh to you._____ your hands, ye sinners; and____ your____ , ye double minded."
5.   "They do always____ in their____ ; and they have not____ my____ ."

The Heart of the Matter

The disposition of the heart, whether filled by the peace, love, and joy of the Holy Spirit or by the things of this world or the flesh, influences greatly our speech, attitudes, and behavior. The psalmist David petitioned God to "Create in me a clean heart, O God, and renew a right spirit within me." This request should be on the lips of every servant of God.

The Heart of the Matter (1)

Old Testament – Proverbs 2:1-2, 6-10, 3:1-5, 4:1-4, 20-23, 8:1-5, 12:8, 20, 23, 14:33, 27:19 Psalms 4:4-8, 13:5-6, 15:1-2, 24:3-5, 32:11, 51:10 Deuteronomy 5:29, 8:2, 13:1-4

New Testament – Matthew 5:8, 28, 6:21, 12:35, 15:16-20 Acts 5:3-4, 8:18-22, 1 John 3:18-21 James 4:8

The Heart of the Matter (2)

Old Testament – Ecclesiastes 11:9-10, 5:18-20, 3:18-18 Nehemiah 9:7-8, 1 Kings 8:57-58 Joshua 24:23 Proverbs 23:26, 22:11, 21:1-2 Psalms 119:32, 36, 111, 112:5-8, 86:11-12, 57:7, 33:15

New Testament – Hebrews 3:7-12, 15 James 1:26, 3:14-15, 5:5 Romans 2:28-29 Ephesians 3:17, 1 Peter 3:15, 2 Peter 1:19

The Heart of the Matter (3)

Old Testament – Ecclesiastes 9:3 Deuteronomy 30:6, 28:47-48, 1 Samuel 13:13-14, 16:7, 1 Chronicles 16:10, 29:17-20, 1 Kings 8:65-66, 10:23-24, 11:4, 9 Jeremiah 15:16 Psalms 19:8, 44:20-21, 64:10, 105:2-3

New Testament – Matthew 11:29, 13:19 Hebrews 4:12, 10:22, 13:9 Acts 13:22, 11:23, 1 Thessalonians 3:12-13, 2 Thessalonians 3:5

The Heart of the Matter (4)

Old Testament – Ecclesiastes 3:11 Deuteronomy 4:9, 29, 39, 10:14-16 Jeremiah 4:4, 14, 18, 5:23-24, 17:5, 9-10, 22:17 Proverbs 24:12 JoeL 2:12-13 Isaiah 44:18-20 Ezekiel 13:22-23, 14:3-8, 33:31, 44:6-9 Psalms 78:36-38, 125:4, 141:3-4

New Testament – Mark 4:15, 7:6 John 5:42 Luke 16:15, 21:34, 1 Corinthians 4:5, 1 Thessalonians 2:4 Revelations 2:23

The Heart of the Matter (5)

Old Testament – Ecclesiastes 2:9-15, 22-23, 1 Kings 2:1-4, 2 Chronicles 15:1-2, 17, 17:1-6, 30:17-20, 31:20-21, 34:1-3, 27-31 Ezra 7:10 Psalms 10:17, 37:31, 66:18 Proverbs 16:1 Job 11:12-14

New Testament – Acts 15:8 Romans 8:27, 5:5, 2 Corinthians 1:21-22, 4:6 Galatians 4:6 Philippians 4:7 Colossians 2:2, 3:15

The Love of God

The Love of God (1)

"Because he hath set his love on Me, therefore will I deliver him: I will set him on high, because he hath known My name." Ps 91:14 "But if any man love God, the same is known of Him." (1 Corinthians 8:3)

The Love of God (2)

"If any man love not the Lord Jesus Christ, let him be Anathema Maranatha." "Jesus said unto them, If God were your Father ye would love me... (1 Corinthians 16:22, John 8:42)

The Love of God (3)

"...because the love of God is shed abroad in our hearts by the Holy Ghost which is given unto us...But God commendeth His love toward us, in that, while we were yet sinners, Christ died for us...we shall be saved from wrath through him. (Romans 5:5-9)

Discussion Questions

1. Can the love of God make a significant impact on those around us? Explain.
2. How did God demonstrate His love for all of mankind?
3. Explain 1 Corinthians 8:3.

4. What is the new commandment that Christ has given to those who follow him?
5. Explain Romans 8:28.

Fill in the Blanks

1. "The ____ of the Lord Jesus Christ, and the ____ of ____, and the communion of the Holy Ghost, be with you all. Amen.
2. "But I know you, that ye have not the ____ of ____ in you."
3. "And hope maketh not ashamed; because the ____ of ____ is shed abroad in our hearts by the Holy Ghost which is given unto us."
4. "But if any man____ God, the same is____ of him."
5. "And we know that ____ ____work together for good to them that____ ____ ."

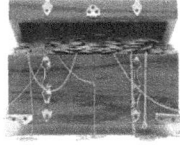

The Love of God

There is a lodging place deep within the innermost recesses of the heart and soul of a Child Of God that enthrones God alone. It is reserved for Him alone. In Matthew 22:37-38, "Jesus said unto him, Thou shalt love the LORD with all thy heart, and with all thy soul, and with all thy mind. This is the first and great commandment." The Love of God inspires, motivates and propels His children to great heights, and to do great works in the kingdom of Christ. It strengthens and emboldens them to overcome all the challenges prevalent on the time side of life. It is imperative that all Christians possess the Love of God first and foremost.

The Love of God (1)

Old Testament – Deuteronomy 5:6-10, 6:4-6, 10:12-15, 13:1-5 Joshua 23:11, 24:23, 1 Samuels 7:3, 12:20, 13:13-14 Psalms 97:10, 91:14, 70:4, 69:34-36, Hosea 11:1, 4, Jeremiah 31:3

New Testament – Mark 12:32-34, John 5:42, Luke 11:42, 1 John 3:16-17

The Love of God (2)

Old Testament – Exodus 20:3-6 Deuteronomy 5:29, 11:1, 13-14, 22-23, 19:9, 30:6, 17-20, 1 Samuel 13:13-14, 2 Samuel 12:24, 1 Kings 3:3, 11:1-4, 9-11 Psalms 5:8-11 Psalms 5:5-8, 18:1, 40:16 Jeremiah 32:17-19

New Testament – John 21:15-18, 17:26, 15:9-14, 14:15, 21-24, 8:42 Acts 13:21-22, 1 Corinthians 2:9

The Love of God (3)

Old Testament – Deuteronomy 33:12 Joshua 22:1-5 Numbers 15:38-39, 1 Kings 8:57-58 Judges 5;31 Nehemiah 1:1-6 Daniel 9:2-5, 19-23, 10:18-19 Psalms 146:8-9, 145:20, 122:6, 119:126-132, 116:1-2, 31: 23

New Testament – Romans 8:28, 35-39, 5:5, 8, 2 Corinthians 5:14, 2 Thessalonians 3:5, 1 John 3:16-18

The Love of God (4)

Old Testament – Hosea 3:1-5, 9:1, 10:2 JoeL2:12-14 Micah 6:8i Isaiah 63:7-9, 61:8, 56:4-6, 38:12-17 Psalms 119:132, 159, 163, 165, 167

New Testament – John 8:42, 16:27, 1 Corinthians 8:3, 16:22 James 1:12, 2:5 Ephesians 1:4, 2:4-5, 3:17-19, 5:1-2, 6:24 Titus 3:1-6

The Love of God (5)

Old Testament – Exodus 19:4-6 Deuteronomy 23:3-5, 32:10 Zechariah 2:8 Zephanian 3:17 Isaiah 49:15-16, 43:3-4 Psalms 36:10, 139:17-18

New Testament – John 3:16-19, 13:1, 34-35, Matthew 10:37, 22:37 Galatians 2:20, 5:6, 2 Timothy 1:13, 4:8 Hebrews 12:5-6 Revelation 1:5, 3:19

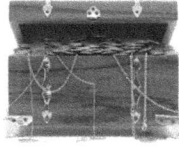

His Divine Nature

His Divine Nature (1)

"He is the Rock, His work is perfect: for all His ways are judgement: a God of truth and without iniquity, just and right is He." (Deut 32:4)

His Divine Nature (2)

"Behold therefore the goodness and severity of God: on the which fell, severity; but toward thee, goodness, if thou continue in His goodness: otherwise thou also shalt be cut off. (Romans 11:22)

His Divine Nature (3)

"For Our God is a consuming fire." (Hebrews 12:29)

Discussion Questions

1. What description of God is given in Deuteronomy 32:3-4?
2. Explain Deuteronomy 4:24.
3. What command is given in Matthew 5:48?
4. What are we exhorted to do in 2 Peter 3:14?
5. Explain 1 John 3:1-3.

Fill in the Blanks

1. "For the Lord thy God is a____ , even a jealous God."

2. "For the Lord thy God is a____ God; he will not forsake thee, neither destroy thee."
3. "And the Lord passed by before him, and proclaimed The Lord, The Lord God, ____ and, ____ , ____and abundant in____ and____."
4. "Beloved, let us____ one another: for____ is of God; and every one that____ is born of God, and____ God."
5. "Be ye therefore ____of____ , as dear children."

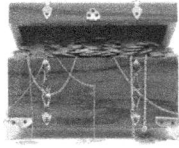

His Divine Nature

We all should strive to obtain the characteristics and attributes of God. God is holy; therefore, we should strive to be holy (1 Peter 1:14). As we allow His word to have free course in our lives, through our submission and obedience, we will become more and more like Him in our demeanor (Luke 6:40).

His Divine Nature (1)

Old Testament – Deuteronomy 32:3-4, 4:24, 31 Exodus 33:18-23, 34:5-8 Job 34;10-15, 21-33 Numbers 14:18-21, 23:19 Hosea 11:9 Isaiah 14:24 Jeremiah 32:17 Psalms 115:3, 97:2-6 Daniel 4:35-37

New Testament – Ephesians 1:11, 5:1-5, 2 Peter 1:2-12 Hebrews 6:17-20, 12:18-29

His Divine Nature (2)

Old Testament – Exodus 15:11, 13 Leviticus 11:44, 19:2, 11-18, 34-37 Zechariah 8:16-17 Ezekiel 22:12-14 Jonah 4:1-2 Psalms 5:4-7, 71:19, 73:1, 27, 86:15, 103:6-14, 17, 130:6-14, 17, 130:3-4, 7-8 Nahum 1:2-7 JoeL 2:12-14

New Testament – Romans 2:4, 11:22-23 Jude 1:21, 1 John 3:1-3, 4:8, 16 Ephesians 4:22-24

His Divine Nature (3)

Old Testament – Deuteronomy 7:9-10 Micah 7:18-20 Habakkuk 1:12-17, 2:1-4 Joshua 24:14, 19-20 Psalms 11:7, 18:25-28, 76:7-12, 86:5, 89:7, 14, 18, 97:10, 119:64-65, 68, 75, 118-119, 156, 145:8-9, 18, 20, 146:9

New Testament – Romans 8:2-8, 1 Corinthians 8:3, 10:13, 1 Peter 1:15-17

His Divine Nature (4)

Old Testament – Jeremiah 29:11-13, 18:7-11 Isaiah 40:15, 17, 18, 21-26, 2:3, 13-20, 1 Samuel 2:30 Malachi 1:6-14 Ps 29:2, 33:5, 90:11, 102:25-28, 119:89-91, 136:1-9 Amos 5;14-15

New Testament – Hebrews 11:6 Romans 9:15-26 James 1:17-18 Philippians 2:13, 1 John 4:7-13

His Divine Nature (5)

Old Testament – Numbers 23:19 Job 9:2-4, 32-33, 11:5-6 Ezra 9:3-6, 13 Nehemiah 9:29, 31 Lamentations 3:22-25, 1 Samuel 15:29 Jeremiah 10:6-7, 10 Isaiah 64:1-4, 66:1-2 Psalms 10:14-18, 27:10, 50:18-21, 103:13-14 Malachi 3:6

New Testament – Hebrews 6:17-18, 4:13, 1 John 1:5-10, 2 Timothy 2:12-13 James 1:13

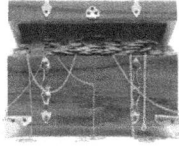

Overcoming

Overcoming (1)

"He that overcometh shall inherit all things; and I will be his God and he shall be My son." (Revelation 21:7)

Overcoming (2)

"...yea, let God be true, but every man a liar; as it is written , That thou mightest be justified in thy sayings, and mightest overcome when thou art judged." (Romans 3:4)

Overcoming (3)

"Ye are of God, little children, and have overcome them: because greater is He that is in you, than he that is in the world." (1 John 4:4)

Discussion Questions

1. What did Jehoshaphat mean in his prayer to God when he said "our eyes are upon thee?"
2. What happens when iniquity abounds and what are we expected to do?
3. What was the testimony of Daniel after being thrown into the lion's den?
4. When Jonah's soul fainted within him, what did he do?

5. Must we go through tribulation before entering into the Kingdom of God?

Fill in the Blanks

1. And because _____shall abound, the ____of____ shall wax____.
2. I can do all things through____which_____me.
3. Ye are of God, little children and have_____them; because_____is he that is in ___, than he that is in the_____.
4. For whatsoever is born of God_____the world; and this is the ____that_____ The world, even our_____.
5. And they_____him by the_____of the_____and by the_____of their _____; and they_____not their lives unto the_____.

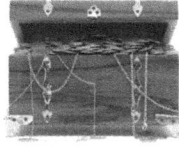

Overcoming

*T*here is much adversity in life. Sometimes, the adversity is within, and, sometimes, the adversity is without. Yet, through it all, it is our faith that will bring us through our trials, holding on to God by our obedience to His Word. Our resolve must be to never give up on God, no matter what we face. This testimony proves the genuineness of our faith, which is precious in God's sight. Without faith, it is impossible to please God, even though, sometimes, we become vexed or saddened by our struggles and trials—yet, He renews our spirit and helps us to overcome.

Overcoming (1)

Old Testament – Genesis 30:6-8, 32:24-28, 49:19, 22-26, 50:20 Numbers 22:6, 11-12, 2 Kings 13:14-19, 16:5 Jeremiah 1:19, 5:22, 15:20, 20:7-11, 38:22 Psalms 9:19, 12:1-5, 13:3-5, 49:5, 69:2, 14-15, 35-36

New Testament – Romans 8:28-39, 12:21, 2 Corinthians 2:14, 1 Corinthians 15:57-58 Revelation 2:7, 11, 17

Overcoming (2)

Old Testament – Numbers 13:27-31 Deuteronomy 7:17-24, Exodus 17:11, 2 Chronicles 20:1-12, 14:11 Zechariah 4:6, 1 Samuel 2:9-10 Isaiah 31:5, 49:8 Psalms 3:1-3, 41:1-2, 60: 12, 61:2-3, 65:2-3, 94:17-18, 118:6, 121:3-8, 124:1-6, 129:1-2

New Testament – John 10:27-29 Matthew 10:16-26, 24:9-13, 1 Corinthians 10:13 Romans 3:4 Revelation 21:7

Overcoming (3)

Old Testament – Deuteronomy 9:1-3, 11:22-25 Daniel 6:11-28, 2 Samuel 22:40, 48--49, 1 Chronicles 22:18 Psalms 18:16-18, 32:7, 10, 56:1-6, 9, 57:1-4, 81:13-15, 98:1 Isaiah 7:1, 16:12, 40:29-31, 42: 13

New Testament – Luke 1:37 John 16:33, 1 John 2:12-14, 4:4, 5:1-5

Overcoming (4)

Old Testament – 1 Samuel 10:19, 1 Chronicles 5:2 Ecclesiastes 4:9-12 Job 15:20, 24, 19:20, 26 Psalms 27:12-14, 94:17, 119:92, 142:3-7

New Testament – Matthew 17:20, 21:21, 2 Peter 2:18-20 Romans 8:18 Acts 14:22, 19:11-16 Revelation 3:4-5, 10-12, 20-21, 11:3-8, 12:7-11, 13:1-8, 15:2, 17:14

Overcoming (5)

Old Testament – Jonah 2:1-10 Lamentations 3:52-58, 2 Samuel 22:5-7, 17-19 Isaiah 50:6-10, 43:2-7, 41:10-13 Job 36:15-16, 2 Chronicles 13:16-18, 16:8, 1 Chronicles 5:18-20 Psalms 18:39, 47, 27:1-3, 47:3, 144:1-2

New Testament – Luke 11:21-22 Matthew 24:12-13 Philippians 4:13 Hebrews 11:33, 2 Timothy 4:16-18, 1 Peter 5:10

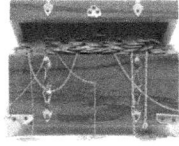

The Book

The Book (1)

"And Ezra opened the book in the sight of all the people;(for he was above all the people;) and when he opened it, all the people stood up:)...So they read in the book in the law of God distinctly, and gave the sense, and caused them to understand the reading." (Nehemiah 8:5, 8)

The Book (2)

"Seek ye out of the book of the LORD, and read: no one of these shall fail, none shall want her mate: for My mouth it hath commanded, and His spirit it hath gathered them." (Isaiah 34:16)

The Book (3)

"...every man that heareth the words of the prophecy of this book, if any man add...God shall add unto him the plagues that are written in this book:..if any man take away...God shall take away his part in the book of life... (Rev 22:18-19)

Discussion Questions

1. What instructions were given to Joshua in Joshua 1:8?
2. What instructions were given to kings in Deuteronomy 17:18-19?
3. What instructions are given in 2 Timothy 3:15-17?

4. Explain Acts 17:11.
5. Discuss John 20:30-31.

Fill in the Blanks

1. "This is the____ of the generations of Adam..."
2. "And the priest shall____ these curses in a____ , and he shall blot them out with the____ ____ ."
3. "For whatsoever things were____ aforetime were____ for our____ ."
4. "Then said I, Lo, I come (in the____ of___ ____ it is written of me)."
5. "Blessed is he that____ , and they that hear the____ of this____ prophecy, and keep those things which are____ therein."

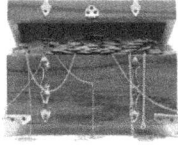

The Book

O n many occasions, God instructed the prophets to write in a book and have his people read, study, and observe. This book is the Holy Bible we now have.

> "Seek ye out of the book of the Lord, and read: no one of these shall fail, none shall want her mate: for my mouth it hath commanded, and his spirit it hath gathered them." (Isaiah 34:16).

The Book (1)

Old Testament – Genesis 5:1 Numbers 5:23, 21:14 Exodus 17:14, 24:3-4, 7, 34:27-28 Nahum 1:1 Ezra 2:62, 4:15, 6:18 Nehemiah 7:5, 64, 8:1-9, 18, 9:3, 12:23 Jeremiah 30:2 Psalms 40:7, 87:6

New Testament – Luke 4:16-20 Matthew 4:4-10 Romans 15:4 Galatians 3:10 Hebrews 9:19, 10:7, 12:23, 2 Peter 1:19-21, 1 John 5:13

The Book (2)

Old Testament – Deuteronomy 31:9, 24-26, 30:9-10, 29:18-21, 27, 28:58-61, 17:18-20, 9:14, 2 Kings 11:12, 2 Chronicles 34:14-31 Joshua 8:31-35, 10:13, 18:9, 23:6, 24:24-26 Isaiah 30:8, 8:1, 16, 20

New Testament – John 20:30-31, 21:24-25 Romans 4:23-24 Acts 1:20, 7:42, 13:33-40, 1 Corinthians 10:7, 11, 14:36-37

The Book (3)

Old Testament – Joshua 1:8 Daniel 10:21 Ezekiel 2:8-10, 3:1-4, 13:9, 24:2 Zechariah 5:1-4, 1:4-6, 1 Kings 11:41, 14:19, 29 Isaiah 34:16 Proverbs 30:16 Jeremiah 15:16, 25:13, 30, 36:2-32, 45:1-5, 51:60-64

New Testament – Luke 24:27, 32, 45 Matthew 22:29, 2 Timothy 3:15-17 Acts 17:1-2, 11 Colossians 4:16, Philippians 4:3, 1 Thessalonians 5:27 Revelation 22:18-19

The Book (4)

Old Testament – Exodus 17:13-14 Numbers 33:1-2, 1 Samuel 10:25, 2 Kings 22:8-16, 23:1-3, 21, 24, 28 Hosea 8:12 Job 19;23-24, 31:35 Nehemiah 13:1-3, 9:1-3 Ezra 6:18, 10:1-3 Daniel 9:2-13, 2 Chronicles 35:26-27 Esther 10:2 Isaiah 29:11-14

New Testament – 1 Corinthians 4:6, 2 Thessalonians 2:15, 3:14 Revelation 1:3, 11, 3:5, 13:8, 17:8

The Book (5)

Old Testament – Daniel 7:10, 12:1-4 Exodus 32:31-33 Psalms 139:16, 109:13-15, 69:26-28, 56:8 Malachi 3:16 Isaiah 4:3 Habakkuk 2:2 Ecclesiastes 12:10 Proverbs 22:20-21, 1 Kings 4:30-32

New Testament – Luke 1:1-4, 10:20, 16:31, John 5:47, 1 Thessalonians 2:13, 2 Peter 3:15-16, 1 Timothy 4:13, 3:14-15 Revelation 20:11-15, 21:27

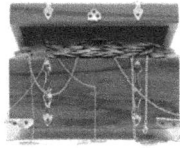

A Covenant Relationship

a Covenant Relatonship (1)

"Know therefore that the LORD thy God, He is God, the faithful God, which keepeth covenant and mercy with them that love Him and keep His commandments... (Deuteronomy 7:9)

a Covenant Relationship (2)

"All the paths of the LORD are mercy and truth unto such as keep His covenant and testimonies." "The secret of the LORD is with them that fear Him; and He will shew them His covenant." (Psalm 25:10, 14)

a Covenant Relationship (3)

"Behold, the days come, saith the LORD, that I will make a new covenant..Not according to the covenant that I made with their fathers..But this shall be the covenant ...I will put My law in their inward parts, and write it in their hearts; (Jeremiah 31:31-33)

Discussion Questions

1. What transpired in Exodus 24:7-8?
2. Explain 2 Kings 23:1-3?
3. What conditions were mentioned in Exodus 19:5?
4. Explain Hebrew 8:6-18.
5. Explain Galatians 4:21-31.

Fill in the Blanks

1. "And I have also____ my____ with them, to give them the land of____ ."
2. "For this is my____ unto them, when I shall take away their____ ."
3. "They shall ask the way to____ with their faces____ , saying, Come, and let us join____ to the____ in a____ ____ that shall not be____ ."
4. "And to Jesus the____ of the new____ , and to the____ ____ of____ , that speaketh better things than that of____ ."
5. "But they like men have____ the____ : there have they dealt treacherously against me."

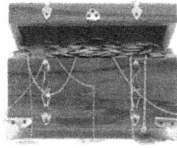

A Covenant Relationship

*T*he word covenant is "a set agreement having complete terms determined by the initiating party, which also is fully affirmed by the one entering the agreement." God enters a covenant relationship with those who are His people.

a Covenant Relatonship (1)

Old Testament – Genesis 6:18-22, 9:8-17, 17:1-21, 26:1-5, 35:9-13 Exodus 2:23-24, 6:2-5, 19:5-6, 24:3-8 Deuteronomy 5:2-22, 27-33, 7:6-12, 29:9- 15 Nehemiah 1:2-9, 9:7-8, 2 Kings 13:22-23

New Testament – Luke 1:68-73 Acts 3:24-26, 7:1-8 Romans 4:8-18, 11:25-27

a Covenant Relationship (2)

Old Testament – Deuteronomy 4:12-13, 23, 31, 8:11-18, 9:4-19, 17:2-5, 31:16-19 Psalms 105:6-10, 103:17-18, 78:10, 37, 1 Chronicles 16:14-18 Judges 2:20 Isaiah 24:5-6 Hosea 6:7 Jeremiah 31:31-33, 33:14-22, 50:4-5

New Testament – Hebrews 8:6-18 Galatians 3:6-29, 4:21-31 Romans 9:1-5, 25-33

a Covenant Relationship (3)

Old Testament – Daniel 9:3-11, 2 Chronicles 6:10-14, 7:16-18, 13:5, 21:5-7, 34:30-31 Isaiah 24:5, 28:14-18, 42:1-6, 49:7-8, 54:8-10, 55:3, 59:20-21, 61:8-11 Ezekiel 34:23-25, 37:24-28

New Testament – Luke 1:30-33, 1 Corinthians 11:23-25 Acts 2:22-36, 2 Corinthians 3:3-14 Revelation 11:15, 19

a Covenant Relationship (4)

Old Testament – Judges 2:1-5 Haggai 2:1-5, 2 Kings 17:13-15, 23:1-3, 21 Jeremiah 11:1-11, 22:1-9, 23:5-8 Psalms 132:9-12, 111:5, 9, 103:17-18, 89:1-7, 20-28, 34, 50:5, 16-17, 25:10, 14

New Testament – Matthew 26:26-29 Hebrews 9:1-4, 14-24, 10:16-29, 12:22-24, 13:20-21

Covenant Relationship (5)

Old Testament – Numbers 30:2-16 Malachi 2:4-14 Job 31:1-4 Proverbs 2:11-17 Ezekiel 16:8, 58-62, 17:12-19, 20:33-37, 44:5-7 Hosea 2:18-20, 6:5-7, 8:1-3 Zechariah 11:10-14 Jeremiah 32:37-41 Psalms 44:17, 106:43-45

New Testament – Romans 1:29-31, 7:1-4 Hebrews 7:17-22 James 5:12

The Potter and the Clay

The Potter and the Clay (1)

"...Shall the thing formed say to Him that formed it, Why hast thou made me thus? Hath not the potter power over the clay, of the same lump to make one vessel unto honour, and another unto dishonour?" (Romans 9:20-21)

The Potter and the Clay (2)

"Know ye that the LORD He is God. it is He that hath made us, and not we ourselves; We are His people, and the sheep of His pasture. (Psalms 100:3)

The Potter and the Clay (3)

"For by him were all things created, that are in heaven, and that are in earth, visible and invisible, whether they be thrones, or dominions, or principalities, or powers: all things were created by him, and for him." (Colossians 1:16)

Discussion Questions

1. God can remake the marred vessels of clay if they would do what?
2. How does God create a clean heart and a right spirit in us?

3. Is it wrong to strive with our Maker? If so, why do many people do so?
4. What passage says God's ways are past finding out?
5. What passage says that if any man be in Christ, he is a new creature?

Fill in the Blanks

1. "Therefore hath he_____ on whom he will have____ , and whom he will he___ ."
2. "A new____ also will I give you, and a new____ will I put within you."
3. "Whereunto I also____ , striving according to his____ , which____ in me mightily."
4. "Now unto him that is____ to do exceeding____ above all that we ask or____ , according to the____ that____ in us."
5. "If a man therefore ___himself from these, he shall be a____ unto____ , sanctified, and____ for the____ ____ , and prepared unto every____ ____ ."

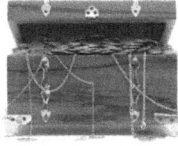

The Potter and the Clay

*T*he imagery of the potter and the clay is our lives in the hands of our God. When we humble ourselves and submit to His holy and divine will, when we maintain our faith, our trust, and our reliance on Him by diligently keeping His commands, God can mold and fashion any of us to be a vessel to be used by Him. A choice vessel.

The Potter and the Clay (1)

Old Testament – Jeremiah 18:1-11, 13:11, 5:22-24, 1:5, 10 Job 4:17-21, 9:4-10, 31:13-15, 36:3, 24-33 Pr 14:31, 22:2 Psalms 95:4-6, 100:3, 119:73, 138:8, 139:13-18, 149:2

New Testament – Romans 9:18-23 Acts 7:49-50, 17:26-31 Ephesians 3:8-9, 1:11, 2 Timothy 2:21

The Potter and the Clay (2)

Old Testament – Isaiah 29:15-16, 22-24, 41:24-25, 45:7- 13, 18, 22, 64:5-9 Lamentations 4:1-2 Zechariah 11:10-14 Jeremiah 19:1-4, 10-11 Job 10:8-13, 26:5-14, 33:6-13, 38:1-14 Psalms 2:1-9, 51:7-12, 144:3-4

New Testament – Hebrews 2:5-8 Colossians 1:16-17, 2 Corinthians 4:6-7 Philippians 2:13-15

The Potter and the Clay (3)

Old Testament – Ecclesiastes 1:13, 15, 7:13, 8:7-8 Job 9:12, 11:10, 12:7-10, 23:13-14, 38:28-41, 39:1-5, 19-30, 42:2 Psalms 147:3-11, 115:3, 46:8-10, 24:1-2

New Testament – Romans 1:20, 11:33-36 Hebrews 13:20-21, 1 Peter 4:19

The Potter and the Clay (4)

Old Testament – Genesis 2:7, 5:2 Proverbs 20:12, 24 Psalms 148:5, 146:5-9, 104:23-30, 102:17-18, 94:3-11 Ecclesiastes 7:29, 12:1 Amos 3:6, Isaiah 40:26-28, 41:17-20, 57:19 Malachi 2:10

New Testament – Ephesians 2:10, 4:24 Colossians 3:8-10 Revelation 4:11

The Potter and the Clay (5)

Old Testament – Deuteronomy 10:14 Nehemiah 9:6 Jonah 1:9, 1 Samuel 2:6-10 Hosea 8:4, 8, 13:14-15, Isaiah 54:16, 30:12-14 Jeremiah 22:24, 28, 25:34, 48:11, 38, 51:34 Psalms 2:9-11, 31:12, 33:12-15 Proverbs 25:4

New Testament – Acts 9:13-15, 1 Thessalonians 4:3-4, 2 Timothy 2:20-21 Revelation 2:26-27

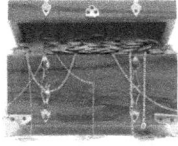

Spiritual Warfare

Spiritual Warfare (1)

"For though we walk in the flesh, we do not war after the flesh; (For the weapons of our warfare are not carnal, but mighty through God to the pulling down of strongholds;)(2 Cor 10:3-4)

Spiritual Warfare (2)

"No weapon that is formed against thee shall prosper; and every tongue that shall rise against thee in judgement thou shalt condemn. This is the heritage of the servants of the LORD, and their righteousness is of Me, saith the LORD. (Isaiah 54:17)

Spiritual Warfare (3)

"This charge I commit unto thee, son Timothy, according to the prophecies which went before on thee, that thou by them mightest war a good warfare;" (1 Timothy 1:18)

Discussion Questions

1. Explain the prophecy found in Genesis 3:15. 135 Spiritual Warfare
2. How are we to overcome our adversary according to 1 Peter 5:8-9?
3. How were thy able to overcome in Revelation 12:7-12?

4. Explain John 8:44.
5. Explain John 10:10.

Fill in the Blanks

1. "And they overcame him by the____ of the___ , and by the word of their____ ."
2. "And the Lord said unto___ , The Lord____ thee, O____ ."
3. "For though we walk in the____ , we do not____ after the____ ."
4. "And said, O full of all____ and all____ , thou child of the____ , thou enemy of all , wilt thou not cease to____ the right ways of the____ ?"
5. "They shall put you out of the : yea, the time cometh, that whosoever____ you will think that he doeth____ service."

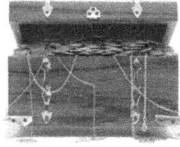

Spiritual Warfare

*T*hose who are Christians are at war with the Devil and his angels. The Christian has to put on the whole armor of God; he has to fight the good fight of faith to gain the victory. The weapons of our warfare are spiritual. These passages give us insight into the battle that is waged against us.

Spiritual Warfare (1)

Old Testament – Genesis 3:15, 4:7-8 Daniel 7:21-28 Zechariah 3:1-2 Proverbs 29:27 Psalms 140:1-4, 120:5-7, 68:3, 57:4, 6, 55:18-21, 37:12-15, 32

New Testament – John 16:2, 7:7 Luke 22:31-32 Acts 20:28-31, 13:10 Romans 16:17-20, 1 Peter 5:8-9, 1 Timothy 5:14-15, 1 John 3:12, 1 Thessalonians 2:18, 3:5 Revelation 13:6-8

Spiritual Warfare (2)

Old Testament – Judges 2:21-23 Deuteronomy 20:1-4, 30:6-7 Numbers 24:9 Exodus 23:22, Isaiah 54:17 Jeremiah 1:19 Proverbs 18:3, 24:15-16 Psalms 11:2, 38:12, 20, 56:1-9, 64:1-10, 71:13, 24, 119:150, 161

New Testament – Philippians 1:28-29, 1 John 4:4-6, 3:7-8 Galatians 1:6-9 Romans 11:26, 28 Revelation 3:9, 12:7-12, 17

Spiritual Warfare (3)

Old Testament – Genesis 15:1 Deuteronomy 28:7, 2 Kings 6:16-18, 2 Chronicles 14:11, 20:15, 17, Isaiah 41:10-12, 42:13 Zechariah 4:6 Psalms 17:4, 27:2-3, 44:5-7, 4/:6-11, 69:4, 9, 125:3

New Testament – John 15:18-25 Romans 8:31-39, 7:22-25 Galatians 5:16-17, 1 Timothy 1:18, 2 Timothy 2:3-5, 2 Corinthians 10:3-6 Ephesians 6:10-18 Revelation 19:11-21

Spiritual Warfare (4)

Old Testament – Daniel 8:23-26, 1 Chronicles 21:1 Job 1:6-12, 2:3-7 Proverbs 29:10, 1 Samuel 24:13, Isaiah 59:18-20 Nahum 1:8 Psalms 9:3-6, 14:4-5, 22:16-21, 68:21 Joshua 10:25

New Testament – Matthew 4:1-11, 16:21-23, 1 Corinthians 7:5 Acts 5:1-11, 2 Timothy 2:24-26 James 4:1-7, 1 Peter 2:11

Spiritual Warfare (5)

Old Testament – 2 Chronicles 20:17, 29, 32:7-8 Psalms 18:16-21, 39, 48, 34:7, 35:1-3, 37:17-20, Isaiah 31:4-5 Jeremiah 15:20-21 Zechariah 10:4-5, 14:3-9

New Testament – Luke 10:18 Matthew 13:36-41, 16:22-23 John 8:40-47, 10:10, 1 Corinthians 9:25-27, 2 Corinthians 2:6-11, 4:3-4, 1 John 5:18-19

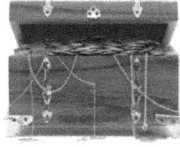

Life's About Choices

Life's About Choices (1)

"And Elijah came unto the people, and said, How long halt ye between two opinions? if the LORD be God follow Him: but if Baal, then follow him. And the people answered him not a word." (1 Kings 18:21)

Life's About Choices (2)

"He that hath my commandments and keepeth them, he it is that loveth me:.. He that loveth me not keepeth not my sayings: and the Word which ye hear is not mine, but the Father's which sent me." (Jn 14:21, 24)

Life's About Choices (3)

"And if it seem evil unto you to serve the LORD, choose you this day whom ye shall serve...but as for me and my house, we will serve the LORD... And Joshua said unto the people, Ye are witnesses against yourselves that ye have chosen you the LORD (Josh 24:15, 22)

Discussion Questions

1. What were the choices given to Adam and Eve in Genesis 3:1-13, and what consequences did they face?
2. What was Peter's response when he was given a choice in John 6:66-69?
3. What are the choices given in Romans 6:12-18?

4. Explain the choices made in Mark 10:17-22.
5. Explain John 14:21-24.

Fill in the Blanks

1. "I call heaven and earth to record this day against you, that I have____ before you____ and death, and____: therefore____ that both thou and thy seed may____ ."
2. "And this is the____ , that light is come into the world, and____ loved____ rather than____ , because their deeds were____ ."
3. "But if not, be it known unto thee, O king, that we will ____ serve thy____ , nor____ the____ ____ which thou hast set up."
4. "In all thy ways____ ____ , and he shall____ thy____ ."
5. "He that is unjust, let him be____ still: and he which is____, let him be____ still: and he that is , let him be still: and he that is____, let him be____ still."

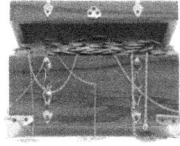

Life's About Choices

When man was created and placed in the Garden of Eden, he was given the freedom of choice. Consequences for the decisions and choices we make have always been a part of life.

> "For he that soweth to his flesh shall of the flesh reap corruption; but he that soweth to the Spirit shall of the Spirit reap life everlasting" (Galatians 6:8).

> "Therefore, since we know this to be a true axiom about life, let us strive to choose wisely, in accordance to the Word of God, which is the sword of the Spirit" (Ephesians 6:17).

Life's About Choices (1)

Old Testament – Genesis 3:1-7, 4:3-7, 13:4-13 Exodus 32:25-28 Deuteronomy 11:26-29, 30:15-21 Judges 10:6, 14- 16, 1 Kings 18:21 Jeremiah 5:30-31, 21:8-9 Psalms 125:4-5 Micah 4:5

New Testament – Luke 12:15-21, 16:13, 19-25 Matthew 12:33, 10:37-39 Mark 10:17-23, 8:36-37 James 1:8

Life's About Choices (2)

Old Testament – Genesis 19:17, 26 Daniel 3:1-30 Joshua 24:14-15, 22, 2 Kings 5:9-15, 1 Kings 13:7-24, 1 Samuel 24:1-12 Numbers 22:11-12, 17-18

Ruth 1:8-18 Jeremiah 44:16-22 Malachi 3:13-18, Isaiah 3:10-11 Psalms 32:8-9, 34:12-14 Proverbs 11:19, 14:16

New Testament – Luke 14:26-27, 18:28-30 Matthew 13:44-46 John 3:19-21, 6:66-69, 14:21-24 Revelation 3:15-16

Life's About Choices (3)

Old Testament – Job 15:2-5, 27:2-6, 29:1-9, 25, 34:1-4, 31-35, 1 Chronicles 21:9-13, Isaiah 7:13-16, 55:3, 7, 56:4-5, 58:5-13, 66:3-4 Jeremiah 7:22-24 Psalms 81:11-16, 97:10, 119:30, 32, 104, 173

New Testament – 2 Timothy 2:19 Romans 12:9, 1 Thessalonians 5:21-22 Ephesians 5:7-13, James 3:13-18, Galatians 5:16-17, Revelation 22:11

Life's About Choices (4)

Old Testament – Leviticus 10:8-10 Ezekiel 20:11-13, 22:26, 33:30-32, 44:5-8, 15, 23 Psalms 25:12, Isaiah 1:17-20 Proverbs 1:22-29, 3:31, 10:17, 13:8, 15:24, 32, 19:27

New Testament – Luke 10:38-42 Matthew 21:28-32 Acts 7:51, 53 Romans 6:12-18, 10:16, 21 Hebrews 12:25, 10:26-29

Life's About Choices (5)

Old Testament – Isaiah 1:27-29, 26:10, 30:15, 48:18-19 Ecclesiastes 11:3 Ezekiel 3:27 Jeremiah 6:16-19, 18:11-12, 35:15, 17 Psalms 34:12-14, 58:4-5, 81:11-16 Proverbs 12:28, 14:32

New Testament – John 8:47, 10:1-5, 25-27, 14:21-24, Philippians 1:22-24, 3 John 1:11, 1 Peter 3:10-11

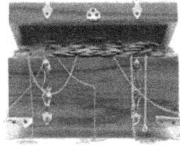

Our Sin Problem

Our Sin Problem (1)

"For there is not a just man upon earth, that doeth good and sinneth not."
"As it is written, There is none righteous, no, not one:"...that every mouth
may be stopped, and all the world may become guilty before God..."
"For all have sinned and come short of the glory of God." (Ecclesiastes
7:20 Romans 3:23)

Our Sin Problem (2)

"Behold, the LORD's hand is not shortened, that it cannot save; neither
His ear heavy, that it cannot hear: But your iniquities have separated
between you and your God, and your sins have hid His face from you,
that He will not hear." (Isaiah 59:1-2)

Our Sin Problem (3)

"For the ways of man are before the eyes of the LORD, and He pondereth
all his goings. His own iniquities shall take the wicked, and he shall be
holden with the cords of his sins." (Prov 5:21-22)

Discussion Questions

1. How do we receive the forgiveness of sin?
2. Can sin be forgiven without the shedding of blood? Explain.
3. Explain Hebrews 2:1-3?

4. What happens if we say we have no sin?
5. What does it mean to be the propitiation for sin (1 John 2:2)?

Fill in the Blanks

1. "The next day John seeth____ coming unto him and saith, Behold the____ of____ , which taketh away the____ of the world."
2. "I said therefore unto you, that ye shall ____in your____ : for if ye____ not that I am___ , ye shall___ in your____ ."
3. "For____ have____ and come____ of the____ of God."
4. "Whosoever committeth sin_____ also the____ : for ____is the ____of the law."
5. "If we say that we have____ ____ , we____ ourselves and the____ is not in us."

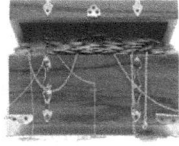

Our Sin Problem

The Bible states in Ecclesiastes 7:20, "For there is not a just man upon earth, that doeth good, and sinneth not." Sin means "to violate God's command, to go contrary, to transgress, to wander, to offend, to miss the mark, and to fall short." Sin separates us from our God (Isaiah 59:2).

Our Sin Problem (1)

Old Testament – Genesis 3:1-17, 4:7, 6:5-6 Leviticus 16:2-16, 21-22, 30 Exodus 32:30-34 Numbers 15:27-31, 32:23 Ecclesiastes 7:20, 8:11-13, 9:2, 18 Proverbs 5:22, 10:16, 14:34, 20:9 Psalms 119:11, 32:1-2, 25:7, 18

New Testament – John 1:29 Romans 4:6-8, 5:11-21 Hebrews 9:18-24, 10:14-23, 1 John 1:8-10, 1:1-2

Our Sin Problem (2)

Old Testament – Hosea 9:9, 8:11-13, 7:1-2 Jeremiah 17:1, 14:7-10, 5:25, 2 Chronicles 6:36-39 Psalms 130:3-8, 103:8-14 Job 15:14-16, 14:4, 13:23-27, 10:14-15 Micah 6:7-8, Isaiah 53:6-12, 59:1-20, 64:6-9

New Testament – Ephesians 2:1-8 John 3:16-17, 8:21-24, 9:39-41 Romans 3:9-26, 6:1-14, 7:7-25

Our Sin Problem (3)

Old Testament – Leviticus 26:13-24, 39-42, 1 Kings 8:31-39 Daniel 9:3-21, Isaiah 1:4, 16-18, 33:14, 38:17, 40:2, 43:25-26, 44:22 Jeremiah 18:7-11 Ezekiel 14:13-14, 18:4, 20-28 Psalms 19:12-13, 69:5, 90:3, 8

New Testament – Luke 13:2-5, 15:1-7 Acts 26:18, 2 Corinthians 5:17-21 Colossians 2:9-14, 2 Peter 1:9 Hebrews 10:24-31, 2:1-3, 14-17 Revelations 1:5

Our Sin Problem (4)

Old Testament – Genesis 13:13, 18:20-33 Numbers 16:1-5, 20-32 Joshua 7:1, 11-12, 19-26, 2 Samuel 12:7-13 Job 36:17-21, Isaiah 58:1 Ezekiel 33:10-19, 21:24-27 Micah 7:16-20

New Testament – Luke 1:76-77 Acts 2:38, 13:38-39 Romans 6:1-23, 8:1-4, 11:26-27 Hebrews 8:12, 11:24-25, 1 Timothy 5:22, 24 Revelation 18:4-5

Our Sin Problem (5)

Old Testament – 2 Kings 21:1-16, 2 Chronicles 33:10-13, 28:9-13, Isaiah 30:1, 1 Samuel 15:16-26 Proverbs 29:1, 6, 23:17-18, 13:21, 1:10 Ecclesiastes 5:6 Psalms 32:1-6, 51:12-13

New Testament – Romans 5:8-9 Galatians 2:17, 1:4 Hebrews 12:1-3 James 4:8, 17, 1 Peter 4:1-5, 18, 1 John 3:4-10, 4:10 Colossians 1:12-14 Ephesians 1:7

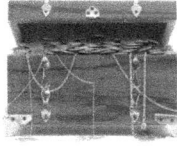

Deceit

Deceit (1)

"He feedeth on ashes: a deceived heart hath turned him aside, that he cannot deliver his soul, nor say, Is there not a lie in my right hand?" "Thine habitation is in the midst of deceit; through deceit they refuse to know Me, saith the LORD." (Isaiah 44:20, Jeremiah 9:6)

Deceit (2)

"For if a man think himself to be something, when he is nothing, he deceiveth himself. "Be not deceived; God is not mocked: for whatsoever a man soweth, that shall he also reap." (Galatians 6:3, 7)

Deceit (3)

"And Jesus answered and said unto them, Take heed that no man deceive you. For many shall come in my name...and shall deceive many...For there shall arise false Christs, and false prophets...insomuch that, if it were possible, they shall deceive the very elect." (Matthew 24:4-5, 24)

Discussion Questions

1. How did Satan deceive Eve in Genesis 3:1-5, 13?
2. What did Jesus encounter in Luke 20:20?
3. What deception was used in Nehemiah 6:1-14?
4. Discuss Proverbs 26:18-26.

5. What deception transpired in Jeremiah 23:16-26?

Fill in the Blanks

1. "And he taught daily in the temple. But the____ ____ and the____ and the____ of the people____ to ____him."
2. "The wisdom of the____ is to understand his way: but the folly of fools is____ ."
3. "But I fear, lest by any means, as the serpent____ Eve through his____ , so your minds should be____ from the____ that is in Christ."
4. "Be not____ : evil____ ____ good manners."
5. "That we henceforth be no more children, tossed to and fro, and carried about with every ____of____ , by the____ of men, and____ ____ , whereby they lie in wait to____ ."

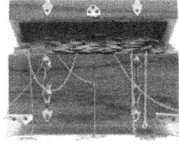

Deceit

*D*eceit involves trickery and the clever use of disguises to twist, turn, and manipulate. It involves crookedness and possessing a hidden agenda, usually masked to avoid detection. It portends to encapsulate or con, in order to take advantage of its desired target by seeking to be undetected, undiscovered, and remaining unexposed.

Deceit (1)

Old Testament – Genesis 3:1-7, 13 Joshua 9:3-23, 1 Kings 13:7-24 Proverbs 14:8, 20:17, 26:4-5, 9-10 Psalms 26:4-5, 9-10, 101:7, 119:118, Isaiah 44:20 Jeremiah 9:2-8, 11:19, 1 Samuel 12:2-5

New Testament – Luke 20:20, 23 Matthew 12:14-15, 26:3-4, 2 Corinthians 2:9, 11, 7:2, 11:3, 12-15, 12:17-19 Revelation 12:9-11

Deceit (2)

Old Testament – Genesis 27:8-13, 34-35, 29:25, 31:6-7, Leviticus 19:11-13, 1 Kings 21:1-19 Micah 6:10-13 Job 5:12-13, 13:4-7, 15:2-5, 31-35 Psalms 35:19-20, 36:1-4, 52:1-5, 72:13-14 Proverbs 11:18

New Testament – 1 Corinthians 15:33, 6:8-10 Galatians 6:3, 7 James 1:22, 26 Ephesians 4:17-22 Hebrews 3:13, 2 Timothy 3:13

Deceit (3)

Old Testament – Hosea 12:1, 7, 11:12 Nehemiah 6:1-14 Obadiah 1:6-7 Zephaniah 1:9 Job 12:16-25 Ezekiel 14:9 Jeremiah 4:10, 5:26-27, 8:5-7, 14;14, 17:9-10, 20:7-11, 23:25-29 Proverbs 12:5, 17, 20

New Testament – Matthew 24:4-5, 11, 24, 2 Thessalonians 2:3-12, 1 John 3:7-8, 2 Peter 2:12-13

Deceit (4)

Old Testament – Deuteronomy 11:16, 13:1-10 Job 31:1-6, 9-12, 26-28, 24:15-17 Proverbs 27:6 Psalms 5:6, 28:3, 38:12, 43:1, 55:11-14, 22-23, 78:55-57, 120:2 Ezekiel 11:2, 5, Isaiah 19:13-14 Jeremiah 48:10, 29:8-9, 30-32, 18:18-19

New Testament – Luke 19:47 Galatians 2:4-6 Romans 3:13, 16:18 Ephesians 5:6, 4:14

Deceit (5)

Old Testament – 1 Samuel 21:10-15 Judges 3:14-29, 4:18-22, 16:4-18 Proverbs 7:21-27, 10:18, 23:1-3, 6, 29:13, 30:20 Micah 2:1-2 Psalms 12:2-3, 32:2, 41:6-9, 50:16-20, 109:2-3

New Testament – 1 John 1:8-9, 2:21-26, 2 John 1:7-11, 3 John 1:9-11, 1 Timothy 4:1-3, Colossians 2:4, 6, 8, 18, 2 Peter 2:1-3, 18

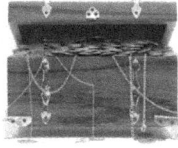

Glimpses of Heaven

Glimpses of Heaven (1)

I beheld till the thrones were cast down, and the Ancient of days did sit, whose garment was white as snow...His throne was like the fiery flame... ten thousands times ten thousands stood before Him: the judgement was set, and the books were opened. (Dan 7:9-10)

Glimpses of Heaven (2)

"Lord, who shall abide in thy tabernacle? who shall dwell in thy holy hill? He that walketh uprightly, and worketh righteousness, and speaketh the truth in his heart. He that backbiteth not with his tongue, ...He that doeth these things shall never be moved. Ps 15:1-5

Glimpses of Heaven (3)

"For he looked for a city which hath foundations, whose builder and maker is God...and confessed that they were strangers and pilgrims on the earth...But now they desire a better country, that is, an heavenly;... for He hath prepared for them a city." Heb 11:8-16

Discussion Questions

1. Explain Daniel 7:13-14.
2. What prerequisites were given in Psalms 15:1-5?
3. Are there tears in heaven? Discuss.

4. Explain Revelation 22:14-15.
5. What are the prerequisites given in Matthew 25:31-46?

Fill in the Blanks

1. "I beheld till the thrones were cast down, and the____ ____ of days did sit, whose garment was_____ as____ , and the hair of his head like the____ ____ : his throne was like the____ ____ , and his wheels as____ ____ ."
2. "And he that sat was to look upon____ ____ a____ ____ and a____ ____ ____ , in sight like unto an____ ."
3. "And God shall away all from their ; and there shall be no more , neither , nor , neither shall there be any more ."
4. "After this I beheld, and, lo, a great____ , which no man could____ , of all____ , and____ , and____ , and____ , stood before the____ , and before the____ , clothed with____ , and_____ in their hands."
5. "In the year that King Uzziah died I saw also the Lord sitting upon a____ , high and lifted up, and his train filled the____ ."

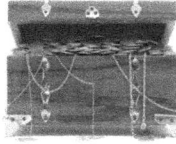

Glimpses of Heaven

*T*he following are passages where the Bible gives us glimpses of what heaven is like. Heaven is a wonderful place Jesus has prepared for those who follow Him. It's beauty and loveliness is beyond man's imagination and comprehension. It is reserved for those who love God and whose names are written in God's Book of Life (Luke 10:20, Revelations 3:5, 20:15, 21:7). We all should strive wholeheartedly to make heaven our eternal home.

Glimpses of Heaven (1)

Old Testament – Daniel 7:9-14, 21-22, 12:2-4 Proverbs 30:4, 15:24 Psalms 5:4-5, 11:4, 7, 15:1-5, 29:9, 45:6-8, 50:1-4, 84:1-4, 10, 97:1-9, 104:1-4, 113:4-6, 115:16, 140:13, 1 Chronicles 16:27

New Testament – Luke 20:34-36 Matthew 19:14, 18:3, 10, 5:20, John 14:2-3 Revelation 4:1-11, 5:11-14

Glimpses of Heaven (2)

Old Testament – Genesis 28:12, 17, 2 Kings 2:1, 11, 1 Kings 22:19-23 Ezekiel 1:1-5, 22-28, 10:1-8, 17-22 Zechariah 6:1-8, 12-15 Job 22:12-14, 13:16 Psalms 18:6-16, 33:13-15, 68:1-2, 15-18, 89:6-8, 14, 110:1-2

New Testament – John 1:51 Ac 1:9-11, 7:55-56 Hebrews 1:1-14, 8:1-2 Revelations 20:11-15

Glimpses of Heaven (3)

Old Testament – Exodus 24:9-11 Deuteronomy 4:11-12, 15, 24, 33:2 Habakkuk 3:3-11, Isaiah 6:1-11, 33:14-17, 37:16, 57:15, 63:15, 64:1-2 Psalms 16:11, 20:6, 65:2, 4, 140:13, 1 Samuel 2:10

New Testament – Hebrews 11:9-16, 12:18-29 Revelation 5:1-9, 21:1-27, 22:1-7, 11-15

Glimpses of Heaven (4)

Old Testament – Zechariah 1:7-16, 2:1-5, 4:9-14 Ezekiel 8:1-6, 9:3-11, 40:1-4, 43:1-7, 10-12 Daniel 4:13-17, 34-35, Isaiah 40:22-26, 66:1-2 Psalms 144:5-7, 103:19-21, 50:2-7

New Testament – Revelation 3:12, 21, 7:9-17, 10:1-11, 11:1-2, 16-19, 14:6, 13, 20:11-15

Glimpses of Heaven (5)

Old Testament – Psalms 2:2-4, 18:6-16, 47:8, 57:2-3, 73: 25, 76:8-9, 80:14-19, 115:2-3, 123:1 Habakkuk 2:19-20 Micah 1:2-4 Jonah 2:7 Job 28:24-28 Nahum 1:6-9

New Testament – Luke 12:8-9, 15:10 Matthew 25:31-34 Acts 7: 48-49, 1 Peter 3:18, 22

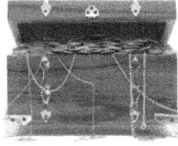

The Spirit of God

The Spirit of God (1)

"A new heart also will I give you, and a new spirit will I put within you: and I will take away the stoney heart... And I will put My Spirit within you, and cause you to walk in My statutes, and keep My judgements, and do them." (Ezekiel 36:26-27)

The Spirit of God (2)

"But if ye be led of the Spirit, ye are not under the law...But the fruit of the Spirit is love, joy, peace, longsuffering, gentleness, goodness, faith, Meekness, temperance: against such there is no law." (Galatians 5:18, 22-23)

The Spirit of God (3)

"And he that keepeth his commandments dwelleth in him, and he in him. And hereby we know that he abideth in us, by the Spirit which he hath given us. (1 John 3:24)

Discussion Questions

1. Discuss Genesis 1:2.
2. What observations are made in Romans 8:1-16?
3. Can we be children of God without having the Spirit of God? Explain.

4. What requirement is needed in order to obtain the Spirit of God according to Acts 2:38 and Acts 5:32?

5. Explain John 6:63.

Fill in the Blanks

1. "For we through the____ wait for the hope of____ by faith."
2. "Now if any man have not the____ of____ , he is none of his."
3. "The____ of____ hath made me, and the breath of the Almighty hath given me____ ."
4. "But God hath revealed them unto us by____ ____ : for the____ searcheth all things, yea, the____ ____ of God."
5. "Whither shall I go from thy____ ? or whither shall I flee from thy____ ?"

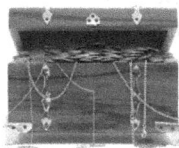

The Spirit of God

*T*his is a wonderful and fascinating study on the Spirit of God, showing how He works in all of God's creation.

The Spirit of God (1)

Old Testament – Genesis 1:2, 2:7 Job 33:4, 27:3-4, 26:13 Psalms 139:7-10,
104:29-31, Isaiah 40:12-13, 42:1, 44:3, 48:16, 59:19-21, 61:1-3 JoeL2:27-29,
Zechariah 12:10

*New Testament – Luke 4:16-20, John 3:5-6 Acts 2:16-1838, 5:32, 1 Corinthians
12:13 Romans 8:1-16 Jude 1:17-20*

The Spirit of God (2)

Old Testament – Genesis 41:38 Job 32:8 Daniel 5:11-14 Micah 3:8, 2
Chronicles 24:20 Ezekiel 11:5, 3:24-27, 2:2, 7

*New Testament – Act 6:3-5, 7:51-55, Matthew 10:19-20 John 7:38-39, 16:13-14,
20:21-22, 1 John 4:6-13, 1 Corinthians 2:4-16, 3:16, 12:3 Romans 15:13-16, 2
Corinthians 1:22, 5:5 Ephesians 5:9-10*

The Spirit of God (3)

Old Testament – Exodus 31:3, 35:31 Numbers 11:25, 27:18-21, 1 Samuel
10:6, 9-10, 16:13-14, Ezekiel 36:26-27 Psalms 51:9-11, 143:10 Micah 2:7,
Isaiah 11:1-4, 30:1, 32:15-18 Zechariah 4:6

New Testament – Luke 12:10-12, 1:13-15 John 16:7-8 Acts 1:1-2, 19:2-5, 1 Peter 1:9-12, 2 Peter 1:20-21, 1 John 3:24, 1 Corinthians 6:19

The Spirit of God (4)

Old Testament – 1 Kings 18:3-15, 46, 2 Kings 2:9-16, 2 Chronicles 15:1-2, 18:23-24, 20:14-15, Isaiah 63:11-14 Nehemiah 9:20 Ezekiel 39:25-29, 37:3-5, 9-14 Haggai 2:5

New Testament – Matthew 3:16-17 John 3:34, 6:63, 14:17, 26 Romans 5:1-5 Philippians 3:3 Galatians 3:1-5, 4:6, 1 Peter 3:18 Titus 3:3-6, 1 Timothy 3:16 Colossians 1:5-8

The Spirit of God (5)

Old Testament – Judges 3:9-10, 6:33-34, 11:29, 13:24-25, 14:5-6, 19, 15:14-17 Numbers 24:1-7, 2 Sa 23:1-4 Proverbs 1:23

New Testament – Luke 24:49 Acts 1:8, 8:14-17 Romans 8:22-27, 2 Corinthians 3:3-6, 17-18, 1 Corinthians 6:11, 17 Ephesians 4:3-4, 6:17 Galatians 5:5, 16-25 Revelation 2:7, 11, 17, 29, 22:17

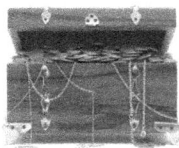

The Ways of the Lord

The Ways of the Lord (1)

"Wherefore I was grieved with that generation, and said, They do always err in their heart; and have not known My ways. So I sware in My wrath, They shall not enter into My rest." (Hebrews 3:10-11)

The Ways of the Lord (2)

"Let the wicked forsake his way and the unrighteous man his thoughts... For My thoughts are not your thoughts, neither your ways My ways... For as the heavens are higher than the earth, so are My ways higher than your ways, and My thoughts than your thoughts." (Isaiah 55:7-13)

The Ways of the Lord (3)

"And many people shall go and say, Come ye, and let us go up to the mountain of the LORD...and He will teach us His Ways, and we will walk in His paths: for out of Zion shall go forth the law, and the word of the LORD from Jerusalem." (Isaiah 2:3)

Discussion Questions

1. Explain Deuteronomy 32:4.
2. After a disciple is fully trained, who will he be like?
3. What was the problem noted in Hebrews 3:8-10?

4. Are God's thoughts and ways the same as our thoughts and ways? Discuss.
5. Explain Matthew 22:16.

Fill in the Blanks

1. "He is the____ , his work is perfect: for all his____ are judgment: a God of ____and without____ ____ , and____ is he."
2. "Talk no more so____ ; let not____ come out of your____ : for the Lord is a God of____ , and by him actions are____ ."
3. "O the depth of the riches both of the____ and____ of God! How____ are his____ , and his____ past finding out!"
4. "God is not a man, that he should; neither the son of man, that he should____ ."
5. "Be ye therefore____ of God, as dear____ ."

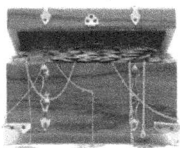

The Ways of the Lord

The Psalmist writes in Psalms 25:4-5, "Shew me thy ways, O Lord; teach me thy paths." As children of God, our hearts must be inclined to walk in the ways of God. This is indeed a much-needed study.

The Ways of the Lord (1)

Old Testament – Deuteronomy 32:4, 10:17-21, 7:9-10, 1 Samuel 2:3, 6-10 Job 35:6-14, 23:13, 9:4-16 Psalms 31:19, 23, 33:4-15, 34:7-9, 65:4-11 Micah 7:18-20, Isaiah 64:4-5, 63:7, 25:1

New Testament – Mark 10:18 Luke 6:35-36, 40 Matthew 7:11 James 1:17, 5:11 Hebrews 3:10-11

The Ways of the Lord (2)

Old Testament – Exodus 9:27, 2 Chronicles 12:6 Daniel 9:7-14 Lamentations 1:18 Je 12:1, 23:6 Habakkuk 1:13 Job 35:2-3, 8:3, 6, 4:17-21, Isaiah 54:17, 46:13, 45:22-25 Psalms 145:17, 132:9, 89:14, 34, 11:7, 7:9

New Testament – Romans 3:3, 21-23, 10:3-4, 2 Corinthians 5:21 Philippians 3:9, 2 Timothy 2:13

The Ways of the Lord (3)

Old Testament – Exodus 33:19, 34:5-8 Numbers 14:18 Nehemiah 9:13-17 Daniel 4:34-37 Joel 2:12-13 Zechariah 10:6, Isaiah 61:8, 55:7-13, 30:18

Jeremiah 32:17-19, 33:6 Lamentations 3:22 Zephaniah 3:5 Hosea 11:9-12, 1 Samuel 15:29 Psalms 31:5, 42:8, 145:8-9, 146:7-9

New Testament – 2 Corinthians 13:11 Philippians 4:9 Ephesians 1:11, 4:31-32, 1 John 4:8, 16

The Ways of the Lord (4)

Old Testament – Genesis 18:25 Job 34:10, 12, 2 Chronicles 19:7 Numbers 23:19 Deuteronomy 1:17, 4:23-24, 9:3 Exodus 14:3 Psalms 9:3-4, 16, 18:25-34, 39, 24:8, 45:3-4, 50:3-6, 92:12-15, 97:3

New Testament – Matthew 22:16 Hebrews 12:28-29, 10:26-27, 2 Timothy 2:12-13 Revelation 6:1-2, 19:11-16

The Ways of the Lord (5)

Old Testament – Deuteronomy 30:15-16, 28:9, 26:17, 11:22-25 Judges 2:21-22 Joshua 22:5, , Isaiah 2:2-3, 58:2-13 Psalms 25:20, 84:5, 85:13, 111:7-8, 119:1-3, 15, 128 Proverbs 10:29 Hosea 14:9

New Testament – Luke 1:76, Matthew 3:3 Acts 2:28, 13:6-10 Revelation 15:3

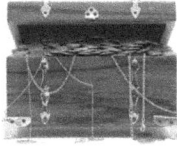

The Need for Correction

The Need for Correction (1)

"My son, despise not the chastening of the LORD; neither be weary of His correction:For whom the LORD loveth He correcth;...""Behold, happy is the man whom God correcteth: therefore despise not thou the chastening of the Almighty." (Pr 3:10-11 Job 5:17)

The Need for Correction (2)

"Woe to her that is filthy and polluted.. the oppressing city! She obeyed not the voice; she received not correction; she trusted not in the LORD; she drew not near to her God....every morning He bring His judgement to light, 1.. but the unjust knoweth no shame." (Zep 3:1-2, 5)

The Need for Correction (3)

"All scripture is given by inspiration of God, and is profitable for doctrine, for reproof, for correction, for instruction in righteousness." "As many as I love, I rebuke and chasten: be zealous therefore, and repent." (2 Tim 3:16 Rev 3:19)

Discussion Questions

1. Why do some despise chastisement or correction?
2. What is the reasoning for God's chastisement or correction?
3. Explain Hebrews 12:6-8.

4. Explain Psalms 119:67, 71, 75.
5. Explain Matthew 10:14-15.

Fill in the Blanks

1. "Before I was _____I went ____but____ have I kept thy____ ."
2. "Now no____ for the present seemeth to be joyous, but____ .
   Nevertheless____ it____ the____ fruit of____ unto them which
   are exercised thereby."
3. "But if ye be without_____ whereof all are_____ , then are
   ye____ and not sons."
4. "Oh Lord, are not____ ____ upon the truth? Thou hast____
   them but they have not____ , thou hast_____ them but they
   have____ to receive____ ; they made their faces than a , they
   have refused to ."
5. "I tell you, Nay, but except ye____ , ye shall all likewise____ ."

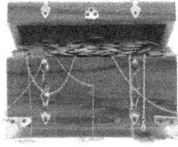

The Need for Correction

*W*e must recognize that we are not perfect and that we all fall short in many ways; in our thoughts, in our views, in our actions, and in our conversing one with another. We all stand in need of consistently being corrected by the Word of God as we strive to live the Christian life. In so doing, we grow to maturity and are made to become more and more like our Lord and Savior, Jesus Christ.

The Need for Correction (1)

Old Testament – Deuteronomy 8:5-6, 21:18-21, 2 Samuel 7:14 Psalms 38:1, 39:11, 94:10-13, 118:18, 119:67, 71, 75 Proverbs 1:30-32, 3:11-12, 10:17 Job 5:17 Jeremiah 30:11, 7:28, 5:3 Zephaniah 3:2

New Testament – Hebrews 12:5-11, 1 Corinthians 11:28-32, 2 Timothy 3:16-17

The Need for Correction (2)

Old Testament – 1 Samuel 2:22-25, 34 Exodus 32:33 Psalms 6:1, 78:37-39, 141:5 Jeremiah 10:24, 4:18 Lamentations 3:27-33, 39 Ezra 9:13-15, Isaiah 57:16-18 Zephaniah 3:2-8 Proverbs 6:23, 8:33, 15:5, 10, 31-33 Amos 5:10

New Testament – John 7:7 Matthew 22:29, 11:15-20, 10:34, 2 Thessalonians 3:14-15 Revelation 3:19

The Need for Correction (3)

Old Testament – Hosea 13:6-9 Jeremiah 6:8, 22:13-19, 32:31-33, 46:28 Job 11:5-6, 13:10-11, 22:3-4, 33:14-19, 34:31-33, 37:9-13 Habakkuk 1:12-13 Proverbs 19:25, 27, 29, 21:11, 27:22

New Testament – 2 Corinthians 10:5-6 Hebrews 2:1-3, 10:25-31 Titus 1:10-13

The Need for Correction (4)

Old Testament – Amos 4:4-12 Lamentations 3:1-3, 40-50 Hosea 5:9, 15, 7:1-2, 11:9-11 Psalms 60:1-3, 83:13-16, 88:7-13, 103:9-14 Proverbs 5:3-13, 7:4-5, 19-22, 19:18, 20, 22:15, 23:13-14, 29:15, 17

New Testament – Colossians 3:25 Romans 2:8-9, 19-24 Hebrews 12:25, 29, 2 Peter 2:21

The Need for Correction (5)

Old Testament – Ecclesiastes 7:5 Proverbs 1:5, 7, 9:7-9, 10:8, 13, 13:1, 14:9, 23:9, 24:7, 9, 25:12, 26:3-5, 29:1, 9 Psalms 32:8-9, 50:16-21, 89:30-32 Jeremiah 2:19-22, 13:10-14 Hosea 4:4-7

New Testament – Matthew 7:6, 10:14-15 John 9:41, 2 Corinthians 5:11 Acts 17:10-11, 22-32 Galatians 2:11-17 James 4:11, 15-17

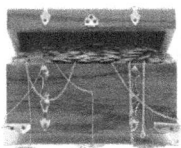

Troublesome Times

Troublesome Times (1)

"And at that time shall Michael stand up, the great prince for the children of thy people: and there shall be a time of trouble, such as never was...and at that time thy people shall be delivered, every one that shall be found written in the book." (DanieL12:1)

Troublesome Times (2)

"Know therefore and understand that from the going forth of the commandment to restore and to build Jerusalem unto the Messiah the Prince...the street shall be built again, and the wall even in troublous times. (Daniel 9:26)

Troublesome Times (3)

"Therefore the prudent shall keep silence in that time; for it is an evil time." (Amos 5:13)

Discussion Questions

1. Explain Genesis 18:20-33.
2. Explain Romans 1:18-32.
3. Is it in man to direct his own steps?
4. What happens to those that choose to live ungodly lives?

5. What are those that have named the name of Christ instructed to do in 2 Timothy 2:19?

Fill in the Blanks

1. "Nevertheless the____ of God standeth sure, having this, The Lord knoweth them that are his. And, Let everyone that____ the____ of Christ_____ from ____."
2. "The Lord also will be a____ for the oppressed, a refuge in____ of____ ."
3. "Save yourselves from this____ generation."
4. "And because _____shall_____ , the love of many shall____ ____ ."
5. "And delivered just____ , vexed with the____ ____ of the wicked."

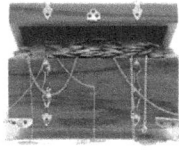

Troublesome Times

*W*hen God made the world, he made it very good (Genesis 1:31). God set man in paradise. However, when sin entered the world through Adam and Eve's transgressions, man's every imagination of the thoughts of his heart was only evil continually (Genesis 6:5). Thus, troublesome times are the direct outcome of man's waywardness and desire to do evil.

Troublesome Times (1)

Old Testament – Daniel 12:1-9 Job 3:26, 5:6-7, Jeremiah 14:8, 19, 30:7 Psalms 25:17, 22, 27:5, 37:39, 41:1, 46:1, 50:14 is 33:2, Proverbs 11:8, 12:13, 15:6, 16 Nahum 1:7

New Testaments 2 Corinthians 1:3-4, 2 Thessalonians 1:6-9, 2:1-2, Galatians 5:10-12, Hebrews 12:14-15

Troublesome Times (2)

Old Testament – Daniel 9:20-25, 11:35 Amos 6:1-3, 5:13, 4:9-12 Micah 2:1-3, Isaiah 10:1-3, 24:21-22, 57:1, 20-21 Job 31:14, 27:8-9, 15:20-24 Psalms 9:9, 10:1, 20:1-2, 22:11, 37:18-19, 59:16

New Testament – Matthew 24:3-14, 36-39, 16:2-4 John 17:14-16 Hebrews 11:35-40

Troublesome Times (3)

Old Testament – Deuteronomy 31:16-17, 21-22, 32:32-35, 2 Chronicles 15:3-6 Habakkuk 3:3-6, 10-16 Jeremiah 2:28-29, 8:12-15, 18:8-13, 23:12, 50:31, 51:6, 33, 78:33-34, 77:2-5, 60:11

New Testament – Acts 2:40, 3:19-21 Ephesians 5:15-16, 6:13, 1 John 5:18-19

Troublesome Times (4)

Old Testament – Exodus 32:20-35 Hosea 7:1-2, 9:7-9 Ezra 9:7, 13-15 Nehemiah 9:25-27, 32-33 Ezekiel 5:5-9, 7:1-7, 14:13-21 Zephaniah 1:12-15, Isaiah 17:9-14, 22:4-5, 26:16, 2 Chronicles 29:5-8 Psalms 107:6, 102:2, 88:1-3, 86:7

New Testament – John 16:33 Acts 14:22, 2 Corinthians 4:8-11, 7:5-6

Troublesome Times (5)

Old Testament – Genesis 47:7-8 Ecclesiates 12:1, 11:8, 9:12, 3:1-8, Isaiah 37:1-3, 15-17, 29 Job 38:22-23, 34:20, 3:17 Jeremiah 15:11 Psalms 13:2-4, 31:7-9, 69:15-17, 81:5-7, 91:14-15, 107:9- 13, 17-19, 24-22, 116:3-6, 138:7

New Testament – 2 Timothy 3:1, 12 Revelation 7:13-14, 2:9-10

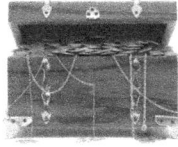

Honour

Honour (1)

"A son honoureth his father, and a servant his master: if then I be a father, where is mine honour? and if I be a master, where is My fear? saith the LORD of hosts unto you....for I am a great King, saith the LORD of hosts, and my name is dreadful among the heathen." (Malachi 1:6, 14)

Honour (2)

"But in a great house there are not only vessels of gold and of silver, but of wood and of earth; and some to honour, and some to dishonour. If a man purge himself from these, he shall be a vessel unto honour, sanctified ....and prepared unto every good work." (2 Timothy 2:20-21)

Honuor (3)

"The good man is perished out of the earth: and there is none upright among men:..The best of them is as a brier: ...For the son dishonoureth the father, the daughter riseth up against her mother...a man's enemies are the men of his own house." (Micah 7:2-6)

Discussion Questions

1. What command did King Ahasuerus give in Esther 1:20?
2. According to Psalms 26:8, where is the place where God's Honour dwelleth?

3. Explain Proverbs 3:9.
4. Explain 1 Peter 3:7?
5. Discuss Colossians 2:23.

Fill in the Blanks

1. _____thy father and thy mother: that thy days may be_____ upon the_____which The LORD thy God giveth thee.
2. I receive not _____ from _____.
3. How can ye believe, which receive _____one of another, and seek _____ the_____ that cometh from God _____?
4. Be kindly_____one to another with _____love; in_____ preferring one another.
5. Honour_____men. Love the_____, Fear God. Honour the_____.

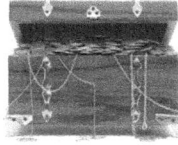

Honour

*I*n 1 Peter 2:17, the Bible states that we are to honour all men. We are obligated to give all men due respect and noble treatment. This is the code of conduct for the Christian.

Honour (1)

Old Testament – Exodus 14:4, 17-18 Ecclesiastes 6:1-2, 1 Samuel 2:29-30, 1 Chronicles 16:27-29, 29:11-13 Malachi 1:6-14 Proverbs 3:9, 14:31, 15:33, 18:12, 21:21 Psalms 15:1-4, 26:8, 66:2, 71:8

New Testament – John 5:23, 40-44, 12:26 Romans 12:10, 1 Peter 2:17

Honour (2)

Old Testament – Leviticus 19:32 Numbers 27:18-20 Exodus 20:12, 18:21, 1 Samuel 9:6, 15:28-30 Ecclesiastes 10:1 Proverbs 5:7-9, 26:1, 8 Lamentations 5:12, 4:16 Hosea 9:7-9 Micah 7:4, 6, Isaiah 1:2-4, 26, 9:14-16, 23:9, 58: 13

New Testament – Matthew 13:57, 15:4-6 John 8:48-49, 54 Acts 23:5, 2 Peter 2:10, 1 Timothy 5:17, 6:1

Honour (3)

Old Testament – Genesis 49:6 Numbers 22:37-38, 24:11-13 Leviticus 19:15, 2 Samuel 6:20-22, 23:15-19, 1 Chronicles 4:9-10, 11:20-25, 1 Kings 3:7-13, 2 Kings 5:1 Proverbs 27:18, 13:18 Psalms 149:9

New Testament – Luke 14:7-9 Acts 6:3, 5, 1 Corinthians 4:10, 15:41-43, 2 Timothy 2:19-21

Honour (4)

Old Testament – Deuteronomy 5:16, 21:18-21, 26:18-19 Judges 4:4-9, 9:8-15, 2 Chronicles 26:14-19 Nahum 3:8-10 Esther 1:15-21, 6:1-3, 8-9, 9;16-17 Proverbs 11:16, 25:2, 31:10-12, 23-25 Psalms 149:4, 9

New Testament – Acts 13:49-52, 1 Timothy 5:3-6 Ephesians 6:1-3, 5:25, 33 Hebrews 13:4

Honour (5)

Old Testament – Jeremiah 33:6-9, 15-16 Psalms 91:14-15, 111:1-3, 112:9, 145:3-5, Isaiah 42:21 Proverbs 3:13-16, 4:8, 8:14-18

New Testament – Romans 12:10, 1 Thessalonians 4:1-4 Hebrews 2:6-9, 3:3, 5:1-4, 2 Peter 1:16-17, 1 Timothy 1:17, 6:14-16 Revelation 4:11, 5:13, 19:7-9, 21:22-24

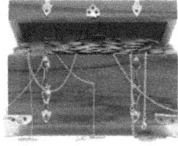

My Meditation

My Meditation (1)

"Blessed is the man that walketh not in the counsel of the ungodly, nor standeth in the way of sinners, nor sitteth in the seat of the scornful. But his delight is in the law of the LORD; and in His law doth he meditate day and night. (Psalm 1:1-2)

My Meditation (2)

"Till I come, give attendance to reading, to exhortation, to doctrine... Meditate upon these things; ...Take heed unto thyself, and unto the doctrine; continue in them: for in doing this thou shalt both save thyself, and them that hear thee. (1 Timothy 4:15-16)

My Meditation (3)

"I will meditate also of all thy work, and talk of thy doings." "I will meditate in thy precepts, and have respect unto thy ways." "Mine eyes prevent the night watches, that I might meditate in thy word."Psalms 77:12, 119:15, 148

Discussion Questions

1. Explain Exodus 24:63.
2. What was the command given to Timothy in 1 Timothy 4:15?
3. What transpires in Psalms 1:1-2?

4. What is pondered in Psalms 77:12?
5. What is meditated upon in Psalms 119:48, 78, 97?

Fill in the Blanks

1. "O how love I thy____! It is my____ all the day."
2. "____ upon these things; give thyself____ to them; that thy____ may appear to all."
3. "But his____ is in the law of the Lord; and in His law doth he ____day and night."
4. "And Isaac went out to____ in the field. . ."
5. "Finally, brethren, whatsoever things are , whatsoever things are , whatsoever things are ; whatsoever things are____ , whatsoever things are____ , whatsoever things are of ____ ____; if there be any____ , and if there be any , ____ on these things."

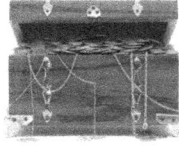

My Meditation

*M*editation is an essential part of Christianity. It allows us to muse on those things written in the pages of God's inspired Word. It invokes us to ponder, to reflect, to render deep thought and reasoning as we study to gain an understanding so that we may do God's will.

My Meditation (1)

Old Testament – Genesis 24:63 Ecclesiastes 1:12-17, 2:1, 11, 15-16, 7:13-14 Job 37:14 Psalms 1:1-2, 4:4, 5:1-3, 64:9, 77:6-12, 104:34, 119:15-16, 23, 95

New Testament – Luke 12:27-28 Philippians 4:8, 2 Corinthians 10:4-5, 2 Peter 1:10-13 Hebrews 10:32-35, 12:3-4

My Meditation (2)

Old Testament – Joshua 1:8, Deuteronomy 6:5-9, 11:18 Psalms 19:14, 37:30-31, 39:3-4, 119:78-80, 97-99, 148, 143:5 Micah 2:1 Jereremiah 4:1 Ezekiel 11:2-4, Pr 3:29, 14:22, 16:30

New Testament – Luke 2:18-19, 51, 6:45, 1 Timothy 4:6, 13-15

My Meditation (3)

Old Testament - Job 22:22 Proverbs 12:20, 15:28, 24:1-2 Ecclesiastes 1:16-18 Psalms 49:3, 11, 64:6-9, 78:1, 119:48, 59, 140:1-2, 141:4, 1 Chronicles 29:17-18 Hosea 7:2, 15, Isaiah 41:19-20, 26:3

New Testament – Hebrews 4:12, 10:16 Philippians 2:5, 1 Corinthians 2:16 Colossians 3:16

My Meditation (4)

Old Testament – Numbers 15:38-40 Deuteronomy 4:39, 8:5, 32:29 Haggai 1:5, 7 Job 34:24-27, 23:14-15, 1 Samuel 12:24 Psalms 8:3-4, 9, 13:2-3, 25:15, 63:5, 6, 123:2, 139:17 Proverbs 16:3, 21:5, 28:26

New Testament – Mark 7:21-22 Matthew 9:4 Romans 12:2, 8:5-8 Ephesians 4:22-23, 27

My Meditation (5)

Old Testament – Deuteronomy 17:18-19, 32:46-47, 1 Chronicles 16:15 Ecclesiastes 8:5-7, 9-13, 16-17, 7:25, 29 Psalms 119:34, 36, 111-112, 107:40-43, 105:39-45, 73:22-28 Proverbs 23:26, 22:17-18, 4:20-22, Isaiah 33:5-6, 17-18

New Testament – Luke 11:39, 12:21-22 Matthew 6:19-20 Colossians 3:2 Philippians 3:19-20

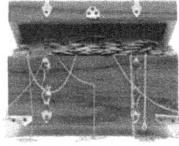

Power

Power (1)

"Ah Lord God! behold, thou hast made the heaven and the earth by thy great power and stretched out arm, and there is nothing too hard for thee:" "God hath spoken once; twice have I heard this; that power belongeth unto God." (Jeremiah 32:17, Psalm 62:11)

Power (2)

"Let every soul be subject unto the higher powers. For there is no power but of God: the powers that are ordained of God. Whosoever therefore resisteth the power, resisteth the ordinance of God: and they that resist shall receive to themselves damnation". (Romans 13:1-2)

Power (3)

"These words spake Jesus, and lifted up his eyes to heaven and said, Father, the hour is come; glorify thy Son, that thy Son also may glorify Thee: As thou hast given him power over all flesh, that he should give eternal life to as many as thou hast given him." (John 17:1-2)

Discussion Questions

1. Explain John 19:11.
2. Discuss 1 Chronicles 29:11-12.
3. Discuss Matthew 28:18.

4. Discuss Matthew 9:6-8.
5. Discuss Jeremiah 51:15-16.

Fill in the Blanks

1. "Both riches and honour come of thee, and thou reignest over all; and in thine hand is ____and____ .
2. "Who knoweth the____ of thine anger? even according to thy fear, so is thy wrath. 393 Power
3. "He giveth____ to the faint; and to them that have no____ he increaseth____ .
4. "And Jesus came and spake unto them, saying, All____ is given unto me in____ and in____ .
5. "The Lord is slow to____ , and great in____ , and will not acquit the____ .

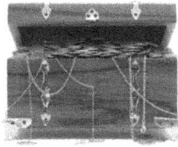

Power

*P*ower is translated from the Greek word *dunamis*. It references author-ity, might, dominance, control, and capability. God has all power, and He gives delegated authority to men.

Power (1)

Old Testament – 1 Chronicles 29:11-12, 2 Chronicles 20:6, 25:8, Isaiah 33:13, 40:26, 29 Jeremiah 27:5, 32:17 Job 24:22, 26:11-14, 36:22-33 Psalms 21:13, 62:11, 66:3-7, 90:11, 111:6, 145:11

New Testament – Romans 13:1-2, 1:16 Matthew 28:18 John 17:2, 10:18, 1:12

Power (2)

Old Testament – Genesis 32:24-28 Hosea 12:2-6 Deuteronomy 8:11-17 Ezra 8:22 Ecclesiastes 5:19, 6:1-2, 8:8 Job 26:23, 2 Samuel 22:33 Proverbs 3:27 Micah 2:1 Ps 37:35-36, 68:35

New Testament – John 19:10-11, 2 Corinthians 4:7, 12:9 Colossians 1:10-13, 2 Timothy 1:7-8, 2 Thessalonians 1:11 Ephesians 6:10, 1 Corinthians 4:19

Power (3)

Old Testament – Exodus 15:6 Deuteronomy 4:33-37, 32:34-36 Leviticus 26: 37-42, 2 Chronicles 20:12, 14:11, 2 Kings 19:24-26 Psalms 22:20, 49:14-15 Zechariah 4:6

New Testament – Luke 1:35, 4:14, 10:19, 22:69, 24:49 Mark 2:10, 11 Acts 1:8 Romans 1:4, 16, 15:13, 19, 16:25, 1 Corinthians 1:18, 24, 2:4, 1 Thessalonians 1:5 Ephesians 3:20

Power (4)

Old Testament – Nahum 1:3-6 Habakkuk 3:3-4 Micah 3:8 Psalms 59:16, 63:1-2, 79:11 NewTestament-Hebrews 1:1-3, 2:14, 6:4-6, 7:14-16 Philippians 3:10, 2 Corinthians 6:3-7, 13:4, 10, 1 Corinthians 6:12-14, 9:9-12, 18

New Testament – 1 Peter 1:3-5, 2 Peter 1:3, 16, 2 Timothy 3:1-5 Revelation 12:10-12

Power (5)

Old Testament – Proverbs 18:21 Leviticus 26:19-21 Jeremiah 15:15-16 Psalms 29:3-4, 106:7-8, 110:1-3, 147:3-5

New Testament – Matthew 22:29, 24:27-30 Ephesians 1:17-19, 2:1-2, 3:7 Acts 8:9-11, 26:15-18, 2 Thessalonians 2:6-10 Colossians 2:10, 1 Peter 3:22 Revelation 20:6

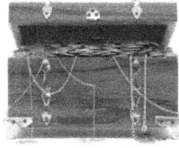

Light Versus Darkness

Light Versus Darkness (1)

"Unto the upright there ariseth light in the darkness: he is gracious, and full of compassion, and righteous." "The entrance of thy words giveth light; it giveth understanding unto the simple. (Psalm 112:4, 119:130)

Light Versus Darkness (2)

"For ye were sometimes darkness, but now are ye light in the Lord: walk as children of light:...And have no fellowship with the unfruitful works of darkness, but rather reprove them." (Eph 5:8, 11)

Light Versus Darkness (3)

"...God is light, and in Him is no darkness at all. If we say that we have fellowship with Him and walk in darkness, we lie...But if we walk in the light, as He is in the light, we have fellowship.." (1 John 1:5-7)

Discussion Questions

1. What is the relationship between the entrance of God's Word and light?
2. Who is the Light of the World?
3. If we walk in darkness, can we say we have fellowship with God? Explain.
4. Why are we to let our lights shine before others?

5. Who creates the light and makes the darkness?

Fill in the Blanks

1. "And this is the condemnation, that light is come into the____ , and men____ darkness rather than____ , because their deeds were____ ."

2. "Woe unto them that call evil____ , and good____ ; that put____ for light, and____ for darkness."

3. "If we say that we have____ with him and walk in____ , we lie, and do not the____ ."

4. "The way of the____ is as____ : they know not at what they____ ."

5. "And have no____ with the____ works of ____, but rather reprove them."

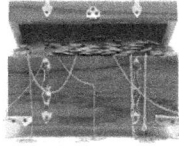

Light Versus Darkness

*T*hese two words are antipodal in nature—one illuminates, and the other dispels illumination. Spiritually, we use the following contrasts: good and evil, right and wrong, God and the Devil. We also learn of two spiritual realms engaged in warfare. The "children of light" are portrayed as those that walk in the light of God's Word or according to God's Word; the "children of darkness" are those who choose to walk contrary to His word.

Light Versus Darkness (1)

Old Testament – Ezekiel 1:4, 27-28, 10:4 Habakkuk 3:3-4, 10-11 Hosea 6:5, Isaiah 51:4, 45:7, 2:5 Proverbs 6:23 Psalms 36:9, 43:3, 97:11, 112:4, 119:105, 130

New Testament – Luke 1:79 John 1:4-9, 3:19-21, 12:35-36, 46, 1 John 1:5-7

Light Versus Darkness (2)

Old Testament – Ecclesiastes 6:3-4 Job 12:22-25, 18:5-6, 18, 21, 24:13-17, 29:2-3, Isaiah 5:20, 8:20, 59:7-10 Proverbs 2:11-13, 13:9, 20:20 Psalms 18:28, 27:1, 37:5-6

New Testament – Acts 26:18 John 8:12, 2 Corinthians 4:3-6 Romans 13:12

Light Versus Darkness (3)

Old Testament – Ecclesiastes 2:12-14, 11:7-8, 1 Samuel 2:9 Amos 5:18-20 Nahum 1:8, Isaiah 10:17, 50:10-11 Job 21:17 Psalms 49:18-19, 56:13, 74:20, 82:5

New Testament – Matthew 5:14-16 Luke 22:53, 2 Corinthians 6:14, 1 Thessalonians 5:4-5 Colossians 1:12-13 Ephesians 5:8-14

Light Versus Darkness (4)

Old Testament – Judges 5:31, 2 Samuel 23:34, 21:17, 1 Kings 11:36, 2 Kings 8:19 Proverbs 16:15 Amos 5:8, 4:13 Job 38:15-19 Psalms 89:15, 104:1-2, 107:9-14, Isaiah 9:2, 6

New Testament – Mt 4:16-17, 6:22-23 Ac 22:6-8 1 Tm 6:14-16

Light Versus Darkness (5)

Old Testament – Job 25:2-3, 33:27-30, 34:22, 37:19-22 Lamentations 3:2 Jeremiah 13:16-18, 31:35-36 Isaiah 42:6-7, 16, 58:6-10, 60:1-3, 18-20, 62:1-2 Psalms 4:6, 13:3 Proverbs 4:18-19

New Testament – 2 Peter 1:19, 1 John 2:8-11 Ephesians 4:17-18 Revelation 21:22-25

Truth

Truth (1)

"He is the Rock, His work is perfect: for all His ways are judgement: a God of truth and without iniquity, just and right is He." "Into thine Hand I commit my spirit...O LORD God of truth." (Deuteronomy 32:4, Psalms 31:5)

Truth (2)

"I have not written unto you because you know not the truth, but because ye know it.. no lie is of the truth." "God is a Spirit and they that worship Him must worship Him in Spirit and in Truth." "Sanctify them through thy truth, Thy word is truth." (1 John 2:21, John 4:4, 17:17)

Truth (3)

"I have chosen the way of truth: thy judgements have I laid before me." "Thou art near, O LORD; and all thy commandments are truth." "But I will shew thee that which is noted in the scripture of truth..." (Psalms 119:30, 151, Daniel 10:21)

Discussion Questions

1. Explain John 18:37-38.
2. Why is truth that which will make us free (John 8:31-32)?
3. What does it mean to err from the truth?

4. Why is God referred to as a God of truth in Deuteronomy 32:4?
5. Why is truth a prerequisite for worshipping God?

Fill in the Blanks

1. "God is a____: and they that him must him in____ and in____ ."
2. "Sanctify them through thy____: thy____ is____."
3. "Every one that is of the____ heareth my____ ."
4. "Seeing ye have purified your souls in____ the____ through the Spirit."
5. "Thy righteousness is an____ , and thy law is the____ ."

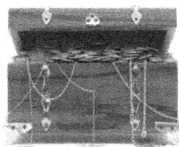

Truth

A lethia in the Greek is translated *truth* in English. This word entails not only the veracity of what is spoken, but also absolute certainty and reality—factual, without corruption, deceit, or pretense. The Bible defines *truth* as the Word of God (John 17:17).

Truth (1)

Old Testament – Deuteronomy 32:4 Exodus 34:5-6 Psalms 119:142, 160 , 96:11-13, 85:10-13, 61:6-7, 43:3, 31:5 Daniel 10:21 Hosea 4:1 Jeremiah 5:1, 9:3

New Testament – John 18:37-38, 17:17, 14:6, 16-17, 8:31-32, 1:1, 14, 17, 1 Corinthians 5:7-8, 1 John 5:6

Truth (2)

Old Testament – 1 Kings 2:1-4 Psalms 145:18, 119:29-32, 151, 111:7-8, 51:6, 40:9-11 Proverbs 8:6-7, 12: 17, 19, 22, 13:5

New Testament – John 8:43-45, 4:23-24, 3:20-21 Matthew 22:16 Acts 26:24-25, 2 Corinthians 4:1-2, 6:3-7 Galatians 2:14, 4:16, 1 Timothy 2:7, 3:15, 1 John 2:21-27

Truth (3)

Old Testament – Joshua 24:14, 1 Sa 12:24, 2 Kings 20:3-6 Psalms 25:5, 26:1-3, 33:4, 45:3-4, 54:3-5, 57:2-3, 10 Proverbs 16:6, Isaiah 26:2 Zephaniah 3:13

New Testament – Hebrews 10:26-27, 2 Thessalonians 2:7-12 Ephesians 4:14-15, 21, 25, 6:14-16

Truth (4)

Old Testament – Daniel 8:12, Isaiah 48:1, 59:13-15, 65:16 Jeremiah 4:2, 7:28 Zechariah 8:3, 15-19 Micah 6:9-13, 7:2-4, 19-20 Psalms 60:1-4, 69:13, 89:13-14 Proverbs 22:17-21

New Testament – 1 Peter 1:22-23 James 1:17, 3:14-15, 5:19-20 Titus 1:1-2, 10-14

Truth (5)

Old Testament – Daniel 4:37, 9:13, 2 Samuel 7:28 Exodus 18:21, 1 Kings 17:24 Proverbs 3:3, 20:28 , 23:23 Psalms 91:4, 100:5, 108:4, 138:2-4 Malachi 2:6

New Testament – Romans 1:18, 25, 1 Timothy 4:1-3, 6:3-5, 2 Timothy 2:15-18, 3:1-8, 4:1-4, 2 Corinthians 13:8, 2 Peter 1:10-12, 2:1-2

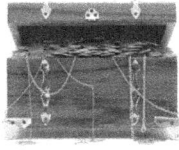

Snares

Snares (1)

"For man also knoweth not his time: as the fishes that are taken in an evil net, and as the birds that are caught in the snare; so are the sons of men snared in an evil time, when it falleth suddenly upon them." (Ec 9:12)

Snares (2)

"And the servant of the Lord must not strive: but be gentle unto all men, apt to teach, patient...And that they may recover themselves out of the snare of the devil, who are taken captive by him at his will." (2 Timothy 2:24-26)

Snares (3)

"Make no friendship with an angry man; and with a furious man thou shalt not go:Lest thou learn his ways, and get a snare to thy soul." (Proverbs 22:24-25)

Discussion Questions

1. What is the warning given in Exodus 23:33?
2. What entanglement is mentioned in Luke 9:62?
3. Explain Proverbs 6:1-5.
4. What are the hindrances described by Jesus in Matthew 13:19, 22? 147 Snares

5. Explain Proverbs 22:24-25.

Fill in the Blanks

1. "But they that will be rich fall into____ and a____ ."
2. "Moreover he must have a good____ of them which are without; lest he fall into____ and the____ of the_____ ."
3. "Let them alone: they be_____ leaders of the_____ . And if the lead_____ the_____ , both shall fall into the_____ ."
4. "The____ of____ was with my God; but the prophet is a____ of a_____ in all his ways, and____ in the house of his God."
5. "For I know this, that after my____ shall____ ____ enter in among you, not_____ the flock."

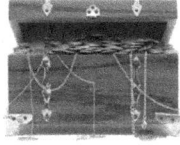

Snares

*I*n the Greek, the word *pagis* is translated "snares." It is defined as "a trap, that which entangles, holds fast, fastens, or impedes." Figuratively, it conveys that which binds and robs someone of their spiritual liberties or potential.

Snares (1)

Old Testament – Exodus 23:30-33, 34:11-12, Judges 2:1-4 Jeremiah 11:19 Psalms 7:14-16, 9:15-16, 10:2-13, 21:8-13, 140:5-8 Proverbs 1:10-19, 5:22-23, 12:13

New Testament – Luke 9:62, 20:20, 21:34-36, 1 Corinthians 10:12- 13, 1 Timothy 6:9-10 Hebrews 10:38-39

Snares (2)

Old Testament – Deuteronomy 7:16, 25 Joshua 23:11-13 Judges 8:27, 1 Samuel 18:20-21 Proverbs 28:10, 26:27, 22:5, 7:5-23, 6:1-6 Ecclesiastes 7:26, 10:8 Psalms 11:5-6, 36:1-4, 1 Chronicles 21:1-3, 7

New Testament – 1 Timothy 3:5-7, 2 Timothy 2:24-26 Ephesians 6:11 2 Corinthians 2:11 Romans 11:7-11

Snares (3)

Old Testament – Deuteronomy 12:29-30 Job 34:29-30, 18:5-10 Ecclesiastes 9:12 Proverbs 13:14, 20:25, 22:24-25, 29:6, 8, 25 Psalms 18:4-5, 37:7, 12-15, 38:12, 57:6, 119:85, 110 Jeremiah 18:22-23 Ezekiel 13:20-23

New Testament – Matthew 13:19-23, 6:13 Galatians 2:4-5, 5:7-9

Snares (4)

Old Testament – Daniel 6:1-9, 15-22, 2 Samuel 3:19, 25-27 Hosea 6:8-9, Isaiah 42:22, 29:20-21, 28:7, 13 Jeremiah 5:26-31, 11:19, 20:7-11, 48:42-44, 50:24 Lamentations 3:47-50 Amos 3:5-7 Psalms 41:5-6, 56:6, 62:4

New Testament – 2 Peter 3:16-17, 2:18-21 Ephesians 4:14, 17-21

Snares (5)

Old Testament – Job 5:12-16 Psalms 17:11-13, 35:7-8, 64:5-8, 124:6-7, 141:9-10, 142:1-4 Pr 24:15-16, 18:7, Isaiah 32:7, 24:17-18, 8:13-15 Ezekiel 12:13, 17:12-20 Hosea 9:7-8

New Testament – Matthew 7:15, 15:14, 23:13-15, 24:4-5, 24 Acts 20:29-31

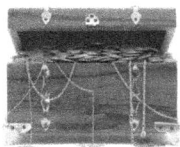

Life With Wings

Life With Wings (1)

"As an eagle stirreth up her nest, fluttereth over her young, spreadeth abroad her wings, taketh them on her wings: So the LORD alone did lead..Dt 32:11-12"

Life With Wings (2)

"But unto you that fear My name shall the Sun of righteousness arise with healing in his wing; and ye shall go forth, and grow up as calves of the stall." (Malachi 4:2)

Life With Wings (3)

"But they that wait upon the LORD shall renew their strength; they shall mount up with wings as eagles; they shall run, and not be weary; and they shall walk, and not faint. (Isaiah 40:31)

Discussion Questions

1. Where is the place of refuge found in Psalms 91:1-4?
2. Explain the imagery found in Deuteronomy 32:11-14.
3. What happens to those that fear God's name in Malachi 4:2?
4. What was the consequence for Jerusalem's rejection of Jesus in Matthew 23:37?
5. Discuss Revelation 12:14.

Fill in the Blanks

1. ...how often would I have gathered thy_____together, even as a ____gathereth Her chickens under her____, and ye would not!

2. And I said, Oh that I had____like a ____! for then would I fly away and be at rest.

3. The LORD_____thy work, and a full reward be given thee of the LORD God of _____, under whose _____ thou art come to trust.

4. And to the woman were given two ____ of a great ____, that she might fly into the Wilderness....

5. Our soul is _____ as a _____ out of the snare of the fowlers: the snare is broken, and We are escaped.

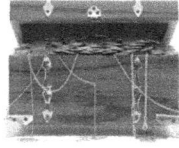

Life With Wings

"As an eagle stirreth up her nest, fluttereth over her young, spreadeth abroad her wings, taketh them, beareth them on her wings: So the LORD alone did lead him, and there was no strange god with him. He made him ride on the high places of the earth..." (Deuteronomy 32:11-13)

*W*hat wonderful and fascinating imagery that is portrayed. God alone was able to take His people to great heights, to ride on the high places of the earth. He bore them on the wings of an eagle. Metaphorically, eagles are noted as amazing, unique, and majestic birds that soar to high altitudes. When one is truly obedient to God, he will have high morals, high principles, high and noble endeavors. He will strive for excellence, he will reach for the sky in his dreams, visions and upright ways.

The psalmist writes in Psalms 18:35, "...thy right hand holden me up, and thy gentleness hath made me great." Life does not have to be lived in the doldrums of despair, self-pity, futility, or that which is base or vile. We can do much better than that through the God of heaven empowering us and directing us by His Word. We can soar, and we can live a life with wings—if we allow Him to lead us.

Life With Wings (1)

Old Testament – Deuteronomy 33:26-29, 32:11-14, 28:1-10, 4:7-9, 36-37
Exodus 19:4-6 Psalms 18:9-10, 27:5-6, 55:5-7, 61:1-4, 75:6-7, 102:6-7, 124:7
Ezekiel 17:2-14, Isaiah 38:14, 31:5

New Testament – Matthew 10:29-31, 23:37, 24:28

Life With Wings (2)

Old Testament – Malachi 4:2, Isaiah 40:29-31, 46:3-4, 9-11, 58:14, 60:8-9, 64:4 Psalms 11:1, 12:5, 18:47-48, 36:7, 68:13, 74:19-23, 84:3-5, 103:1-5

New Testament – Luke 12:24 Matthew 8:20 Mark 1:9-11 Ephesians 1:3, 17-21

Life With Wings (3)

Old Testament – Isaiah 10:14, 11:11-16, 16:2, 19:1, 34:8-15 Obadiah 1:3-4 Proverbs 23:4-5, 26:2, 27:8, 30, 30:17 Jeremiah 4:13, 8:7, 12:9, 17:11, 22:23, 48:28-30, 49:16, 22

New Testament – Revelation 12:14, 17, 14:6-7, 19:17-18

Life With Wings (4)

Old Testament – 2 Chronicles 3:10-13, 5:7-8, Isaiah 6:1-3, 8:8, 18:1, 57:15 Ruth 2:12 Lamentations 3:52-58, 2 Samuel 22:10-20 Hosea 9:8-11, 8:1, 7:11-12 Psalms 91:1-9, 139:9-17

New Testament – Luke 17:31-37, 1 Thessalonians 4:16-18 Revelation 18:2

Life With Wings (5)

Old Testament – Hosea 11:9-11 Job 39:13-18, 26-28, 28:7 Song of Solomon 5:2, 6:9 Psalms 104:1-3, 16-17, 63:7-8, 57:1, 17:8 Ecclesiastes 9:12, 10:20 Proverbs 6:1-5

New Testament – Matthew 13:31-32 Romans 1:20-23, 1 Corinthians 15:39

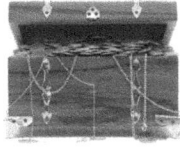

Comfort of the Scriptures

Comfort of the Scripture (1)

"...he expounded unto them in all the scriptures the things concerning himself...And they said to one another, Did not our heart burn within us...while he opened to us the scriptures?" (Luke 24:27, 32)

Comfort of the Scripture (2)

"This is my comfort in my affliction: for thy word hath quickened me..I remember thy judgements of old...and have comforted myself.""Unless thy law had been my delights, I should then have perished in mine affliction." (Psalms 119:50, 52, 92)

Comfort of the Scripture (3)

"For whatsoever things were written aforetime were written for our learning, that we through patience and comfort of the scriptures might have hope." (Romans 15:4)

Discussion Questions

1. Explain Zechariah 1:17.
2. What is conveyed in Romans 15:4?
3. What encouragement is given in Matthew 5:4?
4. Explain John 14:16-18.
5. What was the response in Luke 24:32?

Fill in the Blanks

1. "For whatsoever things were____ aforetime were_____ for our learning, that we through____ and____ of the____ might have ____."
2. "Comfort ye, ____ ye my____ , saith your God."
3. "Thy words have_____ him that was falling, and thou hast____ the feeble____ ."
4. "Blessed are they that____ : for they shall be_____ ."
5. "Walking in the____ of the Lord, and in the____ of the____ ____ , were multiplied."

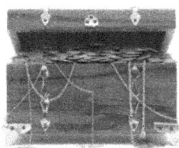

Comfort of the Scriptures

"This is my comfort in my affliction, for thy word hath quickened me" (Psalms 119:50).

*A*s we experience the vicissitudes of life, we must recognize that God has given us His Word as a source of strength and comfort for our very souls. His word refreshes us, restores us, and renews us so that we may continue to meet the challenges we face from day to day.

Comfort of the Scripture (1)

Old Testament – Zecharia 1:13, 17, Isaiah 64:4-5, 61:1-3, 10-11, 50:4-5, 8-11, 40:1-2, 21-31, 3:10-11 Psalms 22:24, 23:1-6, 30:5, 11, 85:8, 119:50, 52

New Testament – Luke 24:27, 32 Romans 15:4-5 Acts 15:30-31, 2 Corinthians 1:3-7, 7:4-7, 13

Comfort of the Scripture (2)

Old Testament – Job 29:2, 25, Isaiah 35:3-7, 43:1-8, 49:13-16, 51:1-12, 52:1-3, 9, 57:16-18, 66:10-13 Psalms 137:1-6, 119:76-82, 92, 107, 175, 102:13-21, 48:11 Daniel 10:10-11, 21

New Testament – 2 Timothy 3:16-17, 1 Thessalonians 5:9-11, 4:13-18, 2:11

Comfort of the Scripture (3)

Old Testament – Job 2:11, 6:8-10, 16:2-7, 21:34, 23:1-7, 12, 42:10-12 Psalms 71:19-21, 77:1-6, 86:17, 94:19, 119:111, 114-118, 143, 161-170 Jeremiah 8:18, 15:16

New Testament – Matthew 5:1-4, 9:22 Acts 9:31 Philippians 2:1-2 Colossians 4:7-8

Comfort of the Scripture (4)

Old Testament – Ezekiel 20:11, 21, 14:20-23 Job 15:11-13, 11:14-20 Jeremiah 6:10 Proverbs 13:13 Psalms 103:13, 119:14-16, 24, 35, 47-48, 70, 72, 147:15-20 Isaiah 12:1, 54:9-17

New Testament – John 7:38, 10:35, 14:15-18 James 2:8-9, 1 Corinthians 10:5-11

Comfort of the Scripture (5)

Old Testament – 1 Chronicles 7:22-23, 19:1-8, 19 Job 5:6-16, 7:13-15, 22:21-26 Psalms 1:1-2, 4:3-8, 56:10-11, 80:17-18, 119:25, 40, 88, 93, 154, 159

New Testament – John 6:63 Mark 12:10-11 Acts 18:24-28 Romans 16:25-26

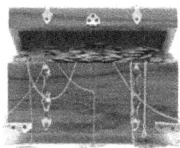

Voice of Pride

Voice of Pride (1)

"The pride of thine heart hath deceived thee...that saith in his heart, Who shall bring me down to the ground? Though thy exalt thyself as the eagle and though thou set thy nest among the stars, thence will I bring thee down, saith the LORD.Obad 1:3-4

Voice of Pride (2)

"Love not the world. neither the things in the world. If any man love the world, the love of the Father is not in him. For all that is in the world is the lust of the flesh.. lust of the eyes...pride of life" (1 Jn 2:15-16)

Voice of Pride (3)

"A man's pride shall bring him low: but honor shall uphold the humble in spirit." "Pride goeth before destruction, and an haughty spirit before a fall." "Only by pride cometh contention:.." "When pride cometh, then cometh shame :.." (Prov 29:23, 16:18, 13:10, 11:2)

Discussion Questions

1. What observations are made in Isaiah 47:7:10?
2. Discuss Proverbs 16:18.
3. What message is being conveyed in Luke 14:8-11?
4. Discuss Job 41:15-34

5. Explain 1 Corinthians 4:6-7.

Fill in the Blanks

1. "We have heard of the____ of Moab; he is very____ : even of his haughtiness, and his____ , and his____ : but his____ shall not be so."
2. "And whosoever shall____ ____ shall be abased; and he that shall____ ____ shall be exalted."
3. "Knowledge____ up, but charity____ ."
4. "For all that is in the____ , the lust of the____ , and the lust of the____ , and the____ of life, is not of the Father, but is of the world."
5. "O God, the____ are risen against me, and the____ of violent men have sought after my____ ; and have not set____ before them."

Voice of Pride

P ride has a distinctive voice. There is self-exaltation in its tone. There are enunciations of disdain. There is the pointing of the finger in disgust. There is malice in the heart. And there is the condemnation of others that do not meet their self-excogitated standards.

Voice of Pride (1)

Old Testament – Obadiah 1:1-4, 12, Isaiah 10:12-16, 33, 14:13-19, 25:10-12, 28:1-3, 47:7-10 Ezekiel 7:10, 16:49-50, 56, 28:2-9, 30:6, 31:10-18 Daniel 4:29-37 Proverbs 16:18, 14:3 Psalms 10:2-7, 59:12, 94:2

New Testament – Matthew 23:12 Luke 1:50-52, 14:8-11

Voice of Pride (2)

Old Testament – Exodus 5:2 Nehemiah 9:10 Deuteronomy 8:11-17 Daniel 5:18-30, Isaiah 2:9-17, 9:8-11, 13:11, 16:6-7, 23:9, 51:22-23, 1 Samuel 2:3 Proverbs 6:16-19, 11:2, 18:12, 21:4, 24, 29:23 Psalms 119:21, 86:14, 36:11-12

New Testament – 1 John 2:16, 1 Timothy 3:6, 2 Thessalonians 2:4 Galatians 6:3

Voice of Pride (3)

Old Testament – Leviticus 26:19, 2 Kings 14:8-15 Ezekiel 35:13-15, Isaiah 3:16-26 Job 35:12, 38:15, 41:15, 24, 34 Psalms 123:4, 73:5-19, 40:4, 31:18-20, 17:10 Proverbs 6:16-19, 8:13, 13:10, 15:25, 16:5

New Testament – John 7:8 Galatians 2:6 Acts 5:36, 12:21-23

Voice of Pride (4)

Old Testament – Habakkuk 2:4-10, Isaiah 3:5, 9, 5:8, 14-16, 21 Hosea 5:3-5, 7:8-10 Zephaniah 2:10-15, 3:11 Zechariah 9:6, 10:11, 11:3 Job 33:14-17, 40:2, 11-12 Proverbs 28:25 Psalms 119:51, 69, 78, 85, 122

New Testament – 1 Timothy 6:3-5, 2 Timothy 3:2-5 Romans 1:29-30 James 4:6

Voice of Pride (5)

Old Testament – 1 Kings 20:1-11, 28, 2 Kings 18:19-23, 29-35, 19:22-28, Isaiah 31:1-3, 22:16-19 Jeremiah 50:29-32, 48:26, 29, 42, 13:15-18, 9:23-24 Exodus 18:11 Psalms 138:6, 101:5, 18:27 Malachi 3:13-15, 4:1

New Testament – 1 Peter 5:5, 1 Corinthians 8:1-3, 4:6-7, 18-19

A Worthy Manner

A Worthy Manner (1)

"And ye shall not walk in the manners of the nation, which I cast out before you..." "That ye might walk worthy of the Lord unto all pleasing, being fruitful in every good work and increasing in the knowledge of God. (Lev 20:23, Colossians 1:10)

A Worthy Manner (2)

"Do not they blaspheme that worthy name by the which you are called." "...But behold, there cometh one after me, whose shoes of his feet, I am not worthy to loose." (James 2:7, Acts 13:25)

A Worthy Manner (3)

"I therefore...beseech you that ye walk worthy of the vocation wherewith ye are called, .. "...which is a manifest token of the righteous judgement of God, that ye may be counted worthy of the kingdom of God, for which ye also suffer. (Eph 4:1, 2 Thess 1:5)

Discussion Questions

1. Discuss Matthew 10:13.
2. Why did Peter and the apostles rejoice in Acts 5:41?
3. Explain Acts 13:46.

4. According to 1 Corinthians 11:27-32, what happens if communion is taken in a unworthy manner?
5. Explain Luke 3:8.

Fill in the Blanks

1. I will call upon the ____, who is _____ to be praised: so I shall be save from my enemies.
2. And into whatsoever city or town ye shall enter, enquire who in it is _____: and There _____ till ye go thence.
3. He that loveth father or mother more than me is not _____ of me: and he that loveth son or daughter more than me is not _____ of me.
4. And he that taketh not his _____, and followeth after me is not _____ of me.
5. Thou art _____, O Lord, to receive glory and honour and power: for thou hast created all things, and for thy pleasure they are and were created.

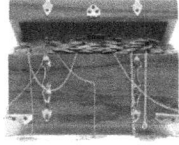

A Worthy Manner

*I*n Colossians 1:10, the apostle Paul writes, "That ye might walk worthy of the Lord unto all pleasing, being fruitful in every good work, and increasing in the knowledge of God."

This is an admonition for all Christians as they strive to find acceptance before the Lord. To whom much is given, much is required. May we never take lightly or insignificantly all the blessings bestowed upon us by our Lord and Savior, Jesus Christ. Let us strive wholeheartedly in doing His will. Let us always remember that He died for us, that we may live for Him.

A Worthy Manner (1)

Old Testament – Genesis 32:9-10 Leviticus 10:3, 10, 20:22-23 Numbers 15:14-16 Ruth 4:1-7, 11, 14, 1 Samuel 2:30 Psalms 18:3, 29:2 Malachi 1:6, 11-14

New Testament – Luke 3:7-8, 7:1-10, 9:52-56, 21:36, 1 Peter 3:4-5 Acts 13:44-46 Ephesians 4:1-2 Colossians 1:9-10.

A Worthy Manner (2)

Old Testament – Leviticus 10:12-13 Numbers 28:1-2, 1 Chronicles 13:1-12, 15:11-13, 16:27-29 Psalms 68:29, 72:10-11, 76:11, 93:5, 96:8-9

New Testament – Matthew 10:37-38, 22:1-13 Luke 15:11-19, 22, 32, 20:34-35, 1 Corinthians 5:8 Revelation 3:4, 4:11, 5:11-12

A Worthy Manner (3)

Old Testament – Genesis 17:1 Deuteronomy 18:9-13, 10:18 Ezekiel 44:23, 22:26, 11:9-12 Proverbs 15:8-9

New Testament – Philippians 1:27, 2 Timothy 2:19-21 Ephesians 5:3-12 Romans 1:28-32, 8:18 Hebrews 10:28-29, 1 Corinthians 11:26-29 James 2:7, 1 Thessalonians 2:10-12, 2 Thessalonians 1:11-12 Titus 2:1-3

A Worthy Manner (4)

Old Testament – Exodus 14:4, 17-18, 19:22 Leviticus 26:11-16, 27-28, 40-42, 1 Samuel 15:11, 22-26, 2 Samuel 12:14 Nehemiah 5:1-9 Psalms 50:8-23, 18:25-26 Proverbs 21:3

New Testament – Matthew 3:4-8, 11 Acts 5:38-41, 1 Peter 4:13-16 Hebrews 11:35-38, 1 Timothy 6:1

A Worthy Manner (5)

Old Testament – Numbers 28:2, 6 Leviticus 3:5 Ezra 6:7, 10, 2 Samuel 24:22-24, Isaiah 43:21-24 Jeremiah 6:20, 7:1-12, 23 Hosea 6:6 Psalms 51:16-17, 40:6-9 Ezra 20:40-41, 44:5-9

New Testament – Hebrews 3:1-3, 10:6-12, 12:22-29, 2 Corinthians 2:15-16 Philippians 4:18 Revelation 16:5-6

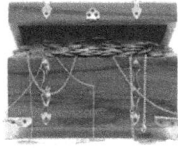

A People of Renown

A People of Renown (1)

"For thou art a holy people unto the LORD thy God, and the LORD hath chosen thee to ne a peculiar people unto Himself, above all the nations that are upon the earth." (Deut 14:2)

A People of Renown (2)

"And the LORD hast avouched thee this day to be His peculiar people... And to make thee high above all nations which He hath made, in praise, and in His name and in honor and that thou mayest be an holy people unto the LORD thy God... (Dt 26:18-19)

A People of Renown (3)

"But ye are a chosen generation, a royal priesthood, an holy nation, a peculiar people; that ye should shew forth the praises of him who hath called you out of darkness into his marvelous light;(1 Peter 2:9)

Discussion Questions

1. What is meant by His workmanship as noted in Ephesians 2:10?
2. Explain Deuteronomy 4:5-8.
3. What does it mean to be part of a holy priesthood?
4. Explain Titus 2:14.

5. Who will we be like, as mentioned, in 1 John 3:2?

Fill in the Blanks

1. "And hath made us____ and____ unto____ and His____ ; to him be and for ever and ever."
2. "For thou art an____ people unto the____ thy____ : The Lord thy God hath chosen thee to be a____ people unto himself, above all_____ that are upon the____ of the____ ."
3. "Ye also, as lively stones, are built up a____ ____ , an____ ____ to offer up____ ____ , acceptable to____ by Jesus Christ."
4. "Who gave himself for us, that he might redeem us from all____ , and purify unto himself a____ ____ , zealous of____ ____ ."
5. "And every man that hath this____ in him____ himself, even as he is____ ."

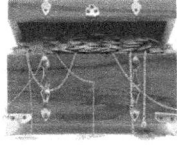

A People of Renown

G od has always had the highest and noblest of intentions for His people. His desire is that we be lights to the world. People will observe that we are a peculiar people. We walk in His ways. We possess the divine attributes of love, kindness, honesty, faithfulness, wisdom, loyalty, and integrity. These remarkable characteristics should abound among those who name the name of Christ.

A People of Renown (1)

Old Testament – Genesis 17:7-9 Deuteronomy 4:5-8, 20, 7:6-9, 10:12-15, 14:2, 26:15-19, 28:7-14, 29:9-13 Hosea 2:19-23 Jeremiah 2:3 Psalms 92:13, 111:6-10, 135:4-7

New Testament – Revelation 1:6 Ephesians 2:10, 5:8-10, 1 Peter 2:4-12, 1 Corinthians 3:9, 16 Philippians 2:15

A People of Renown (2)

Old Testament – Exodus 6:6-7, 15:13-18, 19:3-6 Leviticus 11:45, 26:12-13, 2 Sa 7:23-24 Numbers 22:12 Joshua 2:9-11, Isaiah 35:8-10, 43:1-7, 19-21, 54:17 Psalms 105:5-15, 43-45 Zechariah 2:8

New Testament – Romans 2:28-29, 11:1-24 Ephesians 1:3-7 Titus 2:14, 3:3-8

A People of Renown (3)

Old Testament – Genesis 35:10-11 Deuteronomy 4:32-37, 6:17-18, 32:10-14, 33:1-3, 26-29 Numbers 6:24-27, 23:19-24 Psalms 33:12-19, 68:33-35

New Testament – John 10:27-28, 15:16, 19 Luke 1:17 Acts 15:14 James 2:5, 1 Peter 1:14-22 Revelation 5:10, 7:9-17

A People of Renown (4)

Old Testament – Ezekiel 16:7-14, 34:23-29, 36:23-28, 37:22-27, Isaiah 62:1-5, 12, 61:6-11, 51:4, 16, 28:5-6 Jeremiah 24:6-7, 31:31-33, 32:37-41

New Testament – John 11:49-52, 17:6-26, 2 Corinthians 11:2, Ephesians 1:10-14, 2 Thessalonians 2:13 Revelation 21:2-3

A People of Renown (5)

Old Testament – Genesis 12:1-3, 46:1-3 Exodus 13:14-17 Leviticus 20:26, 1 Chronicles 16:19-22, 17:21-22, 1 Kings 3:8-9, Isaiah 44:23, 55:5, 60:21 Ezekiel 39:7, 13 Daniel 9:15 Psalms 3:8, 28:9

New Testament – Matthew 5:13-14, 1 Corinthians 3:9-10, 16-17 Romans 9:25-26, 8:1, 9, 14-17

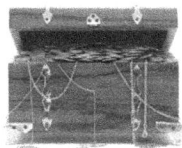

Endurance

Endurance (1)

"For His anger endureth but a moment; in His favour is life: weeping may endure for a night, but joy cometh in the morning." (Psalm 30:5)

Endurance (2)

"Behold, we count them happy which endure. Ye have heard of the patience of Job, and have seen the end of the Lord..." "In your patience possess ye your souls." (James 5:11, Luke 21:19)

Endurance (3)

"For whom the Lord loveth He chasteneth, and scourgeth every son whom He receiveth. If ye endure chastening, God dealeth with you as sons..." (Heb 12:6-7)

Discussion Questions

1. Explain Matthew 24:12-13.
2. What problem existed concerning endurance in Mark 4:17?
3. Discuss Mark 13:13.
4. What did the Apostle Paul commend the Thessalonians for, in 1 Thessalonians 1:4?
5. What instructions did Paul give Timothy in 2 Timothy 2:3?

Fill in the Blanks

1. Thou therefore _____ hardness, as a good _____ of Jesus Christ.
2. Therefore I ____ all things for the _____ sakes, that they may obtain the salvation which is in Christ Jesus with eternal glory.
3. For the time will come when they will not ____ sound _____; but after their own lusts shall they heap to themselves teachers, having itching ears;
4. But watch thou in all things, ____ afflictions, do the work of an evangelist, make full proof of thy ministry.
5. If ye ____ chastening, God dealeth with you as sons; for what son is he whom the father chasteneth not?

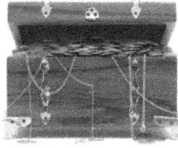

Endurance

"My bone cleaveth to my skin and to my flesh, and I am escaped with the skin of my teeth." (Job 19:20).

*P*erhaps this is a most graphic illustration of what endurance means. Whatever challenge, whatever adversity, whatever trial, whatever impediment, struggle, difficulty, or unmitigated circumstance should be met by faith, unwavering resolve, relentlessness, and tenacity.

The psalmist writes "...for thou hast considered my trouble; thou hast known my soul in adversities" (Psalm 31:7). Endurance in the face of travail, sometimes, can be used as a measure of the depth of loyalty and devotion.

Endurance (1)

Old Testament – Job 6:11-12, 17:9, 27:3-6 Esther 8:6 Proverbs 10:3, 24:10, 27:24 Ezekiel 21:6-7, 15, 22:14 Psalms 9:7-9, 30:5, 72:1-7, 111:3, 112:1-9 Malachi 3:13-18

New Testament – Matthew 10:22, 24:12-13, 1 Corinthians 10:13 Acts 14:22 James 5:11, 1:12

Endurance (2)

Old Testament – Numbers 21:4-5, 11:11-17 Exodus 18:18-23 Job 31:23, 13:15 Psalms 107:23-30, 119: 160, 135:13, 138:7-8, 145:11-13

New Testament – John 6:27 Mark 4:14-17 Luke 21:19 Galatians 6:9 Hebrews 12:1-3, 10:32-37, 6:11-15, 2 Timothy 2:3

Endurance (3)

Old Testament – Ecclesiastes 9:11 Job 1:6-12, 20-22, 2:1-6, 9-10, 16:6-16, 19:8-20, 26-27, 23:10-12 Psalms 16:8, 17:3, 5, 19:9-10, 26:1, 136:1-4, Isaiah 42:1-4

New Testament – Hebrews 12:5-11, 1 Peter 2:19-21, 1:25, 2 Timothy 4:2-5, 2 Thessalonians 1:4-5

Endurance (4)

Old Testament – Genesis 49:19, 32:24-28 Jeremiah 20:8-11, 15:20, 12:5, 1:19, Isaiah 40:29-31, 50:6-7, 1 Samuel 2:9 Ezekiel 2:6, 3:8-9 Psalms 52:1, 89:29, 100:5, 102:8-12, 104:31

New Testament – 2 Corinthians 1:5-6, 4:1, 8-17, 11:24-30, 12:10, 2 Timothy 2:10

Endurance (5)

Old Testament – Genesis 49:14-15 Job 7:1-2, 13-15, 20, 6:8-10, 30, 5:6-8, 19 Psalms 119:80-81, 87, 92, 101-102, 109, 157, 111:10

New Testament – Luke 18:1, 1 Corinthians 9:12 Romans 2:7-8, 9:22-23 Hebrews 3:5-6, 4:14, 6:6, 10:23 Revelation 2:1-3, 3:8, 11

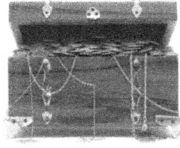

Hidden

Hidden (1)

"...I thank thee, O Father, Lord of heaven and earth, because thou hast hid these things from the wise and prudent, and hast revealed them unto babes. (Mt 11:25)

Hidden (2)

"Again, the kingdom of heaven is like unto treasure hid in a field; the which when a man hath found, he hideth, and for joy thereof goeth and selleth all that he hath, and buyeth that field." (Matt 13:44)

Hidden (3)

"Behold the LORD's hand is not shortened, that it cannot save; neither his ear heavy, that it cannot hear: But your iniquities have separated between you and your God, and your sins have hid His face from you, that He will not hear." (Isaiah 59:1-2)

Discussion Questions

1. Discuss Proverbs 28:12.
2. What are your thoughts concerning the question asked in Psalm 13:1?
3. Explain Psalm 27:5.
4. What is suggested in Isaiah 26:20?

5. Explain James 5:20.

Fill in the Blanks

1. For thou hast ___ their _____ from understanding: therefore shalt thou not exalt them.
2. Lord, all my desire is before thee; and my _____ is not ___ from thee.
3. Thy ____ have I ___ in my heart, that I might not sin against thee.
4. But if our _____ be ___, it is ___ to them that are lost:
5. For ye are ____, and your life is ___ with Christ in God.

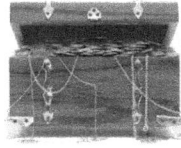

Hidden

*T*he Prophet Isaiah wrote in Isaiah 45:15, "Verily thou art a God that hidest thyself, O God of Israel, the Saviour."

> "And, behold, the LORD passed by, and a great and strong wind rent the mountains, and brake in pieces the rocks before the LORD; but the LORD was not in the wind: and after the wind an earthquake; but the LORD was not in the earthquake: and after the earthquake a fire; but the LORD was not in the fire: and after the fire a small still voice. And it was so. And behold came a voice unto him, and said, 'What doest thou here, Elijah?'" (1 Kings 19:11-13).

Our God is real. Our God is alive. Yet He hides Himself in plain view. We see His works, and we see His creation—but how many of us see Him? Perhaps if we listen to carefully and observe closely the life of Christ and the words of Christ, we can see, know, and understand God (John 14:8-13).

Hidden (1)

Old Testament – Ecclesiastes 1:13, 3:11, 7:13, 23-24, 8:16-17, 11:5 Job 5:8-16, 11:7-12, 23:8-9, 37:23-24 Psalms 147:5, 145:3, 139:5-6, 92:5, 36:6, 10:1-5, Isaiah 45:15

New Testament – Matthew 11:25, 1 Corinthians 2:6-11, 4:5, 1 Peter 1:10-12 Romans 11:33

Hidden (2)

Old Testament – Deuteronomy 29:29 Daniel 2:20-22, 47, Job 12:22, 26:6, 36:24-26 Jeremiah 23:24, 16:17, Isaiah 40:27-28, 29:14-15, 8:17 Ezekiel 39:25-29 Psalms 13:1-3, 25:14, 27:9, 30:7, 37:12-13, 51:9-12 Micah 3:4

New Testament – 2 Corinthians 4:2-6 James 5:20 Ephesians 3:4-9

Hidden (3)

Old Testament – Deuteronomy 31:15-18 Psalms 89:46, 88:14-18, 69:14-17, 55:1, 44:24-26 Habakkuk 1:2-4, 13 Zephaniah 2:1-3, Isaiah 64:6-7, 59:1-2, 57:16-17, 54:6-8, 1:15 Lamentations 3:55-56

New Testament – Luke 19:41-42, 9:43-45, 1 Timothy 5:24-25 Hebrews 4:12-13

Hidden (4)

Old Testament – Deuteronomy 30:11-13, 33:18-19 Job 15:8-11, 20, 17:2-4, 24:1-6, 28:11-23, 29:2-4, 9-25 Proverbs 3:32, 28:12 Hosea 13:12-14 Psalms 17:13-15, 32:5-7, 40:10, 51:6, 119: 11, 19

New Testament – Matthew 13:44 Romans 16:25-26 Colossians 1:26, 2:2-3 Ephesians 1:9

Hidden (5)

Old Testament – Job 10:12-13 Amos 3:4-8, 9:1-3 Obadiah 1:6-8 Psalms 17:8, 27:5, 31:20, 64:2-5, 119:114, 143:9, Isaiah 2:10, 26:20, 32:2

New Testament – Mark 4:22 John 18:20 Matthew 13:17, 35 Ephesians 3:3-5, 9, 6:18-19 Colossians 4:3, 1 Peter 3:1-4, Revelation 2:17

Healing the Hurt

Healing the Hurt (1)

"In the day of my trouble I sought the Lord: my sore ran in the night, and ceased not: my soul refused to be comforted." "Oh LORD my God, I cried unto thee and thou hast healed me." (Psalms 77:2, Psalms 30:2)

Healing the Hurt (2)

"I said, LORD, be merciful unto me: heal my soul; for I have sinned against thee..All that hate me whisper together against me; against me do they devise my hurt." "Heal me, O LORD, and I shall be healed; save me and I shall be saved:... (Psalms 41:4, 7 Jeremiah 17:14)

Healing the Hurt (3)

"Confess your faults one to another, and pray for one another that ye may be healed. The effectual fervent prayer of a righteous man availeth much. (James 5:16)

Discussion Questions

1. In Psalms 147:2-3, who builds up, who gathers the outcasts, who heals the brokenhearted, and who binds up their wounds?
2. Explain Romans 8:28.
3. What invitation did Jesus give in Matthew 11:28-30?

4. Explain Philippians 4:4-7.
5. What does it mean to "rely on God "?

Fill in the Blanks

1. "Heal me, O Lord, and I____ be____ ; save me, and I__ be____ : for thou art my praise."
2. "Blessed be God, even the Father of our Lord Jesus Christ, the Father of____ , and God of____ ____ ."
3. "Moreover the light of the moon shall be as the light of the sun... In the day that the Lord____ up the____ of His people, and ____the stroke of their____."
4. "I can do all through____ which____ me."
5. "Is it nothing to you, all ye that pass by? behold, and see if there be any____ like unto my____."

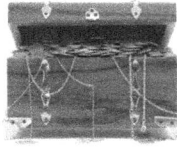

Healing the Hurt

I venture to say that there is a vast multitude of people who struggle within and without with hurts, pains, sorrows, loneliness, and vexations of both heart and spirit. They stand in need of someone who would heal, comfort, strengthen, and restore them. This can truly come only from the God of all comforts (2 Corinthians 1:3-5).

Healing the Hurt (1)

Old Testament – Psalms 147:2-3, 109:21-26, 107:13-20, 84:11, 34:17-22 Exodus 15:22-26 Jeremiah 6:7-8, 14 Malachi 4:2-3 Ecclesiastes 11:10 Proverbs 17:22, 14:10, 12:25, Isaiah 35:1-7

New Testament – Matthew 11:28-30, 12:15 Luke 4:18, Philippians 4:6-7

Healing the Hurt (2)

Old Testament – Genesis 26:28-29, 31:7 Joshua 24:20 Deuteronomy 32:36-40 Proverbs 20:30, 27:6 Job 35:8 Psalms 141:5, 119:67, 75 Jeremiah 10:19, 24, 15:18-21, 30:9-17, Isaiah 53:4-6 Zechariah 13:6

New Testament – Luke 4:23 Acts 10:38, 5:14-16 James 5:16, 1 Peter 2:21-24

Healing the Hurt (3)

Old Testament – Jeremiah 8:9-11, 18-22, 14:19, 33:6-9, 51:8-9 Nahum 3:18-19 Lamentations 1:12-16, 20-22, 3:19-22 Job 24:12, 5:17-18, Isaiah 1:4-6, 6:10, 19:19-22, 30:2 Psalms 30:2-3, 41:4, 7

New Testament – Matthew 10:7-8, 4:23-24 Acts 4:13-14

Healing the Hurt (4)

Old Testament – Exodus 15:26, 23:25, Numbers 12:10-14, 2 Kings 20:1-5, 2 Chronicles 7:14, Isaiah 38:14-16, 57:15-18, 65:25 Hosea 5:13-15, 6:1-2, 14:1-6 Ezekiel 34:14-16 Psalms 42:9-11, 43:5, 67:1-2

New Testament – Luke 4:18, 7:22-23 Matthew 11:28-30

Healing the Hurt (5)

Old Testament=Ecclesiastes 3:1-3 Proverbs 3:7-8, 4:20-22, 12:18, 13:17, 15:13, 16:24, Isaiah 11:6-10, 66:9-14 Lamentations 2:10-13 Jeremiah 17:14 Ezekiel 47:6-12 Psalms 85:6, 103:1-5, 119:50, 92

New Testament – Luke 10:30-37 Matthew 11:28-30 Revelation 22:1-2

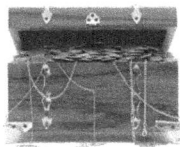

Day by Day

Day by Day (1)

"For which cause we faint not; but though our outward man perish, yet the inward man is renewed day by day." (2 Corinthians 4:16)

Day by Day (2)

"So teach us to number our days, that we may apply our hearts unto wisdom". (Psalm 90:12)

Day by Day (3)

"Day unto Day uttereth speech, and night unto night sheweth knowledge. There is no speech nor language, where there voice is not heard." (Psalms 19:2-3)

Discussion Questions

1. What does it mean to number our days?
2. Explain James 4:13-15.
3. What task was given in 1 Chronicles 23:30?
4. What are Christians instructed to do in Hebrews 3:13?
5. What transpired in Acts 2:46?

Fill in the Blanks

1. "And to stand____ ____ to thank and praise the Lord, and like-wise at even."
2. "Take therefore no thought for the____ : for the____ shall take thought for the____ of itself. Sufficient unto the____ is the____ thereof."
3. "This is the____ which the Lord hath made; we will____ and be____ in it."
4. "And____ in the____ , and in every house, they ceased not to____ and____ Jesus Christ."
5. "In the____ also he led them with a cloud, and all the____ with a light of fire."

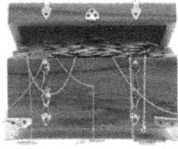

Day by Day

*M*any people wonder and worry about what will happen tomorrow, next year, or some other time in the future. Yet, when that day comes, they are unfortunately not there. We must resolve to live our lives one day at a time, treasure and enjoy today, and give thanks on a daily basis while hope lies ahead in the future.

Day by Day (1)

Old Testament – Psalms 19:2, 39:4-6, 50:1-2, 74:16, 90:12, 119:84, 139:16 Job 14:1-5, 18-20, 23:14, 36:11-12 Proverbs 27:1 Ecclesiastes 7:14, 11:6-8, 12:1 Genesis 47:9

New Testament – Matthew 6:34 James 4:13-15, 2 Corinthians 4:16 Ephesians 5:15-16

Day by Day (2)

Old Testament – Exodus 13:21-22, 16:4, 21, 29:36-39, 30:7-8, 36:3 Leviticus 6:12-13, 1 Kings 8:59, Isaiah 28:16-19, 33:2, 50:4 Lamentations 3:22-23 Psalms 5:3, 68:19, 72:15, 92:1-2, 113:3 Malachi 1:11

New Testament – Luke 9:23, 11:3, 19:47 Acts 5:42, 17:11

Day by Day (3)

Old Testament – 1 Chronicles 23:30, 16:23, 12:22, 2 Kings 25:27-30 Joshua 1:8, Isaiah 21:11-12, 17:14 Job 7:1-6 Psalms 39:5, 61:8, 71:15, 24, 74:16, 90:4, 113:3, 118:24

New Testament – Mark 1:35 Luke 21:37-38 John 8:1-2 Acts 20:31 Romans 13:12, 14:5-8

Day by Day (4)

Old Testament – Deuteronomy 28:15, 64-67 Nehemiah 1:4-6, 8:18 Ezra 6:9-10, 3:4, Isaiah 58:1-2, 6-8 Jeremiah 21:12, Job 36:20 Psalms 22:2, 30:5, 42:7-8, 44:8, 55:17, 86:3, 96:2

New Testament – Hebrews 3:13, 1 Corinthians 15:30-31 Acts 2:46-47, 2 Peter 2:4-8

Day by Day (5)

Old Testament – Deuteronomy 33:12 Zephaniah 3:5 Job 7:17-18, 8:9, 9:25-26, 1 Chronicles 29:15 Proverbs 27:1, 24:10 Ecclesiastes 7:14, 11:6-8, Isaiah 21:6-8 Psalms 130:6, 103:15- 16, 102:11-12, 90:5-6 Jeremiah 33:25-26

New Testament – John 9:4, 11:9-10, 2 Timothy 1:3

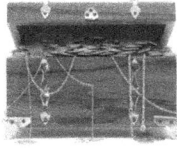

Diligently Seek Him

Diligently Seek Him (1)

"God hath made the world and all things therein...and hath made of one blood all nations of men for to dwell on the face of the earth..That they should seek the Lord...though he be not far from every one of us: (Acts 17:24-27)

Diligently Seek Him (2)

"When thou saidst, Seek ye my face; my heart said unto thee, Thy face, LORD, will I seek. Hide not thy face far from me;.. (Psalm 27:8-9)

Diligently Seek Him (3)

"But without faith it is impossible to please Him; for he that cometh to God must believe that He is, and that He is a rewarder of them that diligently seek Him." (Hebrews 11:6)

Discussion Questions

1. Is our desire to seek God based on how precious God is to us? Explain.
2. If we value the things of this world more than the knowledge of God, will that divided loyalty cause problems for us.
3. Discuss Matthew 13:44-46.
4. Explain John 4:23.

5. Explain Galatians 1:10.

Fill in the Blanks

1. "Sow to yourselves in_____ , reap in_____ ; break up your fallow ground: for it is time to_____ the Lord."
2. "But_____ ye_____ the kingdom of God, and his righteousness."
3. "I have not spoken in secret, in a dark place of the earth: I said not unto the seed of_____ , _____ ye me in_____ ."
4. "And that he is a_____ of them that diligently_____ him."
5. "But the hour cometh, and now is, when the_____ _____ shall worship the Father in_____ and in_____ : for the Father_____ such to_____ him."

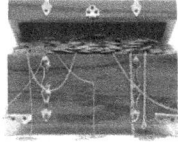

Diligently Seek Him

*I*t is only by diligent search, done with all our heart, soul, and strength, as those that prospect for gold, silver, and precious metal, that we can truly find and know God (Jeremiah 29:11, Deuteronomy 4:29, Hebrews 11:6).

Diligently Seek Him (1)

Old Testament – Hosea 10:12, 6:1-3 Amos 5:4-6, 14-15, 2 Chronicles 31:20-21, 30:18-20, 26:3-5, 15:2, 13, 11:16-17 Deuteronomy 4:27-29, Isaiah 45:19 Psalms 27:8-14, 73:25-28, 105:3-6 Proverbs 28:5

New Testament – Hebrews 11:6 Acts 17:24-27 James 4:8 Matthew 7:7-8

Diligently Seek Him (2)

Old Testament – 1 Chronicles 16:11-12, 28:9 Lamentations 3:25 Hosea 5:14-15 Psalms 10:4, 14:2-3, 27:4, 8-9, 63:1-5, 69:32 Zephaniah 2:3 Jeremiah 29:13 Proverbs 17:11, 19

New Testament – Acts 15:17 Matthew 11:25-26, 13:44-46 Luke 12:29-31 John 7:17-18, 20:15

Diligently Seek Him (3)

Old Testament – Job 23:3, 8-9, 35:13-14, 1 Kings 19:11-16, Isaiah 58:2-5, 55:6-9, 51:1, 34:16 Psalms 9:10, 40:16, 70:4, 77:16-19, 119:2, 10, 45, 94 Zechariah 8:21-23 Zephaniah 1:6-8

New Testament – Romans 1:20, 3:11 John 4:23-24, 1 Peter 1:8-12

Diligently Seek Him (4)

Old Testament – Job 21:14-15, 22:17-18, 34:26-27, 35:10-11 Psalms 50:18-22, 78:34, 83:16, 2 Chronicles 16:12, 12:13-14, 7:14 Hosea 7:10, 5:4, 6 Proverbs 1:27-28 Jeremiah 45:1-5 Micah 3:4 Ezra 8:22

New Testament Hebrews 11:13-14, 13:14 Matthew 6:33 Colossians 3:1

Diligently Seek Him (5)

Old Testament – 2 Chronicles 14:7, 17:3-4, 19:2-3, 1 Chronicles 22:19, Isaiah 26:9, 11:10, 8:17, 19 Leviticus 19:31 Job 8:5-7 Psalms 24:5-6, 22:24-26, 5:2-3 Jeremiah 5:1 Proverbs 11:27

New Testament – John 6:26, 7:32-36, Galatians 1:10, 2:17, 1 Thessalonians 2:4-6, 1 Corinthians 10:33

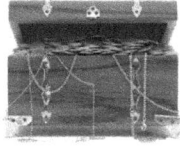

Run Your Race

Run Your Race (1)

"...let us lay aside every weight, and the sin which doth so easily beset us, and let us run with patience the race that is set before us." (Hebrews 12:1)

Run Your Race (2)

"..communicated unto them that gospel which I preach among the Gentiles...lest by any means I should run, or had run, in vain." "Ye did run well; who did hinder you that ye should not obey the truth" (Galatians 2:2, 5:7)

Run Your Race (3)

"Not as though I had already attained, either were perfect: but I follow after, if that I may apprehend...but this one thing I do, forgetting those things which are behind...I press toward the mark for the prize of the high calling of God in Christ Jesus. (Philippians 3:10-14)

Discussion Questions

1. Why is it important that the road we take in life be the narrow way and not the broad way?
2. What hindered those from running in Galatians 5:7?
3. Explain Philippians 2:16.
4. Explain 1 Corinthians 9:24-27.

5. Explain 2 Timothy 4:7.

Fill in the Blanks

1. "I returned, and saw under the sun, that the_____ is not to the_____ , nor the battle to the_____ ."
2. "____ ye to and fro through the____ of Jerusalem, and see now, and know, and seek in the broad places thereof."
3. "Ye did_____well; who did_____you that ye should not_____the_____?"
4. "But none of these things move me, neither count I my life dear unto , so that I might my with ."
5. "And I went up by revelation, and communicated unto them that gospel which I preach among the Gentiles...lest by any means I should____ , or had____ , in____ ."

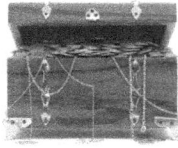

Run Your Race

"Wherefore seeing, we also are compassed about with so great a cloud of witnesses, let us lay aside every weight, and the sin which doth so easily beset us, and let us run with patience the race that is set before us" (Hebrews 12:1).

The Christian life is indeed comparable to the race of athletes who run in order to obtain a prize. There is a need to rid oneself of anything that will encumber or weigh one down as he completes his course. Do not let anything or anyone keep you from running your race.

Run Your Race (1)

Old Testament – Ecclesiastes 9:11 Amos 2:14-16, Isaiah 40:29-31 Job 17:9 Psalms 11:1, 18:29, 32-36, 19:1-5, 27:13-14, 42:1, 63:8, 119:32, 59 Proverbs 3:21-23, 4:11-16, 24:16 Micah 7:8

New Testament – Hebrews 12:1-3, 1 Corinthians 6:18, 9:24-27, Galatians 5:7-10

Run Your Race (2)

Old Testament – Numbers 11:27-30, 2 Kings 4:22-26, 1 Samuel 21:2, 8, 1 Chronicles 12:8, 38 Habakkuk 3:19, Isaiah 5:18-19, 26-27, 18:1-2, 59:7-8 Proverbs 1:15-16, 6:16-19 Jeremiah 5:1-5 Psalms 147:15

New Testament – Luke 14:21-22 Matthew 28:19-20 Acts 8:3-4, 20:18-24

Run Your Race (3)

Old Testament – 1 Kings 18:46, 19:1-3, 9-15 Jonah 1:1-3, 6-10, 3:1-4, 2 Kings 5:20-27 Psalms 139:7-13 Jeremiah 12:5, 23:21-22, 49:3, 51:30-31, Isaiah 33:1-4, 55:3-5 Habakkuk 2:2-3 Zechariah 2:1-4, 4:8-10

New Testament – Romans 3:13-15, 9:15-16, Galatians 2:2 Philippians 2:12-16

Run Your Race (4)

Old Testament – Daniel 12:1-4, 10 JoeL2:1-4, 7-11 Amos 8:11-12, 7:12-15, 6:12-14, 5:18-19, Isaiah 30:15-18 Proverbs 28:1, 18:10 Psalms 58:3-7, 59:1-4, 64:2-8, 119:136, 143:9

New Testament – R2 Timothy 2:22, 1 Timothy 6:11-12, 1 Peter 4:3-4

Run Your Race (5)

Old Testament – Exodus 12:11, 33 Esther 3:13-15, 8:13-14 Jeremiah 1:9-12 Psalms 119:60, 31:11

New Testament – Matthew 24:14-20, 26:31, 56, 28:1-8 Romans 10:14-18 Galatians 6:9 Hebrews 6:1, 18, 10:35-37 Philippians 3:12-14, 2 Timothy 4:6-7

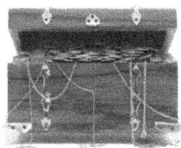

Sing Your Song

Sing Your Song (1)

"The LORD is my strength and my shield; my heart trusted in Him, and I am helped: therefore my heart greatly rejoiceth; and with my song will I praise Him." (Psalm 28:7)

Sing Your Song (2)

"Behold, God is my salvation; I will trust, and not be afraid: for the LORD JEHOVAH is my strength and my song; He also is become my salvation." (Isaiah 12:2)

Sing Your Song (3)

"For there they that carried us away required of us a song; and they that wasted us required of us mirth; saying, Sing us one of the Songs of Zion. How shall we sing the LORD's song in a strange land?" (Psalm 137:3-4)

Discussion Questions

1. According to Psalms 28:7, what happens when we sing our songs to Him?
2. Where is the melody to be made according to Ephesians 5:19? 165 Sing Your Song
3. Explain Hebrews 13:15.

4. What did Paul and Silas do, according to Acts 16:25, while they were in prison?

5. What did Jesus and His disciples do according to Matthew 26:30?

Fill in the Blanks

1. "I will be glad and rejoice___ ____ : I will____ praise to thy____ , O thou most____ ."

2. "While I___ will____ I the Lord: I wil___l praises unto my God while I have any being."

3. "I will____ with the spirit, and I will ____with the____ also."

4. "Saying, I will declare thy name unto my____ , in the midst of the church will I____ ____ unto thee."

5. "Teaching and admonishing one another in____ and____ and ____, ____with grace in your hearts to the Lord."

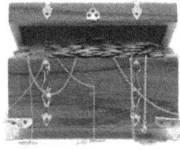

Sing Your Song

*A*ll throughout the Bible, songs of praise and adoration are to be sung from our heart to the great and awesome God of heaven. In our spirits, we are made to rejoice, as the outpouring flows from the depths of our souls, that we are indeed grateful, appreciative, and truly long for our God and our King. Christian, sing your song.

Sing Your Song (1)

Old Testament – Psalms 7:17, 9:1-2, 28:7, 30:4, 47:6-7, 66:1-5, 8 Deuteronomy 31:19, 22, 32:1-3, 43-44 Judges 5:1-3, 12 Numbers 21:16-17 Ezra 3:11, 1 Chronicles 6:31-32, 9:33 Nehemiah 12:45-47

New Testament – Luke 2:9-14 Matthew 26:30 James 5:13, 1 Corinthians 14: 15

Sing Your Song (2)

Old Testament – Job 38:4, 7, 35:10 Psalms 146:1-2, 119:54, 104:33-34, 96:1-4, 95:1-3, 77:6, 68:4, 32-35, 42:7-8, Isaiah 30:29 Jeremiah 33:10- 11 Hosea 2:15, 19-20

New Testament – Hebrews 13:15 Ephesians 5:19-20 Acts 16:25 Romans 15:9-11

Sing Your Song (3)

Old Testament – Exodus 15:1-2, 21, Isaiah 12:1-6, 35:1-2, 10, 42:10-12, 44:23, 51:11, 65:13-14 Proverbs 29:6 Psalms 138:1-5, 135:1-3, 106:11-12, 105:1-3, 101:1, 40:3, 32:7, 9:11 Job 29:12-13

New Testament – Hebrews 2:12 Colossians 3:16 Revelations 15:3

Sing Your Song (4)

Old Testament – 1 Chronicles 13:5-13, 15:2, 13, 16:8-9, 23-25, 2 Chronicles 29:27-30, 30:21 Psalms 149:1-7, 137:1-4, 92:1, 13:7 Amos 5:21-24, 6:3-7, 8:10 Ezekiel 26:13

New Testament – Luke 19:37-40, 1 Corinthians 14:7-9, 26 Revelation 18:21-22

Sing Your Song (5)

Old Testament – Ezra 2:64-65 Jeremiah 20:13, 31:7, 11-12 Pr 25:20 Isaiah 24:16, 26:2, 49:13, 55:12 Psalms 21:13, 59:16-17, 65:13, 67:4, 69:30, 100:2, 126:1-3 Zephaniah 3:14-17 Zechariah 2:10

New Testament – Luke 7:31-32 Revelation 5:7-9

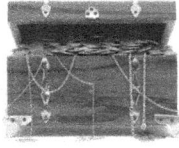

He Leadeth Me

He Leadeth Me (1)

"From the end of the earth will I cry unto thee, when my heart is overwhelmed: lead me to the rock that is higher than I." (Psalm 61:2)

He Leadeth Me (2)

"To him the porter openeth; and the sheep hear his voice: and he calleth his own sheep by name, and leadeth them out. And when he putteth forth his own sheep, he goeth before them, and the sheep follow him: for they know his voice. (John 10:3-4)

He Leadeth Me (3)

"I have taught thee in the way of wisdom; I have led thee in right paths. When thou goest, thy steps shall not be straitened;and when thou runnest, thou shalt not stumble." (Proverbs 4:11-12)

Discussion Questions

1. What message is conveyed in Psalm 23:1-6?
2. Explain Job 12:17, 19.
3. What warning is conveyed in Proverbs 16:29?
4. Why are there few people that find the way unto life in Matthew 7:14?
5. Explain John 10:3.

Fill in the Blanks

1. Or despisest thou the riches of his goodness and forebear-
   ance and longsuffering; Not _____ that the goodness of God
   _____ thee to _____?
2. To him the porter openeth; and the sheep hear his voice: and
   he calleth his own _____ by name, and _____ them out.
3. Thus saith the LORD, thy Redeemer, the Holy One of Israel;
   I am the LORD thy God Which _____ thee to profit, which
   _____ thee by the way that thou _____ go.
4. He _____ my soul: He _____ in the paths of _____ for
   his name's sake.
5. I have seen his ways, and will ____ him: I will _____ him also,
   and restore comforts Unto him and to his mourners.

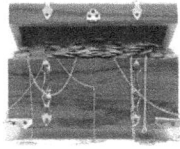

He Leadeth Me

"The LORD is my shepherd; I shall not want. He leadeth me besides the still waters. He restoreth my soul: he leadeth me in the paths of righteousness for his name's sake. Surely, goodness and mercy shall follow me all the days of my life" (Psalms 23:1-6).

*W*hat a wonderful caption of thought that highlights the benefits of those that are being led by God. He protects us, He provides for us, even in the midst of our enemies, even though we find ourselves walking through the valley of the shadow of death. He is right there with us. He will never leave or forsake us. How can anybody not want to follow God?

What a true and remarkable Shepherd.

He Leadeth Me (1)

Old Testament – Exodus 13:17-22, 14:19, 15:11-13, 29:45-46 Deuteronomy 1:30-33, 8:2-6, 11-16, 32:9-12, Isaiah 31:5, 63:7-14 Psalms 23:1-6, 68:4-8, 78:50-53, 80:1, 105:37-43, 107:4-7

New Testament – Matthew 7:13-14 Luke 13:24 John 10:1-5, 27

He Leadeth Me (2)

Old Testament – Genesis 24:27, 48, 28:20-21 Deuteronomy 29:5-6 Jeremiah 10:23 Psalms 119:133 Proverbs 16:9, 20:24, 21:1, 23:26 Job 12:17-19 Psalms 37:23, 48:14, 77:20, 139:5-10, 143:8, 10

New Testament – Matthew 4:18-20, 8:19-22 Luke 24:50-51

He Leadeth Me (3)

Old Testament – Isaiah 11:6, 40:10-11, 42:16, 48:20-21, 49:7-10, 55:11-12, 57:15-18, 58:10-11 Psalms 5:8, 25:5, 31:3, 61:2, 63:8, 85: 13, 139:23-24 Job 23:11

New Testament – Luke 22:33-34 John 21:18-19 Revelation 14:4, 7:17

He Leadeth Me (4)

Old Testament – 1 Samuel 9:6-8 Nehemiah 9:7-12 Deuteronomy 1:6-8 Exodus 32:30-34 Leviticus 26:21-24 Hosea 6:1-3, 11:9-11 Lamentations 3:1-2 Jeremiah 2:5-6, 17, 23:5-8 Psalms 27:11, 43:3, 60:9-10, 125:5 Proverbs 4:11-12

New Testament – John 12:26 Luke 9:57-62 Matthew 10:37-38

He Leadeth Me (5)

Old Testament – Exodus 3:12-16, 33:11-17 Numbers 27:15-23 Deuteronomy 4:23-29, 1 K8:46-50, 18:21 Ezekiel 13:3-4, Isaiah 3:12, 9:16, 48:17 Proverbs 8:20 Psalms 32:8-9, 73:24

New Testament – Matthew 6:13, 15:12-14 Romans 8:14 Galatians 5:18, 2 Peter 3:17, 1 Timothy 2:1-3

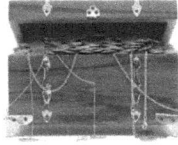

The Land Mourns

The Land Mourns (1)

"The field is wasted, the land mourneth:..Gird yourselves and lament.. call a solemn assembly, gather the elders and all the inhabitants of the land into the house of the LORD your God and cry unto the LORD." JoeL1:10-14

The Land Mourns (2)

"..the LORD hath a controversy with the inhabitants of the land, because there is no truth, nor mercy, nor knowledge of God in the land, By swearing and lying, and killing, and committing adultery, they break out..Therefore shall the land mourn (Hos 4:1-4)

The Land Mourns (3)

"The field is wasted, the land mourneth :..Gird yourselves and lament.. call a solemn assembly, gather the elders and all the inhabitants of the land into the house of the LORD your God and cry unto the LORD." JoeL1:10-14

Discussion Questions

1.   What was God's concern in Genesis 4:9-11?

2. All across this land today, what is the cry that comes before the throne of God concerning the atrocities of its inhabitants? Give a Bible verse that expresses this cry.
3. Explain Genesis 18:20-33.
4. What did Jesus describe in Matthew 24:1-13.
5. Explain Luke 13:1-5, 34-35

Fill in the Blanks

1. "The earth also is_____ under the inhabitants thereof; because they have____ the_____, changed the_____, broken the everlasting_____."
2. "Arise, go to Nineveh, that great city, and ____against it; for their____ is come up____ ____."
3. "And when he was come near, he____ the city, and ____over it."
4. "Wherefore come out from____ them, and be ye____, saith the Lord, and touch not the____ ____; and I will receive you."
5. "For we know that the whole creation___ and ____in pain together until now."

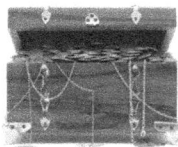

The Land Mourns

What is the condition of the world we live in? How safe are we? What type of social ebbs are we experiencing? Are there injustices, abuses of power, corruption, and unfairness in the land? God has always viewed sin as a reproach unto any people or nation.

The Land Mourns (1)

Old Testament – Genesis 4:9-12, 6:5-6, 11-12, Isaiah 5:18-26, 24:1-7, 20-21, 33:9-15 JoeL1:10- 14 Ezekiel 14:13-23, 2 Chronicles 7:13-14 Job 38:12-13 Haggai 2:6-7 Zechariah 12:11-12

New Testament – Luke 10:12-15, 19:41-44, 21:23, 26

The Land Mourns (2)

Old Testament – Genesis 18:20-33 Leviticus 18:24-30, 20:22-23 Numbers 35:34 Psalms 106:34-43 Habakkuk 3:6-12, Isaiah 59:7-15, 3:5-9, 15-26, 1:7-28 Amos 3:4-11 Jeremiah 2:1-7, 12:4, 14:2-9, 16:17-18 Lk 13:34-35

New Testament – Romans 8:22 Hebrews 6:7-8

The Land Mourns (3)

Old Testament – 2 Chronicles 15:5-6, 34:21-25 Hosea 4:1-10, 9:7-9 Amos 9:5-10, 8:4-11, 5:12-17 Je 10:10-18, 25:13-17, 27-38 JoeL3:11-19 Job 31:38-40, 37:10-13 Psalms 27:13, 60:1-3

New Testament – 2 Peter 2:6-8 Hebrews 11:8-16 Revelation 11:18

The Land Mourns (4)

Old Testament – Deuteronomy 4:25-26, 11:16-17, 18:9-14, 24:1-4 Joshua 23:11-13, 1 Kings 15:11-12, 22:42-46 Jeremiah 4:14-20, 27-28, 6:6-8, 9:17-21, Ezekiel 33:24-29 Zechariah 7:4-14

New Testament – Matthew 24:12-13, 1 Corinthians 5:1-13, 2 Corinthians 6:14-18

The Land Mourns (5)

Old Testament – Amos 1:1-2, 4:6-13 Ezekiel 22:24-31, 16:49-50 Micah 1:2-8 Lamentations 5:15-16, 2:5, 1:4, 8-12 Jeremiah 31:1-19, 32:37-43 Proverbs 14:34, 28:2, 29:2, 4 Psalms 82:1-5, 11:5

New Testament – John 16:20-22 Luke 23:27-31 Revelation 18:1-8,

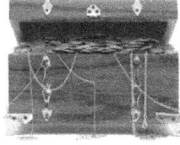

Teach Them

Teach Them (1)

"And Philip ran thither to him, and heard him read the prophet Esaias, and said, Understandest thou what thou readest? And he said, How can I, except some man should guide me? And he desired Philip that he would come and sit with him." (Acts 8:30-31)

Teach Them (2)

"And a certain Jew named Apollos..an eloquent man, and mighty in Scriptures..This man being fervent in spirit and taught diligently the things of the Lord.. when Aquila and Priscilla had heard..expounded unto him the way of God more perfectly." (Acts 18:24-26)

Teach Them (3)

"Go ye therefore and teach all nations, baptizing them in the name of the Father..Son..Holy Ghost:Teaching them to observe all things what-soever I have commanded you:.. (Matt 28:19-20)

Discussion Questions

1. What instructions did Christ give to his disciples in Matthew 28{18-20?
2. What information is made known in Acts 1:1-2?
3. Discuss Ezra 7:10, 25.

4. What admonishment is given in 1 Timothy 1:3?
5. What message is conveyed in Psalms 32:8?

Fill in the Blanks

1. And the servant of the Lord must not _____; but be gentle unto all men, apt to _____, patient
2. These things command and _____.
3. And daily in the temple, and in every house, they _____ not to _____ and _____Jesus Christ.
4. For the _____ _____ shall teach you in the same _____ what ye ought to say.
5. For his God doth _____ him to discretion, and doth _____ him.

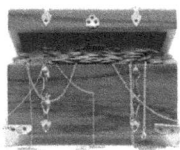

Teach Them

*T*here is a grave and awesome responsibility placed on those who teach. He must give an understanding of the will of God to an audience of students whose very lives will be fashioned by those things taught to them. Jesus specifically made known to all his disciples to teach them whatsoever he has commanded (Matthew 28:20). It is to be done without addition or subtraction (Revelations 22:18-19).

Teach Them (1)

Old Testament – Deuteronomy 5:31, 11:18-19, 33:8-10 Leviticus 10:8-11, 2 Chronicles 17:8-9, 30:22, 35:2-3 Ezra 7:10, 25 Nehemiah 8:5-12 Malachi 2:4-7 Psalms 25:4-5, 8-9, 12, 86:12, Isaiah 54:14, 2:2-3

New Testament – John 3:1-2, 8:26-28 Matthew 28:18-20 Acts 1:1-2

Teach Them (2)

Old Testament – Exodus 4:10-15, 24:12 Deuteronomy 4:5-10, 20:18, 1 Samuel 12:23, 1 Kings 8:35-36, Isaiah 28:9, 40:13-15, 50:4 Proverbs 1:5, 9:9, 16:21-23 Psalms 119:66, 99, 102

New Testament – John 6:45 Matthew 13:54, 7:29 Luke 24:27, 32 Acts 18:25-28, 8:30-31

Teach Them (3)

Old Testament – Genesis 30:27, 18:18-19 Judges 13:6-8, 2 Kings 17:25-28 Exodus 35:30-34 Nehemiah 9:20 Hosea 11:3, 10:11 Job 8:9-10, 32:7-9, 36:22, 40:2-5 Psalms 94:10, 119:33, 171, 143:10

New Testament – John 14:21, 1 Corinthians 2:10-13, 1 John 2:27 Romans 15:4

Teach Them (4)

Old Testament – Ecclesiastes 12:9 Psalms 16:7, 32:8-9, 71:17-18, 119:7, 26, 73, 132:12 Proverbs 4:1-4, 10-13, 5:1-2, 10-13, 22:6, 31:1-9 Ezekiel 22:26, 44:21-23, Isaiah 30:20-21, 48:17

New Testament – John 8:28 Matthew 22:16, 2 Timothy 3:14-17 Ephesians 6:4

Teach Them (5)

Old Testament – Habakkuk 2:18-19, Isaiah 29:10-13 Zephaniah 3:7 Jeremiah 35:13, 32:33, 31:31-34, 29:30-32, 28:16, 9:1-5, 13-14

New Testament – Matthew 15:7-9 Galatians 1:6-12 Titus 1:4-9, 1 Timothy 1:3 Colossians 2:6-8 Hebrews 5:12-14 Romans 2:17-24, 2 Peter 3:15-18 Ephesians 4:11-14

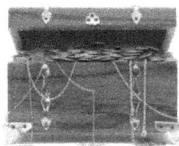

Before Him

Before Him (1)

"For God giveth to man that is good in His sight wisdom, and knowledge and joy :but to the sinner he giveth travail, to gather and to heap up, that he may give to him that is good before God.." (Ecclesiastes 2:26)

Before Him (2)

"Watch ye therefore, and pray always, that ye may be accounted worthy to escape all these things that shall come to pass, and to stand before the Son of man." (Luke 21:36)

Before Him (3)

"Who can stand before His indignation? and who can abide in the fierceness of His anger? His fury is poured out like fire... The LORD is good, a strong hold in the day of trouble; and He knoweth them that trust Him." (Nahum 1:5-7)

Discussion Questions

1. Discuss 1 John 2:28.
2. What is conveyed in Jude 1:24.
3. What are the imperatives in Ephesians 1:4?
4. In Job 13:16, what type person cannot come before him?
5. Discuss Daniel 7:9-14.

Fill in the Blanks

1. And they were both _____ before ___, walking in all His commandments and Ordinances of the Lord blameless.
2. Thou art of purer eyes than to _____ evil, and canst not ____ on iniquity:....
3. But why dost thou judge thy brother? Or why dost thou set at _____ thy Brother? For we al shall stand _____ the judgement seat of Christ.
4. Wherewith shall I come _____the LORD, and bow myself _____ the high God? Shall I come _____ Him with burnt offerings, with calves of a year old?
5. Gather my saints together ____ me; those that have made a _____ with Me by sacrifice.

Before Him

T he Bible mentions in Ephesians 1:4, "According as he hath chosen us in him before the foundation of the world, that we should be holy and without blame before him in love."

We should always be eternally grateful for our Lord and Savior, Jesus, for his dying for all of mankind and for his being our propitiation when we obeyed the gospel. Also, every day we must be cognizant of living in a way that brings glory to his name. Truly, we must live before Him in love.

Before Him (1)

Old Testament – Genesis 17:1 Ecclesiastes 2:26, 3:14, 5:1-2, 8:11-13 Job 13:15-16, 23:3-7, 26:6, 35:13-14, 41:1-10 Habakkuk 1:12-13, 2;4, 20, 3:3-6 Psalms 97:3-5, 68:1-4 Micah 6:6-8

New Testament – Luke 1:70-76 Hebrews 9:24, 12:22-29 Jude 1:24

Before Him (2)

Old Testament – Deuteronomy 31:10-13, 29:9-15, 26:10, 16:16, 5:7 Ezekiel 14:1-6, 20:1-7, 22:30, 44:12-16 Hosea 7:1-2, Isaiah 59:7-12 Nhm 1:5-7 Psalms 65:4, 76:11, 90:8, 95:2, 6, 100:2, 119: 168

New Testament – Ephesians 1:4, 7, 1 John 2:28

Before Him (3)

Old Testament – Genesis 6:11-13, 7:1, 13:13, 18:20-21, 19:13, 24, Isaiah 1:9-18, 40:10, 17, 41:1, 57: 16, 66:4, 1 Chronicles 16:27-33 Psalms 42:1-2, 50:3-5, 54:2-3, 62:8, 72:9-11

New Testament – Luke 21:36, 1 John 3:18-19

Before Him (4)

Old Testament – Daniel 7:9-14, Deuteronomy 33:1-3 Psalms 18:6-23, 73:20-23, 85:13, 96:6, 9, 114:2-7, 119: 169-170, 141:2, 2 Kings 22:19, 1 Kings 2:2-4, 9:3-7, Isaiah 30:27-30

New Testament – Luke 1:5-6, 1 Corinthians 1:27-29 Romans 14:10, 22 Revelation 20:11-12

Before Him (5)

Old Testament – Deuteronomy 4:7-15 Leviticus 10:1-3, 21:17, 23 Psalms 106:23 Haggai 2:11-14 Jeremiah 2:22, 5:22-23, 6:7, 7:9-10, 15:1, 19, 31:35-36 Zechariah 2:10-13 Zephaniah 1:7-12

New Testament – Matthew 25:31-33 Revelation 3:2-6, 7:9-15, 14:2-5, 15:4

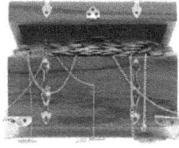

The Shepherd and His Sheep

The Shepherd and His Sheep (1)

"The words of the wise are as goads, and as nails fastened by the masters of assemblies, which are given from one shepherd." (Ecclesiastes 12:11)

The Shepherd and His Sheep (2)

"I am the good shepherd: the good shepherd giveth his life for the sheep"...My sheep hear my voice, and I know them, and they follow me." (Jn 10:11, 27)

The Shepherd and His Sheep (3)

"Now the God of peace, that brought again from the dead our Lord Jesus, that great Shepherd of the sheep, through the blood of the everlasting covenant, " (Heb 13:20)

Discussion Questions

1. Explain Ecclesiastes 12:11.
2. Why was Jesus moved with compassion in Matthew 9:36?
3. What observations are made in John 10:1-16, 26-30?
4. Explain 1 Peter 5:1-4?
5. Explain Hebrews 13:17.

Fill in the Blanks

1. "The words of the wise are as goads, and as nails fastened by the masters of____ , which are given from one____ ."
2. "I am the good____ : the good____ giveth his life for the____ ."
3. "For ye were as ____going astray: but are now returned unto the____ and____ of your souls."
4. "Thou leddest thy people like a____ by the hand of Moses and Aaron."
5. "But when He saw the multitudes, he was moved with compassion on them, because they____ , and were____ abroad, as sheep having no____ ."

The Shepherd and His Sheep

"He shall feed his flock like a shepherd: he shall gather the lambs with his arm, and carry them in his bosom, and shall gently lead those that are with young" (Isaiah 40:11).

*W*hat a wonderful portrait of how Jesus cares for those in His flock. These passages highlight the tenderness, the affection, the nurturing, and the guidance that Jesus provides for those who belong to Him—His flock.

The Shepherd and His Sheep (1)

Old Testament – Ecclesiastes 12:9-11 Genesis 49:24is 40:11, 63:8-14 Jeremiah 13:20 Ezekiel 34:1-23, 30-31, 37:24-28 Psalms 100:3, 80:1, 78:50-52, 77:20

New Testament – John 10:1-16, 26-30 Hebrews 13:20, 1 Peter 2:25, 5:1-4

The Shepherd and His Sheep (2)

Old Testament – Numbers 27:15-18, 2 Samuel 5:1-2, 7:7-8, Isaiah 63:11-14 Micah 4:8, 5:2-5, 7:14 Zechariah 13:6-7, 9:16 Jeremiah 13:17, 20

New Testament – Luke 12:32 Matthew 18:10-14, 26:31-32 John 21:15-17 Acts 20:17, 28-30 Revelation 7:13-17

The Shepherd and His Sheep (3)

Old Testament – Hosea 13:6, 9, 4:16, 1 Kings 22:17 Psalms 44:11, 74:1, 79:11-13, 95:6-7, 119:176, JoeL 1:18-20, Isaiah 13:6-14, 53:6-12, Jeremiah 31:9-12 Micah 2:12-13

New Testament – Matthew 9:35-36 Romans 8:36-39 Acts 8:32-35 Hebrews 13:20-21

The Shepherd and His Sheep (4)

Old Testament – Zechariah 10:1-3, 11:1-17, Isaiah 56:10-12, 9:16 Ezekiel 36:37-38 Jeremiah 2:8, 3:14-15, 12:10, 23:1-6, 25:34-36, 33:12-17, 50:6-8, 17-19, 45 Proverbs 27:23 Psalms 107:40-41

New Testament – Matthew 10:16 Ephesians 4:11-15 Hebrews 13:17

The Shepherd and His Sheep (5)

Old Testament – Jeremiah 11:19, 51:22-23 Amos 7:12-15, 3:12 Zephaniah 2:6-7, 14-15, 3:13, Isaiah 5:15-17, 11:6-10, 49:7-10, 60:7, 61:5-6, 65: 10 Psalms 23:1-6

New Testament – Matthew 7:15, 12:11-12, 25:31-33

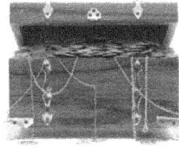

God's Mercy

God's Mercy (1)

"Who is a God like unto thee, that pardoneth iniquity, and passeth by the transgression of the remnant of his heritage? he retaineth not His anger for ever, because He delighteth in mercy. (Micah 7:18)

God's Mercy (2)

"Let the wicked forsake his way, and the unrighteous man his thoughts: and let him return unto the LORD, and He will have mercy upon him; and to our God, for He will abundantly pardon.

God's Mercy (3)

"For I will be merciful to their unrighteousness, and their sins and their iniquities I will remember no more." (Heb 8:12)

Discussion Questions

1. Discuss 1 Timothy 1:12-16.
2. What observations are made in Micah 7:18-19
3. Explain 1 Peter 2:10.
4. Explain Jeremiah 31:18-20.
5. Explain James 2:13.

Fill in the Blanks

1. "For I will be____ to their_____ , and their sins and their iniquities will I____ no____ ."
2. "Blessed be the God and Father of our____ ____ , which according to his____ ____ hath begotten us again unto a lively hope by the____ of Jesus Christ from the dead. ."
3. "O give thanks unto the Lord; for He is____ ; for His____ endureth for ever."
4. "It is of the Lord's____ that we are not____ , because His _____fail not."
5. "Be ye therefore____, as your Father also is_____ "

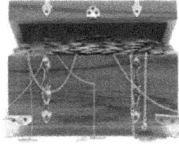

God's Mercy

"The Lord is good to all: and his tender mercies are over all his works" (Psalms 145:9).

It is because of God's mercy and compassion that we are able to live from day to day. He is able to save to the uttermost of those who come to Him. He truly is an awesome God.

God's Mercy (1)

Old Testament – Exodus 34:5-8, 15:13 Numbers 14:18-19 Nehemiah 9:13-33 Micah 7:18-20, 2 Samuel 24:14, Isaiah 55:6-7 Jeremiah 3:12 Psalms 143:1-2, 12, 130:3-7, 57:10, 52:8, 33:18, 25:10, 15

New Testament – Luke 1:49-50, 6:36 Hebrews 4:14-16 James 2:13

God's Mercy (2)

Old Testament – Deuteronomy 7:9-12, 5:10 Jeremiah 31:18-20, Isaiah 60:10, 54:7-10, 49:10-13 Jonah 4:2 Psalms 119:41, 58, 76-77, 132, 116:5, 108:4, 103:11-18, 86:5, 13, 15, 32:10 Proverbs 28:13

New Testament – Titus 3:5-6 Jude 1:21, 1 Peter 2:10 Romans 15:9

God's Mercy (3)

Old Testament – Deuteronomy 4:31 Proverbs 16:6, 14:22, 3:3-4 Hosea 14:3, 12:6, 2:23, 2 Chronicles 30:9 Joel 2:12-13 Lamentations 3:22, 1 Kings 8:22-23 Psalms 89:14, 145:8-9, 147:11

New Testament – Matthew 9:13 Romans 9:15-18, 11:30-32 Ephesians 2:4-7, 1 Timothy 1:12-16 Hebrews 8:12

God's Mercy (4)

Old Testament – Daniel 9:8-9, 18 Ezra 9:9, 13, 1 Chronicles 16:34 Zechariah 10:6 Psalms 90:14, 85:10-13, 66:20, 51:1, 33:22, 31:7-9, 16, 25:6-7, 21:7, 13:5, 6:2-4, 5:7, 4:1

New Testament – 2 Corinthians 1:3-4, 1 Peter 1:3 Hebrews 10:28-29 Galatians 6:14-16

God's Mercy (5)

Old Testament Exodus 33:19 Deuteronomy 32:43, Isaiah 16:4-5 Habakkuk 3:2 Jeremiah 42:11-12, 31:20 Hosea 6:4-6 Micah 6:8 Psalms 119:64, 124, 117:2, 109:21-26, 89:1-2, 57:1-3, 18:25

New Testament – Matthew 23:23, 12:7 Luke 10:30-37, 2 Timothy 1:16-18 Hebrews 2:17

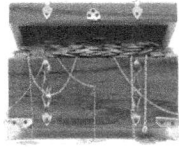

Deliverance

Deliverance (1)

"..thou hast been displeased.. Thou hast made the earth to tremble;thou hast broken it: heal .. for it shaketh. Thou hast shewed thy people hard things: thou hast made us to drink the wine of astonishment..That thy beloved may be delivered;...hear me. (Ps 60:1-5)

Deliverance (2)

"And when the LORD saw that they humbled themselves, the word of the LORD came to Shemaiah, saying, They have humbled themselves; therfore I will not destroy them, but I will grant them some deliverance..." (2 Chronicles 12:7)

Deliverance (3)

"O wretched man that I am! Who shall deliver me from this body of death?I thank God through Jesus Christ..." "Who hath delivered us from the power of darkness , and hath translated us into the kingdom of His dear Son":(Rom 7:24, 25&CoL1:13)

Discussion Questions

1. Discuss Romans 11:24.
2. What was prophesied in Joel 2:32?
3. Who delivered Paul in 2 Timothy 3:11?

4. Who is the delivered one in 2 King 17:39?
5. Discuss Luke 1:68-74.

Fill in the Blanks

1. "Thou also hast_____ me from the_____ of my people, thou hast____ me to be head of the_____ ."
2. "_____ me in thy_____ and cause me to_____ : incline thine ear unto me and_____ me."
3. "And_____ them who through fear of_____ were all their life-time subject to bondage."
4. "Because the creature itself also shall be_____ from the bond-age of corruption into the glorious liberty of the_____ of_____ ."
5. "That he would grant unto us, that we being_____ out of the hand of our enemies might _____him without fear."

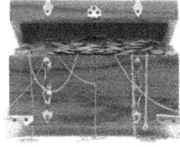

Deliverance

*T*here are many instances in the Bible where men and women cried unto God for deliverance. In dire circumstances beyond their strength and beyond their capability, they sought the God of heaven, and He delivered them. God's help provided a testimony of the goodness of God in their very souls.

Deliverance (1)

Old Testament – 2 Samuel 22:1-4, 44-49 Psalms 71:1-5, 9-12, 60:1-5, 50:15, 40:1-3, 12-17, 34:4-7, 17-19, 32:7, 17:7-13, 12:5, 7 Proverbs 21: 31 JoeL2:32

New Testament – Romans 11:26 Galatians 1:3-4 Hebrews 2:14-15, 1 Thessalonians 1:10 Colossians 1:13-14

Deliverance (2)

Old Testament – Judges 3:9, 10:15, 2 Kings 17:39, 13:14-19 Nehemiah 9::25-33 Daniels 3:17-29, 1 Samuel 17:32-37, 46-51, 2 Chronicles 12:7, 32:11-23 Ezra 9:13-15 Psalms 41:1-2, 43:1, 70:5 Proverbs 11:6, 8

New Testament – 2 Timothy 3:11, 4:18, 2 Corinthians 1:9-10, 2 Peter 2:7-9

Deliverance (3)

Old Testament – Genesis 45:7 Exodus 3:7-8, 18:10-11 Daniel 6:19-27 Jeremiah 20:13 Psalms 18:47-50, 35:10, 40:13-17, 69:11-18, 72:11-12, 82:1-4 Job 36:15 Proverbs 10:2, 23:13-14

New Testament – Matthew 6:13 Romans 4:20-25, 7:24-25, 15:30-31

Deliverance (4)

Old Testament – Job 22:29-30, 1 Samuel 12:20-21, Isaiah 42:22-25, 43:13, 46:1-4, 64:1-4 Micah 5:8 Psalms 6:1-4, 7:1-7, 37:39-40, 56:9-13, 91:1-6, 97:10, 142:3-6

New Testament – Luke 1:68-74 Acts 26:15-18, 2 Thessalonians 3:1-2 Jude 1:3.

Deliverance (5)

Old Testaments-Genesis 32:11-12, 1 Samuel 24:15-18, 26:23-25 Ecclesiastes 8:8, 9:13-15 Proverbs 11:4, 9 Psalms 25:20-21, 31:1-2, 15, 39:8, 59:1-2, 119:134, 153, 154, 170, 144:7-11

New Testament – Matthew 24:6-9, 13, 27:41-43 Romans 8:18-21

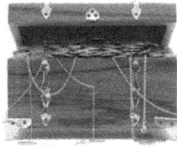

Trouble

Trouble (1)

"Although affliction cometh not forth of the dust, neither doth trouble spring out of the ground. Yet man is born unto trouble, as the sparks fly upward.""Man that is born of a woman is of a few days and full of trouble." (Job 5:6-7, 14:1)

Trouble (2)

"For my sighing cometh before I eat, and my roarings are poured out like the waters. For the thing which I greatly feared is come unto me. I was not in safety, neither had I rest, neither was I quiet; yet trouble came." (Job 3:24-26)

Trouble (3)

"But we would not, brethren, have you ignorant of our trouble ...we were pressed out of measure, above strength ...we despised even of life ...But we had the sentence of death in ourselves that we should not trust in ourselves but in God.. (2 Cor 1:8-9)

Discussion Questions

1. How do we overcome the trouble of this world?
2. Discuss John 14:27.
3. Discuss Job 5:6-7.

4. Explain Acts 14:22.
5. Discuss 2 Corinthians 4:8-12.

Fill in the Blanks

1. "The____ is delivered out of___ , and the____ cometh in his stead."
2. "Let not your heart be____ : ye believe in God, believe also in____ ."
3. "The wicked is snared by the____ of his lips: but the____ shall come out of ____."
4. "And behold at eveningtide____ ; and before the morning he is not. This is the portion of them that____ ____ , and the lot of them that____ ____ ."
5. "But in the time of their____ they will say, Arise, and save us."

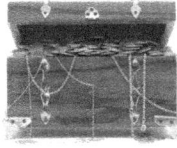

Trouble

In Jeremiah 8:15, the prophet states, "We looked for peace, but no good came; and for a time of health, but behold trouble!" Many of us can identify with the characterization of his situation, comparing it to that of our own. Trouble is everywhere, and even sometimes at our front door. We live in a troubled world.

Trouble (1)

Old Testament – Job 5:6-7, 14:1-5, 23:8-14 Genesis 47:9 Ecclesiastes 7:14, 11:5-8 Hosea 5:15 Jeremiah 8:15 Psalms 50:15, 78:33-35, 90:3-15, 119:50, 67, 71, 143, 142:1-7, 143:11

New Testament – John 14:1, 16:33 Acts 14:22 Romans 8:35-39, 1 Peter 5:8-9

Trouble (2)

Old Testament – Job 3:24-26, 27:8-9, 2 Kings 19:3, Nehemiah 9:26-27 Habakkuk 3:16 Nahum 1:7, 2 Chronicles 4:6-7 Psalms 9:9-13, 22:11, 24, 27:5, 31:7-9, 32:7, 37:39-40, 41:1-2

New Testament – Luke 10:38-42, 8:22-25, 2 C4:8-12, 17, 2 Thessalonians 1:6-8

Trouble (3)

Old Testament – Proverbs 11:8, 29, 12:13, 15:6, 16, 25:19, Isaiah 17:12-14, 26:16, 33:1-2 Jeremiah 30:7 Psalms 30:7, 54:6-7, 60:11, 77:2-12, 88:2-4, 91:14-15, 138:7

New Testament – Acts 17:5-8, 2 Timothy 4:17-18, 2 Corinthians 7:5-7, 1:3-10

Trouble (4)

Old Testament – Job 34:20-21, 21:4 Jeremiah 14:8, 16:19, Isaiah 25:4, 30:20-21, 32:1-2, 10-11 Psalms 116:3-6, 108:12, 107:5-30, 86:7, 10, 46:1-7

New Testament – John 14:27 Galatians 6:15-17, 2 Thessalonians 1:6-9, 1 Peter 3:12-14

Trouble (5)

Old Testament – Deuteronomy 31:16-17, 32:35, 1 Kings 18:17-18 Joshua 7:25-26 Proverbs 24:21-22 Zc 10:2 Jeremiah 2:27-28 Lamentations 1:20-22, 2:11, 3:31-40 Zephaniah 1:14-16 Psalms 25:17-22, 34:6, 17, 71:20

New Testament – Matthew 24:6-13, 1 Corinthians 7:28, 2 Timothy 2:8-9, 2 Corinthians 1:3-6

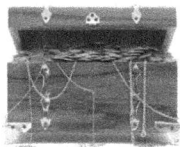

Walk In Peace

Walk In Peace (1)

"Follow peace with all men and holiness, without which no man shall see the Lord: Looking diligently lest any man fail of the grace of God; lest any root of bitterness springing up trouble you, and thereby many be defiled;(Heb 12:14-15)

Walk In Peace (2)

"But the wisdom that is from above is first pure, then peaceable, gentle, and easy to be entreated, full of mercy and good fruits, without partiality and without hypocrisy. And the fruit of righteousness is sown in peace of them that make peace. (James 3:17-18)

Walk In Peace (3)

"I create the fruit of the lips; Peace, peace to him that is afar off. .But the wicked are like the troubled sea, when it cannot rest, whose waters cast up mire and dirt." "There is no peace, saith the LORD, unto the wicked." (Isaiah 57:19-20, 48:22)

Discussion Questions

1. Must peace be pursued in order to obtain it? Explain.
2. What does it mean to be peace makers?
3. Is peace an attribute produced by the Holy Spirit? If so, how?

4. Is it important that we bridle our tongue if we strive to have peace? Explain.
5. Are we commanded to strive to be at peace with all men? How is that problematic?

Fill in the Blanks

1. "Blessed are the_____ : for they shall be called the____ of____ ."
2. "Follow____ with_____ , and____ , without which no man shall see the Lord."
3. "And the_____ of God, which passeth all_____ , shall keep your hearts and _____through Christ Jesus."
4. "Thou wilt keep him in_____ , whose mind is _____on____ : because he____ in thee."
5. "But the wisdom that is from____ is first____ , then____ , gentle, and easy to be intreated, full of____ and____ fruits, without partiality, and without_____ ."

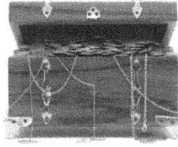

Walk In Peace

A major challenge that all Christians face is to walk daily in the path of peace. This can only be done by walking in the footsteps of the Prince of Peace, as we study His mannerisms, His responses, and His demeanor when He lived on the earth.

Walk In Peace (1)

Old Testament – Malachi 2:4-6 Psalms 34:14-18, 37:37, 120:5-7, Isaiah 26:3, 30:15, 20-21, 57:1-2, 19-21, 59:6-8

New Testament – Matthew 5:9, 23-26, 44-48 Hebrews 12:1-3, 11, 14 Philippians 4:6-9, 1 Pt 2:19-23 Ephesians 4:1-3, 32, 1:2-4

Walk In Peace (2)

Old Testament – Psalms 85:8-13, 119:165, Isaiah 26:10, 12, 32:17-18, 33:20, 48:17-22 Job 3:17-18, 25:2 Proverbs 15:18, 22:10 Ecclesiastes 9;17-18

New Testament – Galatians 5:15, 22, 1 Thessalonians 4:9-11, 2 Thessalonians 3:6-7, 11-16 James 3:14-18 Colossians 3:12-15

Walk In Peace (3)

Old Testament – Deuteronomy 20:10-12, 29:19-20 Leviticus 26:3-6, Isaiah 27:1-5, 45:7, 54:13, 55:12, 66:12-14 Psalms 55:18-23 Proverbs 16:7, 12:20 Job 22:21

New Testament – Matthew 10:11-14 John 14:27 Romans 12:18, 14:17-19, 1 Timothy 2:1-3, 2 Timothy 2:22

Walk In Peace (4)

Old Testament – Numbers 6:26, 25:10-13, 1 Kings 2:33, 1 Chronicles 22:9 Haggai 2:7-9, Isaiah 9:6-7, 52:7, 53:1-5 Nahum 1:15 Jeremiah 29:11, 33:6 Psalms 29:11, 37:11, 72:3, 7, 128:6, 147:14 Micah 5:4-5

New Testament – Romans 5:1 Ephesians 2:12-15 Philippians 4:6-7

Walk In Peace (5)

Old Testament – 2 Chronicles 15:5-6, 12-19 Ezekiel 7:25-27, 13:8-10, 17, 22, 34:23-25, 37:21-26 Jeremiah 4:10, 14, 6:13-14, 8:15, 16:5, 23:5-6 Psalms 28:3, 122:6-8, 125:5

New Testament – Luke 19:41-42 John 16:33, 2 Peter 3:14, 2 Corinthians 13:11

The Blessed Life

"The Blessed Life" (1)

"Blessed is the man that walketh not in the counsel of the ungodly... But his delight is in the law of the LORD; and in His law doth he meditate day and night. And he shall be light a tree planted by the rivers of water..." (Psalms 1:1-3)

The Blessed Life (2)

"The curse of the LORD is in the house of the wicked: but he blesseth the habitation of the just." "A faithful man shall abound with blessings..." (Proverbs 3:33, 28:20)

The Blessed Life (3)

"Not rendering evil for evil, or railing for railing: but contrariwise blessing; knowing that ye are thereunto called, that ye should inherit a blessing. For he that will love life and see good day, let him refrain his tongue from evil and his lips that they speak no guile" (1 Pet 3:9-10)

Discussion Questions

1. What are the benefits of those that acquire wisdom?
2. What was Jesus's response in Luke 11:28?
3. What were the benefits found in Deuteronomy 28:1-13?

4. Where are all spiritual blessings found according to Ephesians 1:3-10?

5. What are the blessings found in Revelation 22:14?

Fill in the Blanks

1. "_____ are they that___ his_____ , that they may have the right to the____ of____ , and may____ in through the gates of the city."

2. "The____ of the____ is in the house of the____ : but he____ the____ of the____ ."

3. "And____ these____ shall come on thee, and____ thee, if thou hearken unto the____ of the____ thy____ ."

4. "The____ cometh not, but for to____ , and to____ , and to____ : ____I am come that they might have____ , and that thy might have it more____ ."

5. "O that there were such an____ in them, that thy would fear___ , and____ all my____ always, that it might be____ with them."

The Blessed Life

*T*he word *blessed* comes from the Greek word *makarios*, which means "happy, fortunate, recipient of benefits and advantages." There are certain divine principles that, if obeyed, will be conducive to our having a life of abundant blessings from God.

The Blessed Life (1)

Old Testament – Ecclesiastes 5:18-20 Proverbs 8:12-19, 32-36 Psalms 1:1-6, 34:2-4, 12-16, 37:4-9, 22-28, 40:4, 84:4-5, 12, 119:1-7, 128:1-6, 147:11-13, Lamentations 3:25-26

New Testament – Luke 11:27-28 John 8:51, 10:9-10, 13:15-17

The Blessed Life (2)

Old Testament – Genesis 22:2, 15-18, 18:17-19, 12:1-3 Deuteronomy 28:1-13 Job 29:2-13 JoeL2:12-14 Psalms 3:8, 24:3-5, 106:3 Proverbs 11:11, 24:24- 25, 28:20

New Testament – Matthew 5:1-12 Lk 14:12-15 James 1:21-25 Romans 4:6-9, 15:29

The Blessed Life (3)

Old Testament – Ecclesiastes 2:24-26 Amos 5:14-15 Jeremiah 17:7-8, 22:3-5, 1 Chronicles 4:9-10, 2 Chronicles 27:6-9 Malachi 3:8-10 Ezekiel 44:30 Psalms 21:1-6, 34:8, 41:1-2 Proverbs 22:9, 20:21 Deuteronomy 32:46-47

New Testament – Luke 12:37-40, 10:19-20 Revelation 1:3, 22:7, 14

The Blessed Life (4)

Old Testament – Exodus 23:25-28 Deuteronomy 7:12-15, 5:29 Numbers 6:22-27, 22:11-12, 23:19-23 Psalms 5:12, 29:11, 67:1-7, 72:17, 112:1-4, 115: 12-18 Proverbs 30:11, 10:6-7, 3:33

New Testament – Romans 12:14-17, 1 Peter 3:8-10 James 3:9-10

The Blessed Life (5)

Old Testament – Deuteronomy 30:19-20, 11:26-29 Proverbs 20:7, 31:27-30 Job 1:6-10, 42:12, Isaiah 30:15, 18, 21-26, 48:17-19 Ezekiel 34:23-31 Psalms 2:12, 4:4-8, 33:12, 65:4

New Testament – Galatians 3:8-14 Acts 3:25-26 Ephesians 1:3 Revelation 16:15, 19:7-9

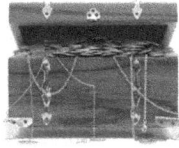

The Will

The Will (1)

"In whom we have obtained an inheritance, being predestinated accordance to the purpose of Him who worketh all things after the counsel of His own will." (Ephesians 1:11)

The Will (2)

"For whosoever shall do the will of my Father which is in heaven, the same is my brother, and sister, and mother." (Matt 12:50)

The Will (3)

"For I came down from heaven, not to do mine own will, but the will of Him that sent me." (John 6:38)

Discussion Questions

1. What is conveyed in Ephesians 1:11?
2. What was the meat Jesus referenced in John 4:34?
3. What requirement did God place on Israel in Jeremiah 7:23?
4. Discuss John 6:38-40.
5. What is conveyed in John 5:30?

Fill in the Blanks

1. Thy Kingdom come, Thy ____ be done on earth, as it is in _____.
2. And that servant which knew his lord's _____ and prepared not himself, neither did According to his ____, shall be beaten with many stripes. For ye have need of _____, that, after ye have done the ____ of God, ye might Receive the _____.
3. Of his own ____ begat He us with the word of _____, that we should be a kind of _____ of His creatures.
4. Which were born, not of blood, nor of the ____ of the flesh, nor of the ____ of man, But of God.
5. For whosoever shall do the ____ of my Father which is in heaven, the same is my _____ and ____, and ____.

The Will

T *helema* is the Greek word for *the will* in English. It connotes a determination, purpose, choice, desire, want, or wish. In Luke 22:42, Jesus submitted his will to the Father's Will. This is precisely what is needed from those of us who desire fellowship with God. We must recognize His preeminence and His authority.

> "For the word of the LORD is right; and all His works are done in truth" (Psalms 33:4).

> "He is the Rock. His work is perfect; all His ways are judgement. A God of truth and without iniquity, just and upright is He" (Deuteronomy 32:4).

The Will (1)

Old Testament – 1 Daniel 4:17, 25, 35 Proverbs 19:21 Isaiah 14:24, 46:10 Psalms 40:8, 119:7, 8, 15, 16, 32, 46-47, 143:10

New Testament – Mark 3:31-35, Matthew 6:10, 7:21, 26:39-42 John 4:34, 5:30, 9:31 Acts 13:22 Hebrews 10:7-10 Ephesians 1:11, 1 John 2:16-17

The Will (2)

Old Testament – Leviticus 19:5, 22:29, 26:12-24, 40-42 Job 13:15, 27:5 Psalms 26:6, 11, 34:1, 54:6, 77:12, 101:1-4, Isaiah 8:17, 63:7

New Testament – 2 Peter 1:21 James 1:18 John 1:12-13, 6:38-40 Matthew 21:28-31, 1 Corinthians 9:17 Ephesians 5:17, 6:6 Hebrews 10:36

The Will (3)

Old Testament – Exodus 25:2, 35:5, 21, Ezra 7:13-18, 1 Chronicles 29:3-5, 9-14, 17, 28:9 Judges 5:2, 8:23-25 Psalms 110:3, 104:33, 9:1-2

New Testament – Philemon 1:14 Hebrews 13:20-21 Acts 21:14 John 7:17 Colossians 1:9 Romans 12:2, 2 Corinthians 8:12, 1 Peter 5:2, 1 John 5:14

The Will (4)

Old Testament – Deuteronomy 18:18-20, Isaiah 22:23-25, 45:13 Psalms 89:3-5, 23-29, 34-35, 95:7-11

New Testament – Hebrews 3:7-8, 14-15 Acts 13:33-36, 3:22-23 Romans 8:27, 9:15-28 Galatians 1:4, Colossians 4:12, 1 Thessalonians 4:3, 5:18, 1 Peter 2:15, 3:17, 4:1-2

The Will (5)

Old Testament – Genesis 28:20-21, 31:3, Isaiah 66:1-2 Jeremiah 7:22-23, 11:2-4, 24:6-7, 30:17-22, 31:1, 33, 32:37-38 Ezekiel 36:26, 28 Hosea 2:19-23 Zechariah 13:9

New Testament – Luke 12:47 Philippians 2:12-15, 2 Corinthians 6:16-18 Hebrews 8:10-12 Matthew 12:50 Acts 22:14 Revelation 21:6-7

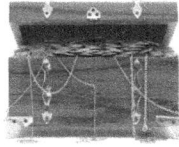

Knowing Him

Knowing Him (1)

"..Let not the wise man glory in his wisdom, neither let the mighty man glory in his might, let not the rich man glory in his riches:But let him that glorieth glory in this, that he understandeth and knoweth Me .." (Jeremiah 9:23-24)

Knowing Him (2)

"for the LORD hath a controversy with the inhabitants of the land, because there is no truth, nor mercy, nor knowledge of God in the land..My people are destroyed for lack of knowledge: ..." (Hosea 4:1, 6)

Knowing Him (3)

"Take my yoke upon you, and learn of me; for I am meek and lowly in heart: and ye shall find rest unto your souls." (Matthew 11:29)

Discussion Questions

1. Discuss Exodus 5:2.
2. Explain 2 Thessalonians 1:7-9.
3. What error is presented in Hebrews 3:10?
4. What problem exists in Isaiah 55:3-9 concerning God and man?387 Knowing Him
5. Discuss 2 Timothy 2:19.

Fill in the Blanks

1. "For I bear them record that they have a zeal of____ , but not____ to____ ."
2. "Casting down____ , and every high thing that exalteth itself against the____ of____ , and bringing into captivity____ ____ to the____ of Christ."
3. "Jesus answered and said unto them, ____ do____ , not knowing the____ , nor the ____of____ ."
4. "That all the people of the____ may____ that the____ is God, and that there is none____ ."
5. "Be still, and____ that I am God: I will be____ among the____ , I will be____ in the____ ."

Knowing Him

"Thus saith the Lord, let not the wise man glory in his wisdom, neither let the mighty man glory in his might, let not the rich man glory in his riches: But let him that glorieth glory in this, that he understandeth and knoweth me, that I am the Lord which exercise lovingkindness, judgment, and righteousness, in the earth: for in these things I delight, saith the Lord" (Jeremiah 9:23-24).

*T*his is a profound passage of Scripture that we should all take note of. Our lives should be punctuated with reading, studying, meditating, and praying as we strive to know more about God, doing His will, and doing that which pleases Him.

Knowing Him (1)

Old Testament – Exodus 5:2, 7:5, 17, 8:16-19, 14:18, 18:1, Isaiah 19:21-22, 1 Kings 8:57-60 Nahum 1:7, 1 Samuel 2:3, Job 18:17-21 Psalms 46:10, 79:6, 83:13-18, 135:5, 147:18-20

New Testament – 1 Thessalonians 4:1-5, 2 Thessalonians 1:7-8 Ephesians 4:18-20 Hebrews 3:10

Knowing Him (2)

Old Testament – Judges 2:10, Isaiah 1:2-4, 5:13 Jeremiah 2:8, 4:22, 5:1-6, 8:7-9, 9:23-24, 10:21-25, 22:16 Hosea 6:6-7, 5:4, 4:1, 6 Daniel 11:32-35

New Testament – Matthew 11:27-29, 7:22-23, 1 John 2:3-5, 13-14, 3:6, 24, 4:5-8, 13, 16

Knowing Him (3)

Old Testament – Isaiah 58:2-8, 55:8-9, 45:4-6, 20, 44:18- 20, 40:28-31, 12:5, 11:9, 2 Chronicles 30:22 Jeremiah 31:33-34 Psalms 36:10, 48:1-3, 67:1-2, 91:14, 98:2

New Testament – John 7:28-29, 8:54-55, 15:21, 16:1-3, 1 John 5:20

Knowing Him (4)

Old Testament – 1 Kings 18:36-37, Isaiah 52:5-6, 64:1-2, 66:13-14 Jeremiah 29:11 Psalms 9:10, 16 Ezekiel 39:6-7, 21-22, 36:11, 23, 35-38, 34:27-30, 20:38-42

New Testament – Matthew 22:29, 1 Corinthians 1:21, 2:9-14, 8:3, 15:34 Galatians 4:8-9 Philippians 3:8-10

Knowing Him (5)

Old Testament – Exodus 6:3 Hosea 11:3, 2:8, 1 Kings 20:13, 1 Samuel 17:46, 2 Chronicles 33:11-13, Isaiah 49:26, 37:20 Ezekiel 6:14, 7:4, 12:14-16 Psalms 95:10, 100:3, 119:66, 79, 125, 152

New Testament – John 17:3-8 Romans 10:2-3, 2 Corinthians 10:5, Colossians 1:9-10, 2 Peter 1:2-8

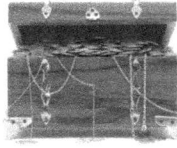

Faith

Faith (1)

"But without faith it is impossible to please Him: for he that cometh to God must believe that He is, and that He is a rewarder of them that diligently seek Him." (Hebrews 11:6)

Faith (2)

"Most men will proclaim every one his own goodness: but a faithful man who can find?" "...Nevertheless when the Son of man cometh, shall he find faith on the earth." (Prov 20:6, Lk 18:8)

Faith (3)

"For whatsoever is born of God overcometh the world: and this is the victory that overcometh the world, even our faith." (1 John 5:4)

Discussion Questions

1. Explain 2 Timothy 2:11-13.
2. Does faith in God cause us to behave differently from the world?
3. In what ways can faith be tested?
4. Explain Revelation 2:10, 13.
5. Explain Psalms 101:6.

Fill in the Blanks

1. "Now____ is the____ of things hoped for, the____ of things not seen."
2. "But they could find none occasion nor fault; forasmuch as he was_____, neither was there any error or fault____ in him."
3. "Know ye therefore that they which are of____, the same are the____ of____."
4. "If we believe not, yet He abideth_____; he cannot deny Himself."
5. "Moreover it is required in stewards, that a man be found_____."

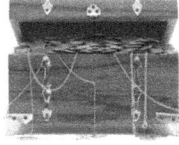

Faith

*F*aith is defined as "belief, firm persuasion, assurance, and firm conviction." Without faith, it is impossible to please God. We are tested to prove our faith to be genuine (Hebrews 11:6, 1 Peter 1:7). This is indeed a much-needed study.

Faith (1)

Old Testament – Deuteronomy 32:4-6, 20, 2 Chronicles, 20:20, Isaiah 11:1-5, 25:1, 1 Samuel 26:23 Lamentations 3:22-23 Hosea 2:20, 11:12 Psalms 143:1, 119:75-77, 90, 89:1-8, 20-24, 33 Habakkuk 2:1-4

New Testament – Galatians 3:7-11, 22-26 Hebrews 11:1-13 , 10:23 Romans 10:4-8, 17, 5:1-2

Faith (2)

Old Testament – 2 Chronicles 19:8-9, 31:11-12, 34:10, 12, 2 K22:7 Proverbs 13:17, 20:6, 25:13, 19, 28:20, 29:14 Psalms 31:23

New Testament – 2 Timothy 2:2, 13 Philippians 2:16-17 Revelation 2:10-13 Matthew 24:45-46, 25:21 Luke 16:10-12 Acts 16:15, 1 Corithians 4:2, 17, 7:25

Faith (3)

Old Testament – 1 Samuel 2:35, 22:14, 2 Samuel 20:19 Daniel 6:3-4 Proverbs 13:17, 11:13 Isaiah 8:2, 49:7 Psalms 101:6, 119:75, 90 Deuteronomy 7:9

New Testament – Luke 7:8-9, 17:5, 18:8 Hebrews 3:5-6, 11:33-39, 1 Timothy 1:12, 1 John 5:4, 1 Peter 1:7 Revelation 19:11, 21:5

Faith (4)

Old Testament – Isaiah 1:21 Jeremiah 23:28-29 Psalms 12:1, 36:5, 40:10, 92:1-2, 119:86, 138

New Testament – Jude 1:3 Titus 1:4-6, 9-13 Colossians 1:21-23, 2:5-7, 2 Corinthians 13:5, 1 Timothy 5:8, 6:10, 20-21, 2 Timothy 2:16-18, 3:8, 4:7 Ephesians 4:5, 13 Romans 16:25-26

Faith (5)

Old Testament – Numbers 12:6-7 Nehemiah 7:1-2, 9:7-8, 13:13

New Testament – Matthew 17:17-20 Luke 5:17-20, 7:47-50, 22:31-32 Ephesians 6:16, 3:12, 17, 2:8 Philippians 1:27, 3:9 Galatians 2:20 Romans 1:5-8, 17, 3:3-4, 27-31, 4:5, 9-20, 16:26 Revelation 13:10, 14:12

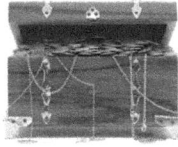

God Is Able

God Is Able (1)

"If it be so, our God whom we serve is able to deliver us from the fiery furnance, and He will deliver us out of thine hand O king." (Daniel 3:17)

God Is Able (2)

"By faith Abraham, when he was tried, offered up Isaac..Accounting that God was able to raise him up, even from the dead; from whence also he received him in a figure. (Heb 11:17-19)

God Is Able (3)

"Wherefore he is able also to save them to the uttermost that come unto God by him, seeing he ever liveth to make intercession for them." (Heb 7:25)

Discussion Questions

1. What was Daniel's response to the question asked him in Daniel 6:20, and what was the response of the king in Daniel 6:26?
2. Explain 2 Timothy 1:12.
3. Discuss Hebrews 7:25.
4. What observations are made in Revelation 5:1-5?
5. What observations are made in Ezekiel 37:11-14?

Fill in the Blanks

1. "If it be so, our God whom we serve is____ to deliver us from the____ ____ ____ , and he will deliver us out of thine hand, O King."
2. "My Father, which gave them me, is greater than all; and no man is____ to pluck them out of my____ ____ ."
3. "For in that he himself hath____ being tempted, he is____ to____ them that are tempted."
4. "Now unto Him that is____ to do____ ____ above all that we ask or think, according to the____ that worketh in us."
5. "There is one lawgiver, who is able to___ and to____ : who art thou that judgest another____ ____? To his own master he standeth or ____. Yea, he shall be ____up: for God is ____ to make him stand."

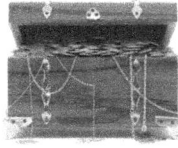

God Is Able

"For with God nothing shall be impossible" (Luke 1:37).

*W*hat an awesome passage about the God we serve. We can turn over to God all of our troubles, our hardships, our problems, and all the other things that are beyond our reach or ability to resolve because we know God is able to work out whatever challenge we face.

God Is Able (1)

Old Testament – Daniel 2:26-28, 3:15-17, 6:18-22, 2 Kings 3:16-18, 20:1-5, 9-11 Numbers 23:19-20 Jeremiah 32:17, 10:10

New Testament – Matthew 3:7-9, 10:28, 19:26, 22:46 Luke 1:37, 21:14-15 Acts 6:8-10, 20:32, 2 Corinthians 1:8- 10, 9:8, 2 Timothy 1:12

God Is Able (2)

Old Testament – Genesis 18:14 Deuteronomy 1:9, 17, 11:25 Joshua 23:8-11, 14:7-12, Isaiah 36:13-21, 37:23-29, 38, 1 Samuel 14:6, 17:33, 37, 45-47, 2 Chronicles 20:12, 25:5-9

New Testament – John 10:29 Romans 4:20-21, 8:31-39, 11:21-23 Hebrews 5:7 Jude 1:24-25

God Is Able (3)

Old Testament – Genesis 40:8, 41:16, 25 Daniel 2:47, 4:18, 35 Proverbs 19:21 Jeremiah 32:27 Job 42:2, 41:10-11 Ecclesiastes 8:17, 1 Chronicles 29:11-12, 2 Chronicles 14:11, 20:6 Joshua 10:8-14 Judges 8:3

New Testament – 1 Corinthians 10:13 Hebrews 2:18, 7:25 Ephesians 3:20, 6:11, 13, 16

God Is Able (4)

Old Testament – Nehemiah 9:20-21 Psalms 68:9-10, 81:10, 105:40-41, 107:9, 145:14-16 Ezekiel 37:1-5, 11-14, 33:10-12

New Testament – Luke 18:37, 19:40, Mark 9:23 Matthew 26:61-65, 2 Timothy 3:15 James 1:21, 5:12 Hebrews 10:4, 7-12

God Is Able (5)

Old Testament – Numbers 13:30-31, 14:24 Leviticus 26:3-9, 1 Kings 20:21-28 Isaiah 40:15, 17, 41:10-14-20, 43:1-5 Psalms 46:6-7, 18:18-19, Zechariah 4:6-7 Hosea 11:9-11

New Testament – Acts 5:39 Romans 14:4 Philippians 3:20-21, 2 Corinthians 3:5-6 Titus 1:9 Revelation 5:1-5, 6:17

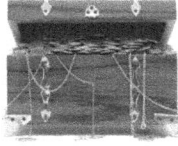

Evil Hearts of Unbelief

Evil Hearts of Unbelief (1)

"Take heed, brethren, lest there be in any of you an evil heart of unbelief, in departing from the living God ..So we see that they could not enter in because of unbelief . (Hebrews 3:12, 19)

Evil Hearts of Unbelief (2)

"For unto us was the gospel preached as well as unto them: but the word preached did not profit them, not being mixed with faith in them that heard it.. Let us labour therefore to enter into that rest, lest any man fall after the same example of unbelief." (Heb 4:2, 11)

Evil Hearts of Unbelief (3)

"Those by the way side are they that hear; then cometh the devil, and taketh away the word out of their hearts, lest they should believe and be saved." (Luke 8:12)

Discussion Questions

1. Explain Psalms 78:10-12, 22.
2. What problem existed in Luke 18:9?
3. Explain John 8:24.
4. What did Jesus marvel at in Mark 6:6?
5. Explain Mark 16:16.

Fill in the Blanks

1. "But these are____, that ye might____ that Jesus is the____, the____ of____; and that____ ye might have____ through his____."
2. "Take heed, brethren, lest there be in any of you an____ heart of____, in departing from the living God."
3. "And He____ because of their____. And he went round about the villages, ____."
4. "For what if some did not____? shall their____ make the faith of God without ____?"
5. "He that____ and is____ shall be; but he that____ ____ shall be____.

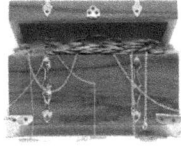

Evil Hearts of Unbelief

*O*ne of the primary reasons many will be lost is the result of unbelief. In spite of the preponderance of evidence presented by historians, by the testimony found in both Old Testament and New Testament, and despite the declarations made by faithful Christians who have been guided by His Word and His Spirit, still many refuse to acknowledge Jesus as Lord. They refuse to submit to His will. They reject the Son of God, and they reject God because of evil hearts of unbelief.

Evil Hearts of Unbelief (1)

Old Testament – Exodus 4:1-9 Numbers 14:11 Deuteronomy 1:30-32 Psalms 106:21-24, 94:6-10, 78:9-12, 18-22, 32, 10:6-13 Jeremiah 5:12-14, 7:8-11, 23-28 Zephaniah 1:12 Ecclesiastes 8:11-12

New Testament – Hebrews 3:12-19, 4:1-6, 11, 10:38-39 Romans 3:3-4, 2 Corinthians 4:3-4

Evil Hearts of Unbelief (2)

Old Testament – Numbers 20:7-12 Deuteronomy 9:23, 32:20 Ezekiel 8:12, 12:21-28, Isaiah 47:7-15 Psalms 14:1-3, 73: 11-24 Job 21:13-15, 28-31

New Testament – Mark 6:4-6, 9:23-24, 16:11-16 John 1:10-12, 6:40, 64-69, 8:24 Romans 11:20-23, 30-33

Evil Hearts of Unbelief (3)

Old Testament – Genesis 3:1-4, 19:14, 17, 26 Proverbs 14:9, 26, 1 Kings 18:21, 2 Kings 7:1-2, 18-20, 17:13-14, Isaiah 7:9-14, 28:16, 53:1-2 Hosea 8:12 Jeremiah 6:10

New Testament – Luke 22:67-71, 8:12 John 5:38, 8:43-45, 10:26, 37-38, 1 Timothy 1:12-13

Evil Hearts of Unbelief (4)

Old Testament – Zechariah 7:8-12, 1:4, Isaiah 30:8-14, 2 Chronicles 36:14-16, 30:7-10 Ezekiel 9:9, 20:45-49, Isaiah 44:18-20, Jeremiah 8:6-9, 12, 26:8-16, 28:13-17, 44:4-11 Psalms 82:5

New Testament – John 12:37-41, Luke 12:45-46, 2 Corinthians 6:14-15 Philippians 1:29 Revelation 21:8

Evil Hearts of Unbelief (5)

Old Testament – Exodus 19:9 Jeremiah 22:21, 29 Psalms 81:11, 13

New Testament – John 14:9-13, 16:8-9, 30, 17:20-21, 20:25-31, 2 Thessalonians 1:7-10, 2:8-12, 1 Corinthians 7:12-15 Acts 13:48, 14:1-2, 26:27-29 Titus 1:15-16, 1 Peter 2:7-8, 1 John 5:10, 2 Timothy 2:13

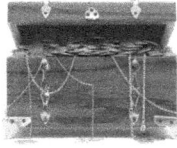

Be Content

Be Content (1)

"But godliness with contentment is great gain. For we brought nothing into this World and it is certain we can carry nothing out. And having food and raiment let us be therewith content." (1 Timothy 6:6-8)

Be Content (2)

"Hell and destruction are never full; so the eyes of man are never satisfied." (Proverbs 27:20)

Be Content (3)

"...For I have learned, in whatsoever state I am, therewith to be content. I know how to be abased and I know how to abound: everywhere and in all things I am instructed both to be full and to be hungry, both to abound and to suffer need." (Phillipians 4:11-12)

Discussion Questions

1. Discuss Ecclesiastes 5:10-11.
2. What warning did Jesus give in Luke 12:15?
3. Is discontentment a reason for those that murmur?
4. What is conveyed in 1 Timothy 6:6-8?
5. Explain Philippians 4:11-12

Fill in the Blanks

1. "Not that I speak in____ of want: for I have____ , in whatsoever state I am, therewith to be____ ."
2. "Lay not up for yourselves____ upon____ , where moth and rust doth corrupt."
3. "Love not the____ , neither the____ that are in the____ . If any man____ the world, the love of the Father is ___in____ ."
4. "The young lions do____ , and suffer____ : but they that seek the Lord shall not____ any____ ____ ."
5. "I have coveted no man's____ , or gold, or _____."

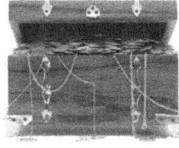

Be Content

C ontentment is a great challenge for many whose lives are centered on material things, social status, money, jobs, or things of this world. But there is a contentment that comes from the Spirit of God and from having a right relationship with God that transcends the ebb and flow of this world's amenities.

Be Content (1)

Old Testament – Ecclesiastes 5:10-11, 4:8, 3:10-12, Proverbs 30:8-9,15-16, 21-23, 27:15-26, 20, 26:21, 19:23, 17:1, 14:14, 12:11,14, Isaiah 5:8, Jeremiah 22:13-17, Nehemiah 5:1-13

New Testament – Luke 12:15, 3:10-14, 1 Timothy 6:6-8

Be Content (2)

Old Testament – Leviticus 10:16-20 Exodus 2:16-21, 16:2-20 Numbers 11:1-10, 18-20, 31-34, 12:1-15, 14:26-29, 35-37 Nehemiah 9:21-26 Proverbs 25:16, 22:10,18: 6, 18, 17:14, 15:16 Psalms 36:7-8, 65:4, 107:9, 145:16

New Testament – John 6:43, 1 Corinthians 10:6-11 James 5:9, 4:1-7

Be Content (3)

Old Testament – Joshua 7:7-11 Exodus 14:11-12, 17:1-4,7 Psalms 78:18-32, 34:9-10 Isaiah 5:1-5, 56:10-11 Hosea 4:6, 10 Ecclesiastes 1:7-8, 2:9-11, 24, 6:9 Proverbs 13:25, 16:8, 17:1, 23:4-5, 25:27

New Testament – Philippians 2:14-15 Hebrews 13:5 James 4:1-4

Be Content (4)

Old Testament – Judges 17:6-11, 2 Kings 5:21-27, 6:1-3 Job 6:25-28,20:19-23, 28-29, 27:13-14, 2 Samuel 12:8-12 Proverbs 5:15-20, 13:7, 11, 21:25-26, 22:16, 28:16 Psalms 63:5

New Testament – Phillipians 4:11-13 Acts 20:33-35, 2 Corinthians 12:20-21 Luke 9:25

Be Content (5)

Old Testament – Micah 2:1-10, 6:10-15 Haggai 1:6,9 Amos 1:13, 8:4-8 Ezekiel 7:19, 27 Proverbs 18:10-11, 18-19 Isaiah 26:3, 28:12-13, 30:15, 43:19-20, 48:22, 55:1-2, 58:6-11 Jeremiah 31:14, 25, 50:19

New Testament – 3 John 1:9-11, 2 Corinthians 12:20-21, 9:8-10 Philippians 4:19 James 3:14-18, 1 Thessalonians 4:11-12, 1 Timothy 2:1-2

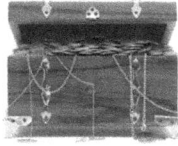

Hope

Hope (1)

"If in this life only we have hope in Christ, we are of all men most miserable." (1 Corinthians 15:19)

Hope (2)

"For there is hope for a tree, if it is cut down, that it will sprout again... but man dieth, and wasteth away; yea, man giveth up the ghost, and where is he?" "Happy is he that hath the God of Jacob...whose hope is in the LORD his God." (Job 14:7-10, Ps 146:5)

Hope (3)

"Hope deferred maketh the heart sick: but when the desire cometh, it is a tree of Life." (Proverbs 13:12)

Discussion Questions

1. Explain Lamentations 3:16-24.
2. According to Romans 15:4, can we have the hope of heaven without obeying the Scriptures? What is the hope of the hypocrite?
3. What happens when hope is deferred?
4. Explain Romans 5:2-4.
5. Discuss 1 Corinthians 15:19.

Fill in the Blanks

1. "The Lord is my portion, saith my____ ; therefore will
   I____ in him."
2. "Which____ we have as an____ of the____ , both____ and____ ,
   and___ which entereth into that within the veil."
3. "For whatsoever things were____ aforetime were____ for
   our____ , that we through patience and comfort of the____
   might have hope."
4. "That at that time ye were without____ , being____ from the
   commonwealth of Israel, and strangers from the covenants of
   promise, having____ ____ , and without____ in the____ ."
5. "Paul, an apostle of____ ____ by the____ of God our Saviour,
   and Lord Jesus Christ, which is____ ____ .

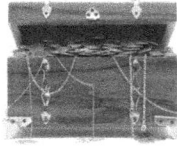

Hope

*H*ope is the anchor of the soul. It enables the Christian to be steadfast and unmovable even in the midst of storms, chaos, and confusion. Hope opens our eyes to see that which is far off, beyond our present world, beyond our present circumstances.

> "For we are saved by hope; but hope that is seen is not hope: for what a man seeth, why doth he yet hope for? But if we hope for that we see not, then do we with patience wait for it" (Romans 8:24-25).

Hope (1)

Old Testament – Psalms 16:8-9, 22:9-10, 31:24, 42:5-8, 43:3-5, 71:5-14, 130:5-7, 141:1-3 Lamentations 3:17-29

New Testament – Acts 2:25-26 Romans 15:4, 12:12, 8:24-25, Hebrews 6:16-19, Titus 1:1-2, 1 Corinthians 15:16-19

Hope (2)

Old Testament – Zechariah 9:9, 12 JoeL3:16 Hosea 2:15 Psalms 38:15, 39:6-7, 78:5-7, 146:5 Proverbs 13:12, 14:32 Job 11:14-20, 14:7-10, 17:11-15

New Testament – Titus 3:4-7 Romans 15:13, 8:16-25 Ephesians 2:11-13, 1 Timothy 1:1, Hebrews 3:6

Hope (3)

Old Testament – Job 4:6-9, 5:15-16, 6:11-13, 7:6-7, 27:3-8, 31:24-28 Psalms 42:11, 119:49, 166, 147:11

New Testament – Romans 4:17-18 Acts 26:6-7, 28:20 Galatians 5:5, 1 Peter 3:14-15

Hope (4)

Old Testament – Proverbs 10:28, 11:7, 14:32, 19:18, 23:15, 18, 24:13-14 Jeremiah 2:25-26, 18:11-12, 31:16-17, Isaiah 38:17-18 Psalms 33:16-18, 119:80-81

New Testament – 2 Thessalonians 2:16 Philippians 1:20 Romans 5:1-5, 1 Thessalonians 5:8 Titus 3:5-7

Hope (5)

Old Testament – Ruth 1:12-13 Job 8:11-15, 20:4-5, 41:1, 9 Proverbs 26:12, 29:20 Psalms 9:18, 62:5, 119:114, 116 Jeremiah 14:8-9, 17:7

New Testament – Ephesians 4:4 Colossians 1:23, 27, 1 John 3:2-3, 1 Peter 1:3, 13 Titus 2:11-13, 2 Corinthians 3:12-14, 1 Corinthians 13:4-7, 13

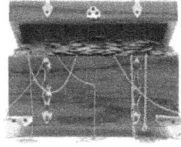

The Cry for Justice

The Cry for Justice (1)

So I returned, and considered all the oppressions that are done under the sun: and behold the tears of such as were oppressed and they had no comforter, and on the side of their oppressers there was power; but they had no comforter. (Ecc 4:1)

The Cry for Justice (2)

"None calleth for justice, nor any pleadeth for truth: they trust in vanity and speak lies..And judgement is turned away backward and justice standeth afar off..and the Lord saw it and it displeased Him that there was no judgement. (Is 59:4, 14, 15)

The Cry for Justice (3)

"To do justice and judgement is more acceptable to the LORD than sacrifice." (Proverbs 21:3)

Discussion Questions

1. What happened in Exodus 2:23-25?624 The Spiritual Treasure Trove
2. Explain Isaiah 28:17.
3. Explain Isaiah 61:8.
4. What will happen in Colossians 3:25?

5. What was the complaint of the prophet Amos in Amos 5:10-15?

Fill in the Blanks

1. "And shall not____ avenge his own, which____ day and night unto him, though he bear____ with them?"
2. "And the Lord said, I have surely seen the____ of my people which are in Egypt, and have heard their___ by reason of their____ ; for I know their____ ."
3. "Vengeance is ____; I will____ , saith the Lord."
4. "For the____ of the poor, for the____ of the needy, now will I arise, saith the Lord; I will____ him in____ from him tha____t at him."
5. "Then said Paul unto him, ___ shall smite thee, thou ___wall: for____ thou to____ me after the law, and____ me to be____ contrary to the law?"

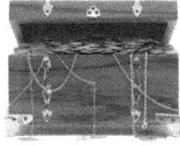

The Cry for Justice

*I*n a culture of oppression, collusion, unfairness, abuse, perverseness, and evil, there is a desperate cry for justice. God's very nature is to render to every man according to his works. God is a righteous judge who sits high and looks low. He declares to all men, "Vengeance is mine; I will repay." These are indeed words of comfort and reassurance to those who carry deep hurts, burdens, and heartaches. They are now free to live life without anger, bitterness, rage, unrest, and vindictive feelings because they know God will answer their cry in due time. God will render justice on their behalf.

The Cry for Justice (1)

Old Testament – Deuteronomy 10:17-18, 16:18-20, 32:4, 2 Chronicles 19:5-10, Ecclesiastes 4:1, 5:8, 8:5-6, Lamentations 3:58-65, Job 19:7, 16:16-20, Psalms 7:6-9, 9:19, 10:16-18, 12:5, 82:1-5, 89:14-15

New Testament – Luke 18:1-8, James 5:4-9, Revelation 6:9-10

The Cry for Justice (2)

Old Testament – Habakkuk 1:2-4, 2:1-7, Ecclesiastes 3:16-18, Zechariah 7:9-14, 8:16-17, Ezekiel 18:5-9, 45:9, Isaiah 59:4-15, 56:1, Amos 5:11-15, 24, Jeremiah 21:12, 22:3, 15-17, 23:5-6, Psalms 33:4-5, 37:28

New Testament – 1 Peter 4:5, James 4:2-6, 13, Colossians 3:25

The Cry for Justice (3)

Old Testament – Genesis 16:5, 31:50-53, Exodus 18:21-22, 26 Numbers 27:3-5, Judges 11:27, 2 Samuel 23:3, 8:15 Job 8:3-4, 37:23-24, Isaiah 1:16-17, 10:1-3, 26:10 Psalms 119:121, 140:12 Pr 8:12, 15

New Testament – Romans 9:14, John 7:24, 5:30

The Cry for Justice (4)

Old Testament – Deuteronomy 33:20-21, 24:14-17 Leviticus 19:13, 15, 25:17, 1 Samuel 12:3-5 Zephaniah 3:5 Proverbs 28:5, 16, 29:27, 31:4-9, Isaiah 28:17 Job 34:24-28, 35:8-14 Psalms 86:14-17

New Testament – Matthew 10:29-31 Luke 16:8-10 Romans 12:19

The Cry for Justice (5)

Old Testament – Exodus 22:22-27, 23:6-9, Micah 2:1-3, 3:9-12, 6:8-9, Ezekiel 22:7-11, 24-29, 9:4-11 Malachi 3:5 Proverbs 22:22-23, 21:3, 14:31 Psalms 103:6, 68:5 Jeremiah 7:5-7, 31:23

New Testament – Acts 25:7-11, 25, 1 Timothy 1:9 Romans 2:1-11

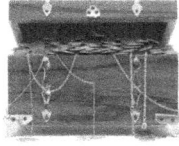

Preach

Preach (1)

"For the preaching of the cross is to them that perish foolishness; but unto us which are saved it is the power of God. (1 Corinthians 1:18)

Preach (2)

"And I saw another angel fly in the midst of heaven, having the everlasting gospel to preach unto them that dwell on the earth, and to every nation, and kindred, and tongue, and people (Revelations 14:7)

Preach (3)

"I charge thee therefore before God and the Lord Jesus Christ... Preach the word; be instant in season and out of season; reprove, rebuke, exhort... For the time will come when they shall not endure sound doctrine; but after their own lusts..." (2 Tim 4:1-3)

Discussion Questions

1. What observations are made in Isaiah 6:8-11?
2. Is preaching the Word of God a way of getting men to repent?
3. Explain the role of a preacher, noted in 2 Timothy 4:1-2.
4. Discuss 1 Corinthians 9:16-17, 27.
5. Discuss Jeremiah 23:16-22, 28-32.

Fill in the Blanks

1. "And they went out, and ____ that men should repent."
2. "And I saw another angel fly in the midst of heaven, having the____ ____ to____ unto them."
3. "____ the kingdom of God, and____ those things which concern the Lord Jesus Christ, with al____l , no man____ him."
4. "And now, behold, I know that ye all, among whom I have gone____ the____ of____ ."
5. "For though I____ the____ , I have nothing to glory of: for necessity is laid upon me; yea, ____ is unto me, if I____ ____ the____ !"

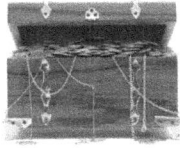

Preach

"And he said unto them, 'Go ye into all the world, and preach
the gospel to every creature'" (Mark 16:15).

*T*he word *preach* in the New Testament comes from the Greek word
kerusso, which means "to proclaim" according to *Strong's Greek
Concordance*. God has always sent men to publicly proclaim, "Thus
says the Lord." His will must be made known to all mankind, and His
gospel must be preached to all nations.

Preach (1)

Old Testament=Jonah 1:1-2, 3:2-10, Isaiah 6:8-11, 41:25-27, 52:7, 58:1, 61:1-3,
Nahum 1:15 Malachi 3:1, 4:5

*New Testament – Luke 1:76-80, 3:3-18, 4:43-44, 7:25-35 Acts 11:19-20, 14:6-7,
16:10, Romans 10:14-15, Colossians 1:23-29, Revelation 14:6-7*

Preach (2)

Old Testament – Numbers 22:38, 24:13 Ezekiel 2:1-10, 3:1-4, 10-11, Isaiah
40:6-9 Ecclesiastes 1:12-13, 7:27-29, 12:9-11

*New Testament=Matthew 4:17, 10:7, 27, 11:1 Mark 16:15-16, 2 Peter 2:4-5, 1 Peter
4:11, 1 Thessalonians 2:4-8, 1 Corinthians 1: 18-21, Galatians 1:6-12, 1 Timothy 4:1-2*

Preach (3)

Old Testament – Jeremiah 1:16-17, 7:28, 25:3-4, Amos 3:6-8, 2 Chronicles 36:15-16 Ezekiel 33:2-16, 3:1-4, 8-11, 2:7-10

New Testament – Acts 28:20-31, 20:19-27, 13:32-42, 10:34-36, 42-43, 9:17-20, 8:4-5, 12, 25-40, 3:13-21, 1 Corinthians 15:1-4

Preach (4)

Old Testament – Lamentations 2:14, Jeremiah 23:16-18, 22, 28-32, 20:7-11, 15:16, 1:4-9, Hosea 9:7-8, Isaiah 30:8-11, Amos 5:10 Micah 3:5-8

New Testament – Luke 6:26 John 7:7, 17:14 Acts 17:2-3, 2 Timothy 4:17, 1 Corithians 15:14, 9:16, 27, 2:1-4

Preach (5)

Old Testament – Nehemiah 6:6-8, 12, Isaiah 8:16, 20, Jeremiah 5:26-31, 26:2-6, 42:4, Ezekiel 13:2-4, 16:2, 23:36-37, 33:7-9, 30-33

New Testament – Luke 8:1, 9:1-6, 60, 11:32, 24:45-47, Acts 5:42, 8:12, 14:12-15, Romans 1:15-16, 16:25-27, 2 Corinthians 4:5

Rejoice

Rejoice (1)

"...but rather rejoice, because your names are written in heaven."
(Luke 10:19-20)

Rejoice (2)

"I rejoice at thy word, as one that findeth great spoil." (Psalms 119:162)

Rejoice (3)

"But let all those that put their trust in thee rejoice: let them ever shout
for joy, because thou defendest them: let them also that love thy name
be joyful in thee." (Psalm 5:11)

Discussion Questions

1. When the heart is heavy-laden, what are the results?
2. What happens when we speak good and kind words to others?
3. In Acts 8:35-39, what made the eunuch rejoice after his discourse with Phillip?
4. What are the fruits of the Spirit?
5. Why should we rejoice even when men hate us for being a Christian?

Fill in the Blanks

1. "A____ heart doeth ____like a____ : but a____ spirit____ the bones.
2. ____in the____ alway; and again I say, ____ ."
3. "Notwithstanding in this rejoice____ , that the spirits are____ unto you; but rather ____, because your____ are written in____ ."
4. "The____ of the eyes____ the heart: and a good ____maketh the bones____ ."
5. "And ye now therefore have____ : but I will see you____ , and your heart shall____ , and your____ no man taketh from you."

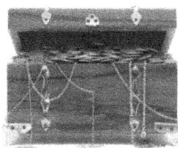

Rejoice

*G*od never intended for His people to be unhappy, dismayed, or conflicted, but rather to be joyous. Rejoicing in His goodness, His mercy, and His kindness, Christians are a glad, radiant, and cheerful people—not because of the world they presently live in, but because of the God of Heaven Who lives within them, and because of His Spirit Who dwells within their hearts.

Rejoice (1)

Old Testament – Ecclesiastes 3:11-12, 5:18-20, 11:7-10, 1 Chronicles 16:10, 31-32, Psalms 9:2, 14, 20:5, 21:1, 28:7, 31:7, 119:111, 162, Jeremiah 15:16, 1 Samuel 2:1, Isaiah 64:5, Habakkuk 3:17-18

New Testament – Luke 10:20, John 3:29, Hebrews 3:6, 1 Peter 1:3-8 Acts 5:41-42

Rejoice (2)

Old Testament – Deuteronomy 12:7, 12, 14:26, 26:10-11, 28:47-48, Isaiah 61:10-11, 51:3, 41:13-16, 35:1-4, 10, 25:9, Psalms 126:6, 107:42-43, 105:3, 70:4, 28:7

New Testament – Luke 1:11-14, 26-33, 41-47, 6:20-23 John 5:35, Matthew 5:9-12

Rejoice (3)

Old Testament – Leviticus 23:40, Deuteronomy 16:10-11, 27:6-7, 2 Chronicles 23:18, 6:40-41 Nehemiah 12:43 Job 8:20-21, Isaiah 29:19, 65:17-19, Psalms 68:3-4, 71:23, 89:16, 90:14, 97:12, 149:2, 5

New Testament – Luke 15:3-10, 19:36-39, John 4:34-36, 16:22

Rejoice (4)

Old Testament – JoeL1:12, 2:21-27, Zechariah 2:10-13, 4:10, 9:9, 10:6-7, Zephaniah 3:14-17, Isaiah 9:2-6, Proverbs 29:2, 6, 28:12, 27:9, 14:7, Psalms 13:5-6, 16:8-9, 32:11

New Testament – Matthew 18:10-13 Acts 2:25-26 Romans 5:12 James 1:9 Philippians 3:1-3

Rejoice (5)

Old Testament – Isaiah 66:10-14, 65:13-14, 62:5, Jeremiah 31:11-13, 32:41-42 Micah 7:8-9 Psalms 2:10-12, 5:8-11, 13:3-5, 14:7, 30:1, 86:4, 104:31, 34, 106:4-5

New Testament – 1 Peter 4:12-15, Romans 15:8-10, 1 Corinthians 13:4-6, Galatians 4:26-27, Revelation 19:7

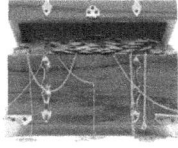

God's Love

God's Love (1)

"The LORD hath appeared of old unto me, saying, Yea, I have loved thee with an everlasting love: therefore with lovingkindness have I drawn thee. (Jer 31:3)

God's Love (2)

"As the Father hath loved me, so also have I loved you: continue ye in my love. If you keep my commandments, ye shall abide in my love; even as I have kept my Father's commandments and abide in His love. (John 15:9-10)

God's Love (3)

"Herein is love, not that we loved God, but that He loved us and sent His Son to be the propitiation for our sins. Beloved, if God loved us, we ought also to love one another. (1 John 4:9-10)

Discussion Questions

1. Can the love of God make a significant impact on those around us? Explain.
2. How did God demonstrate His love for all of mankind?
3. Explain 1 Corinthians 8:3.

4. What is the new commandment that Christ has given to those who follow him?
5. Explain Romans 8:28.

Fill in the Blanks

1. "For God so____ the world, that he gave his only____ ____ , that whosoever____ in him should not perish but have____ ____ ."
2. "Keep yourselves in the____ of____ , looking for the____ of our Lord Jesus Christ unto____ ____ ."
3. "The Lord did not____ his____ upon you, nor choose you, because ye were more in number than any people."
4. "But if any man___ God, the same is____ of him."
5. "And we know that____ ____ work together for good to them that____ ____ ."

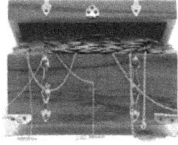

God's Love

*T*he love that God has is matchless and beyond comprehension. It abounds in mercy, kindness, forgiveness, compassion, loyalty, and endearment. Ancient Greek culture used the term *agape* in referring to the highest form of love that originates with God. In Luke 6:35-36, we are instructed to "love ye your enemies and do good, and lend, hoping for nothing again; and your reward shall be great, and ye shall be the children of the Highest: for he is kind unto the unthankful and to the evil. Be ye therefore merciful, as your Father also is merciful." Again, we read, "Beloved, let us love one another: for love is of God; and everyone that loveth is born of God, and knoweth God" (1 John 4:7).

God's Love (1)

Old Testament – Deuteronomy 4:37, 7:6-10, 23:3-5, 33:3, 1 Kings 10:9, 2 Chronicles 2:11-12, 9:7-8, Malachi 1:2, 5, 2:11, Jeremiah 31:3-4

New Testament – John 3:16-19, 15:9-12, 17-19, 17:23-26, Romans 5:1-5, 8:37-39, Galatians 2:20, Ephesians 2:4-7, 5:1-2, 25, 28

God's Love (2)

Old Testament – Deuteronomy 10:14-19, Exodus 19:4-6, 23:22 Numbers 14:8 Hosea 11:3-4, Isaiah 40:11, 43:4, 48:12-15, 49:15-16, Jeremiah 29:11-13, Zephaniah 3:17, Psalms, 5:11, 36:10, 139:17-18

New Testament – Matthew 5:44-48, John 13:34-35, 1 Chronicles 2:9, 1 John 4:7-12, 16-21

God's Love (3)

Old Testament – Proverbs 3:11-12, 12:22, 15:9, 2 Chronicles 16:9, Psalms 11:7, 17:7, 18:30, 26:3, 33:5, 37:28, 45:7, 47:4, 91:4, 2 Samuel 12:24, 1 Kings 3:3 Nehemiah 13:26

New Testament – John 14:21-31, 15:9-10, 17:22-26 Jude 1:21, Romans 8:28

God's Love (4)

Old Testament – Zechariah 2:8, Deuteronomy 33:12, 26-29, 32:9-20 Hosea 1:2-7, 3:1, 11:8-12, Ezekiel 16:5-19, 30-43, 60-63, Isaiah 5:1-7, 54:5-8, Psalms 78:37-38, 25:6

New Testament – 2 Corinthians 5:14, 17, Ephesians 1:3-6, 3:17-19, Romans 1:6-7, 9:25, 11:26-27, 1 Thessalonians 1:4

God's Love (5)

Old Testament – Daniel 9:23, 10:11, 19 Joshua 23:11, Judges 5:31, 2 Chronicles 19:2-3, Isaiah 63:7 Nehemiah 1:5, Psalms 4:2-3, 60:4-5, 87:2, 91:14, 97:10, 103:13- 18, 122:6, 145:20, 146:8

New Testament – John 16:27, 15:9-10, 1 Corinthians 8:3, 1 John 3:1-2, 5:3

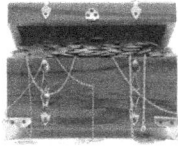

Jealousy and Envy

Jealousy and Envy (1)

"Wrath is cruel, and anger is outrageous; but who is able to stand before envy?" (Prov 27:4)

Jealousy and Envy (2)

"For he knew that the chief priests had delivered him for envy." (Mark 15:10)

Jealousy and Envy (3)

"..for love is strong as death; jealousy is cruel as the grave: the coals thereof are coals of fire, which hath a most vehement flame." (Song of Solomon 8:6)

Discussion Questions

1. Explain Ecclesiastes 4:4.
2. Are envy and jealousy fruits of the flesh? Explain.
3. Why did the chief priests deliver Jesus to Pilate?468 The Spiritual Treasure Trove
4. Explain 1 Corinthians 3:3.
5. Does love envy others?

Fill in the Blanks

1. "____ suffereth____ , and is kind:____ envieth____ ."
2. "For he knew that the____ ____ had delivered him for ____."
3. "For ye are yet____ : for whereas there is among you____ , and____ , and____ , are ye not____ , and____ as men?"
4. "____ , murders, ____ , revellings, and such like: of the which I tell you before, as I have told you in time past, that they which do such things shall____ inherit the____ of____ ."
5. "But when the____ saw the____ , they were filled with____ , and spake against those things which were____ by____ ."

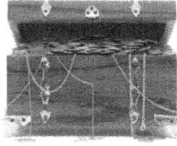

Jealousy and Envy

*J*ealousy is a term derived from the Greek word *zelos*. It engenders selfish ambition, conflict, strife, anger, wrath, rage—all types of negative emotional expressions because of greed or covetousness in the heart. It could be desire for another's wealth, good fortune, social status, talent, skills, recognition, youth, clothes, opportunities, or privileges. Envy is derived from the Greek word *pythonos*. It is the feeling of displeasure produced by witnessing or hearing of the prosperity or success of others. Envy desires to and seeks to deprive another of what he has.

> "Wrath is cruel, and anger is outrageous; but who is able to stand before envy?" (Proverbs 27:4).

Jealousy and Envy (1)

Old Testament – Proverbs 27:4, 24:1-2, 19-20, 23:17, 14:30, 3:31-32 Job 5:2, Psalms 37:1-2, 73:3, 18-20, Ecclesiastes 4:4, 9:3, 6

New Testament – Matthew 27:12, 18, Acts 7:9, 17:5, James 4:4-5, 3:14-16, Philippians 2:3, 1:15-18, Galatians 5:19-20, 26

Jealousy and Envy (2)

Old Testament – Genesis 26:11-14, 37:5-11, 1 Kings 21:1-19, 1 Samuel 18:6-9, Psalms 35:11-16, 19-21, 40:14-15, Ezekiel 36:1-7, Isaiah 11:9-13, 26:11-12

New Testament – John 12:17-19, 11:47-48, 53, 57, Mark 15:10, Acts 13:45 Titus 3:3-7

Jealousy and Envy (3)

Old Testament – Genesis 29:30-32, Song Of Solomon 8:6, Exodus 20:17, Proverbs 6:30-35 2 Samuel 12:1-12, Numbers 5:12-31 Ezekiel 16:2-20, 30-38, 35:10-15

New Testament – Romans 1:28-32, 1 Peter 2:1-3, 1 Corinthians 3:1-3, 4:10-14, 2 Corinthians 10:10-18, 12:20-21

Jealousy and Envy (4)

Old Testament – Exodus 34:14, Deuteronomy 4:24, 5:6-110, 6:14-15, 32:15-22, Joshua 24:17-23, Job 31:26-28, Jeremiah 2:3-11, 18:13-17, Isaiah 42:13, Nahum 1:2, Zechariah 1:14, 8:2, Psalms 79:4-5, JoeL2:18

New Testament – 1 Corinthians 10:19-22, 2 Corinthians 11:2-3, Romans 10:19

Jealousy and Envy (5)

Old Testament – Genesis 4:3-8, 16:1-6, 26:9-14, 30:1-2, 22-24, 31:1-12, 1 Samuel 1:1-8, 20, Daniel 6:1-14, Obadiah 1:9-15, 1 Kings 14:22, Ezekiel 8:1-6, 38:19, 39:25

New Testament – Romans 13:13, 11:11-14, 1 John 3:12, 1 Corinthians 13:4-5, 1 Timothy 6:3-4

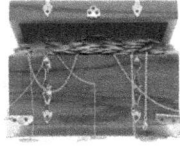

Overcoming the Devil

Overcoming the Devil (1)

"And they overcame him by the blood of the Lamb, and by the word of their testimony: and they loved not their lives unto the death. (Revelation 12:11)

Overcoming the Devil (2)

"Put on the whole armour of God that ye may be able to stand against the wiles of the devil...taking the shield of faith.. to quench all the fiery darts of the wicked." (Eph 6:11, 16)

Overcoming the Devil (3)

"Concerning the works of men, by the word of thy lips I have kept me from the paths of the destroyer." (Psalms 17:4)

Discussion Questions

1. How did the Devil allure Eve in Genesis 3:1-4, 11-15?684 The Spiritual Treasure Trove
2. What transpired in 1 Chronicles 21:1-13?
3. Explain Romans 16:17-20.
4. Explain 2 Corinthians 12:7-10.
5. Explain John 8:34-47.

Fill in the Blanks

1. "Ye are of your father the____ , and the____ of your father ye will ____"
2. "And the Lord said unto, The Lord rebuke thee, O _____."
3. "Ye shall know them by their. Do men gather grapes of, or figs of____ ?"
4. "As saith the proverb of the ancients, ____ proceedeth from the_____ ."
5. "But the Lord is____ , who shall stablish you, and keep you from____."

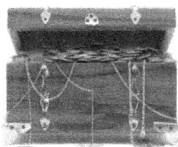

Overcoming the Devil

*T*he greatest challenge we face on the time side of life is overcoming the Devil. He has schemes, he has devices, and he has evil allurements and enticements, all designed to separate us from the love and fellowship of God.

Overcoming the Devil (1)

Old Testament – Genesis 3:1-4, 11-15 Deuteronomy 32:15-22, 1 Chronicles 21: 1-13 Zechariah 3:1-7, Isaiah 14:9-15 Job 1:6-12, 2:1-10

New Testament Matthew 4:1-11, 15:22-28, 17:18, Luke 8:12, 22:3-4, 31-32, 1 John 3:7-10, 4:4, 5:18-19, Revelation 12:7-11, 17

Overcoming the Devil (2)

Old Testament – Daniel 11:27-32, 8:11-12, 24-25, Isaiah 14:19, Psalms 17:4, 36:11-12, 37:20, 94:20-23

New Testament – Acts 13:6-11, 19:13-17, 26:18, Ephesians 2:2, 4:27-32, 6:10-18, James 2:19, 3:14-15, 1 John 2:13-17, Revelation 20:10

Overcoming the Devil (3)

Old Testament – Leviticus 17:7, 19:31 Deuteronomy 18:10-14, 29:26-27, 1 Samuel 28:3-13, Psalms 106:34-37

New Testament – 1 Corinthians 10:19-21, Acts 8:9-24, 5:1-5, John 14:30, 8:37-49, 2 Corinthians 4:1-4.2:9-11, 1 Timothy 5:13-15 Revelation 16:13-14, 19:19-20

Overcoming the Devil (4)

Old Testament – Job 1:6-12, 2:6-10, 15:20-35, 18:5-14, 20:12-29, 21:28-34, 27:13-21, Habakkuk 2:5 Proverbs 27:20, Psalms 9:17

New Testament – Revelation 20:1-3, 19:19-20, 12:12-17, Matthew 16:18, 22-23, Hebrews 2:11-15, 1 Thessalonians 2:18 Luke 4:13

Overcoming the Devil (5)

Old Testament – Ezekiel 28:1-19, 31:7-16, Isaiah 5:14-16, 8:20-22

New Testament – Matthew 13:37-42, Romans 16:19-20, 1 John 3:11-12, 2 Corinthians 11:1-4, 12-15, 12:7, 1 Peter 5:8-10, 1 Timothy 3:5-7, 1 Thessalonians 3:5 James 4:7, 2 Timothy 2:24-26, Revelation 2:10, 13, 24

Our Thoughts

Our Thoughts (1)

"For My thoughts are not your thoughts, neither are your ways my ways, saith the LORD. For as the heavens are higher than the earth, so are my ways higher than your ways, and my thoughts than your thoughts. (Isaiah 55:8-9)

Our Thoughts (2)

"Casting down imaginations and every high thing that exalteth itself against the knowledge of God and bringing into captivity every thought to the obedience of Christ." (2 Cor 10:5)

Our Thoughts (3)

"O Jerusalem, wash thine heart from wickedness, that thou mayest be saved. How long shall thy vain thoughts lodge within thee?" (Jeremiah 4:14)

Discussion Questions

1. Discuss Proverbs 12:5.
2. Explain Romans 1:21.
3. What is conveyed in 2 Corinthians 10:3-5?
4. What is conveyed in Isaiah 55:7-9?
5. Discuss Hebrews 4:12-13.

Fill in the Blanks

1. "Commit thy works unto the____, and thy____ shall be established."
2. "Let the wicked forsake his way, and the____ man his____."
3. "And bringing into____ every____ to the of Christ."
4. "And God saw that the____ of man was great in the earth, and that ____ ____of the____ of his heart was only evil continually."
5. "Curse not the king, no not in thy ____."

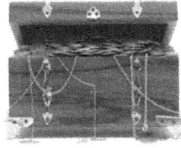

Our Thoughts

*A*rguably, one of the biggest challenges we face as Christians is relying on the Word of God as opposed to our own thoughts, ways, and preconceived notions. It is not in man to direct his own steps. Our steps must be directed by his Word (Jeremiah 10:23, Psalms 119:133, Isaiah 55:7-9, Philippians 2:5).

Our Thoughts (1)

Old Testament – Proverbs 23:7, 16:3, 25, 15:26, 28, 3:5, Psalms 119:113, 133, 94:11, 19, 50:18-21, 1 Chronicles 28:9, 2 Kings 5:11-15, Isaiah 55:7-9 Jeremiah 10:23 Micah 4:12

New Testament – 1 Corinthians 3:18-20, 4:6, 8:2, 10:12, 13:4-5, 11 Romans 12:3 Ephesians 3:20

Our Thoughts (2)

Old Testament – Jeremiah 4:14, Judges 5:15, 1 Chronicles 29:17-18 Job 4:13-21, 17:11-12, 20:2, Zechariah 8:17, 7:9-10 Proverbs 24:23, 6:16-18, 12:5, 20, 20:5, 21:2, 5, 24:2, 9, 12 Psalms 139:1-2, 119:59

New Testament – Luke 7:7-9, 9:47-48, Philippians 4:6-9

Our Thoughts (3)

Old Testament – Genesis 6:5, 8:21, 50:20 Psalms 10:4, 36:1-4, 38:12, 49:11, 64:6-9, Jeremiah 7:23-24, 18:11-13, 23:17-18, 26, Isaiah 59:7-8, 65:2, 66:18 Ezekiel 38:10

New Testament Mark 7:21-23, 1 Timothy 6:4-5, Romans 1:21, 7:22-25, 2 Corinthians 10:4-5

Our Thoughts (4)

Old Testament – Ecclesiastes 10:20, Amod 4:13, Proverbs 30:32-33, Daniel 2:27-30, 5:1-6, 10-17, Job 42:2, 7:11 Psalms 146:3-4, 139:23-24, 48:9-10, Isaiah 26:3, Jeremiah 29:11, 3:15-17, Zechariah 8:14-15 Lk 2:34-35

New Testament Matthew 6:25-34, Hebrews 4:12 Acts 8:20-22

Our Thoughts (5)

Old Testament – Genesis 20:3-11, 38:15, 26 Deuteronomy 15:9, Numbers 24:11, 33:55-56, Nehemiah 5:19, 6:14, Jeremiah 6:19 Micah 2:1, Zechariah 1:5-6, Psalms 36:4, 56:5, 140:1-2 Pr 24:8-9, 4:26

New Testament Matthew 10:19, John 16:2 Acts 26:9-11, James 2:1-4

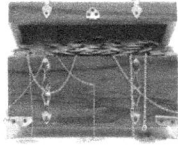

Encouragement

Encouragement (1)

"But charge Joshua, and encourage him and strengthen him: for he shall go over before this people..." (Deut 3:28)

Encouragement (2)

Strengthening the disciples and encouraging them to remain true to the faith. "We must go through many hardships to enter the kingdom of God," (Acts 14:22, NIV)

Encouragement (3)

"...If thou be kind to this people, and please them, and speak good words to them, they will be your servants for ever." (2 Chronicles 10:7)

Discussion Questions

1. Who gave the prophet Isaiah the ability to encourage those that are weary?
2. In Acts 4:36-37, who was called the "son of encouragement"?
3. Explain Proverbs 12:25.
4. Explain Proverbs 17:22.
5. Explain the invitation given in Matthew 11:28.

Fill in the Blanks

1. "And the night following the____ stood by him, and said, Be of____ , Paul."
2. "But charge____ , and ____him, and strengthen_____ ."
3. "Then David said unto the messenger, Thus shalt thou say unto____ ____ ... make thy battle more____ against the city, and overthrow it: and____ thou him."
4. "They____ themselves in an ____matter."
5. "Notwithstanding the Lord____ with me, and me; that by ____the preaching might be____ known, and that all the____ might hear: and I was____ out of the____ of the____ ."

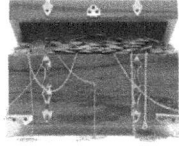

Encouragement

The Greek word for encourage is *parakaleo*; it appears 105 times in the New Testament and means "to call someone aside so that they may be comforted, strengthened, helped, taught, refreshed, or revitalized." As Christians, our lives should be punctuated with words and acts of encouragement to others.

Encouragement (1)

Old Testament – Deuteronomy 1:30, 37-38, 3:27-28, 31:6-8, 1 Chronicles 22:13, Psalms 94:19, 68:7-9, 23:4, Isaiah 66: 13, 61:1-3, 57:18, 28:5, 12, Jeremiah 31:10-14, 25

New Testament – Matthew 11:28-30 John 14:27, Galatians 6:9, Hebrews 10:24-25, 3:13, 1 Peter 3:14

Encouragement (2)

Old Testament – Proverbs 12:25, 15:13, 17:22, 18:14, 19:22 Deuteronomy 24:5, Joshua 1:5, 9, 10:25, Isaiah 40:1-2, 41:10, Psalms 27:2-5, 28:7, 71:21, 119:76

New Testament – John 16:33, 2 Corinthians 1:3-4, 2:4-8, 7:5-7, 13 Romans 14:19 Colossians 4:6, 1 Thessalonians 5:11

Encouragement (3)

Old Testament – 2 Chronicles 35:2, 2 Samuel 11:14-25 Psalms 64:2-5, 69:20, 119:28, 50, 52, Nehemiah 2:2-3, 18, 8:10, 1 Chronicles 16:27, Proverbs 10:22, 12:18, 25:11, Job 6:14, 16:1-6

New Testament – Romans 14:13, 17-18, 15:1-2, 1 Peter 3:8, Ephesians 4:29, Philemon 1:7, 20

Encouragement (4)

Old Testament – Proverbs 10:11, 21, 15:23, 28, 2 Chronicles 10:6-7 Ruth 2:12-13, 1 Samuel 1:12-18, Job 22:29, Psalms 3:1-3, 119:82, 92, Isaiah 51:11, 50:4-7, 49:13-16, 41:17-20, 3:10

New Testament – Hebrews 13:5-6, 1 Thessalonians 5:11, 2:11, 2 Thessalonians 3:13, 16

Encouragement (5)

Old Testament – Joshua 23:6, Ezra 10:4, Isaiah 41:6.2 Samuel 10:12, 9:1-13 Psalms 51:8, 31:24, 30:11, 16:8-9, Proverbs 15:15, 11:25

New Testament – Romans 1:11-12, 12:10, 16:1-16, 1 Corinthians 10:23-24, 14:3, 26, 2 Corinthians 10:8, Ephesians 6:21-22, Colossians 1:1-2, 4:7-8

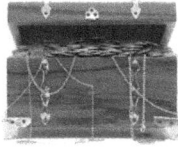

Salvation

Salvation (1)

"Look to Me, and be ye saved, all the ends of the earth: for I am God, and there is none else." (Isaiah 45:22)

Salvation (2)

"Though he were a Son, yet learned he obedience by the things which he suffered; And being made perfect, he became the author of eternal salvation unto all them that obey him;" (Hebrews 5:8-9)

Salvation (3)

"Neither is there salvation in other: for there is none other name under heaven given among men, whereby we must be saved." (Acts 4:12)

Discussion Questions

1. Why do we all stand in need of salvation?
2. Who decides how we are to be saved, man or God?
3. Explain Acts 4:12.
4. Explain Isaiah 59:16-20.
5. Explain Matthew 1:21.

Fill in the Blanks

1. "And she shall bring forth a son, and thou shall call his name_____ : for he shall____ _____ his people from their_____ ."
2. "Behold, the____ hand is not shortened, that it cannot____ ."
3. "Neither his ear_____ , that it cannot____ ."
4. "For God sent not his_____ into the to_____ the world; but that the world through him might be____ ."
5. "And being made perfect, he became the_____ of____ ____ unto all them that____ him."

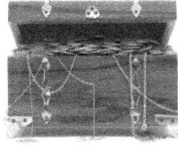

Salvation

*T*his topic unveils the truth that all of mankind stands in need of salvation. Salvation is provided by God through his Beloved Son, Jesus.

Salvation (1)

Old Testament – Genesis 49:10-11, 18 Zechariah 9:9, Isaiah 59:1-2, 16-17, 53:1-12, 52:7-10, Psalms 98:1-3, 119:41, 155, 166, 174, 73:24-28

New Testament – John 1:1-5, 10-14, 29, 36, 3:14-21, 8:24, 51 Hebrews 5:9, 1 Thessalonians 5:9-10, 1 John 2:1-2, 4:14

Salvation (2)

Old Testament – Isaiah 26:1-2, 46:13, 51:4-8, 52:10, 60:16, 18, 61:10-11, 63:5, 8-9, Psalms 3:8, 21:1, 85:7-9, 89:20-26, 91:14-16

New Testament – Luke 1:68-77, Matthew 1:21, 16:15-16 Acts 2:47, 4:12, 16:17, 28-33

Salvation (3)

Old Testament – Jeremiah 3:23, 8:20, 17:13-14 Lamentations 3:26is 45:15, 17, 56:1, Psalms 40:16, 50:23, 62:7, 74:12 Habakkuk 3:17-18

New Testament – John 12:47, 10:9, 5:34, Luke 13:23-28, Acts 2:36-40, Romans 5:8-10, Ephesians 5:23, Titus 3:3-6, 1 Peter 4:17-18

Salvation (4)

Old Testament – Isaiah 12:2-3, 17:7-10, 33:20-22 Job 13:13-16 Psalms 106:4, 35:3, 9, 27:1, 25:5, 24:3-5, 20:5, 14:7

New Testament – Romans 11:26-31, 10:1-4, 9-16, 5:9-10, 1:16, 1 Corinthians 1:18, 10:32-33, 15:1-2, 2 Corinthians 2: 15-17

Salvation (5)

Old Testament – Zechariah 9:16-17, Micah 7:7, 2 Samuel 22:3, 36, 47, 51, 23:5, Isaiah 25:8-9, 64:5 Psalms 119:81, 94, 123, 146, 118:14-15, 21, 116:13

New Testament – Luke 8:11-12, 18:26-27 Acts 11:13-14 Philippians 2:12, 15, 1 Tmothy 4:16, 2 Timothy 3:14-15

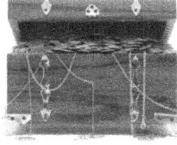

Prosperity

Prosperity (1)

"..But his delight is in the law of the LORD; and in his law doth he meditate day and night. And he shall be like a tree planted by the rivers of water that bringeth forth his fruit in his season; his leaf also shall not wither; and whatsoever he doeth shall proper. (Ps 1:2-3)

Prosperity (2)

"And in every work that he began in the service of the house of God, and in the law, and in the commandments, to seek his God, he did it with all his heart and prospered." (2 Chron 31:21)

Prosperity (3)

"Save now, I beseech thee, O LORD: O LORD, I beseech thee, send now prosperity." (Ps 118:25)

Discussion Questions

1. Does God desire that we be prosperous and have an abundant life? Explain.
2. What is taught in Proverbs 11:25?
3. Explain Jeremiah 29:11.
4. What is taught in Matthew 6:28-33?
5. What is conveyed in Psalms 34:12-15?

Fill in the Blanks

1. "And in every work that he began in the service of the house of____ , and in the____ , and in the____ , to seek his God, he did it with all his heart, and____ ."
2. "And____ we ask, we receive of him, because we keep his____ , and do_____ that are____ in his sight."
3. "I am come that they might have____ , and that they might have it more_____ ."
4. "And I will make thee exceeding_____ , and I will make nations of thee, and ____shall come out of thee."
5. "Keep therefore the words of this covenant, and_____ , that ye may_____ in all that ye do."

Prosperity

*P*rinciples must be learned that can lead us to be prosperous and
successful. Certain demeanors and behaviors must also be corrected
and purged, or they will lead to our failure and our demise.

Prosperity (1)

Old Testament – Ecclesiastes 5:18-20, 7:14, 11:6-10 Psalms 1:1-3, 25:12-13,
35:27, 106:3-5, 122:6-9 Proverbs 11:25, 19:8, 2 Kings 18:1, 5-7, 2 Chronicles
31:20-21, 20:20

New Testament – Luke 18:28-30, 6:38, 2 Corinthians 9:8-11 Ephesians 3:20

Prosperity (2)

Old Testament – Genesis 12:2-3, 17:1-9, 22:15-18, 24:42-50, 56 Joshua
1:7-8, Deuteronomy 29:9, 17:14-20, 1 Chronicles 22:9-13, 1 Kings 2:1-3, 2
Chronicles 26:3-5, 27:6 Psalms 34:10-15, 36:7-8

New Testament – Matthew 6:28-33, 7:7-11 Philippians 4:19, 1 Peter 3:10-12

Prosperity (3)

Old Testament – Isaiah 55:10-11, 58:7-12 Micah 2:7 Psalms 144:10-15,
125:1-4, 37:3-7 Job 8:5-7, 42:10-16 Proverbs 3:1-4, 9-10 Malachi 3:10-11
Haggai 1:5-13, 1 Chronicles 29:11-12, 23-25, Ezra 5:8

New Testament – John 4:14, 10:10, 3 John 1:2-5

Prosperity (4)

Old Testament – Genesis 39:1-6, 20-23, 41:50-52, 50:20 Daniel 6:3, 28 Job 22:21-28 Leviticus 26:3-12 Deuteronomy 7:11-14, 28:15, 29 Numbers 14:41 Psalms 89:16-18, 118:25, 128:1-6, Zechariah 8:12, Jeremiah 29:11

New Testament – Romans 15:13, 1 Thessalonians 4:1, 3:12

Prosperity (5)

Old Testament – Jeremiah 12:1, 5:27-28 Psalms 73:3-12, 16-20 Job 12:6, 16, 20:4-5, 21:7-13, 28-30, 36:10-12 Proverbs 28:13, Isaiah 54:17, 2 Chronicles 13:12, 18:11-17, 24:20, Nehemiah 1:7-11, 2:18, 20

New Testament – 1 John 3:22, James 1:17, 1 Corinthians 3:7

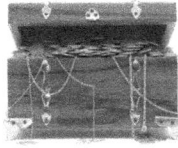

Confess and Repent

Confess and Repent (1)

"...Repent, and turn yourselves from all your transgressions; so iniquity shall not be your ruin. Cast away from you all your transgressions, whereby ye have transgressed; and make you a new heart and a new spirit:.. (Ezekiel 18:30-31)

Confess and Repent (2)

"Blessed is he whose transgression is forgiven, whose sin is covered...I acknowledge my sin unto thee and mine iniquity have I not hid. I said I will confess my transgressions unto the LORD; and thou forgavest the iniquity of my sin." (Psalm 32:1, 5)

Confess and Repent (3)

"If we confess our sins, He is faithful and just to forgive our sins and to cleanse us from all unrighteousness. If we say that we have not sinned, we make Him a liar, and His word is not in us." (1 John 1:9-10)

Discussion Questions

1. Are confession and repentance prerequisites for forgiveness of sins? Explain.
2. Why did Jesus say in Luke 13:3 and 5 that unless we repent, we shall all likewise perish?

3. Are there to be fruits of repentance? Explain.
4. What happens when we confess Christ before men?
5. Explain Proverbs 28:13.

Fill in the Blanks

1. "If they shall____ their ____, and the____ of their fathers, with their ____which they_____ against me, and that they have walked____ unto____ ."
2. "I____ my ____unto thee, and mine____ have I not____ . I said, I will_____ my____ unto the Lord; and thou____ the iniquity of my sin."
3. "____ ye therefore, and be____ , that your sins may be____ out."
4. "From that time Jesus began to preach, and to say, ____ : for the kingdom of heaven is at hand."
5. "____ your____ one to another, and____ one for another."

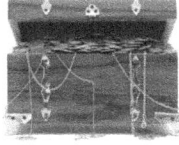

Confess and Repent

*T*he Greek word to confess is *omologeo*. It means "to concede, to declare, to admit one's self guilty of what one is accused of." In the biblical sense, we all must be willing to admit we are wrong when we see ourselves walking in a way that is contrary to the teaching of our Lord and Savior Jesus Christ. The Greek word for repent is *metanoeo*. It means "to change the mind, a change in the inner man." There are to be fruits that bear witness to a changed life, a change in behavior and speech that is reflective of a life devoted to that which pleases God rather than pleasing ourselves. As Christians, confession and repentance are imperative as we strive to walk in accordance to God's Word.

Confess and Repent (1)

Old Testament – Leviticus 26:40-42, Numbers 14:18-20, Daniel 4:27, Ezekiel 14:6-8, 18:21-24, 30-32, 1 Samuel 7:3 Jeremiah 3:12-15, 14:20, 25:5-9 Hosea 5:14-15, 6:1-3

New Testament – Luke 13:3-5, Acts 2:36-41, 3:19, Revelation 2:5, 21-23

Confess and Repent (2)

Old Testament – Ezra 10:1-3, 10-12, 2 Chronicles 30:17-22, 33:9-15, Joshua 7:11, 19, Daniel 9:3-23, Jonah 3:1-10, Lamentations 3:39-50

New Testament – Luke 3:3, 7-14, 19:8-9, 24:45-47 Acts 5: 30-31, 8:18-22, 17:30-31, 26:19-20

Confess and Repent (3)

Old Testament – Leviticus 5:1-6, 16:21-22, Numbers 5:6-7, 1 Chronicles 21:1, 8 Job 33:27-30, 1 Kings 8:33-36, Psalms 32:1-5, 38:18, 51:1-4, 9

New Testament – Matthew 4:17 Mark 6:7, 12, 9:43-48 Luke 5:32, 15:7, Acts 20:20-21, 1 John 1:9-10, Revelation 3: 19.

Confess and Repent (4)

Old Testament – Numbers 23:19 Psalms 68:19-21, Proverbs 29:1, 1 Samuel 15:24-31, 2 Samuel 12:13, JoeL 2:12-14, Jeremiah 2:22, 35, 18:8-11, 36:2-3, Isaiah 30:15, Ezekiel 33:8-19

New Testament – Hebrews 10:26, 2 Peter 3:9, 2 Timothy 2:24-26, Romans 2:3-6, 2 Corinthians 7:9-10, Revelation 2:16

Confess and Repent (5)

Old Testament – Exodus 32:7-12 Job 31:33, 40, 42:7-10, Proverbs 16:6, 28:13 Psalms 85:1-4, Isaiah 44:22, 55:7 Micah 7:18-19, Jeremiah 50:20

New Testament – John 20:21-23, Matthew 11:21-23, Romans 10:10, James 5:16, Acts 8:18-22, 11:16, Revelation 9:20-21

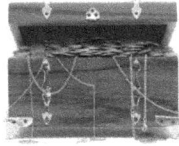

Wisdom

Wisdom (1)

"But where shall wisdom be found? and where is the place of understanding?...Behold, the fear of the LORD, that is wisdom; and to depart from evil is understanding." (Job 28:12, 28)

Wisdom (2)

"Doth not wisdom cry? and understanding put forth her voice?..For wisdom is better than rubies; and all the things that may be desired are not compared to it..For whosoever findeth me findeth life and favor of the LORD. (Proverbs 8:1-36)

Wisdom (3)

"The way of life is above to the wise, that he may depart from hell beneath." (Proverbs 15:24)

Discussion Questions

1. Discuss Ecclesiastes 12:11.
2. What observations are made in Proverbs 1:20-33?
3. What observations are made in Matthew 25:1-12?
4. Discuss Proverbs 8:15-31.
5. Discuss James 3:13-18

Fill in the Blanks

1. "Daniel answered and said, Blessed be the name of God for ever and ever: for___ and ____are his."
2. "____ crieth without; she____ her voice in the streets."
3. "If any of you lack____ , let him ask of____ , that giveth to all men liberally, and ____not; and it shall be given him."
4. "Say unto____ , Thou art my____ ; and call____ thy____ ."
5. "And they were not able to____ the____ and the ____by which he spake."

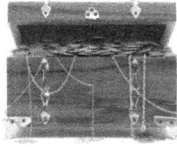

Wisdom

*P*erhaps Job gives the best definition of wisdom in Job 28:28, when he says, "And unto man he said, Behold, the fear of the Lord, that is wisdom; and to depart from evil is understanding." Let us grow in a way that we may have hearts of wisdom.

Wisdom (1)

Old Testament – Job 28:12-28, Ecclesiastes 12:11, 9:13-18, 8:1, 7:19, 2:26, Daniel 2:20-21, 12:3, 10, Deuteronomy 4:5-6, Psalms 119:98, 51:6, 37:30-31, 19:7, Proverbs 2:6-11, 3:13, 19, 19:8, 24:3, 7

New Testament – James 1:5 Colossians 1:9, 28, 2:1-3, 4:5, 2 Timothy 3:15

Wisdom.2

Old Testament – Proverbs 1:20-33, 4:5-11, 8:1-12, 32-36, 1 Chronicles 22:11-12 Ex 28:3, 31:3, 6, 36:2, 2 Chronicles 1:9-12, 9:1-7, 22-23, Job 38:36, 12:13, 9:4, Isaiah 33:5-6 Ezra 7:25

New Testament – Matthew 10:16, Luke 11:31, 21:15 Acts 6:10 Romans 11:33

Wisdom (3)

Old Testament – Ecclesiastes 1:13-17, 10:1-3, Job 32:7-9 Micah 6:9 Deuteronomy 32:28-29, Jeremiah 4:22, 8:8-9, 9:23-24, 10:12-15, Proverbs 22:17- 18, 21:12, 20:26, 15:24, 14:6, 8, 16, 33, 8:14-31

New Testament – Ephesians 1:17, 3:10, Romans 12:16, 16:19, James 3:13-18

Wisdom (4)

Old Testament – Jeremiah 49:7, Isaiah 5:21, Job 39:16-17, 22:2, Proverbs 9:8-12, 10:8, 13-14, 21, 23, 16:16, 20-23, 18:15, 19:20, 21:22, 30, 29:3, 15, 30:24-28, Psalms 90:10-12

New Testament – Matthew 25:1-12, 11:16-19, 7:24-27, 1 Corinthians 3:18-19

Wisdom (5)

Old Testament – Deuteronomy 34:9, 2 Samuel 14:17-20, 1 Kings 2:5-6, 3:16-28, Isaiah 11:1-2, 29:11-14, 47:10 Jeremiah 51:15-17, Hosea 14:9, Proverbs 7:4, 12:15, 13:10, 14, 20, 17:16, 24, 28, 31:26-30

New Testament – Matthew 13:54-55, Luke 16:8, 1 Corinthians 1:20-30, 2:1-13

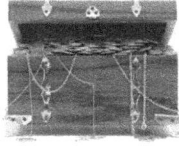

Things to Avoid

Things to Avoid (1)

"Enter not into the path of the wicked and go not in the way of evil men. Avoid it, pass not by it, turn from it, and pass away." (Proverbs 4:14-15)

Things to Avoid (2)

"My son, if sinners entice thee, consent thou not...My son, walk not thou in the way with them; refrain thy foot from their path." (Proverbs 1:10, 15)

Things to Avoid (3)

"Go from the presence of a foolish man, when thou perceivest not in him the lips of knowledge." (Proverbs 14:7)

Discussion Questions

1. What were the instructions given by Jesus in Matthew 7:6?
2. What advice is given in Proverbs 1:10-19 ?
3. What are the admonitions mentioned in Psalms 1:1?
4. What did God command in Deuteronomy 18:9?
5. What were the instructions of 2 Corinthians 6:14-17?

Fill in the Blanks

1. But when they _____ you in this city, _____ ye into another:

2. And whosoever shall not receive you, nor hear your words, when ye _____ out of That house or city, _____ off the _____ of your feet.

3. Having a form of _____ but denying the power there of: from such ____ away.

4. Go from the _____ of a foolish man, when thou _____ not in him the lips of _____.

5. I have _____ my feet from every ____ way, that I might keep thy _____.

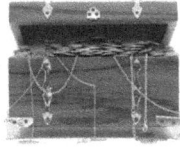

Things to Avoid

*T*here are some situations, and perhaps even some people, that warrant our avoidance in order to maintain our peace, composure, and tranquility of mind.

> "A prudent man foresees evil and hideth himself: but the simple pass on and are punished." "Make no friendship with an angry man: and with a furious man thou shalt not go" (Proverbs 22:3, 24)

Things to Avoid (1)

Old Testament – Exodus 34:12 Deuteronomy 18:9, 12:30, 7:3-4, 1 Kings 11:1-3, Proverbs 1:10-19, 4:14-17, 14:7, 16, 22:3, 24-25, 23:1-3, 6-9, 20-21, Psalms 1:1, 101:3-8, 144:11

New Testament – Matthew 7:6, 10:14, Romans 16:17, 2 Corinthians 6:14-17, Ephesians 5:3-12

Things to Avoid (2)

Old Testament – 2 Samuel 16:5-13, 19:15-23, 1 Kings 2:8-10, 36-46, Isaiah 29:20-22, 50:6-10, Jeremiah 11:19-23, Psalms 37:1-10, 32-40, 38:12-15, 39:1-2, 9, 11, Proverbs 26:17-26, 24:29, 19:11

New Testament – 2 Timothy 4:14-15, 2:23, Romans 12:17

Things to Avoid (3)

Old Testament – Exodus 23:2, 7, Proverbs 11:21, 12:16, 26, 16:29, 22:5, 24:19-25, Job 11:14, 36:18, Psalms 26:4-6, 28:3, 55:6-16, 119:101, 140:4-5, 141:9-10

New Testament – Matthew 10:23, 1 Timothy 6:20-21, Titus 3:9-10 Colossians 2:8 Philippians 3:2-3

Things to Avoid (4)

Old Testament – Ecclesiastes 7:21-22 Proverbs 30:10, 28:28, 26:12, 21:9, 19, 23, 20:3, 19, 22, 18:1, 18, 17:1, 9, 14, 15:1, 18, 14:3, 10, 29, 9:6 Psalms 120:2, 7, 31:18-20, 27:5

New Testament – 1 Thessolonians 5:22, 1 Peter 3:13-18, 2:12, Ephesians 1:4

Things to Avoid (5)

Old Testament – Ecclesiastes 7:26 Proverbs 2:11-19, 5:8-23, 8:13, 13:20, 21:16, 29:5-6, 9-12 Psalms 119:63, 115, 25:3-5, 139:19-22

New Testament – 1 Thessalonians 4:3-5, 11, 1 Timothy 4:7, 16, 5:22, 1 John 2:26-29, 2 Peter 2:18-22 Galatians 1:6-9, 2 John 1:8-11

The Voice of the Lord

The Voice of the LORD (1)

"But this thing commanded I them, saying, Obey my voice and I will be your God, and ye shall be My people: and walk ye in all the ways that I have commanded you, that it may be well unto you. (Jeremiah 7:23)

The Voice of the LORD (2)

"Hear attentively the noise of His voice and the sound that goeth out of His mouth...God thundereth marvellously with His voice; great things doeth He which we cannot comprehend. (Job 37:2, 5)

The Voice of the LORD (3)

"See that ye refuse not him that speaketh.For if they escaped not who refused him that spake on earth much more shall not we escape if we turn from Him that speaketh from heaven:whose voice shook the earth:.. (Heb 12:25-26)

Discussion Questions

1. Discuss the fall of man in Genesis 3:1-11, 17.
2. Discuss Deuteronomy 8:3.
3. Explain John 18:37.
4. Discuss Deuteronomy 28:1-2, 13-15
5. Explain Luke 8:21.

Fill in the Blanks

1. "Why do ye not____ my speech? even because ye____ ___ my ____."
2. "Obey my____ , and I will be____ ___ , and ye shall be___ ___ ."
3. "And a stranger will they____ ____ , but will ____from him: for they know ___the____ of strangers."
4. "Ye shall walk after the Lord your God, and fear him, and keep his____ , and obey his____ ."
5. "He that is of God heareth____ ____ : ye therefore____ them____ , because ye are not of God."

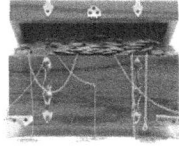

The Voice of the Lord

*T*here are many voices in the world today, saying many different things, expressing many different views, enunciating many different beliefs. But Jesus says in John 10:27, "My sheep hear my voice, and I know them, and they follow me." Those who belong to Christ follow Christ because they are His sheep, they hear His voice, and they hear not the voice of strangers.

The Voice of the LORD (1)

Old Testament – Deuteronomy 4:12-15, 33-36, 5:22-29 Job 37:1-12, Psalms 18:13-15, 29:3-9, 46:6-8, 68:32-35, 81:8-16, Zephaniah 3:1-2, Amos 1:2 Hosea 11:7-11, Zechariah 6:11-15, Ezekiel 43:2

New Testament – Matthew 3:16-17, 17:1-6, John 12:28-30, 50

The Voice of the LORD (2)

Old Testament – Genesis 3:1-4, 8-17, 22:15-18, 26:4-5, Exodus 5:2, 19:3-5, Deuteronomy 8:3, 19-20, 13:1-4, 30:19-20, 1 Samuel 15:1, 18-23, Jeremiah 7:23, 51:15, 16, Job 40:9

New Testament – Hebrews 12:25-29, 3:7-15, 1:1-2, Matthew 17:5, John 18:37

The Voice of the LORD (3)

Old Testament – Exodus 24:7, Joshua 24:24, Micah 6:9, Jeremiah 42:6, 38:20, 26:13, 18:7-11, 7:28, Haggai 1:12-13, Isaiah 1:19-20, Psalms 119:13, 72, 103:20, 95:7-8, 81:11-12

New Testament – Jn 5:25-29, 37-39, 10:1-5, 16, 27, 1 John 4:6

The Voice of the LORD (4)

Old Testament – JoeL2:11, 3:16 Jg 2:20-23, Isaiah 30:30-31, 42:13, 65:12, 66:1-6, Jeremiah 25:27-31, 40:3, 43:1-4, 44:16-17, 22-23, Daniel 9:9-14, Zechariah 7:7-13

New Testament – John 8:43-47, Acts 26:13-19, 1 Peter 1:16-18

The Voice of the LORD (5)

Old Testament – Deuteronomy 28:1-2, 13-15 Exodus 23:20-22, 20:18-19, Psalms 62:11, 85:8, Joshua 5:6, Jeremiah 6:10, 19:3, 1 Samuel 3:10-11, Isaiah 28:23-29, 32:9, 17, 50:10

New Testament – Luke 8:19-21, 11:27-28, Matthew 7:24-27, Acts 11:7-9, Revelation 3:20

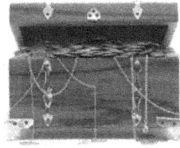

Gracious Words

Gracious Words (1)

"Pleasant words are as an honeycomb, sweet to the soul and health to the bones"

"A word fitly spoken is like apples of gold in pictures of silver" (Proverbs 16:24, 25:11)

Gracious Words (2)

"And all bare witness and wondered at the gracious words which proceeded out of his mouth ..",

"And they said one to another, Did not our heart burn within us while he talked with us by the way and while he opened to us the scriptures." (Luke 4:22, 24:32)

Gracious Words (3)

"Let your speech be alway with grace, seasoned with salt, that ye may know how ye ought to answer every man." (Colossians 4:6)

Discussion Questions

1. Have you ever been hurt, discouraged, or offended by unkind and untrue words?

2. Will God judge us for every word we speak?
3. What was the response in Luke 4:22 to the words spoken by Jesus?
4. What is the command given in Colossians 4:6?
5. What problem existed in James 3:10?

Fill in the Blanks

1. "But I say unto you, That every____ ____ that men shall speak, they shall give_____ thereof in the___ of_____ ."
2. "For by thy____ thou shalt be____ , and by thy____ thou shalt be____ ."
3. "Out of the same____ proceedeth____ and____ . My brethren, these things ought____ so to be."
4. "The words of wise men are____ in quiet more than the_____ of ____that ruleth among____ ."
5. "There is that ____like the____ of a____ : but the____ of the_____ is____ ."

Gracious Words

"A word fitly spoken is like apples of gold in pictures of silver" (Proverbs 25:11).

*I*n order to uplift, strengthen, edify, and encourage others, we must use gracious words.

Gracious Words (1)

Old Testament – Ecclesiastes 9:17, 10:12, 12:10-11 Genesis 49:21, 50:21, Isaiah 50:4, 40:1-2 Job 4:4, 16:3-5, 33:1-3 Hosea 14:2 Zechariah 1:13 Proverbs 8:6-8, 12:18, 25, 15:23, 26, 28, 16:24, 22:17-18, 25:11

New Testament – Luke 4:22, 24:32 John 7:46

Gracious Words (2)

Old Testament – Deuteronomy 32:1-3 Job 29:21-23, 12:11, 6:25-30, 1 Kings 12:6-7, 13-19 Ecclesiastes 5:2, 6 Proverbs 8:13, 10:11, 19-21, 31-32, 16:1, 13, 23-24, 17:27-28

New Testament – John 6:63, 68 Luke 21:14-15 Acts 5:20, 6: 10, 11:13-14

Gracious Words (3)

Old Testament – Psalms 141:3-4, 119:171-172, 71:8, 15, 23-24, 63:3, 5, 59:2-7, 12, 52:1-6, 37:30 Job 27:3-4, 42:7-9 Proverbs 18:6-7, 20:15, 22:11, 23:9, 16, 31:26

New Testament – Matthew 12:34-37 Ephesians 4:15, 29, Colossians 4:6, Philippians 1:27

Gracious Words (4)

Old Testament – 2 Chronicles 18:12-13, Jeremiah 17:15-16, Micah 2:6-7 Malachi 2:6-7, Isaiah 35:3-4, 51:16 Job 34:2-4, Proverbs 21:23, 18:21, 17:7, 15:1-2 Psalms 109:3, 94:3-6, 55:21, 36:3, 31:18

New Testament – James 3:8-13, Galatians 5:15, 2 Timothy 2:23-26

Gracious Words (5)

Old Testament – Deuteronomy 33:3, Psalms 138:4, 119:13, 46,103, 108, 109:30, 50:19-23, 39:1, 34:13, 19:14, 17:3, Isaiah 57:19-21, Job 15:2-6, Proverbs 19:1, 9, 12:6, 14

New Testament – Hebrews 13:15-16, James 1:26, 4:11, 1 Peter 2:21-22, 3:10

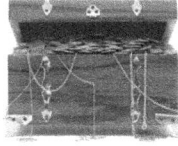

Difference Makers

Difference Makers (1)

"I have chosen the way of thy commandments :thy judgements have I laid before me...I will run the way of thy commandments, when thou shalt enlarge my heart." (Ps 119:30, 32)

Difference Makers (2)

"Thou hast rebuked the proud that are cursed, which do err from thy commandments.""Thou hast trodden down all them that err from thy statutes: for their deceit is falsehood." (Psalms 119:21, 118)

Difference Makers (3)

"A man that hath friends must shew himself friendly: and there is a friend that sticketh closer than a brother." (Proverbs 18:24)

Discussion Questions

1. What was the difference maker that was missing in Israel according to Deuteronomy 5:29?
2. What are the difference makers found in 2 Peter 1:5-11?
3. What is the difference maker found in 1 Corinthians 8:3?
4. What are the difference makers in Hebrews 11:6?
5. What are the difference makers found in Joshua 1:8-9?

Fill in the Blanks

1. "Yea doubtless, and I count ____ ____but loss for the excellency of the____ of____ ____ my Lord: for whom I have suffered the loss of all things, and do count them____ ____ , that I may____ Christ."

2. "But he said, Yea rather, blessed are they that____ the word of God, and____ it."

3. "A man's pride shall bring him____ : but honour shall _____ the____ in_____ ."

4. "But if any man____ ____ , the same is____ of him."

5. "For to be_____ ____ is death; but to be____ ____ is life and peace."

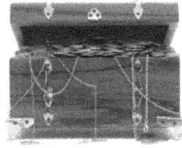

Difference Makers

*T*he attributes of honesty, integrity, godliness, kindness, faithfulness, wisdom, discernment, courage, patience, and love are difference makers. These are the attributes Christians are to add to their faith as they grow spiritually, in order to be pleasing to God.

Difference Makers (1)

Old Testament – Malachi 3:18, Exodus 8:23, 11:3 Deuteronomy 4:5-9, 5:29, Esther 4:14, Jeremiah 7:23, Isaiah 66:2, 57:15, Psalms 4:3, 33:12, 50:5, 23, Proverbs 29:23, Joel 2:12-14

New Testament – Romans 3:21-26, 5:8-11, 6:3-5, 22, 1 John 2:1-2, Ephesians 3:12, Revelation 12:11

Difference Makers (2)

Old Testament – Leviticus 10:8, 10, 20:26, Ezekiel 22:26, Malachi 2:7, Joshua 1:8-9, 7:13, 14:8, Deuteronomy 20:1-4, Exodus 23:22, 1 Chronicles 22:13, 2 Chronicles 24:20, Psalms 44:3-5

New Testament – 1 John 3:22, 5:4, Romans 8:28, 1 Corinthians 8:3, 2 Corinthians 2:14-17, Hebrews 11:6

Difference Makers (3)

Old Testament – Ecclesiastes 9:14-18, Job 36:5-12, Proverbs 13:20-21, 28:25, Psalms 122:6, 106:3-5, 68:6, 37:11, 1:13, 2 Kings 18:5-7, 1 Samuel 18:14, 1 Chronicles 22:11-13

New Testament – 1 Timothy 4:8, 2 Timothy 4:16-18, 2 Peter 1:5-7

Difference Makers (4)

Old Testament – 2 Chronicles 27:6, 26:5, Proverbs 3:33, 14:2, 28:14, 31:30, Ecclesiastes 8:12-13, 7:18, Jeremiah 17:7-8, Psalms 146:5, 128:1-6, 119:1-3, 41:1-3, 37:4-8, 34, 5:12

New Testament – James 1:22-25, John 13:17, Luke 11:28, Hebrews 10:36, Romans 8:6

Difference Makers (5)

Old Testament – Genesis 6:8, 22, 39:2-3, 20-21, 41:38-40, 28:20-21, 1 Chronicles 4:10, Joshua 2:8-14, 1 Samuel 20:19-22, 15:21, Ruth 1:16-17

New Testament – Luke 22:33, 18:28-30, 14:25-33, 7:8-9, 5:11, 27-28, Philippians 3:8, Mark 10:17-22

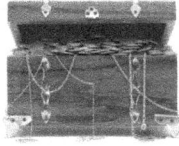

A Spiritual House

A Spiritual House (1)

"But ye are come unto mount Sion, and unto the city of the live God, the heavenly Jerusalem, and to an innumerable company of angels, To the assembly and church of the firstborn, which are written in heaven, and to the God the Judge of all, and to the spirits of just men made perfect..." (Hebrews 12:22-23)

A Spiritual House (2)

"Ye also, as lively stones, are built up a spiritual house, an holy priesthood, to offer up spiritual sacrifices, acceptable to God by Jesus Christ. (1 Peter 2:5)

A Spiritual House (3)

"We have an altar, whereof they have no right to eat which serve the tabernacle."

Discussions Questions

1. Who is the builder of the spiritual house?
2. Are we to be co-workers in the building of God's spiritual house? Explain.90 The Spiritual Treasure Trove
3. How can we be vessels of honor in God's spiritual house (2 Timothy 2:20-21)?

4. Is Christ head over this spiritual house (as noted in Hebrews 3:4-6)?

5. Can there be any other foundation than Jesus Christ that the church is built on?

Fill in the Blanks

1. "Except the____ build the____ , they labour in____ that build it: except the____ keep the city, the watchman waketh but in____ ."

2. "For other____ can no____ lay than that is____ , which is____ ____ ."

3. "And I say also unto thee, That thou art Peter, and upon this rock I will____ my____ ;"

4. "And he is the____ of the____ , the : who is the beginning, the firstborn from the dead; that in___ things He might have the____ ."

5. "And there was a given me a____ like unto a____ : and the angel stood, saying, ____ , and____ the____ of God, and the____ , and____ that____ therein."

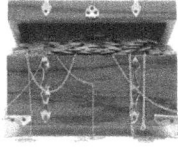

A Spiritual House

The House of God is spiritual. The foundation of the house of God is Jesus Christ. Jesus, in Matthew 16:18, said, "Upon this rock, I will build my church" (Matthew 16:18). We are to conduct ourselves in a worthy manner in the household of God, which is the church of the living God (1 Timothy 3:15). The apostle Peter reminds us that Christians are lively stones that are being built up as part of this spiritual house to offer up spiritual sacrifices acceptable to God by Jesus Christ (1 Peter 2:4-5).

A Spiritual House (1)

Old Testament – Psalms 127:1, Exodus 20:24, 25:8-9, 40, 1 Kings 11:38, Isaiah 56:5-7, 60:7, 11-13, 18, 65:25, 66:20, Joel 3:16-18

New Testament – Luke 1:68-69, Matthew 21:13, 16:18, 1 Timothy 3:15, Hebrews 3:4-6, 10:19-21, 12:22-28, 13:10, 15-16, 1 Peter 4:17

A Spiritual House (2)

Old Testament – Deuteronomy 12:5, 8, 32, Leviticus 21:10-12, 1 Samuel 2:29-30, 2 Chronicles 6:1-2, 20:8-9, 23:19, Psalms 5:7, 26:8, 89:7, Zechariah 2:1-5, 10-13, 4:7-9, 8:20-23

New Testament – 1 Corinthians 3:9-17, 2 Corinthians 6:16, 2 Timothy 2:19-21, Ephesians 2:19-22

A Spiritual House (3)

Old Testament – Ecclesiastes 5:1-2, Psalms 122:1, 9, 111:1, 42:4, Isaiah 2:2-5, 8:13-14, 28:16, Zechariah 3:7-8, 6:12-13, Jeremiah 23:5-6, Amos 9:11, Obadiah 1:17-18

New Testament – Hebrews 1:8, Acts 4:10-12, 15:13-18, Ephesians 3:9-11, 21, 1 Corinthians 6:19, 1 Peter 2:4-10

A Spiritual House (4)

Old Testament – Haggai 1:2, 8, 14, 2:3-9, Ezra 5:1-3, 9, 11, 16-17, 7:23, Jeremiah 7:1-14, 33:15-18, Psalms 84:1-4, 10, Ezekiel 37:24-28, 44:4-9

New Testament – Luke 1:31-33, Hebrews 3:1-3, 2:9-13, Revelation 1:13, 20, Ephesians 1:17-23, Acts 20:28

A Spiritual House (5)

Old Testament – 1 Chronicles 17:9-14, 24-27, 22:5-10, 28:10, 20, 29:1

New Testament – John 2:17-22, Matthew 12:6, Hebrews 8:1-2, 10, 10:5, 10, Romans 7:4, 12:1-5 Acts 7:44-50, 17:24-25, 1 Corinthians 12:13-27, Ephesians 4:4, 11-16, 5:23-32, Revelation 21:2-3

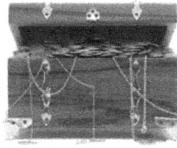

Take Me to the Water

Take me to the Water (1)

"And Elisha sent a messenger unto him, saying , Go and wash in Jordan seven times, and thy flesh shall come again to thee, and thou shalt be clean."

"Then when he went down, and dipped himself seven times in Jordan, according to the saying of the man of God: and his flesh came again like unto the flesh of a little child, and He was clean." (2 Kings 5:10, 14)

Take me to the Water (2)

"And as they went on their way, they came unto a certain water: And the eunuch said, See, here is water; what doth hinder me to be baptized?" "And he commanded the chariot to stand still: and they both went down into the water; both Philip and the eunuch; and he baptized him." (Acts 8:36, 38)

Take me to the Water (3)

"And Jesus, when he was baptized, went up straightway out of the water: and lo, the heavens were opened unto him, and he saw the Spirit of God descending Like a dove, and lighting upon him:" (Matthew 3:16)

Discussion Questions

1. How many times did Naaman have to be dipped, and where was he commanded to dip before being healed of leprosy?
2. Is baptism a burial? If so, explain.
3. Explain Acts 22:16.
4. Why was Jesus baptized?
5. Explain Mark 16:16.

Fill in the Blanks

1. "Jesus answered, Verily, verily, I said unto thee, ____ a man be____ of____ and of the____ , he cannot____ into the of____ ."
2. "In that day there shall be a____ opened to the____ of____ and to the ____of____ for sin and for____ ."
3. "And were____ ____ unto____ in the____ and in the____ ."
4. "And a fountain shall come forth of the____ of the____ , and shall____ the Valley of Shittim."
5. "But the Pharisees and lawyers____ the of God against them-selves, being____ ____ of him."

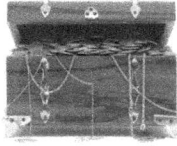

Take Me to the Water

The Ethiopian eunuch in Acts 8:35-36, when Jesus was preached to him, enunciated, "See, here is water; what doth hinder me to be baptized?" He looked for water, he found water, and he was baptized upon hearing Jesus preached unto him. Take me to the water.

Take Me to the Water (1)

Old Testament – Exodus 14:13-14, 21-27, Joshua 4:5-7, 21-24, Isaiah 43:1-4, 19-20, 49:10, 32:1-2, 13-15

New Testament – 1 Corinthians 10:1-4, Matthew 3:13-17, 21:23-27, Acts 8:29, 35-39, 2:17-21, 36-41, John 3:5, 22-27

Take Me to the Water (2)

Old Testament – 2 Kings 5:1-14, Ecclesiastes 30:17-21, Isaiah 1:16, Psalms 51:2-7, Zechariah 13:1, Joel 3:18

New Testament – Ephesians 5:26, Luke 3:3, 7-18, 21-22, Acts 22:16, 16:30-33, 1 Peter 3:20-21, Titus 3:3-7, Hebrews 10:22, 1 Corinthians 6:8-11

Take Me to the Water (3)

Old Testament – Ezekiel 47:1-9, Zechariah 14:8-9, Psalms 36:8-9, 23:1-3, Jeremiah 33:6-18, 17:7-8, 13-14, 2:13

New Testament – Galatians 3:26-27, Romans 6:3-5, Mark 16:14-16, Matthew 28:18-20, Acts 19:1-5, Colossians 2:12-14

Take Me to the Water (4)

Old Testament – Isaiah 12:2-3, 41:17-20, 44:1-5, 48:18-19, 55:1-2, 58:11, 66:10-13

New Testament – Matthew 5:6, John 4:7-15, 6:35, 53-57, 63, 7:37-39, 19:34, 1 John 5:6-8

Take Me to the Water (5)

Old Testament – Psalms 143:6, 65:9-13, 63:1-5, 8, 46:3-5, 42:1-3, 1:1-3, Ezekiel 34:23-31

New Testament – Acts 16:13-15, 18:8, 1 Corinthians 12:13, Revelation 7:13-17, 21:6, 22:1-3, 17

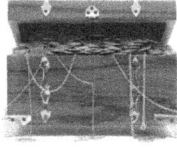

The Church

The Church (1)

"And I say also unto thee, That thou art Peter, and upon this rock I will build my church, and the gates of hell shall not prevail against it." (Matthew 16:18)

The Church (2)

"And he hath put all things under his feet, and gave him to be the head over All things to the church" (Ephesians 1:22)

The Church (3)

"Praising God, and having favour with all the people. And the Lord added to the church daily such as should be saved." (Acts 2:47)

Discussion Questions

1. Did the establishment of the church come from the mind of man or the mind of God?
2. Who is the head of the church?
3. In what city was it prophesied that the church was to be established?
4. Who is the Lawgiver of the church?
5. In what way or ways is the church Christ's body?

Fill in the Blanks

1. "Praising God, and having favour with all the people. And the____ added to the_____ daily such as should be_____ ."
2. "Take heed therefore unto yourselves, and to all the flock, over the which the ____ ____hath made you overseers, to feed the_____ of God, which he hath_____ with his own____ ."
3. "And many people shall go and say, Come ye, and let us go up to the mountain of the____ , to the____ of the God of Jacob; and he will____ us of his ways, and we will____ in His paths: for out of ____shall go forth the____ , and the word of the Lord from_____ ."
4. "And I say also unto thee, That thou art Peter, and upon this rock___ will build my____; and the gates of____ shall not____ against it." 6.
5. "And he is the____ of the_____ , the____ : who is the beginning, the firstborn from the_____ ; that in____ things he might have the____ ."

The Church

The Bible denotes the church in prophecy in the Old Testament. The New Testament reveals the church as it comes to fruition. All of the saved were added to the church (Acts 2:47). Jesus is the one who built the church (Matthew 16:18). Jesus is the one who purchased the church with His blood (Acts 20:28). Therefore, this topic is valuable to study.

The Church (1)

Old Testament – Deuteronomy 18:15, 18:18-19, Isaiah 9:6-7, 28:16-18, 53:1-11, Zechariah 1:16-17, 6:12-13

New Testament – Matthew 21:42-46, Acts 3:22-26, 4:10-12, Colossians 1:13-14, 18-24, 28

The Church (2)

Old Testament – Isaiah 2:2-3, 8:14-17, 11:1-5, 11:10-12, Daniel 2:44, 7:13-14, Jeremiah 23:5-8, Psalms 2:6-12

New Testament – Luke 1:30-33, Matthew 16:13-20, 1 Corinthians 10:4, Romans 9:33, 15:12, Revelation 5:5-14, 22:16, 2:25-29

The Church (3)

Old Testament – Ezekiel 37:15-28, Micah 4:1-2, Joel 2:28-32, Amos 3:7

New Testament – John 11:51-52, Acts 2:5-12, 16-21, 37-41, 2:47, 20:28, 1 Corinthians 12:12-13, Ephesians 1:19-23, 4:4-6, 5:23-32, Romans 16:16-18

The Church (4)

Old Testament – Isaiah 48:3, Ezekiel 34:11-16, 34:23-24, Jeremiah 32:37-41, Psalms 127:1

New Testament – Hebrews 3:1-6, Acts 13:38-41, 13:48, Matthew 12:25, 1 Corinthians 1:10-13, 3:10-11, Philippians 3:16-19, 1 Peter 2:4-10, Revelation 1:9-20, 1 Timothy 2:5

The Church (5)

Old Testament – Psalms 89:19-37, Isaiah 40:9-11, 42:1-7

New Testament – Matthew 12:15-21, John 10:2-6, 17:20-23, Hebrews 13:20-21, 2 Corinthians 11:1-4, Galatians 1:6-12, Revelation 21:1-3, 21:9-14, 21:22-27

The Apple of God's Eye

The Apple of God's Eyes (1)

"He found him in a desert land, and in the waste howling wilderness; he led him about, he instructed him, he kept him as the apple of His eye." (Deuteronomy 32:10)

The Apple of God's Eyes (2)

"Keep me as the apple of the eye, hide me under the shadow Of thy wings." (Psalm 17:8)

The Apple of God's Eyes (3)

"Their heart cried unto the Lord, O wall of the daughter of Zion, Let tears run down like a river day and night: give thyself norest; let not the apple of thine eye cease." (Lamentations 2:18)

Discussion Questions

1. Daniel was a servant in captivity, yet what did the angel Gabriel say of him in Daniel 9:23?
2. The world hated Jesus, but what did God say about Him in Matthew 17:3?
3. According to 1 Corinthians 8:3, how does God view those that love Him?
4. What was Jesus's admonition in Luke 12:32?

5. How did God demonstrate His love for all of us according to Romans 5:7?

Fill in the Blanks

1. "Keep me as the____ of the_____ , hide me under the shadow of thy____ ."
2. "He found him in a desert land, and in the waste howling wilderness; he____ him about, he____ him, he____ him as the____ of his____ ."
3. "While He yet spake, behold, a bright cloud_____ them: and behold a voice out of the cloud, which said, This is my____ Son, in whom I am____ ____ ; hear ye____ ."
4. "For the____ himself____ you, because ye have____ me, and have____ that I came____ from____ ."
5. "And to know the ____of ____, which passeth____ , that ye might be_____ with all the fulness of____ ."

The Apple of God's Eye

*T*he "apple of the eye" is a term of endearment, something to be prized and treasured, to be looked upon with intense love. Apostle Peter reminds the church in 1 Peter 2:9, "But you are a chosen people, a royal priesthood, a holy nation for God's own possession." This is good news for Christians. The world we live in may not put significance or value on the Christian life. But God views His children as the "salt of the earth, " "a city that is set on a hill, " and "the light of the world." We indeed are the apple of God's eye. We should rejoice in that fact every day.

The Apple of God's Eye (1)

Old Testament – Deuteronomy 32:9-10, 26:18-19, Numbers 14:8, 2 Chronicles 16:9, Proverbs 11:20, 12:22, 15:8, Daniel 10:11-12, 19 Psalms 32:8, 37:4-5, 145:19-20

New Testament – John 3:16, 15:13, Romans 5:5-8, 11:33, 2 Thessalonians 3:5, 1 John 3:16, 4:19, Jude 1:21

The Apple of God's Eye (2)

Old Testament – Exodus 19:4-5, Deuteronomy 14:2, Psalms 17:8, 84:11, 91:14-16, 135:4, 1 Chronicles 29:3, Nehemiah 9:20, Zechariah 2:8, Zephaniah 3:17, 1 King 8:53, Jeremiah 31:3, Hosea 11:1-4, Isaiah 49:15-16

New Testament – John 14:21, 15:9, 16:27, Ephesians 2:4-5, 3:19, 1 Corinthians 8:3, Titus 2:14, 1 John 4:7-8, 5:1-3

The Apple of God's Eye (3)

Old Testament – Proverbs 7:1-2, 4:1-5, Psalms 119:16, 24, 35, 47, 70, 77, 174, 147:19-20, Deuteronomy 33:3, 12, 11:13-15, 10:15, 7:6-9, Job 22:22-26, 23:11-12, Isaiah 26:7-9, 42:21

New Testament – John 5:38, 42, 1 Corinthians 16:22, 2:9, James 2:5, 1 John 2:15

The Apple of God's Eye (4)

Old Testament – Genesis 12:2-3, Exodus 15:13-17, 23:20, 27, Numbers 22:12, 23:21-23, Ezekiel 16:10-14, Song of Solomon 8:6-7, 2 Samuel 7:23, Isaiah 43:20, 65:9-10, 13-15, 21-24, Psalms 31:19, 23, 65:4, 101:6, 106:4-5

New Testament – Romans 8:28, 33, 38-39, 1 Peter 2:9-10, James 2:23, Matthew 12:18

The Apple of God's Eye (5)

Old Testament – Isaiah 5:1-7, Jeremiah 11:15-17, 12:7, 14-15, 1 Chronicles 16:20-22, Song of Solomon 3:10, Psalms 5:11, 11:7, 34:7, 15, 60:4-5, 108:5-6, 119:132, 146:8

New Testament – Luke 20:9-15, 9:35, Ephesians 1:6, Romans 1:7, 9:25, 2 Thessalonians 2:13, 2 Peter 3:14

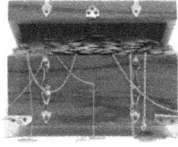

Path of Life

Path of Life (1)

"Thou wilt shew me the path of life: in thy presence is fulness of joy; at thy right Hand there are pleasures for evermore." (Psalms 16:11)

Path of Life (2)

"My son attend to my wisdom, and bow down thine ear to my understanding: That thou mayest regard discretion, and that thy lips may keep knowledge. For the lips of a strange woman drop as an honeycomb... Her feet go down to death; her steps take hold of hell. Lest thou shouldest ponder the path of life, her ways are moveable, that thou canst not know them. (Proverbs 5:1-6)

Path of Life (3)

"Concerning the works of men, by the word of thy lips I have kept from the paths of the destroyer. Hold up my goings in thy paths, that my footsteps slip not." (Psalm 17:4-5)

Discussion Questions

1. Discuss Proverbs 12:26.
2. Explain Isaiah 35:8-9.
3. What was proclaimed by a damsel in Acts 16:17?
4. Explain Proverbs 16:25.

5. What are we to live by, according to Matthew 4:4?156

Fill in the Blanks

1. "They are those that rebel against the____ ; they____ ____ the ways there of, nor abide in the____ thereof."
2. "He that followeth me shall not____ in ____, but shall have the light of___ ."
3. "The labour of the____ tendeth to____ : the fruit of the wicked to____ ."
4. "Jesus saith unto him, I am the____ , the___ , and the____ : no man cometh unto the Father, but by___ ."
5. "Because____ is the gate, and____ is the ____, which leadeth unto____ , and ____there be that find it."

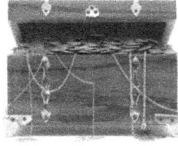

Path of Life

There is a path or trail, unknown and unforeseen by many. In the book of Job, mention is made of it.

> "There is a path which no fowl knoweth, and which the vulture's eye hath not seen: The lion's whelps have not trodden it, nor the fierce lion passed by it.... God understandeth the way thereof, and He knoweth the place thereof" (Job 28:7, 8, 23).

Path of Life (1)

Old Testament – Psalms 16:11, 17:4-5, 85:13, 86:11, 119:1, 3, 30-35, 59, 139:23-24 Deuteronomy 30:15-20 Leviticus 20:22-23, Job 23:11, Isaiah 48:15-17, Proverbs 3:19-23, 15:24, 16:9, 25

New Testament – Matthew 4:4 John 6:63, 68, 8:51, 14:6 Acts 16:17

Path of Life (2)

Old Testament – Deuteronomy 5:32-33, 11:22-28 Job 28:7-8, 23-25, Proverbs 2:11-20, 3:6, 4:18-19, 8:20, 32-36 Jeremiah 6:16, 10:23, Ps 119:133, 37:23, 27:11, 25:4-5, 23:3

New Testament – John 10:1, 9, 27-28, 8:12, 1 John 1:6-7, 2 Peter 2:1-2

PathOfLife.3 Old Testament – Isaiah 30:21, 35:8-10, 40:3, 42:16 Jeremiah 21:8, 31:21, 42:1-3, 50:5 Ezra 8:21 Psalms 26:1-3, 9-12, 31:3, 32:8-9 Proverbs 12:28.11:19, 10:16

New Testament – Luke 1:16-17 Matthew 7:13-14, 16:24-25, 19:27-29 Revelation 14:4-5

Path of Life (4)

Old Testament – Exodus 33:13, 18:20, 1 K8:35-36, 1 Samuel 12:23 Psalms 44:18, 77:13-, 19-20, 107:4-7, Jeremiah 31:8-9 Isaiah 40:13-14, 26:7-8, 2:2-3 Proverbs 23:19

New Testament – Luke 13:24, 4:4, 3:4-5, 1:74-75, 79 Matthew 3:3 Acts 2:28, 24:14

Path of Life (5)

Old Testament – Isaiah 62:10, 49:7-11, 30:8-11, 11:15-16 Psalms 143:8, 10, 125:5, 119:101-105, 128, 81:13-16, 65:9-11, 37:23, 5:8 Job 8:11-13, 24:13 Proverbs 5:5-6, 7:25-27

New Testament – Colossians 2:6, Hebrews 10:19-20, Romans 3:15-17

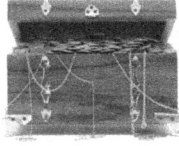

God's Promises

God's Promises (1)

"Now I say that Jesus Christ was a minister of the circumcision for the truth of God, to confirm the promise made unto the fathers."

"And this is the promise that he hath promised us, even eternal life." (Romans 5:8, 1 Jn 2:25)

God's Promises (2)

"For the Son of God, who was preached among you by us, even by me and Silvanus and Timotheus, was not yea and nay, but in him was yea. For all the promises of God in him are yea, and in him Amen, unto the glory of God by us." (2 Cor 1:19-20)

God's Promises (3)

"Hearken, my beloved brethren, Hath not God chosen the poor of this world rich in faith, and heirs of the kingdom which he hath promised to them that love him?" (James 2:5)

Discussion Questions

1. Discuss Joshua 23:5, 10, 14-15.
2. Discuss Hebrews 6:9-20.
3. What observations are made in Romans 9:1-8?

4. Explain Galatians 3:13-22, 29.
5. Discuss Jeremiah 32:40-42.

Fill in the Blanks

1. "And ye know in all your hearts and in all your_____ _____, that not_____ _____hath_____ of all the good things which the Lord your God spake_____ _____."
2. "For the_____, that he should be_____ _____the of the world, was not to Abraham, or to his seed, through the_____, but through the_____ of_____."
3. "My covenant will I not_____, nor the thing that is gone out of _____."
4. "Whose voice then shook the earth: but now he hath_____, saying, Yet once more I _____not the earth only, but also heaven."
5. "Which he had_____ afore by his prophets in the holy scriptures."

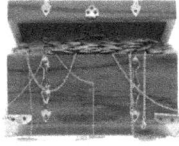

God's Promises

*T*he Christian has blessed assurance because of the promises of God. God is faithful. It is impossible for God to lie; therefore, we can have strong consolation, and our very souls can be anchored because we know with absolute certainty that God will do what He said He will do. God will keep all that He has promised.

God's Promises (1)

Old Testament – Genesis 22:15-18 Deuteronomy 1:11, 6:1-3, 9:27-28, 10:8-9, 15:5-6 Numbers 23:19 Joshua 23:5, 10, 14-15, 21:43-45 isaiah 42:8-9, 46:9-11, 48:3 Psalms 89:34-35, 105:30-42

New Testament – Romans 4:13-21 Hebrews 6:9-20 Titus 1:1-2

God's Promises (2)

Old Testament – Exodus 6:8 Deuteronomy 23:23, 26:18, 27:1-3 Joshua 22:1-4 Numbers 30:2, 14:34, 39-43 Hosea 10:4, 6:7 Ecclesiastes 5:4-5 Leviticus 5:4-5 Micah 7: 20

New Testament – Acts 2:29-30, 39-42, 13:22-23, 26:6-7 Romans 1:1-3, 9:3-11 Ephesians 3:5-6 GaLatians 3:13-22, 29 Hebrews 10:23, 36

God's Promises (3)

Old Testament – Genesis 28:20-22, 31:13 Deuteronomy 12:20-21, 23:21 Psalms 65:1, 76:11 Ezekiel 12:25, 28, 2 Chronicles 1:8-9, 6:10, 15-17, 21:7, 1 Kings 5:12, 8:19-20, 56, 9:1-5 Jeremiah 32:37-42, 33:14-17, 25-26

New Testament – Luke 1:30-33, 68-73 Acts 3:20-26 Hebrews 11:8-17, 33, 8:6-10, 2 Peter 1:4 Ephesians 1:13

God's Promises (4)

Old Testament – Leviticus 19:12, 6:1-5, 1 Samuel 30:15-16, 2 Chronicles 36:11-13 Judges 11:30-35 Nehemiah 5:9-13, 10:28-30, 13:23-25 Psalms 119:106

New Testament – Matthew 5:33-37, 14:1-9, 26:69-75 Hebrews 4:1, 3:18-19 Romans 15:8, 2 Corinthians 1:19-20, 7:1, 1 John 2:25

God's Promises (5)

Old Testament – 1 Samuel 15:29, 2 Samuel 7:28, Jeremiah 1:11-12, 4:28 Isaiah 14:24, 45:23-25, 55:10-11, 66:22-24, 2 Kings 20:9-11 Zechariah 1:5-6 Psalms 77:7-8, H Ezekiel 13:1-4, 16-22

New Testament – Luke 24:49 Acts 1:4, 2:33, 13:32-33, 26:6-7 Ephesians 3:3-6, 2 Peter 3:9, 13 Hebrews 9:15, 12:25-26 James 2:5, 1:12, 2 Peter 2:18-20

Humility

Humility (1)

"If my people, which are called by my name, shall humble themselves, and pray, and seek my face, and turn from their wicked ways; then will I hear from heaven, and will forgive their sin, and will heal their land." (2 Chronicles 7:14)

Humility (2)

"Whereupon the princes of Israel and the king humbled themselves; and they said, The LORD Is righteous. And when the LORD saw that they humbled themselves, the word of the LORD came to Shemaiah, saying, They have humbled themselves; therefore I will not destroy them, but I will grant them some deliverance; and my wrath shall not be poured out upon Jerusalem by the hand of Shishak." (2 Chronicles 12:6-7)

Humility (3)

"Humble yourselves in the sight of the Lord, and he shall lift you up." (James 4:10)

Discussion Questions

1. Discuss 2 Chronicles 7:14.
2. What was God's response in 2 Chronicles 34:27?
3. Explain Proverbs 29:23.

4. Discuss 2 Corinthians 12:20-21.
5. Discuss 1 Peter 5:5-7.

Fill in the Blanks

1. "_____ yourselves therefore under the mighty____ of God, that he may____ you in due time."
2. "Now I Nebuchadnezzar____ and____ and ____the King of heaven, all whose works are____, and his ways____ : and those that____ in ____he is able to____ ."
3. "If I then, your____ and____ , have washed your feet; ye also ought to wash____ ____ ____ ."
4. "And being found in fashion as a man, he____ ____ , and became____ unto death, even the death of the cross."
5. "Now the man Moses was very____ , above all the men which were upon the____ of the____ ."

Humility

*H*umility is the disposition of the soul and mind that seeks to serve rather than to exalt oneself. From a Christian perspective, it is the making of oneself small and subjugated, so that God may have the glory, the preeminence, and that His will be done above our own. It necessitates total reliance and trust in God.

> "Whosoever therefore humble himself as this little child, the same is greatest in the kingdom of heaven" (Matthew 18:4).

Humility (1)

Old Testament – 2 Chronicles 7:14, 12:6-7, 32:24-26, 33:9-13, 34:24-28, Jonah 3:4-10, Leviticus 26:40-42, Proverbs 16:5, 19, 18:12, 1 Samuel 2:1-3, Daniel 4:37, Psalms 149:4, 147:6, 138:6

New Testament – Matthew 11:28-29, 18:4, 23:12 John 13:14-15, Luke 22:25-27

Humility (2)

Old Testament – Exodus 3:11 Numbers 12:3 Genesis 18:27, 32:9-10, Judges 6:15, 1 Samuel 9:21, 15:17, Jeremiah 1:6, Amos 7:14-15, Job 5:11, 22:29, 42:4-5, Proverbs 29:23, 22:4, Psalms 8:2

New Testament – Luke 1:50-52, Matthew 11:25, 23:12, Ephesians 3:8, 2 Corinthians 12:7-9, Colossians 3:12, James 4:6-10

Humility (3)

Old Testament – Zephaniah 2:3, 1 Kings 21:29, Jeremiah 13:18, Joel 1:8, Lamentations 2:10, 3:19-20, Job 40:12, Daniel 9:3, Psalms 22:26, 25:9, 34:2, 18, 37:11, 45:4, 69:30-32, Deuteronomy 8:2-3

New Testament – Matthew 5:5, Philippians 2:8, Titus 3:1-2, Ephesians 4:1-2, 1 Peter 3:8, 5:5-7

Humility (4)

Old Testament – Proverbs 3:34 6:1-3, 11:2, Daniel 5:20-22, Ezekiel 21:25-26, Job 24:24-25, Isaiah 2:11-12, 17, 22, 5:15-16, 13:11, Jeremiah 6:26, 25:34, 48:28-29, Malachi 4:1, Zechariah 11:2-3, Psalms 35:9-14

New Testament – James 1:9-10, 1 Timothy 6:11, 2 Timothy 2:24-25, Galatians 5:22-23

Humility (5)

Old Testament – 1 Chronicles 29:14, 1 Kings 3:7, 2 Chronicles 12:6-7, 11-13, Job 10:15, Psalms 9:12, 10:12, 17, 113:5-6, 131:2, Isaiah 10:33, 38:14, 57:15, 66:2, Ezra 9:3-6, 13, Jeremiah 44:4, 10

New Testament – Luke 10:13, Matthew 15:25-28, 2 Corinthians 12:20-21

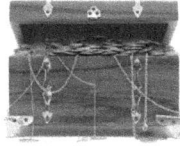

Identifying Problem Areas

Identifying Problem Areas (1)

"O that there were such a heart in them, that they would fear Me, and keep all My commandments always, that it might be well with them, and with their children for ever! (Deuteronomy 5:29)

Identifying Problem Areas (2)

"For I say unto you, That except your righteousness shall exceed the righteousness of the scribes, and Pharisees; ye shall in no case enter into the kingdom of heaven." (Matthew 5:20)

Identifying Problem Areas (3)

"Jesus answered and said unto them, Ye do err, not knowing the scriptures, nor the power of God." (Matthew 22:29)

Discussion Questions

1. What was the problem area in Deuteronomy 5:29?
2. What was the problem area in Deuteronomy 28:47-48?
3. How big of a problem is unbelief in the heart of man?
4. In what ways is ignoring, rejecting, or changing the Word of God a problem area for man?
5. Is being carnally minded or worldly minded a problem area? If so, explain.

Fill in the Blanks

1. "One____ thou____ : go thy way, sell whatsoever thou hast, and give to the poor, and thou____ have____ in____ : and come, take up the cross, and____ me. And he was____ at that____ , and_____ grieved: for he had____ possessions."

2. "Take heed, brethren, lest there be in any of you an_____ of____ , in departing from the____ God."

3. "For unto us was the_____ as well as unto them: but the word____ did not____ them, not being____ with____ in them that heard it."

4. "To whom shall I speak, and give warning, that they may____ ? behold, their ear is____ , and they cannot____ : behold, the____ of the Lord is unto them a____ ; they have_____ in it."

5. "O that there were such an____ in them, that they would_____ , and____ all my____ always, that it might be____ with____ , and with their children for ever!"

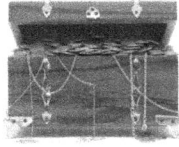

Identifying Problem Areas

*A*ll of us are imperfect creatures. We all fall short in many ways and in many areas. All of us stand in need of being corrected at some time. We must examine ourselves daily to see whether or not we are going contrary to the Word of God; none of us are above correction. Once an error is found, we must confess and repent, and the blood of Christ will cleanse us from all sin (Galatians 3:26-27, 1 John 1:8-10).

Identifying Problem Areas (1)

Old Testament – Deuteronomy 5:27-29, Deuteronomy 28:47-48, Ezekiel 33:30-33, Hosea 4:1-2, 6, 12 Jeremiah 6:10, Jeremiah 23;32 Ecclesiastes 10:5-7, Isaiah 3:12, 9:16, 28:7 Amos 2:4 Psalms 51:16-17, 95:10 Proverbs 14:22, 19:27

New Testament – Matthew 5:20, Matthew 18:2-3, 22:29 John 3:3-6, John 5:38-42, Romans 10:13

Identifying Problem Areas (2)

Old Testament – Deuteronomy 7:22 Joshua 6:18, 7:6-12, 20-26 Amos 5:18-24, Isaiah 59:1-8, 12-15, 58:1-10, Isaiah 55:7, 44:18-20 Jeremiah 9:3-6, 23-24, 2:11-35 Psalms 50:18-23 , 78:36-39, 56-59, Hosea 8:1-4, 12-14, 4:1-2, 6, 12

New Testament – Hebrews 3:7-14, Hebrews 4:1-3, Hebrews 12:14-15, 1 Corinthians 13:1-8, 15:34 Mark 10:17-27

Identifying Problem Areas (3)

Old Testament – Leviticus 18:24-30 Deuteronomy 12:30-33, Deuteronomy 8:2-6, 10-20, Numbers 21:4-9 2 Kings 17:7-12, 15, 1 Samuel 8:5-7, 2 Chronicles 36:14 Psalm 2:1-6, 106:34-35, Hosea 13:9-12, Joel 3:11-14 Jeremiah 10:1-2, Ezekiel 23:30, 36:28-29, 37:21-28 Amos 3:3, Micah 6:1-8

New Testament – Acts 4:24-30, 11:18, Galatians 3:8

Identifying Problem Areas (4)

Old Testament – Genesis 44:4-6, 10, 16-17, 22 Deutoronomy 32:4-5, 20, 28-29, 31:17-18, 9:23-24, 2 Chronicles 7:14-15, Isaiah 30:1-3, 8-13, 48:18, 55:8-9 Jeremiah 2:29-32, 35-37, Jeremiah 5:1-5, Jeremiah 6:16-19

New Testament – lMatthew 23:37-39 Hebrews 3:10, 12, 4:1-7, Romans 3:3-4, 11:20-23

Identifying Problem Areas (5)

Old Testament – Job 42:7-9, 1 Samuel 2:12 Jeremiah 22:1-5, 8-10, 15-23, 29, 23:32

New Testament – Acts 17:2-11, 1 Corinthians 1:21 Matthew 13:19-23, 18:21-35 Galatians 5:7-10, 14-26, 3:12 Peter 3:14-18

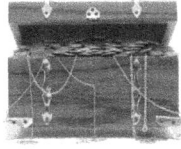

The Poor

The Poor (1)

"The wicked in his pride doth persecute the poor: let them be taken in the devices that they have imagined" (Psalm 10:2)

The Poor (2)

"He that hath pity upon the poor lendeth to the LORD: and that which he hath given will he pay him again." (Proverbs 19:7)

The Poor (3)

"But when thou makest a feast, call the poor, the maimed, the lame, the blind:" (Luke 14:13)

Discussion Questions

1. What message did Jesus convey in Mark 12:42-43?
2. What transpired in Matthew 19:21-25, that caused amazement among even the disciples?
3. What does it mean to be poor in spirit, as mentioned in Matthew 5:3?
4. What warning was given in James 2:1-9?
5. Discuss James 2:15-16.

Fill in the Blanks

1. For it hath pleased them of _____ and_____ to make a certain contribution for the _____ which are at Jerusalem.
2. The righteous _____ the cause of the _____: but the wicked regardeth not to know it.
3. Better is the _____ that walketh in his _____, than he that is perverse in his ways, though he be rich.
4. He hath dispersed, he hath given to the ____; his righteousness endureth for ever; his horn shall be exalted with _____.
5. Only they would they we should remember the ____; the same which I also was forward to do

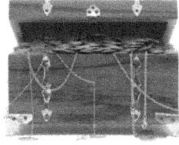

The Poor

C ompassion for the poor has always been a part of God's plan. The rich and the poor meet together; the LORD is the maker of them all (Proverbs 22:2).

> "But when thou makest a feast, call the poor, the maimed, the lame, the blind: And thou shalt be blessed; for they cannot recompense thee: for thou shalt be recompensed at the resurrection of the just" (Luke 14:13-14).

God loves and cares for all His creation. He uses us as instruments or vessels to minister to the poor of the land. He considers them as being our brethren. There is no partiality with God—however, that is not the case with many of us. Those who belong to Christ must seek to do that which God greatly desires.

The Poor (1)

Old Testament. Deuteronomy 15:7-11, 24:12-15, 1 Samuel 2:7-8 Ecclesiastes 5:8, 4:13 Poverbsr 29:7, 28:6, 21:13, 19:17, Job 29:11-16, 5:12-16 Psalms 9:18-20, 12:5

New Testament. Matthew 11:3-5, 19:21-26, 29 Luke 12:12-24, 1 Corinthians 1:26-29, 2 Corinthians 8:9

The Poor (2)

Old Testament – Exodus 22:22-25, 23:3 Leviticus 19:9-10, 25:35, 39 Job 36:5-6, 15 Psalms 34:6, 35:4-10, 37:14-15, 40:16-17, 41:1-2 Ezekiel 16:49-50, 18:12-13, 22:29 Isaiah 3:14-15

New Testament – James 5:1-7, 2:2-7, 15-16, 1 John 3:17

The Poor (3)

Old Testament – Ecclesiastes 4:1, 9:13-16 Deuteronomy 10:16-18, 14:28-29 Job 13:13-23, 30:25, 22:2, 9, 16, 22-23, 19:1, 4, 7, 22, 18:23, 17:5 Isaiah 1:17-23, 3:13-15, 10:1-2 Amos 2:6-7, 5:11-13

New Testament. James 1:27 Galatians 2:9-10 John 12:3-8

The Poor (4)

Old Testament. Daniel 4:27, Isaiah 58:6-11, 41:17 29:19, 25:1-4, 14:30-32, 11:4 Amos 8:4 Habakkuk 3:13-14 Jeremiah 5:27-29 Zechariah 7:9-14 Psalms 10:12-18, 72:11-14, 82:1-4, 140:12-13

New Testament – Luke 6:20-25, 19:5-8 Mark 12:38-44

The Poor (5)

Old Testament. Leviticus 19:15 Job 34:21, 28, 24:2-10 Proverbs 10:15, 13:7, 28:27, 30:8-9 Psalms 14:4-6, 40:16-17, 68:10, 69:29-33, 74:21, 107:39, 41, 109:31, 132:13-15

New Testament – Matthew 25:34-44 Romans 15:26 Acts 11:29

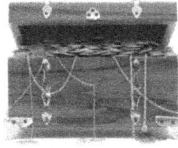

Relationships: Good and Bad

Relationships: Good and Bad (1)

"Set me as a seal upon thine heart, as a seal upon thine arm: for love is strong as death; jealousy is cruel as the grave : the coals thereof are coals of fire, which hast a most vehement flame." (Song Of Solomon 8:6)

Relationships: Good and Bad (2)

"It is better to dwell in the wilderness than with a contentious and an angry woman." (Proverbs 21:19)

Relationships: Good and Bad (3)

"Likewise , ye husbands, dwell with them according to knowledge, giving honour unto the wife, as unto the weaker vessel, and as being heirs together of the grace of life; that your prayers be not hindered." (1 Peter 3:7)

Discussion Questions

1. Why did God make Adam a help meet for him?
2. What are the attributes of a virtuous woman?
3. What can be said of the character of both Elisabeth and Zacharias?
4. What does the instruction "to dwell with his wife according to knowledge" mean?

5. If any man has a quarrel with us, what are we to do?

Fill in the Blanks

1. "And the Lord God said, it is not good that the man should___
   ____ ; I will make him an____ ____ for him."
2. "Wherefore they are no more twain, but____ flesh. What
   therefore God hath joined____ , let not___ put____ ."
3. "Marriage is____ in all, and the bed ___: but____ and____ God
   will____ ."
4. "A ____woman is a crown to her____ : but she that maketh____
   is as___ in his____ ."
5. "It is better to dwell in the____ , than with a____ and an
   ____woman.

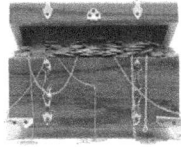

Relationships: Good and Bad

O ver the course of our lives, we form relationships. Normally, these relationships fall into two categories—those that are beneficial, helpful, uplifting, and encouraging, and those that we find to be detrimental, hurtful, unfavorable, or less than desirable. The relationship that man has with God is always a highly esteemed, highly treasured, most profitable relationship. We are to use discernment as we enter into relationships with others.

Relationships: Good and Bad (1)

Old Testament – Genesis 2:18, 21-25, 5:2, 29:18, 20, 34:3, 8 Song of Solomon 1:7, 3:1-4, 8:6-7 Ecclesiastes 9:9 Proverbs 12:2'4 19:14, 30:18-19, 31:10-31 Psalms 11:2, 5

New Testament – Matthew 19:4-12 Luke 1:5-6 Ephesians 5:22-28, 1 Corinthians 11:8-12

Relationships: Good and Bad (2)

Old Testament – Deuteronomy 24:5, 20:7, Proverbs 5:18 Genesis 26:8, 15, 1 Samuel 1:8, 25:2-3, 25 Judges 16:4, 16-18 Proverbs 5:1-13, 20-23, 14:1, 25:19, 30:21-23, 31:2 Ecclesiastes 7:26, 1 K21:25

New Testament – 1 Peter 3:1-7, 1 Corinthians 7:1-16, Colossians 3:18-22

Relationships: Good and Bad (3)

Old Testament – Genesis 16:5-6, 21:9-11 Exodus 4:24-26 Esther 1:8-19, 2:1-9, 17, 4:13-14, 1 Kings 1:1-4, Ruth 1:8-18, 3:7-11 Psalms 128:1-6, 119:63 Proverbs 11:29, 18:22, 22:14, 23:27-28

New Testament – 1 Corinthians 7:2-5, 10-16, 39, 2 Corinthians 6:14-18, Titus 2:1-8, 1 Thessalonians 4:1-8

Relationships: Good and Bad (4)

Old Testament – Ecclesiastes 4:9-12, 1 Samuel 18:1-3, 20::12-17 Proverbs 18:24, 26:18-26, 27:14-17 Job 16:1-6, 20, 17:5 Psalms 35:11-15, 41:6-7, 55:12-14 Zechariah 13:6 Mica 7:5-6

New Testament – 1 Corinthians 6:15-20, 15:33, Eph 5:11 James 4:14, 2 Corinthians 11:2-4, Revelation 19:7-10, Hebrews 13:4

Relationships: Good and Bad (5)

Old Testament – Dt 17:17-14-17, 1 K11:1-4 Ezra 10:1-4, 9-12 Nehemiah 13:23-27 Jeremiah 44:13-28 Malachi 2:11-16 Amos 3:3 Psalms 50:18-23, Proverbs 29:24, 28:27, 18:19, 11:14-18

New Testament – Matthew 10:34-36, 12:12:48-50, 1 Cor 5:6-13

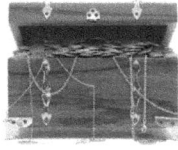

Our Father

Our Father (1)

"Have we not one father? Hath not God created us? Why do we deal treacherously every man against his brother, by profaning the covenant of our fathers? (Malachi 2:10)

Our Father (2)

"As obedient children not fashioning yourselves according to the former lusts in your ignorance... And if you call on the Father... pass the time of your sojourning here in fear." (1 Peter 1:14, 17)

Our Father (3)

"...Father, if thou be willing, remove this cup from me: nevertheless not my will, but thine, be done." (Luke 22:34)

Discussion Questions

1. What were the conditions put forth by God in 2 Corintinians 6:15-18, that determined whether or not He would be their Father or not?
2. What determining factors were mentioned in Romans 8:14-16, that was indicative of God being their Father?
3. What transpired in Deuteronomy 32:1-6?
4. Discuss Proverbs 30:4.

5. Discuss Matthew 5:44-45.

Fill in the Blanks

1. I speak that which I have seen with my _____: and ye do that which ye have seen with your _____.
2. For if ye forgive men their trespasses, your ____ ____ will also forgive you.
3. Not every one that saith unto me, Lord, Lord, shall enter into the kingdom of _____: but he that doeth the will of my _____ which is in heaven.
4. For ye are all ____ of God by ___ in Christ Jesus.
5. For whom the LORD loveth he _____: even as a _____ the son in whom he _____.

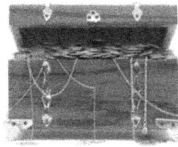

Our Father

The recognition of God as "Our Father" is an expression of endearment spoken by those who belong to Him and who are considered to be "children of God." This ascribes to a relationship rather than the ritualistic detachment so often found in religious expressions today. Not only is there a sense of reliance and submission to Him, but there is also a tone of love and adoration denoted.

Our Father (1)

Old Testament – Deuteronomy 32:1-6, 8:3-5 Exodus 4:22-23 Jeremiah 31:9, 20 Hosea 11:1, 4, 1:10 Proverbs 30:4 Malachi 1:6-7, 2:10 Psalms 68:3-5, 27:10

New Testament Matthew 5:9, 16, 44-48, 6:1-9 John 1:11-12 Romans 8:14-16, 9:8, 26 Hebrew 12:5-11, 2 Corinthians 6:14-18

Our Father (2)

Old Testament – Deuteronomy 1:30-33, 32:7-15 isaiah 1:2-4, 43:1-6, 46:3-4, 63:7-9, 15-16, 64:6-8 Hosea 13:12-14 Jer 3:4-5, 12-19 Proverbs 3:12, 4:1, 17:2

New Testament 1 John 3:1-3, Matthew 6:14-18, 30:33, 7:9-11, 21, 10:16-20, 26-29

Our Father (3)

Old Testament – 2 Samuel 7:12-14 isaiah 9:6-7, 22:21-25 Zechariah 12:10 Psalms 2:7-12, 89:3-4, 23-26

New Testament John 8:38, 42, 10:23-30 Matthew 7:21, 10:32-33, 12:50, 16:13-20, 22:41-46, 23:9 Hebrews 1:1-5, 3:6 Acts 2:29-36 GaLatians 4:4-6, 3:26

Our Father (4)

Old Testament – Genesis 6:1-2 Deuteronomy 14:1 Exodus 22:29 Job 1:6, 2:1, 38:4-7

New Testament Matthew 17:5 Luke 2:49, 22:41-42, 23:34 John 4:34, 5:17-45, 6:44-45, 57, 17:1-26, 1 Peter 1:13-17, 2:21-23, 2 Corinthians 1:5-9 Ephesians 2:3-18, 1:2-17, 1 John 1:1-3

Our Father (5)

Old Testament – Psalms 149:2, 127:3, 103:13-14, 82:5-7 Deuteronomy 32:18-20

New Testament John 8:18-19, 28-29, 38-44, 1 John 3:7-10, 2:1, 15-16, 22-24, 2 John 1:3-4, 1 Corinthians 8:3-6 James 1:17, 27

The Big If

The Big If (1)

"And the LORD said unto Cain, Why art thou wroth? And why is thy countenance fallen? If thou doest well, shalt thou not be accepted? And if thou doest not well, sin lieth at the door. And unto thee shall be his desire, and thou shalt rule over him." (Genesis 4:6-7)

The Big If (2)

"Then said Jesus to those Jews which believed on him, If ye continue in my word, then ye are my disciples indeed:" (John 8:31)

The Big If (3)

"Verily, verily, I say unto you, If a man keep my saying, he shall never see death." (John 8:51)

Discussion Questions

1. What would have happened if Cain would have heeded the advice given by God in Genesis 4:7?
2. What were the conditions given by Joshua to the children of Israel in Joshua 24:20-24?
3. What were the conditions given in 2 Chronicles 15:2?534 The Spiritual Treasure Trove

4. What factor given in John 14:15-21 determines whether or not we will keep Christ's commandments?
5. What are the results to expect, given in Revelation 22:18-19, if we should add to or take away from the Word of God?

Fill in the Blanks

1. "___ ye keep my____ , ye shall abide in my____ .
2. "Then said Jesus to those Jews which____ on Him, If ye____ in my____ , then are ye my____ indeed.
3. "For___ ye thoroughly____ your____ and your____ ; if ye thoroughly execute____ between a man and his____ .
4. "___ we suffer, we shall also____ with him:__ we deny , he also will___ ___ ."
5. "But___ ye do not____ , neither will your____ which is in____ ___ your____ .

The Big If

*T*he word *if* is a conditional particle or conjunction. It consists of only two alphabetical letters, yet it is the causation for many failures, many tragedies, much regret, and much devastation: "If only I knew, " "If only I had done this, " "If only I had done that, " "If only I would have followed good advice, " "If only I would have listened." In this topic, we have selected Scriptures about Biblical events and circumstances that were conditional and pivotal and based on the *Big If*.

The Big If (1)

Old Testament – Genesis 4:6-7 Deuteronomy 28:1-2, 15 Exodus 19:5 Joshua 24:20 Jeremiah 4:1-4 Ezekiel 33:10-16, 2 Chronicles 7:13-14, 6:36-39

New Testament – John 8: 31, 51, 14:15, 15:6-7, 10-14, 2 Peter 1:2-11

The Big If (2)

Old Testament – 1 Samuel 12:14-15, Malachi 3:10, Isaiah 58:10-14, 1 Kings 18:21 Job 11:13-19, 8:3-7, Zechariah 3:7, 2 Chronicles 15:2, Ecclesiastes 10:10, Proverbs 1:10-18

New Testament.2- Matthew 5:28-30, 39-48, 6:14-15, 10:12-14, 12:26-30, Luke 23:31

The Big If (3)

Old Testament Genesis 13:9, 18:23-32 Numbers 32:13-15, 1 Samuel 2:25, 24:17-19 Hosea 6:1-3, Nehemiah 1:7-9, Proverbs 16:31, 23:15, 24:10-12

New Testament Mark 11:24-26 John 3:1-12, 7:16-17, 9:31-33, 41 10:9, 37-38

The Big If (4)

Old Testament – Deuteronomy 4:29, 1 Chronbicles 28:9, Jeremiah 17:24-27, 26:4-6, Jonah 3:6-9, Haggai 2:12-14, Malachi 2:2, Amos 5:18-19, Psalms 81:8, 95:1-8, Isaiah 1:19-20, 8:20

New Testament – - Matthew 21:18-22 Romans 6:5-8, 2 Corinthians 5:17-18, Hebrews 10:38, Revalation 22:7, 18-19

The Big If (5)

Old Testament – Numbers 15:22-31, 22:18, 35:16-24, Joshua 23:11-13, Jeremiah 12:5, 1 Kings 18:21, Deuteronomy 32:41, Psalms 7:11-12, 11:3, 124:1-3, 130:3-4

New Testament – Luke 16:31, 23:31, Hebrews 10:26-27, 6:3-6, 1 Corinthians 6:4-10, 3:17-18, 1 Peter 4:18

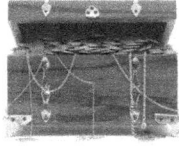

Stand

Stand (1)

"Thus saith the LORD: Stand in the court of the LORD's house and speak unto all the cities of Judah, which come to worship in the LORD's house, all the words that I command thee to speak unto them; diminish not a word:" (Jer 26:2)

Stand (2)

"Therefore being justified by faith, we have peace with God through our Lord Jesus Christ: By whom also we have access by faith into this grace wherein we stan, and rejoice in hope of the glory of God." (Rom 5:1-2)

Stand (3)

"Put on the whole armour of God, that you may be able to stand against the wiles of the devil." (Ephesians 6:11)

Discussion Questions

1. Discuss Jeremiah 26:2.
2. Explain Psalms 1:1-5.
3. What is conveyed in 1 Corinthians 16:13?
4. Explain Ephesians 6:11-14.
5. Discuss Exodus 14:13.

Fill in the Blanks

1. "The wicked are overthrown, and are not: but the house of the____ shall____ ."

2. "Put on the whole armor of God, that ye may be____ to____ against the____ of the devil."

3. "____therefore, having your____ girt about with____ , and having on the____ of ____."

4. "Therefore the shall not____ in the judgment, nor sinners in the____ of the____."

5. "Be not hasty to go out of his sight:____ not in an evil____ ; for he doeth____ ____ him."

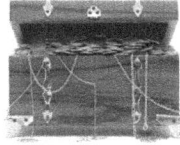

Stand

"To stand" involves being set to defend, to resist, or to withstand opposition. It means "to establish one's position, refusing to be swayed, moved back, manipulated or pushed away, not to give in or quit." As Christians, we stand on the Bible truths. We have convictions, principles, and values that we will not compromise with the world.

Stand (1)

Old Testament – Jeremiah 26:2, 15:16-19, 7:2-7, Ezekiel 2:1-5, 13:5, 22:29-30, Ezra 9:15, Nehemiah 8:4-9, 9:3, Psalms 1:1-5, 4:3-4, 5:4-5, 20:7-8, 24:3-5, Proverbs 12:7, 19:21, 22:29, Job 37:14

New Testament – Romans 5:1-2, 9:11, 14:4, 10, Revelation 20:12

Stand (2)

Old Testament – Deuteronomy 5:31, 11:22-25, 27:9-13, Joshua 7:11-13, Exodus 33:21, Psalms 27:5, 30:7, 33:8, 35:1-2, 40:1-2, Zechariah 4:11-14, 14:3-4, Isaiah 51:20-23, 28:18, 11:10

New Testament – Philippians 4:1, 1:27, Colossians, 4:12, 1 Corinthians 15:1-2, 2:3-5, James 5:9

Stand (3)

Old Testament – Daniel 10:8-11, 1 Samuel 6:20, Malachi 3:2, Nahum 1:5-7, 2:8, Jeremiah 49:19, 46:21, 15:1, Ezekiel 44:15-16, 24, Zechariah 3:1-8, Micah 5:4-5, Isaiah 46:9-10, 48:13, 51:17, 20, 1 Kings 8:22-23

New Testament – 2 Timothy 4:16-17, 1 Thessalonians 3:8, 2 Thessalonians 2:15, Galatians 5:1, Ephesians 6:11-14

Stand (4)

Old Testament – Exodus 3:5-6, 9:13, 14:13, Joshua 1:3-5, 3:8, 13, 5:13-15, 10:8, 13, 23:9-11, Daniel 12:1, 5-7, Psalms 147:17-20, 135:1-2, 134:1-3, 122:1-2

New Testament – 1 Peter 5:11-12, Romans 11:20, 1 Corinthians 16:13, Acts 5:20, 23:11, 26:6, 27:23

Stand (5)

Old Testament – Ecclesiastes 8:2-3 Job 8:13-15, 41:10, Leviticus 26:37, 2 Chronicles 29:11, 1 Chronicles 23:28, 30, 1 Samuel 12:6-7, 9:27, Numbers 9:6-8, Jeremiah 6:16, Isaiah 40:8, 14:24, 8:10, Psalms 111:7-8, 109:30-31

New Testament – 1 Corinthians 10:12, Luke 13:25, Revelation 3:20, 6:17, 10:5-6

Higher Ground

Higher Ground (1)

"From the end of the earth will I cry unto thee, when my heart is over-whelmed: lead me to the rock that is higher than I." {Psalm 61:2)

Higher Ground (2)

"Even when we were dead in sins, hath quickened us together with Christ, (by grace ye are saved;) And hath raised us up together in heavenly places in Christ Jesus." (Ephesians 2:5-6)

Higher Ground (3)

"The way of life is above to the wise, that he may depart from hell beneath." (Proverbs 15:24)

Discussion Questions

1. Explain Psalms 61:2.
2. What does God say that He will do for His people according to Psalms 27:6?
3. What is Christ's desire according to John 10:10?654 The Spiritual Treasure Trove
4. Explain Ephesians 1:3.
5. What were the conditions for success in Deuteronomy 28:1, 12-13?

Fill in the Blanks

1. "And it shall come to pass, if thou shalt____ ____ unto the voice of the Lord thy God to____ and to do____ which I command thee this day, that the____ thy____ will set thee on____ above all nations of the____."
2. "And hath____ us up together, and made us sit together in____ places in____ ."
3. "But thou shalt remember the Lord thy God; for it is he that____ thee to get____ , that He may____ His covenant."
4. "Humble ____in the sight of the Lord, and he shall____ you up."
5. "The Lord God is my____, and he will make my feet like hinds' feet, and he will make me to walk upon mine____ ____."

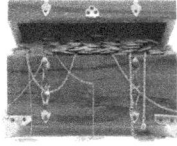

Higher Ground

*I*t has always been God's desire for His people to be a people of renown—a people with high morals, high standards, high aspirations, and even a high and noble view of life itself. His Word, when obeyed, will propel us to higher levels and higher ground.

Higher Ground (1)

Old Testament – Psalms 61:1-3, Psalms 31:19-20, Psalms 27:5-6, Psalms 18:33, Deuteronomy 32:13-14, Deuteronomy 28:1, 12-13, Deuteronomy 26:18-19, 1 Samuel 2:7-8, 2 Samuel 22:48-51, Proverbs 25:6-7, Isaiah 35:8-9

New Testament – Luke 18:10-14, Luke 14:10-11, Matthew 19:27-28, Ephesians 2:6-7, Ephesians 1:19-23

Higher Ground (2)

Old Testament – Numbers 20:17, Habakkuk 3:19, Proverbs 16:17, Isaiah 62:10, Isaiah 58:11-14, Isaiah 57:15, Isaiah 49:11-13, Isaiah 40:3-4, Isaiah 19:23-25, Isaiah 11:1-5, 15-16, Job 5:11, Job 22:23, 29-30

New Testament – Ephesians 1:3, James 1:9-10, James 4:6, 10, 1 Peter 5:6-7, Revelation 5:9-10

Higher Ground (3)

Old Testament – 2 Samuel 7:8-10, 1 Ch 14:2 Daniel 4:17, Daniel 2:20-21, Psalms 75:4-7, Psalms 83:1-5, 12-18, Psalms 91:14, Psalms 107:40-43, Job 12:16-25, Job 34:24-25, Ezekiel 17:22-24, Jeremiah 27:5

New Testament – John 3:27, John 19:10-11, 1 Corinthians 4:7, Romans 13:1, Romans 8:28, 31

Higher Ground (4)

Old Testament – Deuteronomy 8:18, Deuteronomy 15:6, Deuteronomy 30:4-10, Leviticus 26:13, Proverbs 11:11, 14:11, 15:24, 28:10 Psalms 18:23-26, 37:3-4, 23-24, Psalms 41:10-13, Psalms 44:1-8, Psalms 69:14-18, 29

New Testament – Luke 1:52, 16:25 John 3:12, 316:33, 8:23, 1 John 4:5

Higher Ground (5)

Old Testament – Genesis 27:29, 37:5-11, 49:22-26, 1 Chr 5:2, Job 36:7, Psalms 119:116-118, Psalms 18:43-50, 27:6, 45:7, 47:1-4, 113:5-8, Proverbs 24:7, 29:33, Isaiah 33:15-16, 48:15-22

New Testament – Matthew 6:33, Colossians 3:1-5, James 3:14-18, 1 Corinthians 15:45-49 Phillipians 3:20

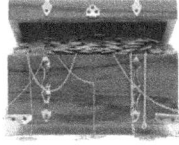

The Way

The Way (1)

"And thou shalt teach them ordinances and laws, and shalt show them the way wherein they must walk, and the work that they must do." (Exodus 18:20)

The Way (2)

"The same followed Paul and us, and cried saying, These men are servants of the most high God, which shew us the way of salvation." (Acts 16:17)

The Way (3)

"Having therefore brethren, boldness to enter into the holiest by the blood of Jesus, By a new and living way, which he hath consecrated for us, through the veil, that is to say, his flesh." (Hebrews 10:19-20)

Discussion Questions

1. What observations are made in Psalms 119:1, 9, 14, 27-37?
2. Discuss Isaiah 35:8.
3. Explain Acts 16:17.
4. Discuss Proverbs 10:17.
5. Discuss Proverbs 15:24.

Fill in the Blanks

1. "Lead me, O Lord, in thy____ because of mine_____ ; make thy____ ____ before my face."
2. "I have chosen the way of____ ."
3. "I will run the____ of thy_____ ."
4. "Jesus saith unto him, I am the____ , the____ and the____ ."
5. "There is a____ that seemeth right unto a man, but the thereof are the____ of____ .

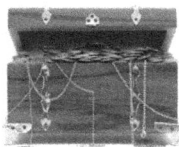

The Way

"I will instruct thee and teach thee in the way which thou shalt go: I will guide thee with mine eye" (Psalms 32:8).

*T*here is a way given by God in which his people must go. It is the "highway, " where only the redeemed walk. It is the way of salvation. It is the way of truth. This is a delightful and very interesting study.

The Way (1)

Old Testament – Genesis 18:19, Exodus 18:20, 23:20-21, 33:13, Psalms 5:8, 18:21, 32, 25:8-9, 32:8-9, 37:34, 77:13, Isaiah 2:2-3, 30:21, 35:8-9, Proverbs 4:11, 6:23, 8:20, 9:6, Job 28:7, 23

New Testament – John 14:6, Luke 1:78-79, Matthew 22:16, Acts 16:17

The Way (2)

Old Testament – Deuteronomy 1:30-33, Numbers 21:4, Nehemiah 9:19, Psalms 67:1-2, 1:6, Proverbs 2:8, Jeremiah 50:5, 42:1-3, 32:39, 23:22, 10:23, 6:16, 5:3-4, Isaiah 40:25-27, Job 12:24, 22:25-28

New Testament – Matthew 3:3, 7:13-14, 2 Peter 2:1-2, 15, 21, 1 Corinthians 12:31

The Way (3)

Old Testament – Genesis 24:48, 28:20-22, Deuteronomy 14:24-25, 31:29, Numbers 22:32-33, Proverbs 13:15, 15:24, 16:25, Psalms 107:40, 119:1, 9, 14, 27-37, 101, 128, 139:23-24, Isaiah 26:7-8, 48:17, 53:6, 55:7

New Testament – Acts 2:28, 18:25-26, 24:14

The Way (4)

Old Testament – Numbers 21:22, Judges 5:9-10, 18:6, Proverbs 10:17, 29 Job 17:9, 21:29-31, Jeremiah 12:1 Isaiah 59:8, Psalms 36:4, 37:34, 143:8, 146:9, Nahum 1:3

New Testament – Acts 9:1-2, 19:8-9, 23, 22:4, 24:22-25

The Way (5)

Old Testament – Ezra 8:21, 1 Samuel 9:6-8, Psalms 107:7, Jeremiah 6:27, 10:2, Malachi 2:6-8, Hosea 2:6, 10:13, Amos 2:6-7, Isaiah 56:11, 57:9-10, 14, Jonah 3:8-10, Ezekiel 33:8-11, 15, 17, 36:17-19

New Testament – John 1:23, Hebrews 5:1-2, 9:6-8, 10:19-20, 12:13

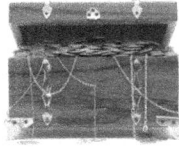

How?

How? (1)

"And Moses spake before the LORD, saying, Behold, the children of Israel have not hearkened unto me; how then shall Pharaoh, hear me, who am of uncircumcised lips?" (Exodus 6:12)

How? (2)

"For if the word spoken by angels was steadfast, and every transgression and disobedience received a just recompence of reward; How shall we escape, if we neglect so great salvation; which at the first began to be spoken by the Lord, and was confirmed unto us by them that heard him;" (Hebrews 2:2-3)

How? (3)

"But if thine eye be evil, thy whole body shall be full of darkness. If therefore the light that is in thee be darkness, how great is that darkness!" (Matthew 6:23)

Discussion Questions

1. What is inferred in 1 John 4:20-21?
2. What is being conveyed in Isaiah 52:7?
3. What is the Apostle Paul stating in Romans 3:5-6)?
4. Discuss Romans 6:1-2.

5. Explain Proverbs 20:24.

Fill in the Blanks

1. I know it is of a ____: but ____ should man be just with God?
2. In the LORD put I my ____: ____ say ye to my soul, Flee as a bird to your mountain?
3. Or ___ wilt thou say to thy brother, Let me pull the mote out of thine eye; and, behold, a beam is in thine own ____?
4. He that spared not his own son, but delivered him up for us all, ___ shall he not with ____ also freely give us all things?
5. And the LORD said unto Moses, ___ long will this people provoke me? And ___ ____ will it ere they believe me, for all the signs which I have showed among them?

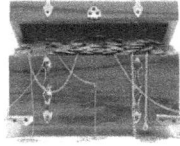

How?

*T*his particular topic delves into the *interrogative expressions*, or expressions of inquiry noted in the Bible, pertaining to various subjects, manners, and means. As we ponder, excogitate, and meditate, our reasoning will compel us to dig deeply and reflectively in order to comprehend or to reach an understanding.

How? (1)

Old Testament – Exodus 6:12, 30, 10:3, 7, 11:6-7 Deuteronomy 18:21-22, 32:29-30, Job 9:2, 11-14, 13:23, 15:14-16, 22:12-19, 25:2-6

New Testament – John 3:4-12, 5:44-47, 6:51-53, 9:14-16, 14:5-6, Acts 8:30-31 Hebrews 2:1-3, 1 John 4:20-21.

How? (2)

Old Testament – Numbers 23:8, 19-21, 24:5, 9 Exodus 19:4, 18:8, 1 Samuel 12:24, Proverbs 15:11, 20:24, Ezekiel 33:10-11, Hosea 11:8-9, Psalms 137:4-5, 119:9, 84, 90:13-14, 89:50-51

New Testament – Matthew 12:34-37, 16:11-12, 18:12-14, 21-23, 22:12-15

How? (3)

Old Testament – Exodus 9:29-30, 16:28, Numbers 14:11, 27, Joshua 18:3, 1 Kings 18:21, Habakkuk 1:2-4, 13, 2:6-9, Zechariah 1:12-16, Psalms 4:2-3, 6:3-4, 13:1-3, 35:17-22, Job 8:2-6, 19:1-4

New Testament – Matthew 17:17-18, John 10:24-28, Romans 6:2-4, Revelation 6:10

How? (4)

Old Testament – Jeremiah 47:5-7, 12:4-5, Esther 8:6, Ecclesiastes 10:15, Judges 13:8, 12, 16:15-17, Job 26:2-4, 34:16-19, Proverbs 1:22, 5:7-12, 6:9-11, 16:16, 21:27, Psalms 74:10-12, 22

New Testament – Luke 12:54-56, Matthew 6:23, 7:3-4, 11, 10:25, 23:33

How? (5)

Old Testament – Isaiah 52:7, 38:2-3, 6:8-11, 1:21, Jeremiah 49:25, 50:23, 51:41, Job 21:17-21, 4:17-19 Psalms 11:1, 3, 21:1, 36:7, 66:3-5, 92:5, 119:97, 103, 159

New Testament – Romans 3:5-6, 6:1-2, 8:31-32, 10:14-15

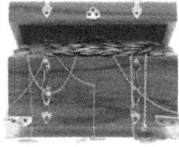

The Spirit of Man

The Spirit of Man (1)

"For what knoweth the things of man, save the spirit of man which is in him? Even so the things of God knoweth no man, but the Spirit of God." (1 Corinthians 2:11)

The Spirit of Man (2)

"But there is a spirit in man: and the inspiration of the Almighty giveth them understanding." (Job 32:8)

The Spirit of Man (3)

"He that hath knowledge spareth his words: and a man of understanding is of an excellent spirit." (Proverbs 17:27)

Discussion Questions

1. Explain Proverbs 20:27.
2. What transpired in Genesis 2:7?
3. What are the attributes of those that walk in the Spirit of God according to Galatians 5:22-23?
4. Explain Romans 8:1-17.
5. What happens if we do not have the Spirit of Christ in us?

Fill in the Blanks

1. "The itself_____ beareth_____ with our_____ , that we are the_____ of God."
2. "And we are His witnesses of these things; and so is also the_____ , whom God hath given to them that_____ ."
3. "But he that is joined unto the_____ is one_____ ."
4. "Now if any man have not the_____ of_____, he is none of his."
5. "Who knoweth the_____ of man that goeth_____ , and the spirit of the beast that goeth_____ to the earth?"

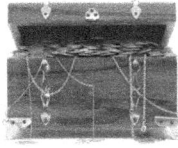

The Spirit of Man

"But there is a spirit in man: and the inspiration of the Almighty giveth them understanding" (Job 32:8).

There is a spirit in man that is given by God. These passages give us insight concerning the spirit of man.

The Spirit of Man (1)

Old Testament – Genesis 2:7, Zechariah 12:1, Proverbs 20:27, 17:27, Ecclesiastes 3:21, 11:5, 12:6-7, Job 27:3-4, 32:8, 18, 33:3-4, 34:12-15, Ezekiel 37:5-14, Malachi 2:14-16

New Testament – 1 Corinthians 14:32, 6:17-20, 2 Corinthians 7:1, Hebrews 4:12, 1 Peter 3:1-4, Mark 14:38, Acts 7:59

The Spirit of Man (2)

Old Testament – Numbers 14:24, 27:16-19, 32:10-12, Isaiah 26:8-9, 29:24, 57:15-16, 66:2, Deuteronomy 2:28-30, 2 Chronicles 36:22, 2 Kings 2:9-10, Job 26:4 Proverbs 25:28, 16:2, 32

New Testament – Luke 9:55, 1 John 4:1, 6, 2 Corinthians 12:18, 4:13, 1 Corinthians 2:11-16, 4:21

The Spirit of Man (3)

Old Testament – Exodus 35:21, 29-31, Daniel 6:3, 5:11-14, Ezekiel 11:17-20, 18:31, 36:26-28, Micah 2:7, Isaiah 63:11, 14, Psalms 143:3-10, 51:10-12, 17, Proverbs 1:23, 16:18-19, Zechariah 4:6, Nehemiah 9:20

New Testament – Ephesians 1:16-17, 4:22-24, 2 Timothy 4:22

The Spirit of Man (4)

Old Testament – Ecclesiastes 7:8-9, Psalms 32:2, Joel 2:28-29, Zechariah 12:9-10, Isaiah 11:1-2, 32:13-15, 38:16-17, 42:1-4, 44:3, Ezekiel 39:26-29

New Testament – Acts 2:1-4, 16-18, 5:32, 19:1-6, 1 John 3:24, Romans 8:1-17, Galatians 5:16-25

The Spirit of Man (5)

Old Testament – 1 Samuel 1:15, 16:13-23, Exodus 6:9, Daniel 7:1, Hosea 4:11-12, 5:3-4, Job 6:4, 7:11, 15:12-13, Psalms 142:3, 78:5-8, Proverbs 29:23, 18:14, 15:4, 11:13

New Testament – Acts 17:16-17, 2 Thessolonians 2:1-2, 2 Corinthians 11:2-4, Revelations 16:13-14, Matthews 12:43-45

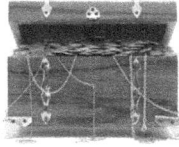

Chasing the Wind

Chasing the Wind (1)

"What profit hath a man of all his labour which he taketh under the sun? One generation passeth and another cometh..The wind goeth toward the south, and turneth about unto the north; it whirleth about continually, and the wind returneth. to his circuits. Ec 1:3-6

Chasing the Wind (2)

"...turn not aside from following the LORD, but serve the LORD with all your heart; And turn ye not aside: for then should ye go after vain things, which cannot profit nor deliver; for they are vain. (1 Sam 12:20-21)

Chasing the Wind (3)

"They are as stubble before the wind, and as chaff that the storm carrieth away." (Job 21:18)

Discussion Questions

1. What conclusion did Solomon make in Ecclesiastes 1:12-17?
2. What did Jesus admonish us to seek first?
3. Explain Matthew 16:26.
4. What observations are made in Mark 10:23-30?
5. Explain Proverbs 22:8

Fill in the Blanks

1. "For all that is in the____ , the____ of the____ , and the____ of the____ , and the____ of life, is not of the____ but is of the____ ."

2. "Surely men of____ degree are____ , and men of high____ are a____ ."

3. "Behold, thou hast made my days as an____ ; and mine age is as____ before thee: verily every____ at his____ is alto-gether____ ."

4. "Whereas ye know not what shall be on the ____. For what is your life? It is even a____ , that____ for a____ and then van-isheth____ ."

5. "Let us hear the of the____ : Fear____ and keep His _____: for this is the____ ____ of man.

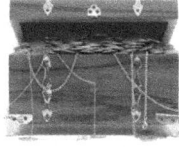

Chasing the Wind

To pursue those things that are vain and unprofitable, to devote oneself wholeheartedly to that which is insignificant, frivolous, or that which will one day perish, to grasp after that which only deteriorates—this is to grasp after the wind.

> "And this also is a sore evil, that in all points as he came, so shall he go: and what profit hath he that hath laboured for the wind?" (Ecclesiastes 5:16).

Chasing the Wind (1)

Old Testament – Ecclesiastes 5:15-16, 2:11, 16, 21, 1:3-6, 13-18 Job 30:15, 22, 21:17-18, 15:2-3, 12-13, 21-30 Proverbs 27:15-16, 11:29 Psalms 1:4, 35:1-5, 48:7, 78:26, 37-39, 83:13, 16, 103:13-16 Isaiah 26:17-18, 27:6-8

New Testament – John 6:27 Luke 12:20-21, 16:25 Ephesians 4:14-15 James 1:5-6

Chasing the Wind (2)

Old Testament – Ecclesiastes 6:1-9, 4:4-8, 15-16 Proverbs 11:7, 28:19, 1 Samuel 12:20-21, 8:1-3 Psalms 4:2, 39:5-6, 49:11, 17, 62:9 Job 7:7-10, 20:4-8, 27:12-21 Isaiah 41:16 Ezekiel 27:22-27 Haggai 1:6, 9 Hosea 8:7

New Testament – Mark 8:36, 1 Timothy 5:6, 6:7

Chasing the Wind (3)

Old Testament – Ecclesiastes 8:9-10, 5:10-11 Proverbs 23:4-5 Job 9:25-29, 11:11-12, 37:14-17, 38:24, 39: 13-16 Jeremiah 4:11-14, 18:17, 22:22, 51:1-2 Isaiah 40:7-8 Psalms 148:8-14, 147:15-18, 135:7, 104:1-3

New Testament – John 3:8 James 4:14-15 Jude 1:11-13

Chasing the Wind (4)

Old Testament – Ecclesiastes 11:3-4, 6, 9:1-3, 6, 11-13, 8:11-14, 17, 3:9-18 Proverbs 14:32, 30:4 Job 13:23, 25, 18:5-18, 21:13-18, 37:5-9 Psalms 4:2, 58:9 Hosea 12:1 Isaiah 40:22-24, 17:12-13

New Testament – Matthew 3:11-12, 1 Peter 1:24-25, 2 Peter 2:17-21

Chasing the Wind (5)

Old Testament – Ecclesiastes 1:8-11, 2:1-9, 12-15, 7:2, 8, 14, 12:8, 13-14 Jeremiah 17:11 Habakkuk 2:6-7 Isaiah 47:7-11, 41:24, 29 Proverbs 10:2, 23:17-18 Psalms 49:6-9, 12-15, 31:6, 24:3-4 Jonah 2:8 Hosea 13:15 Job 36:18- 19

New Testament – Matthew 6:19-21, 13:22-23, 1 Timothy 6:8-10

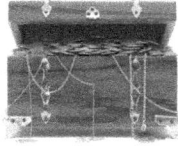

Discernment

Discernment (1)

"Give therefore thy servant an understanding heart to judge thy people, that I may discern between good and bad:"... (1 Kg 3:9)

Discernment (2)

"But the natural man receiveth not the things of the Spirit of God: for they are foolishness unto him: neither can he know, because they are spiritually discerned. (1 Corinthians 2:14)

Discernment (3)

"For the word of God is quick and powerful and sharper than any twoedged sword...and is a discerner of the thoughts and and intents of the heart. (Heb 4:12)

Discussion Questions

1. What was the request Moses made to God in order to find grace in His sight?
2. Can our eyes be blinded and hearts hardened even though the Word of God is spoken to us? Explain.
3. In 1 Kings 3:16-28, how did King Solomon determine which woman was the child's mother?

4. Should every Christian examine himself to see if he is truly walking in accordance to God's will? If so, why is it necessary to do so?
5. What passage of Scripture tells us that the Word of God a discerner of the thoughts and intents of the heart?

Fill in the Blanks

1. "Enter ye in at the____ gate: for___ is the gate, and ____is the____ , that leadeth to____ , and many there be which go in thereat."
2. "Who is____ , and he shall____ these things?____ , and he shall ___them? for the ways of the Lord are____ , and the____ shall____ in them: but the____ shall fall therein."
3. "To the____ and to the____ : if they speak not____ to this____ , it is because there is no____ in them."
4. "But if they had stood in my____ , and had caused___ ____ to hear my____ , then they should have____ them from their____ way, and from the____ of their doings."
5. "For the____ of God is quick, ____and____ , and than any twoedged sword, piercing even to the____ asunder of____ and ____, and of the joints and marrow, and is a____ of the____ and of the____ ."

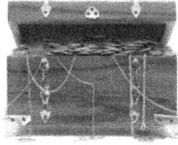

Discernment

*D*iscernment is greatly needed because of the vast number of decisions we make in a lifetime. Some decisions we make lead to failure. Wisdom enables us to perceive, and to differentiate, in order to ascertain the best course of action and make intelligent, reasonable, and sound decisions. The Word of God can and will empower us and direct our steps as we make decisions in life.

Discernment (1)

Old Testament – Exodus 33:12-17 Judges 6:13-23, 36-40, 7:2-7, 1 Kings 3:8-12, 16-28 Job 6:25-30 Jonah 4:1-7, 10-11is 7:13-16 Ezekiel 44:23-24 Psalms 119:66 Proverbs 2:10-11, 14:8, 12, 18: 17, 27:12

New Testament – Matthew 7:13-20, 16:1-4, 24:4-5, 24-27 Luke 10:21-24, 1 C2:11-14 Philippians 1:9-11

Discernment (2)

Old Testament – Genesis 18:21-33, 24:4-8, 21, 37-58, 27:21-24, 30-35 Numbers 11:23-25, 13:17-20, 15:29-36 Judges 14:12-18, 1 Kings 10:1-8, 2 Samuel 14:16-17, 19:34-35 Pr 4:19, 25:8, 26:24-26, 30:18-20

New Testament – Luke 9:55-56, 12:54-56, 13:23-25, 2 Corinthians 13:5, 1 John 2:19, 26, 29

Discernment (3)

Old Testament – Exodus 16:4 Leviticus 27:14 Deuteronomy 1:12-17, 39, 17:8-11, 19:15-19, 21:1-5 Judges 2:20-22, 3:1-4, 18:1-6, 1 Chronicles 12:32 Proverbs 25:2, 18:18, 16:33 Malachi 3:17-18

New Testament – Hebrews 4:12, 5:12-14 Ephesians 4:11-14, 5:13, 1 Timothy 5:21-25, 3:10

Discernment (4)

Old Testament – Exodus 21:13-14 Deuteronomy 1:42-44, 17:12-13, 18:18-22, 29:29 Isaiah 8:20, 34:16 Jeremiah 23:13-18, 22, 26, 29, 36 Psalms 19:13, 119: 101, 104, 118, 128, 136

New Testament – John 5:38, 6:63, 68, 8:31, 42-47 Acts 3:22-23, 17:11, 1 Thessalonians 2:13, 2 Peter 2:9-10 Galatians 1:6-12, 2 John 1:8-11

Discernment (5)

Old Testament – Exodus 6:5-7, 7:5, 8:16-19, 14:18 Numbers 16:1-5, 25-29, 32, 1 Samuel 1:6-9, 19-20, 1 Kings 20:23, 28-29 Jeremiah 8:8-9, 16:20-21, 44:16-17, 26-28 Psalms 83:13-18 Hosea 14:9 Proverbs 20:24-25

New Testament – Ephesians 1:18 Colossians 2:8, 20-23, 1 Job 4:5-6, 5:13, 20, 3 John 1:11

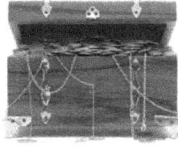

One to Another

One to Another (1)

"Let all bitterness, and wrath and anger, and clamour and evil speaking be put away from you.. And be ye kind one to another, tenderhearted, forgiving one another, even as God for Christ's sake hath forgiven you." (Eph 4:31-32)

One to Another (2)

"To speak evil of no man, to be no brawlers but gentle, shewing all meekness unto all men. For we ourselves also were foolish, disobedient, deceived, serving divers lusts and pleasures, living in malice and envy, hateful and hating one another. Butafter..Titus 3:2-4

One to Another (3)

"Follow peace with all men, and holiness, without which no man shall see the Lord: Looking diligently lest any man fall short of the grace of God; lest any root of bitterness springing up trouble you, and thereby many be defiled." (Heb 12:14-15)

Discussion Questions

1. Explain Psalms 133:1.
2. What is conveyed in Romans 13:8-10?
3. What warning is given in Galatians 5:13-15?

4. What transpired in Obadiah 1:10-15?
5. Explain James 2:15-16

Fill in the Blanks

1. "Forbearing___ ____ , and forgiving___ ____ , if any man have a quarrel against any: even as Christ ____you, so also do ye."
2. "For my____ and____ sakes I will now say, Peace be within thee."
3. "And this is his_____ , That we should believe on the name of his Son Jesus Christ, and____ ____ ____ , as he gave us ____."
4. "Charity suffereth long, and is____ ; charity____ not; charity_____ not itself, is not____ up."
5. "Ye shall not therefore_____ ____ ____ ; but thou shalt fear thy God: for I am the Lord your God."

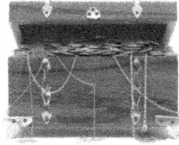

One to Another

The terms *brother* and *sister* take on a special connotation in Christ. These not only are terms of endearment, but also descriptive of how we are to treat one another. We belong to the same family of God. When one rejoices, we all should rejoice with that one. When one is made sad, we should sit in sorrow with that one, also. These passages display the relationship we should have one to another.

One to Another (1)

Old Testament – Genesis 4:9, 13:1-9 Psalms 133:1, 122:8-9, 55:11-14, 19-23, 35:13-16 Job 6:14, 30:25, 31:15-22, 29-32 Zc 7:9-10

New Testament – Romans 13:8-10, 12:5-16 Ephesians 4:24-32 Colossians 3:9-15 Hebrews 13:1-3, 12:14-15, 1 Corinthians 13:1-7, 16:14 John 13:3-15, 34-35

One to Another (2)

Old Testament – Genesis 11:3-6 Deuteronomy 15:7-11 Leviticus 19:13-18 Exodus 20:13-17, 22:7-15, 23:4-8 Numbers 15:15-16 Zechariah 8:16-17, 1 Samuel 20:14-17 Proverbs 19:22, 16:27-30 Psalms 101:4-5

New Testament – Matthew 5:20-45 Luke 6:31, 10:29-37, 17:1-4, 1 Thessalonians 3:12, 4:1-9 Galatians 5:13-15 Titus 3:2-5

One to Another (3)

Old Testament – Genesis 42:1, 11, 21, 43:33 Psalms 145:4, 71:18 Ezekiel 33:30-31 Obadiah 1:10-15 Numbers 32:6-9 Malachi 2:10 Isaiah 3:5, 58:4-10 Proverbs 22:2, 14:31

New Testament – James 4:11-12, 5:9, 16 Romans 15:2, 5-7, 14:1-19, 1 Peter 3:8-9 Luke 24:17, 32 Philippians 2:1-5

One to Another (4)

Old Testament – 4 Leviticus 25:17, 43, 46, 53 Jeremiah 7:5-7, 22:13 Isaiah 11:6-10, 2:2-4 Zephaniah 3:13

New Testament – Mark 9:50 Acts 7:26 Matthew 18:6-7, 15-17, 13:41-42 Philippians 1:10, 27, 1 Timothy 3:15, 2 Timothy 2:24-26, 1 Thessalonians 2:7-12, 5:14-15 Titus 2:1-15 James 1:19-20, 3:13, 17, 18, 1 John 1:7, 2 Corinthians 13:11

One to Another (5)

Old Testament – Numbers 20:14-21 Deuteronomy 23:7-9 Exodus 23:4-9 Esther 9:17-22 Proverbs 3:28-30, 10:12, 15:17, 17:8, 18:19, 24, 19:6, 25:17, 27:10

New Testament – John 15:12-17 Matthew 25:31-46 James 3:17, 23, 1 Corinthians 12:25-26 Galatians 6:1-2, 10

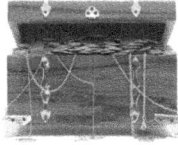

A Place of Refuge

A Place of Refuge (1)

"God is our refuge and strength, a very present help in trouble." (Psalms 46:1)

A Place of Refuge (2)

"That by two immutable things, in which it was impossible for God to lie, we might have a strong consolation, who have fled for refuge to lay hold upon the hope set before us:" (Hebrews 6:18)

A Place of Refuge (3)

"For thou hast been a strength to the poor, a strength to the needy in his distress, a refuge from the storm, a shadow from the heat, when the blast of the terrible ones is as a storm against the wall." (Isaiah 25:4)

Discussion Questions

1. Who did Jesus invite in Matthew 11:28-30?
2. Can the gates of hell prevail against Christ's church? Explain.
3. Explain Matthew 23:37-38.
4. Will God leave or forsake us? Explain.
5. What does it mean to abide in Christ?

Fill in the Blanks

1. "And a man shall be as an____ place from the____ , and a____ from the tempest."

2. "Come unto me, ____ ____ ye that____ ____ and are heavy____ , and I will give you____ ."

3. "And I say also unto____ , That thou art Peter, and upon this____ I will build my____ ; and the____ of____ shall not____ against it."

4. "There is therefore now no____ to them which are in____ ____ , who walk not ____the flesh, but after the____ ."

5. "The Lord also will be a____ ____ for the____ ____ , a____ ____ in times of____ ."

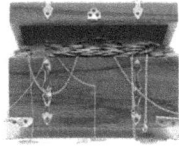

A Place of Refuge

*I*n the face of natural disaster, we all seek a place of safety, a shelter from rain, storm, or danger. Spiritually, God is viewed as the high tower, the rock in a weary land, our hope, our fortress, our covert from the storm, our shadow from the heat, and our hiding place when the waters of life overflow us.

A Place of Refuge (1)

Old Testament – Psalms 121:5-8, 141:8-10, 62:5-8, Proverbs 18:10, 29:25 Isaiah 32:1-3, 18-20, 8:14-17, 4:2-6, 2:1-3, 10 Ezekiel 34:12-16, 25-31

New Testament – Luke 1:68-71, Matthew 11:28-30, 23:37, John 16:33, Romans 5:9, Hebrews 6:18-20, Colossians 3:3

A Place of Refuge (2)

Old Testament – Exodus 33:20-23, Isaiah 11:10, 26:20, Jeremiah 16:19, 17:13-17, Psalms 142:3-5, 96:6, 71:7, 46:1-11, 31:20, 27:5, 9:9-10, Joel 3:16, Zechariah 2:4-5, 8:20-23, 1 Chronicles 16:27

New Testament – Matthew 1:23, 16:18, Acts 2:47, Hebrews 12:22-29, John 3:36, 5:24, 15:4-10

A Place of Refuge (3)

Old Testament – 2 Samuel 22:2-4, 47-51, Proverbs 14:26, Isaiah 28:16-17, 25:3-4, Psalms 3:1-5, 4:8, 5:3-7, 11-12, 31:1-3, 32:7, 57:1, 61:1-4, 68:20, 29-31, 72:17, 144:1-2

New Testament – John 11:25, 14:1-3, Hebrews 13:5-6, Ephesians 2:1-8, Romans 8:1, 10, 1 John 4:9

A Place of Refuge (4)

Old Testament – Deuteronomy 33:27-29, Hosea 2:18-20, Jeremiah 23:5-6, Isaiah 33:20-21, 35:9-10, 60:18, 21, 65:9-10, Psalms 143:9, 119:114, 94:22, 91:2-9, 84:11, 64:2-9

New Testament – John 5:40, Colossians 1:13-14, 21-23, 28, 1 John 5:11-12, 19-20

A Place of Refuge (5)

Old Testament – Deuteronomy 33:12, Proverbs 2:6-8, Job 11:13-18, Isaiah 51:12-16, Lamentations 4:18-20, Psalms 14:4-6, 17:8, 27:5, 32:7, 37:7, 17, 48:1-3, 59:15-16, 63:7, 116:6-7, 132:13-18

New Testament – Luke 13:34-35, John 14:2-3, Hebrews 11:8-10, 4:1-5, Colossians 3:3

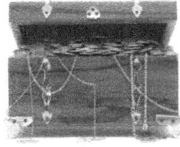

Acceptance

Acceptance (1)

"Wherefore we receiving a kingdom which cannot be moved, let us have grace, whereby we may serve God acceptably with reverence and godly fear:" (Hebrews 12:28)

Acceptance (2)

"If thou doest well, shalt thou not be accepted? And if thou doest not well, sin lieth at the door, . And unto thee shall be his desire, and thou shalt rule over him." (Genesis 4:7)

Acceptance (3)

"But in every nation he that feareth him, and worketh righteousness, is accepted with him." (Acts 10:35)

Discussion Questions

1. Discuss Leviticus 1:2-4.
2. Why was Cain's offering rejected?
3. Why was the worship mentioned in Mark 7:7-9 rejected?
4. Explain Hebrews 12:28.
5. Discuss Acts 10:34-35

Fill in the Blanks

1. "But to do_____ and to communicate forget not: for with such sacrifices God is_____ _____ ."

2. "The lips of the_____ know what is_____ : but the mouth of the_____ speaketh_____ ."

3. "I beseech you therefore, brethren, by the mercies of God, that ye_____ your bodies a_____ _____ , holy, _____ unto God, which is your_____ _____ ."

4. "Study to show thy self _____unto God, a workman that_____ not to be_____ ."

5. "That ye might walk_____ of the Lord unto all_____ , being_____ in every good_____ , and_____ in the_____ of_____ ."

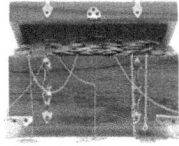

Acceptance

In this particular study, passages are listed that show God's acceptance and rejection of things presented by man.

Acceptance (1)

Old Testament – Leviticus 1:2-4, 7:18, 10:1-3, 16-20, 19:5-7, 22:18-25, Genesis 4:3-7, Psalms 119:21, 118, Jeremiah 6:20, 30, 14:10-12, Job 42:7-9, Proverbs 10:32, 21:3

New Testament – Mark 7:8-9, 13, 2 Timothy 2:15, Acts 10:34-35, Ephesians 1:6, Hebrews 12:28, 6:7-8

Acceptance (2)

Old Testament – Deuteronomy 33:8, 11, 24, Exodus 28:2, 30-38, Ezekiel 14:1-3, 20:3, 40-41, Isaiah 60:7, 56:7, Ecclesiastes 9:7, Psalms 5:12, 19:14, 69:13, Proverbs 12:2, 8:33-35, 3:3-4

New Testament – 2 Corinthians 5:9, 1 Peter 2:5, 20, 1 Timothy 5:4, 2:1-3, Philippians 4:18, Ephesians 5:9-10, 1 John 3:22

Acceptance (3)

Old Testament – Ezekiel 43:4-12, 27, 44:5-10, Malachi 1:7-13, Isaiah 1:11-17, Hosea 8:2, 12-13, 6:6, 1 Samuel 15:22-23, Amos 5:22, Micah 6:6-8, Psalms 51:16-19, 80:19, 119:58, 108, 135, 155

New Testament – 2 Corinthians 10:18, Romans 12:1-2, 14:17-18, 15:16, Hebrews 13:16

Acceptance (4)

Old Testament – Daniel 4:27, 1 Samuel 13:9-14, Isaiah 58:2-9, 56:4-5, 49:8, Jeremiah 7:2-10, 23, Hosea 9:1-4, Job 22:21-28, Psalms 65:4, 30:7, 4:3-5

New Testament – Luke 21:36, 2 Corinthians 13:5-7, 7:1, Hebrews 13:9-10, 12:14, 4:1, 11, Colossians 1:19-23

Acceptance (5)

Old Testament – Ecclesiastes 12:10, Numbers 11:11-15, Exodus 33:12-17, 1 Samuel 15:25-26, 2:26, 18:5, Job 10:12, 33:26, Psalms 20:1-4, 41:11, 44:3, 106:4, Isaiah 26:10, Proverbs 18:5, Hosea 8:2-4, 13

New Testament – Galatians 2:6, 2 Corinthians 6:1-2, 1 Timothy 1:15-16, 4:9-10

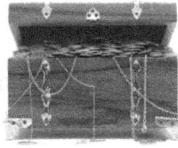

Character Traits

Character Traits (1)

"Lo, this only have I found, that God made man upright: but they have sought out many inventions." (Ecclesiastes 7:29)

Character Traits (2)

"Only let your conduct be as it becometh the gospel of Christ:..." (Philippians 1:27)

Character Traits (3)

"These were more noble than those in Thessalonica, in that they received the word with all readiness of mind, and searched the scriptures daily, whether those things were so." (Acts 17:11)

Discussion Questions

1. What did God say about the character of Job in Job 2:3?
2. Describe the character of Ruth in Ruth 3:10-11.
3. What are the character traits Christians are instructed to have in Colossians 3:5-13?
4. Explain James 3:13-18.
5. What character traits are noted in Matthew 5:3-12?

Fill in the Blanks

1. "The____ is not above his master: but every one that is____ shall be as his____ ."
2. "Lo, this only have I found, that God hath made man____ ; but they have____ ____ many inventions."
3. "And now, my daughter, fear not; I will do to thee all that thou requirest: for all the city of my ____doth know that thou art a____ ____ ."
4. "Blessed are the merciful: for they shall obtain ____."
5. "And they were both____ before God, walking in all the____ and ____of the Lord____ ."

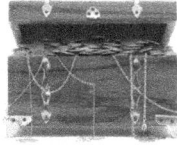

Character Traits

*E*thos is a Greek word which means character, the sum of qualities defines a person. It is considered to be the imprint of the soul. It is who we really are inside. There are traits, good or bad, that are associated with our character.

Character Traits (1)

Old Testament – Ecclesiastes 7:29, Job 2:3, 6:28-30, 27:3-6, 31:4-6, Ruth 3:10-11, Proverbs 31:10-31, 12:4, 11:3, Isaiah 26:10, 32:6, Psalms 141:3-5, Genesis 6:9, 17:1

New Testament – Luke 6:40, 9:55-56, 2 Peter 1:3-8, 3:14, 1 Peter 1:14-16, Philippians 1:27

Character Traits (2)

Old Testament – 2 Samuel 20:19, 22:22-24, Psalms 119:1-3, 11, 101:1-7, 26:1-12, 7:3-5, 1:1-3, 1 Samuel 18:14-16, Job 29:11-17, Isaiah 33:15-16, 38:1-3, Zechariah 7:9-10, Micah 4:5

New Testament – 1 Timothy 4:12, 1 Thessalonians 2:3-12, James 3:13-18, Acts 17:11

Character Traits (3)

Old Testament – Genesis 6:22, 18:19, Daniel 6:3-4, 1 Samuel 29:3, 6, 1 Kings 15:5, Isaiah 50:5-6, 57:15, 66:2, Jonah 1:9, Psalms 84:2, 5, 119:30, 32, 130:5, 13, 1:2, 141:8

New Testament – Matthew 5:3-12, 18:3, 1 Peter 3:2-4, 4:8-9, Colossians 3:12-14, Ephesians 4:24-32

Character Traits (4)

Old Testament – Genesis 18:27, 32:10, Ezra 9:5-6, Jeremiah 3:25, Isaiah 57:15, 2 Chronicles 7:14, 33:12-13, 1 Kings 21:29, Psalms 131:1-2, 85:9, 50:23, 49:11-12, 16-20, 25:14, Isaiah 50:5-7

New Testament – John 13:4-15, Matthew 5:3-12, 18:3-4, Philippians 2:5-9

Character Traits (5)

Old Testament – Job 13:15, 23:10, 23:4, Daniel 3:12-18, Joshua 24:14, 1 Kings 18:21, Micah 4:5, Psalms 71:14-16, 5:3, 62:5, 119:74, 81, 130:5, Isaiah 26:8, 64:4

New Testament – James 5:15-18, Luke 9:55-56, 22:39-46, Hebrews 4:14-16, 10:39

Man Up

Man Up (1)

"Watch ye, stand fast in the faith, quit you like men, be strong." (1 Corinthians 16:13)

Man Up (2)

"Be strong and quit yourselves like men..." (1 Samuel 4:9)

Man Up (3)

"I go the way of all the earth: be thou strong therefore and show thyself a man." (1 Kings 2:2)

Discussion Questions

1. Whose image was man created in?
2. Discuss 1 Corinthians 11:3-12.
3. What instructions are given in Ephesians 5:25-33?
4. Explain 1 Timothy 5:8.
5. What expectations were given Timothy in 2 Timothy 2:1-7?

Fill in the Blanks

1. "Thou therefore endure____ , as a good soldier of Jesus Christ."

2. "Wherefore, brethren, look ye out from____ you seven ____ of____ report, full of the____ ____ and____ ."

3. "But as for___ and my____ , we will serve the Lord."

4. "For the____ is the____ of the wife, even as____ is the____ of the____ ."

5. "So ought men to____ their____ as their own bodies. He that ____his wife loveth____ ."

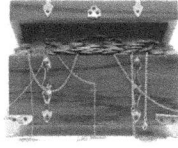

Man Up

G od has placed in man the instinct to protect, provide, and care for his family. There is a sense of fulfillment and completeness as he carries out these responsibilities. His role must be tempered with love, wisdom, patience, and perseverance.

Man Up (1)

Old Testament – Genesis 1:26-27, 2:7-8, 19, 3:17-19, Ecclesiastes 7:29, 9:10, Job 7:1-3, 17-18, 10:11-15, Job 28:24-28, 38:3-17, 40:7-14, 42:5-6, Psalms 8:4-9

New Testament – 1 Corinthians 11:3-12, 13:11, 16:13, Luke 12:35-36, 1 Timothy 3:4-5, 5:8

Man Up (2)

Old Testament – Genesis 5:1-2, 12:11-20, 26:6-10, Joshua 1:1-9, 14, 18, 8:3, 10:7-8, Judges 6:12, 14, 16, 1 Samuel 4:9, 18:17, 26:15, Nehemiah 4:14, 5:13, 7:1-2, Proverbs 31:1-3, 8-9

New Testament – Acts 6:3-6, 2 Timothy 2:1-7, 2 Thessalonians 3:6-10, 15, 1 Corinthians 7:32-33

Man Up (3)

Old Testament – Exodus 23:17, Numbers 1:1-3, 45, 2 Samuel 10:12, Joshua 24:15, 1 Samuel 30:1-19, 1 Kings 2:2, 20:1-11, 21, Judges 7:3-7, Isaiah 19:16, Jeremiah 51:30, 50:35-37, 5:1, Ezekiel 22:27-30

New Testament – 1 Timothy 5:22, 3:7-15, 2:8-15, 1 Corinthians 14:34-38, 2 Thessalonians 3:14-15

Man Up (4)

Old Testament – Jeremiah 5:16, Joel 2:7, 3:9-11, 16, Zechariah 10:4-12, 1 Chronicles 7:5, 12:20-21, 25, 30-33, 38, 26:6, 8, 31-32, 2 Chronicles 13:3, 2 Samuel 23:8-17, Nehemiah 9:27, Proverbs 27:17, Jeremiah 46:15, 21, 28

New Testament – 1 Corinthians 6:5-8, 2 Corinthians 10:4-5, 1 Timothy 1:18, 4:12

Man Up (5)

Old Testament – 1 Samuel 9:1-2, 13:13-14, 16:18, 1 Chronicles 12:21, 26:6, Proverbs 29:8, 25:6, 22:29, 20:29, 18:16, 13:20, Psalms 9:20, Lamentations 1:15

New Testament – Luke 1:21-22, 1 Corinthians 14:20, 1 Timothy 6:3-11, Acts 21:10-13, 20:24-26, 15:22, 25-6, 8::2, 4:13

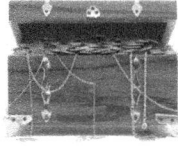

The Heaven Bound

The Heaven Bound (1)

"Lord, who shall abide in thy tabernacle? Who shall dwell in thy holy hill? He that walketh uprightly and worketh righteousness and speaketh the truth in his heart. He that backbiteth not with his tongue, nor doeth evil to his neighbor, nor taketh up a reproach against his neighbor. In whose eyes a vile person is contemned; but he honoureth them that fear the Lord. He that sweareth to his own hurt, and changeth not. He that putteth not out his money to usury, nor taketh a reward against the innocent. He that doeth these things shall never be removed. (Psalm 15:1-5)

The Heaven Bound (2)

"Blessed are they that do his commandments that they may have the right to the tree of life and may enter in through the gates of the city." (Revelation 22:14)

The Heaven Bound (3)

"To him that overcometh will I grant to sit with me in my throne, even as I overcame, And am set down with my Father in his throne." (Revelation 3:21)

Discussion Questions

1. Explain Psalms 15:1-5.

2. What requirement did Jesus give in John 8:31 that determines whether or not we are his disciple?
3. What is required in Hebrews 12:14?
4. Explain Matthew 25:31-46.
5. Does God reward those that diligently seek Him? Explain.

Fill in the Blanks

1. "Lord, who shall____ in thy____? Who shall____ in thy holy hill? He that walketh____, and worketh_____, and speaketh the_____ in his____ ."
2. "Know ye not that the _____shall not inherit the_____ of____ ?"
3. "I tell you, ____ : but, except ye____ , ye shall____ ____ ____ ."
4. "Except a man be ____again, he cannot see the_____ of_____ ."
5. "Take____ unto___ , and unto the_____ ; continue in them: for in____ this thou shalt both____ ____ , and them that hear thee."

The Heaven Bound

*E*numerated in Scripture are passages that pertain to character traits of those who travel on the path that leads to heaven.

> "And when Jesus saw that he answered discreetly, he said unto him, Thou art not far from the kingdom of God" (Mark 12:34).

The Heaven Bound (1)

Old Testament – Psalms 15:1-5, 24:3-5, 50:23, 106:3-5, 139:1-6, 23-24, Ezekiel 18:4-13, 21-28, Isaiah 26:19, 33:14-17, 66:1-2, 3:10-11

New Testament – John 10:9-10, 27-28, 8:51, Matthew 28:18-20, 1 Corinthians 6:9-11, Revelation 20:11-15

The Heaven Bound (2)

Old Testament – Daniel 12:1-3, 10, Genesis 6:8-9, 22, 5:24, Deuteronomy 10:12-20, Micah 6:8, Numbers 12:3, 7, Job 1:1, 8, Proverbs 28:18, Psalm 33:13-18, 85:9, 91:14-16, 149:4

New Testament – Matthew 5:3, 10, 20, 7:21, 13:41-43, 49-50, Mark 12:28-34, Revelation 3:4

The Heaven Bound (3)

Old Testament – Proverbs 15:24, 11:7, Psalm 11:7, 17:15, 37:18, 69:32, 36, 73:24, 118:19-21, 119:155, 166, 140:13

New Testament – John 6:68, 8:21, Acts 3:22-23, 16:17, 1 Timothy 4:16, Hebrews 12:14-15,

2 Peter 1:2-11, 1 John 5:11-13, Galatians 5:14, 18, 22-26, Romans 8:1

The Heaven Bound (4)

Old Testament – Isaiah 26:2, 64:4-5, Psalms 11:7, 31:19, 65:4, 76:7-12, 101:6-7, Proverb 12:28, Nahum 1:3-7, Zechariah 9:9, 16

New Testament – Matthew 1:21, 16:18, Acts 2:47, Ephesians 5:23, 1 Peter 4:18, Revelation 20:12-15, 21:27, 22:14-15

The Heaven Bound (5)

Old Testament – Zechariah 8:16-17, Jeremiah 7:3-7, Psalm 1:5-6, 5:4-5, 37:27-29, 41:12, 49:13-15, 61:4-5, 103:15-18, 112:1, 6, Isaiah 25:8-9, 54:14-17

New Testament – Matthew 19:16-29, 24:12-13, Luke 13:3-5, Romans 2:7-10, Revelation 2:7, 10, 3:21

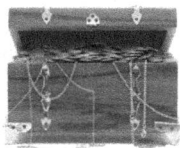

The Sovereignty of God

The Sovereignty of God (1)

"Have ye not known? Have ye not heard? Hath it not been told you from the beginning? Have ye not understood from the foundations of the earth? It is he that sitteth upon the circle of the earth, and the inhabitants thereof are as grasshoppers; that stretchest out the heavens as a curtain, and spreadeth them out as a tent to dwell in: That bringeth the princes to nothing: he maketh the judges of the earth as vanity.... and he shall blow upon them, and they shall wither, and the whirlwind shall take them away as stubble." (Isaiah 40:21-24)

The Sovereignty of God (2)

"O my God, make them like a wheel; as the stubble before the wind... That men may know that thou, whose name alone is JEHOVAH, art the most high over all the earth." (Psalm 83:13, 18)

The Sovereignty of God (3)

"Behold, I am the Lord, the God of all flesh: is there any thing too hard for me?" (Jeremiah 32:27)

Discussion Questions

1. What conclusion did king Nebuchadnezzar make in Daniel 4:35-37?

2. Explain 1 Corinthians 11:3.
3. What does it mean to submit to the rule and the authority of God?
4. Explain Colossians 1:15-18.
5. Why is it necessary that we serve God acceptably as noted in Hebrews 12:28?

Fill in the Blanks

1. "But I would have you know, that the head of every man is Christ; and the head of the woman is____; and the head of Christ is____ ."
2. "See that ye____ ____ him that speaketh."
3. "For if they escaped____ ____ who refused him that spake on earth, much more shall not____ ____ ____ , if we turn away from him that____ from____ ."
4. "God forbid: yea, let God be____ ____ , but every man a____ ; as it is written, That thou____ be____ in thy sayings, and mightiest____ when thou art____ ."
5. "In whom also we have____ ____ an inheritance, being____ according to the____ of him who worketh all things after the ____of his____ ____ ."

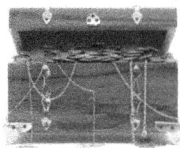

The Sovereignty of God

*T*his topic bespeaks the awesome power and reign of God. God created all things, God is above all things, and God has the ultimate rule over all things. To him be glory and dominion for ever and ever. Amen (1 Peter 5:11).

The Sovereignty of God (1)

Old Testament – Isaiah 40:21-31, Psalms 145:1-14, 20, 96:4-10, 94:1-15, 51:15-17, Job 12:13-25, Jeremiah 32:27, Hosea 11:9, Numbers 23:19,

New Testament – John 5:17-30, 1 Corinthians 11:3, Colossians 1:15-18, Philippians 2:10-17, Hebrews 12:25-29, 13:15-16, Revelation 4:11

The Sovereignty of God (2)

Old Testament – 2 Chronicles 20:5-9, 1 Chronicles 29:11-15, 16:25-36, Exodus 15:18, Isaiah 52:7, 32:1-3, 24:21-23, 2:10-21, Malachi 1:14, Psalm 146:10, 99:1-5, 97:1-10, 47:7-9

New Testament – Hebrews 1:3-14, Romans 3:3-4, Revelation 11:15-19, 19:5-6, 15

The Sovereignty of God (3)

Old Testament – Daniel 7:9-14, 4:35-37, Psalms 103:19, 100:3, 89:11-17, 36:5-10, Isaiah 66:1-2, Job 23:13-15, 24:22-25, Micah 7:18-20, 1 Samuel 15:29

New Testament – John 4:24, Romans 13:1-2, 1 Corinthians 8:3-6, 2 John 1:9-11, Hebrews 10:26-31

The Sovereignty of God (4)

Old Testament – Habakkuk 3:3-6, Isaiah 46:3-5, 9-10, 45:12-15, 22-25, Job 11:10-20, 38:3-18, 39:9-30, 40:9-14, Micah 6:6-9, Jeremiah 13:1-11, Psalm 147:3-11, 95:3-8

New Testament – Luke 1:51-54, 74-75, Acts 5:38-39, Romans 14:11, Ephesians 1:11

The Sovereignty of God (5)

Old Testament – Job 25:2-3, Psalm 115:3, 76:12-17, 58:10-11, 21:8-13, Isaiah 37:22-38, 41:1-5, 66:2, Jeremiah 2:19, 5:22-24, 10:6-7, 32:37-40

New Testament – Luke 1:37, Matthew 19:26, Romans 9:15-26, Hebrews 2:1-4, 4:11-13

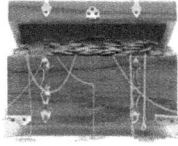

Prayer

Prayer (1)

"My voice shalt thou hear in the morning, O LORD; in the morning will I direct my prayer unto thee, and will look up." (Psalm 5:3)

Prayer (2)

"Confess your faults one to another, and pray one for another, that ye may be healed. The effectual fervent prayer of a righteous man availeth much." (James 5:16)

Prayer (3)

"Go, and say to Hezekiah, Thus saith the LORD, the God of David thy father, I have heard thy prayer, I have seen thy tears, : bejold I will add unto thy days fifteen years." (Isaiah 38:5)

Discussion Questions

1. List several things that hinder our prayers.
2. What does the word supplications mean?
3. List several times when we should pray. Explain your answers.
4. In Whose name should we pray?
5. How do we know that the Spirit of God makes intercession on our behalf when we pray?

Fill in the Blanks

1. "Likewise the____ also helpeth our infirmities: for we know not what we should____ for as we ought: but the Spirit itself maketh____ for us with groanings which cannot be____ ."
2. "After this manner therefore____ ye: Our____ which art in____ , ____ be thy____ ."
3. "If ye in me, and my abide in you, ye shall what ye will, and it shall be unto you."
4. "But your____ have____ between you and your God, and your____ have hid his____ from you, that he will____ hear."
5. "Likewise, ye husbands, dwell with them____ to____ , giving____ unto the wife, ... that your____ be not____ ."

Prayer

*P*rayer is the lifeline of a child of God. Through prayer, we show our reliance. Through prayer, we demonstrate our humility. Through prayer, we attest to the sovereignty, the awesomeness, and the preeminence of God. Let us all bow down. Let us all pray each and every day. God is our Father, and He desires that we, His children, walk with Him, talk with Him, and have sweet fellowship with Him throughout our life. What a wonderful privilege that He has given unto us.

Prayer (1)

Old Testament – Job 11:13-15, 18, 22:21-27, 33:23-29, Proverbs 15:8, 29, 28:9, Psalms 3:4-5, 5:1-3, 39:12-13, 54:2-4, 55:1-8, 109:4, 118:5, 138:3, 142:1-2

New Testament – Luke 18:1, 7, 21:36, 22:31-32, 40, 46, 1 Thessalonians 5:17, 25, 1 Peter 3:12

Prayer (2)

Old Testament – Exodus 2:23-25, 3:7-10, 22:22-24, Deuteronomy 24:14-15, 1 Samuel 1:13-17, 26-28, 2 Kings 5:17-19, Daniel 6:4-14, 26-27, 9:3-23, Psalms 34:15-17, 61:1-5, 88:1-3, 11-13

New Testament – Matthew 21:21-22, 26:36, 41, Luke 6:12, Hebrews 5:7, Acts 1:13-14

Prayer (3)

Old Testament – Lamentations 3:8, 44, Micah 3:4, Zechariah 7:13, Proverbs 21:13, Psalms 80:4, 86:6, 107:27-28, Isaiah 59:1-2, Jeremiah 7:16-17, 11:14, 14:10-12, 29:10-12, 2 Chronicles 33:12-13, Job 9:15-16

New Testament – Luke 11:1-4, 9-13, Acts 10:1-4, Colossians 4:2-3, 1 John 5:14-15

Prayer (4)

Old Testament – Nehemiah 1:3-11, 2:1-4, 18, 2 Samuel 12:15-23, 1 Kings 13:4-6, 8:22-30, 54-59, Kings 6:15-20, 2 Chronicles 30:17-20, 2 Chronicles 32:19-21, Isaiah 38:1-5, Psalms 6:2, 8-10, 17:1, 28:1-6, 31:21-24

New Testament – John 14:13-16, 16:23-26, 17:9, 15, 20

Prayer (5)

Old Testament – Ezra 9:5-15, 10:1, Job 16:15-20, Psalms 143:6, 141:2, 119:169-170, 102:1-2, 62:8, 55:17, 18:4-6, 9:10-12

New Testament – Philippians 4:6, Romans 1:9, 8:26, 15:30, Ephesians 6:18, 1 Timothy 2:1-8, 5:5, 2 Timothy 1:3, Revelation 5:8, 8:3-4

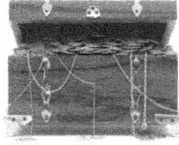

Get an Understanding

Get an Understanding (1)

"Get wisdom, get an understanding: forget it not; neither decline from the words of my mouth.... Wisdom is the principal thing; therefore get wisdom: and with all thy getting get understanding." (Proverbs 4:5, 7)

Get an Understanding (2)

"The eyes of your understanding being enlightened: that ye may know what is the hope of his calling, and what the riches of the glory of his inheritance in the saints," (Ephesians 1:18)

Get an Understanding (3)

"A fool hath no delight in understanding, but that his heart may discover itself." (Proverbs 18:2)

Discussion Questions

1. Explain Proverbs 4:5-7.
2. Can an understanding be aided by wise counsel? Discuss.
3. Explain Ephesians 5:17.
4. Explain Ephesians 4:17-20.
5. According to Jeremiah 9:23-24, what are we allowed to boast about?

Fill in the Blanks

1. "But let him that glorieth____ in this, that he____ and____ me."
2. "Wisdom is the____ thing; therefore get____ : and with all thy getting get_____ ."
3. "Having the____ darkened, being alienated from the ____ of____ through the_____ that is in them, because of the____ of their____ ."
4. "Without____ , covenantbreakers, without____ ____ , implacable, ____ ."
5. "He that getteth_____ loveth his own_____: he that keepeth____ shall find good.

Get an Understanding

*T*he Greek word *sunesis* is translated *understanding* in English. It necessitates critical thinking in order to reach a meaningful conclusion. Understanding is essential in our communications and interactions with one with another and also in our reasoning and discernment. It involves the cognitive, the spiritual, and the moral.

Get an Understanding (1)

Old Testament – Proverbs 4:5-7, 1:5-6, 14:6-8, 29, 33, Psalms 119:98-100, 104-105, 130-131, 111:10, Job 28:12-28, 36:26-33, 37:2-5, Jeremiah 9:23-24

New Testament – Matthew 13:14-23, Acts 8:30-40, 2 Peter 3:14-17, Ephesians 1:16-17

Get an Understanding (2)

Old Testament – 1 Samuel 25:3, 12:7, Nehemiah 8:2-3, 6-8, 11-12, Deuteronomy 4:5-10, 1 Kings 3:7-12, 10:1-9, 24, Daniel 5:11-12, Hosea 14:2-9, Isaiah 1:18, Proverbs 2:1-11, Psalms 119:34, 73, 144

New Testament – Luke 24:32, 45, Ephesians 5:17, Acts 17:2-3, 11

Get an Understanding (3)

Old Testament – Proverbs 8:1-17, 10:13-14, 23, 16:16, 21-23, 24:3-7, 30-34, 28:5, 15-16, Psalms 49:20, Psalms 19:7-13, Job 32:7-9, Ecclesiastes 5:1

New Testament – Ephesians 4:17-20, 1 Corinthians 14:14-20, Luke 10:21-24, John 8:43-49, 9:39-41

Get an Understanding (4)

Old Testament – Daniel 11:33-35, 12:8-10, Job 17:4, 39:13-17, Proverbs 18:2, 15, 17:16, 24, 27-28, Micah 4:12, Deuteronomy 32:17-22, 27-28, Isaiah 44:9-20, Psalms 115:4-8

New Testament – Acts 17:18-33, Romans 1:18-23, Hebrews 5:9-14, 2 Timothy 3:5-8

Get an Understanding (5)

Old Testament – Isaiah 28:9-10, 29:14-16, 24, 32:2-4, 3:13-22, 13:15, 19:8, 25, 21:16, Psalms 94:8-12, 119:27, 119: 27, 130, 169

New Testament – Matthew 15:16-20, 1 Corinthians 2:14, 2 Timothy 2:7, 1 John 5:20

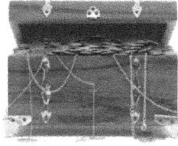

The Eyes

The Eyes (1)

"For God doth know that in the day ye eat thereof, then your eyes shall be opened, and ye shall be as gods, knowing good and evil. And when the woman saw that the tree was good for food, and that it was pleasant to the eyes...she took of the fruit thereof, and did eat, and gave also unto her husband...And the eyes of them both were opened, and they knew that they were naked..." (Genesis 3:5-7)

The Eyes (2)

"For all that is in the world, the lust of the flesh, the lust of the eyes, and the pride of life, is not of the Father, but is of the world." (1 John 2:16)

The Eyes (3)

"Let thine eyes look right on, and let thine eyelids look straight before thee." (Proverbs 4:25)

Discussion Questions

1. What did Jesus mean in Matthew 5:29, concerning the eye?
2. What is being conveyed in Ephesians 1:18?
3. How can a covenant be made with the eyes, mentioned in Job 31:1?
4. Explain 2 Peter 2:14.

5. What thoughts are expressed in Psalms 146:8?

Fill in the Blanks

1. Thefts, covetousness, _____, deceit, lasciviousness, an evil ___, blasphemy, ____, foolishness.
2. The light of the body is the___: therefore when thine ___ is single, thy whole body also is full of light; but when thine ___ is evil, thy body also is full of darkness." (Luke 7:34)
3. In those days there was no king in Israel, but every man did that which was right in his own ____.
4. Consider and hear me, O Lord my God: lighten my ____, lest I sleep the sleep of _____;
5. There is no _____ of ____ before their _____.

The Eyes

*T*he eyes provide vision so that we may be able to view all the things that surround us. They are a fascinating gift from God. It is vital to us, as we perform the many different tasks, activities, and duties associated with everyday life. Yet metaphorically, there is enlightenment that comes from God's word through the windows of the soul that enable us to view life and the things in life from a heavenly perspective.

> "For with thee is the fountain of life: in thy light we see light." "The entrance of thy words giveth light: it giveth understanding to the simple" (Psalms 36:9, 119:130).

The passages in this study gives us insight pertaining to the physical eyes and the spiritual aspects of the eyes.

The Eyes (1)

Old Testament – Gen 3:5-7, 13:7-10, 13, Numbers 15:37-39, Deuteronomy 12:18, 16:19, 29:2-4, 2 Kings 6:15-20, Psalms 119:18, 37, 148, 101:3, 6, 25:15, Proverbs 3:7, 4:25, 16:29-30, 20:8, 23:6

New Testament – Matthew 6:22-23, 7:3-5, Mark 7:18-23, 1 John 2:16

The Eyes (2)

Old Testament – Genesis 21:15-19, 24:63-67, Song of Solomon 6:5, 13, Numbers 24:15-17, Deuteronomy 6:4-8, 15:9, Judges 17:6, Ezra 9:5-8, Psalms 13:3, 15:1-4, 19:8, Proverbs 30:12-13, 17, 27:20

New Testament – Matthew 5:29, 20:13-15, Acts 26:17-18, 1 John 2:11

The Eyes (3)

Old Testament – Zechariah 9:1, 2 Chronicles 20:12, Psalms 146:8, 145:15, 141:7-8, 123:1-2, 26:2-3, Isaiah 17:9, 29:18, 32:1-3, 33:14-15, 17, 20, 35:4-5, 40:26, 42:1-7, 43:8-9

New Testament – Luke 7:19-23, Revelation 3:18, Acts 28:25-27, Ephesians 1:17-18

The Eyes (4)

Old Testament – Ecclesiastes 2:14, 6:9, 11:9, Job 31:1-4, 7-11, 24:15-25, 11:20, Jeremiah 5:20-23, 7:11-14, 22:15-17, Ezekiel 12:2, 24:16-24, 44:5-9, Psalms 69:23-27, 73:7-12

New Testament – Luke 10:22-24, 16:22-23, 18:10-13, 19:41-42

The Eyes (5)

Old Testament – Numbers 22:31-35, Exodus 24:17, Micah 4:11-12, Isaiah 52:8-10, Zechariah 11:17, Job 16:18-20, 32:1, Proverbs 16:2, 17:24, 21:2, 22:9, 23:31-33, 28:22, 27, 29:13, Lamentations 3:50-51

New Testament – Luke 11:34, John 4:35, 2 Peter 2:14, Romans 3:18, 1 Corinthians 2:9

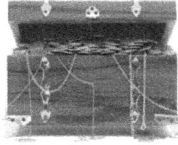

According to the Pattern

According to the Pattern (1)

"And let them make Me a sanctuary; that I may dwell among them. According to all that I shew thee, after the pattern of the tabernacle, and the pattern of all the instruments thereof, even so shall ye make it." (Exodus 25:8-9)

According to the Pattern (2)

"Thou son of man, shew the house to the house of Israel, that they may be ashamed of their iniquities: and let them measure the pattern." (Ezekiel 43:10)

According to the Pattern (3)

"Who serve unto the example and shadow of heavenly things, as Moses was admonished of God when he was about to make the tabernacle: See, saith he, that thou make all things according to the pattern shewed to thee in the mount." (Hebrews 8:5)

Discussion Questions

1. What instructions were given in Exodus 25:8-9, 40?
2. What happened in Revelation 10:1-3?
3. What type pattern is mentioned in 1 Timothy 1:16?
4. Explain Philippians 3:16-18.

5. What warning is given in Revelation 22:18-19?

Fill in the Blanks

1. "Brethren, be_____ together of me, and____ them which walk so as ye have___ for an____ ."
2. "Be ye followers of____ , even as I also am of____ ."
3. ".... For, See, saith he, that thou make all things according to the____ shewed to thee in the mount."
4. "This book of the law shall not ____out of thy____ ; but thou shalt ____therein day and night, that thou mayest observe to do ____to all that is ____ ____."
5. "Teaching them to observe____ things whatsoever I have____ you."

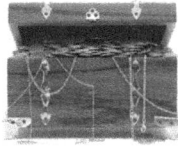

According to the Pattern

*G*od has always given man instructions as to the performing of various tasks that were commanded by Him. They were to follow those plans with complete adroitness without addition, subtraction, or any deviation.

According to the Pattern (1)

Old Testament – Exodus 25:8-9, 40, 26:30, 27:8, 35:10, 39:42-43, Leviticus 10:1-3, 9-11, Joshua 1:7-8, 17-18, 1 Chronicles 13:6-13, 1 Chronicles 15:11-15, Proverbs 30:6

New Testament – 1 Corinthians 3:9-17, 1 Timothy 1:16, 2 Timothy 1:13-14, 2:2, 5 Philippians 3:16-19, Galatians 1:6-12, Revelation 22:18-19

According to the Pattern (2)

Old Testament – Genesis 6:14-16, 22, 7:1-5, Exodus 29:35, 41, 30:37, 31:11, 32:28-29, 36:11, 32:28-29, 36:1, 38:21, 39:5, 14, 32 Psalms 78:72, 106:45, 119:9, 28, 41, 65, 90-91

New Testament – Acts 13:17-23, Hebrews 8:4-6, 9:23-24, Titus 2:7-8, 1 John 5:14, James 2:8

According to the Pattern (3)

Old Testament – Deuteronomy 4:2, 12:8, 32, 17:11, 14-20, Exodus 12:49-50, 40:12-16, 1 Chronicles 28:9-12, 18-19, 1 Samuel 13:6-14, Ezra 3:4, 6:14, 7:10-14 Psalms 119: 158, 169 Isaiah 8:20

New Testament – John 12:48-50, Acts 1:1-2, Ephesians 2:20-22, 1 Peter 1:1-3, 2 Thessalonians 3:6-9, 1 Thessalonians 1:6-7, 2:13-14

According to the Pattern (4)

Old Testament – Isaiah 5:24, 11:10-12, 49:22-23, 51:4-11, 16, 59:19-21, 62:10-12, Jeremiah 50:2, 51:12, 27 Zechariah 9:16, 12:10, Psalms 20:5, Psalms 60:4

New Testament – Matthew 11:2-6, 17:4-5, John 3:14-15, 4:25-26, , 8:28-29, 12:32, 14:6, Luke 24:32, 44-47, Acts 7:37, 1 Peter 2:21, 1 John 3:2-3, Colossians 3:10

According to the Pattern (5)

Old Testament – Joshua 22:26-28, 2 Kings 16:10-11, 1 Kings 6:1-9, 38, Ezekiel 40:2-6, 41:1-4, 13-15, 42:15-20, 43:10-13, 44:5-11, Psalms 127:1, 102:16-17, 69:35-36, 51:18-19

New Testament – Mark 14:58, Matthew 26:61, 16:18, 1 Peter 2:3-10, Hebrews 7:12-16, 24, 13:10-16, Revelation 11:1-2, 21:14-17

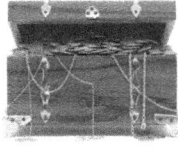

Strengthen Thou Me

Strengthen Thou Me (1)

"I can do all things through Christ which strengtheneth me." (Philippians 4:15)

Strengthen Thou Me (2)

"Wisdom strengthen the wise more than ten mighty men which are in the city." (Ecclesiastes 7:19)

Strengthen Thou Me (3)

"Notwithstanding the Lord stood with me, and strengthen me; that by me the preaching might be fully known, and that all the Gentiles might hear: and I was delivered out of the mouth of the lion." (2 Timothy 4:17)

Discussion Questions

1. What command is given in 1 Chronicles 16:11?
2. What transpired in 2 Timothy 4:17?
3. Explain 2 Corinthians 12:8-10.
4. When the soul gets weary, how is it to be strengthened according to Psalms 119:28?
5. Why did Paul feel he could do all things as expressed in Philippians 4:13?

Fill in the Blanks

1. "My soul___ for thy salvation: but I ___ in thy___ ."
2. "He staggered not at the___ of God through unbelief;   but was___ in faith, giving glory to God."
3. "I can do all things through Christ which___ me."
4. "Finally, my brethren, be___ in the Lord, and in the___ of His might."
5. "A wise man is___ ; yea, a man of knowledge increaseth___ ."

Strengthen Thou Me

"Lord, make me to know mine end, and the measure of my days, what it is; that I may know how frail I am" (Psalms 39:4).

*T*his realization causes us to cry out "strengthen thou me." At times, we are overwhelmed by the vicissitudes of life, and we come to greatly appreciate God in our lives. We come to attest to the beautiful names that refer to God in the Hebrew and Greek languages.

- Chyahluth—My strength (Psalms 22:19)
- Elohim Yakol—God the most able (Daniel 3:17)
- Jehovah Azar—The Lord my helper (Psalms 30:10)
- Jehovah-Raphe—The Lord who hears (Exodus 15:22)
- Jehovah Tsur—The Lord my strength (Psalms 144:1)
- RAB—Lord, Nourisher (Daniel 2:10)
- RUMN RO'SH – The one who lifts my head (Psalms 3:3)

When I am weak, He is strong in me, and He strengthens me through His awesome power.

Strengthen Thou Me (1)

Old Testament – 1 Chronicles 16:11, Psalms 22:14-15, 39:4, 13, Zechariah 10:6, 12, 1 Samuel 15:29, Deuteronomy 33:25, Isaiah 40:25 30, 41:10, 25:6-9, Job 9:19, 36:5-6, Habakkuk 3:19, Psalms 119:28, 138:3

New Testament – 2 Timothy 4:17, Philippians 4:13, 1 Peter 5:10, Ephesians 3:16

Strengthen Thou Me (2)

Old Testament – Exodus 15:13, Psalms 105:24, 84:7, 77:14, 71:16, 33:16-22, Jeremiah 50:34, 1 Chronicles 29:12, Daniel 10:15-19, Isaiah 35:3-4, 12:2, Job 6:11-13, 17:9, 26:2

New Testament – Luke 1:49-51, Romans 5:6, 2 Corinthians 1:8-9, 4{7, 12:7-10, 1 Corinthians 1:25

Strengthen Thou Me (3)

Old Testament – Deuteronomy 3:28, 1 Samuel 2:4, Isaiah 45:24, Nehemiah 6:9, 8:10, Job 4;3-5, 16:4-5, Hosea 7:15-16, Psalms 18:32, 39, 27:14, 29:11, 31:24, 68:35, 89:20-21

New Testament – Luke 22:31-32, 41-43, Romans 4:20, 15:1, Acts 18:23

Strengthen Thou Me (4)

Old Testament – Exodus 13:14, 16, 15:2, Numbers 23:22, Judges 16:28-30, Jeremiah 16:19-21, Psalms 20:5-7, 27:1, 28:7-8, 43:2, 73:26, 140:7, 147:10-13, Job 9:19, 12:21, Joel 2:11

New Testament – 2 Corinthians 13:4, 9, 10:10, 1 Corinthians 2:1-5, Colossians 1:10

Strengthen Thou Me (5)

Old Testament – 1 Chronicles 16:27-28, 2 Samuel 22:33, Job 23:3-6, 36:5, Proverbs 10:29, 24:5, 10, Ecclesiastes 7:19, Psalms 37:39, 46:1, 52:6-7, 59:16-17, 81:1, 96:6, 105:4, 118:14

New Testament – Ephesians 6:10, 1 Corinthians 16:13, 2 Timothy 2:1, 1 John 2:14

Our Cry

Our Cry (1)

"In my distress I called upon the LORD and cried unto my God: He heard my voice out of his temple and my cry came before Him, even into His ears. Then the earth shook and trembled; the foundations of the hills moved and were shaken, because He was wroth." (Psalms 18:6-7)

Our Cry (2)

"...He forgetteth not the cry of the humble." (Psalms 9:12)

Our Cry (3)

"And shall not God avenge his own elect, which cry day and night unto him, though He bear long with them?" (Luke 18:7)

Discussion Questions

1. What is the difference between crying out to God and praying to God?
2. What manner and how often did the Psalmist cy out to God in Psalms 55:17?
3. What was the reason given for Israel crying out to God in Exodus 2:23?
4. What are your thoughts concerning Hebrews 5:5-7?
5. What transpired in Psalms 106:43-45?

Fill in the Blanks

1. And he answered and said unto them, I tell you that, if these hold their _____, the stones would immediately ___ .
2. If thou afflict them in any wise, and they ___ at all to Me, I will surely _____ their ___.
3. O earth, cover not thou my blood, and let my _____ have no place.
4. Hear, O LORD, when I ___ with my voice: have _____ also upon me, and answer me.
5. Whoso stoppeth his ears at the ___ of the poor, he also shall ___ himself, but shall not be heard.

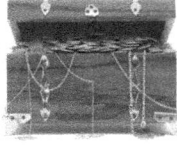

Our Cry

S a'ak in the Hebrew language means *to cry out*. It also means to summon or appeal. It conveys more than uttering mere words out of the mouth, but to make a petition or request from the depth of the soul or heart.

> "Out of the depths have I cried unto thee, O LORD. LORD, hear my voice: let thine ears be attentive to the voice of my supplications" (Psalms 130:1-2).

Our Cry (1)

Old Testament – Exodus 2:23-25, 3:7, 9, 22:23, Deuteronomy 26:5-8, Judges 3:9, 15, 4:3-9, 10:9-16, Psalms 106:43-45, 61:1-2, 55;17, 22, 18:6-17, 9:9-12, Job 16:15-20, 3:24-26, Lamentations 2:18-19, 3:48-56

New Testament – Luke 18:7, 19:40, Hebrews 5:5-7

Our Cry (2)

Old Testament – Genesis 4:8-10, 18:20-33, 19:13, Hosea 7:1-2, 13-14, 8:2-3, Ezekiel 9:4-9, 21:6-12, Jonah 1:2, 3:4, Isaiah 58:1, 42:13-16, 40:6-8, Psalms 56:9, 57:2-3, 69:1-3, 86:1-2

New Testament – Matthews 20:29-34, 23:37-38, Luke 4:33-36, 9:37-42

Our Cry (3)

Old Testament – 1 Chronicles 5:18-22, 2 Chronicles 14:11-13, 18:31, 20:9, 32:19-22, Isaiah 12:6, 19:19-20, 24:13-14, 30:19, Psalms 22:4-5, 30:2-8, 34:6, 15-19, 40:1-3

New Testament – Matthews 14:30-31, 15:22-28, 20:30-34, 21:9-11

Our Cry (4)

Old Testament – Habakkuk 1:4, 2:1-11, Micah 3:4, 4:9-13, Jeremiah 18:20-22, 20:7-11, Job 19:7, 24:12, 27:8-9, 35:12-13, 88:1-4, 102:1-12, 107:5-30

New Testament – Mark 4:37-41, 6:45-51, 9:17-24, Luke 18:38-43

Our Cry (5)

Old Testament – Judges 6:6-10, Joel 1:8-14, 1 Samuel 7:9, 1 Kings 17:17-22, 2 Chronicles 13:14-18, Zephaniah 1:10-14, Isaiah 14:31-32, 15:3-5, Jeremiah 4:5-8, 7:13-16, 11:11, 14:1-12, Lamentations 3:6-8, 55-56, 4:12-15, Psalms 130:1-2, 119:145-146

New Testament – Acts 7:59-60, Romans 8:15, Galatians 4:27, Matthews 25:6-13

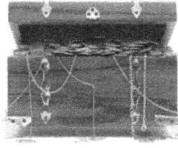

The Watchman and His Warnings

The Watchman and his Warnings (1)

"Son of man, I have made thee a watchman unto the house of Israel: therefore hear the word at my mouth, and give them warning from Me." (Ezekiel 3:17)

The Watchman and his Warnings (2)

"Set up the standard upon the walls of Babylon, make the watch strong, set up the watchmen, prepare the ambushes: for the LORD hath both devised and done that which He spake against the inhabitants of Babylon." (Jeremiah 51:2)

The Watchman and his Warnings (3)

"Obey them that have the rule over you, and submit yourselves: for they watch for your souls, as they must give account, that they may do it with joy, and not with grief: for that is unprofitable for you." (Hebrews 13:17)

Discussion Questions

1. What was supposed to happen to the watchman that saw danger approaching yet did not warn the people?
2. Are there to be watchmen in the church today who watch for the souls of men and must be accountable to God? If so, who are they?

3. Must those in the church submit to the rule of the watchman without grief? If so, why?
4. Was Ezekiel a watchman for Israel? If so, explain his duties.
5. Was Ephraim a watchman? If so, what passage of Scripture mentions his role?

Fill in the Blanks

1. "And appoint____ of the inhabitants of____ , every one in his____ , and every one to be over against his____ ."
2. "____ them that have the____ over you, and ____yourselves: for they watch for your____ , as they that must give____ , that they may do it with____ , and not with____ ."
3. "For thus hath the____ said unto me, Go, set a ____, let him____ what he seeth."
4. "The watchman of____ was with my____ ."
5. "Also____ set watchmen____ you, saying, ____to the sound of the____ . But they said, We will not____ ."

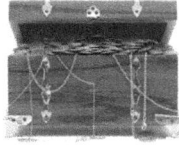

The Watchman and His Warnings

*T*hroughout the Bible, God has assigned certain men to be watchmen for His people. God's people were His flock that obeyed and followed His commands. The watchman's responsibility was to issue warnings to the flock concerning perils or dangers. The watchman was to be vigilant and observant as he carried out his job. The flock's responsibility was to heed the cautionary warnings of its watchmen.

The Watchman & His Warnings (1)

Old Testament – Isaiah 21:4-12, 29:18-20, 52:1-8, 8-11, 62:6-12, Ezekiel 3:17-21, 25-27, 7:1-6, 11:2-8, 13:1-10, 22-23, 14:1-6, 12-14, 33:2-9, Psalms 141:3-4, 127:1

New Testament – Acts 1:1-2, 10:42, 20:25-31, 2 Timothy 4:1-5, 1 Timothy 1:3-7, 18-20, 4:1-7, 16, 1 Thessalonians 5:14-15

The Watchman & His Warnings (2)

Old Testament – Nehemiah 4:4-9, 12-15, 18:-23, 7:1-3, 13:15-19, 2 Kings 9:17-24, 11:1-8, Ezekiel 44:1-9, 43:5-12, 2 Chronicles 19:7-10, 20:24-30, 23:1-6, 36:15-16, Psalms 141:3

New Testament – Mark 13:33-37, 14:34, 38, 41, Matthews 26:41, Luke 21:34-36

The Watchman & His Warnings (3)

Old Testament – 1 Samuel 14:16, 2 Samuel 13:22-34, 18:5-15, 19-27, 31-33, Jeremiah 6:10-13, 16-19, 7:24-29, 9:25-26, 31:1, 6-9, 28, 51:10-12, 27-31, Lamentations 2:18-19, Isaiah 31:1-6, Habakkuk 2:1-4, Micah 7:7-11, 4:4-8, Psalms 130:6-9, 48:12-14

New Testament – Luke 12:37-40, Matthew 24:42-44, Ephesians 6:18, Colossians 4:2

The Watchman & His Warnings (4)

Old Testament – Daniel 4:13-14, 17, 23-25, Zechariah 1:8-21, Job 7:12-21, Hosea 9:7-8, 8:1-8, Joel 2:1-3, Isaiah 58:1-2, 2510-12, Amos 3:6-10, 7:12-17, Jeremiah 4:5-17, 6:27-30, Psalms 48:11-14, 55:10-11, 59:5-9, 14-17

New Testament – Hebrews 13:17, 1 Peter 4:7, 1 Thessalonians 5:6, 1 Corinthians 16:13

The Watchman & His Warnings (5)

Old Testament – Song of Solomon 5:7, 1:5-6, 2 Kings 11:5-8, 11, 17:6-9, 15, 18:1-8, Ezekiel 2:1-7, 3:1-11, 11:25, 33:7, 30-33, Zephaniah 1:14-16, 3:1-7, Lamentations 4:16-17, Proverbs 8:1-4, 34

New Testament – Luke 2:8, 1 Peter 5:1-2, 8-9, Revelations 3:2-3, 11, 16:15

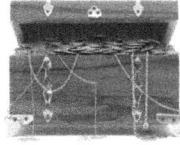

The River Runs

The River Runs (1)

"He brought streams also out of the rock, and caused waters to run down like rivers." (Psalms 78:16)

The River Runs (2)

"And he shewed me a pure river of water of life, clear as crystal, proceeding out of the throne of God and of the Lamb. In the midst of the street of it, and on either side of the river, was the tree of life, which bare twelve manner of fruits, and yielded her fruit every month: and the leaves of the tree were for the healing of the nations." (Revelation 22:1-2)

The River Runs (3)

"I will open rivers in high places, and fountains in the midst of the valleys: I will make the wilderness a pool of water, and the dry land springs of water." (Isaiah 41:18)

Discussion Questions

1. What transpired in 1 Corinthians 10:1-4?
2. What is the living water mentioned in John 4:10-14?
3. Discuss Revelation 21:6.
4. What is conveyed in Proverbs 18:4?
5. What thoughts are conveyed in Psalms 90:3-12?

Fill in the Blanks

1. And he shall be like a tree planted by _____ of _____, that bringeth forth his fruit in his season;

2. In that day there shall be a fountain opened to the house of _____ and to the _____ of Jerusalem for sin and uncleanness.

3. Jesus answered, Verily, Verily, I say unto thee, Except a man be born of the water, and of the Spirit, he cannot enter into the kingdom of God. (John 3:5)

4. Afterward he measured a thousand and it was a ____ that I could not pass over:

5. And though thy people shall be as the sand of the ___, yet a remnant of them shall return: the consumption decreed shall overflow with righteousness." (Isaiah 10:22)

The River Runs

"Thou visitest the earth, and watereth it: thou greatly enrichest it with the river of God, which is full of water: thou preparest them corn, when thou hast provided for it" (Psalms 65:9).

*W*hat a wonderful, powerful and thought-provoking passage of Scripture. Notice the imagery. What is the river of God? Does the Psalmist speak metaphorically from life observations, or is there a meaning much deeper than that? An examination of this collage of verses will provide clarity to a great degree.

The River Runs (1)

Old Testament – Psalms 78:14-16, 65:9-13, 46:4-5, 36:8-9, 23:2, Isaiah 66:10-12, 48:18-22, 41:17-18, 33:20-24, Ezekiel 47:1-12

New Testament – Revelation 22:1-3, 1 Corinthians 10:1-4, John 4:10-14

The River Runs (2)

Old Testament – Ecclesiastes 1:7, Psalms 80:8-11, 14, 15, 17, 90:5-6, 104:10-13, 105:41-43, 119:136, Job 27:20-23, 20:17-19, 14:11-12, 19-22, Isaiah 32:1-2, 27:12, 2:2-3, Zechariah 13:1, 14:8-9

New Testament – Acts 1:5, John &;37-38, Hebrews 10:22

The River Runs (3)

Old Testament – Joel 1:18-20, 3:12-18, Isaiah 8:6-8, 10:22, 23:10, 28:15-17, 35;6-7, 41:17-18, 43:2, 44:3-4, 58:11, Jeremiah 31:10-112, Zechariah 9:9-10, 10:11, Psalms 107:31-33, 89:20, 25, 72:6-8

New Testament – Jude 1:12, Revelation 7:16-17, 21:6

The River Runs (4)

Old Testament – Ezekiel 29:3-16, 31:2-7, 32:2, 6, 34:13-15, Psalms 1:1-3, 23:1-2, 74:12-15, 137:1-5, Habakkuk 3:8-15, Jeremiah 46:6-10, 31:9, 17:13, 9:1-2, 2:12-13, Hosea 13:12-15

New Testament – Mark 1:4-5, 9, Luke 3:7, Acts 2:36-38

The River Runs (5)

Old Testament – 1 Samuel 20:1-3, 25-27, 31, 2 Samuel 12:22-23, 1 Chronicles 29:14-15, 1 Kings 2:1-2, 10, Job 30:22-23, 9:25-26, 4:18-20, Psalms 89:47-48, Proverbs 27:1

New Testament – Hebrews 9:27, 1 Corinthians 15:26, 51-57, John 14:1-4, 8:51, James 4:14

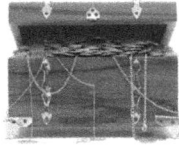

Joy and Gladness of Heart

Joy and Gladness of Heart (1)

"A merry heart maketh a cheerful countenance: but by sorrow of the heart the spirit is broken." (Proverbs 15:13)

Joy and Gladness of Heart (2)

"Serve the LORD with gladness: come before His presence with singing." (Psalm 100:2)

Joy and Gladness of Heart (3)

"And they, continuing daily with one accord in the temple, and breaking bread from house to house, did eat their meat with gladness and singleness of heart." (Acts 2:46)

Discussion Questions

1. Explain Deuteronomy 12:7.
2. Explain Deuteronomy 28:47-48.
3. What is the benefit of having a merry heart or a heart that resonates with joy and gladness mentioned in Proverbs 15:13?
4. Explain Proverbs 17:22.
5. What are the fruit of the Spirit?

Fill in the Blanks

1. "But the___ of the___ is___ , ___ , ___ , ___ , ___, ___, ___ ."
2. "And thou shalt___ in every___ which the Lord thy___ hath given unto___ , and unto___ ___ ."
3. "Your father___ rejoiced to see my day: and he saw it, and was___ ."
4. "Who, when he came, and had seen the ___of God, was___ , and___ them all, that with___ of___ they would___ unto the___ ."
5. "And ye now therefore have___ : but I will see you again, and your___ shall___ , and your___ no man taketh from you."

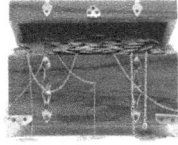

Joy and Gladness of Heart

O ne of the prerequisites for worshiping God is to have a heart of joy and gladness as you reflect upon His goodness, His provision, His protection, His kindness, and His mercy toward all of us. He blesses us in spite of our waywardness, flaws, and shortcomings. We should always be eternally grateful.

Joy and Gladness of Heart (1)

Old Testament – Deuteronomy 12:4-7, 10-12, 16:11-15, 28:47-48, Malachi 2:13 Zephaniah 3:14-17, Psalms 100:1-2, 105:1-3, 43, Joel 2:21-23, Isaiah 61:10-11, Proverbs 15:13

New Testament – Luke 1:46-55, Acts 2:46-47, 8:35-39, Philippians 3:1-3, 4:4

Joy and Gladness of Heart (2)

Old Testament – Deuteronomy 26:8-11, 33:29, Psalms 4:3-7, 9:1-2, 16:8-11, 21:1-6, 48:11, 67:4, 70:4, 144:14-15, 1 Samuel 2:1-2, Habakkuk 3:17-18, Proverbs 17:22, 28:14, 29:18

New Testament – Luke 10:19-20, John 16:33, 13:15, 17 Romans 5:1-2, 11, Galatians 5:22-23, Acts 13:47-52

Joy and Gladness of Heart (3)

Old Testament – 1 Kings 10:8=9, Psalms 45:6-8, 51:6-8, 96:9-12, 97:1, 8-12, 104:33-34, 126:5-6, Isaiah 66:5, 10, Jeremiah 7:30, 34, 15:16-17, 16:9-11, 25:10, 31:9-13, 33:8-11 Nehemiah 8:1-12

New Testament – Matthew 2:9-11, Luke 1:8-14, 46-47, John 8:56, 1 Peter 1:3-8

Joy and Gladness of Heart (4)

Old Testament – Deuteronomy 12:17-18, 2 Chronicles 6:41, 7:10, 1 Kings 8:66, Proverbs 15:15, Ecclesiastes 9:7, Jeremiah 30:17-19, Isaiah 25:9, 51:3, 11, , 61:7, 10, Psalms 30:11, 89:15-16, 95:1-3

New Testament – John 16:20-22, Matthew 5:11-12, 25:21 Acts 2:28, 11:21-23,

Joy and Gladness of Heart (5)

Old Testament – 1 Chronicles 29:6-9, 2 Chronicles 29:28-30, 36, 30:22-23, 26, Zechariah 8:1-6, 19, Esther 9:17-23, Psalms 31:7, 40:16, 64:10, 118:24

New Testament – Acts 8:5, 8, 1 Thessalonians 1:6, 2:19-20, 3:8-9, Philemon 1:7, 20, 2 Timothy 1:3-4, 1 Peter 4:12-13

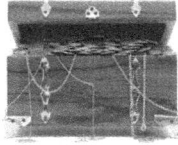

The Wrath of God

The Wrath of God (1)

"He that beliveth on the Son hath everlasting life: and he that believeth not the Son shall not see life; but the wrath of God abideth on him." (John 3:36)

The Wrath of God (2)

"But fornication, and all uncleanness, or covetousness, let it not be once named among you, as becometh saints; ...Let no man deceive you with vain words: for because of these things cometh the wrath of God upon the children of disobedience." (Ephesians 5:3, 6)

The Wrath of God (3)

"God is jealous, and the LORD revengeth; the LORD revengeth, and is furious; the LORD will take vengeance on His adversaries, and He reserveth wrath for his enemies. (Nahum 1:2)

Discussion Questions

1. Why did God destroy the earth in the Genesis account? Explain.
2. Did Jesus, in His earthly ministry, foretell of a future day of wrath? If He did, what Scriptural basis can you give?

3. Does being in Christ save us from the wrath to come? Explain whether or not you think this is true according to Scripture.
4. Is God both good and severe? If so, give a passage of Scripture to back up your thoughts.
5. List five ways that we are encouraged to live.

Fill in the Blanks

1. "And GOD saw that the____ of man was great in the earth, and that every____ of the thoughts of his heart was only____ continually. And it____ the Lord that he had made man on the earth, and it____ him in his heart."
2. "But of that____ and____ knoweth no man, no, not the angels of heaven, but my Father____ ."
3. "There is therefore now___ condemnation to them which are in____ ____ who walk not after the____ , but after the Spirit."
4. "In flaming fire taking____ on them that____ not God, and that____ not the gospel of our Lord Jesus Christ."
5. "Much more then, being now justified by his ____, we shall be____ from ____through Him."

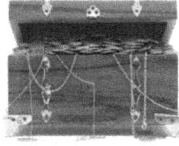

The Wrath of God

The Psalmist writes in Psalm 7:11, "God judgeth the righteous, and God is angry with the wicked every day." It is in Christ that all of mankind can make peace with God. In Christ, there is forgiveness of sins and the propitiation required to enjoy fellowship with God. There are terrible consequences for those who reject God's Gift. God will judge and inflict punishment and righteous indignation upon the children of disobedience. This is a very interesting study that reveals both the goodness and the severity of God.

The Wrath of God (1)

Old Testament – Genesis 6:5-8, 18:20-33, Exodus 15:3-7, Deuteronomy 4:23-24, 0:7-8, 13-14, 18-29, 29:19-28, Numbers 16:41-48, 25:1-11, Lamentations 2:1-11, 3:19-40, Habakkuk 3:2, Nahum 1:2-8, Psalms 2:1-5, 10-12, 21:7-9, 38:1-10, 18, 21

New Testament – Matthew 3:5-8, John 3:35-36, Luke 12:4-5, Romans 1:18, 28-32, 2:1-9, 5:8-9

The Wrath of God (2)

Old Testament – Leviticus 10:1-6, Joshua 1, 10-13, 19-26, 22:20. 2 Samuel 24:1-4, 10-17, 25, 1 Chronicles 27:23-24, 2 Chronicles 17:1-7, 12, 19:1-3, 8-10, 24:17-20, 28:7-11, Isaiah 5:20-24, 9:16-19, 10:5-6, 13:9-13, 26:21, Psalms 7:11-17, Job 36:11-13, 18, Proverbs 11:4-5, 23, 29:8

New Testament – Matthew 24:36-39, Hebrews 10:26-31, Romans 9:18-23, 12:17-19

The Wrath of God (3)

Old Testament – 2 Kings 22:8-13, 16-20, 23:1-3, 25-26, Jeremiah 36{1-7, 16-23, 27-32, 44:1-8, 15-23, 27-29, 50:4-13, Ezra 5:8-12, 7:21-23, 8:21-23, 10:1-3, 10-14, Psalms 59:12-13, 78:31-34, 38-39, 79:4-6, 102:9-13

New Testament – Ephesians 2:1-5, 5:1-6, 1 Thessalonians 5:5-9, Revelations 12:7-12, 14:6-10, 17-19

The Wrath of God (4)

Old Testament – Deuteronomy 11:16-17, Numbers 1:52-53, 11:4-10, 30-34, 18:1-5, 1 Chronicles 13:1-12, 15:11-13, 2 Chronicles 12:1-7, 12, Hosea 5:3-10, 13:5-13, Psalms 110:5-7, 90:3-12, 89:46-52, 88:7-17, 85:1-4, 7

New Testament – Romans 11:17-22, 13:1-5, Hebrews 3:7-11, 4:1-3, Revelation 6:13-17, 11:16-19, 18:1-5, 17, 21

The Wrath of God (5)

Old Testament – 2 Chronicles 29:1-10, 30:6-11, 32:23-26, 34:1-3, 21-33, 36:11-16, Proverbs 29:1, Job 19:29, 21:29-31, Zephaniah 1:14-18, Jeremiah 7:23-29, 10:10, 18:19-22, 21:3-6, 32:36-42, Zechariah 7:8-14, 8:13-17

New Testament – 2 Peter 2:9, Colossians 3:5-6, 1 Thessalonians 1:8-10, 2:14-16, Revelation 19:11-15

Sorrow

Sorrow (1)

"Rejoice, O young man, in thy youth; and let thy heart cheer thee in the days of thy youth, and walk in the ways of thine heart, and in the sight of thine eyes; but know thou, that for all these things God will bring thee into judgement. Therefore remove sorrow from thy heart, and put away evil from thy flesh: for childhood and youth are vanity. (Ecclesiastes 11:9-10)

Sorrow (2)

"A merry heart maketh a cheerful countenance: but by sorrow of the heart the spirit is broken." (Proverbs 15:13)

Sorrow (3)

"But I would not have you to be ignorant, brethren, concerning them which are asleep, that ye sorrow not, even as others which have no hope." (1 Thessalonians 4:13)

Discussion Questions

1. How does godly sorrow work repentance, as mentioned in 2 Corinthians 7:10?
2. What did Jesus convey to his disciples in John 16:20?
3. What was the curse placed on the woman in Genesis 3:16?

4. What was the curse placed on man in Genesis 3:17?
5. Why did sorrow of heart pose a problem for the king in Nehemiah 2:2?

Fill in the Blanks

1. How long shall I take counsel in my soul, having _____ in my ____ daily? How long shall mine enemy be exalted over me?
2. The blessing of the ___, it maketh rich, and he addeth no _____ with it.
3. Just because I have said these things unto you, _____ hath filled your _____.
4. Give them _____ of heart, thy ____ unto them.
5. Is it nothing to you, all ye that pass by? Behold, and see if there be any ____ like unto my _____, which is done unto me, wherewith the LORD hath afflicted me in the day of His fierce anger.

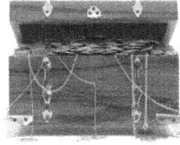

Sorrow

The KJV Dictionary defines sorrow as "the uneasiness or pain of mind which is produced by the loss of any good, or of frustrated hopes of good, or expected loss of happiness; to grieve; to be sad." It causes heaviness of heart that can cause the spirit of man to be broken and the soul of man to be cast down. Yet it can be beneficial to us by producing remorseful feelings in us that prompt us to repent of our sins and transgressions. Therefore, it can be useful at times, and, at times, it can be detrimental to us.

Sorrow (1)

Old Testament – Genesis 3:16-17, 4:3-7, 1 Chronicles 4:9, Leviticus 26:14-16, Deuteronomy 28:15, 65-66, Job 3:3-10, 6:1-10, 17:7, Lamentations 1:12, 18, Psalms 13:1-2, 16:4, 18:4-6, 32:10, 39:1-4, 107:33-39, 43

New Testament – 2 Corinthians 2:1-7, 7:5-13, Philippians 2:25-28

Sorrow (2)

Old Testament – Ecclesiastes 1:16-18, 2:22-24, 11:8-10, Proverbs 10:10, 22, 12:25, 14:13, 15:13, 18:14, Job 9:28-33, 21:17, Lamentations 3:64-65, Jeremiah 8:18-22, Psalms 69:29, Zephaniah 3:16-19, Isaiah 53:1-5,

New Testament – John 14:1, 27, 16:20-22, Matthew 24:6-8, 1 Timothy 6:10

Sorrow (3)

Old Testament – Nehemiah 2:2, Ezra 9:5-7, 13-15, Hosea 13:12-13, 8:8-10, Jeremiah 51:29, 49:22-24, 45:3, Isaiah 29:1-2, Ecclesiastes 7:3, Proverbs 14:10, Psalms 90:7-10, 69:20, 43:2, 5, 42:5, 38:17-18

New Testament – Luke 22:41-45, Romans 9:1-3, 1 Thessalonians 4:13, Revelation 18:7

Sorrow (4)

Old Testament – Genesis 44:27-34, Exodus 3:7, 15:11-14, Deuteronomy 26:6-9, 1 Samuel 1:9-17, 2 Samuel 16:5-12, Esther 9:20-22, Jeremiah 30:15-19, 31:25, Isaiah 14:3, 35:10, 50:11, 51:11, 65:13-14

New Testament – Luke 18:22-24, Matthew 26:36-41, Acts 20:36-38, 2 Corinthians 6:3-10

Sorrow (5)

Old Testament – Job 30:28-31, 22:21, 29, Nehemiah 8:10, 2 Chronicles 6:28-30, Lamentations 3:31-33, Isaiah 17:10-11, 22:4-5, Psalms 30:2-5, 31:10, 19, 34:19, 22, 51:8-12, 61:2, 119:92, 165, 127:2, 147:3

New Testament – 1 Peter 2:19, Romans 8:18-22, Revelation 18:7, 21:4

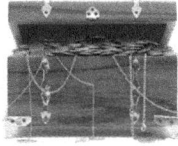

Paradoxes

Paradoxes (1)

"They are corrupt and speak wickedly concerning oppression: they speak loftily. They set their mouth against the heavens, and their tongue walketh through the earth...And they say, How doth God know? And is there knowledge in the most High? Behold, these are the ungodly, who prosper in the world; they increase in riches." (Psalms 73:8-12)

Paradoxes (2)

"Jesus answered and said unto him, Verily, verily, I say unto thee, Except a man be born again, he cannot see the kingdom of God." (John 3:3)

Paradoxes (3)

"He that believeth on me, as the scripture hath said, out of his belly shall flow rivers of living water." (John 7:38)

Discussion Questions

1. What did David observe about the prosperity of the wicked?
2. What did Jesus mean when He said, "He that findeth his life shall lose it and he that loseth his life for my sake shall find it"?
3. What does it mean to carry your cross?

4. What is living water (those that drink it will never thirst again but it springs up into everlasting life)?
5. What did Jesus mean when He said, "Except a man be born again he cannot see the kingdom of God"?

Fill in the Blanks

1. "And he said, Go, and tell this people, ____ye indeed, but____ not; and ____ye ____, but____ not."
2. "He that____ his life shall____ it; and he that____ his life in this world shall ____it unto____ ____ ."
3. "Behold, his soul which is lifted up is not____ in him: but the just shall____ by his____ ."
4. "And the world passeth away, and the____ thereof; but he that____ the will of____ abideth____ ."
5. "But the____ man receiveth____ the things of the____ of____ ; for they are____ unto him; neither can he____ them, because they are____ ____ ."

Paradoxes

*T*he word *paradox* is from the Greek word *paradoxon*, which means "contrary to common thought, view or perception." It is contrary to our opinion, our expectations, our analysis, or our belief. The command given by Moses to stand still while God parted the Red Sea was paradoxical. It defied logic and understanding. It even defied nature. The command for Naaman to dip seven times in the Jordan River contradicted the accepted view of how healing from leprosy was to be done, yet through Naaman's obedience, he was healed. The Bible is replete with many paradoxes we may not understand. But out of faith in God, we obey God, and God accomplishes His divine will.

Paradoxes (1)

Old Testament – Psalms 73:12-20, 78:34, 119:67, 71, Jeremiah 5:26-28, 12:1-2, 44:16-19, Job 20:5-8, Ecclesiastes 3:16-18, 7:14, 8:14, 17, 9:1-3, Isaiah 6:9-10, Proverbs 27:20

New Testament – Luke 16:25, John 12:24-26, Matthew 10:36-39, 1 Corinthians 15:31, 2 Corinthians 12:15

Paradoxes (2)

Old Testament – Deuteronomy 29:5-6, 32:30, Joshua 23:10, 10:12-14, Job 9:4, 22:2-3, 35:7, 41:11, Jeremiah 14:8-9, 51:51, Habakkuk 1:1-4, 7-17, 2:1-4

New Testament – Luke 14:11, 6:20-35, 1 Corinthians 1:27-29, John 3:3-8, 4:10-15, 6:53-63, 7:38, 12:24-25, 18:33-37

Paradoxes (3)

Old Testament – Daniel 4:17, Psalms 75:6-8, 17:13-14, Isaiah 45:7, Lamentations 3:38, Amos 3:6, Proverbs 16:4, Job 21:7-20, 29-31, 33:27-30, Ezekiel 18:4, 21-23

New Testament – Mark 9:43-48, 1 John 2:15-17, Matthew 16:26, 5:3-16, Romans 9:13-23, 12:14-21, 2 Timothy 2:20-21

Paradoxes (4)

Old Testament – Psalms 8:4-6, 9:19-20, 39:4-6, 62:9, 103:14-16, 130:3-4, Job 4:15-21, 7:17-18, 9:20, 10:9-15, 15:14-16, Ecclesiastes 8:8, Nehemiah 9:6, Ezekiel 34:31

New Testament – 1 Corinthians 2:14, 3:7, 21, Galatians 6:3, 2 Corinthians 1:9, 12:9-10, 2 Timothy 2:11-12

Paradoxes (5)

Old Testament – Ecclesiastes 11:1-3, 5:15-16, 2:21, 1:5-9, Psalms 90:3-6, 104:23-30, 115:16, 146:9, 2 Kings 21:11-13, Isaiah 24:1, 29:15-18

New Testament – Acts 17:2-6, 5:27-28, 2:32-36, Matthew 7:6, 22-23, 19:30, 23:11, 15, 26:41, John 9:41, Luke 6:46, Revelation 3:17-19

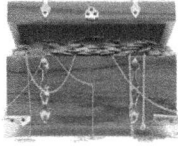

Doing What Pleases God

Doing What Pleases God (1)

"I will praise the name of God with a song, and will magnify him with thanksgiving. This also shall please the LORD better than an ox or bullock that hath horns and hoofs." (Psalms 69:30-31)

Doing What Pleases God (2)

"For do I now persuade men, or God? Or do I seek to please men? For if I yet pleased men, I should not be the servant of Christ." (Galatians 1:10)

Doing What Pleases God (3)

"And whatsoever we ask, we receive of him, because we keep his commandments, and do those things that are pleasing in his sight." (1 John 3:22)

Discussion Questions

1. Both Cain and Abel offered sacrifices. Which one found acceptance? Which one did not find acceptance?
2. What did Jesus tell the Samaritan woman about the worship of God?
3. Why did Saul fall into disfavor with God?
4. Are good works and sharing a means of pleasing God? Explain.

5. Can those who walk in the flesh please God?

Fill in the Blanks

1. "I know also, my God, that thou triest the heart, and hath pleasure in____ ."
2. "For whosoever shall do___ ___ of my Father which is in heaven, the same is my brother, and sister, and mother."
3. "Children, obey your parents in all things: for this is___ ___ unto the Lord."
4. "For do I now persuade men, or God? or do I____ to___ men? For if I yet___ men, I should not be the____of Christ."
5. "But if any man ____God, the same is___ of him."

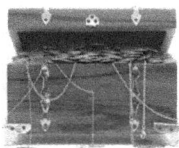

Doing What Pleases God

*T*he Bible reveals that which is acceptable before God and that which is unacceptable before God. As Christians, our aim and our desire should always be to live in a way, worship in a way, and walk in a way that pleases God. This can only be done through our Lord and Savior, Jesus Christ, the perfect example, about Whom God said, "This is My Beloved Son, in whom I am well pleased; hear ye him" (Matthew 17:5).

Doing What Pleases God (1)

Old Testament – Genesis 4:3-7, 5:21-24, 6:9, 17:1-2, 18:18-19, Leviticus 10:1-3, 17-19, Numbers 23:19-21, 27, 24:1-7, Psalms 69:30-31, 50:7-14, 23, Proverbs 16:7

New Testament – Matthew 12:4, Matthew 12:8-50, John 8:29, Luke 3:21-23, Acts 10:34-35, Hebrews 11:5-10, 13:20-21, Galatians 1:10, 15-17, 1 John 3:22

Doing What Pleases God (2)

Old Testament – 1 Samuel 12:22, 13:5-14, 15:10-26, 16:1, 7, 13, 1 Kings 15:4-5, 1 Chronicles 29:17, Proverbs 3:3-4, 12:2, 14:9, Psalms 115:1-3, 135:5-6, Daniel 4:35, Jonah 1:14, Ecclesiastes 2:26

New Testament – Colossians 1:9-10, Colossians 3:20, Romans 8:1-8, 14:17-18, 1 Corinthians 7:31-32

Doing What Pleases God (3)

Old Testament – Job 22:2-3, 21-30, 34:21-27, 36:11-12, Isaiah 42:21, 46:9-10, 58:5-13, 61:8-11, 64:4-5, 66:1-2, Psalms 5:4-7, 35:27, 41:11-13, 51:18-19, 111:2

New Testament – Luke 12:12-31-34, Ephesians 1:4-5, Philippians 4:16-18, 1 Thessalonians 4:1-8, 2:1-4

Doing What Pleases God (4)

Old Testament – Malachi 1:6-10, 14, 1 Kings 3:9-10, 12, Ecclesiastes 7:25-26, 8:1-3, Ezra 10:10-12, 1 Chronicles 17:25-27, Haggai 1:7-8, Hosea 8:8-12, Isaiah 2:5-6, 44:22-28, 48:14, 55:10-11, 56:4-5, Psalms 40:6-13, 103:21, 147:10-11, 149:4

New Testament – 1 Corinthians 1:21, 10:5-12, 12:18, 15:34-38, Philippians 2:12-13

Doing What Pleases God (5)

Old Testament – Ecclesiastes 5:4, Ezekiel 18:23, 30-32, 33:10-11, Psalms 145:19, 37:4-5, Jeremiah 34:12-16, 48:36-38, 53:1-10

New Testament – Matthew 12:18, 17:5, Romans 15:2-3, 1 Peter 3:2-4, 2 Corinthians 12:7-10, 2 Thesslonians 1:11, 2:2:10-12, I Timothy 5:6, Hebrews 10:4-6, 8, 38, 1 Peter 1:17, Revelation 4:11

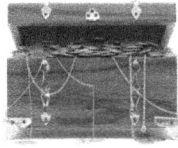

Why Men Are Lost

Why Men are Lost (1)

"Then said one unto him, Lord, are there few that be saved? And he said unto them, Strive to enter in at the strait gate: for many, I say unto you, will seek to enter in, and will not be able." (Luke 13:23-24)

Why men are lost (2)

"Behold the Lord's hand is not shortened, that it cannot save; neither his ear heavy that it cannot hear: But your iniquities have separated between you and your God, and your sins have hid his face from you, that he will not hear." (Isaiah 59:1-2)

Why men are Lost (3)

"Jesus answered and said unto him, Verily, verily I say unto thee, Except a man be born again, he cannot enter the kingdom of God." (John 3:3)

Discussion Questions

1. What separates us from God even to the point that He will not hear us?
2. What can take away our sins and restore us to our God?
3. What happens if we die in our sins?
4. What happens if we refuse to repent?

5. Can we walk in the flesh and still enter the kingdom of God? Explain.

Fill in the Blanks

1. "Then GOD saw that the ____of man was great in the____ , and that every____ of the____ of his heart was only____ continually. And the Lord ____was that He had made____ on the earth and He was____ in His____ ."
2. "But your____ have ____between you and your God, and your ____have hid his____ from you, that he will not ____."
3. "Jesus answered and said unto___ ___ him, Verily, verily, I say unto , a man be born ____, he____ see the kingdom of God."
4. "I said therefore unto you, that ye shall___ in your____ ; for if ye believe___ that I am He, ye shall___ in your___ ."
5. "For God____ not his Son into the world to____ the world; but that the world through ____might be____ ."

Why Men Are Lost

W hy some men are lost is a very interesting topic that warrants careful consideration. What does God see in us that will cause Him to cast us away eternally from His presence? Although He loves us and He created us, why are some men saved—and some men will be lost?

Why Men Are Lost (1)

Old Testament – Isaiah 59:1-11, 45:22, 30:9-15, 5:1-7, 14-24, Jeremiah 4:14, Jeremiah 6:16-19, 8:9, 1 Samuel 8:6-7, Hosea 4:6, Proverbs 28:18, Psalms 125:4-5, 101:6-7

New Testament – John 1:10-13, John 3:16-21, John 8:43-47, 2 Corinthians 4:3-4, 2 Timothy 4:2-5, 2 Thessalonians 2:10-12

Why Men Are Lost (2)

Old Testament – Genesis 6:5-9, Ecclesiastes 8:11-13, Jeremiah 50:6, 44:16-17, 18:12, Zephaniah 3:1-2, Ezekiel 18:21-23, Isaiah 3:8-12, 57:17, Proverbs 28:26, Psalms 73:27

New Testament – Hebrews 3:10-11, John 3:3-6, Matthew 5:20-30, 6:14-15, 7:13-23

Why Men Are Lost (3)

Old Testament – Exodus 9:30, Deuteronomy 5:29, Jeremiah 5:22-24, 44:10, Job 6:14, 15:4-6, 21:7-9, 14-20, Psalms 36:1, 55:19, 85:9, 119:118, 155, 158, 147:11, Malachi 3:5, Proverbs 1:29, Isaiah 57:11, 66:2

New Testament – Matthew 10:28, Romans 3:10-18, Jude 1:12, Luke 13:3, 5

Why Men Are Lost (4)

Old Testament – Jeremiah 23:1, 9-18, 22, 25-32, 9:6, 8:5-6, 7:23-24, 5:25-31, Isaiah 56:10-11, 9:16, Proverbs 20:17, Ezekiel 13:22, Ezekiel 18:31

New Testament – 2 Peter 2:1-3, 19, 21, 3:17, Matthew 15:13-14, 23:13-33, 24:4-5, John 8:24, 2 Corinthians 11:2-4, 1 John 2:3-6

Why Men Are Lost (5)

Old Testament – Deuteronomy 32:28-29, Proverbs 1:23-25, 30, Psalms 1:1-6, 5:10, 81:10-12, 107:11-12, Isaiah 30:1, Hosea 11:6, Micah 4:11-12

New Testament – Acts 3:23, Hebrews 3:12, 4:11, 6:4-6, 10:26-27, 12:14-17 Galatians 5:19-21, 1 Corinthians 6:9-10, 3:17, 2 Thessalonians 1:7-8

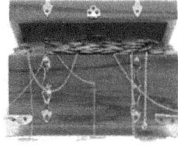

Jesus: Prophecy and Fulfillment

Jesus: Prophecy and Fulfillment (1)

"The sceptre shall not depart from Judah, nor a lawgiver from between his feet, until Shiloh come; and unto him shall the gathering of the people be. (Genesis 49:10)

Jesus: Prophecy and Fullment (2)

"I shall see him, but not now: I shall behold him, but not now: there shall come a Star out of Jacob, and a Sceptre shall rise out of Israel, and shall smite the corners of Moab, and destroy all the children of Sheth. (Numbers 24:17)

Jesus: Prophecy and Fulfillment (3)

"And he shall send Jesus Christ, which before was preached unto you: Whom the heaven must receive until the times of restitution of all things, which God hath spoken by the mouth of all the prophets since the world began." (Acts 3:20-21)

Discussion Questions

1. What passages of Scripture mention that Jesus was born of a virgin?
2. In what passages of Scripture did Moses speak concerning Jesus?

3. Where in the Bible can you find that Jesus was God's beloved son?.

4. List Bible references that teach that Jesus is the Word of God. In what ways do those verses teach that all men should obey Him?

5. What does it mean when the Bible says that Jesus is the propitiation for the sin of the entire world?

Fill in the Blanks

1. "That at the name of____ every knee should____ ."

2. "I know that____ cometh, which is called____ : when he is come, he will tell us____ things."

3. "For unto us a child is____ unto us a son is____ : and the government shall be upon his____ and his name shall be called___ , ___ , ___, ___ , ___ ."

4. "And when he putteth forth his ___, he goeth____ them, and the sheep____ him, for they know his____ ."

5. "And he was____ with a vesture dipped in____ ; and his name is called____ ____ ."

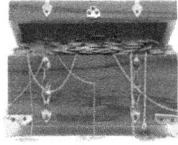

Jesus: Prophecy and Fulfillment

*B*efore the foundation of the world, after the counsel of His own will, God determined that in Christ all spiritual blessings in heavenly places would reside. It was determined that, in Christ, all of mankind would be saved. Indeed, He is the Savior of the world; there is salvation in no other name. (Ephesians 1:1-11, 1 John 4:14, Acts 4:12). All in Christ are to walk before Him in love and without blame. Amazingly, the prophets foretold of His grace, His salvation, and His coming (1 Peter 1:10-12). This indeed is a much needed and fascinating study that will strengthen both the faith and resolve of all Christians.

Jesus: Prophecy & Fulfillment (1)

Old Testament – Genesis 49:10, Numbers 24:16-17, Isaiah 7:14, 9:6-7, 11:1-10, 59:20, 61:1-3, Jeremiah 31:22, Zechariah 9:9, 13:6-7, Psalms 45:6-7, 89:3-4, 132:7-18

New Testament – Matthew 1:18-23, 21:2-11, Luke 1:26-33, 24:27, 32, 44-47, John 5:39, 8:58, Acts 13:24-26

Jesus: Prophecy & Fulfillment (2)

Old Testament – Amos 3:7, Daniel 7:13-14, 9:25-26, Malachi 4:5, 3:1, Jeremiah 31:31-33, 32:40, Isaiah 40:9-11, 53:1-12, 54:7-9, Psalms 89:20-37, 40:6-8, 22:13-18

New Testament – Matthew 26:31-32, Mark 14:58-62, Luke 1:13-17, Galatians 3:6-9, 13-18, 26-29, Romans 16:20, 1 John 3:1-15, Revelation 11:15, 12:1-17

Jesus: Prophecy & Fulfillment (3)

Old Testament – Numbers 21:6-9, Isaiah 8:14-15, 28:16, 32:1-2, 47:4, 49:26, Job 19:5, Zechariah 11:10-13, Psalms 118:22-23, 110:1-4, 69:21, 22:1, 16

New Testament – John 4:24, 6:38-40, 10:1-16, 26-29, 1 Corinthians 10:4, 1 Peter 2:6-8, Hebrews 13:20, Ephesians 1:7, Revelation 5:9

Jesus: Prophecy & Fulfillment (4)

Old Testament – Deuteronomy 18:15, Ecclesiastes 12:11, Ezekiel 34:23, 37:24, Psalms 80:1, 23:1, 16:8-10, 2:1-12, Proverbs 30:4, Isaiah 52:12-15, 42:1-7

New Testament – John 4:25-26, 6:14, 14:6-12, Acts 3:18-26, 1 Peter 2:21-25, Romans 4:23-25, 8:32, Hebrews 10:20, Revelation 17:14, Revelation 19:11-16

Jesus: Prophecy & Fulfillment (5)

Old Testament – Genesis 3:15, 2 Samuel 7:12, 16, Psalms 18:50, 31:5, 41:7-9, 109:8, Isaiah 9:1-2, Micah 5:2-4

New Testament – Luke 24:47, Acts 2:5-12, Acts 2:39-47, 13:47-49, Matthew 16:18-21, 22:41-46, Romans 10:9-13, 1 Corinthians 15:54-55, Revelation 21:4

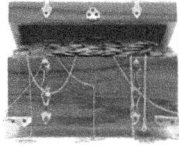

The Blessings and the Curses

The Blessings and the Curses (1)

"Behold, I set before you this day a blessing and a curse; A blessing, if ye obey the commandments of the LORD your God, which I command you this day: And a curse if ye will not obey the commandments of the LORD your God, but turn aside out of the way which I command you this day, to go after other gods, which ye have not known." (Deuteronomy 11:26-28)

The Blessings and the Curses (2)

"For thou, LORD, wilt bless the righteous; with favour wilt thou compass him as with a shield." (Psalm 5:12)

The Blessings and the Curses (3)

"But he said, Yea rather, blessed are they that hear the word of God, and keep it." (Luke 11:28)

Discussion Questions

1. God set before Israel a blessing and a curse. What did this have to do with His commandments?
2. What happens if we sin willfully?
3. When all nations stand before Christ in His glory, how will He separate them?

4. According to Ephesians 1:3, where did God place all spiritual blessings that were in the heavenly places?
5. What is the spirit that works in the children of disobedience?

Fill in the Blanks

1. "The____ of the Lord is in the____ of the____ , but he____ the habitation of the____ ."
2. "These shall stand____ ____ upon to bless."
3. "And these shall stand upon____ ____ to curse."
4. "Blessed be the God and Father of our Lord Jesus Christ, who hath____ us with all ____ ____in heavenly places in____ ."
5. "Blessed is he whose____ is forgiven, whose ____is____ ."

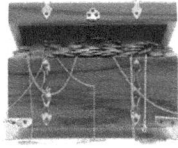

The Blessings and the Curses

*W*e will be blessed tremendously by living a life of obedience to God. In His Word are principles of success for all mankind, provided we walk therein. Unfortunately, there are things that lead to our demise or failure. The life of sin, a life that is contrary to His will, may be pleasurable for a season, but the wages of sin is death.

The Blessings and the the Curses (1)

Old Testament – Gen 12:1-3, 17:1-7, 18:17-19, 22:1-18, Numbers 22:1-12, 18, 23:3-13, 19-26, 24:1-7, 15-23, Deuteronomy 7:9-16, 11:26-29, 23:5, 27:12-13, 28:1-15, 30:15-20, Psalms 5:11-12, 112:1-2, 119:1, 2, 21, Proverbs 3:33

New Testament – Matthew 5:1-12, 13:10-16, 25:31-36, 41-44, Luke 11:27-28, Galatians 3:6-14

The Blessings and the the Curses (2)

Old Testament – Numbers 6:22-27, Leviticus 9:22-24, Deuteronomy 10:1-4, 8, 16:15, 24:19, 29:16-21, Joshua 6:16-18, 8:30-35, Proverbs 8:32-36, 10:6, 22, 11:11, 26, 20:7, 21, Psalms 62:3-4, 65:4, 94:12, 106:3, 109:16-19, 28

New Testament – Matthew 5:44-45, Ephesians 1:3, Romans 12:14, 1 Corinthians 4:12-13, 1 Peter 3:9

The Blessings and the the Curses (3)

Old Testament – Genesis 3:9-19, 5:29, 9:19-27, 49:5-7, Leviticus 24:10-16, 23, Deuteronomy 27:15-26, 28:16-37, Job 1:6-12, 20-22, 2:1-6, 9-10, 5:1-3, 24:2-18, 29:1-13, 31:19-22, 29-30, 42:7-13 Proverbs 30:10-11, Psalms 29:11, 100:4, 128:1, 4

New Testament – Luke 6:28, Acts 3:25-26, Romans 4:6-9, Hebrews 6:7-14

The Blessings and the the Curses (4)

Old Testament – Exodus 34:42-43, Joshua 22:1-7, Leviticus 26:3-12, 14-19, 40-42, Isaiah 19:21-25, 65:8, Jeremiah 17:5-8, 24:1-9, 25:13-18, 26:2-6, Lamentations 3:64-65, Daniel 9:11-14, Zechariah 8:9-13, Haggai 2:4-7, 17-19, Psalms 67:1-7, 103:1-2, 20-22, 115:12-13

New Testament – Luke 1:68, 2:25-34, 7:19-23, Revelation 22:7, 14-19

The Blessings and the the Curses (5)

Old Testament – 1 Chronicles 4:9-10, Isaiah 30:17-18, 32:17-20, 51:1-2, 56:1-2, 61:8-9, Ezekiel 34:21-26, 29-31, Joel 2:12-14, Malachi 3:8-10, Psalms 1:1, 2:12, 32:1-2, 33:12, 72:11-10, 84:4-5, 12, 147:11-147:11-13

New Testament – 1 Timothy 6:5, James 1:12, 25, Revelation 1:3, 14:13, 16:15, 19:9, 20:6

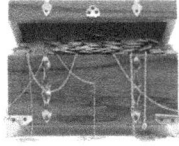

Judge or Judge Not

Judge or Judge Not (1)

"Judge not according to appearance, but judge righteous judgement." (John 7:24)

Judge or Judge Not (2)

"Judge not, that ye be not judged. For with what judgement ye judge, ye shall be judged: and with what measure ye mete, it shall be measured to you again." (Matthew 7:1-2)

Judge or Judge Not (3)

"And Laban said to Jacob, Behold this heap, and behold this pillar, which I cast betwixt me and thee....The God of Abraham, and the God of Nahor, the God of their father, judge betwixt us. And Jacob sware by the fear of his father Isaac.: (Genesis 31:51-53)

Discussion Questions

1. What was the charge given by God to those who were selected to be judges among His people?
2. Explain John 7:24.
3. In 1 Corinthians 5: 1-7, did the apostle Paul judge someone? Explain.
4. Explain James 5:9.

5. Explain Matthew 7:1-5

Fill in the Blanks

1. "And I____ your judges at that time, saying, ____ the causes between your____ , and____ ____ between every man and his____ , and the____ that is with him."
2. "But with me it is a very small thing that I should be____ of you, or of man's____ : yea, I ____not mine own self."
3. "Who art thou that ____another man's____ ? to his own____ he standeth or____ . Yea, he shall be____ up: for God is__ to make him stand."
4. "For I verily, as absent in body, but present in____ , have____ already, as though I were____ , concerning him that hath so____ this____ ."
5. "____ not according to the____ , but ____righteous____ ."

Judge or Judge Not

*T*o judge means "to form an opinion, to give a conclusion." It means "to render an assessment; to sift, to select, to value, to decide." Can we make choices, use discernment, observe? Do we have the right to determine anyone's eternal destination and treat them in a scornful and contemptible manner based on our view of them? What standard should we use in our judgement of others?

Judge or Judge Not (1)

Old Testament – Genesis 15:12-14, 16:3-5, 31:36-37, 48-53, 49:16, Deuteronomy 1:9-17, 16:18-20, 25:1-3, 27:19, Zechariah 8:16-17, Psalms 75:1-2, Isaiah 11:1-4

New Testament – John 5:30, 7:24, 46, 51, 8:15-18, 18:28-38, 19:6-16, 1 Corinthians 4:2-5, 2:15-16, Romans 14:1-4, 10-13

Judge or Judge Not (2)

Old Testament – Exodus 2:11-15, 5:1-9, 20-21, 18:13-24, Leviticus 19:15, 35-37, 2 Chronicles 19:5-7, Ecclesiastes 5:8, Proverbs 31:4-5, 8-9, Isaiah 10:1-3, Jeremiah 22:3, 13-16, Job 34:16-23, 26-28, Micah 3:1-2, 9-12, Psalms 82:1-8, 75:4-7, Joel 3:11-14

New Testament – Matthew 7:1-5, Romans 2:1-5, 16-27, 1 Timothy 1:8-11, James 2:8-13

Judge or Judge Not (3)

Old Testament – Genesis 18:23-25, Deuteronomy 32:35-36, 40-43, Judges 11:27, 1 Samuel 2:10, 24:12-20, 1 Chronicles 16:30-33, 2 Chronicles 6:22-23, 20:9-12, Job 9:11-15, 21:22-26, 31, 22:12-13, 23:2-7, 31:23-28, Psalms 7:6-13, 50:3-6, 58:10-11, 67:4, 94:1-2, 14-17

New Testament – Luke 18:1-8, John 12:47-48, Acts 4:15-20, 10:38-42, 17:30-31, Revelation 18:1-8

Judge or Judge Not (4)

Old Testament – Deuteronomy 17:6-11, 19:16-21, 21:1-9, 24:17, Exodus 21:5-6, 23:1-2, 6-8, 1 Samuel 2:12-17, 22-25, 8:1-5, 12:1-5, Proverbs 28:5, 29:14, Isaiah 26:9-10, Jeremiah 10:24, Psalms 9:4-8, 10:14-18

New Testament – John 5:22-24, 1 Corinthians 5:1-7, 12-13, 6:1-11, James 4:11-12, 5:9

Judge or Judge Not (5)

Old Testament – 1 Kings 3:6-12, 28, Isaiah 2:4, 33:20-22, 51:4-5 Proverbs 16:10 Jeremiah 5:23-28, 11:20 Ezra 7:23, 25-26 Ezekiel 33:18-20, 34:12-17, 20-23 Psalms 2:10-12, 72:2-4, 96:10-13, 98:9, 110:5-6, 135:13-14

New Testament – Acts 13:46, Hebrews 12:22-23, 10:26-30, Romans 3:3-4, 1 Peter 1:17, 2:21-23, 4:5-6 Revelation 20:11-13

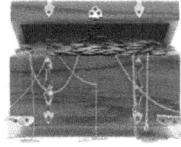

Redemption

Redemption (1)

"Be merciful, O LORD, unto thy people Israel, whom thou hast redeemed, and lay not innocent blood unto thy people of Israel's charge. And the blood shall be forgiven them." (Deuteronomy 21:8)

Redemption (2)

"Blessed be the Lord God of Israel; for He hath visited and redeemed His people," (Luke 1:68)

Redemption (3)

"For I know that my redeemer liveth, and that he shall stand at the latter day upon the earth:" (Job 19:25)

Discussion Questions

1. Discuss Hosea 13:14.
2. Explain Mark 10:45.
3. What observations are made in Hebrews 9:11-15?
4. Discuss Revelation 5:9.
5. What observations are made in Isaiah 35:8-10?

Fill in the Blanks

1. "Blessed be the Lord God of Israel; for he hath____ and____ His people."
2. "Who gave____ a____ for all, to be testified in due time."
3. "For their ____is mighty; he shall____ their cause with thee."
4. "Who gave____ for us, that He might_____ us from all____ , and purify unto himself a peculiar people, ____ of good works."
5. "He sent ____unto His people: he hath commanded his ____for ever; holy and reverend is____ ____ "

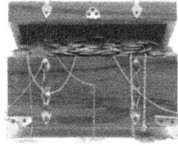

Redemption

*T*he *Strong's Greek Lexicon* defines redemption as "a release effected by payment of ransom; deliverance." Literally, it means "to bring back from or to win back from." The apostle Paul notes in Romans 7:14 (NIV), "But I am unspiritual, sold as a slave to sin." Perhaps this is the best characterization of our spiritual lives. A price had to be paid to redeem us or ransom us from the bondage of sin. Jesus paid that price (Acts 20:28, 1 Corinthians 6:20, 1 Corinthians 7:23).

Redemption (1)

Old Testament – Exodus 6:6-8, 30:12, Hosea 13:14, Isaiah 51:9-11, 43:3, 14-16, 41:10-14, 35:8-10, Proverbs 21:18, 23:11, Jeremiah 50:34, Job 19:22-25, Psalms 19:14

New Testament – Luke 1:68-69, 2:34-38, Mark 10:45, Romans 7:9-14, Hebrews 9:11-15

Redemption (2)

Old Testament – Deuteronomy 7:8, Nehemiah 5:1-12, Ruth 4:3-8, Psalms 49:7-9, 15, 69:18, 72:12-14, 111:7-9, 130:7-9, 1 Chronicles 17:21-22, Isaiah 52:3, 19, 47:4, 29:22-24

New Testament – Luke 21:21:27-28, Romans 3:24, 8:21-23, Titus 2:14, Hebrews 2:14-15, 1 Timothy 2:3-6

Redemption (3)

Old Testament – Deuteronomy 21:8, 9:26, 2 Samuel 7:23-24, Nehemiah 1:10-11, Micah 6:1-4, 4:9-10, Psalms 31:5, 34:22, 71:23, 74:2, 77:15, 78:34-35, 103:1-4, 107:2, Isaiah 59:20, 62:12

New Testament – 1 Corinthians 1:30, 6:20, Acts 20:28, 1 Peter 1:18-19, Revelation 14:3-4

Redemption (4)

Old Testament – Job 36:18-19, 33: 18, 24, 5:18-20, Isaiah 50:2-3, 49:6-8, 24-26, 48:17, 20, 44:6, 22-24, 38:16-17, 1:26-27 Jeremiah 15:21, Psalms 106:10

New Testament – Galatians 5:1, 4:3-5, 2:19-20, Colossians 1:12-14, Revelation 5:9

Redemption (5)

Old Testament – Leviticus 25:47-48, Deuteronomy 15:15, Job 6:21-23, 17:3, Isaiah 54:5, 8, 60:14-16, 63:9, 16, Psalms 25:22, 26:11, 44:6, 26, 136:24, 1 Kings 1:29-30, Lamentations 3:58, Zechariah 10:8

New Testament – Matthew 26:28, 1 Corinthians 7:23, Ephesians 1:7, 13-14, 4:30, Revelation 1:5-6

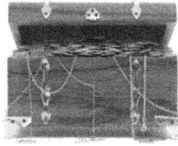

Obedience

Obedience (1)

"But this thing commanded I them, saying, Obey my voice, and I will be your God, and ye shall be my people: and walk in all the ways that I have commanded you, that it may be well unto you." (Jeremiah 7:23)

Obedience (2)

"And we are his witnesses of these things: and so is also the Holy Ghost, whom God hath given to him them that obey Him." (Acts 5:32)

Obedience (3)

"Ye shall walk after the LORD your God, and fear Him, and keep His commandments, and obey His voice, and ye shall serve Him, and cleave unto Him." (Deuteronomy 13:4)

Discussion Questions

1. What observations are noted in Deuteronomy 4:29-31?
2. Discuss Acts 5:29, 32.
3. Explain 2 Corinthians 10:5.
4. Discuss Ezekiel 33:30-32.
5. Discuss Romans 13:1-2.

Fill in the Blanks

1. "And being made perfect, he became the____ of eternal salvation unto all them that____ him."
2. "For to this end also did I____ , that I might know the____ of you, whether ye be____ in all things."
3. "Ye shall walk after the Lord your God, and fear him, and____ his____ , and his , and ye shall serve him, and cleave unto him."
4. "If ye be____ and____ , ye shall eat the good of the land."
5. "Ye did run well; who did hinder you that ye should not____ the ____?"

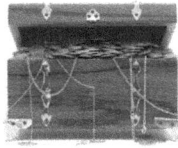

Obedience

O bedience necessitates that we submit ourselves to the will of another. At that point, our wills become imbued or intertwined in such a way that oneness is accomplished. Having oneness with God is a wonderful thing; thus, His will is accomplished.

Obedience (1)

Old Testament – Exodus 19:3-6, 24:7, Deuteronomy 13:4, 11:26-28, 5:27-29, 4:29-31, Daniel 7:27, 9:8-11, Joshua 24:20-24, Jeremiah 7:23, 28, 11:1-4, 7-8, 22:21, Psalms 119:2-10, 17, 21, Ezekiel 36:27-28, Nehemiah 9:24-26, 30-35

New Testament – Luke 6:46-49, Hebrews 2:1-3, John 14:21, 24, Acts 5:29, 32, Romans 2:6-9, 2 Thessalonians 1:6-8, 3:14

Obedience (2)

Old Testament – Deuteronomy 8:13-20, 27:9-10, 28:1-2, 15, 30:1-3, 19-20, Job 36:5-12, 23:11-12, 1 Samuel 12:14-15, 13:11-14, 15:19-24, Psalms 78:5-11 Ezekiel 33:30-32, Proverbs 30:17, 25:12, 7:1-3, 4:1-4

New Testament – John 15:10 Acts 6:7, Romans 1:1-5, 18, 29-30, 5:19, 10:13-17, 16:25-26 Colossians 3:5-6

Obedience (3)

Old Testament – Deuteronomy 8:3, 6, 18:18-22, Joshua 22:1-4, Jeremiah 35:2-10, 14-19, 26:12, 18:7-13, Zephaniah 3:1-5, Psalms 81:10-16, 119:2-10, 21, 53

New Testament – 2 Corinthians 10:3-5, 2:9, Acts 3:20-23, Titus 1:16, 3:1-3, Ephesians 5:3-6, 1 Timothy 1:9-10, 2 Timothy 3:1-2

Obedience (4)

Old Testament – Jeremiah 42:5-6, 20-22, 38:19-20, 32:33, 6:16-19, Leviticus 26:27-28, 40-42, Nehemiah 9:13-17, 2 Chronicles 19:7, Psalms 78:5-8, Isaiah 1:16-20, 42:23-25, 50:10

New Testament – Hebrews 5:8-9, 13:17, Romans 13:1-2, 6:12-18, Luke 6:46-49

Obedience (5)

Old Testament – Genesis 22:18, 26:4-5, Exodus 23:20-22, Deuteronomy 8:10-11, 19-20, 1 Samuel 28:16-28, 2 Chronicles 11:3-4, Zechariah 6:11-15, Psalms 18:43-44

New Testament – Luke 8:25, 11:27-28, 17:6-10 John 8:51, Philippians 2:5-8, 12, Philemon 1:21, 2 Corinthians 7:15, 1 Peter 4:17, 1:14, Ephesians 2:2

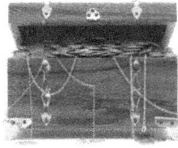

It Is All about God

It Is all about God (1)

"Thou art worthy, O Lord, to receive glory and honour and power: for thou hast created all things, and for thy pleasure they are and were created." (Revelation 4:11)

It Is all about God (2)

"Behold, the heaven and the heaven of heavens is the Lord's thy God, the earth also, with all that therein is." (Deuteronomy 10:14)

It Is all about God (3)

"For of Him, and through Him, are all things: to whom be glory for ever. Amen. (Romans 11:36)

Discussion Questions

1. What observations were made in Daniel 4:34-35?
2. Discuss Isaiah 40:21-26.
3. Explain Hebrews 12:28-29.
4. What observations are mentioned in Job 38:4-13?
5. Explain Romans 11:36.

Fill in the Blanks

1. "Behold, the____ and the____ of____ is the Lord's thy God, the____ also, with all that therein is."

2. "In whom also we have____ an____ , being predestinated according to the____ of him who worketh all things after the____ of his own will."

3. "And Jesus looking upon them saith, With men it is____ , but not with____ : for with God all things are_____ ."

4. "Thou art____ , O Lord, to receive glory and honour and power: for thou hast_____ all things, and for____ ____ they are and were____ ."

5. "O house of Israel, cannot I do with you as this____ ? saith the Lord. Behold as the ____is in the____ hand, so are ye in____ ____ , O house of Israel."

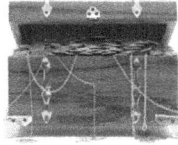

It Is All about God

"Thine, O Lord, is the greatness, and the power, and the glory, and the victory, and the majesty: for all that is in the heaven and in the earth is thine; thine is the kingdom, O Lord, and thou art exalted as head above all. Both riches and honour come of thee, and thou reignest over all; and in thine hand is power and might; and in thine hand it is to make great, and to give strength unto all" (1 Chronicles 29:11-12).

"For thou art great, and doest wondrous things; thou art God alone" (Psalms 86:10).

*M*ay we always remember, in our worship, in our praise, in our thanksgiving, in our adoration, and even in our living, that it is all about God. To Him alone belong the praise, honor, and glory. An outpouring from our soul, mind, and spirit should testify about the goodness of God. It is truly all about God.

It Is All about God (1)

Old Testament – Daniel 4:34-35, 2:20, Deuteronomy 10:14, 17, 20-21, 32:2-3, Exodus 15:2, Leviticus 25:23, Haggai 2:8, Psalms 50:7-12, 86:10, 115:3, Jeremiah 27:5, Isaiah 45:12-13, 44:24, 43:21, 37:16

New Testament – 1 Corinthians 10:26, 28, Romans 11:36, Colossians 1:16-17, Galatians 1:10

It Is All about God (2)

Old Testament – Exodus 15:11, Lamentations 3:37, Micah 7:18, 2 Samuel 22:31-32, Deuteronomy 4:7-8, Proverbs 30:4, 16:4, 1 Kings 8:53, Isaiah, 40:18, 63:3, Job 26:6-14, 38:4-13, 41:11, Psalms 90:2, 135:6

New Testament – 1 Corinthians 1:29-31, 3:21, 2 Corinthians 4:7, Ephesians 3:9, Colossians 3:10, Revelation 4:11, 10:6

It Is All about God (3)

Old Testament – 1 Samuel 3:18, 2 Samuel 10:12, 15:26, 24:14, Leviticus 10:3, Numbers 18:29, 32, Proverbs 3:9, Psalms 68:29, 72:9-11, 76:11, 89:6-8, 2 Chronicles 32:23, Malachi 1:11, 14, Isaiah 60:3-7, 17, 21, 40:21-26, 14:25-27

New Testament – Ephesians 1:11, Hebrews 12:28, Romans 9:16

It Is All about God (4)

Old Testament – Genesis 18:14, Deuteronomy 27:8-11, 1 Samuel 14:6, 2 Samuel 7:18-19, Hosea 11:9, 2 Kings 3:17-18, Isaiah 8:10, 40:15-17, 41:10, 46:9-10, Jeremiah 20:11, 32:17, 27, Job 42:2, Psalms 56:9, 60:12, Zechariah 4:6

New Testament – Mark 10:27, Romans 8:31, Acts 5:39, 1 Corinthians 10:22

It Is All about God (5)

Old Testament – Jeremiah 18:2-10, Lamentations 4:2, Job 4:17-19, 10:8-9, Isaiah 29:16, 2 Chronicles 20:12, Psalms 145:15, 141:8, 123:1-2, 121:1-2, 42:1, 35:3, 25:15, Nehemiah 9:6

New Testament – Romans 9:19-23, Ephesians 2:10, Colossians 1:10, Hebrews 11:5, 13:16, 1 John 3:22, John 8:29

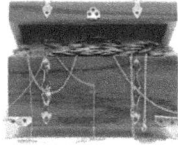

The Inheritance

The Inheritance (1)

"To an inheritance incorruptible, and undefiled, and that fadeth not away, reserved in heaven for you." (1 Peter 1:4)

The Inheritance (2)

"House and riches are the inheritance of fathers: but a prudent wife is from the LORD." (Proverbs 19:14)

The Inheritance (3)

"And now, brethren, I commend you to God, and to the word of his grace, which is able to build you up, and to give you an inheritance among all them that are sanctified." (Acts 20:32)

Discussion Questions

1. Discuss Psalms 16:5-6.
2. What observations are made in Genesis 15:7-14?
3. Explain Acts 26:18.
4. Explain Proverbs 11:29.
5. Discuss Ephesians 5:5.

Fill in the Blanks

1. "Save thy people, and bless thine____ : feed them also, and lift them up for ever."
2. "Then shall the____ say unto them on his right hand, Come, ye____ of my Father, ____the kingdom prepared for you from the____ of the world."
3. "To open their eyes, and to turn them from____ to____ , and from the power of____ unto God, that they may receive ____of sins, and ____among them which are____ by faith that is in me."
4. "Knowing that of the Lord ye shall receive the reward of the____ : for ye serve the Lord Christ."
5. "Giving thanks unto the Father, which hath made us meet to be____ of the____ of the____ in light."

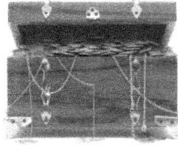

The Inheritance

"That in the dispensation of the fulness of times he might gather together in one all things in Christ, both which are in heaven, and which are on earth; even in him: In whom also we have obtained an inheritance" (Ephesians 1:10-11).

These words of assurance were framed to encourage and enlighten those who are in Christ. As we journey through the present world in which we now exist, this affirmation gives us hope that we will inherit the promises of God. We have an inheritance that God gives to those who belong to Him.

The Inheritance (1)

Old Testament – Deuteronomy 4:20, 37-38, 9:26-29, 32:9, 1 Samuel 10:1, 2 Samuel 14:16, 1 Kings 8:51-53, Psalms 16:5-6, 28:9, 33:12, 74:2, 106:40, 135:12, Jeremiah 10:16

New Testament – Matthews 19:27-29, Acts 20:32, Acts 26:15-18, Colossians 1:12, 3:24

The Inheritance (2)

Old Testament – Genesis 12:7, 15:7-14, 25:5, 28:3-4, Exodus 23:29-30, 32:13, Leviticus 20:22-24, Numbers 18:20-21, Joshua 1:6, 14:9, Psalms 2:7-10, 37:9-11, 111:6, Isaiah 60:21

New Testament – Matthew 5:5, 19:29, 1 Corinthians 2:9, 6:9-10, Romans 4:13, Romans 8:17, Titus 3:7

The Inheritance (3)

Old Testament – Deuteronomy 3:27-28, 12:10-12, Numbers 27:1-11, Joshua 11:23, Proverbs 11:29, 13:22, 17:2, 19:14, 20:21, Psalms 37:18, 78:70-71, 106:4-5

New Testament – Luke 12:13-15, Mark 10:17-24, Ephesians 1:9-11, 5:5, Galatians 3:18, 29, 4:30, 5:19-21, Revelation 21:7

The Inheritance (4)

Old Testament – Ezekiel 22:16, 44:15, 27-28, 1 Samuel 2:8-9, Isaiah 19:23-25, 49:8, 54:3, 57:11-13, 63:17, 65:8-9, Zechariah 2:12, Ecclesiastes 7:11, Psalms 37:29, 34, 47:1-4, 61:5, 69:34-36, 105:6-11

New Testament – James 2:5, Matthew 25:34-40, Hebrews 6:12, 9:15, 11:8, 10

The Inheritance (5)

Old Testament – Ezekiel 33:21-24, 35:10-15, Lamentations 5:1-2, Malachi 1:3, Jeremiah 3:17-18, 12:14-15, 16:17-18, 50:8-11, 51:19, Job 27:13-14, Proverbs 8:20-21, 3:35, Psalms 119:111, 136:16-21

New Testament – Hebrews 12:14-16, 1 Peter 1:2-4, 3:9, 5:2-3

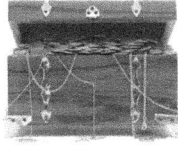

Our Days

Our Days (1)

"And Jacob said unto Pharoah, The days of the years of my pilgrimage are an hundred and thirty years: few and evil have the days of the years of my life been, and have not attained unto the days of the years of my fathers in the days of their pilgrimage." (Genesis 47:9)

Our Days (2)

"For our days are passed away in thy wrath: we spend our years as a tale that is told...So teach us to number our days, that we may apply our hearts unto wisdom." (Psalms 90:9, 12)

Our Days (3)

"Walk in wisdom toward them that are without, redeeming the time." (Colossians 4:5)

Discussion Questions

1. Discuss Proverbs 16:31.
2. Discuss Ephesians 5:15-16.
3. What observations did Solomon make in Ecclesiastes 11:7-10?
4. Explain 1 Thessalonians 5:4-8.
5. Discuss the days mentioned in Acts 3:24.

Fill in the Blanks

1. "Because to every purpose there is____ and____ , therefore the____ of man is great upon him."
2. "Walk in_____ toward them that are without, ____ the time."
3. "Surely____ and ____shall follow me all the days of my___ : and I will dwell in the house of the____ for ever."
4. "Because he hath appointed a ____, in the which he will____ the world in righteousness by that man whom he hath ordained."
5. "This know also, that in the last____ ____ times shall come."

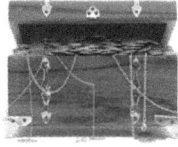

Our Days

"For all our days are passed away in thy wrath: we spend our years as a tale that is told" So teach us to number our days that we might apply our hearts unto wisdom" (Psalms 90:9).

*T*he Psalmist gives a profound and thought-provoking view of life and exhorts us not to live haphazardly or frivolously, but to number our days. We should invoke the help of God to assist us in living from day to day.

Our Days (1)

Old Testament – Genesis 3:17, 6:3, 47:9, Ecclesiastes 2:3-11, 16-23, 5:15-20, 6:3-7, 12, Psalms 34:12-16, 90:3-12, Job 7:7-10, 17-18, 23:13-14, 32:7-9, 119:100, Proverbs 16:31, 9:10-11

New Testament – Luke 1:68-75, Ephesians 1:4, 5:15-16, Colossians 4:5

Our Days (2)

Old Testament – Ecclesiastes 11:8-10, 9:9-10, 8:5-13, 7:14-18, Deuteronomy 4:9-10, 40, 5:33, 6:1-2, 11:26-32, Psalms 1:1-2, 21:1-4, 23:6, 27:4, 37:18-19, 39:4-7

New Testament – Luke 12:15-23, 16:19-25, 17:20-30, 2 Peter 3:18-14, Acts 17:31

Our Days (3)

Old Testament – Job 29:2-4, 17-18, 30:16, 27, 36:6-11, Ecclesiastes 2:3, 16, 12:1, Proverbs 3:1-2, 13-16, 10:27, 15:15, 24:10, 27:10, 31:10-12, Psalms 103:15-18, 89:47-48, 1 Chronicles 29:15

New Testament – James 4:13-15, 1 Thessalonians 5:4-8, Acts 3:24, 2 Corinthians 5:15

Our Days (4)

Old Testament – 1 Kings 3:10-14, 4:21, 8:37-40, 15:4-5, 2 Chronicles 15:15, 17, 24:2, 34:33, Joshua 24:31, Psalms 128:1-5, 94:11-13, 72:1-7, 49:3, 5, 44:1-2, 8 Isaiah 65:19-22

New Testament – Mark 2:19-20, Hebrews 5:7-9, 8:8-13, Romans 13:11-14

Our Days (5)

Old Testament – Job 7:1, 9:25, 14:1-9, 15:20, 30-33, Psalms 37:35-36, 55:23, 72:7, 94:9-13, 102:11, 24-28, 128:1, 5, 144:4, Isaiah 65:19-23, 1 Kings 8:38-40, 15:4-5

New Testament – Galatians 2:20, Romans 14:7-8, Hebrews 10:16, 2 Timothy 3:1-5, 1 Timothy 4:1

Be Ye Holy

Be Ye Holy (1)

"Speak unto all the congregation of the children of Israel, and say unto them, Ye shall be holy: for I am holy: for I the LORD your God am holy." (Leviticus 19:2)

Be Ye Holy (2)

"According as he hath chosen us in him before the foundation of the world, that we should be holy and without blame before him in love:" (Ephesians 1:4)

Be Ye Holy (3)

"Who hath saved us, and called us with an holy calling, not according to our works, but according to his own purpose and grace, which was given us in Christ Jesus before the world began," (2 Timothy 1:9)

Discussion Questions

1. Explain Hebrews 10:10-14, 29.
2. Explain Colossians 1:19-22.
3. Can we be holy in God's eyesight without the blood of Christ to atone for our sins? Discuss.
4. What does it mean to be part of a royal priesthood according to 1 Peter 2:9?

5. Discuss Leviticus 19:2.

Fill in the Blanks

1. "According as he hath chosen us in him before the foundation of the____, that we should be____ and without____ before
   Him in____."
2. "For thou art an____ people unto the Lord thy God, and the
   Lord hath chosen thee to be a ____people unto____, above all
   the nations that are upon the____."
3. "Give unto the Lord the____ due unto His name; worship the
   Lord in the beauty of____."
4. "Who shall ascend into the hill of the Lord? or who shall____
   in his____ ____?"
5. "He sent redemption unto his people: he hath commanded
   His covenant for ever: ____and____ is his name."

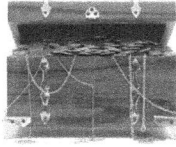

Be Ye Holy

"Be ye holy; for I am holy" (1 Peter 1:16).

*W*e must always recognize that the God we serve and follow is holy. Therefore, with all our might, we strive to be partakers of His divine nature by rising above the evil allurements, the sinful passions and temptations, and any encumbrance that is contrary to the character and holiness of God. In this struggle, we do not win every battle, but—thanks be to God—because of the blood of Christ, we are cleansed when we fall short and able to overcome whatever challenges we face in living a holy life.

Be Ye Holy (1)

Old Testament – Leviticus 19:2, 11:45, 10:10-11, Deuteronomy 28:9-10, 26:18-19, 23:14, 14:2, 7:6, 1 Samuel 2:2, 6:20, Psalms 24:3-4, 119:9, Isaiah 4:2-3

New Testament – 2 Timothy 1:9, 2:19, 1 Thessalonians 4:7, Ephesians 1:4, 2:19-21, 5:27, 1 Peter 1:15-19, 2:9, 2 Peter 3:9-11

Be Ye Holy (2)

Old Testament – Exodus 19:6-8, 22:31, 28:36, 38, Zechariah 14:20-21, 1 Chronicles 16:29, 2 Chronicles 20:21, 23:6, 30:27, 31:14-18, Psalms 65:4, 86:2, 93:5

New Testament – Luke 1:68-75, Romans, 6:18-19, 12:1-2, Hebrews 3:1-2, 7:24-26, 12:10, 14, 2 Corinthians 7:1, 1 Timothy 2:8

Be Ye Holy (3)

Old Testament – Numbers 6:1-8, 21, 15:37-40, Leviticus 27:26-33, 22:1-10, 20-32, 21:1-8, Exodus 19:10, 14, 22, 29:43-44, Proverbs 9:10, 20:25, Psalms 29:2, 96:9, 111:9

New Testament – Hebrews 2:9-11, 10:10-14, 29, Colossians 1:19-22, 3:12, Ephesians 4:22-24

Be Ye Holy (4)

Old Testament – Exodus 3:3-5, Joshua 5:13-15, 24:19-24, Isaiah 63:15-19, 62:8-12, 52:1, 35:8-9, 17:7, Ezekiel 20:37-41, 36:17-38, 43:7-12, Psalms 22:3, 30:4, 43:3, 93:5, 145:17, 21

New Testament – Revelation 22:11, 19, 15:4, 4:8, 1 Corinthians 3:17

Be Ye Holy (5)

Old Testament – Deuteronomy 33:8-10, Leviticus 20:22-26, Ezekiel 22:24-26, 44:5-8, 13-15, 23, Haggai 2:11-14, Proverbs 30:2-3, Jeremiah 11:14-15, Hosea 11:9, Zephaniah 3:11, Ezra 8:28, 9:8, Psalms 97:12, 99:3, 5, 9, Zechariah 8:3, 2 Kings 4:9

New Testament – 2 Peter 1:21, 3:2, Acts 3:21, Romans 1:1-2.

Abide

Abide (1)

"He that dwelleth in the secret place of the most High shall abide under the shadow of thy wings. Selah." (Psalms 91:1)

Abide (2)

"The fear of the LORD tendeth to life: and he that hath it shall abide satisfied, he shall not be visited with evil." (Proverbs 19:23)

Abide (3)

"If ye keep my commandments, ye shall abide in my love; even as I have kept my Father's commandments and abide in His love." (John 15:10)

Discussion Questions

1. According to Psalms 15: 1-6, what types of individuals will abide in God's holy tabernacle?
2. Discuss 1 Samuel 22:23.
3. Discuss John 15:4-10.
4. Explain 1 Timothy 1:3.
5. Explain 2 John 1:9.

Fill in the Blanks

1. "Who can stand before his____ ? and who can____ in the fierceness of his anger?"
2. "For he____ to the Lord, and ____not from following him, but kept His____ , which the Lord commanded Moses."
3. "And I will pray the Father, and he shall give you another____ , that he may____ with you for ever."
4. "Thy____ is unto all generations: thou hast established the earth, and it____ ."
5. "And now___ faith, hope, charity, these three; but the greatest of these is ____."

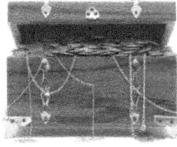

Abide

O nce knowledge of the will of God is ascertained, we must abide in God's commands. We must be anchored by them. We must not allow anything or anyone to sway us from the teachings of our Lord and Savior, Jesus Christ. To stay put, to hold fast, to cling, and to dwell within the will of God differentiates us, molds us, and fashions us as Christians.

Abide (1)

Old Testament – Psalms 15:1-6, 16:8, 61:2-4, 7, 62:2-6, 91:1-2, 1 Samuel 22:23, 19:2, 1:22, Isaiah 50:10, 54:17, Job 24:13, Proverbs 7:11, 19:23, Deuteronomy 10:20, 13:4

New Testament – John 15:4-10, 14:15-16, 1 John 2:6, 10-14, 24-28, 3:6, 14-15, 24

Abide (2)

Old Testament – Nehemiah 1:6-10, Malachi 3:1-2, Joel 2:11, Judges 9:8-15, Isaiah 3:12, Jeremiah 13:11, Joshua 23:6-8, Deuteronomy 11:22-25, 2 Samuel 16:8, 2 Kings 18:5-6, Micah 5:2-4, Psalms 125:1, 112:6, 21:7

New Testament – John 12:46, Acts 11:21-23, Romans 11:21-23, 12:9, 1 Corinthians 3:9-14.

Abide (3)

Old Testament – Ecclesiastes 8:15, Numbers 31:21-23, 53, Joel 2:11-14, Job 39:9-10, 26-28, 38:38-41, Psalms 49:12-13, 55:19, 119:90, 2 Samuel 22:19-22, Isaiah 48:2, 10:20, Jeremiah 32:40, 31:35-36, Proverbs 27:8, 21:16

New Testament – John 3:36, 8:34-36, 12:24, 34-36, Jude 1:21

Abide (4)

Old Testament – Deuteronomy 4:3-4, 30:19-20, Joshua 22:2, 5, 23:11-12, Numbers 2:5, 1 Samuel 5:6-7, 1 Kings 8:13, 27, 1 Chronicles 29:13-15, Jeremiah 21:8-9, 10:10, Isaiah 26:20, Lamentations 4:20, Psalms 63:7-8, 57:1, 119:31

New Testament – Matthew 23:37, John 5:38, 2 Timothy 2:13, Hebrews 7:1-3, 3:12-14

Abide (5)

Old Testament – Genesis 22:5, 14, Leviticus 8:33-35, Deuteronomy 3:19, 2 Samuel 15:19-21, 2 Chronicles 25:19-20, 32:10-15, 21, Jeremiah 26:19, 42:10-16, 44:26-29, 50:40, Psalms 18:18, Isaiah 14:1, Proverbs 4:20-21, 27, 15:31

New Testament – 1 Timothy 1:3, 2 John 1:9, 1 Corinthians 7:20, 24, 13:8, 13

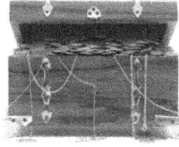

The Door/Gate

The Door/Gate (1)

"Continue in prayer, and watch in the same with thanksgiving; Withal praying also for us, that God would open unto us a door of utterance, to speak the mystery of Christ, for which I am also in bonds:" (Colossians 4:2-3)

The Door/Gate (2)

"Have mercy upon me. O LORD; consider my trouble which I suffer of the that hate me, thou that liftest me up from the gates of death: That I may shew forth all thy praise in the gates of the daughter of Zion: I will rejoice in thy salvation. (Psalms 9:13-14)

The Door/Gate (3)

"Blessed are they that do his commandments, that they may have the right to the tree of life, and may enter through the gates into the city." (Revelation 22:14)

Discussion Questions

1. What observations are made in John 10:1-7?
2. Explain Luke 13:24-28.
3. Discuss Psalms 24:7-10?
4. What transpires in Matthew 25:1-10?

5. Explain Revelation 3:7-8, 20.

Fill in the Blanks

1. "If thou doest___ , shall thou not be____ ? and if thou doest not well, sin lieth at the____ . And unto thee shall be his desire, and thou shalt____ over him."
2. "Behold, I stand at the___ , and ___: if any man hear my___ , and open the door, I will come in to him and will sup with him, and he with me."
3. "Enter ye in at the____ ____ : for wide is the____ , and broad is the way, that leadeth to destruction, and many there be which go in thereat."
4. "She crieth at the____ , at the entry of the city, at the coming in at the____ ."
5. "I am the____ : by me if any man____ ____ , he shall be____ , and shall go in and out, and find____ ."

The Door/Gate

"Enter into his gates with thanksgiving, and into his courts with praise: be thankful unto him, and bless his name" (Psalms 100:4).

"And I will give her vineyards from thence, and the valley of Achor for a door of hope" (Hosea 2:15).

*G*od has always provided a way or entrance into God's holy habitation or domain. Jesus Himself is the Door, the Way, the Portal, the Gate that all mankind must enter in order to have eternal life.

The Door/Gate (1)

Old Testament – Genesis 4:7, 28:12, 17, 2 Chronicles 23:19, 29:3-5, 1 Chronicles 9:21-23, Malachi 1:10, Ezekiel 44:1-11, Isaiah 62:10, 60:11, 26:2, 20, Psalms 147:12-13, 122:2, 7, 118:19-20, 100:4, 84:10, 24:7-10

New Testament – John 10:1-7, Matthew 7:13-14, Luke 13:24-28

The Door/Gate (2)

Old Testament – Zechariah 11:1-2, 8:16, Jeremiah 1:15, 7:2-7, 14:2, 17:19-21, 22:1-4, 26:10-15, Isaiah 24:5-12, Amos 5:10-12, Micah 1:12, Proverbs 1:20-23, 8:3-9, 34-36, 22:22-23, 31:10, 23, 31

New Testament – 2 Peter 1:10-11, Revelation 22:14, 4:1, 3:7-8, 20

The Door/Gate (3)

Old Testament – Genesis 22:17, 24:60, Exodus 32:26-27, Deuteronomy 23:14-17, 22:23-24, 21:18-21, Numbers 15:32-36, 2 Kings 6:32-33, Lamentations 1:4, 4:12, 18, Isaiah 45:1-3, Hosea 2:15, Psalms 87:1-3

New Testament – Hebrews 13:10-13, 1 Corinthians 16:9, 2 Corinthians 2:12, Revelation 21:9-25

The Door/Gate (4)

Old Testament – Exodus 12:7, 21-23, Deuteronomy 6:4-9, 11:16-20, 12:15-18, Leviticus 12:42-46, 24:10-14, Joshua 20:1-4, Ruth 4:1-2, 10-11, Job 38:8-11, Lamentations 5:12, 14, 2:9-10, Isaiah 3:26, 14:31, Psalms 9:13-14

New Testament – Colossians 4:2-3, Acts 14:27, 5:19-20, James 5:9

The Door/Gate (5)

Old Testament – Deuteronomy 17:2-5, 28:47-52, Ezekiel 21:1-15, 26:10, 38:10-11, Judges 5:8-11, Nahum 3:13, Jeremiah 15:7, 51:58, Nehemiah 2:1-3, 12-18, 3:1, 3, 6, 13-15, 32, 4:1-3, 12:25, 30, Proverbs 14:19

New Testament – Luke 5-10, Matthew 25:1-10, John 10:9-10

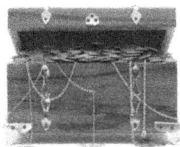

Children of God

Children of God (1)

"Ye are the children of the LORD your God: ye shall not cut yourselves, nor make any baldness between your eyes for the dead. (Deuteronomy 14:1)

Children of God (2)

"For as many as are led by the Spirit of God, they are the sons of God:" (Romans 14:1)

Children of God (3)

"Blessed are the peacemakers: for they shall be called the children of God." (Matthew 5:9)

Discussion Questions

1. Discuss Acts 2:38-39.
2. What observations are made in Galatians 4:4-7, 28-31?
3. Discuss Genesis 6:1-4.
4. Discuss Isaiah 9:6.
5. Explain Luke 20:34-36.

Fill in the Blanks

1. "Ye are the____ of the____ your____ : ye shall not cut your-selves, nor make any baldness between your eyes for the ____."

2. "The____ itself beareth witness with our____ , that we are the ____of ____.

3. "Ye are all the children of____ , and the children of the____ : we are not of the____ nor of____ ."

4. "In this the____ of ____are manifest, and the____ of the____ : whosoever doeth not____ is not of____ , neither he that loveth not his____ ."

5. "I have said, Ye are gods; and all of you are____ of the most____ ."

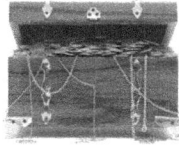

Children of God

O ne of the greatest distinctions a man can ever have is to be known as a child of God. It is a most notable and praiseworthy accomplishment. This relationship should be revered and treasured by all who obey the gospel of our Lord and Savior Jesus Christ.

> "But as many as received him, to them gave he power to become the sons of God, even to them that believe on his name" (John 1:12).

Children of God (1)

Old Testament – Deuteronomy 14:1, 8:5-6, Exodus 4:22, Isaiah 43:5-7, 45:11-12, 63:16, Jeremiah 3:18-19

New Testament – Romans 8:14-21, Matthew 3:9, 5:9, 6:6, 9, 13:36-38, 17:25-26, 18:3-7, John 1:10-12, Acts 2:38-39, 3:22-25, Galatians 4:4-7, 28-31.

Children of God (2)

Old Testament – Genesis 6:1-4, Job 1:6, 2:1, 38:4, 7, Exodus 22:29, Psalms 149:2, 127:3, 103:13-14, 89:27, 30-36, Isaiah 8:18

New Testament – Hebrews 12:5-11, 2:9-15, Romans 9:1-8, 24-27, Acts 10:34-36, 13:23-26, 33-39, 2 Corinthians 6:17-18, Revelation 21:5-7.

Children of God (3)

Old Testament – Hosea 11:7, 10, 13:13, Isaiah 1:2-4, 3:4, 12, 29:22-24, 54:1, 13-17, 63:7-8, Psalms 68:4-6, 82:6, Malachi 2:10

New Testament – Matthew 12:47-50, Luke 6:35, 11;11-13, 16:8-9, 1 Thessalonians 5:5, 1 Peter 2:9-10, Ephesians 2:2, 5:1, 6, 8

Children of God (4)

Old Testament – Hosea 1:10, Isaiah 64:8, Psalms 27:10, Jeremiah 31:1, 9, 20, 3:14, 20, Deuteronomy 32:5-6, 20

New Testament – John 8:38-44, 47, 1 John 3:1-2, 7-10, 18, 4:4, 5:1-4, 18, 1 Peter 1:14, 17, Colossians 3:5-6, Philippians 2:14-15, Acts 17:28-30

Children of God (5)

Old Testament – Psalms 2:7, 12, 1 Chronicles 17:11-13, Isaiah 22:21-25

New Testament – Luke 1:13-17, 7:31-35, 20:34-36, Matthew 9:15, 15:26-27, 19:13-14, Mark 10:23-24, John 11:49-52, 13:33, Galatians 3:7, 26-29, 4:19, 28-31, 1 John 2:28, Acts 13:33

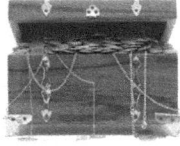

Because

Because (1)

"Because I will publish the name of the LORD: ascribe ye greatness unto our God." (Deuteronomy 32:3)

Because (2)

"Because strait is the gate, and narrow is the way, which leadeth unto life, and few there be that find it." (Matthew 7:14)

Because (3)

"The world cannot hate you; but me it hateth, because I testify of it, that the works thereof are evil." (John 7:7)

Discussion Questions

1. What observations are made in Deuteronomy 32:3, 46-47?
2. Discuss John 7:7.
3. Explain Proverbs 1:24-29.
4. Explain Isaiah 8:20.
5. Discuss Hebrews 4:4-6.

Fill in the Blanks

1. "Because____ is the gate, and____ is the way, which leadeth unto ____, and few there be that____ it."
2. "And ____iniquity shall abound, the____ of many shall wax___ ."
3. " ____sentence against an evil work is not executed____ , therefore the heart of the sons of men is fully set in them to do____ ."
4. "The robbery of the____ shall destroy them; ____they refuse to do____ ."
5. "The world cannot hate you; but me it____ , because I testify of it, that the works thereof are____ ."

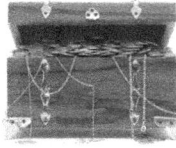

Because

With this particular topic, passages of Scripture are listed as explanations for why things transpire the way they do.

> "My people are destroyed for lack of knowledge: because thou hast rejected knowledge, I will also reject thee..." (Hosea 4:6).

Because (1)

Old Testament – Deuteronomy 32:3, 46-47, 28:47-48, 23:2-5, 18:9-12, 8:19-20, 1 Kings 21:29, 2 Kings 22:18-20, Ecclesiastes 8:6, 11, 13, 10:15, 12, 9, Psalms 91:9-10, 107:17, 116:1-2

New Testament – Matthew 7:14, Luke 10:19-20, 13:2-3, John 7:7, 3:18-19

Because (2)

Old Testament – Jonah 1:7-10, Daniel 3:29, 6:23, Hosea 4:1, 6, 10, 8:7, 11, 10:9, 13, 11:5-6, Amos 4:11-12, Psalms 5:8, 11, 13:3-6, 14:4-6, 16:8, 18:16-19, 119:53-56, 62, 74, 100, 136, 158, 164

New Testament – Matthew 9:36, 11:20, 25, 12:41, 18:7

Because (3)

Old Testament – Proverbs 1:24-29, 21:7, 27:20, Isaiah 5:11-14, 24, 8:20, 17:9-10, Jeremiah 2:35, 4:4, 18-19, 27-28, 5:6, 12-14, Psalms 78:19-22, 60:4, 59:8-9, 45:4

New Testament – John 15:19-21, 16:1-3, Romans 1:21-22, 6:15-16, 1 Timothy 4:10

Because (4)

Old Testament – Numbers 14:24, 20:10-13, 25:10-13, 1 Samuel 13:13-14, 15:23-24, Jeremiah 6:19, 30, 8:14-15, 9:13-15, 12:11, 13, 17:13, 19:15, 21:12, Lamentations 1:16, 3:22

New Testament – Matthew 13:10-13, 58, 17:19-20, Hebrews 3:12, 4:4-6

Because (5)

Old Testament – Genesis 2:23, 3:20, 32:24-32, 39:23, 1 Chronicles 4:9-10, Deuteronomy 4:36-37, 7:7:8, 1 Kings 10:9, 15:4-5, 2 Kings 17:26, 18:11-12, 19:28, 21:14-15, Psalms 28:4-7, 33:21

New Testament – Matthew 19:3-8, 24:12, 1 John 3:1, 9, 12, 14, 22, 4:4, 9, 13

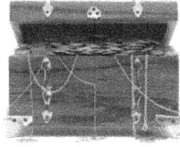

Vanity

Vanity (1)

"Favour is deceitful, and beauty is vain, : but a woman that feareth the LORD, she shall be praised." (Proverbs 31:30)

Vainity (2)

"I do not frustrate the grace of God: for if righteousness come by law, then Christ died in vain." (Galatians 2:21)

Vanity (3)

"We then, as workers together with him, beseech you also that ye receive not the grace of God in vain." (2 Corinthians 6:2)

Discussion Questions

1. Explain Matthew 16:26.
2. What is the prevailing thought in Ecclesiastes 3:11-12, 22?
3. Explain Deuteronomy 32:21, 46-47?
4. Explain 1 Samuel 12:20-21.
5. Explain Matthew 15:9

Fill in the Blanks

1. "Surely every man walketh in a ___shew: surely they are___ in ___: he heapeth up riches, and knoweth not who shall gather them."
2. "But avoid foolish___ , and___ , and___ , and ___about the law; for they are unprofitable and___ ."
3. "I hate ___thoughts: but thy law do I___ ."
4. "Except the Lord build the house, they labour in___ that build it."
5. "And again, The Lord knoweth the thoughts of the___ , that they are___ ."

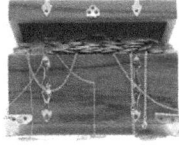

Vanity

"Vanity of vanities, saith the preacher; all is vanity" (Ecclesiastes 12:8).

*M*any are baffled by this statement that the wise man Solomon made as he gave careful thought and consideration to the ways of man—man tabernacled on the earth. Solomon observed the comings and the goings of all mankind. What mankind pursued, what mankind valued, what mankind treasured and esteemed highly, and what mankind devoted himself wholeheartedly to—his affections, his loyalties, his goals, his visions—were analyzed by Solomon. What he saw from his panoramic view led him to conclude that all of man's strivings and efforts were focused on that which will one day perish or vanish away and that which has no eternal significance whatsoever. He saw from a distance the consummation of all things, when we all shall appear before the judgment seat of God, when we all shall give an account for the deeds done and the life we lived, and when a decision will be made about our eternal destination. He saw that what really matters in life at that most crucial point is whether or not we obeyed God and kept His holy commandments. Everything else was inconsequential. Everything else was also vanity, vexation of spirit, and chasing the wind.

Vanity (1)

Old Testament – Ecclesiastes 1:2, 13-14, 3:17-19, 7:14-17, 9:9-10, Job 7:1-3, 13-16, 9:29, 10:15, 11:11-12, 15:27-35, Jeremiah 9:23-24, 2:4-5, 1 Samuel 12:20-21, Psalms 62:8-10, 39:5-6

New Testament – Matthew 16:26, Galatians 4:8-11, Philippians 2:14-16

Vanity (2)

Old Testament – Deuteronomy 32:21, 46-47, Leviticus 26:15-20, Malachi 3:13-16, 2 Kings 17:15, 1 Kings 16:13-14, 25-26, Jonah 2:7-8, Haggai 2:13-18, 1:5-9, Psalms 2:1-4, 78:33-35, 108:10-12, 119:37, 113

New Testament – Acts 4:24-26, 14:15, Titus 3:8-9, 2 Timothy 2:16

Vanity (3)

Old Testament – Jeremiah 4:14, 22, 30, 6:29, 8:8-9, 19-22, 10:3-5, 8, 14:22, 23:14-16, Lamentations 2:13-15, 4:17, Zechariah 10:2, Isaiah 1: 13-17, 17:4-11, 30:7, 27-28, 49:4, Psalms 127:1-2

New Testament – Romans 1:20-21, Colossians 2:8, 18, Ephesians 4:17-20

Vanity (4)

Old Testament – Proverbs 31:30, 30:7-9, 28-19, 21:6, 13:11, 12:11, 10:17, Ecclesiastes 5:7, 10, 6:1-4, 9-12, Job 15:2-4, 16:3, 22, 21:34, 27:8-12, 35:13-16

New Testament – 1 Corinthians 3:20, 15:1-2, 10-17, 58, Galatians 2:21, 3:1-4, 2 Corinthians 6:1

Vanity (5)

Old Testament – Ecclesiastes 4:4-8, 8:6-14, 11:8-10, 12:8-13, Isaiah 5:18-19, 40:17-23, 41:28-29, 57:13, 58:4-9, 59:1-4, Ezekiel 13:4-10, 22-23, 21:28-29, Psalms 144:11

New Testament – Matthew 15:9, Ephesians 5:6, 1 Timothy 1:5-6, 6:20-21, 1 Thessalonians 3:5, 2:1

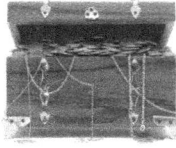

The Tongue

The Tongue (1)

"And the tongue is a fire, a world of iniquity: so is the tongue among our members, that it defileth the whole body, and setteth on fire the course of nature; and it is set on fire of hell." (James 3:6)

The Tongue (2)

"Death and life is in the power of the tongue: and they that love it shall eat the fruit thereof." (Proverbs 18:21)

The Tongue (3)

"For thy mouth uttereth thine iniquity, and thou choosest the tongue of the crafty." (Job 15:5)

Discussion Questions

1. Discuss Psalms 120:2-7.
2. Discuss Matthew 12:34-37.
3. Explain Isaiah 50:4.
4. Explain James 1:26.
5. Discuss Ephesians 4:29-31.

Fill in the Blanks

1. "Thou shalt hide them in the secret of thy ____from the pride of man: thou shalt keep them ____in a____ from the____ of____ ."

2. "There is that speaketh like the____ of a____ : but the____ of the____ is____ ."

3. "For he that will love____ , and see____ days, let him ____ refrain his____ from evil, and his lips that they____ no guile."

4. "For thy ____uttereth thine____ , and thou choosest the____ of the crafty."

5. "Though I speak with the____ of men and of angels, and have not____ , I am become as____ ____ or a tinkling____ ."

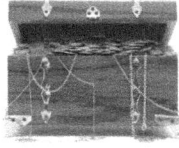

The Tongue

*M*etaphorically, the tongue represents our choice of words, our vernacular. Our words can be coarse, offensive, insulting, full of ridicule and disdain. They can also be gracious, encouraging, uplifting, kind, edifying, comforting, and soothing. As Christians, we must use our tongues to promote that which incites good in others.

The Tongue (1)

Old Testament – Leviticus 19:16 Exodus 20:16 Ecclesiastes 5:2, 10:11, Hosea 7:16, Jeremiah 9:3-8, Job 16:2-5, Isaiah 54:17, Zephaniah 3:13, Psalms 12:1-4, 15:1-3, 31:18-20, 57:2-4, 58:4-7, 64:2-8, 119:171-172, 120:2-7, 140:3, Proverbs 12:18-19, 30:14

New Testament – Matthew 5:11-12, 12:34-37, James 3:2-10, 4:11, Titus 3:2

The Tongue (2)

Old Testament – Proverbs 18:21, 15:2, 4, 23, 28, 10:18, 20, 31, 6:16-19, 23-24, Isaiah 59:3-4, 50:4, 45:23, 41:17, 35:4-6, Job 33:1-3, 27:4-5, 15:2-5, 6:22-30, Psalms 101:5-8, 141:3

New Testament – Ephesians 4:29-31, 1 Timothy 3:8, James 1:26, Romans 3:13-14, 14:11

The Tongue (3)

Old Testament – Jeremiah 6:28, 12:6, 18:18, 20:10, Ezekiel 3:25-27, Amos 6:10-11, Esther 7:4, Micah 6:12-13, Habakkuk 1:12-13, Isaiah 30:27-31, 3:8-11, Zechariah 14:12, Psalms 27:12, 31:13, 39:1, 55:9, 109:1-2, 17-20, 139:4

New Testament – Acts 6:9-15, 1 Peter 4:4, 11, 3:10-16, 2:1, 12.

The Tongue (4)

Old Testament – Proverbs 31:10, 26, 28:23, 26:20-28, 25:15, 23, 21:6, 23, 17:4, 20, Psalms 73:8-12, 36-37, 52:1-5, 51:14, 50:16-19, 41:5-7, 37:30-37, 34:13, 10:4-7, 5:9

New Testament – 1 Corinthians 13:1, 8, 2 Corinthians 12:19-21, Galatians 5:15, Colossians 4:6, James 5:9

The Tongue (5)

Old Testament – Isaiah 32:4-8, 28:11-15, 11:15-16, Job 20:12-16, 15:2-5, 5:17, 21, Proverbs 2:11-17, 16:1, 28, Psalms 137:6, 126:1-2, 71:23-24, 68:21-23, 66:16-17, 35:27-28, 22:15-20

New Testament – Acts 2:25-26, Philippians 2:9-11, 1 John 3:18, Luke 6:45

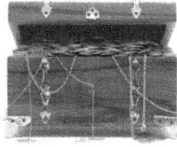

Offenses

Offenses (1)

"Then said he unto the disciples, it is impossible but that offenses will come: but woe unto him, through whom they come! (Luke 17:1)

Offenses (2)

"Now I beseech you, brethren, mark them which cause divisions and offenses contrary to the doctrine which ye have learned; and avoid them." (Romans 16:17)

Offenses (3)

"Great peace have they which love thy law: and nothing shall offend them." (Psalms 119:165)

Discussion Questions

1. Discuss Proverbs 18:19.
2. Discuss Matthew 13:34-42.
3. Discuss Paul's testimony in 2 Corinthians 6:3-10.
4. Explain Matthew 24:10-13.
5. Explain Romans 5:17-21.

Fill in the Blanks

1. "Giving no___ in any thing, that the____ be not____ ."
2. "Then said he unto the disciples, It is____ but that ____will come: but woe unto him, through whom they____ !"
3. "And if thou sell ought unto thy____ , or buyest ought of thy neighbour's hand, ye shall not____ one another."
4. "For in many things we____ all. If any man____ not in word, the same is a____ ____ , and able also to____ the whole body."
5. "And herein do I exercise myself, to have____ a conscience void of____ toward God, and toward men."

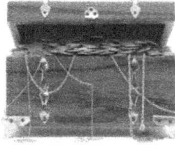

Offenses

*B*y definition, offenses are those things that impugn, insult, denigrate, annoy, disturb, or create unrest, displeasure, pain, and sorrow in others. Lives have been ruined, careers destroyed, character tarnished, integrity questioned, and relationships broken by offenses perpetrated by individuals who refuse to walk in love, kindness, and consideration for others as our Lord has commanded.

> "Ye know not what manner of spirit ye are of. For the Son of man is not come to destroy men's lives, but to save them" (Luke 9:55).

Offenses (1)

Old Testament – Proverbs 26:18-19, 18:19, Job 24:2-10, 34:31, Leviticus 25:14, 17, 19:33, Deuteronomy 23:15-16, 27:17-19, Psalms 7:11, 16, 10:14, 18, 17:8-9, 119:122, 134, Lamentations 3:59-64

New Testament – Luke 6:22, 17:1-4, Matthew 5:29-30, 38-44, 13:37-42

Offenses (2)

Old Testament – Exodus 20:16-17, 23:1-9, Leviticus 19:9-18, 33-36, Numbers 35:16-21, Deuteronomy 25:1-3, 24:10-17, 23:24-25, Obadiah 1:10-15, Proverbs 24:28

New Testament – Matthew 18:15-18, Acts 24:16, 1 Corinthians 10:32-33, 9:19-23, 2 Corinthians 11:7, 6:3-10, Philippians 1:8-10, Romans 16:17

Offenses (3)

Old Testament – Exodus 21:22-36, 22:1-16, 1 Samuel 12:3-5, Proverbs 17:13, 22:22, 28:8, Amos 4:1-2, Micah 2:2, Zechariah 7:9-10, Jeremiah 7:6-7, Isaiah 33:1, 24:16, 3:14-15, Psalms 18:47-48

New Testament – Matthew 24:10-13, 13:20-21, 1 Corinthians 6:8-10, 8:9, 13, Romans 14:21

Offenses (4)

Old Testament – Hosea 13:1, 5:14-15, Exodus 22:18-24, Deuteronomy 15:9, 18:9-14, Numbers 15:29-36, Isaiah 11:9-10, 29:20-21, 51:21-23, Malachi 3:5, 2:8-16, Job 20:4-7, 12-19, 1 Samuel 25:2-13, 31

New Testament – 1 Thessalonians 4:6, Acts 25:8, 11, Galatians 5:11-13, James 2:10, 3:2

Offenses (5)

Old Testament – Job 16:10, 20, 19:2, 22, 29, 21:27, 42:8, Isaiah 50:6-10, Lamentations 2:15-16, 3:27-30, Ezekiel 3:8-11, Psalms 94:1-7, 69:20-21, 35:15-26, Jeremiah 2:3

New Testament – Matthew 11:6, 26:31, 67, 27:26-31, Luke 23:28, 34, Hebrews 12:1-4, 1 Peter 2:19-23

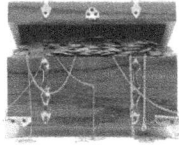

Hearers

Hearers (1)

"Be ye doers of the word, and not hearers only, deceiving your own selves. (James 1:22)

Hearers (2)

"(For not the hearers of the law are just before God, but the doers of the law shall be justified)." (Romans 2:13)

Hearers (3)

"To whom shall I speak, and give warning, behold their ear is uncircumcised, and they cannot hearken: behold, the word of the LORD is unto them a reproach; they have no delight in it." (Jeremiah 6:10)

Discussion Questions

1. Explain Jeremiah 6:10, 19.
2. Discuss Jeremiah 22:29.
3. Discuss John 8:43-47.
4. Explain Hebrews 2:1-3.
5. Discuss Amos 8:11

Fill in the Blanks

1. "The ear that____ the reproof of life abideth among ___ ____."
2. "For Moses truly said unto the fathers, A____ shall the Lord your God____ up unto you of your_____ , like unto me; him shall ye____ in ___ ____whatsoever he shall say unto you."
3. "Every one that is of the___ ___ my voice."
4. "A wise man will ____, and will increase learning; and a man of ____shall attain unto wise ____."
5. "Take heed unto thyself, and unto the____ ; continue in them: for in doing this thou shalt both____ thyself, and them that____ ____ ."

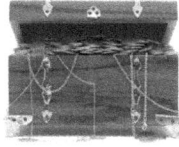

Hearers

"My sheep hear my voice, and I know them, and they follow me" (John 10:27).

*T*his verse delineates a unique aspect of those who belong to the Lord. They hear His voice. They follow Him. May we strive always to be hearers of the words of Christ and doers of His will as we follow Him.

Hearers (1)

Old Testament – Jeremiah 6:10, 19, 7:2, 10:1-2, 13:10-11, 15, 22:29, 23:22-29, Isaiah 48:16-19, 51:1, 4, 7, Psalms 81:13-16, Proverbs 15:31-32, 19:20, 27, 20:12, 22:17-21

New Testament – John 6:60-68, 8:43, 47, 18:37, Hebrew 2:1-3, James 1:19-25

Hearers (2)

Old Testament – Deuteronomy 4:9-10, 5:1, 27, 6:3, 12:28, 32:1-3, Numbers 9:8, 24:13, Psalms 85:8, 95:6-8, Ezekiel 2:1-7, 3:4-11, 17, 37:1-4, 10, Jeremiah 9:19-21, Amos 8:11

New Testament – Luke 8:18-21, 9:35, 10:24, 11:27-28, Acts 3:22-23, Romans 10:13-21

Hearers (3)

Old Testament – Deuteronomy 26:15-17, 30:12-14, 31:12-13, Joshua 24:27, 1:18, Isaiah 28:23-29, 34:1-2, 42:18-23, 51:1, 4, 7, Zechariah 7:7-13, 1:4-6, Hosea 9:17, Proverbs 29:24, Ezekiel 33:30-33

New Testament – Acts 7:51-54, Hebrews 4:1-2, 2:1-3, 1 Timothy 4:16, 2 Timothy 1:13

Hearers (4)

Old Testament – Ecclesiastes 5:1, 7:5, 9:17, Proverbs 1:5, 32-33, 4:10, 8:33, 10:8, 23:19, Psalms 49:1-3, 66:16, 138:4, 143:8, Isaiah 18:3, 6:9-11, 1:2, 10

New Testament – Matthew 13:13-23, 7:24-27, Luke 10:16, 1 John 4:5-6, Revelation 1:3, 2:17, 22:17-19

Hearers (5)

Old Testament – 1 Samuel 3:7-11, 2 Kings 21:12, Jeremiah 19:1-3, 15, 25:8-9, 35:17, 36:11-32, 44:16-24, Proverbs 5:7, 8:6-8, 28:9, 29:1, Psalms 58:4-5, 62:11, 119:149

New Testament – Matthew 17:5, Luke 10:38-39, 42, 16:31, John 5:24-25, 10:27, Romans 2:13

Idolatry

Idolatry (1)

"Mortify therefore your members which are upon the earth, fornication, uncleanness, inordinate affection, evil concupiscence, and covetousness, which is idolatry:" (Colossians 3:5)

Idolatry (2)

"For rebellion is as the sin of witchcraft, and stubbornness is as iniquity and idolatry. Because thou hast rejected the word of the LORD, he hath rejected thee from being king." (1 Samuel 15:23)

Idolatry (3)

"Wherefore. my dearly beloved, flee from idolatry.... What say I then? That the idol is any thing, or that which is offered in sacrifice to idols is any thing? But I say, that the things which the Gentiles sacrifice, they sacrifice to devils, and not to God: and I would not that ye should have fellowship with devils." (1 Corinthians 10:19-20)

Discussion Questions

1. What command is given in Exodus 20:2-6?
2. What was the apostle Paul's response when he saw idolatry in Acts 17:16-31?
3. Explain Ezekiel 14:3-8.699 Idolatry

4. Will all idolaters be lost?
5. What transpired in Acts 19:23-41?

Fill in the Blanks

1. "Their____ are silver and gold, the work of men's____ ."
2. "Neither is ____with men's____ , as though he needed any thing, seeing he giveth to all life, and____ , and all____ ."
3. "For this ye know, that no____ , nor____ person, nor____ man, who is an____ , hath any inheritance in the ____of Christ and of God."
4. "Howbeit then, when ye knew not God, ye did____ unto them which by nature are____ ____ ."
5. "He tha____t unto any god, save unto the Lord____ , he shall be utterly____ ."

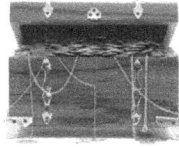

Idolatry

*I*dolatry is "to worship or serve an image." God has forbidden his people to make them, bow down to them, call on their names, follow them, or be a part of any devotion to them.

> "Wherefore, my dearly beloved, flee from idolatry" (1 Corinthians 10:14).

Idolatry (1)

Old Testament – Exodus 20:2-6, 22:18, 20, 32:1-14, 19-28, Genesis 31:30-37, 35:1-4, Deuteronomy 32:16-22, 28-29, 1 Samuel 5:1-12, 1 Kings 12:27-33, 13:1-6, 18:17-40, Psalms 81:8-16

New Testament – 1 Corinthians 10:14-28, 2 Corinthians 6:14-18, Acts 17:16-31, Revelation 9:20

Idolatry (2)

Old Testament – Exodus 34:12-17, Leviticus 17:7, 26:1, 30, 2 Kings 5:15-19, 2 Chronicles 15:1-9, 16, Psalms 106:28-40, Jeremiah 2:8-13, 22-29, 44:9-20, 45:15-16, 20-22, 46:1-2, 6-8

New Testament – 1 John 5:21, 1 Corinthians 12:2, Acts 12:21-23, Acts 10:25-26, Romans 1:20-23

Idolatry (3)

Old Testament – Psalms 115:4-8, 97:7-9, 96:4-5, 81:8-12, Hosea 3:1, 4:12-19, 8:4-6, 9:10, 14:1-4, Habakkuk 2:18-20, Micah 1:7, Amos 5:26-27, Jeremiah 19:13-15, 25:6-7, 44:15-22

New Testament – Colossians 3:5, Ephesians 5:5, Galatians 5:19-21, 1 Corinthians 8:4-13, Revelation 21:8

Idolatry (4)

Old Testament – Deuteronomy 13:1-9, Daniel 3:1-7, 12-29, 5:1-6, 23-31, Ezekiel 6:1-7, 8:7-18, 14:3-8, 16:35-38, Isaiah 2:6-9, 17-22, 19:1-4, 19-22, Nahum 1:14, Zechariah 10:2, 13:1-4, Micah 5:10-15

New Testament – Acts 7:40-54, 14:11-18, 19:23-41

Idolatry (5)

Old Testament – 2 Kings 17:7-18, 27-34, 19:16-19, 1 Kings 11:4-11, 14:22-24, 15:11-14, 22:41-46, Jeremiah 2:5-8, 10:1-10, 14-16, Jonah 2:8, Isaiah 31:6-7, 57:3-5, 13

New Testament – Galatians 4:8-9, 1 Corinthians 5:7-11, 6:9-10, 1 Thessalonians 1:9-10, Revelation 2:14

Giving

Giving (1)

"Honour the LORD with thy substance, and with the firstfruits of all thine increase: So shall thy barns be filled with plenty, and thy presses shall burst out with new wine." (Proverbs 3:9-10)

Giving (2)

"I have shewed you all things, how that so labouring ye ought to support the weak, and to remember the words of the Lord Jesus, how he said, it is more blessed to give than to receive." (Acts 20:35)

Giving (3)

"And this stone, which I have set for a pillar, shall be God's house: and of all that thou shalt give me I will surely give the tenth unto thee." (Genesis 28:22)

Discussion Questions

1. Explain Proverbs 11:25.
2. What instructions are given in Matthew 5:42?
3. What happens when a cup of cold water is given to Christ's disciple?
4. Explain Luke 14:12-14.
5. What did Jacob vow in Genesis 28:22?

Fill in the Blanks

1. "Thou shalt not delay to ___the first of thy___ ___ , and of thy____ ."
2. "He that___ unto the poor shall not____ : but he that hideth his eyes shall have many a____ ."
3. "And whosoever shall___ to drink unto one of the little ones a ___of____ water only in the name of a____ , verily I say unto you, he shall in no ___lose his reward."
4. "But this I say, He which____ sparingly shall____ also ____; and he which bountifully shall reap also____ ."
5. "But whoso hath this world's good, and seeth his brother____ ____ and shutteth up his bowels of compassion from him, how____ the____ of____ in him?"

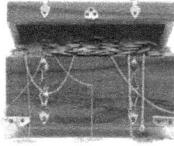

Giving

*G*iving feely from the heart is a true expression of one's love, reflecting the emotional sentiment within us.

"Honour the Lord with thy substance, and with the first fruits of all thine increase" (Proverbs 3:9).

Giving (1)

Old Testament – Proverbs 3:9-10, 11:24-25, Genesis 4:3-7, 14:17-20, Exodus 22:29, 23:16, 19, 25:1-2, 1 Chronicles 16:29, 29:9, 17, 2 Chronicles 31:4-5, 10, Deuteronomy 16:13-17

New Testament – Matthew 5:20, 42, 6:1-4, 19-21, 2 Corinthians 8:1-15, Acts 20:35, 4:32-37

Giving (2)

Old Testament – Deuteronomy 15:7-11, Leviticus 19:9-10, Proverbs 14:31, 19:16, 21:13, 22:9, 16, 28:27, Ecclesiastes 11:1-2, 6, Ezekiel 18:7-9, Isaiah 58:6-12, Job 31:16-23

New Testament – Luke 6:38, 14:12-14, 21:1-4, Matthew 10:42, 19:21-22, 25:31-46, 26:7-11

Giving (3)

Old Testament – Genesis 28:22, Deuteronomy 14:22-29, 26:1-16, Leviticus 27:30-33, Nahum 10:35-39, Haggai 1:3-11, 2:15-19, Ezra 2:68-69, 7:16-28, 8:24-30, Amos 4:4-5, 12, Malachi 3:10-12

New Testament – Matthew 23:23, 1 Corinthians 16:1-2, 2 Corinthians 9:5-15, Hebrews 13:16, 7:5-12

Giving (4)

Old Testament – Deuteronomy 24:19-22, Proverbs 13:23, 28:3, 8, 31:10, 20, Psalms 41:1, 112:9, Job 29:11-17, 24:2-10, 22:5-10, Isaiah 32:5-8, Jeremiah 22:13-17, Micah 2:1-3, Proverbs 22:22-23

New Testament – Luke 16:19-25, James 2:15-18, 1 Timothy 6:17-19, 1 John 3:17

Giving (5)

Old Testament – Nehemiah 13:10-12, 2 Chronicles 31:11-14, 1 Chronicles 29:14, Haggai 2:8, Psalms 24:1, 50:10-12, 54:6, 144:13-15, 145:15-16, Micah 4:13

New Testament – 1 Peter 4:9-10, Romans 12:10-13, Galatians 2:10, Philippians 4:15-19, Luke 11:40-41, 12:33, 19:8

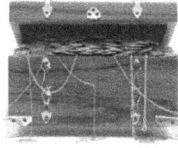

Oneness

Oneness (1)

"Hear, O Israel: The LORD our God is one LORD:" (Deuteronomy 6:4)

Oneness (2)

"And I will give them one heart, and one way, that they may fear me for ever, for the good of them, and of their children after them:" (Jeremiah 32:39)

Oneness (3)

"Neither pray I for these alone, but for them also which shall believe on me through their word; That they all may be one; as thou, Father, art in me, and I in thee, that they also may be one in us: that the world may believe that thou hast sent me." (John 17:20-21)

Discussion Questions

1. What was God's response toward division among his people in Ezekiel 37: 15-28?
2. What instruction was given in Romans 15:6?
3. Explain Ephesians 4:4-6.
4. How is unity viewed in Psalms 133:1?
5. What command was given in 1 Corinthians 1:10?

Fill in the Blanks

1. "That ye may with____ ____ and____ ____ glorify God, even the Father of our Lord Jesus Christ."
2. "Nevertheless, whereto we have already attained, let us____ by the ____rule, let us____ the same____ ."
3. "Behold, how____ and how____ it is for brethren to____ together in____ !"
4. "As we said before, so say I now again, If any man____ any other____ unto you than that ye ____, let him be ____."
5. "There is____ body, and____ Spirit, even as ye are called in____ hope of your calling. ____Lord, ____ faith, ____ baptism, ____ God and Father of all, who is above all, and through____ , and in you____ ."

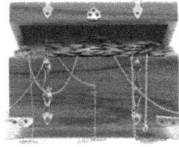

Oneness

"Hear, O Israel: the Lord our God is one Lord" (Deuteronomy 6:4).

"And I will give them one heart, and one way..." (Jeremiah 32:39).

"The words of the wise are as goads, and as nails fastened by the masters of assemblies, which are given from one shepherd" (Ecclesiastes 12:11).

*I*t must be duly noted that God is a God of Oneness, as mentioned in this series of passages.

Oneness (1)

Old Testament – Deuteronomy 6:4, 4:33-35, 18:18-20, Genesis 49:10, Leviticus 7:7, 2 Samuel 7:23, 19:8-14, Ecclesiastes 12:11, Jeremiah 32:37-40, Psalms 89:34, Isaiah 55:11, 33:22

New Testament – Romans 15:5-6, James 4:12, 1 Timothy 2:5, Acts 4:12, John 17:11, 20-23, John 12:48-50, John 10:16, 30, Mark 12:29-31

Oneness (2)

Old Testament – Genesis 2:21-24, 11:6, Micah 5:2, Isaiah 2:1-2, 60:7, 22, Zechariah 2:11, 8:20-23, 14:9, Ezekiel 11:19, 34:23, 37:15-28

New Testament – John 11:49-52, Acts 2:41, 47, 4:32, Ephesians 5:29-32, 4:4-6, 3:8-9, 21, 2:11-18, 1:10, 22-23, 1 Timothy 2:5, Revelation 15:4

Oneness (3)

Old Testament – 2 Chronicles 30:12, 1 Chronicles 12:38, Isaiah 45:22-23, 8:16, 20, Jeremiah 20:11, 51:5, Proverbs 30:5-6, Malachi 2:10

New Testament – Galatians 3:16, 20, 26-28, Romans 10:12, 1 Corinthians 12:11-25, 6:16-17,

2 Corinthians 11:2-4, Philippians 1:27, 2:2, 3:15-19, 1 John 5:7-8

Oneness (4)

Old Testament – Hosea 10:2-3, 11:9, Judges 6:16, 20:1-8, 11, 48, Isaiah 1:24, 5:19, 10:17, 20, 12:6, 17:7, 19:20, 29:19, 23, 30:11, 12, 15, Psalms 133:1, 125:5, 119:21, 130, 133, Ecclesiastes 9:18

New Testament – John 8:50, Matthew 12:6, 25-30, Acts 3:23, Romans 3:29-30, 1 Timothy 1:3, 1 John 2:19, Galatians 1:9, 1 Corinthians 14:33, 2 Corinthians 4:13, 10:5

Oneness (5)

Old Testament – 2 Chronicles 32:12, 18:12-13, 1 Chronicles 17:21, 2 Samuel 19:11-14, Numbers 15:15-16, 24:13, Exodus 12:49-50, Judges 20:1, 8, 11, Hosea 1:10-11

New Testament – Mark 10:18, Acts 17:26-31, 1 Peter 4:11, Titus 3:10-11, 1 Corinthians 1:10-13, 3:3-7, 15:39 Matthew 23:8-10, 1 Timothy 6:3-5

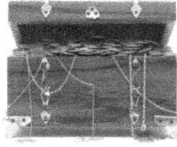

Atonement

Atonement (1)

"For the life of the flesh is in the blood: and I have given it to you upon the altar to make atonement for your souls: for it is the blood that maketh an atonement for the soul. (Leviticus 17:11)

Atonement (2)

"And the blood shall be to you for a token upon the houses where ye are: and when I see the blood, I will pass over you, and the plague shall not be upon you to destroy you, when I smite the land of Egypt." (Exodus 12:13)

Atonement (3)

"But God commendeth his love toward us , in that, while we were yet sinners, Christ died for us. Much more then, being now justified by his blood, we shall be saved from wrath through him." (Romans 5:8-9)

Discussion Questions

1. Explain Numbers 15:25.
2. Why do we need atonement for our sins to find acceptance with God?
3. What is mentioned in John 1:29?
4. Explain Ephesians 2:12.
5. What observations are made in Romans 5:1-21?

Fill in the Blanks

1. "But your___ have separated between you and your God, and your____ have hid his face from you, that he will____ ____ ."
2. "Behold the____ of God, which taketh___ the____ of the____ ."
3. "Wherefore he is able also to____ ____ to the____ that come unto God by him, seeing he ever____ to make____ for them."
4. "And he is the____ for our sins: and not for ours only, but also for the___ of the whole____ ."
5. "For I delivered unto you first of all that which I also received, how that____ died for our ____according to the____ ."

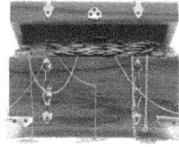

Atonement

*B*y definition, atonement means "to cause to be covered, to be restored, to favor, to appease in order to be reconciled." This atonement can only come through our Lord and Savior Jesus Christ. We can enjoy peace with God because He is the atonement for our sins.

Atonement (1)

Old Testament – Numbers 15:22-36, 8:9-12, 19, 21, Leviticus 16:3-11, 14-30, 17:11, 23:26-28, Exodus 29:31-33, 36-37, 30:10, 15-16, Psalms 51:1-4, 9, 65:3-4, 79:8-9, Isaiah 59:1-2, 53:1-12

New Testament – John 1:29, Romans 5:1-21, Hebrews 13:10-16

Atonement (2)

Old Testament – Leviticus 1:1-4, 4:13-26, 7:7, 27, Deuteronomy 12:20-25, 21:8-9, 32:43, Exodus 12:5-13, 32:1-6, 30-35, Ezekiel 16:63, 2 Samuel 21:1-6, Proverbs 16:6

New Testament – Acts 15:28-29, 10:15, Colossians 1:19-23, 2:13-17, Ephesians 1:7, 2:4-18, Romans 3:21-26

Atonement (3)

Old Testament – Leviticus 6:12-13, 30, 9:7, 22-24, Numbers 5:12-31, 6:1-8, 31:48-50, Daniel 9:5-11, 24, 4:27, 2 Chronicles 29:5-8, 21-24, Ezekiel 45:15-20, Job 42:7-9, Psalms 32:1-6, 49:5-9, 15

New Testament – Hebrews 2:9-17, 7:25-28, 9:11-28, 1 John 2:1-2

Atonement (4)

Old Testament – Isaiah 43:22-28, 27:2-9, 22:12-14, 1 Samuel 2:25, 28-36, 3:14, 10:8, 13:8-14, 15:17-26, Psalms 4:5, Proverbs 15:8, Hosea 8:13-14, 9:4-7

New Testament – 1 John 1:5-9, John 11:49-52, Hebrews 10:5-12, 16-31, Acts 20:28, 1 Peter 1:18-19

Atonement (5)

Old Testament – Exodus 29:32-37, Numbers 6:9-11, 25:11-13, Jeremiah 5:25, 33:8, 14-18, Isaiah 1:11-16, 52:2-3, 9-15, 56:7-8, Amos 5:21-27, Psalms 50:7-15, Micah 6:6-8

New Testament – 1 Corinthians 15:3, 17, 1 John 4:9-10, Titus 2:11-15, 1 Peter 3:18, 1 Timothy 2:5-6

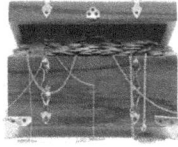

God Has the Record

God Has the Record (1)

"Also now, behold, my witness is in heaven, and my record is on high."
(Job 16:19)

God Has the Record (2)

"Thou tellest my wanderings: put thou my tears into thy bottle: are
they not in thy book?

God Has the Record (3)

"Fear them not therefore: for there is nothing covered, that shall not be
revealed; and hid that shall not be known...Are not two sparrows sold
for a farthind? And one of them shall not fall on the ground without
your Father. But the very hairs of your head are numbered." (Matthew
10:26, 29, 30)

Discussion Questions

1. Explain Job 16:19.
2. Explain Psalms 56:8.
3. What observation does God make in Malachi 2:13-14?
4. What was written in the books mentioned in
   Revelation 20:12?
5. Explain Hebrews 4:12-13.

Fill in the Blanks

1. "Also now, behold, my___ is in___, and my___ is on high."
2. "___ them not therefore: for there is___ covered, that shall not be___; and ___, that shall not be known."
3. "But even the very___ of your head are all___ ."
4. "Neither is there any creature that is not___ in his___: but all things are___ and ___unto the eyes of him with whom we have to___ ."
5. "For if our heart___ us, God is greater than our heart, and___ all."

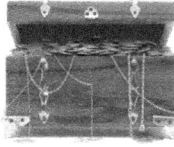

God Has the Record

A record exists on high of every tear that is shed, every deed that is done, and every word that is spoken. Nothing escapes His notice. Therefore, we are both reassured and encouraged as we strive to live before Him in an acceptable way.

God Has the Record (1)

Old Testament – Job 10:12-17, 16:19, 19:23-25, Hosea 13:12, 7:2, Amos 8:7, Jeremiah 17:1, 16:17-18, Psalms 10:4-15, 25:7, 56:8, 139:1-18, Ezekiel 11:5

New Testament – Matthew 10:26, 28-31, Hebrews 4:12-13, 12:15-29, Revelation 20:11-15, 22:6-12

God Has the Record (2)

Old Testament – Proverbs 15:3, 5:21, Isaiah 40:26-27, Ecclesiastes 12:14, 11:9, 3:17, Job 21:27-31, 34:11, 19-27, Jeremiah 23:23-24, 32:19, Psalms 69:19, 130:3-4, Exodus 17:14, 32:31-33, Malachi 3:13-16

New Testament – 1 Corinthians 4:5, Matthew 12:36, Acts 3:19, Luke 12:2

God Has the Record (3)

Old Testament – Genesis 31:50, Micah 1:2, Malachi 2:13-14, 1 Samuel 2:3, 12:5, 20:23, Judges 11:10, Jeremiah 42:5, Numbers 30:2, Ecclesiastes 5:2, 4-6, Deuteronomy 23:21, Proverbs 26:18-19, Psalms 90:8, 64:5-8

New Testament – 2 Corinthians 1:23, 5:10, 1 John 3:20, 1 Timothy 5:24-25

God Has the Record (4)

Old Testament – Ezekiel 8:12, 9:9, Zephaniah 1:12, Amos 5:12, 9:2-4, 8-10, Psalms 59:7-9, 12-13, 50:19-21, 44:20-21, Isaiah 5:18-19, 29:15, Job 14:5, 22:12-21, 31:1-5, 14

New Testament – John 2:24-25, Romans 1:18, 2:1-3, 16, 14:7-8

God Has the Record (5)

Old Testament – Jeremiah 2:22, 25, 29:23, Nahum 1:2-5, 9-12, Proverbs 23:10-11, 18, 13:21, Isaiah 3:10-11, Psalms 139:2-4, 15-16, 38:9, 20-21, 33:13-20, Job 36:5-7, 15-18, 37:20-24

New Testament – Hebrews 6:10, Matthew 6:3-4, 16:27, Revelation 11:18

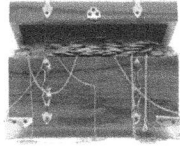

The Hypocrite/Backslider

The Hypocrite/Backslider (1)

"Ah sinful nation, a people laden with iniquity, a seed of evildoers, children that are corrupters: they have forsaken the LORD, they have provoked the Holy One of Israel unto anger, they have gone backward." (Isaiah 1:4)

The Hypocrite/Backslider (2)

"For what is the hope of the hypocrite, though he hath gained, when God taketh away his soul? (Job 27:8)

The Hypocrite/Backslider (3)

"Thou hypocrite, first cast out the beam out of thyine own eye; and then shalt thou see clearly to cast out the mote out of thy brother's eye.? (Matthew 7:5)

Discussion Questions

1. What is a hypocritical nation (Isaiah 10:6-7)?
2. What commandment did Christ give in Matthew 6:1-4?
3. Explain Isaiah 1:4, 21-23 and Israel's spiritual condition.
4. What admonition was given in Matthew 12:33-35?
5. Explain Jeremiah 49:4, 16.

Fill in the Blanks

1. "For what is the____ of the____ , though he hath gained, when God taketh away_____ ?"
2. "For it had been better for them____ to have____ the way of righteousness, than, after they have ____it, to turn from the_____ ___ delivered unto them."
3. "They profess that they know___ ; but in works they___ him, being___ , and____ , and___ unto every good work___ ."
4. "That the___ reign not, lest the people be ____."
5. "Thou therefore which____ another, ___ thou not thyself? thou that___ a man should not___ , does thou____ ?"

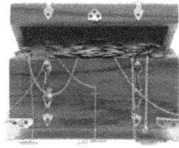

The Hypocrite/Backslider

B oth of the terms *hypocrite* and *backslider* denote a negative disposition of the soul of man. The hypocrite pretends to be that which he is not. He is one that operates behind a mask. The hypocrite cannot tarry in God's sight (Job 13:16). The backslider is one that turns back or turns away or shrinks back.

> "Now the just shall live by faith: but if any man draw back, my soul shall have no pleasure in him" (Hebrews 10:38).

The Hypocrite/Backslider (1)

Old Testament – Isaiah 1:4, 21-23, 9:16-17, Jeremiah 3:10-14, 20-22, 8:4-9, 9:1-9, 12:6, Psalms 12:2, 28:3-4, 78:9-10, 55-57, Job 27:8-10, 13:16

New Testament – Matthew 6:1-8, 16, 7:3-5, 15:1-9, 16:1-4, 23:13-33

The Hypocrite/Backslider (2)

Old Testament – Job 8:11-14, 15:27-35, 20:4-9, Proverbs 26:18-28, 14:14, 11:9, Isaiah 58:1-5, 65:5, Ezekiel 33:31, Psalms 120:1-7, 55:20-21

New Testament – Romans 2:17-29, 12:9, Titus 1:16, 1 John 1:6-10, 3:7-10

The Hypocrite/Backslider (3)

Old Testament – Job 34:26-30, 36:13-14, Ecclesiastes 10:11, Isaiah 5:18-24, 10:6-7, 29:13, 32:6-7, 33:1, 14-16, Amos 5:6-7, 10-24, Obadiah 1:10-15, Psalms 35:11-26

New Testament – Luke 11:39-54, 13:10-17, Hebrews 10:36-39

The Hypocrite/Backslider (4)

Old Testament – Jeremiah 49:4, 16, 44:10-11, 42:20-22, 18:18-20, 14:10-15, 7:8-16, Malachi 3:7, Psalms 5:4-6, 9, 50:17-23, 52:1-5

New Testament – Matthew 24:46-51, James 3:10, 2 Peter 2:3, 12-22, 3:5, 16, John 12:3-6

The Hypocrite/Backslider (5)

Old Testament – Jeremiah 2:5, 11-13, 19, 21, 27, 5:5-6, 31, 6:12-15, 13:23-25, 22:13-19, 31:21-25, Isaiah 31:6-7, 1 Samuel 15:11, Hosea 11:3-7

New Testament – 1 Timothy 4:1-3, 2 Timothy 3:5-7, Galatians 2:11-18, Matthew 12:33-35, Luke 6:42

Lift Him Up

Lift Him Up (1)

"The lofty looks of man shall be humbled, and the haughtiness of men shall be bowed down, and the LORD alone shall be exalted in that day." (Isaiah 2:11)

Lift Him Up (2)

"Be thou exalted, LORD, in thine own strength: so we will sing and praise thy power." (Psalms 21:13)

Lift Him Up (3)

"And I, if I be lifted up from the earth, will draw all men unto me." (John 12:32)

Discussion Questions

1. Explain Psalms 29:2.
2. According to Romans 11:36, who made all things?
3. What does it mean to be preeminent in all things? (Colossians 3:17-18).
4. Explain John 8:28.
5. Explain 1 Peter 4:11.

Fill in the Blanks

1. "O magnify the___ with me, and let us____ his name___ ."
2. "For of___, and through___, and to___ , are all___ : to whom be____ for ever."
3. "And I, if I be___ up___ the___ , __will___ all men unto__ ."
4. "I will praise thee, O___ my____ , with all my___ : and I will___ thy name for evermore."
5. "By ___therefore let us offer the____ of praise to God___ , that is, the___ of our lips giving thanks to His ___."

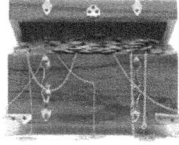

Lift Him Up

"And I, if I be lifted up from the earth, will draw all men unto me" (John 12:32).

The world is looking for answers to the many questions they ponder. Many are looking for love, someone who truly cares for their soul and their wellbeing. Many are looking for direction, many are looking for help, and many are looking for healing for their sin-sick souls. The world must come to know that Jesus is the answer to all they go through. Jesus can fill the void in their life and give them peace and joy that surpass all understanding. Jesus is the One they can trust. He will never forsake them or let them down. Jesus is the anchor of our souls, the One who must be lifted up to the world.

Lift Him Up (1)

Old Testament – Psalms 29:1-2, 34:1-3, 63:1-7, 107:1-9, 32, 116:1-9, 17, 144:15, 1 Chronicles 16:21-31, 29:10-13, 2 Samuel 22:1-20, 2 Chronicles 20:17, 29-30

New Testament – Ephesians 3:14-21, 1 Timothy 1:17, 2:8, 6:15-16, Romans 11:36

Lift Him Up (2)

Old Testament – Isaiah 2:11-12, 5:15-17, 25:1, 4, 8-9, Psalms 2:10-12, 9:1-2, 9-14, 21:13, 22:25-31, 142:3-7, 145:1-21, Jeremiah 17:14, Deuteronomy 10:21

New Testament – Hebrews 13:15-16, Jude 1:25, Revelation 4:11, 19:1, 5-6

Lift Him Up (3)

Old Testament – 2 Samuel 22:47, Job 36:22-26, 37:5-14, Jeremiah 32:17-20, 26-27, 37-42, 2 Chronicles 32:7-8, Isaiah 42:10-16, Psalms 44:1-8, 57:7-11, 96:1-13, 100:1-5, 108:1-5, 12-13

New Testament – John 8:28, 12:32, Colossians 3:17, 1:16-20

Lift Him Up (4)

Old Testament – 2 Chronicles 20:12, 16-22, Exodus 4:29-31, 15:1-2, 6-11, 1 Samuel 12:22-24, Psalms 5:3-7, 11-12, 40:1-10, 69:15-20, 30-36, 86:12, 95:1-8, 99:1-5, 9, 111:1-6

New Testament – 1 Peter 4:11, 2 Peter 3:17-18, 2 Thessalonians 1:11-12

Lift Him Up (5)

Old Testament – Job 36:24-26, Nehemiah 8:5-6, Isaiah 26:11-13, Psalms 28:2-9, 40:9-11, 46:8-11, 47:1-9, 48:1-5, 9-14, 92:4-8, 105:1-5

New Testament – Acts 13:47-48, Philippians 2:9-11, Revelation 5:11-14, 7:9-12

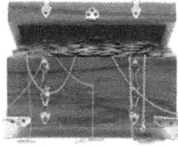

Seeing the Unseen

Seeing the Unseen (1)

"And he said unto me, Son of man, can these bones live? And I answered, O LORD GOD, thou knowest....So I prophesied as he commanded me, and the breath came into them, and they lived, and stood up upon their feet, an exceeding great army." (Exodus 37:5, 10)

Seeing the Unseen (2)

"Nicodemus saith unto him, How can a man be born when he is old? Can he enter a second time into his mother's womb, and be born? Jesus answered. Verily, verily, I say unto thee, Except a man be born of water and of the Spirit, he cannot enter into the kingdom of God." (John 3:4-5)

Seeing the Unseen (3)

"And when the servant of the man of God was risen early, and gone forth, behold, an host compassed the city both with horses and chariots. And his servant said unto him, Alas, my master! How shall we do?.... And Elisha prayed, and said, LORD. I pray thee, open his eyes, that he may see. And the LORD opened the eyes of the young man; and he saw: and, behold, the mountain was full of horses and chariots of fire round about Elisha." (2 Kings 6:15, 17)

Discussion Questions

1. What did God show Ezekiel in Ezekiel 37:1-14 that was to be made known to his people Israel?
2. What did Jesus see that Nicodemus did not understand?
3. Explain Romans 7:15-25.
4. What did Jesus see in Matthew 7:13-14 that many today are unaware of?
5. What did the apostle Paul see in Acts 17:16-31?

Fill in the Blanks

1. "God thundereth ___with his voice; great things doeth he, which we___ ___ ."
2. "For we are___ by hope: but hope that is___ is not___: for what a man___ , why doth he yet___ for?"
3. "The ___things___ unto the Lord our God: but those things which are___ belong unto___ and to our___ for ever, that we may do all the___ of this___ ."
4. "For we___ by___ , not by___ ."
5. "And Jesus said, For___ I am come into this world, that they which___ ___might___ ; and that they which___ might be made___ ."

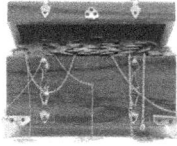

Seeing the Unseen

"While we look not at the things which are seen, but at the things which are not seen: for the things which are seen are temporal: but the things which are not seen are eternal" (2 Corinthians 4:18).

In all of us should be an awareness that the life we live now will someday no longer be, and that the eternal life which we presently do not see will one day be seen by all. Through the Word of God, we are able to glimpse what transpires beyond the grave and this life; therefore, our affections and our focus should be on things that are above and not on things below (Colossians 3:2).

Seeing the Unseen (1)

Old Testament – Ezekiel 37:1-14, Exodus 14:10-31, 2nd Kings 6:8-17, Genesis 18:9-14, Numbers 22:20-35, Job 11:7-12, 37:5, 23, Psalms 33:6-11, Joshua 21:45, Lamentations 3:37-38, Isaiah 14:24, Zechariah 1:6

New Testament – John 3:1-8, Matthew 7:13-14, 2 Corinthians 5:7, Romans 11:33

Seeing the Unseen (2)

Old Testament – Job 12:13-25, 23:8-9, 37:7, 14, 42:5-6, Isaiah 26:11, 29:7-20, 24, 30:20-21, 34:16, 42:9, 16, Daniel 12:3-7, Psalms 91:7-9, 37:10-13, Proverbs 27:19

New Testament – 2 Corinthians 4:18, Romans 8:24-25, 7:15-25, 2:28-29

Seeing the Unseen (3)

Old Testament – Judges 7:1-9, Deuteronomy 3:21-24, Joshua 5:13-14, 6:1-5, 20, 10:6-14, Daniel 5:1-12, 23-31, Ezekiel 39:24-29, Jeremiah 33:3-9, Isaiah 40:27-31, Zephaniah 2:1-3

New Testament – Hebrews 11:13-16, Acts 17:16-3, Ephesians 3:1-5, 17-20, 1 Peter 1:10-12

Seeing the Unseen (4)

Old Testament – Deuteronomy 29:29, 20:1-4, Daniel 3:23-29, Jeremiah 1:8, 18-19, Job 5:8-16, 11:7-11, Daniel 2:20-23, Psalms 139:15-18, 31:19-20, 16:11, Isaiah 64:4

New Testament – Matthew 11:16-27, 13:10-17, John 9:39-41, 1 John 3:2-3, Acts 16:16-17

Seeing the Unseen (5)

Old Testament – Amos 3:4-7, Psalms 25:12-14, 36:9, 119:18, Job 11:13-19, 29:1-3, Isaiah 6:9-10, 29:9-10, 44:18-20, Deuteronomy 29:4, Hosea 14:9

New Testament – John 7:17, 15:15, 20:29-31, Ephesians 3:1-5, 9-11, 2 Corinthians 4:3-4, 1 Corinthians 2:9-16

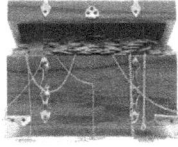

Leadership

Leadership (1)

"The God of Israel said, the Rock of Israel spake to me, He that ruleth over men must be just, ruling in the fear of God." (2 Samuel 23:3)

Leadership (2)

"And the Lord said, Who then is that faithful and wise steward, whom his lord shall make ruler over his household, to give them their portion of meat in due season? Blessed is that servant, whom his lord when he cometh shall find so doing. (Luke 42-43)

Leadership (3)

"And thou, Ezra, after the wisdom of thy God, that is in thine hand, set magistrates and judges, which may judge all the people that are beyond the river, all such as know the laws of thy God; and teach ye them that know them not." (Ezra 7:25)

Discussion Questions

1. In Hebrews 3:5, what leadership quality was acknowledged in Moses?
2. What were the criteria of those selected to lead in Acts 6:3-6?
3. What was wrong with the leaders in Matthew 15:14?
4. What advice was given in Proverbs 31:3-5?

5. Explain 2 Thessalonians 3:7-9.

Fill in the Blanks

1. "But we were____ among you, even as a__ __ her children."
2. "The words of____ men are heard in quiet more than the cry of him that____ among____."
3. "And Moses verily was____ in all his house, as a____, for a____ of those things which were to be spoken after."
4. "Moreover it is____ in__ , that a man be found____ ."
5. "And I thank Christ Jesus our Lord, who hath____ me, for that he____ me____ , putting me into the____."

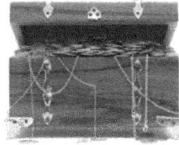

Leadership

*B*iblical leadership patterns itself after the example left by our Lord and Savior, Jesus Christ. It models the vision, the divine attributes, and the willingness to lead by serving others rather than lording over others. A great need exists for genuine, Christlike leadership in the church today.

Leadership (1)

Old Testament – Exodus 3:11-12, 4:10-16, Numbers 11:16-17, 12:1-9, 27:16-23, Joshua 1:1-9, Daniel 2:20-21, 4:17, 5:18-21, 1 Chronicles 28:4, 2 Samuel 23:3, Proverbs 8:12, 15, 16

New Testament – Hebrews 3:5, John 19:11, 1 Peter 2:13-15, Romans 13:1-5, Luke 12:42-43

Leadership (2)

Old Testament – Exodus 18:19-27, Deuteronomy 1:13-18, 16:18-20, 17:8-20, Ezra 7:10, 23-28, 8:17-21, Numbers 20:8-12, Leviticus 10:1-3, Malachi 2:7, 1 Kings 3:7-12, Jeremiah 3:15, 1 Samuel 2:35, Zechariah 3:7

New Testament – Acts 6:3-6, 14:23, 20:28-32, Hebrews 13:17, 1 Peter 5:1-5

Leadership (3)

Old Testament – 2 Samuel 5:1-3, 10, 12, 7:8-9, 1 Samuel 22:14, Nehemiah 7:1-2, 9:7-8, 13:13, Isaiah 8:1-2, Daniel 6:1-4, 2 Kings 12:14-15, 22:7, Psalms 101:6, Proverbs 29:4, 12, 14

New Testament – 2 Timothy 2:2, 20-21, 1 Timothy 1:12-13, 3:1-13, Titus 1:5-9, 1 Corinthians 4:1-2

Leadership (4)

Old Testament – 1 Samuel 13:6-14, 15:11-26, Proverbs 25:19, Isaiah 9:16, 3:12, 1:23-27, Zechariah 11:5, 16-17, Jeremiah 5:13, 26-31, 12:10, 50:6, Lamentations 4:13-16, Hosea 9:7-9, 8:4, Ezekiel 13:1-9

New Testament – Romans 2:17-24, Matthew 15:14, 21:33-46, 23:1-33

Leadership (5)

Old Testament – Leviticus 21:1, 6-15, 1 Samuel 8:4-5, 11-22, 10:25, 12:1-7, 25, Proverbs 31:3-5, 28:15-16, 20:26, 1 Chronicles 29:1, 19-25, Judges 17:6, Ecclesiastes 8:9, 9:17

New Testament – Luke 16:10-12, John 21:15-17, 2 Thessalonians 3:7-9, 1 Thessalonians 5:11-13, 2:7-12, 1:6

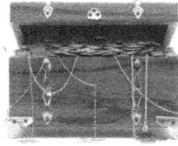

Doctrine

Doctrine (1)

"My doctrine shall drop as the rain, my speech shall distil as the dew, as the rain upon the tender herb, and as the showers upon the grass:" (Deuteronomy 32:2)

Doctrine (2)

"For I give you good doctrine, forsake ye not my law." (Proverbs 4:2)

Doctrine (3)

"Take heed unto thyself, and unto the doctrine; continue in them: for in doing this thou shalt both save thyself, and them that hear thee." (1 Timothy 4:16)

Discussion Questions

1. What warning was given in Proverbs 4:2?
2. What happens if we ignore Jesus's instructions according to Acts 3:23?
3. Explain Mathew 4:4.
4. What were the observations made in 2 John 1:4-11?
5. Explain 1 John 2:3-6, 26-27.

Fill in the Blanks

1. "And many nations shall come, and say, Come, and let us go up to the mountain of the____, and to the____ of the____ of____; and he will____ us of his____, and we will____ in His____."
2. "If any man will do his___, he shall___of the , whether it be of____, or whether I___ of myself."
3. "Take____ unto____, and unto the____; continue in them: for in doing this thou shalt both save____, and them that____ thee."
4. "And they continued____ in the apostles'____ and fellowship."
5. "As I besought thee to abide still at____, when I went into____, that thou mightiest charge some that they____ no other____."

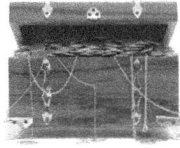

Doctrine

D idache is the Greek word that is translated *doctrine*. It means "teachings, a body of teachings, instructions, beliefs and precepts." The early church continued steadfastly in the apostle's doctrine that was given to them by Christ Himself (Acts 2:42, Acts 1:2, Matthew 28:20). We are admonished to teach only that which originated from Christ and not from men (Galatians 1:6-12, Romans 16:17, 1 Timothy 6:3, 1 Timothy 1:3, 1 Timothy 4:1, Matthew 15:9).

Doctrine (1)

Old Testament – Proverbs 4:2, Deuteronomy 32:2, Isaiah 55:8-11, 54:13, 29:24, 28:9-10, 26, 2:3,

2 Kings 17:27

New Testament – John 7:16-17, 6:44-45, 63, 68, Matthew 28:18-20, 21:23-27, 15:6, 9, 13, 4:4, Acts 1:1-12, 2:42, 3:22-23, 2 John 1:4-11

Doctrine (2)

Old Testament – Exodus 4:12, 18:20, 23, Numbers 22:18, 20, 38, 23:19, Deuteronomy 4:1-2, 14, 18:18, 1 Samuel 12:23, Jeremiah 10:8, Nahum 8:5-8, Ezra 7:10, 25

New Testament – Matthew 22:16, 29, Luke 24:32, 45, John 12:48-50, Acts 17:1-2, 11, 2 Timothy 3:10-17, 1 Timothy 4:1-6, 16

Doctrine (3)

Old Testament – Job 11:4-5, 1 Kings 8:35-36, Psalms 25:4-5, Psalms 32:8-9, Psalms 77:13, Psalms 94:12, Psalms 119:30-33, Malachi 2:6

New Testament – Mark 11:18, John 3:31-34, John 4:25-26, Acts 5:20, 28-29, 42, 1 Timothy 6:1-5, 20-21, 2 Timothy 4:2-5, Titus 1:7-9, Ephesians 4:11-15

Doctrine (4)

Old Testament – Psalms 143:10, 132:12, 119:1-7, 93-94, 128, 168, 89:34, Proverbs 2:6, 30:5-6

New Testament – 2 Peter 1:19-21, Romans 3:3-4, 6:17, 10:17, 15:4, 1 Peter 4:11, Galatians 1:6-12,

1 Corinthians 14:34, Acts 20:28-31, 1 Timothy 5:17, Mark 7:7-9

Doctrine (5)

Old Testament – Isaiah 30:10-13, 9:14-16, 1 Kings 22:8, 16, Ezekiel 13:1-9, Jeremiah 5:30-31, 14:14, 23:16-18, 29:8-9, 21-23, 35:12-15, Deuteronomy 18:20

New Testament – Matthew 7:15-23, 15:14, 24:4-5, 23-26, 1 John 2:3-6, 26-27, 4:1-6, Romans 16:17-18, 2 Peter 2:1-3, 18-21, Revelation 19:19-21

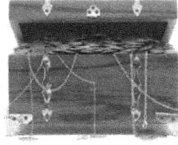

His Marvelous Work

His Marvelous Work (1)

"Remember His marvelous works that He hath done, His wonders, and the judgments of his mouth." (1 Chronicles 16:12)

His Marvelous Work (2)

"In whom we have redemption through his blood, the forgiveness of sins, according to the riches of his grace; wherein he hath abounded toward us in all wisdom and prudence; (Ephesians 1:7-8)

His Marvelous Work (3)

"To wit, that God was in Christ, reconciling the world unto himself, not imputing their trespasses unto them; and hath committed unto us the word of reconciliation." (2 Corinthians 5:19)

Discussion Questions

1. What are the exhortations given in 1 Chronicles 16:23-29?
2. What work does God work in us, according to Hebrews 13:21?
3. What observations are made in Jeremiah 10:12-16?
4. What marvelous work was done in Colossians 2:11-12?
5. Explain Romans 11:33-34.

Fill in the Blanks

1. "Which doeth great things and;___ things without number."
2. "The king's___ is in the hand of the___ , as the rivers of water: he___ it___ he will."
3. "This was the___ doing, and it is___ in our eyes?"
4. "If I do not the___ of my Father, believe me___ ."
5. "Who hath___me, that I should repay him? whatsoever is___ the whole___ is___ ."

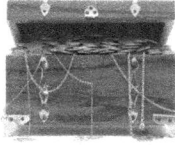

His Marvelous Work

"Remember his marvelous works that he hath done, his wonders, and the judgments of his mouth" (1 Chronicles 16:12).

O ur God is truly an awesome God. If only we would make observations of all He has done and of all that He is doing—the sunshine, the rain, the clouds, the wind, the rivers, the fish, the birds, the skies, the trees, the flowers, the meadows, the mountains, our families, our friends, every good and perfect gift comes from God. We need to take time and meditate on his marvelous work.

His Marvelous Work (1)

Old Testament – 1 Chronicles 16:8-12, 23-29, Psalms 111:1-9, 105:1-5, 43-45, 77:11-20, Proverbs 21:1, 30, Daniel 4:35, 37, Ecclesiastes 3:11-18, 1 Kings 8:56-61, Isaiah 45:5-13, 43:13-19

New Testament – 2 Corinthians 5:17-21, Philippians 2:9-13, Ephesians 1:3-12, Hebrews 13:21

His Marvelous Work (2)

Old Testament – Job 5:7-16, 36:24-33, 42:1-3, Psalms 40:5, 92:4-5, 96:1-4, 136:1-4, Isaiah 25:1, 28:20-21, 29:9-14, Jeremiah 8:6-9

New Testament – 1 Corinthians 1:19-29, John 6:28-29, 10:37-38, Acts 5:38-39, Colossians 1:28-29, 2:11-12

His Marvelous Work (3)

Old Testament – Jeremiah 10:12-16, 32:17-22, 33:1-3, 6-9, Psalms 145:1-21, 139:14-18, 118:22-23, 104:24-34, 90:16-17, 72:18-19, Isaiah 54:16-17, 22:20-25

New Testament – Mark 12:10-12, Romans 9:28, Philippians 2:13, 1 Corinthians 12:6

His Marvelous Work (4)

Old Testament – Job 9:8-10, 11:7-10, 12:13-25, Psalms 19:1-6, 31:21, 33:8-15, 50:1-15, 66:1-9, 71:16-21, 86:9-10, Zechariah 8:1-6

New Testament – Romans 11:33-36, Acts 13:38-41, 1 Peter 2:9, 2 Corinthians 9:8, Revelation 15:3-4

His Marvelous Work (5)

Old Testament – Exodus 34:10, Deuteronomy 4:32-35, Job 23:11-14, 33:13-14, 40:7-14, 41:11, Psalms 78:12-16, 98:1-4, 107:8-15, 126:1-3, Joshua 21:44-45

New Testament – John 5:36, 9:30-33, 10:37, 15:24, Luke 1:49-54, 1 John 5:9

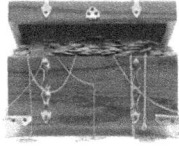

The Man of God

The Man of God (1)

"And this is the blessing, wherewith Moses the man of God blessed the children of Israel before his death." (Deuteronomy 33:1)

The Man of God (2)

"Then the woman came and told her husband, saying, A man of God came unto me, and his countenance was like the countenance of an angel of God, very terrible: but I asked him not whence he was, neither told me his name: (Judges 13:6)

The Man of God (3)

"But thou, O man of God, flee these things; and follow after righteousness, godliness, faith, love, patience, meekness." (1 Timothy 6:11)

Discussion Questions

1. What was the charge given to Solomon in 1 Chronicles 28:8-9?
2. Explain Isaiah 66:2.
3. What instructions did Paul give Timothy in 2 Timothy 2:1-7?
4. What instructions were given in 1 Timothy 4:12-14?
5. Explain 1 Corinthians 4:20-21.

Fill in the Blanks

1. "Mine eyes shall be upon the___ of the land, that they may____ with me: he that walketh in a____ way, he shall____ me."

2. "I give thee____ in the sight of____ , who quickeneth all things, and before Christ Jesus."

3. "That the___ of___ may be perfect, throughly furnished unto all___ works."

4. "Wherefore, brethren, look ye out among you seven men of____ report, full of the____ ____ and___ , whom we may____ over this business."

5. "And she said unto her husband, Behold now, I perceive that this is an____ ____ of____ , which passeth by us continually."

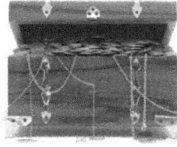

The Man of God

*T*his is a most honored reference or appellation to the man who is commissioned by God, charged by God to perform or accomplish God's divine purpose. It necessitates the utmost adroitness, utmost faithfulness, and utmost austerity in the deliberation of this duty given unto him.

The Man of God (1)

Old Testament – Joshua 14:5-6, Numbers 12:3-8, 1 Chronicles 6:49, 23:14, 28:8-9, 2 Chronicles 8:8-14, 16:9, Zechariah 3:6-7, Exodus 18:19-23, Psalms 101:6, 65:4, Proverbs 20:6, Isaiah 66:2

New Testament – Hebrews 3:1-6, Acts 6:3-6, 11:20-26, 1 Timothy 6:11-12, 2 Timothy 3:10-17, 2:1-10, 19-21

The Man of God (2)

Old Testament – Ezekiel 22:29-30, 24:15-18, Isaiah 6:1-12, 64:7, Jeremiah 1:4-10, 5:1-6, 20:7-18, 1 Samuel 2:21, 26-35, 9:6-10, 17, 21-27, 10:6, Psalms 37:23, 30-31, 147:11, Malachi 2:5-7

New Testament – Acts 10:35, Luke 14:26-27, Titus 1:1, 4-9, James 1:1, Philippians 2:19-22

The Man of God (3)

Old Testament – Genesis 41:38-41, Judges 13:2-25, Numbers 27:18-19, 16:7, 11-31, 14:22-24, 11:14-17 Daniel 6:3, 5:11-14, Nehemiah 7:1-2, 1 Kings 12:17-24, 13:1-31, 17:1-24, 2 Chronicles 9:1-8, 25:1-9

New Testament – John 8:42-47, 1 John 3:7-10, 24, 4:5-6, 1 Timothy 4:12-16

The Man of God (4)

Old Testament – Exodus 7:1-12, 1 Kings 18:1-12, 16- 46, 19:9-18, 20:26-43, Proverbs 31:3-5, 2 Kings 1:1-17 Ecclesiastes 2:26

New Testament – Matthew 10:40-42, James 5:17-18, 1 Corinthians 2:1-10, 1 Corinthians 4:6-17, 1 Timothy 3:1-13

The Man of God (5)

Old Testament – Psalms 1:1-6, 4:3, 86:2, 16, 2 Kings 2:8-15, 23-25, 4:1-44, 5:1-27, 6:1-17, 7:1-20, 8:1-15, 13:14-21, 23:16-18

New Testament – Luke 4:24-30, 6:20-26, Acts 5:38-42, 14:8-18

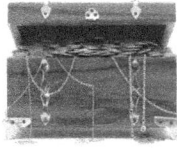

Findeth

Findeth (1)

"He that followeth after righteousness and mercy findeth life, righteousness, and honour. (Proverbs 21:21)

Findeth (2)

"Again, the kingdom of heaven is like unto treasure hid in a field; the which when a man hath found, he hideth, and for joy thereof goeth and selleth all that he hath, and buyeth that field." (Matthew 13:44)

Findeth (3)

"Run ye to and fro throughout the streets of Jerusalem, and see now, and know, and seek in the broad places thereof, if ye can find a man, if there be any thar executeth judgment, that seeketh the truth; and I will pardon it." (Jeremiah 5:1)

Discussion Questions

1. Discuss Psalms 77:2-11.
2. What did the servants of the king search for in Matthew 22?
3. Explain Romans 10:20-21.
4. Discuss Ecclesiastes 3:10-11.
5. Discuss Acts 17:27-28.

Fill in the Blanks

1. "And in their ____was found no guile: for they are without ____before the throne of God."
2. "Ask, and it shall be given to you____;____ , and ye shall____ ; knock, and it shall be opened unto you."
3. "Then shall they call upon me, but I will not ____; they shall seek me____ , but they shall not____ ____ ."
4. "For the work of a____ shall he____ unto him, and ___every man to find___ to his way."
5. "Take my yoke upon you, and____ of___ ; for I am and in heart: and ye shall ____rest unto your souls."

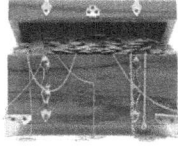

Findeth

"I rejoice at thy word, as one that findeth great spoil" (Psalms 119:162).

"Happy is the man that findeth wisdom, and the man that getteth understandeth" (Proverbs 3:13).

"Again, the kingdom of heaven is like unto treasure hid in a field; the which when a man hath found, he hideth, and for joy thereof goeth and selleth all that he hath, and buyeth that field" (Matthew 13:44).

*M*any of us search, sometimes even for years, for that which will fill the void within us, the longing in our soul that keeps us in a state of unrest and discontent until we find that which will bring joy, peace, fulfilment, completeness, and satisfaction. The Christian finds that which his soul desires in Jesus Christ.

Findeth (1)

Old Testament – Proverbs 18:22, 20:6, 21:21, 31:10, Ecclesiastes 7:14, 24-29, 8:16-17, 9:10, 11:1-2, 12:10, Psalms 119:162, Isaiah 55:6, 65:1, Jeremiah 5:1-4, Ezekiel 22:30

New Testament – Romans 10:20-21, Matthew 22:9-10, 13:44-46, Luke 15:4-10, 18:7-83

Findeth (2)

Old Testament – Genesis 18:26-33, Numbers 32:23, Job 9:2-10, 11:7-8, 23:3-6, 33:10-11, 37:22-24, Ecclesiastes 3:10-11, Proverbs 2: 1-5, Jeremiah 6:16, 29:13-14, Deuteronomy 4:29, Psalms 132:3-5, 32:6, 17:3

New Testament – Romans 11:33, Matthew 10:39, 11:29, 24:46

Findeth (3)

Old Testament – Lamentations 1:3, 6, 2:9-10, Amos 8:11-12, Jeremiah 5:26-28, Proverbs 1:23-28, 3:3-4, 4:20-22, 8:11-12, 17, 34-35, 14:6, Job 17:10, 28:12-13, 34:11

New Testament – Matthew 7:7, 14, 8:8-10, 11:25, John 1:41, 45, 7:31-36, Acts 17:27-28

Findeth (4)

Old Testament – Genesis 6:6, 8, 19:17-19, 33:8, 34:11, 47:25, Numbers 32:5, 2 Samuel 15:25, Ruth 2:2, 13, Judges 6:16-17, Hosea 24:3, 5:6, 2:6-7, Proverbs 17:20, 19:8, 28:23

New Testament – Luke 11:9-10, 19:47-48, 23:4, 13-14, Hebrews 4:14-16, Romans 7:18, 21

Findeth (5)

Old Testament – Nehemiah 9:7-8, Exodus 33:13-17, 34:9, Genesis 41:38, Daniel 1:19-20, 5:11, 14, 6:4, 22-23, 1 Samuel 29:3, 6, 24:17, 19, Psalms 89:20, 2 Chronicles 15:1-4, 19:3, 1 Kings 1:52, Jeremiah 50:20

New Testament – Luke 6:7, John 10:9, 19:4, Acts 17:27, 2 Peter 3:14, Revelation 14:5

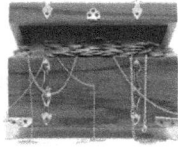

Taste and See

Taste and See (1)

"O taste and see that the LORD is good: blessed is the man that trusteh in Him." (Psalms 34:8)

Taste and See (2)

"If ye then, being evil, know how to give good gifts unto your children, how much more shall your Father which is in heaven give good things to them that ask them? (Matthew 7:11)

Taste and See (3)

"The LORD is good unto them that wait for Him, to the soul that seeketh Him." (Lamentations 3:25)

Discussion Questions

1. What observations are made in Psalms 63:3-8?
2. Explain Romans 8:28, 36-37.
3. What is conveyed in Psalms 34:7-10?
4. Why is it imperative that we have a desire for the sincere milk of the word?
5. Explain 2 Corinthians 2:15-16.

Fill in the Blanks

1. "And walk in____, as Christ also hath___ us, and hath given himself for us an____ and a sacrifice to God for a____ ___ Saviour.
2. "Behold that which I have seen: it is____ and____ for one to eat and to drink, and to enjoy the good of all his____.
3. "Truly God is____ to Israel, even to such as are of a____ .
4. "For the bread of___ is he which cometh down from____ , and giveth____ unto the world.
5. "Then Jesus said unto them, Verily, verily, I say unto you, Except ye____ the of the Son of man, and____ his, ye have no____ in you.

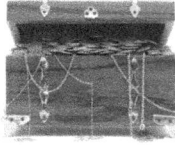

Taste and See

"O taste and see that the Lord is good..." (Psalms 34:8).

"My meditation of him shall be sweet: I will be glad in the Lord" (Psalms 104:34).

"How sweet are thy words unto my taste! yea, sweeter than honey to my mouth!" (Psalms 119:103).

To those who know and love the Lord, He is good, and He is sweet.

Taste and See(1)

Old Testament – Psalms 34:8, 18-19, 63:3-8, 84:2-7, 11-12, 86:5, 10, 13-15, 100:4-5, 119:68, 103, Deuteronomy 8:10-20, Jeremiah 32:38-41, Lamentations 3:25-26

New Testament – Matthew 7:11, 5:43-48, Romans 2:4-10, 11:22, 33-36, James 1:17

Taste and See (2)

Old Testament – Jeremiah 15:16, Ezekiel 3:1-4, Job 23:12, Proverbs 24:13-14, 16:20-24, Psalms 19:7-11, 31:19-24, 145:5-21, Isaiah 7:14-15

New Testament – John 4:31-34, 6:27, 32-35, 53-58, Matthew 26:26-28, 1 Corinthians 11:23-34

Taste and See (3)

Old Testament – Psalms 36:7-10, 42:1-4, 8, 52:1-9, 65:4-5, 9-13, 73:1, Nehemiah 9:15, 20-21, 25, Deuteronomy 12:7, 20-21, 28, Ecclesiastes 3:12-13, 5:18

New Testament – Luke 22:28-30, 14:12-24, 1 Peter 2:1-3, Hebrews 6:4-8

Taste and See (4)

Old Testament – Proverbs 20:17, Proverbs 9:17-18, Deuteronomy 32:30-33, Isaiah 5:20-23, Job 20:12-23, 29, Exodus 15:22-26, Psalms 37:25, Psalms 104:33-34, Psalms 141:4-6, Isaiah 55:1-3, Nahum 1:7

New Testament – Ephesians 5:2, 2 Corinthians 2:14-17, Philippians 4:1

Taste and See (5)

Old Testament – Exodus 15:25, Ezekiel 2:8-10, 3:1-4, Ecclesiastes 11:7, Psalms 60:3, 75:7-8, 104:34, 135:3, 136:1-3, 25, 141:4-6, Proverbs 3:19, 24, 13:19, 27:7, Job 36:11, 16, Isaiah 55:1-3, Jeremiah 31:12, 25-26

New Testament – Matthew 5:6, John 4:14, 6:48, 7:37, Philippians 4:18, Revelation 10:8-10

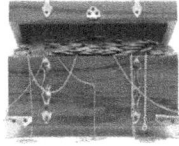

Walk in Love

Walk in Love (1)

"He hath shewed thee, O man, what is good; and what doth the LORD require of thee, but to do justly, and to love mercy, and to walk humbly with thy God?" (Micah 6:8)

Walk in Love (2)

"Be ye therefore followers of God, as dear children; And walk in love, as Christ also loved us, and hath given himself for us as an offering and a sacrifice to God for a sweetsmelling savour." (Ephesians 5:1-2)

Walk in Love (3)

"According as he hath chosen us in him before the foundation of the world, that we should be holy and without blame before him in love." (Ephesians 1:4)

Discussion Questions

1. What was God's requirement in Micah 6:8?
2. Explain Jeremiah 31:3.
3. What are your observations of Romans 12:9-21?
4. Explain 1 Corinthians 8:3.
5. What does love for Christ cause us to do in John 14:15, 21, 23-24?

Fill in the Blanks

1. "And we know that all____ work together for___ to them that____ God, to them who are the called according to his____ ."

2. "And walk in____ , as Christ also hath ____us, and hath given himself for us an offering and a sacrifice to God for a sweet smelling savour."

3. "Cause me to hear thy___ in the morning; for in thee do I trust: cause me to know the____ wherein I should___ ; for I lift up my soul unto you."

4. "He____ righteousness and____ : the earth is full of the____ of the Lord."

5. "A new commandment I give unto you, That you____ one another; as I have____ you, that ye also____ one another."

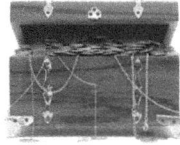

Walk in Love

*P*erhaps the best definition of love (or charity) is the one Paul describes in 1 Corinthians 13:4-7: "Charity suffereth long, and is kind; charity envieth not; charity vaunteth not itself, is not puffed up, Doth not behave itself unseemly, seeketh not her own, is not easily provoked, thinketh no evil; Rejoiceth not in iniquity, but rejoiceth in the truth; Beareth all things, believeth all things, hopeth all things, endureth all things." This depiction of love is a portrait of our Lord and Savior, Jesus. Not only did He exemplify love, but He also commanded us to love as He loved (John 13:34-35). How big a problem is that for us? Is love the badge, the true identifying mark of a Christian? Every day, we must strive to walk in love.

Walk in Love (1)

Old Testament – Micah 6:8, Zephaniah 3:17, 20, Deuteronomy 10:12, 15-19, 7:7-9, 12-14, 33:3, Jeremiah 31:3, Zechariah 2:8, Psalms 143:8, 25:6, 10, 89:14-17

New Testament – 1 John 4:7-13, 16-19, Ephesians 5:1-2, 1:4, 1 Corinthians 13:1-8, 13

Walk in Love (2)

Old Testament – Hosea 11:3-4, Deuteronomy 4:36-40, Leviticus 19:18, 34, Exodus 34:5-8, Jonah 4:2, Joel 2:13, Lamentations 3:22-23, Psalms 63:3, 33:5, 31:23

New Testament – John 13:34-35, 1 Corinthians 8:3, 16:14, Galatians 5:13-14, 22-26, 1 John 3:1-3, 11, 23-24

Walk in Love (3)

Old Testament – Deuteronomy 15:7-14, 18:13, Zechariah 7:8-10, Isaiah 58:6-11, 1:11-17, Jeremiah 22:16-17, Amos 5:11-15, 21-24, Psalms 36:10, 51:15-19, Proverbs 21:3

New Testament – John 3:16-17, 15:12-13, Luke 10:25-37, Romans 13:8-10, 1 John 3:16-19

Walk in Love (4)

Old Testament – Daniel 9:4, Malachi 1:2-3, Deuteronomy 23:5, 13:1-3, 1 Samuel 2:30, Exodus 34:6-8, Psalms 107:8-9, 42-43, 94:14-15, 78:37-39, 67-68, 40:5, 10-11

New Testament – John 14:15, 21, 23-24, 16:27, Romans 5:6-8, 11:22, Jude 1:21

Walk in Love (5)

Old Testament – 1 Kings 3:3, Psalms 145:20, 119:47-48, 127-128, 116:1-2, 97:10, 91:14, 48:9-14, 5:11-12, Isaiah 26:7-10, Proverbs 16:13

New Testament – Romans 8:28, 12:9-21, 1 Corinthians 2:9, 2 Corinthians 13:11, 2 Thessalonians 2:16-17, 1 Peter 1:22, 4:8

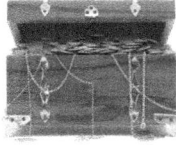

I Shall Not Be Moved

I Shall Not Be Moved (1)

"But none of these things move me, neither count I my life dear unto myself, so that I might finish my course with joy, and the ministry, which I have received of the Lord Jesus, to testify the gospel of the grace of God." (Acts 20:21)

I Shall Not Be Moved (2)

"Therefore, my beloved brethren, be ye stedfast, unmoveable, always abounding in the work of the Lord, forasmuch as ye know that your labour is not in vain in the Lord." (1 Corinthians 15:58)

I Shall Not Be Moved (3)

"And though after my skin worms destroy the body, yet in my flesh shall I see God:" (Job 19:26)

Discussion Questions

1. What are your observations of Daniel 6:8-28?
2. What response did Peter give in John 6:66-69?
3. What type resolve did Paul have in Romans 8:28-39?
4. What was the command given in 1 Corinthians 15:58?
5. What warning is given in Galatians 1:6-9?

Fill in the Blanks

1. "If ye____ in the faith grounded and settled, and be not____ away from the___ of the____ ."
2. "And this word, Yet once more, signifieth the ____of those things that are____ , as of things that are made, that those things which cannot be___ may___ ."
3. "Therefore, my beloved____ , be ye____ , ____, always abounding in the____ of the___ ."
4. "And though after my skin worms___ this____ , yet in my flesh shall I___ ___ ."
5. "Lord, to whom shall we go? thou hast the___ of___ life."

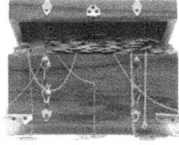

I Shall Not Be Moved

Within us, a declaration concerning what we truly value, what we truly believe in, and what we truly stand for is of utmost importance. It is imperative that our souls be anchored because of the relentless resolve we manifest and the unwavering conviction we have, even to the point of crying out, "I shall not be moved" in spite of opposition.

I Shall Not Be Moved (1)

Old Testament – Proverbs 10:25, 30, 12:3, 7, 23:18, Psalms 21:7, 57:7, 112:5-7, Job 27:3-6, 19:25-27, 14:14, 18-20, 2 Samuel 22:22-24

New Testament – 1 Corinthians 15:58, 16:13, Acts 20:17-21, Acts 21:13-14, Romans 8:28-39, 4:20-25

I Shall Not Be Moved (2)

Old Testament – Psalms 16:8-9, 55:22, 62:5-6, 63:8, 119:110-112, 117, Jeremiah 13:11, 2 Kings 18:5-7, Joshua 23:6-8, Proverbs 21:16-21

New Testament – John 6:66-69, Hebrews 10:35-39, 12:27, 2 Timothy 1:12-14, 2:1-10, 3:10-12

I Shall Not Be Moved (3)

Old Testament – Daniel 6:8-26, 1 Chronicles 16:29-30, Psalms 15:1-5, 20:7-8, 26:1, 30:6-7, 46:1-7, 62:1-2, 108:1, 119:33, 69, 101, 115, 125:1-2

New Testament – Acts 2:25-26, 14:19-22, Matthew 24:8-13, 35, 2 Peter 2:20-21, 3:17

I Shall Not Be Moved (4)

Old Testament – Job 2:3, 9-10, 11:10-15, 13:14-15, 19:20, 25-27, 31:4-6 Psalms 26:8-12, 44:17-19, 61:2-4, 66:8-9, 94:17-18

New Testament – Hebrews 3:12-14, 1 Thessalonians 3:7-8, 1 Timothy 6:20-21, Colossians 1:23, Galatians 1:6-9, Philippians 3:17-20

I Shall Not Be Moved (5)

Old Testament – Isaiah 10:17-20, 26:3, 48:1-2, 50:9-10, 2 Samuel 22:19, Psalms 1;1-3, 13:3-4, 27:10, 13, 119:10, 21,31, 157-158, 176 Jeremiah 17:5-8

New Testament – John 15:1-8, Matthew 13:23, 15:13, Colossians 2:4-8, 18-19, Ephesians 3:13-19, 4:11-16

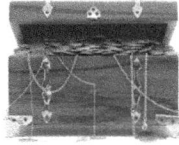

Yield Not to Temptation

Yield Not to Temptation (1)

"There hath no temptation taken you but such as is common to man: but God is faithful, who will not suffer you to be tempted above that ye are able; but with the temptation also make a way to escape, that ye may be able to bear it." (1 Corinthians 10:13)

Yield Not to Temptation (2)

"Thorns and snares are in the way of the froward: he that doth keep his soul shall be far from them." (Proverbs 22:5)

Yield Not to Temptation (3)

"My son, if sinners entice thee, consent thou not." (Proverbs 1:10)

Discussion Questions

1. What caused Eve to give into the temptation of the serpent?
2. Explain 1 Corinthians 10:13.
3. How did Jesus handle the temptation in Matthew 4:1-11, that were hurled at him by Satan?
4. What temptation did Daniel and the three Hebrew boys face in Daniel 1:3-14?
5. Explain Proverbs 19:27.

Fill in the Blanks

1. "There hath no____ taken you but such as is____ to man."
2. "And the Lord God said unto the____ , what is this that thou hast done? And the woman said, The serpent____ me, and I did___ ."
3. "Jesus said unto him, It is___ again, Thou shalt not____ the Lord___ ___ ."
4. "The ___is more excellent than his neighbour: but the____ of the wicked____ them."
5. "For in that____ he hath suffered being____ , he is able to____ them that are____."

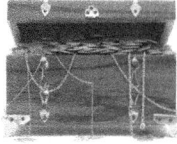

Yield Not to Temptation

L ife is filled with temptations, evil allurements, and seductive ele-
ments that seek to ensnare us and enslave us. We must say no to
that which we know to be wrong. We must not surrender, capitulate,
conform, submit to, or be overcome by that which is evil. The "good fight
of faith" causes us to cling to and follow that which is good, honorable,
and right before God.

Yield Not to Temptation (1)

Old Testament – Genesis 3:1-13, Numbers 22:15-18, Leviticus 18:1-5,
20:22-24, Deuteronomy 7:3-6, 25-26, 13:1-4, 28:14-15, Psalms 106:34-40,
Proverbs 22:5

*New Testament – Matthew 4:1-11, 1 Thessalonians 3:5, 1 Corinthians 7:5, 1 Peter
5:8-9, Revelation 3:10-12*

Yield Not to Temptation (2)

Old Testament – Genesis 39:4-9, 50:15, 19-21, Numbers 20:7-12, Joshua
7:11-26, 2 Samuel 11:1-5, 12:7-13, 1 Kings 11:1-12, Proverbs 20:7-9,
12:26, 6:23-32

New Testament – 1 Corinthians 10:13, James 1:12-15, 2 Peter 2:4-9, 3:1-9, 14-18

Yield Not to Temptation (3)

Old Testament – Jeremiah 35:1-10, 18-19, Daniel 1:3-16, 1 Samuel 13:6-14, 2 Kings 5:15-27, 1 Chronicles 21:1-7, Proverbs 1:10-19, 4:14-19, 16:29-30

New Testament – Matthew 26:41, 69-75, 16:21-23, Galatians 2:11-19, 1 Timothy 5:11-15

Yield Not to Temptation (4)

Old Testament – Daniel 11:32, Psalms 12:1-2, 1 Kings 13:7-29, Proverbs 29:5, 10:17, 19:27, Jeremiah 15:19, 9:8, Hosea 5:4, 7:2, Malachi 2:5-9

New Testament – 1 Corinthians 10:6-11, Hebrews 2:18, 4:14-16, Acts 5:1-6, James 5:4-7, Romans 16:17-18, Philippians 3:16-19

Yield Not to Temptation (5)

Old Testament – Job 2:6-10, 13:14-16, 19:25-27, 27:2-6, Zechariah 3:1-4, Psalms 4:4-5, 7:10-11, 11:5-7, Jeremiah 17:10, 14-16

New Testament – Revelation 2:23, 12:9-12, 17, 1 Peter 2:11-12, 4:12-19, 2 Timothy 2:22-26

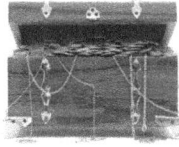

The Slippery Slope
of the Ungodly

The Slippery Slope of the Ungodly (1)

"To deliver thee from the way of evil men, from the man that speaketh froward things; Who leave the paths of uprightness, to walk in the ways of darkness; Who rejoice to do evil, and delight in the forwardness of the wicked; Whose ways are crooked, and they froward in their paths: (Proverbs 2:12-15)

The Slippery Slope of the Ungodly (2)

"Truly God is good to Israel, even to such as are of a clean heart. But as for me, my feet were almost gone; my steps had well nigh slipped. For I was envious at the foolish, when I saw the prosperity of the wicked.... When I thought to know this , it was too painful for me; Until I went into the sanctuary of God; then understood I their end. Surely thou didst set them in slippery places: thou castedst them down into destruction..... as in a moment. (Psalms 73:1-3, 16-19)

The Slippery Slope of the Ungodly (3)

"For the wrath of God is revealed from heaven against all ungodliness and unrighteousness of men, who hold the truth in unrighteousness; (Romans 1:18)

Discussion Questions

1. Do we choose how we live? Discuss.
2. Explain Hebrew 2:1-3.
3. Can we cause others to stumble? Explain.
4. Explain Jeremiah 22:11.
5. Explain why the wicked seemingly prosper at times.

Fill in the Blanks

1. But____ ___ and___ shall wax worse and worse, ____, and being____.
2. But he that doeth____ shall receive for the____ which he hath____.
3. Ye therefore, beloved, seeing ye know these things before, ____ lest ye also, being____ with the____ of the wicked, fall from your our____.
4. His own____ shall take the____ , and he shall be____ with the____ of his____.
5. For a just man falleth____ times, and riseth up again: but the ___shall___ into___ .

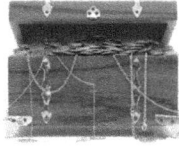

The Slippery Slope
of the Ungodly

*R*eferences in the Bible reveal the path that leads to slippery places where those who choose to live ungodly, disobedient, and rebellious lives place themselves (oftentimes, unknowingly).

> "Surely thou didst set them in slippery places: thou castedst them down into destruction" (Psalms 73:18).

> "Let their way be dark and slippery: and let the angel of the Lord persecute them" (Psalms 35:6).

> "Hold up my goings in thy paths, that my footsteps slip not" (Psalms 17:5).

God's desire for His children is that they travel the path of uprightness.

> "The wicked shall be turned into hell, and all the nations that forget God" (Psalms 9:17).

The Slippery Slope of the Ungodly (1)

Old Testament – Deuteronomy 32:32-35, 2 Chronicles 19:1-2, Job 16:9-11, 17:2-10, 30:8-14, Proverbs 2:12-15, 5:22-23, 16:27, 19:28-29, Psalms 93:3-5, 73:1-12, 14-20, 27-28, 43:1-2, 39:1-2, 37:9-10, 36:11-12, 35:6-8, 28:2-5

New Testament – Matthew 3:10-12, 5:20-22, 13:30, 15:13-14, 23:13-24, 33, Luke 16:20-31, 2 Thessalonians 1:6-10

The Slippery Slope of the Ungodly (2)

Old Testament – 2 Samuel 22:5-7, 17-18, 36-37, 1 Samuel 2:6-9, Psalms 1:1-6, 7:9-16, 10:2-14, 11:2-6, 12:5-8, 17:5-14, 37:17, 20, 28, Jeremiah 23:9-12, 13:16, Isaiah 8:20-22, Job 20:4-5, 12-29, 18:5-18, 21, Proverbs 3:25-26

New Testament – John 12:35, Matthew 8:11-12, 12:34-35, 23:33-35, Jude 1:4, 6, James 4:6-10, 1 Corinthians 10:6-12

The Slippery Slope of the Ungodly (3)

Old Testament – Ecclesiastes 8:8, 10-13, 7:17, Proverbs 14:32, 10:25, 27, 28, 30, Jeremiah 13:23-24, 12:1-4, Job 12:5-6, 21:7-18, 29-31, 27:13-23, Psalms 3:7, 9:16-17, 18:36, 48, 52:1, 5-7, 68:1-2

New Testament – Jude 1:14-21, 1 Peter 4:15-18, 2 Peter 2:1-22, 3:3-14

The Slippery Slope of the Ungodly (4)

Old Testament – Isaiah 5:11-16, 18-24, 19:8-14, 30:7-13, Job 9:24, 29, 10:15, Micah 6:9-16, Proverbs 21:27, 23:17, 25:26, Habakkuk 1:1-4, 7-13, 2:1-4, Psalms 55:22-23, 92:7-9, 94:3-13, 16-23, 121:3-7

New Testament – Hebrews 2:1-3, Colossians 3:25, 2 Timothy 3:13, 2 Peter 3:17, 2 Thessalonians 2:7-12

The Slippery Slope of the Ungodly (5)

Old Testament – Isaiah 3:10-11, 30:7-13, 41:10-13, 16, Proverbs 24:15-16, Job 15:20-35, 34:17-30, Psalms 109:1-3, 16-20, 31, 97:10, 68:21, 38:15-16, 20, 18:35-36

New Testament – Romans 1:18, 28-32, 4:4-8, 5:6-11, Titus 2:12, 2 Timothy 2:15-16, 3:1-8, 1 Peter 2:12-15 Revelation 22:11

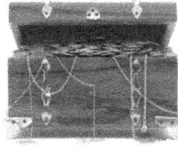

The Remnant

The Remnant (1)

"Then said one unto him, Lord, are there few that be saved? And he said unto them, Strive to enter in at the strait gate: for many, I say unto you, will seek to enter in, and shall not be able." (Luke 13:23-24)

The Remnant (2)

"And it shall come to pass in that day, that the remnant of Israel, and such as are escaped of the house of Jacob, shall no more again stay upon him that smote them; but shall stay upon the LORD, the Holy One of Israel, in truth. The remnant shall return, even the remnant of Jacob, unto the mighty God." (Isaiah 10:20-21)

The Remnant (3)

"Esaias also crieth concerning Israel, Though the number of the children of Israel be as the sand of the sea, a remnant shall be saved:" (Romans 9:27)

Discussion Questions

1. Why were all the nations blessed according to Genesis 22:18?
2. Describe those in Isaiah 35:8-10.
3. What was unique about those listed in Revelation 14:4-7?
4. Explain Zephaniah 3:13.

5. What encouragement was given in Jeremiah 15:11?

Fill in the Blanks

1. "The Lord said, Verily it shall be well with thy_____ ."
2. "Esaias also crieth concerning_____ , Though the number of the_____ of_____ be as the sand of the sea, a_____ shall be_____ ."
3. "So the last shall be_____ , and the first_____: for many_____ be called, but ___chosen."
4. "Because___ is the gate, and narrow is the___, which___unto life, and___ there be that_____ it."
5. "Therefore will he give them up, until the time that she which hath brought forth: then the_____ of his brethren shall_____ unto the children of___ ."

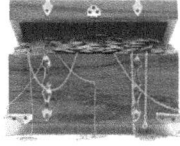

The Remnant

*B*y definition, the word *remnant*, translated from *yether* in the Hebrew, literally means "what is left over." Zechariah 13:9 reads "And I will bring the third part through the fire, and will refine them as silver is refined, and will try them as gold is tried: they shall call on my name, and I will hear them: I will say, it is my people: and they shall say, 'The Lord is my God'"

Notice two-thirds were cut off and perished. What was left over was the remnant. The remnant became acceptable before God. This principle is also noted in New Testament passages, such as "Many are called, but few are chosen" (Matthew 20:16).

The Remnant (1)

Old Testament – Deuteronomy 4:27, 7:7, 26:1-5, 1 Chronicles 16:13-19, 1 Samuel 14:6, Isaiah 1:9, 21-28, 10:20-22, 11:1-5, 11-12, 16, 16:14, 24:5-6, 37:4, 31-32, 46:3-4, Jeremiah 46:1-2, 31-32

New Testament – Luke 13:23-24, Matthew 20:16, 22:14, Romans 9:27

The Remnant (2)

Old Testament – Zephaniah 3:12-13, 2:7-9, Micah 5:2-3, 7-8, 7:18, Zechariah 14:8-9, 13:6-9, 8:6-12, Isaiah 65:8-9, 60:21-22, 46:34, 17:3-6, 11, 2 Kings 19:30-31, Psalms 105:6-12

New Testament – John 11:52, Mark 13:20, 1 Peter 1:2, Romans 11:5, Revelation 12:17

The Remnant (3)

Old Testament – Jeremiah 6:9, 15:11, 23:3-4, 31:7, 39:9, 43:5, 44:28, Joel 2:32, Amos 5:15, Zechariah 10:6-8, Proverbs 2:21-22, Psalms 50:5, 106:47, 147:2, Isaiah 27:13, 56:8

New Testament – 1 Thessalonians 1:4, Colossians 3:12, 2 Timothy 2:10, 1 Corinthians 1:27, Revelation 11:13, 11:13, 17:14

The Remnant (4)

Old Testament – 1 Kings 12:23-24, 14:7-10, 2 Kings 21:12-14, 25:11, Jeremiah 24:8, 40:11-16, 41:16, Ezekiel 6:7-8, 11:13, Psalms 108:10-11, 77:7-9, Nehemiah 1:8-9, 1 Chronicles 30:6

New Testament – Matthew 13:19-23, 1 Peter 4:18, Revelation 14:4-5, 7:13-14, 3:4

The Remnant (5)

Old Testament – Esther 3:8, Ezekiel 36:19-24, 25:16, Isaiah 16:4, 18:7, 28:5, 24-29, Nehemiah 1:3, Micah 2:12-13, 4:6-7, Ezra 9:8-9, 14-15, Amos 9:11-15, Haggai 1:12-14, Psalms 60:1-5

New Testament – Matthew 19:25-29, 18:3, 7:21, 5:20 Revelation 21:27, 22:14

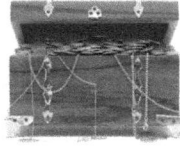

Greatness

Greatness (1)

"I will go in the strength of the Lord God: I will make mention of thy righteousness, even of thine only...Thy righteousness also, O God, is very high, who hast done great things: O God, who is like unto thee! .....Thou increase my greatness, and comfort me on every side." (Psalms 71:16, 19, 21)

Greatness (2)

"Whosoever therefore shall break one of these least commandments, and shall teach men so, he shall be called least in the kingdom of heaven: but whosoever shall do and teach shall be called great in the kingdom of heaven." (Matthew 5:19)

Greatness (3)

"For I say unto you, Among those that are born of women there is not a greater prophet than John the Baptist: but he that is least in the kingdom of God is greater than he." (Luke 7:28)

Discussion Questions

1. Explain Matthew 5:19-20.
2. What observations are made in Deuteronomy 4:5-8, 32-35?
3. Discuss Psalms 119:156, 162, 165.

4. Explain 1 John 4:4.
5. Discuss Daniel 2:45-48.

Fill in the Blanks

1. "And I will make of thee a____ nation, and I will___ thee, and make thy name____ ; and thou shalt be a____ ."
2. "Whosoever therefore shall ___himself as this little____ , the same is____ in the kingdom of heaven."
3. "Ye are of God, little____ , and have overcome them: because____ is he that is in you than he that is in the world."
4. "He shall be____ , and shall be called the Son of the Highest: and the Lord God shall give unto him the throne of his father____ ."
5. "So, David waxed____ and ____: for the Lord of hosts was____ ____ ."

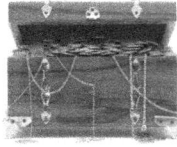

Greatness

"Thou hast also given me the shield of thy salvation: and thy right hand hath holden me up, and thy gentleness hath made me great" (Psalms 18:35).

"Keep therefore and do them; for this is your wisdom and your understanding in the sight of nations, which shall hear all these statutes, and say, Surely this great nation is a wise and understanding people" (Deuteronomy 4:6).

It is absolutely amazing how God can transform any one of us and all of us into greatness by our obedience to His Word and our trust in Him.

Greatness (1)

Old Testament – Genesis 12:1-2, 18:17-19, 22:15-18, 24:34-35, Nehemiah 9:6-8, Ecclesiastes 2:26, 1 Chronicles 29:11-12, 2 Samuel 22:33, 36, Daniel 4:30-32, Job 20:4-9, Psalms 37:35-36, 71:16, 19, 21, 75:4-7

New Testament – Matthew 5:19-20, 8:9-10, 11:7-11, 18:1-4

Greatness (2)

Old Testament – Genesis 37:5-10, 39:9, 41:38-40, 48:16-17, Exodus 11:3, Deuteronomy 4:5-8, 32-35, 34:10, Daniel 2:45-48, Daniel 10:11-12, 18-21, 2 Chronicles 1:7-12, 9:1-8, 1 Chronicles 29:25, Ecclesiastes 2:9, Esther 6:1-11, 9:4, 10:23

New Testament – Matthew 20:25-26, 23:11

Greatness (3)

Old Testament – 1 Chronicles 17:7-8, 11:7-9, 1 Kings 1:37, 47, 2:12, 2 Kings 2:12, 4:8-9, 5:1, 1014, Job 1:1-3, 32:8-9, 33:12, Deuteronomy 32:3-4, Psalms 111:2-3, 112:1-3, 119:156, 162, 165, 145:3-7

New Testament – Matthew 12:6-8, 41, 42, John 8:53-58, 4:12-14

Greatness (4)

Old Testament – Proverbs 18:16, 25:4-6, Ezekiel 31:3-11, 17:2-14, Isaiah 57:10-13, 63:1-3, Deuteronomy 3:24, 1 Chronicles 29:11, Psalms 66:3-7, 86:7, 147:5

New Testament – John 15:13, Ephesians 2:4-5, 1 John 4:4, Hebrews 13:20-21, 2 Corinthians 7:4

Greatness (5)

Old Testament – 1 Chronicles 16:25, Job 5:8-9, 9:4-10, 23:6-7, 36:26, 37:26, Lamentations 3:22-23, Isaiah 63:7, 54:13, 40:26, 32:2, 19:20, 12:6, Psalms 47:2, 48:1-2, 76:1

New Testament – Luke 1:31-32, 49, 7:16, Titus 2:13, Hebrews 4:14, 13:20-21

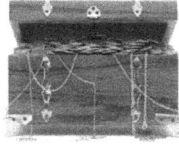

Counsel

Counsel (1)

"There is no wisdom nor understanding nor counsel against the LORD." (Proverbs 21:30)

Counsel (2)

"But the Pharisees and lawyers rejected the counsel of God against themselves, being not baptized of him." (Luke 7:30)

Counsel (3)

"For I have not shunned to declare unto you all the counsel of God." (Acts 20:27)

Discussion Questions

1. Discuss Ephesians 1:11.
2. What oversight was made in Jeremiah 23:18, 22?
3. Discuss Psalms 1:1-2.
4. Explain Proverbs 21:30.
5. What did the Pharisees and lawyers do wrong in Luke 7:30?

Fill in the Blanks

1. "They soon____ his works; they waited not for his counsel."

2. "And now I say unto you, Refrain from these men, and let them alone: for if this____ or this____ be of____ , it will come to nought."

3. "But he forsook the____ of the old men, which they had given him, and____ with the young men that were grown up with him, and which stood before him."

4. "And the spirit of the Lord shall rest upon him, the spirit of wisdom and understanding, the spirit of____ and____ , the spirit of knowledge and of the____ of the____ ."

5. "For who hath known the ____of the Lord? or who hath been his____ ?"

Counsel

"Without counsel purposes are disappointed: but in the multitude of counsellors, they are established" (Proverbs 15:22).

"Thy testimonies also are my delight and my counselors" (Psalms 119:24).

*A*ll of us stand in need of sound advice. We deliberate upon the proper solution or course of action to take. The Word of God is the counsellor for the Christian. God, through His Word, offers wise counsel so that we may have good discernment in our decision making.

Counsel (1)

Old Testament – Exodus 18:19-20, Numbers 27:18-21, Deuteronomy 32:26-28, Hosea 11:4-6, 4:12, Jeremiah 19:7, 23:18, 22, Isaiah 30:1-3, 46:10-11, Proverbs 21:30, Psalms 119:24, 107:11-12, 106:13, 43, 81:11-13

New Testament – Ephesians 1:11, 1 Corinthians 4:5, Acts 5:38, Hebrews 16:18

Counsel (2)

Old Testament – 1 Kings 1:11-12, 12:6-16, 2 Kings 6:8-10, 2 Samuel 15:30-34, 17:7-16, 23, Isaiah 29:15, 28:24-26, 29, 23:8-9, 19:3, 11, 17, 9:6-7, Proverbs 19:21, Psalms 33:11, 73:24

New Testament – Luke 7:30, John 12:10-11, 18:14, Acts 20:27

Counsel (3)

Old Testament – Judges 18:5-6, 20:6-7, 18, 35, Ezra 7:12-14, 21, 10:1-3, 8, Micah 4:9, 12, Zechariah 6:12-13, Isaiah 11:2, 25:1, 40:13-15, Psalms 1:1-2, 2:1-3, Job 5:13, 12:13, 17, 37:10-12, Proverbs 22:20

New Testament – Mark 15:43, Luke 15:43, Revelation 3:18

Counsel (4)

Old Testament – Daniel 4:27, 2:14, Nehemiah 4:15, 1 Samuel 14:37, 28:4-7, 1 Chronicles 10:13-14, Ezekiel 11:2, 7:26, Isaiah 47:11-13, 45:20-21, 41:27-21, Jeremiah 7:23-24, 19:3-7, Proverbs 12:5, 15, 20, 20:5, 18

New Testament – Matthew 22:15, 27:1, 28:11-15, Acts 2:22-23

Counsel (5)

Old Testament – Isaiah 5:18-19, 7:3-6, 8:10, 16:2-3, Nahum 1:11-14, Job 18:5-7, 21:13-16, 22:9-18, Habakkuk 2:9-10, Psalms 64:2-6, 71:10-11, Proverbs 1:5, 24-31, 8:14, 15:22, 24:6

New Testament – Acts 4:26-28, 5:29-33, 9:22-23, Romans 11:34-36

Elders

Elders (1)

"Her husband is known in the gates, when he sitteth among the elders of the land." (Proverbs 31:23)

Elders (2)

"And as they went through the cities, they delivered them the decrees for to keep, that were ordained of the apostles and elders which were at Jerusalem." (Acts 16:4)

Elders (3)

"For this cause left I thee in Crete, that thou shouldest set in order the things that were wanting, and ordain elders in every city, as I had appointed thee:" (Titus 1:5)

Discussion Questions

1. What observations are made concerning elders in Exodus 3:16-18?
2. Explain Hebrews 11:1-2.
3. What command was given in Titus 1:5?
4. Discuss Acts 20:17-32.
5. Discuss 1 Peter 5:1-5

Fill in the Blanks

1. "Obey them that have the____ over____, and____ yourselves: for they____ for your souls, as they that must give____ ."
2. "Let the elders that____ well be counted worthy of double____ , especially they who labour in the___ and____ ."
3. "Her husband is known in the gates, when he sitteth among the____ of the land."
4. "The anger of the Lord hath divided them; he will no more regard them: they____ not the persons of the____ , they favored not the____ ."
5. "But the eyes of their God was upon the____ of the Jews, that they could not cause them to____ , till the matter came to Darius."

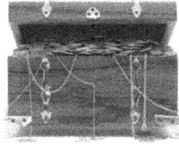

Elders

B aker's *Evangelical Dictionary of Biblical Theology* notes, "In both the Old and New Testament, the term *elder* indicates one of advanced age (Hebrew *zagen*; Greek *presbyteros*) who had an office of leadership within the people of God." The following passages of Scripture unveil God's ordination of the usage of elders in carrying out His will and note their authority and responsibility in this office.

Elders (1)

Old Testament – Genesis 50:7, Exodus 3:16-18, 4:29-31, 17:5-6, 19:7-8, 24:1, 9-11, 14, Ezekiel 8:1, 14:1-8, 20:1-4, 19, 2 Kings 6:32-33, 23:1-2, 1 Kings 8:1-3, Psalms 107:31-32, Proverbs 31:23

New Testament – Hebrews 11:1-2, Acts 16:4, 20:17-32, 21:18, Titus 1:5

Elders (2)

Old Testament – Leviticus 4:13-15, 9:1-2, Numbers 11:16-17, 24-25, 16:17, 24-25, Deuteronomy 5:23-27, 19:11-12, 21:1-6, 18-21, 25:5-9, Ruth 4:1-11, 1 Samuel 15:29-30, Jeremiah 3:15, 23:4-6

New Testament – Ephesians 4:11, 1 Peter 5:1- 5, John 21:15-17, Hebrews 13:17, 1 Thessalonians 5:5, 12, 13

Elders (3)

Old Testament – Deuteronomy 27:1, 31:9-13, 28, Joshua 7:6, 8:10, 33-35, 20:8, 23:1-2, 24:1, Ezra 5:3-11, 6:7-8, 14, 10:8, 14, 1 Chronicles 11:3, 21:16

New Testament – 1 Timothy 5:17-22, 1 Thessalonians 5:12-13, 2 John 1:1, 3 John 1:1-2

Elders (4)

Old Testament – Judges 11:5-11, 21:1-2, 16-23, 1 Samuel 4:3, 11:1-3, 9-11, 30:26, 2 Samuel 5:3, 19:11-14, Joel 1:13-14, 19-20, 2:12-16, Isaiah 37:1-3, Lamentations 1:18-19, 2:8-10

New Testament – Revelation 4:4, 10-11, 7:11-13, 19:4

Elders (5)

Old Testament – Jeremiah 26:14-18, 29:1-7, Lamentations 4:16, 5:12-14, Job 29:7-11, 31:21-23, 1 Kings 20:7-8, 28, Judges 8:4-7, 13-16, Numbers 22:7-12, 1 Samuel 16:4-5, 2 Samuel 12:16-17

New Testament – Matthew 15:1-3, Acts 4:8-12, 11:29-30, 14:21-23, 5:1-6, 23-24

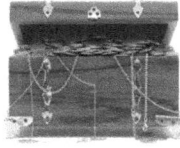

Spiritual Blindness

Spiritual Blindness (1)

"Let them alone: they be blind leaders of the blind. And if the blind lead the blind, both shall fall into the ditch." (Matthew 15:14)

Spiritual Blindness (2)

"But if our gospel be his, it is hid to them that are lost: In whom the god of this world hath blinded the minds of them which believe not, lest the light of the glorious gospel of Christ should shine unto them." (2 Corinthins 4:3-4)

Spiritual Blindness (3)

"The way of the wicked is as darkness: they know not at what they stumble." (Proverbs 4:19)

Discussion Questions

1. How did Paul describe his purpose in Acts 26:16-18?
2. Discuss Isaiah 6:9-10.
3. What observations are made in Jeremiah 5:12-25?
4. Explain 2 Corinthians 4:3-6.
5. Discuss Matthew 15:13-14.

Fill in the Blanks

1. "And thou shalt take no gift: for the gift____ the wise, and____ the words of the____ ."

2. "Therefore speak I to them in____ : because they____ see not; and____ they hear not, neither do they____ ."

3. "In whom the___ of this world hath____ the____ of them which believe not, lest the____ of the glorious gospel of Christ, who is the image of God, should____ unto them."

4. "Let their eyes be____ , that they____ not; and make their loins____ to shake."

5. "And Jesus said, For Judgment I am come into this world, that they which___ ___ might ____; and that they which____ might be made____ ."

Spiritual Blindness

"But he that hateth his brother is in darkness, and walketh in darkness, and knoweth not whither he goeth, because that darkness hath blinded his eyes" (1 John 2:11).

*T*o live in a way that is contrary to the words of Christ is to walk in darkness. Jesus is the Light of the world. We are to be directed by Him in all things. May our hearts always be inclined to seek, to grow in knowledge of His will, and to walk in accordance with that which He has commanded. Otherwise, we will be blinded by our own waywardness and error.

Spiritual Blindness (1)

Old Testament – 1 Samuel 12:3, Deuteronomy 16:19, 28:15, 28-29, 65, 29:2-4, Isaiah 6:1-12, 29:18-19, 35:1-6, 42:1-7, 16-21, 43:6-9, 56:8-11, 59:7-15, Psalms 13:3, 146:8

New Testament – Luke 4:16-21, Matthew 11:2-6, 25-27, 13:10-17, 15:13-14, 16:13-20 Acts 26:13-18

Spiritual Blindness (2)

Old Testament – Deuteronomy 12:8, 28, Judges 17:6, 21:25, Proverbs 12:15, 16:25, 20:6, 12, 21:2, Jeremiah 5:21-25, Lamentations 4:12-14, Isaiah 5:20-21, 25:5-7, 30:8-10, 60:1-5, Psalms 119:18, 63:20-23

New Testament – Luke 6:39, Matthew 23:13-24, 6:22-23, John 9:39-41, 12:37-41, Ephesians 4:17-20, Revelation 3:15-18

Spiritual Blindness (3)

Old Testament – Exodus 23:7-8, 34:29-35, Ezra 9:5-8, 2 Samuel 22:23-29, Job 17:4-7, 34:32, 36:5-10, 37:19-24, 38:15, 36, 37, Isaiah 29:9-18, 32:1-3, Zephaniah 1:17, Zechariah 12:4, 8-10

New Testament – Luke 2:25-32, 2 Corinthians 3:5-16, 4:1-6, Romans 1:20-21, 11:7-12, 25-26, 1 John 2:8-11

Spiritual Blindness (4)

Old Testament – Numbers 22:21-34, 24:15-20, Proverbs 4:18-19, 14:12, 16, 19:2-3, 30:12-14, Psalms 10:4-5, 19:8, 82:2, 5, 107:40-43, Isaiah 9:2, 6-8, 50:10-11, 59:8-21, Micah 3:5-12, Jeremiah 8:7-9, 13:16, 31:8-10

New Testament – John 8:12, 12:35-36, 46, Mark 8:14-18, Romans 2:17-24, 10:1-3, 2 Peter 1:1-9, 19

Spiritual Blindness (5)

Old Testament – Job 5:12-14, 11:20, 12:17-25, 24:1, 13, 17-25, 29:2-3, 15, 42:5, Ezekiel 12:2, Isaiah 65:2, Amos 3:7, 10, Jonah 4:2, 6-11, Jeremiah 22:16-17, Psalms 18:27-28, 36:1-4, 9, Proverbs 29:13, 17:24, 16:30, Ecclesiastes 2:12-14, 10:2, 15, Daniel 2:22-23

New Testament – John 11:9-10, Luke 8:10, 11:34-36, Acts 28:25-28, 1 Corinthians 2:9-15, Ephesians 1:17-18, 2 Peter 2:9-19, 3:5

A Guaranteed Win

A Guaranteed Win (1)

"There is now no condemnation to them that are in Christ Jesus, who walk not after the flesh, but after the Spirit." (Romans 8:1)

A Guaranteed Win (2)

"Ye are of God, little children, and have overcome them: because greater is he that is in you, than he that is in the world." (1 John 4:4)

A Guaranteed Win (3)

"Much more then, being now justified by his blood, we shall be saved from wrath through him." (Romans 5:9)

Discussion Questions

1. Why did Jesus die?
2. Can there be forgiveness of sin without shedding of blood? Explain.
3. What does it mean to abide in Christ?
4. In the New Testament, were the saved added to the church? Is this still true today?
5. Can the gates of hell prevail against the church? Explain.

Fill in the Blanks

1. "These things I have_____ unto you, that in_____ ye might have_____ . In the world ye shall have_____ : but be of good cheer; I have_____ the world."
2. "There is therefore now no_____ to them which are in_____ _____ , who walk___ after the flesh, but after the_____ ."
3. "And they shall___ against___ ; but they shall not_____ against thee; for I am with thee, ___ the___ , to___ thee."
4. "And I say also unto thee, That thou art Peter, and upon this_____ I will build___ ___ ; and the gates of_____ shall not_____ against___ ."
5. "But thanks be to_____ , which giveth us the_____ through our Lord_____ _____ ."

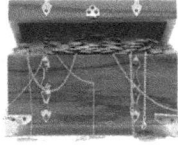

A Guaranteed Win

*D*id you know that the victory over sin and the Devil has already been won? Did you know that if we put on Christ through baptism, if we become a part of His body, if we walk according to His Spirit, there is now no condemnation for those in Christ Jesus? It is a guaranteed win, made possible by the blood of Christ, His atonement, His redemption, His sacrifice. As a Christian, we can rejoice every day because of what Christ accomplished at the cross of Calvary.

A Guaranteed Win (1)

Old Testament – Deuteronomy 1:28-31, 3:21-22, 11:22-25, 20:1-4, 28:1-10, 15, 32:29-31, 39-43, 2 Chronicles 13:12, 32:7-8, 1 Samuel 17:32-37, 42-47, 49-53, Jeremiah 32:17-22, 26-27, Psalms 44:3-8, 46:6-11

New Testament – Romans 8:31, John 8:51, 10:27-30, 16:33, Acts 13:37-41, Hebrews 7:25, 1 Corinthians 15:52-57, 2 Corinthians 2:14, Galatians 5:18-23

A Guaranteed Win (2)

Old Testament – Exodus 14:13-14, 19-31 Joshua 1:1-5, 10:40-42, 23:8-11, Isaiah 8:9-10, 41:8-14, 42:12-13, 43:1-7, 13, Zechariah 10:3-5, 1 Chronicles 29:11, Psalms 80:1-3, 98:1-3, 118:6, 10-17

New Testament – Matthew 12:17-20, John 6:40, 47, 15:3-7, Romans 6:22, 7:21-25, 8;1-6, 33-39, 1 John 5:4-5, 18-20, Revelation 17:14

A Guaranteed Win (3)

Old Testament – Genesis 26:24, 28:12-16, Jeremiah 1:8, 19, 15:20, 30:11, 42:11, 46:28, Ezekiel 34:28-31, Zechariah 8:20-23, Isaiah 63:1-9, Haggai 1:12-13, 2:2-4, Psalms 9:19-20, 34:19, 56:1-13, 60:11-12

New Testament – Matthew 16:18, Mark 1026-27, Acts 2:47, Romans 5:9-11, 18-21, 2 Peter 1:3-11, Revelation 12:7-12, 17, 19:11-21.

A Guaranteed Win (4)

Old Testament – Genesis 12:3, Exodus 23:22, Numbers 10:9, 24:8-9, Deuteronomy 4:30-31, 31:6-8, Joshua 21:43-45, 23:14, Psalms 9:3, 18:47-50, 27:2-6, 34:7, 41:11, 108:13

New Testament – 1 John 4:4, Jude 1:24-25, Colossians 2:10-15, Revelation 6:2, 15:2-4

A Guaranteed Win (5)

Old Testament – Exodus 15:1-3, 6-18, 1 Samuel 2:9-10, Isaiah 54:17, 50:6-11, Micah 7:7-10, Proverbs 21:30-31, 24:15-16, Zechariah 4:6-7, 10:3-5, 14:3-9, 2 Chronicles 20:14-21, 32:7-8, Psalms 2:1-6, 35:1-9

New Testament – Matthew 7:21-27, John 3:14-18, 36, 4:14, 5:24, 6:37-40, Galatians 6:8, Revelation 3:7-13, 20-22

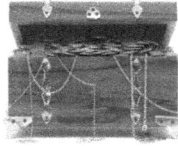

Thus Saith the Lord

Thus Saith the Lord (1)

"For they are impudent children and stiffnecked. I do send the unto them; and thou shalt say unto them, Thus saith the Lord God." (Ezekiel 2:4)

Thus Saith the Lord (2)

"But when I speak with thee, I will open thy mouth, and thou shalt say unto them, Thus saith the Lord; He that heareth, let him hear; and he that forbeareth, let him forbear: for they are a rebellious house." (Ezekiel 3:27)

Thus Saith the Lord (3)

"He that is of God heareth God's words: ye therefore hear them not, because ye are not of God." (John 8:47)

Discussion Questions

1. Explain Ezekiel 2:1-10.
2. Who has the words of eternal life?
3. According to Matthew 4:4, what are we to live by?
4. Explain John 8:51.
5. Explain James 1:27.

Fill in the Blanks

1. "O earth, earth, earth hear the____ of the____."
2. "And go, get thee to them of the captivity, unto the____ of thy, and____ unto them, and tell them, ___ _____ ___ ; whether they will____, or whether they will___ ."
3. "Then Simon Peter answered him, , to whom shall we go? thou hast the____ of___ ___ ."
4. "Verily, verily, I say unto you, If a man keep___ ____ , he shall never see____ ."
5. "Teaching them to____ all things____ I have____ you."

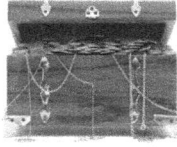

Thus Saith the Lord

*M*any different views say many different things about many different subjects with many different opinions. Yet, when God speaks, he speaks the truth with absoluteness, authority, and incontrovertibility. Our entire lives and that which we follow should be built upon "Thus saith the Lord."

Thus Saith the Lord (1)

Old Testament – Ezekiel 2:1-4, 7, 3:10-11, 27, 37:1-4, 10, Isaiah 59:21, Psalms 33:8-9, 68:11, 89:34, 103:20, Numbers 22:18, 35, 24:13

New Testament – Matthew 4:4, Hebrews 2:1-3, John 5:24-25, 17:6-8, 14, 17, 15:7-11

Thus Saith the Lord (2)

Old Testament – Jeremiah 1:7-9, 17-19, 7:2-3, 25-28, 17:19-23, Ezekiel 21:6-7, 33:7-9, 40:4, Isaiah 6:8-11, 40:5:8, 58:1, Amos 3:6-8

New Testament – Matthew 10:9-20, 27, John 6:63-68, 7:7, 15-18, 8:47, 1 Thessalonians 2:13

Thus Saith the Lord (3)

Old Testament – Jeremiah 15:16, 19, 22:29, 36:1-2, 6, 22-30, 38:20-22, 42:15-18, Zechariah 1:3-6, 12-17, 3:1-7, 4:6, 5:1-4, Isaiah 55:3, 11, Psalms 2:1-5, 50:7, 85:8

New Testament – Matthew 7:24-27, John 5:38, 8:51, 12:47-50, Acts 3:23

Thus Saith the Lord (4)

Old Testament – Deuteronomy 18:18-19, 12:32, Isaiah 8:10-11, 20, Jeremiah 23:16-18, 22, 28-32, 33:19-21, 25-26, Ezekiel 20:2-8, 27, 45-47, 14:12-14, 19-21, 11:16-21

New Testament – Matthew 17:5, 28:20 Acts 13:47-48, Galatians 1:8-12

Thus Saith the Lord (5)

Old Testament – 1 Kings 13:7-9, 18-22, Jeremiah 37:17, 21:1-8, 5:12-14, Amos 7:14-17, Isaiah 49:2, 8, 18, 22, 25, 51:16, Isaiah 59:21, 66:2, Job 23:12, Psalms 78:1, 105:5, 119:72, 88

New Testament – John 3:34, 8:31, 38, 43

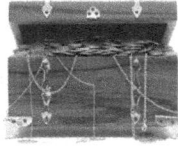

Do Good

Do Good (1)

"Seek good and not evil, that ye may live: and so the LORD, the God of hosts, shall be with you, as ye have spoken. Hate the evil, and love the good, and establish judgment in the gate: it may be that the LORD God of hosts will be gracious unto the remnant of Joseph." (Amos 5:14-15)

Do Good (2)

"And they said, Cornelius the centurion, a just man, and one that feareth God, and of good report among all the nation of the Jews, was warned from God by an holy angel to send for thee into his house, and to hear words of thee." (Acts 10:22)

Do Good (3)

"Beloved, follow not that which is evil, but that which is good. He that doeth good is of God: but he that doeth evil hath not seen God." (3 John 1:11)

Discussion Questions

1. How was Jesus described in Acts 10:38?
2. Explain Amos 5: 14-15.
3. Are we to do good to all men? Discuss.

4. What type of works are we instructed to have in Ephesians 2:10?
5. What instructions are given in 1 Timothy 6:17-18?

Fill in the Blanks

1. "Do____ , O Lord, unto those that be____, and to them that are ____n their____ ."
2. "Beloved, follow not that which is____, but that which is___. He that___ ____ is of God: but he that____ hath not seen God."
3. "Be not overcome of evil, but____ evil with____ ."
4. "That they do, that they be rich in____ ____ , ready to distribute, ___ to____ ."
5. "But the wisdom that is____ above is first____ , then____ , ___ , and____ to be intreated, full of___ and___ ."

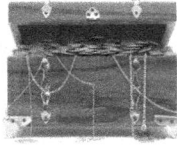

Do Good

*T*he following verses contain exhortations to be kind, to act honorably, nobly, with right behavior and good intentions. These are character traits of those we consider to be "good people." Do good, and you will be good.

Do Good (1)

Old Testament – Amos 5:14-15, Ezra 8:22, Deuteronomy 6:18, 12:28, 2 Chronicles 31:20-21, Psalms 34:13-16, Psalms 37:3, 23, 27-28, 125:4-5, Micah 6:8, Proverbs 20:6

New Testament – Acts 10:38, John 10:11, Matthew 19:16-26, 12:33-35, 3 John 1:11

Do Good (2)

Old Testament – Isaiah 1:16-17, Hosea 10:12-13, Micah 2:7, Proverbs 11:17, 23, 27, 12:2, 14, 13:21, 14:19, 1 Samuel 2:3, 2 Samuel 22:24-28

New Testament – Romans 11:22, 2:5-10, Galatians 6:10, Philippians 4:8-9, John 5:28-29

Do Good (3)

Old Testament – Numbers 24:13, 2 Chronicles 20:31-32, 14:2-4, Isaiah 38:1-5, Esther 10:3, Proverbs 31:10-12, 28:10, 14, 18, 20-22

New Testament – Acts 10:22, 34-35, 11:22-24, Luke 23:50-52, Ephesians 5:7-10, 1 Timothy 6:17-19, Revelation 19:8

Do Good (4)

Old Testament – Ecclesiastes 3:12, 8:12-13, 9:18, Exodus 23:1-2, 7, Zephaniah 2:3, Job 11:14-15, 1 Samuel 12:23, Proverbs 2:20-22, Amos 6:12, Isaiah 5:20

New Testament – Ephesians 2:10, Romans 12:9, 21, Titus 1:16, Luke 17:1-2, 7-10

Do Good (5)

Old Testament – Psalms 143:10, 133:1-3, 119:66, 68, 122, 158, Micah 7:2-3, Proverbs 14:19, 17:20, 26, 28:10, Micah 7:2-4

New Testament – Luke 6:35-36, 8:11-15, 1 Peter 3:10-11, 2:11-12, Matthew 25:21, James 3:17

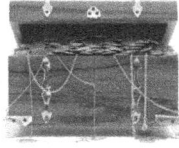

I Will Patiently Wait on God

I Will Wait Patiently on God (1)

"For since the beginning of the world men have not heard, nor perceived by the ear, neither hath the eye seen, O God, beside thee, what he hath prepared for him that waiteth for him. (Isaiah 64:4)

I Will Wait Patiently on God (2)

"In your patience possess ye your souls." (Luke 21:19)

I Will Wait Patiently on God (3)

"My soul, wait thou only upon God; for my expectation is from him." (Psalms 62:5)

Discussion Questions

1. Explain Psalms 40:1-4.
2. Explain Isaiah 64:4.
3. What instructions are given in Luke 21:19?
4. Is waiting on God indicative of trusting God?
5. Explain Hebrews 6:15.

Fill in the Blanks

1. "And so, after he had____ endured, he obtained the____ ."
2. "But that on the good ground are they, which in an___ and____ heart, having heard the____ , keep it, and bring forth fruit with____ ."
3. "Be ye also. Stablish your____: for the coming of the____ draweth nigh."
4. "Therefore turn thou to thy____ : keep mercy and____, and____ on thy God____ ."
5. "Rejoicing in____ ; ____in tribulation; continuing____ in prayer."

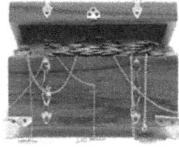

I Will Patiently Wait on God

*I*will patiently wait on God when faced with the challenges and the difficulties of life. We must learn to turn them all over to God, especially when we find ourselves at wit's end. This is learned behavior. We learn to lean on Him, cast our burdens on Him, and then to patiently wait on Him because nothing is too hard for Him.

I Will Patiently Wait on God (1)

Old Testament – Psalms 40:1-4, 37:1-3, 7-11, 46:10-11, Exodus 14:14, Isaiah 64:1-4, 66:13, 30:15-18, Proverbs 14:29, 15:18

New Testament – Luke 21:19, Luke 8:15, 1 Peter 2:19-23, Philippians 4:5-7, Romans 15:5-7, 13, 30-33

I Will Patiently Wait on God (2)

Old Testament – Psalms 25:3, 27:13-14, 33:20-22, 59:9-11, 62:1-8, Isaiah 25:9-12, 40:28-31, 42:13-16, Ecclesiastes 7:8-9, Proverbs 20:22

New Testament – Hebrews 6:15, Romans 12:10-13, 8:24-25, 5:3-5, 2:5-9, Galatians 5:22-23

I Will Patiently Wait on God (3)

Old Testament – Lamentations 3:25-26, Psalms 52:8-9, Psalms 107:27-31, Psalms 119:81-87, Psalms 130:5-8, Jeremiah 14:22, Hosea 12:6, Micah 7:7-10, Isaiah 26:8-9, 20-21

New Testament – James 5:7-8, 2 Peter 3:9, Luke 18:1-8, Colossians 1:11

I Will Patiently Wait on God (4)

Old Testament – Psalms 62:5-8, Psalms 77:2-10, 94:17-19, 143:6-8, Job 14:14, Isaiah 7:2-7, 8:17, Habakkuk 2:2-3, Ecclesiastes 10:4

New Testament – Galatians 6:9, Hebrews 12:1-2, Revelation 2:2-5, 3:10-11

I Will Patiently Wait on God (5)

Old Testament – Psalms 131:1-3, 124:8, 63:1-8, 39:4-7, 38:15-22, 9:9-12, 18-20, Isaiah 35:3-4, 49:8-13, 23, Lamentations 4:17

New Testament – Hebrews 9:27-28, Jude 1:20-21, 1 Corinthians 1:4-8, 2 Peter 3:11-14, Revelation 14:12-13

Reverential Fear

Reverential Fear (1)

"Behold therefore the goodness and the severity of God: on them which fell severity; but toward thee, goodness, if thou continue in his goodness: otherwise thou also shalt be cut off." (Romans 11:22)

Reverential Fear (2)

"God is greatly to be feared in the assembly of the saints, and to be held in reverence of all them that are about Him." (Psalms 89:7)

Reverential Fear (3)

"The God of Israel said, the Rock of Israel spake to me, He that ruleth over men must be just, ruling in the fear of God." (2 Samuel 23:3)

Discussion Questions

1. Explain Ecclesiastes 8:11-13.
2. Why did Moses take off his shoes, when he stood before the burning bush?
3. List several things that happens when men do not have the fear of God.
4. Explain Jeremiah 5:22-24.
5. Explain Romans 11:20-22.

Fill in the Blanks

1. "___ ye not me? saith the Lord: will ye not___ at my...?"
2. "The___ of the Lord is to___ ; pride, and___, and the___ , and the___ mouth, do I hate."
3. "But in every nation he that , and worketh, is with Him."
4. "Behold therefore the___ and___ of God: on them which fell, ___ ; but toward thee, ___ : if thou continue in his___ . Otherwise thou also shall be cut off."
5. "Let all the___ ___ the Lord: let all___ the of the___ stand in___ of Him."

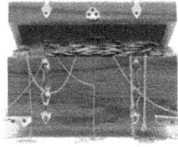

Reverential Fear

> "Wherefore we receiving a kingdom which cannot be moved, let us have grace, whereby we may serve God acceptably with reverence and godly fear" (Hebrews 12:28).

*O*ur God must always be served reverentially. He is to be hallowed by all that seek to worship Him. Our God is a Mighty King and is worthy of our upmost respect and devotion.

Reverential Fear (1)

Old Testament – Exodus 3:3-6, 4:24-26, 19:10-25, 20:7, 18-21, Leviticus 10:1-3, 24:10-16, 23, 1 Chronicles 13:8-13, 15:13, Psalms 119:120, 97:2-5, 89:7

New Testament – Romans 11:20-22, 2 Corinthians 5:11, Revelation 6:12-17, Hebrews 12:18-29

Reverential Fear (2)

Old Testament – Ecclesiastes 8:11-13, 12:13-14, Daniel 5:1-6, 23-31, Jeremiah 2:19, 5:22-24, 10:6-7, Proverbs 8:13, 9:10, 14:26-27, Psalms 96:4-9, 22:23-25, 19:9, 9:20

New Testament – Romans 3:13-18, Luke 12:4-5, 23:27-30, 39-41, James 2:19

Reverential Fear (3)

Old Testament – Genesis 42:10, Psalms 18:4-21, 112:1, 128:1-5, Isaiah 33:6, 14-16, 66:1-2, Deuteronomy 4:23-24, 28:58-61, Nahum 1:5-6, Malachi 3:2-6

New Testament – Luke 1:49-52, Acts 10:34-35, Hebrews 4:1-2, 11-13, Philippians 2:13-16

Reverential Fear (4)

Old Testament – Zephaniah 3:6-8, Isaiah 8:8-14, 13:5-13, 51:7-8, 12-17, Psalms 36:1-4, 76:6-12, 55:15-19, 17:10-15, Proverbs 10:27, Ezekiel 32:2-10, 21-23

New Testament – 2 Corinthians 7:1, Acts 9:31, 18:9-10 Ephesians 6:5-6, 5:21

Reverential Fear (5)

Old Testament – Job 1:1, 8-10, Psalms 66:16, 34:7-16, 33:8, 25:14, Exodus 18:21, 1 Samuel 23:3, 2 Chronicles 19:5-9, Proverbs 16:6

New Testament – Romans 13:1-5, 1 Peter 2:13-18, Jude 1:12-13, 16-21, 2 Thessalonians 1:4-10, Acts 13:16, 26, 40-47

Noteworthy Questions

Noteworthy Questions (1)

"Now when John had heard in prison the works of Christ, he sent two of his disciples, And said unto him, Art thou he that should come, or do we look for another?? (Matthew 11:2-3)

Noteworthy Questions (2)

"Who hath ascended up into heaven? Who hath gathered the wind in his fists? Who hath bound the waters in a garment? Who hath established all the ends of the earth? what is his name, and what is his son's name, if thou canst tell?" (Proverbs 30:4)

Noteworthy Questions (3)

"I tell you that he will avenge them speedily. Nevertheless when the Son of man cometh, shall he find faith on the earth?" (Luke 18:8)

Discussion Questions

1. What is God's name in Exodus 3:13-14?
2. How did God humble Pharaoh?
3. Why did Moses request God's presence to be with him as he led God's people?
4. What will happen when Jesus comes again in His glory?
5. What error was made in Matthew 22:29?

Fill in the Blanks

1. "Then___ ____ answered him, Lord, to whom shall we go? thou hast the____ of____ life."
2. "But to which of the____ said he at any time, Sit on my right hand, until I make thine____ thy____?"
3. "Whom shall he____ knowledge? and whom shall he make to___ ____? them that are____ from the milk, and____ from the____ ."
4. "What shall we then say to these? If God be___ ____, who can be____?"
5. "He that chastiseth the____, shall not He____ ? He that____ man , shall not He____ ?"

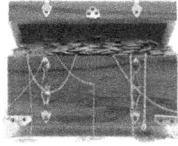

Noteworthy Questions

*I*n these passages of Scripture, a compilation of thought-provoking questions that perhaps many of us have asked is noted.

Noteworthy Questions (1)

Old Testament – Exodus 3:13-15, 5:1-2, 10:3-4, 16-18, 15:11-18, 33:11-17, Proverbs 30:4, 24:8-10, Isaiah 6:8-11, 28:9-12

New Testament – Hebrews 1:5-14, John 8:53-58, 18:33-38, Matthew 8:27, 11:2-11, 16:13-18, 26-27

Noteworthy Questions (2)

Old Testament – Job 7:1-4, 12-21, 31:4-12, 35-40, 38:1-18, 40:1-14, 1 Kings 19:9-16, 2 Kings 6:15-17, Jeremiah 32:27

New Testament – Matthew 20:20-23, John 6:28-35, 60-69, 7:31, 10:24-28, Luke 18:8

Noteworthy Questions (3)

Old Testament – Jeremiah 8:22, 14:8-9, 19-22, 15:12-21, Psalms 13:1-6, 89:46-52, 90:1-13, Lamentations 1:12-17, 2:13-17, 3:32-41, Malachi 4:1-3

New Testament – Hebrews 12:7-13, 2:1-4, John 10:10, 19-21, Romans 8:31-39, 3:3-18

Noteworthy Questions (4)

Old Testament – Genesis 4:9, Ecclesiastes 4:8-10, Psalms 142:2-5, 82:1-5, Proverbs 19:17, Isaiah 58:3-11, Jeremiah 22:15-16, Job 31:13, 23, 31-32, Ezekiel 16:48-50

New Testament – Luke 3:7-15, 14:12-14, 18:18-27, Matthew 25:31-36, 1 John 3:17-18

Noteworthy Questions (5)

Old Testament – Job 28:12-28, Proverbs 4:5-13, 8:1-21, 32-36, 10:23, Ecclesiastes 8:1, 10:10, 12-15, Psalms 94:8-12, Deuteronomy 4:5-10, 1 Kings 10: 1-3, 24

New Testament – Matthew 11:16-19, 15:12-14, 22:29-33, 41-46, 25:1-13, John 9:39-41

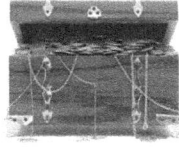

Commitment

Commitment (1)

"Commit thy way unto the LORD; trust also in Him; and He shall bring it to pass." (Psalms 37:5)

Commitment (2)

"But without faith it is impossible to please Him: for he that cometh to God must believe that He is, and that He is a rewarder of them that diligently seek Him." (Hebrews 11:6)

Commitment (3)

"For the eyes of the LORD run to and fro throughout the whole earth, to show himself strong in the behalf of them whose heart is perfect toward Him...." (2 Chronicles 16:9)

Discussion Questions

1. What happens when we commit our ways to the Lord, as noted in Psalms 37:4-5?
2. What was the problem identified in Deuteronomy 5:29?
3. Explain Hebrews 11:6.
4. Explain 2 Chronicles 16:9.
5. What should we seek first according to Matthew 6:33?

Fill in the Blanks

1. "____ thy way unto the____ ; trust also in him; and he____ ____ it to pass."
2. "My son, give me thine____ , and let thine eyes___ my___ ."
3. "But seek ye____ the kingdom of God, and his____ ; and all these things shall be____ unto you."
4. "But without faith it is____ to please him: for he that____ to God must believe the he is, and that___ is a____ of them that____ seek Him."
5. "Not____ in business; ____in spirit;____ the____ ."

Commitment

*C*ommitment is defined as "dedication, devotion, allegiance, faithfulness, and loyalty to something or someone." If there is no commitment to the profession of our faith, we produce only a shallow, half-hearted effort, at best.

Commitment (1)

Old Testament – Psalms 37:4-5, 27:8, 14:2, 119:2, 10, 34, 63, 2 Chronicles 31:21, Proverbs 3:69-70, 16:3, 1 Chronicles 29:9, Genesis 22:10-12, 15-18

New Testament – Matthew 10:37-39, 19:27-29, Luke 9:59-63, Mark 10:17-23, Hebrews 11:6

Commitment (2)

Old Testament – Genesis 28:20-22, Ruth 1:16-17, 1 Samuel 1:8-11, 20-22, 13:13-14, Psalms 63:7-8, 107:31-32, Deuteronomy 5:27-29, 2 Chronicles 16:9, 1 Chronicles 28:8-9

New Testament – Matthew 6:33, 5:20, Revelation 3:14-16, Romans 12:1, 1 John 3:21-22

Commitment (3)

Old Testament – Proverbs 23:26, 4:1-5, Psalms 18:20-26, 119:15-16, 48, 57-60, 80-88, Job 23:11-12, Numbers 14:24, 32:6, 11-12, 1 Samuel 2:30, Hosea 6:4-7, Isaiah 26:7-10

New Testament – John 12:26, 42-43, 15:1-8, Luke 12:29-31, Revelation 3:1-3

Commitment (4)

Old Testament – Jonah 2:1-9, 1 Chronicles 16:8-11, 23-25, 28-29, Psalms 40:8-11, 50:14, 23, 51:12-15, 86:9-12, 116:12-14, 17-19, 118:28-29, 2 Chronicles 15:1-2

New Testament – Hebrews 13:15-16, 6:10-12, Ephesians 6:5-8, James 4:8

Commitment (5)

Old Testament – 2 Kings 10:15-17, 30, Ezra 8:21-22, Amos 5:14-15, Isaiah 43:22-28, Psalms 29:2, 9, 69:30-32, 85:8-13, Malachi 1:6-19

New Testament – Matthew 11:16-19, 12:33, 23:1-15, 24-33, Philippians 3:2-3, Romans 12:11-12

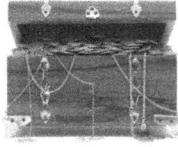

Law of Moses/Law of Christ

Law of Moses/Law of Christ (1)

"For Moses truly said unto the fathers, A prophet shall the LORD your God raise up unto you of your brethren, like unto me; him shall ye hear in all things whatsoever he shall say unto you." (Acts 3:22)

Law of Moses/Law of Christ (2)

"And by him all that believe are justified from all things, from which ye could not be justified by the law of Moses." (Acts 13:39)

Law of Moses/Law of Christ (3)

"For all the prophets and the law prophesied until John." (Matthew 11:13)

Discussion Questions

1. Explain Acts 3:18-26.
2. What was prophesied in Jeremiah 31:31-34?
3. Explain Acts 13:39.
4. Explain Galatians 5:1-6, 14.
5. What contrast did Jesus make between His law and the law of Moses in Matthew 5:20-44?

Fill in the Blanks

1. "But Christ as a son over his___ ___ ; whose____ are we,
   if we _____ the confidence and the rejoicing of the____
   firm__ the end."

2. "Christ is become of ___ ___ unto you, whosoever of you are___
   by the___ ; ye are____ from grace."

3. "And by him all that____ are____ from all things, from which
   ye could not be____ by the___ of___ ."

4. "Then said I, Lo, I come (in the volume of the book it is written of me,)to do thy___ , O___ .... He taketh away the____ , that
   he may___ the____ ."

5. "For the___ was given by___ , but___ and____ came by
   Jesus Christ."

Law of Moses/Law of Christ

*I*n Hebrews 3:1-5, the Bible states a contrast between the house built by Moses and the house built by Christ. Moses gave the law in the house he built. Christ is the lawgiver in his own house (Acts 3:22-26).

Law of Moses/ Law of Christ (1)

Old Testament – Exodus 34:4, 32, Leviticus 27:34, Deuteronomy 4:1-15, 36, 44-45, 5:1-5, 39, 18:15, 18-20, Psalms 78:36-43, Jeremiah 31:31-34

New Testament – Acts 3:18-26, Romans 11:1-23, Hebrews 10:1-10, 15-22, 3:1-6, Luke 16:16, Galatians 3:10-25

Law of Moses/ Law of Christ (2)

Old Testament – Exodus 33:5-11, Nehemiah 9:12-21, 26-35, Jeremiah 32:37-42, Isaiah 2:1-5, 10:20-23, Ezekiel 36:16-29

New Testament – Romans 9:1-8, 30-33, 10:1-9, 4:13-18, Galatians 3:21-26, 2 Corinthians 3:2-18, Hebrews 7:11-25, 8:1-13, 9:11-26

Law of Moses & Law of Christ (3)

Old Testament – Hosea 2:2, Isaiah 50:1, Ezekiel 37:21-28, Zechariah 12:10, Jeremiah 33:14-18, 32:37-42, Malachi 4:4-6

New Testament – Matthew 11:13-14, 17:1-13, John 1:1-17, Romans 7:4-6, Acts 2:14-24, 32-42, 13:22-39, 15:10-11, Colossians 2:11-17.

Law of Moses & Law of Christ (4)

Old Testament – Isaiah 9:6-7, 11:1-12, 56:5, 62:2, Zechariah 9:9, Nehemiah 8:1-8

New Testament – Luke 7:16-23, Philippians 2:8-11, Acts 4:12, 11:26, John 4:25-26, 7:19-26, 8:53-58, 10:27-30, Romans 8:3-4, 3:27-31, Hebrews 1:1-14, Galatians 5:1-6, 14, 18-23.

Law of Moses & Law of Christ (5)

Old Testament – Numbers 15:15-16, 22-36, Leviticus 7:27, 20:9-12, 25-27, Leviticus 24:10-23

New Testament – James 2:7-13, Hebrews 10:26-31, Galatians 6:2, Matthew 5:17-22, 27-30, 38-45, 22:36-40, Romans 13:8-10, Ephesians 2:11-22, 1 Timothy 1:5-11

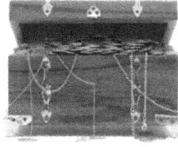

Walk the Walk

Walk the Walk (1)

"And they come unto thee as the people cometh, and they sit before thee as my people, and they hear thy words, but they will not do them: for with the mouth they shew much love, but their heart goeth after their covetousness. And, lo, thou art unto them as a very lovely song of one that hath a pleasant voice, and can play well on an instrument: for they hear thy words, but they do them not." (Ezekiel 33:31-32)

Walk the Walk (2)

"And they were both righteous before God, walking in all the commandments and ordinances of the Lord blameless." (Luke 1:6)

Walk the Walk (3)

"(For we walk by faith, not by sight:)" (2 Corinthians 5:7)

Discussion Questions

1. What should our aim be according to Micah 6:8?
2. What was the problem identified in Ezekiel 33:30-33?
3. What does it mean to walk in the light?
4. Explain Ephesians 2:1-3, 10.
5. Explain Galatians 5:16-25.

Fill in the Blanks

1. "And they were both____ before____ , in all the____ and____ of the Lord____ ."
2. "If we say that we have____ with him, and____ in____ , we lie, and do not the____ ."
3. "I have no greater____ than to hear that my____ walk in____ ."
4. "This I say then, ____ in the Spirit, and ye shall not fulfil the ____of the____ ."
5. "There is therefore now no____ to them which are in Christ Jesus, who____ not after the____ , but after the____ ."

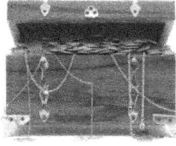

Walk the Walk

*T*his series of Scriptures commands us to walk in a worthy way that pleases God. We all should strive every day to walk in the footsteps of our Lord and Savior Jesus Christ, who set the example as to how we are to behave ourselves in this present world.

Walk the Walk (1)

Old Testament – Ezekiel 33:30-33, Hosea 11:3-4, 7, 5:4, Jeremiah 22:16, Psalms 15:1-5, 26:1-6, 119:1-3, 30-35, Habakkuk 3:19, Proverbs 15:24, Micah 6:8

New Testament – Luke 1:5-6, Romans 6:4, 1 Thessalonians 2:1-12, 4:1-2, 1 John 2:3-6, 11, James 2:1-9

Walk the Walk (2)

Old Testament – Genesis 6:9, 17:1, Jeremiah 7:9-10, 23, 1 Kings 9:4-5, 15:1-5, Isaiah 35:8-10, 26:7, 10, Leviticus 26:11-13, Proverbs 16:9, 17, 25, 29, 4:11-19, 25

New Testament – Ephesians 2:1-3, 10, 1 John 1:5-7, John 8:12, 12:35-36, Colossians 1:9-10, 2:6

Walk the Walk (3)

Old Testament – Psalms 1:1-6, 16:11, 23:1-6, 25:8-15, 84:5-7, 11-12, 89:15-17, 30-36, Isaiah 38:1-5, 1 Kings 8:22-25

New Testament – Ephesians 4:1-3, 17-20, 5:1-12, 15-17, Philippians 3:16-20, Colossians 3:1-7, 4:5

Walk the Walk (4)

Old Testament – Isaiah 65:2, 59:7-9, Psalms 5:8, 32:8-9, 85:13, 86:11, Micah 4:1-2, 5, Proverbs 20:7, 14:2, 3:20-26

New Testament – Acts 9:31, Romans 13:12-14, 8:1-5, Galatians 5:16-25, 3 John 1:2-4, 11

Walk the Walk (5)

Old Testament – Deuteronomy 5:32-33, 6:7, Exodus 18:19-20, Hosea 14:9, Proverbs 10:9, 29-30, 6:12-15, 28-29, Psalms 17:4-5, 101:1-7, 143:8

New Testament – Revelation 3:4, 2 Corinthians 5:7, 2 John 1:4-6, 2 Peter 2:1-10, 14-15, 21

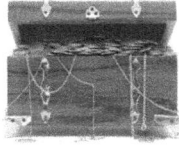

Handling Disappointment

Handling Disappointment (1)

"For I reckon that the sufferings of this present time are not worthy to be compared with the glory which shall be revealed in us. (Romans 8:18)

Handling Disappointment (2)

"What shall we then say to these things? If God be for us, who can be against us?" (Romans 8:31)

Handling Disappointment (3)

"Ye are of God, little children, and have overcome them: because greater is he that is in you, than he that is in the world." (1 John 4:4)

Discussion Questions

1. Can life be lived without disappointing moments? Explain.
2. How are we to handle the disappointing challenges we face?
3. Explain Hebrews 12:1-4.
4. What commands are given in Romans 12:17-21?
5. Explain 1 Corinthians 10:13.

Fill in the Blanks

1. "For consider____ that____ such contradiction of____ against himself, lest ye be____ and___ in your____ ."
2. "Though a sinner do____ an____ times, and his____ be____ , yet surely I know that it shall be____ with them that____ , which____ before____ ."
3. "For which cause we____ not; but though our____ man____ , yet the____ man is____ day by day."
4. "Thou wilt keep him in____ peace, whose____ is stayed on thee."
5. "And because____ shall abound, the____ of ____shall wax____ ."

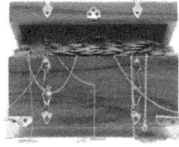

Handling Disappointment

What a wonderful world it would be if everyone obeyed God, walked in love, and treated others the way they would like to be treated. Life would be entirely different. Jesus said in John 16:33, "In the world ye shall have tribulation." Thus, we face difficult situations, disappointments, sorrow of heart, failures, and many things that sometimes cast us down spiritually. These passages address the handling of life's disappointments.

Handling Disappointment (1)

Old Testament – Habakkuk 1:1-4, 12-17, 2:1-4, Jeremiah 12:1-4, 20:7-12, 15:17-21, Jonah 3:1-10, 4:1-11, Psalms 10:1-15, Numbers 32:22, Ecclesiastes 8:11-13

New Testament – Hebrews 4:11-13, Luke 12:6-7, 17:1-2, 2 Corinthians 4:7-18, Romans 8:18, 31, 1 John 4:4

Handling Disappointment (2)

Old Testament – 1 Kings 19:1-16, Psalms 77:1-13, 73:1-21, Isaiah 40:21-31, 64:4, Malachi 3:13-18, Psalms 11:1-7, 17:3-4, 13-15, 37:1-9, 34-40

New Testament – Romans 12:17-21, Matthew 24:12-13, 10:14-22, John 12:25-26

Handling Disappointment (3)

Old Testament – Job 19:19-20, 23:8-12, 27:3-6, Amos 5:10, 13-15, Isaiah 59:4-8, 14-15, Lamentations 3:1-14, 24-29, Psalms 34:17-19, 24:15-16, 42:1-11, 44:14-18

New Testament – John 16:33, Hebrews 12:1-4, 2 Corinthians 1:8-10, 2 Thessalonians 3:1-5, 13, 16, Jude 1:20-21, 24, Philippians 4:13

Handling Disappointment (4)

Old Testament – Genesis 50:16-21, 41:50-52, Psalms 105:17-22, 55:1-8, 12-14, 20-23, 40:13-17, 27:12-14, Micah 7:5-6, Isaiah 26:3-4, 20-21, Jeremiah 30:10-11

New Testament – Romans 8:28, 2 Peter 2:4-9, 1 Corinthians 11:17-19, 10:13

Handling Disappointment (5)

Old Testament – Ruth 1:19-21, 4:13-17, Ecclesiastes 7:13-14, Proverbs 24:10, Psalms 31:7-8, 61:1-4, 40:1-5, 2 Kings 13:14-19

New Testament – Hebrews 10:32-39, 2 Corinthians 12:2-10, 2 Timothy 1:12, 4:16-18, Galatians 6:9

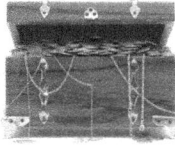

A Glimpse of Hell

A Glimpse of Hell (1)

"And in hell he lift up his eyes, being in torments, and seeth Abraham afar off and Lazarus in his bosom. And he cried and said Father Abraham, have mercy and send Lazarus, that he may dip the tip of his finger in water, and cool my tongue; for I am tormented in this flame." (Luke 16:23-24)

A Glimpse of Hell (2)

"And if thy right eye offend thee, pluck it out, and cast it from thee: for it is profitable for thee that one of thy members should perish, and not thy whole body should be cast into hell." (Matthew 5:29)

A Glimpse of Hell (3)

"And death and hell were cast into the lake of fire. This is the second death." (Revelation 20:14)

Discussion Questions

1. Explain Luke 13:3-5, 23-28.
2. Why was it that the rich man could not send Lazarus to tell others about hell in Luke 16:19-31?
3. Explain Daniel 12:2.

4. Explain the necessity of obeying the gospel as a prerequisite in avoiding hell, 2 Thessalonians 1:6-12.531

5. Will there be many or few that will be destined to hell according to Luke 13:23-28?

Fill in the Blanks

1. "The____ shall be turned into____ , and all the nations that forget God."
2. "And the____ ___ that deceived them was cast into the___ of___ and____ , where the beast and the false prophet are, and shall be____ day and night for ever and ever."
3. "Where their worm ___not, and the fire is not____ ."
4. "How oft is the candle of the____ put out! and how oft cometh their ____upon them! God____ sorrows in His anger."
5. "But whosoever shall say, Thou fool, shall be in___ of____ ____ ."

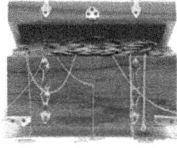

A Glimpse of Hell

*T*he Bible gives a depiction of hell, the horrors of hell, the torments of hell, and the eternal fires of hell. We must all do what is needed to avoid a terrible place like hell.

A Glimpse of Hell (1)

Old Testament – Psalms 9:15-17, 10:4-15, 52:1-7, Isaiah 5:11-24, 8:19-22, 66:24, Proverbs 27:20, 15:3, 9-11, Job 10:21-22, 18:5-21

New Testament – Mark 9:40-48, Luke 13:3-5, 23-28, 16:19-31, Revelation 16:1-11, 15, 19:15-21

A Glimpse of Hell (2)

Old Testament – Numbers 16:21-33, Deuteronomy 32:15-22, Isaiah 14:3-6, 9-20, 24:16-23, 47:5-15, Habakkuk 2:5-20, Job 21:7-21, 26-33, Psalms 55:15, 19-23

New Testament – Matthew 5:20-22, 27-30, 10:28, 25:24-46, 2 Thessalonians 1:6-12, Revelation 20:10-15

A Glimpse of Hell (3)

Old Testament – Daniel 12:2, Isaiah 1:28-31, 26:10-11, Proverbs 9:13-18, 21:16, 29:1, Job 24:13-24, Psalms 73:18-22, 27

New Testament – Matthew 3:12, 13:36-42, 47-50, John 15:1-6, Galatians 5:19-21, Hebrews 10:26-31

A Glimpse of Hell (4)

Old Testament – Psalms 145:20, 119:118-120, 155, 158, 49:11-20, Ezekiel 28:1-19, 31:10-18, 32:18-32

New Testament – Matthew 23:15-15, 29-33, 18:6-10, 16:18-19, 11:23-24, Revelation 21:7-8

A Glimpse of Hell (5)

Old Testament – Amos 5:4-7, 17-20, Micah 1:2-4, Obadiah 1:15-18, Nehemiah 1:2-10, 14-15, Jeremiah 5:29-31, Job 18:5-11, 27:13-23, Psalms 75:2-8, Proverbs 16:4-5

New Testament – Romans 1:28-32, 2:3-11, Jude 1:4-7, 12-13, Hebrews 6:4-8, Revelation 14:6-11

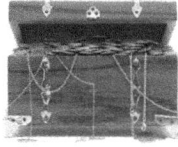

The Sin of Rebellion

The Sin of Rebellion (1)

"I have spread out my hands all day unto a rebellious people, which walketh in a way that was not good, after their own thoughts;" (Isaiah 65:2)

The Sin of Rebelliobn (2)

"Ye stiffnecked and uncircumcised in heart and ears, ye do always resist the Holy Ghost : as your fathers did, so do ye." (Acts 7:51)

The Sin of Rebellion (3)

"And Moses and Aaron gathered the congregation together before the rock, and he said unto them, Hear now, ye rebels; must we fetch you water out of this rock?" (Numbers 20:10)

Discussion Questions

1. Explain Romans 13:1-5.
2. Are we commanded to obey those in the leadership positions in the church?
3. Explain Titus 3:10-11.
4. Who orchestrated the division in Romans 16:17-20?
5. Explain Proverb 17:11.

Fill in the Blanks

1. "An___ man seeketh____ only : therefore a____ messenger shall be sent____ him."
2. "He, that being often____ hardeneth his neck, shall suddenly be____ , and that without____ ."
3. "____ them that have the____ over you, and____ yourselves: for they____ for your____ , as they that must give____ ."
4. "And if any man____ not our____ by this____ , note that man, and have____ ____ with him, that he may be____ ."
5. "Whosoever therefore____ the____ , resisteth the___ of___ : and they that resist shall receive to themselves____ ."

The Sin of Rebellion

In 1 Samuel 15:23, the Bible reads, "For rebellion is as the sin of witchcraft, and stubbornness is as iniquity and idolatry." Rebellion is defined as "an open and avowed renunciation of authority or lawful government." It is to treat established authority with contempt by not obeying laws of proclamation and refusing to adhere to the established order. In biblical terms, it is to sin with a high hand against God.

The Sin of Rebellion (1)

Old Testament – Isaiah 65:2-3, 1:1-5, 19-20, Ezekiel 2:1-10, 3:1-10, 25:27, 1 Samuel 15:22-23, Deuteronomy 21:18-21, Psalms 2:1-5, 66:7, 68:6

New Testament – Acts 7:51-54, Matthew 21:33-41, John 12:48-50, Luke 19:12-14, 27, Titus 3:10-11

The Sin of Rebellion (2)

Old Testament – Proverbs 17:1, 11, 19, 28:4, Jeremiah 28:15-16, Numbers 16:1-5, 19-34, 15:30-36, 12:1-10, Exodus 22:28, Joshua 1:16-18

New Testament – Romans 13:1-5, Hebrews 13:17, Acts 23:1-5, Jude 1:6-10, 14-19, Galatians 5:7-10

The Sin of Rebellion (3)

Old Testament – Deuteronomy 31:26-30, Exodus 16:6-8, Daniel 9:9-12, Ezra 9:5-15, Psalms 5:9-10, 78:5-8, 17-22, 36-39, Isaiah 30:1-3, 63:8-10, 1 Samuel 8:6

New Testament – Titus 1:10-11, 1 Corinthians 10:5-10, 2 Corinthians 12:20-21, Luke 10:16, 1 Thessalonians 4:7-8

The Sin of Rebellion (4)

Old Testament – Hosea 9:7-9, 15, 7:1-4, 11-14, 4:1-9, 18, Zechariah 7:8-14, Jeremiah 29:30-32, 5:20-31, Ezekiel 6:9-14, Proverbs 29:1

New Testament – Romans 1:18-23, 28-32, 16:17-20, 2 Timothy 3:1-9, 2 Thessalonians 3:14, Hebrews 3:7-19

The Sin of Rebellion (5)

Old Testament – Numbers 17:1-10, 20:7-13, 27:12-14, Nehemiah 9:12-17, 26-31, Ezekiel 12:1-3, 8-11, 20:7-11, 21-26, 33-38, Psalms 81:10-16, Lamentations 1:12-20, 3:40-48

New Testament – Acts 20:29-32, 2 Peter 2:10-21, 1 John 4:5-6, 2 Timothy 2:24-26

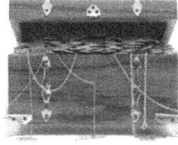

Suffering

Suffering (1)

"Before I was afflicted I went astray: but now have I kept thy word." (Psalms 119:67)

Suffering (2)

"And not only so, but we glory in tribulations also: knowing that tribulation worketh patience;"

Suffering (3)

"For unto you it is given in the behalf of Christ, not only to believe on him, but to suffer for his sake;" (Philippians 1:29)

Discussion Questions

1. Explain Deuteronomy 8:2-6.
2. Explain Matthew 5:1-12.
3. What is the admonition found in 2 Timothy 3:12?
4. Can we rejoice when we suffer for Christ? Discuss.
5. Explain Acts 14:22.

Fill in the Blanks

1. "But and if ye____ for____ sake, happy are___ : and be not____ of their____ , neither be ____."
2. "There hath no _____ taken you but such as is common to ___: but God is____ , who will not____ you to be____ above that ye are able; but will with the_____ ____ also make a____ to____ , that ye may be able to___ it."
3. "He that goeth forth and____ , bearing precious____ , shall doubtless come again with____ , bringing his___ with him."
4. "And because____ shall abound, the love of many shall wax____ ."
5. "As it is____ , For thy sake we are____ all the day long; we are____ as____ for the____.

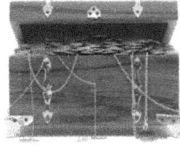

Suffering

S uffering is a topic that resonates with all of mankind. Why is the world filled with so many people who are suffering? Why did Jesus have to suffer? Why is it imperative that Christians suffer for the cause of Christ? We are to share in His sufferings; none of us are exempt. This, indeed, is an interesting study.

Suffering (1)

Old Testament – Genesis 3:15-19, 47:8-9, Job 14:1-2, 5:6-7, 3:23-26, 23:15-15, 33:14-26, 42:1-5, Deuteronomy 8:2-6, 10-20, Daniel 4:29-37, Psalms 119:67, 71, 75

New Testament – Hebrews 11:6, 32-40, 2:10, Romans 5:3-4, 8:18, 28, 2 Corinthians 4:8-11, 16-18

Suffering (2)

Old Testament – Ecclesiastes 7:14, Psalms 30:5, 34:19, 69:7-14, 19-21, 80:4-6, 126:5-6, Jeremiah 20:12-18, 15:10, 12:5-6, Lamentations 3:19-41

New Testament – Matthew 5:1-12, 10:21-39, 20:20-23, 1 Peter 2:19-25, 4:1-2, 12-19

Suffering (3)

Old Testament – Proverbs 1:24-33, Deuteronomy 28:1-2, 15, Psalms 34:12-16, Isaiah 3:10-11, 30:20-21, 43:1-7, Proverbs 24:16, 14:32, Micah 7:8-9

New Testament – 2 Timothy 3:12, 1 Thessalonians 3:1-4, 7-8, 2 Thessalonians 1:4-12, 1 Peter 3:8-18, Acts 14:22

Suffering (4)

Old Testament – Ezekiel 34:12-21, 15:6-8, 6:10-14, Ezra 9:1-15, Habakkuk 3:1-2, 7-19, Proverbs 3:11-12, Jeremiah 10:19-24, 22:21-22, 30:11-19, 31:15-20, 46:28

New Testament – 1 Corinthians 28-32, Hebrews 12:5-14, Colossians 3:23-25, Revelation 3:19

Suffering (5)

Old Testament – Psalms 80:3-7, 88:1-18, 90:3-17, 142:1-7, 44:10-18, 22-26, Deuteronomy 4:27-31, Jeremiah 29:13, Lamentations 2:17-19, Hosea 5:9-15, 6:1-2

New Testament – 1 Corinthians 10:13, 2 Corinthians 12:7-10, Romans 8:36-39, Matthew 24:12-13, James 1:2-4

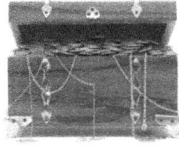

El Roi–the God Who Sees Me

El Roi–the God Who Sees Me (1)

"Neither is there any creature that is not manifest in His sight: but all things are naked and opened unto the eyes of Him with whom we have to do." (Hebrews 4:13)

El Roi–the God Who Sees Me (2)

"For mine eyes are upon all their ways: they are not hid from My face, neither is their iniquity hid from mine eyes." (Jeremiah 16:17)

El Roi–the God Who Sees Me (3)

"And they consider not in their hearts that I remember all their wickedness: now their own doings have beset them about; they are before My face," (Hosea 7:2)

Discussion Questions

1. Does God see all our ways, and does God hear every idle word we speak? How do you know this?
2. Does God know the thoughts and intents of our hearts? How do you know this?
3. Does God know the number of stars in heaven, and can He call them all by their name? How do you know this?

4. Does God know all the things we go through and every tear we shed? How do you know this?
5. Is there any place we can hide from God? How do you know this?

Fill in the Blanks

1. "Whither shall I go from thy___? or whither shall I___ from thy___?"
2. "Talk no more so exceeding___; let not___ come out of your___: for the Lord is a God of___, and by him___ are___."
3. "But the very___ of your___ are all ___."
4. "Thou hast set our___ before___, our___ sins in the___ of thy___."
5. "How long shall the land___, and the herbs of every field___, for the___ of them that dwell therein? the beasts are consumed, and the birds: because they___, He shall___ ___ our last end."

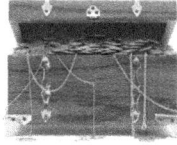

El Roi—the God Who Sees Me

E *l Roi* means "the God who sees me." In Genesis 16:13, Sara's maid, Hagar, fled into the wilderness. She traveled down a very lonely road, perhaps at the lowest point in her life, but an angel dispatched from God was sent to her with instructions that would lead her back to safety. Yet in the midst of it all, despite her lonely state and her sad condition, she recognized that God was a God who saw her even in her affliction. She proclaimed, "God sees me (EI Roi)." We can also make the same proclamation. God sees all of us, even in dire circumstances, even in our affliction, and He can provide for us just as He did for Hagar.

El Roi—the God Who Sees Me (1)

Old Testament – Genesis 16:13, Psalms 147:4-5, Psalms 139:1-12, 16-18, 102:19-28, 90:8, Hosea 7:2, Jeremiah 16:17, 23:23-24, 32:19, Proverbs 5:21

New Testament – Hebrews 4:12-13, Matthew 10:29-31, John 1:43-51, John 8:38, 44, 1 Corinthians 2:10-11

El Roi—the God Who Sees Me (2)

Old Testament – Isaiah 63:15-16, 29:14-17, 18:4-6, Habakkuk 1:13, Psalms 80:14-15, Lamentations 3:50-57, Proverbs 15:3, 11, Job 26:6, 31:4-6, 34:21-25

New Testament – Mark 10:21-22, John 4:17-19, John 29:5, John 5:19-20, 42, Luke 16:15

El Roi–the God Who Sees Me (3)

Old Testament – Jeremiah 16:17, 17:9-10, Job 10:9-16, 23:8-10, 13-17, 38:17-21, 2 Chronicles 16:9, Isaiah 40:27-28, Malachi 2:17, 3:13-18, Psalms 138:6, 37:12-13, 10:4-11

New Testament – 1 Peter 3:12, Matthew 6:1-6, Romans 8:27, 1 Corinthians 4:5

El Roi–the God Who Sees Me (4)

Old Testament – Daniel 2:22, Psalms 11:4-5, 31:7, 33:13-19, 66:7, 13:4-9, Isaiah 53:11, 1 Samuel 16:7, Ezekiel 11:5, 38:10-11, 1

New Testament – Luke 11:34-36, John 2:24-25, 3:11, 32, 13:38, 21:18-

El Roi–the God Who Sees Me (5)

Old Testament – Jeremiah 5:3, 12:4, Psalms 104:32-35, 102:19-21, 101:6, 50:16-23, 44:18-21, 36:9, 1 Samuel 2:3, Ecclesiastes 12:14

New Testament – Matthew 6:26-32, 1 John 3:20-24, John 9:39-41, Revelation 3:17-18

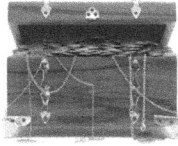

Ebenezer Stone/The Rock of Help

Ebenezer Stone/The Rock of Help (1)

"Then Samuel took a stone, and set it between Mizpeh and Shen, and called the name of it Ebenezer, saying, Hitherto hath the LORD helped us." (1 Samuel 7:12)

Ebenezer Stone/The Rock of Help (2)

"The LORD liveth; and blessed be my rock; and exalted be the God of the rock of my salvation." (2 Samuel 22:47)

Ebenezer Stone/The Rock of Help (3)

"And did all drink the same spiritual drink: for they drank of that spiritual Rock that followed them: and that Rock was Christ." (1 Corinthians 10:4)

Discussion Questions

1. What is the Rock found in Matthew 16:16-18?
2. What is the Rock found in I Corinthians 10:1-4?
3. What is the Rock found in Daniel 2:44-45?
4. Explain Psalms 62:6.
5. Explain the Rock in Isaiah 32:1-3.

Fill in the Blanks

1. "And did all drink the same____ drink; for they drank of that____ ____ that followed them: and that____ was____ ."

2. "And I say unto thee, That thou art Peter, and upon this____ I will build my___ ; and the gates of___ shall not____ against it."

3. "Whosoever cometh to____ , and hearth my sayings, and ___them, I will shew you to whom he is like."

4. "He is like a man which built an house, and digged deep, and laid ____the on a____ : and when the flood arose, the stream beat vehemently upon that____ , and could not shake it: for it was founded upon a____ ."

5. "And a____ of stumbling, and a___ of____ , even to them which____ at the____ , being disobedient."

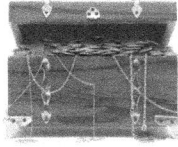

Ebenezer Stone/The Rock of Help

*B*y definition, the Ebenezer Stone is the "stone of help." It commemorated the event where God helped Israel to gain victory over the Philistines at Mizpeh (1 Samuel 7:12). Though we do not have a physical stone to mark events in our life where we can recall God's saving us and giving us the victory, there should always be a remembrance of His constant care and divine intervention in the affairs of men, which attests to our lives that victory belongs to the Lord.

Ebenezer Stone/The Rock of Help (1)

Old Testament – 1 Samuel 7:10-13, Genesis 28:10-22, 35:9-15, Psalms 30:10, 71:1-3, 72:12, 78:34-35, 94:17, 22-23, 95:1, Isaiah 28:16

New Testament – Matthew 21:42-44, 16:16-18, 7:24-27, 1 Corinthians 3:1-10

Ebenezer Stone/The Rock of Help (2)

Old Testament – Genesis 49:24, Deuteronomy 32:4, 15, 18, 31, Isaiah 17:9-11, 26:4, Daniel 2:44-45, Zechariah 12:3, 10, 3:8-10, Psalms 118:22-24, 62:1-2, 6-8, 10:14

New Testament – Acts 4:11, 1 Peter 2:4-8, Ephesians 2:19-22, Romans 9:33

Ebenezer Stone/The Rock of Help (3)

Old Testament – Joshua 4:1-7, 20-24, 24:22-27, Exodus 17:3-7, Isaiah 32:1-3, 1 Samuel 2:1-2, Psalms 146:3, 31:1-3, 27:5, 107:20, 61:1-4

New Testament – 1 Corinthians 10:1-4, 1:22-24, John 10:28-30, Revelation 2:17

Ebenezer Stone/The Rock of Help (4)

Old Testament – 2 Samuel 23:2-4, 22:2-4, 30-33, Psalms 144:1-2, 92:13-15, 89:14, 20-26, 40:1-2, 37:38-40, Isaiah 8:14, 33:16-17

New Testament – Luke 20:17-18, 6:46-49, Ephesians 2:19-22, 2 Timothy 2:19

Ebenezer Stone/The Rock of Help (5)

Old Testament – 1 Kings 19:11-1, Exodus 33:21-23, Isaiah 2:10-12, 25:10-12, 51:1, 12-15, Psalms 18:46-49, 28:1-2, 34:17-19, 78:34-35, 121:1-8, Proverbs 18:10

New Testament – Hebrews 13:5-6, 10:19-23, 4:16, Romans 8:31

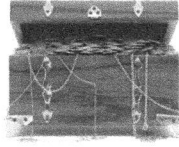

Marriage and Divorce

Marriage and Divorce (1)

"...Because the LORD hath been witness between thee and the wife of thy youth, against whom thou hast dealt treacherously: yet is she thy companion, and the wife of thy covenant. And did not he make one? Yet had he the residue of the spirit. And wherefore one? That he might seek a goodly seed. Therefore take heed to your spirit, and let none deal treacherously against the wife of his youth. For the LORD, the God of Israel, saith that he hateth putting away for one covereth violence with his garment, saith the LORD of hosts: therefore take heed to your spirit, that ye deal not treacherously. (Malachi 2:14-16)

Marriage and Divorce (2)

"Marriage is honourable in all, and the bed undefiled: but whoremongers and adulterers God will judge. (Hebrews 13:4)

Marriage and Divorce (3)

"And unto the married I command, yet not I, but the Lord, Let not the wife depart from her husband: But and if she depart, let her remain unmarried or be reconciled to her husband: and let not the husband put away his wife." (1 Corinthians 7:10-11)

Discussion Questions

1. Explain Genesis 2:24.
2. What did Christ teach concerning marriage in Matthew 19:1-12?
3. Explain Hebrews 13:4.
4. Explain Romans 7:2-3
5. Why was John the Baptist beheaded?

Fill in the Blanks

1. "For John had said unto____ , It is not____ for thee to have thy brother's____ ."
2. "And he saith unto them, ____ shall put away his____ , and , committeth____ against___ ."
3. "And if a____ shall____ ___ her____ , and be____ to____ , she____ ___ ."
4. "For the woman which hath an____ is bound by the ____to her____ so long as he____ ; but if the____ be____ , she is____ from the____ of her____ ." 5."____ is honorable in all, and the___ ____ : but___ and____ God will____ ."
5. Marriage is ____ in all, and the bed _____ : but _____ and adulterers God will judge.

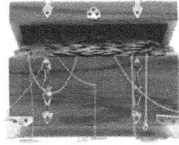

Marriage and Divorce

The divine institution of marriage was formed by God in Genesis 2:24. It is God's will that the marital union that is instituted be treasured and upheld by His Word. There are cautions associated with those who would treat this union treacherously (Matthew 19:6, Malachi 2:14-15).

Marriage and Divorce (1)

Old Testament – Genesis 2:18-24, 3:9-20, 12:1-20 16:1-16 Deuteronomy 24:5, 20:7, Proverbs 5:18-21, Exodus 20:14, 17, Malachi 2:11-16, 3:5, Ecclesiastes 9:9

New Testament – 1 Corinthians 7:1-7, John 2:1-10 Matthew 19:1-12, 5:27-32, Luke 16:18, 1 Thessalonians 4:1-8, 1 Timothy 5:14

Marriage and Divorce (2)

Old Testament – Genesis 20:3, 9-11, 26:6-11, Leviticus 20:10, Exodus 22:16-17, Deuteronomy 7:1-4, 21:10-14, Job 31:9-12, Jeremiah 23:9-12, 29:20-23 Hosea 4:14

New Testament – John 8:2-11, Ephesians 5:3-6, Hebrews 13:4, 1 Corinthians 6:9-20, 2 Corinthians 6:14-18. Galatians 5:19-21

Marriage and Divorce (3)

Old Testament – Genesis 26:34-67, Proverbs 6:23-35, 11:29, 12:4, 14:1, 18:22, 19:14, 30:18-20, 31:10-31, 1 Samuel 25:2-44 Psalms 68:6

New Testament – 1 Corinthians 7:33-39, 1 Corinthians 11:11-12, Romans 7:2-3, 1 Peter 3:1-7, James 2:11

Marriage and Divorce (4)

Old Testament – Genesis 24:18-22, 51-67, Ruth 3:10-11, 4:13-15, Esther 1:4-12, 17-21, 2:1-4, 17, Song of Solomon 8:6-7, Isaiah 62:5, Ezekiel 16:1-38, 60-63

New Testament – Ephesians 5:22-33, 1 Corinthians 13:4-8, Romans 13:9-10, Mark 10:1-12

Marriage and Divorce (5)

Old Testament – Leviticus 21:7-9, 13-15, 18:20, 1 Kings 11:1-4, 9-11, Deuteronomy 24:1-4, 22:22, Isaiah 50:1, 4:1, Jeremiah 3:8, Hosea 2:2-8

New Testament – Matthew 1:18-20, John 4:16-18, Luke 17:26-27, Mark 6:16-27, 1 Corinthians 7:8-28

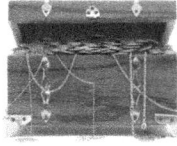

The King and His Kingdom

The King and His Kingdom (1)

"For unto us a child is born, unto us a son is given: and the government shall be upon his shoulder: and his name shall be called Wonderful, Counsellor, The mighty God, The everlasting Father, The Prince of Peace." (Isaiah 9:6)

The King and His Kingdom (2)

"Then Pilate entered in the judgement hall again, and called Jesus, and said unto him, Art thou the King of the Jews?... Jesus answered, My kingdom is not of this world: if my kingdom were of this world, then would my servants fight, that I should not be delivered to the Jews: but now is my kingdom not from hence." (John 18:33, 36)

The King and His Kingdom (3)

"Behold, the days come, saith the LORD, that I will raise unto David a righteous Branch, and a King shall reign and prosper, and shall execute judgement and justice in the earth. In his days Judah shall be saved, and Israel shall dwell safely: and this is his name whereby he shall be called, THE LORD OUR RIGHTEOUSNESS." (Jeremiah 23:5-6)

Discussion Questions

1. Explain Isaiah 9:6-7

2. What did the prophet Daniel foretell in Daniel 2:44?
3. Explain Luke 1:30-35.
4. What will be gathered out of Christ's kingdom in Matthew 13:41-42?
5. Explain Colossians 1:13.

Fill in the Blanks

1. "Who is this___ of____ ? The___ strong and mighty, the___ mighty in___ ."
2. "Then Pilate entered into the___ ___ again, and called___ , and said unto him, Art thou the___ ___ of the___ ?"
3. "Jesus answered, My___ ___ is not of this___ ."
4. "And I will give unto thee the___ of the kingdom of heaven."
5. "And he said unto them, I must___ the___ of___ to other cities also: for therefore am I___ ."

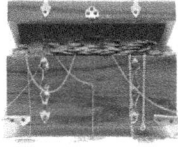

The King and His Kingdom

*H*ave you given much thought to Christ being a king and reigning in his kingdom? Pilate inquired about that in John 18:33. Notice Jesus's response in John 18:36. This study will unveil passages that will shed light on this spiritual kingdom and Christ reigning.

The King and His Kingdom (1)

Old Testament – Isaiah 9:6-7, 16:5, 22:22-25, Daniel 7:13-14, 18, 27, 2:44, 9:24, Ezekiel 37:21-28, 34:23-31, Numbers 24:17

New Testament – Luke 1:30-35, Luke 2:25-40, John 10:14-30, 18:33-38, 19:12-22, Acts 2:29-36

The King and His Kingdom (2)

Old Testament – Psalms 24:7-10, 45:1-11, 47:1-8, 2:1-12, 110:1-7, Zechariah 9:9

New Testament – John 12:12-16, Hebrews 1:1-14, 1 Corinthians 15:23-28, Ephesians 1:13-23, Colossians 1:13-23, Matthew 16:17-20, 13:41-42, Revelation 6:1-2, 15-17

The King and His Kingdom (3)

Old Testament – Psalms 145:1-4, 10-21, 103:17-22, Ezekiel 1:1, 26-28, Jeremiah 33:14-22, Zechariah 6:12-13, Isaiah 11:1-5, 10-12, 6:1-5, Proverbs 30:4

New Testament – Luke 4:41-43, John 5:19-29, Matthew 26:63-64, Revelation 1:4-8, 13-18

The King and His Kingdom (4)

Old Testament – Psalms 72:1-9, 17-19, Zephaniah 3:14-20, Jeremiah 23:5-8, 32:37-41, Micah 5:2-5, 10-15, 4:1-7

New Testament – Matthew 28:17-20, Acts 15:14-19, 2 Peter 1:10-11, Ephesians 5:5, Revelation 3:21, 21:1-7, 22-27

The King and His Kingdom (5)

Old Testament – Isaiah 40:9-11, 54:1-5, 59:16-21, 62:5-22, Jeremiah 3:17-18, Psalms 132:10-18, 89:20-36

New Testament – Luke 7:16-23, 4:40-44, 2 Corinthians 11:2, Revelation 21:9-14, Matthew 22:41-46, Hebrews 8:1-2

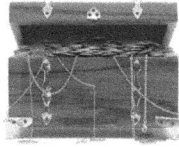

A Word to the Young

A Word to the Young (1)

"Remember now thy Creator in the days of thy youth, while the evil days come not, nor the years draw nigh, when thou shalt say, I have no pleasure in them." (Ecclesiastes 12:1)

A Word to the Young (2)

"Let no man despise thy youth, but be thou an example of the believers, in word, in conversation, in charity, in spirit, in faith, in purity." (1 Timothy 4:12)

A Word to the Young (3)

"Likewise, ye younger, submit yourselves to the elder. Yea, all of you be subject one to another, and be clothed with humility: for God resisteth the proud, and giveth grace to the humble." (1 Peter 5:5)

Discussion Questions

1. Explain Ecclesiastes 12:1-7.
2. What are the youthful lusts mentioned in 2 Timothy 2:22?
3. What was the precaution given in Proverbs 6:20-26?
4. What is the God-given role of parents in regard to their children?
5. Explain 1 Corinthians 7:14

Fill in the Blanks

1. "Let no man despise thy____ ; but be thou an____ of the____ , in___ , in___ , in___ , in___ , in___ , in___ ."
2. "Likewise, ye___ , submit yourselves unto the____ ."
3. "____ up a____ in the___ he should go."
4. "Children, ___ your____ in the____ ."
5. "And ye fathers, ____ not your____ to___ ."

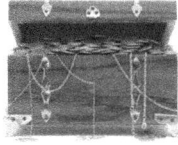

A Word to the Young

*I*n many instances, the Bible is replete with advice for the youth. Many of the difficulties, challenges, and temptations in life can be avoided by the adherence to words of wisdom.

A Word to the Young (1)

Old Testament – Ecclesiastes 12:1-7, 11:9-10, 9:9-10, 4:13, Jeremiah 1:4-7, Isaiah 11:6, 1 Samuel 2:18-21, 1 Samuel 3:16-19, Psalms 131:2

New Testament – Luke 2:43-49, Matthew 18:1-5, 1 Corinthians 14:20, 2 Timothy 3:14-15, 1 Timothy 4:12

A Word to the Young (2)

Old Testament – Psalms 119:9, 71:17-18, 34:11-16, Proverbs 1:8-19, 2:1-8, 3:11-18, 7:1-5, 1 Kings 12:4-16

New Testament – Hebrews 12:8-11, 1 Peter 5:5, Titus 2:1-8, 2 Timothy 2:22, 1 Timothy 5:1-2

A Word to the Young (3)

Old Testament – Proverbs 3:33, 4:1-8, 6:20-26, 128:1-6, Isaiah 48:17-19, 54:13, 2 Chronicles 34:1-3, 8, 26-33

New Testament – John 6:45, 1 Thessalonians 4:9-12, 1 John 2:12-14, 2 John 1:4-6

A Word to the Young (4)

Old Testament – Psalms 37:25, 32:8-9, 27:10, 25:7, Proverbs 5:18—21, Malachi 2:14-16, Jeremiah 31:17-20, 1 Kings 2:1-4

New Testament – Colossians 3:20-21, 3 John 1:4, 11, 1 Corinthians 7:14, 13:11

A Word to the Young (5)

Old Testament – Lamentations 3:27-33, Psalms 123:2, 8:2, Isaiah 40:31-32, Ecclesiastes 9:11, Zechariah 4:6, Proverbs 15:5, 31-32, 20:11, 20, 22:6, 15

New Testament – Matthew 11:25, 15:4-6, Ephesians 6:1-3, Ephesians 4:14, 1 Peter 2:1

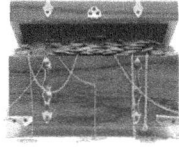

Fight for Family

Fight for Family (1)

"And I looked, and rose up, and said unto the nobles, and to the rulers, and to the rest of the people, Be not afraid of them: remember the LORD, which is great and terrible, and fight for your brethren, your sons, and your daughters, your wives, and your houses." (Nehemiah 4:14)

Fight for Family (2)

"But if any provide not for his own, and specially for those of his own house , he hath denied the faith, and is worse than an infidel.? (1 Timothy 5:8)

Fight for Family (3)

"At the same time, saith the LORD, will I be the God of all the families of Israel, and they shall be my people." (Jeremiah 31:1)

Discussion Questions

1. Explain Psalms 127:1-5.
2. What are the things commanded by God that we are to teach our children?
3. Explain Nehemiah 4:12-14.
4. What happens when children refuse to obey and honor their parents?

5. What happens when parents neglect the training of their children as instructed by God?

Fill in the Blanks

1. "Be not ye afraid of ___ ___ : remember the ___ ___ , which is great and terrible, and ___ ___ for your ___ ___ , your ___ ___ , and your ___ , your ___ , and your ___ ."
2. "At the same time, saith the Lord, will I be the ___ ___ of all the ___ of Israel, and they shall be my ___ ___ ."
3. "In the house of the ___ ___ is much ___ ; but in the ___ of the wicked is ___ ."
4. "A ___ man, and one that ___ ___ ___ ___ with all his ___ , which gave much alms to the people, and prayed to ___ ___ alway."
5. "Train up a ___ in the ___ ___ he should go: when he is ___ , he will not ___ from it."

Fight for Family

*O*ur families find their origins and their purposes in God. God placed us in our families. We are to be loved, nurtured, helped, encouraged, strengthened, disciplined, and guided by those who are dear to us and who are of a kindred spirit. The Bible teaches in Proverbs 3:33 that the curse of the Lord is in the house of the wicked, but He blesses the habitation of the just. We must fight for our families against the evils of this present world that seek to undermine God's will and His instructions regarding our families.

Fight for Family (1)

Old Testament – Nehemiah 4:12-14, Jeremiah 31:1, 15-20, 1:19, Psalms 127:1-5, 78:2-8 Zechariah 14:17, Proverbs 3:33, 15:6, 16-17, Deuteronomy 6:6-9

New Testament – Luke 1:5-6, Matthew 7:24-27, 10:12-13, 34-38, Mark 3:25, Ephesians 3:14-15

Fight for Family (2)

Old Testament – Genesis 18:17-19, 20:1-18, Deuteronomy 28:1-8, 15-20, Proverbs 24:3-4, Proverbs 20:11, 19:13-14, 18, 26, 14:1, 11, 26, Malachi 1:6

New Testament – Acts 10:1-2, 11:1-14, 16:14-15, 24-34, Titus 1:5-11, 2:1-8, 11-15

Fight for Family (3)

Old Testament – 1 Samuel 25:2-13, 32-38, Psalms 128:1-6, 122:6-8, 4:8, Malachi 2:10-16, Proverbs 6:20-24, 11:3-6, 20-22, 29, 25:19-31

New Testament – Ephesians 5:22-33, 6:1-4, 1 Peter 3:1-12, 1 Thessalonians 4:1-8, 2 Timothy 1:2-5

Fight for Family (4)

Old Testament – 1 Samuel 30:1-6, 17-19, Job 1:7-10, 29:2-6, Isaiah 38:1-6, Psalms 107:20, 28-41, Amos 3:1-2, 10, Proverbs 10:1, 17, 30, Malachi 4:5

New Testament – Colossians 3:18-23, 1 Timothy 3:4-5, 11-12, Luke 11:11-13, Matthew 15:3-6

Fight for Family (5)

Old Testament – Ruth 3:10-11, 4:11-17, Proverbs 12:4, 13:22, 17:6, 18:22, 22:6, Song of Solomon 8:6-7, Psalms 103:13, Ecclesiastes 9:9

New Testament – Mathew 18:2-7, Romans 1:28-32, 2 Timothy 3:1-5, 1 Timothy 5:8

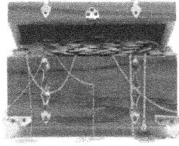

Forgiveness

Forgiveness (1)

"And forgive us our debts, as we forgive our debtors." (Matthew 6:12)

Forgiveness (2)

"So likewise shall my heavenly Father do also unto you, if ye from your hearts forgive not every one his brother their trespasses." (Matthew 18:35)

Forgiveness (3)

"Then said Jesus, Father, forgive them; for they know not what they do. And they parted his raiment, and cast lots." (Luke 23:34)

Discussion Questions

1. Is there any man on earth that doesn't have a sin problem? Explain.
2. Does sin separate us from our God? Explain.
3. Explain Acts 22:16.
4. Can God forgive us for all sin? Discuss.
5. What happens if we die in our sins? Discuss.

Fill in the Blanks

1. "I said therefore unto you, that ye shall___ in your___ ; for if ye____ not that I am he, ye shall___ in your____ ."
2. "Then Peter said unto them, ____ , and be____ every one of you in the___ of Jesus Christ for the____ of___ ___ ."
3. "Wherefore he is able also to____ them to the___ ____ that come unto___ ___ by him, seeing he ever liveth to make____ for them."
4. "To him give all the____ witness, that through his name whosoever___ ___ in him, shall receive___ of___ ___ ."
5. "But the___ hath concluded all under___ ____ , that the promise by faith of ___ ___ ___might be given to them that___ ___ ."

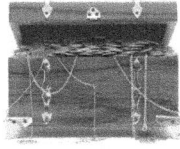

Forgiveness

Forgiveness is defined as the pardoning of sins, letting them go as if they had not been committed. It means to have something sent away, to release someone from indebtedness or offense. What a wonderful thought! All of us sin and fall short of the glory of God, yet God is so loving, so kind, so compassionate in His divine nature that He is willing to forgive all of us for all of our trespasses as if we had never done wrong. This is an awesome blessing for those who are in Christ Jesus and covered by his blood.

Forgiveness (1)

Old Testament – Ecclesiastes 7:20, Proverbs 20:9, Psalms 143:2, 130:3-4, 103:1-4, 10-14, 99:8, 32:1-6, Isaiah 64:6

New Testament – Luke 7:44-50, 18:9-14, John 8:24, 9:41, Hebrews 4:14-16, 7:25

Forgiveness (2)

Old Testament – Leviticus 5:5-6, 16:20-24, 30, 17:11, Exodus 12:13, Psalms 65:1-4, Isaiah 53:4-12, Zechariah 13:1, Micah 7:18-19

New Testament – John 1:29, Matthew 6:12, Hebrews 2:14-18, 9:6-15, 19-28, 10:10, 13:10-13, 1 Peter 2:24

Forgiveness (3)

Old Testament – Daniel 9:8-19, 1 Kings 8:30-40, 46-52, Psalms 86:5-10, 2 Chronicles 33:11-13, Isaiah 38:1-5

New Testament – Galatians 3:22, Acts 2:36-41, 13:38-39, 22:16, James 5:14-16, Revelation 5:9-10

Forgiveness (4)

Old Testament – Isaiah 59:1-3, 12-13, 55:6-7, Isaiah 1:15-20, Psalms 79:8-9, Jeremiah 14:7-10, 3:25

New Testament – Mark 11:25, Matthew 25:28, Acts 10:43, Colossians 3:12-13, 1 John 1:6-10, 2:1-2.

Forgiveness (5)

Old Testament – Proverbs 19:11, 20:22, 24:29, 25:21-22, Leviticus 19:17-18

New Testament – Matthew 18:15-35, Romans 12:17-19, 1 Thessalonians 5:15, 1 John 2:9-11, Ephesians 4:31-32

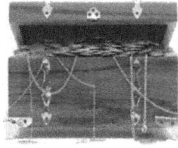

In the Lord

In the Lord (1)

"For now we live, if ye stand fast in the Lord." (1 Thessalonians 3:8)

In the Lord (2)

"Be glad in the LORD, and rejoice, ye righteous: and shout for joy, all ye that are upright in heart." (Psalms 32:11)

In the Lord (3)

"For ye were sometimes darkness, but now are ye light in the the Lord: walk as children of light:" (Ephesians 5:8)

Discussion Questions

1. Explain Psalms 31:24.
2. Explain 1 Corinthians 1:31.
3. Discuss 1 Corinthians 7:39.
4. Discuss 1 Corinthians 15:58.
5. Discuss Galatians 3:26-28.

Fill in the Blanks

1. "Rejoice___ ___ ___ alway: and again, I say, ___ ."

2. "And I will strengthen them___ ___ ___ ___ ; and they shall walk up and down in his name, saith the____ ."
3. "He trusted__ ___ ____ God of Israel; so that after him was none like him among all the kings of Judah, nor any that were before him."
4. "And it was known throughout all Joppa; and many believed in the___ ___ ."
5. "Write, Blessed are the dead which___ in the____ from henceforth."

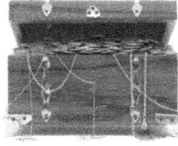

In the Lord

*I*n these passages, thoughts are conveyed concerning how precious it is to be in the Lord. To hope in the Lord, trust in the Lord, rejoice in the Lord, to find strength in the Lord, peace in the Lord, encouragement in the Lord, and help in the Lord—how precious that is!

In the Lord (1)

Old Testament – Psalms 9:2, 32:11, 63:7, 104:34, 149:2, Habakkuk 3:17-18, Isaiah 61:10, 45:17, 22-25, 41:13-16, Zechariah 12:4-5, 10:6-7, 11-12

New Testament – Luke 1:46-47, Philippians 4:4, 1 Corinthians 1:31, 7:22, 15:58, Ephesians 5:8-10, 2:13-21, 1 Thessalonians 3:8

In the Lord (2)

Old Testament – Genesis 15:6, 2 Chronicles 20:20, 1 Samuel 30:6, 2 Kings 18:5-6, Proverbs 16:20, 29:25, Isaiah 58:14, Jeremiah 17:7, Psalms 37:3-7, 118:8, 125:1, 146:5

New Testament – John 14:1, 15:1-7, 10, 16:33, 1 Corinthians 12:3, 15:31, Romans 8:1-2, 38-39, 6:3-5, Revelation 14:13

In the Lord (3)

Old Testament – Zephaniah 3:1-2, Isaiah 30:1-3, 31:1, Jeremiah 13:25, 17:5, Psalms 115:9-11, 112:7, 73:28, 64:10, 52:7-8, 32:10, 31:6, 24, 20:7, 4:5

New Testament – 1 Timothy 1:14, 4:10, 6:17, 2 Corinthians 10:17, 3:4, Ephesians 1:1-3, 7-12, 20, 2:13, 3:6, Romans 3:24

In the Lord (4)

Old Testament – 1 Samuel 2:1-2, Isaiah 25:8-9, 26:4, 29:19, Jeremiah 3:23, 51:7-10, Job 22:21-26, Psalms 2:11-12, 5:11, 21:1-7, 40:3-4, Proverbs 18:10, 28:25

New Testament – 1 Corinthians 7:22, 39, 9:1-2, Galatians 3:26-28, Ephesians 5:8-10, Philippians 1:14, 3:1, 4:1-2, 10

In the Lord (5)

Old Testament – Proverbs 3:5, Joel 2:23, Psalms 11:1-3, 26:1, 33:1, 21-22, 34:2, 35:9, 56:10-11, Haggai 1:13

New Testament – Acts 14:3, 9:42, 1 Thessalonians 5:12-13, Philippians 2:29-30, 1 Corinthians 4:17, Ephesians 6:10, 4:17-21, 2 Thessalonians 3:4-5, Philemon 1:20, 1 Peter 3:15-16, 5:14

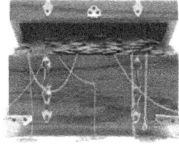

Why?

Why? (1)

"Why do the heathen rage, and the people imagine a vain thing?" (Psalms 2:1)

Why? (2)

"And he saith unto them, Why are ye fearful, O ye of little faith? Then he arose, and rebuked the winds and the sea; and there was a great calm." (Matthew 8:26)

Why? (3)

"Why is light given to a man whose way is hid, and whom God hath hedged in?" (Job 3:23)

Discussion Questions

1. What questions did Habakkuk ask in Habakkuk 1:1-3, 13?
2. What question did Jeremiah ask in Jeremiah 12:1-4?
3. Discuss Matthew 7:3-5.
4. Discuss 1 Corinthians 6:2-10.
5. What questions did Job ask in Job 21:7-13?

Fill in the Blanks

1. "___ do the heathen rage, and the people imagine a vain thing?"
2. "And the disciples came, and said unto him, ___ speakest those unto___ in parables?"
3. "But___ dost thou judge thy brother? Or___ dost thou set at nought___ ___ ? for we shall___ stand before the judgment seat of Christ."
4. "___ do ye persecute me as___ , and are not satisfied with my flesh?"
5. "And I, brethren, if I yet preach circumcision, ___ do I yet suffer___ ___ ? then is the offence of the cross ceased."

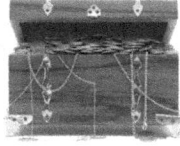

Why?

*W*hy? Perhaps one of the most commonly asked questions in the world is the question "Why?" This word is referenced when the desire is to know the reason, the causation, or the purpose.

Why? (1)

Old Testament – Psalms 2:1-5, 10:1-6, 22:1-6, 52:1-7, Job 21:7-16, 33:13, Habakkuk 1:1-3, 13, 2:1-4, 2 Chronicles 7:21-22, 24:20-25, 25:11-15, 19-22

New Testament – Matthew 7:3-5, 9:11-17, 13:10-17, Luke 5:30-35, Acts 4:24-29, 14:11-15

Why? (2)

Old Testament – Genesis 4:6-7, Exodus 3:3-6, 5:22-23, 6:1-8, Deuteronomy 5:25-27, Judges 5:16-23, 6:13-16, 11:7-11, Jeremiah 2:14, 8:5, 14, 14:7-9, 17-19, 30:15-17, Isaiah 40:27, Psalms 42:5-11

New Testament – Matthew 8:26, 17:14-21, 22:18-22, 26:7-10, 27:46-54

Why? (3)

Old Testament – Exodus 1:15-20, Josh 5:1-4, 7:19-25, Judges 2:1-3, 13:18-21, 1 Samuel 6:3, Psalms 68:15-16, Ezra 7:23, Nehemiah 6:1-3

New Testament – Matthew 6:28-34, 19:7-11, 21:25-27, Mark 2:7-10, 8:12, Romans 3:3-7, 8:24-25, 9:18-21, Galatians 2:14-16, 5:11-14

Why? (4)

Old Testament – Numbers 11:19-23, 31, 20:3-12, Deuteronomy 32:5, 20, Psalms 74:1-2, 11-12, 80:4-12, 88:14-15, 1 Kings 9:7-9, Ezekiel 33:10-11, 18:18-19, Job 19:22-25

New Testament – Luke 5:29-35, Romans 14:7-10, Colossians 2:20-23, 1 Corinthians 4:7, 6:7-10, 15:29-31

Why? (5)

Old Testament – Jonah 1:7-10, Ruth 1:11-16, 19-21, Job 3:23-26, 7:20-21, 27:8-12, Jeremiah 12:1-4, 15:18, 46:15-19, Haggai 1:9-11, Lamentations 3:22, 39, Ezra 9:13, Micah 4:6-9

New Testament – Luke 24:4-8, 36-39, Acts 1:9-11, 9:3-5, 15:10-11, 22:9-16

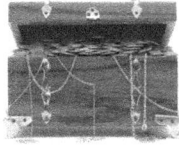

Being Prudent

Being Prudent (1)

"Every prudent man dealeth with knowledge: but a fool layeth open his folly." (Proverbs 13:16)

Being Prudent (2)

"Give not that which is holy unto the dogs, neither cast your pearls before the swine, lest they trample them under their feet, and turn again and rend you." (Matthew 7:6)

Being Prudent (3)

"Therefore the prudent shall keep silence in that time; for it is an evil time." (Amos 5:13)

Discussion Questions

1. Explain Proverbs 14:8.
2. Discuss Proverbs 22:3.
3. Discuss Isaiah 10:13.
4. Discuss Matthew 11:25.
5. Explain 1 Corinthians 1:19.

Fill in the Blanks

1. "A___ wrath is presently known: but a___ man covereth shame."
2. "The___believeth every word: but the___ man looketh well
   to his going."
3. "Wherein he hath abounded toward us in all___ and__ ."
4. "Behold, my servant shall deal____ , he shall be exalted and
   extolled, and be___ ___ ___ ."
5. "I wisdom dwell with___ , and find out____ of witty
   inventions."

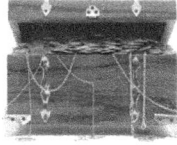

Being Prudent

B eing prudent is to coordinate or to orchestrate one's affairs by the use of sagacity or reasoning. It is to manage with good judgment and good cognitive skills.

Being Prudent (1)

Old Testament – Genesis 25:29-34, 1 Samuel 16:1-5, 18, 21:10-15, 24:1-20, Judges 3:15-30, 4:15-24, 1 Kings 3:16-28, Micah 7:5-6, Proverbs 13:16, 14:8, 15, 18, 15:5, 16:21, 18:17

New Testament – Matthew 7:6, 10:14, 16, 36, 16:6-12, 23:1-5, 15

Being Prudent (2)

Old Testament – Genesis 13:7-12, 16:1-10, 38:11-26, 1 Kings 14:1-13, 2 Samuel 14:1-22, Joshua 9:1-27, Job 15:5, 5:13, Isaiah 26:10, 5:21, Psalms 125:4-5, 18:25-26, Proverbs 2:10-15

New Testament – 2 Corinthians 12:16, 11:3, Ephesians 4:14, Colossians 2:18, Revelation 22:11

Being Prudent (3)

Old Testament – Genesis 25:23, 27:6-13, 30-35, 32:9-21, 33:1-4, 1 Samuel 12:1-12, Judges 19:1-30, 20:6-11, Amos 5:13, Numbers 25:16-18, Proverbs 12:16, 23, 22:3

New Testament – Ephesians 6:11, 5:17, Matthew 24:24, 2 Corinthians 2:11, 11:12-15, Romans 16:18, 2 Peter 3:17

Being Prudent (4)

Old Testament – Genesis 29:18-27, 31:6-13, 36-42, Joshua 8:15-21, 1 Kings 20:35-43, 12:1-16, 2 Kings 10:18-28, Psalms 83:3-5, 39:1, Proverbs 8:12, 19:14, Song of Solomon 8:9-10

New Testament – Luke 21:34-36, Matthew 26:41, Acts 20:31, Ephesians 5:15-17, 1 Corinthians 3:19, 1:19

Being Prudent (5)

Old Testament – Exodus 18:13-24, 4:24-26, 2 Chronicles 35:20-24, Numbers 15:32-36, 25:3-13, Hosea 14:9, Jeremiah 49:7, 20, Isaiah 52:13-15, 10:12-13, 3:1-8, Proverbs 27:12

New Testament – Ephesians 1:8-9, 1 Corinthians 10:12, 23, Titus 3:9, 14, Luke 14:12-14, Philemon 1:10-18

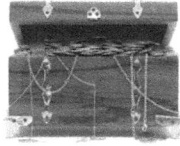

Command Them

Command Them (1)

"Teaching them to observe all things whatsoever I have commanded you: and, lo, I am with you always, even unto the end of the world. Amen." (Matthew 28:20)

Command Them (2)

"And Moses did as the LORD commanded them, so did they." (Exodus 7:6)

Command Them (3)

"So likewise ye, when ye shall have done all those things which are commanded you, say, We are unprofitable servants: we have done that which was our duty to do." (Luke 17:10)

Discussion Questions

1. Discuss Matthew 28:20.
2. Discuss Acts 1:1-2.
3. Discuss John 14:15, 21, 31.
4. Explain Acts 10:33.
5. Discuss Psalms 119:4-6, 10, 21.

Fill in the Blanks

1. "And they answered____ , saying, All that thou_____ us we will do, and___ thou us we will go."
2. "To such as keep his____ , and to those that remember his____ to do them."
3. "For if ye shall diligently keep all these____ which I___ you, to do them, to love the____ ____ your____ , to walk in all his ways, and to____ unto____ ."
4. "So likewise ye, when ye shall have done all those_____ which are____ you, say, We are____ ____ ."
5. "And hereby we do know that we know him, if we___ his____ .

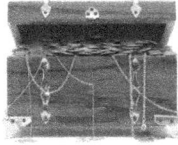

Command Them

C ommand means "to give an imperative, executive or an authoritative order." It is to give a direct order or requirement.

"Observe and hear all these words which I command thee" (Deuteronomy 12:28).

Command Them (1)

Old Testament – Exodus 7:6, 34:32-34, Leviticus 22:31, 10:1-3, Deuteronomy 4:2, Numbers 15:38-40, Ezra 7:23, Jeremiah 26:2, Job 23:12, Isaiah 34:16, 45:12, 48:18, Psalms 103:17-20, Proverbs 19:16

New Testament – Matthew 28:20, John 12:49-50, Acts 1:1-2, 15:24, 1 Thessalonians 4:1-2

Command Them (2)

Old Testament – Genesis 7:5, 9, 18:19, Exodus 18:23, 19:7-9, 24:12, Numbers 23:20, 26, 24:13, Jeremiah 1:7, 17, 7:23, 11:3-4, 8, Proverbs 10:8, 7:2, Psalms 119:4-6, 10, 21

New Testament – Matthew 5:19, 19:17, John 14:15, 21, 31, Acts 10:33, 42, 48, 1 Corinthians 14:34-37

Command Them (3)

Old Testament – Numbers 9:8, 17:11, 32:25, 31, Deuteronomy 6:6-7, 7:9, 11, 12:28, 32, 18:18-20, 26:16-18, 30:15-16, 2 Chronicles 30:12, Psalms 78:5, 89:31-34, 107:25-31, 111:7-10

New Testament – Luke 17:10, John 15:10, Acts 3:22, 13:47, 17:30

Command Them (4)

Old Testament – Deuteronomy 5:30-33, 11:22-23, 13:1-5, Judges 3:1-4, 1 Kings 11:38, 15:4-5, Ezekiel 24:18, 2 Kings 18:1-6, 17:19, Psalms 119:32, 35, 60, 115, 166, 112:1, Proverbs 13:13

New Testament – Romans 16:26, Titus 1:3, 14, 1 John 2:3-4, 3:23-24, 5:2-3

Command Them (5)

Old Testament – Joshua 1:7, 16-18, 11:15, Jeremiah 35:18-19, Job 42:9, Psalms 44:4, 68:28, Ecclesiastes 8:5, 12:13, Lamentations 1:18, 3:37-38

New Testament – Romans 13:8-9, 2 Thessalonians 3:4-12, 2 Peter 3:1-2, 1 Timothy 6:13-14, 1:5, 2 John 4-6, Colossians 2:18-22, Revelation 12:17, 14:12-13, 22:14

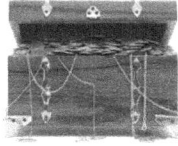

Behold

Behold (1)

"Behold, I will send my messenger, and he shall prepare the way before me: and the LORD, whom ye seek, shall suddenly come to his temple, even the messenger of the covenant, whom ye delight: behold, he shall come, saith the LORD of hosts. But who may abide the day of his coming? And who shall stand when he appeareth? For he is like a refiner's fire, and like fullers' soap." (Malachi 3:1-2)

Behold (2)

"The next day John seeth Jesus coming unto him, and saith, Behold the Lamb of God, which taketh away the sin of the world." (John 1:29)

Behold (3)

"While he yet spake, behold, a bright cloud overshadowed them: and behold a voice out of the cloud, which said, This is my beloved Son, in whom I am well pleased; hear ye him." (Matthew 17:5)

Discussion Questions

1. Discuss Deuteronomy 9:13.
2. Discuss Matthew 17:1-5.
3. What observations are made in Matthew 20:18-19, 30-34?
4. Explain Ecclesiastes 4:1.

5.   Discuss Revelation 3:8-11.

Fill in the Blanks

1.   "The next day John seeth Jesus coming unto him, and saith, ____ the____ of____ , which taketh away the sin of the____ ."
2.   "____ , I lay in Sion a chief corner stone, ___ , ___ : and he that____ on him shall not be____ ."
3.   "I looked on my right hand, and____ , but there was no man that would____ me:____ failed me; no man____ for my soul."
4.   "____ , what manner of love the Father hath bestowed upon us, that we should be called the ____of____ ."
5.   "____ , I come as a____ . Blessed is he that____ , and keepeth his____ , lest he walk naked, and they see his shame.

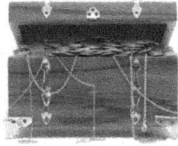

Behold

The Greek word *ide* is translated "behold." This is an imperative command, meaning "to look upon or to gaze upon."

Behold (1)

Old Testament – Genesis 1:31, Ecclesiastes 8:17, 7:27-29, Job 36:5-12, 22-26, 40:4-5, Isaiah 35:4, 40:9-10, 15-17, Numbers 23:9, 20-21, 24:14-17, Zechariah 6:12-13, 8:7-8, 9:9, Psalms 46:8-11, 17:15

New Testament – Matthew 17:5, John 1:29, 36, 12:15, 19, 17:24

Behold (2)

Old Testament – Deuteronomy 1:8, 21, 4:5, 9, 5:22-24, 9:13-16, Numbers 32:14, 23, 25:11-12, 21:5-9, Joshua 5:13-15, Exodus 23:20, 34:30, Isaiah 52:6, 13-15, 55:4-5, 66:12, Malachi 3:1

New Testament – Matthew 20:18-19, 30-34, 23:34-38, 28:2-11, John 1:14

Behold (3)

Old Testament – 1 Kings 19:5-13, 2 Kings 1:9-14, 2:8-21, Joshua 14:10-12, Isaiah 12:2, 28:2-6, 50:9-11, Lamentations 3:50-57, Jeremiah 32:27, 17:14-15, 4:13, 23-26, Proverbs 11:31, Psalms 11:4, 33:13-19, 133:1-3

New Testament – James 5:9-11, Revelation 19:11-16, 16:15

Behold (4)

Old Testament – Ecclesiastes 4:1, Psalms 142:4, 123:2, 121:4-8, Job 16:16-19, 19:7, 23:8-10, 28:24-28, 2 Chronicles 13:12, Zechariah 5:1-7, Ezekiel 8:2-12, 13:8-9, 20-23, 15:1-6, 43:2-5, 10-12

New Testament – Romans 9:33, Revelation 1:7, 18, 3:8-11, 20-22, 6:2

Behold (5)

Old Testament – Deuteronomy 26:10-11, 11:26-29, Jeremiah 14:18-19, 16:14-17, 21, 21:8, 23:5-8, Isaiah 42:1-9, 43:19, 65:17-23, Psalms 84:9-12, 102:19-22, 134:1-3

New Testament – Hebrews 2:9-13, 8:8-10, 1 Peter 2:4-6, 12, 1 John 3:1, Revelation 21:3-5

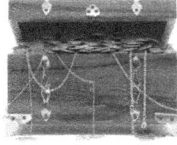

Perspective

Perspective (1)

"He that cometh from above is above all: he that is of the earth is earthly, and speaketh of the earth: he that cometh from heaven is above all." (John 3:31)

Perspective (2)

"He that speaketh of himself seeketh his own glory: but he that seeketh his glory that sent him, the same is true, and no unrighteousness is in him." (John 7:18)

Perspective (3)

"And if ye walk contrary unto me, and will not hearken unto me; I will bring seven times more the plagues upon you according to your sins." (Leviticus 26:21)

Discussion Questions

1. What observations are made in John 8:23, 38-51?
2. Discuss Romans 10:1-3.
3. Explain Romans 14:17-19.
4. Discuss 1 Samuel 16:7.
5. What observations are made in John 5:42, 44?

Fill in the Blanks

1. "A man's heart deviseth his____ : but the Lord directeth his____ ."
2. "Man's goings are of the Lord; how can a man then____ his_____ ?"
3. "This people draweth____ unto me with their____ , and____ me with their lips; but their____ is far from me."
4. "If any man will do his___ , he shall ____of the____ , whether it be of____ , or___ I speak of____ ."
5. "Set your____ on things____ , not on things on the___ ."

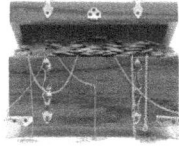

Perspective

*P*erspective is defined as "a viewpoint, an understanding, an observation as we ponder the relative importance of facts, situation, experiences, etc." Our reasoning from our perspective oftentimes becomes the integral basis of our beliefs, customs, and behaviors. It is important to note that God has said in His holy Word, "For my thoughts are not your thoughts, neither are your ways my ways. For as the heavens are higher than the earth, so are my ways higher than your ways, and my thoughts than your thoughts" (Isaiah 55:8-9).

Therefore, it is imperative that we be guided by the divine or heavenly perspective of God as it is revealed in His holy Word. Again, we read where our Lord and Savior Jesus proclaimed, "He that cometh from above is above all: he that is of the earth is earthly, and speaketh of the earth: he that cometh from heaven is above all" (John 3:31).

> "Ye are from beneath; I am from above: ye are of this world;
> I am not of this world" (John 8:23).

> "No man hath seen God at any time; the only begotten Son,
> which is in the bosom of the Father, he hath declared Him"
> (John 1:18).

Jesus's perspective was different from the perspective of man. He is the Shepherd whose voice we must listen to and follow if our aim is to make heaven our home.

Perspective (1)

Old Testament – Leviticus 26:21, 24, Isaiah 1:13-18, 41:24, 43:22-24, 45:12, 20, 22, 58:3-9, 64:6, Ecclesiastes 7:29, Jeremiah 44:16-22, 27, 22:29, 10:23, Psalms 119:133, 37:23, Proverbs 4:19, 16:9, 20:2

New Testament – John 3:31, 8:23, 38-51, Romans 10:1-3

Perspective (2)

Old Testament – Ecclesiastes 5:15-16, 6:1-4, 9:5-6, 12:13-14, Daniel 4:30-37, 1 Kings 20:28, Psalms 39:5-7, 49:6-20, 90:5-9, 94:11, 100:3, 144:4, 15

New Testament – Luke 12:16-21, 16:20-31, John 4:41, 7:18, 12:43, Romans 2:29, Galatians 1:10

Perspective (3)

Old Testament – 1 Samuel 16:7, 2 Chronicles 6:14, 16:9, 1 Chronicles 28:9, Psalms 4:5, 34:15, 50:14, 23, 51:16-17, 116:17, Malachi 1:7-11, 14, Amos 5:14-15, 22-24, Jeremiah 32:19, Proverbs 23:26

New Testament – Matthew 15:8, John 5:42, 44, 4:23, Romans 14:17-19, 8:5-8, 28

Perspective (4)

Old Testament – Judges 21:25, Isaiah 30:21, 25:1, 8:10, Jeremiah 7:23-24, 23:16, 22, Job 18:5-7, Proverbs 12:15, 14:12, 19:20-21, 30:12, Deuteronomy 32:20, 28-29, Psalms 33:11, 81:11-16, 106:13, 43

New Testament – Matthew 21:23-27, John 7:17, 4:34, Luke 16:15

Perspective (5)

Old Testament – 1 Kings 18:21, Joshua 24:15, 5:13-15, Exodus 32:26-28, Ezekiel 33:21, Jeremiah 9:6, Psalms 15:1-5, 16:8, 24:3-5, 65:4, 91:14, Daniel 9:3

New Testament – Colossians 3:1-2, Philippians 3:20-21, 2 Corinthians 4:18, 2 Timothy 2:4, Romans 8:5-8, Matthew 6:33, 12:47-50, John 8:29

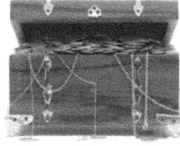

What?

What? (1)

"What is man, that thou shouldest magnify him? And that thou shouldest set thine heart uon him?" (Job 7:17)

What? (2)

"For what is a man profited, if he shall gain the whole world, and lose his own soul? Or what shall a man give in exchange for his soul?" (Matthew 16:26)

What? (3)

"Now when they heard this, they were pricked in their heart, ansd said unto Peter and the rest of the apostle, Men and brethren, what shall we do?" (Acts 2:37)

Discussion Questions

1. Discuss Job 7:17-18.
2. Explain Romans 9:20-24.
3. Explain Acts 2:12, 37-38.
4. Discuss Romans 3:3-4.
5. Discuss Joshua 7:8-12.

Fill in the Blanks

1. "What is___ , that thou art____ of him?"
2. "And Samuel said, ____ hast thou done?"
3. "Now when they heard this, they were____ in their____ , and said unto Peter and to the rest of the apostles, Men and brethren, ____ shall we do?"
4. "And he said, ____ hast thou done? the voice of thy____ ___ crieth unto me from the ground."
5. "By which also ye are saved, if ye keep in memory____ I____ unto you, unless ye have believed in____ ."

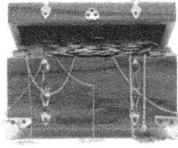

What?

*T*he definition of the word *what* references a word used "to make inquiry concerning causes, identify value, origin, or nature." It is a word used to interrogate.

What? (1)

Old Testament – Job 7:17-18, 9:12-20, 15:14-16, 41:10-11, Psalms 8:4-6, 56:11, 66:16, 89:48, 144:3-4, Ecclesiastes 6:11-12, Isaiah 45:9-13

New Testament – Romans 9:20-24, 11:15-22, James 4:14, John 2:24-25, 6:62-66, 18:37-38, Matthew 11:7-13

What? (2)

Old Testament – 1 Samuel 13:11, 14, 15:14, 22-23, Isaiah 1:11, 17, 5:4-7, 10:3-4, 19:12, 21:11-12, Jeremiah 2:5, 23, 5:30-31, 6:18-20, 8:6-9, Deuteronomy 10:12, 12:32, Micah 6:6-8, Psalms 116:12-19

New Testament – Mark 10:17-22, John 2:5, Matthew 10:27-28, 16:26

What? (3)

Old Testament – Deuteronomy 4:7-9, Exodus 19:4-6, 1 Samuel 7:23-24, Lamentations 5:1-7, Zechariah 13:4-6

New Testament – Luke 20:12-19, 9:51-56, Matthew 8:27, 7:12, Romans 3:3-4, 12:2, 14:17-23, 15:4, 1 Thessalonians 4:1-2, 2:19, 2 Peter 3:11-14, Colossians 3:17, 27, Galatians 6:7-8, Ephesians 5:10, 17

What? (4)

Old Testament – Genesis 31:16, Numbers 9:8, 22:19, 24:13, Ezra 7:23, 1 Kings 22:14, Ezekiel 2:8, Psalms 85:8, Job 37:9-12

New Testament – John 11:21-22, 12:49-50, 1 Corinthians 15:1-2, 10:31, 6:16-17, 3:13, Matthew 19:4-6, 28:20, Luke 5:25-26, 8:28-39, Ephesians 6:8, Philippians 4:8

What? (5)

Old Testament – Genesis 4:10-12, 12:18-20, 26:10-12, 42:28, 44:16, Joshua 7:8-12, Proverbs 4:19, 10:32, 25:8

New Testament – Acts 2:12, 37-38, 4:7-16, 8:30-38, 9:3-6, 17-18, 10:1-6, 47-48, 11:9, 16:30-33, 19:1-5, Romans 6:1-3, 15, 21

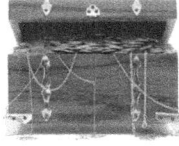

God Is Good

God Is Good (1)

"He loveth righteousness and judgment: the earth is full of the goodness of the LORD." (Psalms 33:5)

God Is Good (2)

"Or despises thou the riches of his goodness and forbearance and longsuffering, not knowing that the goodness of God leadeth thee to repentance?" (Romans 2:4)

God Is Good (3)

"And God saw every thing that he had made, and, behold, it was very good. And the evening and the morning were the sixth day," (Genesis 1:31)

Discussion Questions

1. Discuss Psalms 145:7-9.
2. Explain Lamentations 3:25.
3. Discuss James 1:17.
4. Explain Romans 2:4.
5. Explain Romans 11:22.

Fill in the Blanks

1. "If ye then, being evil, know how to give_____ ___ ___ unto your children, how much more shall your father which is in____ give good___ to them that___ ___?"

2. "And God saw every thing that he had made, and, behold, it was___ ___."

3. "For God giveth to a man that is____ in his sight____, and___, and____."

4. "And he said unto him, Why callest thou me____? there is none but one, that is, _____."

5. "I will mention the of the____ Lord, and the____ of the Lord."

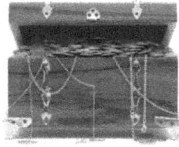

God Is Good

O ne of the amazing attributes of God is that He is good all the time. It is because of the goodness of God that we live from day to day. Even to His enemies, God is good.

God Is Good (1)

Old Testament – Genesis 1:31, Deuteronomy 6:18, 24, 8:16, 26:11, 28:12, Ezekiel 34:26, 36:8-11, Jeremiah 31:12-14, 32:39-42, 33:11, Isaiah 63:7, 58:10-11, Psalms 145:7-9, 135:3, 125:4, 118:1

New Testament – Matthew 19:16-17, 7:11, 5:44-45, Ephesians 5:8-10

God Is Good (2)

Old Testament – Exodus 18:9, Numbers 10:29, 32, 1 Chronicles 16:34, 2 Chronicles 30:18-19, 19:11, Nahum 1:7, Psalms 23:5-6, 25:8, 27:13, 34:8, 54:6, 86:5, 100:5, 119:39, 68, 122

New Testament – Romans 12:2, 8:28, James 1:17, 1 Thessalonians 5:21, 2 Thessalonians 1:11, Galatians 5:22-23

God Is Good (3)

Old Testament – Lamentations 3:25, 38, Job 2:10, 1 Samuel 3:18, Isaiah 39:8, Jeremiah 5:24-25, 2:7, Psalms 84:11, 85:12-13, 107:1, 31, 118:29, 119:66, Ecclesiastes 2:26, 2 Chronicles 7:3, Ezra 3:11, 8:18, Nehemiah 2:17, 5:19

New Testament – Luke 6:38, Romans 2:4, 7:12-16, 11:22

God Is Good (4)

Old Testament – Deuteronomy 30:5, 9, Joshua 24:20, 23:14-16, 1 Chronicles 17:26-27, 2 Chronicles 6:41, 2 Chronicles 7:10, Nehemiah 13:30-31, 1 Samuel 10:12, 1 Samuel 3:18, Amos 5:14-15, Psalms 36:1, 4, 37:23, 106:1-5, 136:1

New Testament – 1 Timothy 4:4-6, Acts 10:38, 11:24, 14:15-16

God Is Good (5)

Old Testament – Hosea 3:4-5, Jeremiah 18:6-11, 24:1-10, Micah 2:7, 6:8, Psalms 97:10, 86:17, 73:1, 69:16, 68:10, 65:4, 52:1, 33:5, 31:19, 27:13, 104:27-28, 109:21, 122:9

New Testament – Hebrews 9:11, James 3:17, Ephesians 6:8, Romans 12:9

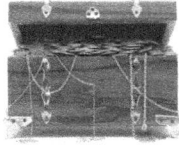

The Throne

The Throne (1)

"But unto the Son he saith, Thy throne, O God, is for ever and ever: a sceptre of righteousness is the sceptre of thy kingdom." (Hebrews 1:8)

The Throne (2)

"And immediately I was in the spirit: and behold, a throne was set in heaven, and one sat on the throne. And he that sat was to look upon like a jasper and a sardine stone: and there was a rainbow round about the throne, in sight like unto an emerald." (Revelation 4:2)

The Throne (3)

"God reigneth over the heathen: God sitteth upon the throne of His Holiness." (Psalms 47:8)

Discussion Questions

1. Discuss Daniel 7:9-14.
2. Discuss Hebrews 1:8.
3. What observations are made in Revelation 7:9-17?
4. Discuss Revelation 20:11-15.
5. What observations were made in Acts 7:55-56?

Fill in the Blanks

1. "Heaven is my____ and earth is my____ ."
2. "It is an____ to kings to commit____ : for the____ is____ by righteousness."
3. "The Lord hath____ his___ ____ in the____ ; and his kingdom ruleth over all."
4. "But unto the Son he saith, Thy____ , is for ever and ever: a sceptre of____ is the sceptre of thy____ ."
5. "Thy seed will I establish for___ ____ , and build up thy____ to all____ ."

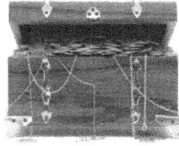

The Throne

A throne is a symbol of sovereignty, authority, power, dignity, and judgment. It symbolizes the place where kings rule in their kingdoms. God is King of kings, and there are many passages depicting Him sitting and ruling on His throne.

The Throne (1)

Old Testament – Daniel 7:9-14, 4:13, 17, 34-37, Deuteronomy 26:15, Ezekiel 1:4, 26-28, 10:1-5, Isaiah 6:1-4, 37:16, 40:22, 63:15, 66:1, Lamentations 5:19, Psalms 9:4-7, 11:4-7, 33:13-15, 103:19, Zechariah 2:13

New Testament – Acts 7:49, 55, 56, 2:30-36, Revelation 20:11-15

The Throne (2)

Old Testament – 1 Kings 22:19, Job 26:6-9, 11, Ezekiel 43:7, 9, Jeremiah 3:17, 14:21, 17:12, Zechariah 8:3, 20-23, Isaiah 24:23, 2:2-5, Psalms 22:3, 45:6, 47:8-9, 80:1, 97:1-2, 99:1-5

New Testament – Hebrews 12:21-29, 4:14-16, Revelation 4:2-11, 5:11-13, 21:5-7

The Throne (3)

Old Testament – Exodus 24:9-11, 25:17-22, 30:1, 6, Numbers 7:89, 1 Samuel 4:4, 1 Samuel 7:12-16, 1 Chronicles 22;9-10, 28:5, 29:23 Haggai 2:22, Zechariah 6:12-13, Isaiah 22:21-23, 9:6-7, Psalms 102:15-19, 132:11-12

New Testament – Hebrews 1:8, 8:1-2, 12:2, Revelation 1:4, 13

The Throne (4)

Old Testament – Deuteronomy 17:18-20, Proverbs 16:12, 20:8, 25:5, 29:14, 1 Samuel 2:8, Job 36:7, Psalms 113:7-8 Isaiah 16:5, 32:1, 47:1, Jeremiah 1:15-16, 22:1-4, 25:30, 29:16-19, 43:8-10

New Testament – Luke 1:30-32, Matthew 19:28, Mark 10:35-40, Revelation 6:14-16, 7:9-17

The Throne (5)

Old Testament – 1 Kings 1:46-48, 2:33, 10:18-20, Jeremiah 33:17-21, Psalms 2:1-12, 89:1-4, 14, 19-36, 93:1-2, 110:1-4, 122:3, 5, Zechariah 6:12-15

New Testament – 1 Peter 2:5-8, 3:22, Hebrews 2:9-18, Matthew 22:41-45, 26:64, Mark 14:60-62, 16:19-20

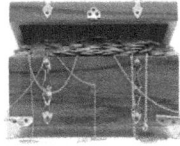

God Is Unique

God Is Unique (1)

"But he is in one mind, and who can turn him? And what his soul desireth, even that he doeth. For he performeth the thing that is appointed for me: and many such things are with him." (Job 23:13-14)

God Is Unique (2)

"O the depth of the riches both of the wisdom and knowledge of God! How unsearchable are his judgments, and his ways past finding out!" (Romans 11:33)

God Is Unique (3)

"In whom also we have obtained an inheritance, being predestinated according to the purpose of him who worketh all things after the counsel of his own will:" (Ephesians 1:11)

Discussion Questions

1. What observations are made in Job 34:29-33?
2. What observations are made in Romans 11:33-36?
3. What observations did Job make in Job 9:4-12?
4. Discuss Revelation 15:4.
5. Discuss Psalms 86:8-10.

Fill in the Blanks

1. "Among the gods there is____ like unto thee, O Lord."
2. "For thou art____ ____ , and doest____ things: thou art____ ____ ."
3. "That by two____ things, in which it was____ for God to____ ."
4. "I am____ and____ , the beginning and the____ , the first and the____ ."
5. "Therefore hath he____ on whom he will have____ and whom he____ he____ ."

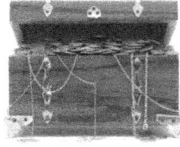

God Is Unique

"But he is unique and who can turn Him? And what His soul desires, that He does" (Job 23:13, NASB).

*T*his verse most vividly portrays our God. God's thoughts are not our thoughts; his ways are not ours. They are far above our comprehension. God works all things after the counsel of His own will. He cannot lie. He is always true and faithful. He does good always. God alone is God.

God Is Unique (1)

Old Testament – Job 23:13-14, 24:22-25, 28:9-11, 24-27, 36:26, 40:9-14, Jeremiah 10:6-7, 16, Isaiah 55:8-9, 46:9-13, 40:22-26, 12:6, Psalms 35:10, 47:2, 71:19, 86:8-10

New Testament – Romans 11:33-36, Ephesians 1:10-11, 1 Timothy 1:17, 6:16

God Is Unique (2)

Deuteronomy 33:26, 32:4, 31, 4:7-8, 32-39, 3:24, Exodus 19:4, 15:11-16, 1 Samuel 7:22-24, Jeremiah 32:27, Isaiah 45:5-8, 21-25, Proverbs 30:4-6, Micah 7:18-19, Psalms 66:5, 16, 95:3-6 New Testament – Luke 1:51-53, Mark 10:17-18, John 17:3, 25, Revelation 15:4

God Is Unique (3)

Old Testament – Ecclesiastes 3:11, 1 Samuel 2:2, Daniel 4:3, Exodus 8:10, 9:14, Psalms 89:6-8, 34, Numbers 23:19, 1 Samuel 15:29, Malachi 3:6, Isaiah 55:10-11, 43:13, 14:27, Psalms 97:3-5, 50:3, 29:3-9, 18:8-15, Habakkuk 3:3-6

New Testament – John 4:24, 1 Corinthians 8:6, 2 Timothy 2:13, Hebrews 6:18

God Is Unique (4)

Old Testament – 1 Kings 8:23, Job 34:29-33, 37:2-15, 41:10-11, Psalms 147:3-5, 139:2-6, 113:5-9, 86:10, 83:18, Isaiah 40:12-18, 44:5-8, 64:4, Jeremiah 50:44, Hosea 7:2

New Testament – Matthew 11:25, Romans 9:18, 11:8-10, 13:1, Hebrews 4:12-13, 1 Corinthians 8:6

God Is Unique (5)

Old Testament – Deuteronomy 32:11-15, 20, Isaiah 45:15, 57:17, 59:1-2, 64:6-7, Ezekiel 39:24-29, Psalms 50:17-21, Job 9:4-12, 19-21, 32, 12:10-14, 25:2-6, Habakkuk 1:13, Psalms 10:1, 28:1, 62:5-6, 11

New Testament – John 6:44, 65, Revelation 1:8, 18, 22:13

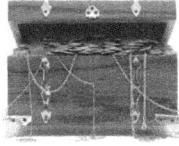

...But God

...But God (1)

"But as for you, ye thought evil against me; but God meant it unto good, to bring to pass, as it is this day, to save much people alive." (Genesis 50:20)

...But God (2)

"For scarcely for a righteous man will one die: yet peradventure for a good man some would even dare to die. But God commendeth his love toward us, in that, while we were yet sinners, Christ died for us." (Romans 5:7-8)

...But God (3)

"But if it be of God, ye cannot overthrow it; lest haply ye be found even to fight against God." (Acts 5:39)

Discussion Questions

1. Discuss 1 Kings 5:4.
2. Discuss Psalms 3:3.
3. What observations are made in Mark 2:7-11?
4. What observations are made in 1 Corinthians 2:1-5?
5. What was shown to the apostle Peter in Acts 10:28?

Fill in the Blanks

1. "But God____ His love toward us, in that, while we were
   yet____ , Christ died for us."
2. "My flesh and my____ faileth: but__ is the strength of my____ ,
   and my portion for ever."
3. "Wherein I suffer trouble, as an evil doer, even unto____ ; but
   the word of____ is not bound."
4. "But if it be of___ , ye cannot____ it; lest haply ye be found even
   to____ against God."
5. "But the____ was with Joseph, and showed him____ , and gave
   him____ in the sight of the____ of the____ ."

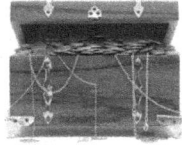

...But God

> "Ye thought evil against me; but God meant it unto good..." (Genesis 50:20).

*I*n the discourse Joseph had with his brothers, he extolled how divine intervention had thwarted their evil plans and wrought blessings instead of his demise. What an awesome God we serve.

...But God (1)

Old Testament – Genesis 50:20, 48:21, 45:7-8, 31:4-7, 29, 20:2-3, 1 Samuel 7:10, 16:7, 12, 23:13-14, 1 Kings 5:4, Isaiah 17:13, Jeremiah 20:10-11, Ecclesiastes 5:7, Psalms 3:3, 73:26, 75:6-7

New Testament – Mark 2:7-11, Luke 12:20-21, 16:15, Romans 5:7-8, 6:17, 23

...But God (2)

Old Testament – Daniel 2:28, Genesis 39:20-21, Deuteronomy 4:3-4, 7:6-8, 22-23, 10:12, 23:5, 1 Samuel 15:25-26, 16:18, 2 Chronicles 20:15, 32:8, 1 Samuel 17:45, Psalms 64:7, 10, 66:18-19, 68:20-21, 86:14-15

New Testament – Matthew 19:26, Acts 3:18, 5:38-39, 7:8-9

...But God (3)

Old Testament – Exodus 1:15-17, 21, 20:19, Leviticus 25:17, 36, 43, Nehemiah 5:15, Proverbs 31:30, Ezra 8:22, 9:7-9, Josh 5:13-15, 23:8-9, 1 Kings 12:22-24, 13:8-9, Psalms 130:3-4, 103:17, 94:22

New Testament – Acts 10:28, 13:29-30, 2 Timothy 2:9, 1 Thessalonians 4:7-9

...But God (4)

Old Testament – 1 Kings 19:11-13, Job 23:8-10, 13, 36:9-12, Psalms 81:8-16, Ezekiel 20:8-11, 21-26, Jeremiah 10:10, 24, Psalms 4:3, 9:7, 18:18, 20:7, 22:9, 37:17, 49:15, 102:12, 27

New Testament – Ephesians 2:4-5, 12-13, 1 Corinthians 3:6-7, 7:15, 10:13, 15:57

...But God (5)

Old Testament – Numbers 22:20, 35, 23:19-26, 24:4-11, 2 Chronicles 18:11-13, 40:8, Zechariah 1:6, Judges 5:31, Proverbs 21:30-31, Psalms 78:37-39, 89:30-33, 92:6-10, 96:5, 118:13, 17-18

New Testament – 1 Corinthians 1:27, 2:1-5, 6:13, 12:24-25, Galatians 6:14, 3:18, 20

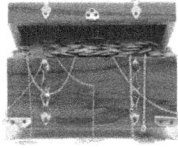

The Fool

The Fool (1)

"A wise man's heart is at his right hand; but a fool's heart is at his left. Yea also, when he that is a fool walketh by the way, his wisdom faileth him, and he saith to every one that he is a fool." (Ecclesiastes 10:2-3)

The Fool (2)

"We are fools for Christ's sake, but ye are wise in Christ;" (1 Corinthians 4:10)

The Fool (3)

"The wise shall inherit glory: but shame shall be the promotion of fools." (Proverbs 3:35)

Discussion Questions

1. Discuss Matthew 5:22.
2. Discuss Ecclesiastes 10:2-3.
3. Explain Romans 1:22.
4. Discuss Proverbs 11:29.
5. Explain Ecclesiastes 5:4.

Fill in the Blanks

1. "I have seen the___ taking root: but suddenly I cursed his____ ."
2. "The wise shall inherit glory: but shame shall be the____ of____ ."
3. "The____ hath said in his heart, There is no God."
4. "For so is the will of God, that with____ ____ ye may put to silence the____ of___ men."
5. "Are ye so____ ? having begun in the____ , are ye now made perfect by the____ ?"

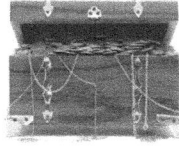

The Fool

*T*he fool is one whose heart is inclined toward that which is senseless or wayward. He lacks wisdom and does not seek to get an understanding, but rather seeks that which is perverse, frivolous, imprudent, silly, and unwise.

The Fool (1)

Old Testament – Job 5:3-5, Hosea 7:11, Jeremiah 17:11, Ecclesiastes 10:2-3, 12-15, 9:17, 5:1-4, Proverbs 1:7, 20-22, 9:6, 13, 10:14, 23, 12:1, 15, 23, 14:6-9, 18:2, Psalms 53:1, 74:18, 107:17

New Testament – Ephesians 5:15-17, Titus 3:3, Matthew 5:22, 1 Corinthians 3:18-20, 4:10

The Fool (2)

Old Testament – 1 Samuel 25:17, 25, 1 Samuel 3:33, 13:12-13, Isaiah 9:17, 32:5-6, Ecclesiastes 4:5, Psalms 92:5-6, Proverbs 3:35, 8:5, 33, 10:21, 14:1, 33, 15:2, 5, 7, 14, 21, 16:22, 19:2, 27, 23:9

New Testament – Luke 11:39-40, 12:16-20, Matthew 23:16-19, Romans 1:22

The Fool (3)

Old Testament – Deuteronomy 32:5-6, 28, Job 30:8, Proverbs 11:29, 13:16, 20, 14:16-18, 24, 17:7, 10, 12, 16, 27-28, 18:6-7, 21:20, 24:7, 26:1-12, 18-19, Isaiah 35:8

New Testament – 2 Corinthians 12:11-13, 11:16-21, 1 Corinthians 15:34-38, 2:14-16

The Fool (4)

Old Testament – 1 Samuel 15:31, Hosea 13:12-13, 9:7, Lamentations 2:14, Isaiah 19:11-13, Ezekiel 13:3-4, 22, Zechariah 11:15, Job 12:16-17, Proverbs 30:21-23, 29:9, 28:26, 27:3, 22, Psalms 49:10-13, 94:8

New Testament – Matthew 7:26-27, 1 Peter 2:15, Ephesians 5:2-3, Galatians 3:1-3

The Fool (5)

Old Testament – Psalms 69:5, 38:5, 2 Chronicles 16:9, 1 Chronicles 21:8, 1 Samuel 26:21, 13:13, Jeremiah 4:22, 5:4-5, 10:8, 14, Proverbs 15:5, 20:3, 22:3, 15, 24:9, 27:12, 29:11, 20

New Testament – Luke 24:25-26, 45, Matthew 25:1-9, 1 Corinthians 1:18-27, 2 Timothy 2:23, Titus 3:9

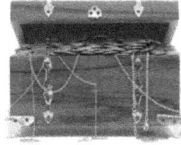

Strife

Strife (1)

"Surely the churning of milk bringeth forth butter, and the wringing of the nose bringeth forth blood: so the forcing of wrath bringeth forth strife." (Proverbs 30:33)

Strife (2)

"For ye are yet carnal: for whereas there is among you envying, and strife, and division, are ye not carnal, and walk as men?" (1 Corintinians 3:3)

Strife (3)

"An angry man stirreth up strife, and a furious man aboundeth in transgression." (Proverbs 29:22)

Discussion Questions

1. Discuss Proverbs 15:18.
2. According to Proverbs 6:12-19, how does God feel about strife?
3. How did Abraham resolve the strife between his herdmen and Lot's herdmen?
4. Discuss Matthew 5:9.
5. Discuss James 4:1-3.

Fill in the Blanks

1. "It is an honour for a man to cease from_____ : but every fool will be___ ."
2. "And the servant of the Lord___ ___ strive; but be_____ unto all men, apt to teach, patient."
3. "For ye are yet_____ : for whereas there is among you_____ , and_____ , and_____ , are ye not carnal, and walk as men?"
4. "For where_____ and_____ is, there is confusion and every___ ___ ."
5. "Better is a dry morsel, and quietness therewith, than a house full of sacrifices with_____ ."

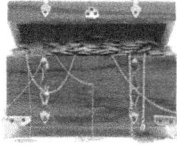

Strife

The Greek word *eris* is translated "strife" in English. It means "to quarrel, to wrangle, to have contention, to be at variance, to have discord, bickering and controversy." Strife is like having to swim in muddy and unpleasant waters. It is the opposite of peace. If we yield to the Spirit of God, we will have peace. By yielding to the flesh, we will have strife.

Strife (1)

Old Testament – Genesis 13:5-9, 21:25-32, 26:18-22, 34:30, Leviticus 19:17-18, Exodus 21:18-22, Proverbs 20:3, 19:11, 17:9, 14, 19, 16:28, 15:16-18, 3:30, Ecclesiastes 7:21-22, Psalms 133:1

New Testament – Matthew 5:9, 39-45, 12:19-20, 2 Timothy 2:23-26, Ephesians 4:26-32

Strife (2)

Old Testament – Genesis 16:3-9, 21:9-12, Leviticus 24:10-16, Job 30:7-10, Jeremiah 6:28, Proverbs 6:12-19, 12:18, 13:10, 15:1, 18:19, Psalms 31:13, 41:7-9, 74:4, 10, 18-23, 101:5

New Testament – Matthew 5:25-26, 10:34-36, 18:15-17, 2 Corinthians 12:20-21, 1 Corinthians 3:3

Strife (3)

Old Testament – Genesis 49:5-7, Exodus 17:1-7, 2 Kings 14:8-12, Numbers 21:21-24, Judges 11:27-32, Proverbs 30:33, 29:22, 28:25, 26:17-21, 25:8-9, 21-24, 24:29, Jeremiah 15:10, 11:19, Isaiah 50:6-7, Psalms 102:8

New Testament – Luke 17:1-2, Romans 12:14-21, Hebrews 12:14-15

Strife (4)

Old Testament – Deuteronomy 1:12, Proverbs 10:12, 17:1, 18:6, 21:23, 22:10, Isaiah 29:20-21, 58:4, Habakkuk 1:3-5, Psalms 80:6-7, 106:32

New Testament – Mark 9:43-48, Matthew 13:41, Acts 24:16, 2 Corinthians 6:3, 1 Corinthians 10:32, 11:16, 1 Timothy 6:3-4, Romans 2:8-9, 16:17, James 3:14-16, Titus 3:9

Strife (5)

Old Testament – Job 3:17, 24-26, 5:21, Psalms 3:1, 27:12, 31:20, 50:20, 55:2-9, 57:4, 120:2-7, Ecclesiastes 9:18, Isaiah 57:20-21, 48:22

New Testament – Matthew 23:13, 24, Romans 1:29-32, 3:13-17, 13:13, James 4:1-3, Philippians 1:15-16, Jude 1:15-16, 1 Corinthians 6:1-10

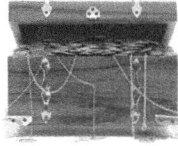

Covetousness

Covetousness (1)

"For from the least of them even unto the greatest of them every one is given to covetousness; and from the prophet even unto the priest every one dealeth falsely." (Jeremiah 6:13)

Covetousness (2)

"And he said unto them, Take heed, and beware of covetousness: for a man's life consisteth not in the abundance of the things which he possesseth." (Luke 12:15)

Covetousness (3)

"But fornication, and all uncleanness, or covetousness, let it not be once named among you, as becometh saints;" (Ephesians 5:3)

Discussion Questions

1. Discuss Ezekiel 16:49.
2. What warnings are given in Matthew 6:19-34?
3. Explain Luke 16:14-15.
4. Discuss Ephesians 5:3,
5. Discuss Ecclesiastes 5:8-15.

Fill in the Blanks

1. "He that loveth silver shall not be____ with____ ; nor he that loveth____ with____ : this is also vanity."
2. "Lay not up for yourselves____ upon earth, where____ and____ doth corrupt, and where____ break through and____ ."
3. "For this ye know, that no____ , nor____ person, nor____ man, who is an____ , hath any inheritance in the____ of____ and of___ ."
4. "Neither shalt thou desire thy___ ___ ___ , neither shalt thou____ thy house, his____ , or his manservant, or his maid-servant, his ox, or his ass, or any____ that is thy____ ."
5. "And he said unto them, take heed, and beware of____ : for a man's life consisteth not in the____ of the____ which he____ ."

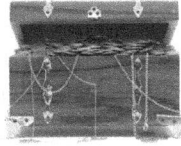

Covetousness

C ovetousness is a widespread and pervasive sin in today's culture. The Merriam-Webster Dictionary defines covetousness as "an inordinate desire often for another's possessions; to be greedy, acquisitive, grasping, avaricious, having or showing a strong desire for, especially material possessions." Many devote their entire lives to are preoccupied with) the accumulation of wealth, big cars, big houses, and a host of worldly possessions that, in time, perish—yet no thought, time, or consideration is given to that which is spiritual and eternal.

Covetousness (1)

Old Testament – Jeremiah 6:13, 8:10, 17:11, 22:17, Haggai 1:2-9, Habakkuk 2:9-10, Obadiah 1:13, Psalms 49:6-20, 52:5-7, 62:9-10, Proverbs 1:19, 15:27, 27:20, 24

New Testament – Matthew 6:19-34, 13:22, 19:21-29, Luke 16:13-15, Acts 8:18-24, 1 Timothy 6:9-19

Covetousness (2)

Old Testament – Deuteronomy 5:21, 7:25-26, Exodus 18:21, Joshua 7:11-26, 1 Samuel 11:2-4, 12:8-10, 1 Kings 21:1-24, Isaiah 5:8, 57:17, Jeremiah 22:13-15, 9:23-24, Micah 2:2, Psalms 119:36, Proverbs 22:16

New Testament – Luke 12:15, Hebrews 13:5, Colossians 3:5, Ephesians 5:3, 5, 1 Corinthians 6:9-10

Covetousness (3)

Old Testament – Exodus 23:4-8, 2 Chronicles 19:5-7, 1 Samuel 12:3-5, 8:1-3, 2:12-17, 22, 29-34, Job 20:15-29, 15:34, Psalms 10:3, 15:5, 26:9-10, Hosea 4:7-10, Amos 5:12, Isaiah 56:10-11, 33:14-15

New Testament – 1 John 3:1-3, 8, 1 Thessalonians 2:5, Ephesians 4:19

Covetousness (4)

Old Testament – Deuteronomy 25:13-16, Leviticus 25:35-37, Hosea 12:7-8, Amos 8:4-8, Micah 7:2-4, 6:9-15, 3:11-12, Ezekiel 18:5-9, 22:12, 28:4-5, Job 31:23-25, Ecclesiastes 5:8-15, Proverbs 28:6, 8, 16, 22, 21:6, 26

New Testament – Matthew 7:20-23, Acts 20:33, 1 Corinthians 5:9-11

Covetousness (5)

Old Testament – Ecclesiastes 6:1-2, 9, 4:6-8, 2 Kings 5:20-27, Nehemiah 5:1-13, Job 36:18-19, 27:16-23, Proverbs 10:2, 13:7-8, 23:4-5, Jeremiah 5:26-29, Ezekiel 33:31, Amos 2:6, Deuteronomy 8:11-14, 17, Psalms 39:6, 17:10-15

New Testament – Matthew 6:19-21, Luke 12:16-21, Romans 13:8-10

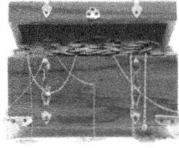

Return to Me

Return to Me (1)

"Come and let us return unto the LORD: for he hath torn, and he will heal us; he hath smitten, and he will bind us up." (Hosea 6:1)

Return to Me (2)

"And the son said unto him, Father, I have sinned against heaven, and in thy sight, and am no more worthy to be called thy son. But the father said unto the servants, Bring forth the best robe, and put it on him; and put a ring on his hand, and shoes on his feet: And bring hither the fatted calf, and kill it; and let us eat, and be merry: For this my son was dead, and is alive again; he was lost, and is found. And they began to make merry." (Luke 15:21-23)

Return to Me (3)

"For ye were as sheep going astray; but are now returned unto the Shepherd and Bishop of your souls." (1 Peter 2:25)

Discussion Questions

1. Discuss Hosea 11:8-11.
2. Discuss Luke 15:14-24.
3. What is conveyed in Isaiah 55:7?
4. Discuss Jeremiah 3:12-33.

5. Discuss Ezekiel 37:11-14.

Fill in the Blanks

1. "I have spread out____ ____ all the day unto a____ ____ , which walketh in a way that was not good, after their own____ ."
2. "Let the wicked his____ , and the man his thoughts: and let him ____unto the Lord, and He will have____ upon him; and to our God, for he will____ ____ ."
3. "For ye were as sheep going____ ; but are now unto the Shepherd and Bishop of your____ ."
4. "Come unto____ , all ye that labour and are heavy laden, and I will give you____ ."
5. "No man can come to me, except the____ which hath sent me____ ____ : and I will raise him up at the____ ____ ."

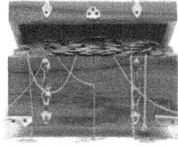

Return to Me

God wants us back when we go astray. The prodigal son who ventured away from his father's house to go into a foreign country was enticed by sin and lawlessness, only to meet his looming demise. But when he came to his senses and desired to return, he found his father eagerly waiting for him. The father's actions demonstrate the love and compassion God has for all of mankind, even those who go astray.

Return to Me (1)

Old Testament – Hosea 11:8-11, 6:1-7, 5:15, 3:1-5, 2 Chronicles 15:1-4, Jeremiah 3:12-23, 15:17-19, 31:1-9, 18-20, 1 Kings 8:46-61, Psalms 119:67, 71, 75-77, 176, Proverbs 21:16

New Testament – Luke 15:14-24, Matthew 11:28-30, Acts 5:31, 26:18-20, 1 Peter 2:25

Return to Me (2)

Old Testament – Isaiah 65:2, 55:7, 45:22, 43:25-26, 31:6, 30:15-19, 1:18, Ezekiel 37:11-14, 36:17-36, 34:16, 23, Zechariah 1:3-6, 16, 10:6, 14:8-9, Psalms 90:3-9, 13

New Testament – Luke 24:44-47, 13:34-35, Acts 3:19-23, 11:21, Romans 11:26

Return to Me (3)

Old Testament – Hosea 14:1-7, 13:4-9, 12:6, Joel 2:12-14, Ezekiel 16:1-23, 58-63, 33:10-11, 39:21-28, 2 Chronicles 7:14-15, Deuteronomy 30:1-6, 4:30-31, Lamentations 3:40, Jeremiah 4:1-2, Psalms 119:36-37, 59

New Testament – James 4:8, Hebrews 4:15-16, 7:25, 2 Peter 2:20-21

Return to Me (4)

Old Testament – Amos 4:4-12, 5:4-8, Isaiah 28:15-22, Jonah 3:5-10, Nehemiah 1:7-9, Malachi 3:7, Job, 22:23-30, 36:8-10, Jeremiah 3:10, 50:4-7, 34, Ezekiel 44:10, 34:5-14, 18:30, 14:10-11, Micah 4:6-7

New Testament – Luke 15:4-7, 19:10, John 6:44, 65-69

Return to Me (5)

Old Testament – Hosea 5:3-4, 4:11-12, 2:9-23, Isaiah 19:22, 44:22, 53:6-12, Zechariah 8:4-8, 12-17, 9:9, 12, 11:10-13, 12:10, 13:6-7, Psalms 22:22-27, 79:9, 11, 85:1-4, 7-13

New Testament – John 3:16-21, 5:39-40, 14:6, Acts 2:32-41.

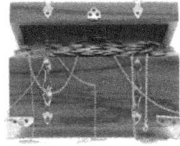

I Am

I Am (1)

"I will not execute the fierceness of mine anger, I will not return to destroy Ephraim: for I am God, and not man; the Holy One in the midst of thee: and I will not enter into the city." (Hosea 11:9)

I Am (2)

"....for I am a great King, saith the LORD of hosts, and my name is dreadful among the heathen." (Malachi 1:16)

I Am (3)

"Jesus said unto them, Verily, verily, I say unto you, Before Abraham was, I am." (John 8:58)

Discussion Questions

1. Discuss Genesis 17:1.
2. Discuss Matthew 16:16.
3. What observations are made in Psalms 145:8-20.
4. Discuss Luke 7:14-23.
5. Discuss Exodus 5:2-3.

Fill in the Blanks

1. "And God said unto Moses, ___ ___ that___ ___: and he said, Thus shalt thou say unto the children of Israel, ___ ___ hath sent me unto you."
2. "Jesus said unto them, ___ ___, I say unto you. Before Abraham was, ___ ___ ."
3. "And God said unto him I am___ ___ ."
4. "Speak unto all the___ of the children of___ , and say unto them, Ye shall be holy: for I the Lord your God___ ___ ."
5. " Alpha and Omega, the___ and the___ , saith the Lord, which is, and which was, and which is to___ , the___ ."

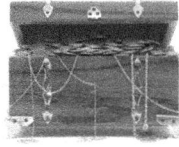

I Am

The proclamation "I am" is profound and emphatic, transcending the boundaries of the cognitive capabilities and perceptions of mortal beings. The God of eternity speaks, and only He can say, "I AM" because all of creation is centered around Him and Him alone.

I Am (1)

Old Testament – Song of Solomon 2:1, Hosea 11:9, Malachi 1:14, 3:6, Exodus 3:6, 14, Genesis 17:1, Isaiah 43:3, 13, 15, 46:9, 48:12, 17, Psalms 145:8-20

New Testament – Matthew 17:5, 16:16, John 4:25-26, 6:35, 8:12, 58, 10:7, 11, 11:25, 14:6, 15:1, Revelation 19:11, 13, 16, 22:16

I Am (2)

Old Testament – Genesis 46:3-4, 35:11, 28:13, 15:1, Deuteronomy 33:29, 5:6-9, 6:13-15, Psalms 35:3, 62:1-2, 99:8, Exodus 5:2-3, 6:2-8, 15:3, 26, Isaiah 9:6, 41:10, 13, 45:3, 21-22

New Testament – Matthew 1:23, John 1:1-4, 29, 7:28-29, 18:4-9, 37, 19:14-22

I Am (3)

Old Testament – Leviticus 19:2, Deuteronomy 7:9, 10:17, 1 Samuel 2:2-3, 5:1-8, 17:4-10, 26, 43-47, Isaiah 42:8, 49:26, Jeremiah 31:9, 32:27, Psalms 18:2, 35:10, 68:5, 84:11, 103:13, 146:5-9

New Testament – John 14:8-11, 13:13, 8:18-24, 6:47-51, Revelation 1:8, 11-18

I Am (4)

Old Testament – Ezekiel 20:19, 34:31, 44:28, Jeremiah 51:19, Nehemiah 9:6-8, Isaiah 36:7-21, 37:15-38, 54:11-17, Psalms 9:20, 46:10, 83:18, 86:10, 100:3, 149:2, Joel 2:27

New Testament – John 3:29, 35-36, 5:43-44, 10:9, 30-38, 12:46, Mark 15:32, 39

I Am (5)

Old Testament – Genesis 16:13, 31:13, 1 Kings 20:13, 28, 2 Kings 5:14-19, Daniel 4:35, 37, Jeremiah 31:3, 23:23-24, Isaiah 40:25-28, 63:16, Psalms 90:2, 115:3, 113:3-9, 95:3-8, 62:5-8, 50:7

New Testament – Luke 7:14-23, John 9:33-38, 20:24-28, Hebrews 1:8-14

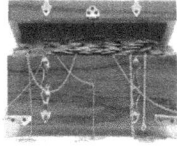

Followers

Followers (1)

"Be ye followers of me. Even as I also am of Christ." (1 Corinthians 11:1)

Followers (2)

"My sheep hear my voice, and I know them, and follow me:" (John 10:27)

Followers (3)

"They also that render evil for good are mine adversaries; because I follow the thing that good is." (Psalms 38:20)

Discussion Questions

1. Discuss Psalms 77:20.
2. What observations are made in John 10:1-16?
3. What command is given in 1 Corinthians 11:1?
4. What warning is given in Philippians 3:17-18?
5. What warnings are given in Acts 20:28-30?

Fill in the Blanks

1. "And when he putteth forth his own____ , he goeth before them, and the____ ____ him: for they know his___ ."
2. "Be ye____ of me, even as I also am of____ ."

3. "Brethren, be____ together of me, and mark them which walk so as ye have us for an____ ."

4. "He restoreth my soul: he____ me in the___ of ____for his name's sake."

5. "The man that____ out of the way of____ shall remain in the____ of the dead."

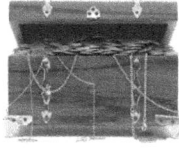

Followers

A s Christians, we are followers of our Lord and Savior, Jesus Christ. He is our Shepherd. We hear His voice, and we follow Him because we are His sheep.

Followers (1)

Old Testament – Exodus 15:13, Deuteronomy 31:8, Isaiah 40:11, 49:10-11, 58:11, Psalms 16:8, 23:1-6, 25:8-10, 31:3, 32:7-10, 48:12-14, 63:8, 80:1

New Testament – 1 Peter 2:25, Matthew 4:18-20, 8:19-22, 16:24, 19:21-29, 20:29-34, 21:9, John 2:26

Followers (2)

Old Testament – Numbers 27:15-21, Exodus 13:21, 23:2, Deuteronomy 5:32-33, 12:28-30, 16:20, 32:11-12, Joshua 14:8-9, 14, Nehemiah 9:12-19, Hosea 6:1-3, Psalms 5:8, 25:4-5, 43:3, 78:70-72

New Testament – Matthew 9:36, John 8:12, 10:1-16, 27, 1 Peter 2:21, Revelation 14:4

Followers (3)

Old Testament – Ezekiel 37:24, Micah 5:4, Isaiah 11:6, 30:21, 42:16, 48:17, 49:10, 63:14, Jeremiah 31:3, Psalms 73:24, 119:30, 32, 35, 143:10

New Testament – Romans 8:14, John 16:13, Galatians 5:18, Ephesians 5:1, 1 Corinthians 11:1, 4:16, 1 Thessalonians 1:6, Hebrews 6:12, 13:7, Matthew 10:37-38

Followers (4)

Old Testament – Deuteronomy 8:2, 15-16, 1 Samuel 12:14, 15:11, Hosea 12:1, 2 Chronicles 25:27, 34:33, Ruth 1:16, Psalms 125:5, 78:52-53, 77:20, Proverbs 3:6, 4:11, 8:20

New Testament – Romans 14:19, Hebrews 12:14, 2 Thessalonians 3:7, 9, 2 Timothy 2:22, 3 John 1:11, Philippians 3:17, 1 Timothy 5:13, 15

Followers (5)

Old Testament – Numbers 15:38-41, Deuteronomy 13:1-4, Leviticus 18:2-5, 20:23, Joshua 23:6, Isaiah 1:1-4, 23, 3:12, 28:14-16, 30:8-11, Amos 7:12-17, Micah 2:11, Proverbs 21:16, 11:19

New Testament – Acts 20:28-30, Galatians 1:6-9, 2 Peter 2:1-3, 15, 21, 1 Timothy 6:3-11, 5:24

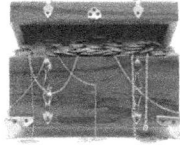

The World

The World (1)

"I have given them thy word; and the world hath hated them, because they are not of the world, even as I am not of the world." (John 17:14)

The World (2)

"For all that is in the world, the lust of the flesh, and the lust of the eyes, and the pride of life, is not of the Father, but is of the world." (1 John 2:16)

The World (3)

"For God so loved the world, that he gave his only begotten Son, that whosoever believeth in him should not perish, but have everlasting life." (John 3:16)

Discussion Questions

1. What was the world like at the beginning when God created it according to Genesis 1:31?
2. What happened in Genesis 6:5-12?
3. Explain Matthew 12:30.
4. Explain John 1:10-13.
5. What observations are made in Isaiah 59:1-21?

Fill in the Blanks

1. "And I will___the world for their____ and the for their____."
2. "The next day John seeth____ coming unto him and saith, behold the Lamb of God, which taketh away the____ of the____."
3. "Go ye therefore, and____ all____, baptizing them in the name of the____ and of the____ and of the_____."
4. "I pray for them: I pray not for the____ but for them which thou hast given me; for they are thine."
5. "They are not of the____, even as I am not of the____."

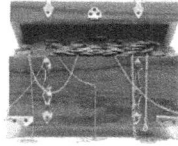

The World

*J*esus, in John 15:18-19 states, "If the world hate you, ye know that it hated me before it hated you. If ye were of the world, the world would love his own: but because ye are not of the world, but I have chosen you out of the world, therefore the world hateth you."

This passage connotes a line of demarcation that exists between those who render obedience and loyalty to God versus those who pursue a course authored by the men or inhabitants of the world. This world embodies world systems, worldly logic, world axioms, world doctrines, world views, world standards, and world values that are in direct opposition to God and the Word of God. Man has to choose to follow either the world or the God Who created us. There is no middle ground.

The World (1)

Old Testament – Genesis 1:31, 6:5-12, Isaiah 13:9-11, 24:4-6, 45:22, Zechariah 1:8-15, 5:1-6, 6:1-13, Jeremiah 23:5-6, Psalms 72:17-19

New Testament – John 1:29, 3:36, 4:25-26, 5:39, 8:12, 23-24, Matthew 3:7, Romans 1:18, 5:7-9, 1 Thessalonians 5:9-10, 1 John 4:3-14, 2:2

The World (2)

Old Testament – Ecclesiastes 3:11, Job 37:10-12, Proverbs 16:4, Jeremiah 6:19, 10:10-12, 22:29, 25:30-33, 2 Chronicles 36:16, Psalms 9:8, 17:13-15, 96:10, 13, 98:7-9

New Testament – Acts 17:24-31, 2:40-47, Mark 16:15-16, John 3:16-20, 2 Corinthians 5:18-20, Colossians 1:13-29

The World (3)

Old Testament – Isaiah 40:22-24, 1 Chronicles 16:14, 30, Psalms 90:2-9, 89:7-11, 49:1-9, 2:1-5, 7:11, 11:3-7, 17:13-14, Ezekiel 22:30, Isaiah 59:16-21, 52:10-15, 53:1-12

New Testament – John 1:10-13, 36, 4:42, 6:14, 33, 51, 8:23-26, Romans 5:9-21

The World (4)

Old Testament – 1 Samuel 2:10, Nahum 1:2-7, Psalms 102:25-26, 98:7-9, 75:8, Job 21:17-20, Jeremiah 25:13-17, 26-29, Isaiah 62:10-12, 34:1-4, 18:3, 11:1-10, 2:10-21

New Testament – Revelation 6:15-17, 14:6-7, 2 Peter 2:4-6, 3:1-14, 2 Thessalonians 1:4-11, Galatians 1:4

The World (5)

Old Testament – Job 26:7, 11, 38:12-13, 9:4-6, Psalms 119:119-120, 34:16

New Testament – Revelation 11:18, 12:10-12, Ephesians 6:12, 2:1-12, 1 Corinthians 11:32, 2:4-16, James 1:27, 4:4, 2 Corinthians 6:17-18, 4:3-7, Colossians 1:13-28, 2:12-14, Matthew 28:18-20, John 17:1-26

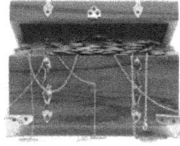

Praise Him

Praise Him (1)

"By him therefore let us offer the sacrifice of praise to God continually, that is, the fruit of our lips giving thanks to his name." (Hebrews 13:15)

Praise Him (2)

"Being filled with the fruits of righteousness, which are by Jesus Christ, unto the glory and praise of God." (Philippians 1:11)

Praise (3)

"Rejoice in the LORD, O ye righteous: for praise is comely for the upright." (Psalms 33:1)

Discussion Questions

1. Discuss Habakkuk 3:3.
2. What is conveyed in Psalms 100:1-5?
3. What transpired in Matthew 21:15-16?
4. What is conveyed in Philippians 1:9-11?
5. Explain Proverbs 28:4.

Fill in the Blanks

1. "And suddenly there was with the____ a____ of the heavenly host, ____ God."
2. "And we have sent with him the brother, whose____ is in the____ throughout all the____ ."
3. "And they sang together by course in____ and____ ____ unto the Lord; because he is good, for his mercy____ for ever toward Israel."
4. "In God I will____ his____ , in God I have put my trust; I will not fear what flesh can do unto me."
5. "And at midnight Paul and Silas prayed, and sang____ unto____ ."

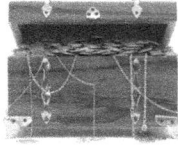

Praise Him

*A*n outflow from the soul of man should come forth with expressions of adoration, thanksgiving, commendation, acknowledgment, and intense longing to the God of heaven. God is a good God. He is worthy of our praise and devotion.

Praise Him (1)

Old Testament – Deuteronomy 10:20-21, Exodus 15:2, 11-13, Jeremiah 17:14, Isaiah 43:21, 42:10-12, 1 Chronicles 29:11-13, 23:26-30, 16:8-11, 27-36, Psalms 100:1-5, 111:1-10, 115:17-18, Proverbs 28:4

New Testament – Luke 2:13-14, 20, 18:35-43, Acts 2:39-47, 3:1-9.

Praise Him (2)

Old Testament – Isaiah 25:1, Jeremiah 20:13, Judges 5:1-3, 1 Samuel 22:48-50, Psalms 145:1-10, 21, 138:1-5, 117:1-2, 116:1-9, 19, 113:1-3, 112:1-4, 109:29-31, 43:3-5, 42:1-11

New Testament – Matthew 21:15-16, Romans 2:28-29, 15:5-11, 1 Peter 2:9

Praise Him (3)

Old Testament – 2 Chronicles 20:9-12, 17-19, Jeremiah 13:11, 31:6-7, Isaiah 12:1-6, 38:18-19, 60:18, 61:1-3, 11, Psalms 50:23, 56:4, 10, 57:7, 63:3-5, 76:10, 119:7, 164, 171, 175

New Testament – Philippians 1:9-11, 4:8, Ephesians 1:6, 12-14, 2 Corinthians 8:18

Praise Him (4)

Old Testament – Habakkuk 3:3, 2 Chronicles 7:3, Nehemiah 12:46, Ezra 3:11, Psalms 7:17, 9:1-2, 11-14, 22:3, 22, 25-26, 35:27-28, 48:1, 10, 51:15, 71:6-8, 14, 86:12, 89:1-5, 104:33-35

New Testament – Hebrews 2:9, 12, 13:15, Luke 24:51-53, Revelation 19:5-6

Praise Him (5)

Old Testament – Deuteronomy 32:1-3, Daniel 2:23, 4:34, Zephaniah 3:16-20, Psalms 108:1, 3, 107:20-32, 106:47-48, 105:1-3, 99:1-3, 96:1-4, 78:4, 74:21, 67:5-7, 66:1-8

New Testament – John 12:42-43, 1 Corinthians 4:5, Acts 16:25, 1 Peter 1:4-7, James 5:13

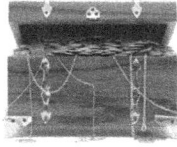

The Quest

The Quest (1)

"All this I proved by wisdom: I said, I will be wise; but it was far from me. That which is far off, and exceeding deep, who can find it out? I applied mine heart to know, and to search, and to seek out wisdom, and the reason of things, and to know the wickedness of folly, even of foolishness and madness:" (Ecclesiastes 7:23-25)

The Quest (2)

"Because strait is the gate, and narrow is the way, which leadeth unto life, and few there be that find it." (Matthew 7:14)

The Quest (3)

"But without faith it is impossible to please him: for he that cometh to God must believe that he is, and that he is a rewarder of them that diligently seek him." (Hebrews 11:6)

Discussion Questions

1. Explain Proverbs 29:18.
2. What observations are made in Job 28:12-28?
3. What does slothful mean?
4. Explain Ecclesiastes 7:25.
5. Discuss John 5:39.

Fill in the Blanks

1. "But where shall____ be found? and where is the____ of____ ?"
2. "Because strait is the____ , and____ is the way, which leadeth unto____ , and few there be that____ it."
3. "But if from thence thou shalt____ the ____ thy___ , thou shalt find him, if thou seek him with all thy____ and with all thy____ ."
4. "That they should____ the Lord, if haply they might feel after him, and____ ____ , though he be not far from every____ of us."
5. "Where is the____ where____ ____ dwelleth? And as for____ , where is the place thereof."

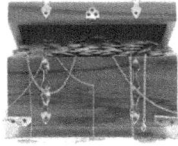

The Quest

*W*hat are your goals? Are you striving to accomplish something in your life? Are they carnal or spiritual pursuits? We must always dream and have visions of doing great things prior to our being successful. We must quest for holy things in our lives.

The Quest (1)

Old Testament – Job 28:12-28, Ecclesiastes 3:11, 7:23-25, 8:5-6, 16-17, Proverbs 8:15-21, 35, 3:1-4, 2:1-11, 1:20-28, Jeremiah 5:1-5, 29:13-14, Isaiah 65:1

New Testament – Matthew 7:14, 11:25, Romans 9:30-32, 10:18-20, 11:7-12, 33-35, Hebrews 4:2, 1 Corinthians 1:20-31

The Quest (2)

Old Testament – Job 23:3-15, 13:18-24, 38:1-4, 40:1-14, 42:1-6, Psalms 34:4-6, 10, 63:1-2, 119:2, 10, 2 Chronicles 33:12-13, 15:3-4, 12-15, Isaiah 26:8-9, 45:15-19, 55:6-7, Deuteronomy 4:29

New Testament – Hebrews 11:6, Acts 17:24-27, John 1:41, 45

The Quest (3)

Old Testament – Zephaniah 2:3, Hosea 10:12, Job 8:5-7, 10:12, Psalms 5:12, 44:3, 80:3, 7, 19, 89:17, 90:17, Proverbs 3:3-4, 8:34-35, 11:27, 12:2, 1 Samuel 15:25-26, Genesis 6:8-9, Exodus 33:11-13

New Testament – Luke 1:28-39, 2:52, Acts 7:44-46, Hebrews 11:5, Romans 9:16

The Quest (4)

Old Testament – Job 38:19-21, Isaiah 45:7, 42:16, 9:2-8, 2:5, 60:19-20, Psalms 119:105, 130, 105:28, 89:15, 56:13, 43:3, 36:9, Jeremiah 13:16

New Testament – Matthew 4:16-17, John 1:3-9, 8:12, 12:35-36, Colossians 1:12-13, 1 John 1:5-7, 2 Corinthians 4:6, Ephesians 5:8

The Quest (5)

Old Testament – Job 37:2-14, 36:22-26, 7:17-18, Psalms 8:3-9, 90:3-12, 104:13-14, 23-24, 115:16, Jeremiah 10:23, Isaiah 30:20-21, 35:8-10, 43:21, 45:8-13, Proverbs 16:4, Micah 6:8, Ecclesiastes 7:29

New Testament – Revelation 4:11, Ephesians 4:24, 3:9, 11, 2:10, 1:4

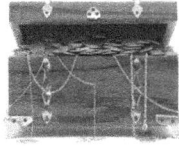

Compassion

Compassion (1)

"And the LORD passed by before him, and proclaimed, The LORD, The LORD, merciful and gracious, longsuffering, and abundant in goodness and truth," (Exodus 34:6)

Compassion (2)

"Finally, be ye all of one mind, having compassion one of another, love as brethren, be pitiful, be courteous:" (1 Peter 3:8)

Compassion (3)

"But though he cause grief, yet will he have compassion according to the multitude of his mercies." (Lamentations 3:32)

Discussion Questions

1. What attributes are noted about God in Exodus 34:6-7?
2. What are we commanded to be and do in Colossians 3:12-13?
3. What invitation is given in Matthew 11:28-29?
4. What was the response of Job's friends in Job 6:14-27?
5. What is conveyed in Luke 10:30-37?

Fill in the Blanks

1. "And Jesus went forth, and saw a great_____, and was moved with_____ toward them, and he healed their sick."
2. "And it shall come to pass, after that I have plucked them out I will____, and have_____ on them."
3. "The Lord is____, and full of_____; slow to____, and of great mercy."
4. "But when he saw the____, he was moved with____ on them, because they____, and were____ abroad, as____ having no____."
5. "Shouldest not thou also have had_____ on thy fellowservant, even as I had_____ on thee?"

Compassion

G od's very nature is one of compassion, love, and concern about the well-being of others. God has a willingness to help and encourage others and feeling sympathetic to others. This characterized the life of Jesus, and it must also be a part of our Christian character. The world has a great need for compassionate people.

Compassion (1)

Old Testament – Exodus 34:6-7, 33:19, John 4:2, 6-11, Hosea 11:1-4, 8-12, 12:6, Jeremiah 31:3, 10-20, 28, Ezekiel 16:1-15, 60-63, Lamentations 1:1-12, 3:14-33, Psalms 103:8-18, 145:8, 147:3, 6, 11

New Testament – Matthew 9:35-36, Luke 19:41-42, Colossians 3:12-13

Compassion (2)

Old Testament – Micah 7:18-19, 2 Chronicles 30:9, Isaiah 1:4-6, 18, 38:14-17, 40:11, 49:15-16, 55:6-7, 63:7, Joel 2:12-13, Hosea 14:3-9, 2 Kings 13:23, Psalms 69:15-20, 86:5, 15-17, 119:77

New Testament – Hebrews 5:1-2, 10:34, Ephesians 4:29-32, James 3:17-18

Compassion (3)

Old Testament – Job 6:14-18, 13:4, 16:2-6, 26:1-4, Psalms 55:1-8, 77:2-9, 142:1-7, Isaiah 54:7-13, 60:10, 63:15, Jeremiah 12:15, 30:15-17, Psalms 25:6, 107:1-15, 43, 111:4

New Testament – 2 Corinthians 1:3-6, Luke 6:36, 1 Peter 3:8, 1 John 3:17, 1 Thessalonians 2:8

Compassion (4)

Old Testament – Zechariah 7:9-11, Nehemiah 9:16-17, Psalms 78:37-39, Psalms 116:5-6, 1 Samuel 23:21, 1 Samuel 9:3-10, Exodus 2:1-6, 22:26-27, Leviticus 19:9-10, Deuteronomy 15:7-11, Proverbs 19:17, 22, 21:13, 29:7, Job 29:7-16

New Testament – Matthew 5:7, 14:14, 18:23-35, Luke 10:30-37

Compassion (5)

Old Testament – 1 Chronicles 21:13, Zechariah 1:12-17, 10:6, Jeremiah 29:11, 42:11-12, Isaiah 57:18, 50:4-5, 40:12, Proverbs 25:11, 15:23, Psalms 25:6, 27:10, 13, 56:8, 112:4, 119:132, 2 Chronicles 36:15

New Testament – Luke 1:50, Matthew 11:28-29, James 5:11, Romans 9:15, 2 Corinthians 2:7

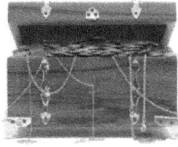

Wedge Issues

Wedge Issues (1)

"And Barnabas determined to take with them John whose surname was Mark. But Paul thought not good to take him with them, who departed from them from Pamphylia, and went not with them to the work. And the contention was so sharp between them, that they departed asunder one from the other: and so Barnabas took Mark, and sailed unto Cyprus;" (Acts 15:37-39)

Wedge Issues (2)

"Am I therefore your enemy, because I tell you the truth?" (Galatians 4:16)

Wedge Issueas (3)

"Only by pride cometh contention: but with the well advised is wisdom." (Proverbs 13:10)

Discussion Questions

1. Explain Genesis 3:15.
2. Explain Proverbs 25:17.
3. What is the wedge issue mentioned in John 6:60-68?
4. What is the wedge issue mentioned in John 7:7?
5. Explain Amos 3:3

Fill in the Blanks

1. "Follow peace with all men, and____ , without which no man shall see____ ."
2. "The world cannot____ you; but me it____ , because I____ of it, that the works thereof are evil."
3. "Can two walk____ , except they be____ ?"
4. "Am I therefore become your____ , because I tell you the____ ?"
5. "Withdraw thy foot from thy____ ____ ; lest he be weary of thee, and so____ ____ ."

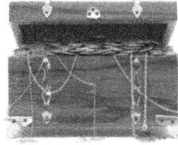

Wedge Issues

*I*ssues, concerns, and differences of opinions separate us, splinter us, and even divide us. It can happen to the best of friends, family members, acquaintances, co-workers, and a host of other individuals. Sometimes, they are trifling, minute matters, insignificant things that are of minor importance, yet they prove to be wedge issues that keep us apart. Love binds us, love unites us, and love keeps us together. According to Hebrews 12:14, wedge issues will keep many from seeing the Lord.

Wedge Issues (1)

Old Testament – Genesis 3:15, 4:3-8, 49:3-4, Exodus 32:25-27, Joshua 24:1, 5, Daniel 3:17-18, Amos 3:3, Psalms 119:63, 78, 85, 139:21, Proverbs 13:10, 25:17, 29:27, 30:15

New Testament – John 7:7, 8:37, 44, 47, 14:23-24, Luke 10:38-42, 1 Corinthians 16:22, 1 John 2:19

Wedge Issues (2)

Old Testament – Proverbs 14:7, 17:9, 14, 20:19, 22:24-25, 25:24, 27:4, Genesis 13:5-11, 26:19-22, 27:6-13, 41, 1 Samuel 13:13-28, 1 Kings 12:1-19

New Testament – John 5:38, 42, 47, 15:18-23, Hebrews 12:14-17, Romans 11:28, Galatians 4:16, 1 Corinthians 5:1-5

Wedge Issues (3)

Old Testament – Genesis 16:1-13, 37:3-8, 18-28, 50:20, Numbers 12:1-14, 16:1-5, 28-33, Amos 5:10, Hosea 9:7-8, Jeremiah 15:10, 11:19, 1 Kings 22:7-8, Psalms 120:5-7, 31:11-18, Proverbs 9:7-8, 15:12

New Testament – John 3:19-20, Acts 15:37-39, Ephesians 5:11, Luke 6:22-28, Galatians 6:14

Wedge Issues (4)

Old Testament – Genesis 31:50-53, Judges 11:27, 1 Samuel 24:9-12, 30:1-6, 18, Jeremiah 20:7-11, Psalms 10:1-8, 69:7-9, 20-26, 55:2-3, 12-14, Proverbs 3:29-30, 13:10, 25:8-10

New Testament – Acts 19:8-9, Romans 15:3, 1 Peter 4:3-5, 14, Galatians 5:7-10, Titus 3:10

Wedge Issues (5)

Old Testament – 2 Chronicles 15:2, Exodus 23:22, Genesis 12:3, 24:49-50, Numbers 24:9, 22:11-12, 17-18, Nehemiah 13:2, 23-31, Proverbs 24:21-25, 22:10, 18:19, 17:20, 16:18, 27-30, 6:16-19

New Testament – John 6:60-68, 12:42-43, Luke 18:25, 1 Timothy 6:3-5

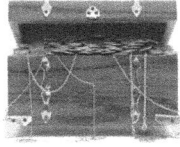

Worship

Worship (1)

"Ye worship ye know not what: we know what we worship: for salvation is of the Jews. But the hour cometh, and now is , when the true worshipper shall worship the Father in spirit and in truth: for the Father seeketh such to worship him. God is Spirit: and they that worship Him must worhip Him in spirit and in truth." (John 4:22-24)

Worship (2)

"And now, behold, I have brought the firstfruits of the land, which thou, O LORD, hast given me. And thou shalt set it before the LORD thy God, and worship before the LORD thy God." (Deuteronomy 26:10)

Worship (3)

"Give unto the LORD THE GLORY DUE UNTO His name; worship the LORD in the beauty of holiness." (Psalms 29:2)

Discussion Questions

1. Explain Matthew 15:1-14.
2. What thoughts are conveyed in Hebrews 12:18-28?
3. Explain Leviticus 10:1-3.
4. What was wrong in those that worshipped in Acts 17:16-32?
5. Explain John 4:20-28

Fill in the Blanks

1. "But in vain they do____ me, teaching for doctrines the_____ of men."
2. "Exalt ye the Lord our God, and____ at His____ ; for he is holy."
3. "God is a____ : and they that____ him must____ him in____ and in____ ."
4. "For as I passed by, and beheld your____ , I found an altar... Whom therefore ye ignorantly_____ ."
5. "For we are the____ , which____ God in the____ , and rejoice in____ ____ , and have no confidence in the flesh."

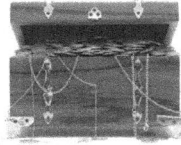

Worship

*P*roskuneo in the Greek is translated *worship* in English. It means "to fall down, to prostrate oneself, to adore on one's knees, to do obeisance, to outstretch the hands with a kiss." These are all physical gestures that denote worship, but worship must be in the heart of man to be categorized as true and acceptable before God.

Worship (1)

Old Testament – Psalms 99:5, 9, 86:9, 66:4-5, 57:7, 9, 11, 47:2, 6-9, 1 Chronicles 16:29-31, Exodus 20:24, 34:14, Deuteronomy 26:10, 12:5-14, 26-32, 16:16-17, Genesis 4:3-7, Leviticus 10:1-3

New Testament – Hebrews 10:23-31, 12:18-28, 13:10-16, Acts 17:16-32

Worship (2)

Old Testament – Haggai 1:8, Exodus 25:8-9, 36:1-5, Psalms 150:1, 138:1-2, 134:2-3, 132:7, 96:6-10, 95:1-6, 72:5-11, 54:6, 5:7, Isaiah 66:23, 43:21-26

New Testament – Hebrews 8:1-5, 9:1-3, 6-11, 24, Ephesians 2:13-22, 1 Peter 2:4-5, Revelation 7:9-12, 15:4

Worship (3)

Old Testament – Deuteronomy 31:11-13, 4:1-2, Nehemiah 8:1-8, 2 Chronicles 17:3-8, Jeremiah 36:4-8, 7:1-11, 1:15-17, Isaiah 58:1-2, 2:1-5, Ezekiel 43:7, 10-12, 44:5-9, Ecclesiastes 5:1-2, 1 Kings 12:27-30, 13:1-6

New Testament – Luke 4:16-22, 28, Acts 15:21, John 4:20-28, Philippians 3:3

Worship (4)

Old Testament – Ezra 7:10-18, 23-26, 2 Chronicles 30:12, 18-20, Psalms 22:22-29, 26:5-8, 29:2, Proverbs 15:8, Malachi 1:6-14, 2:13-16, Jeremiah 26:2-6, Hosea 6:6, Zechariah 2:9-14, Isaiah 29:13-14

New Testament – Matthew 15:1-14, Colossians 2:4-8, 18-23, 1 Corinthians 14:23-37, Acts 2:41-47, 20:7

Worship (5)

Old Testament – 2 Chronicles 34:15-21, 24, 27, 30-31, 29:29-30, Daniel 9:3-19, 3:28, 1 Kings 8:22-50, 54, 1 Chronicles 29:19-20, Exodus 4:28-31, 12:25-27, Nehemiah 9:1-3, Isaiah 27:13, Psalms 5:7

New Testament – Matthew 4:19, Acts 18:7, 24:14, Revelation 11:16, 22:8-14.

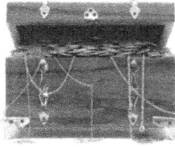

Admonitions

Admonitions (1)

"He that being often reproved hardeneth his neck, shall suddenly be destroyed, and that without remedy." (Proverbs 29:1)

Admonitions (2)

"For whatsoever things were written aforetime were written for our learning, that we through patience and comfort of the scriptures might have hope." (Romans 15:4)

Admonitions (3)

"As many as I love, I rebuke and chasten: be zealous and repent." (Revelation 3:19)

Discussion Questions

1. What warning is conveyed in Genesis 18:32?
2. What is conveyed in Numbers 15:27-36?
3. What admonitions are given in Matthew 11:20-24?
4. What admonishment is given in Isaiah 8:20?
5. Explain Hebrews 12:5-11.

Fill in the Blanks

1. "But fornication, and all uncleanness, or covetousness, let it not be____ among you, as becometh____ ."
2. "He, that being often____ hardeneth his neck, shall suddenly be____ , and that without____ ."
3. "He that turneth away his____ from hearing the law, even his____ shall be____ ."
4. "For this ye know, that no____ , nor____ person, nor____ man, who is an____ , hath any inheritance in the____ of Christ and of____ ."
5. "As many as I love, I___ and____ : be zealous therefore, and____ ."

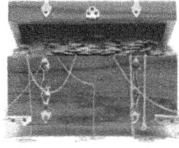

Admonitions

*T*here are many warnings, reprimands, rebukes, and reproofs in the Bible that should make us beware and use caution as we live in God's presence. The following passages of Scripture are admonitions.

Admonitions (1)

Old Testament – Daniel 10:21, Amos 3:7, Genesis 2:16-17, 3:6-12, 24, 18:17, 32, 19:17, 26, Joshua 6:18, 7:20-26, Deuteronomy 18:9, 12-13, 2 Kings 17:7-12, Daniel 9:11-19, Numbers 15:27-36, Jeremiah 36:1-6, 16-32

New Testament – Hebrews 2:1-3, 3:7-19, Romans 15:4, 14

Admonitions (2)

Old Testament – Ezekiel 2:3-10, 3:4-11, Jeremiah 44:4-5, 16-17, 35:15-17, 11:6-8, 7:25-28, 22:29, Isaiah 3:8-9, 22:12-14, 22, 30:1, 8, 2 Chronicles 36:15-16, Proverbs 29:1, 28:9, 24:20-22

New Testament – Acts 7:51-54, Matthew 11:20-24, 23:37

Admonitions (3)

Old Testament – Genesis 4:3-7, 20:3-7, 31:24, 29, 1 Chronicles 16:21-22, Amos 5:10, 18-24, 6:1-8, 8:9-11, Isaiah 34:16, 8:20, Jeremiah 17:5-6, 29:15-21, 44:27-29

New Testament – Luke 6:24-26, Matthew 23:13-15, 33, Acts 20:27-32, 3:20-23

Admonitions (4)

Old Testament – Zephaniah 3:1-2, 8, 2:3-5 Amos 3:1-3, Jeremiah 48:10, 13:27, 2:19-22, 29-31, Isaiah 5:18-24, 33:1, Hosea 7:1-13, Micah 2:1-3, Proverbs 17:15, 10:23-25

New Testament – 1 Corinthians 9:16, 10:6-11, Ephesians 5:3-7, Hebrews 4:1-2, 11, 2 Peter 3:17, Revelation 14:6-7

Admonitions (5)

Old Testament – Nehemiah 5:1-12, 2 Samuel 7:14, Ecclesiastes 7:5, Job 33:27-29, 10:14-15, 5:17-18, Proverbs 3:11-12, 5:3-14, 6:23, 12:1, Psalms 141:5, 94:12-13

New Testament – Matthew 16:21-26, John 5:14, 8:11, Galatians 2:11-18, Hebrews 12:5-11, Revelation 3:19, 12:12

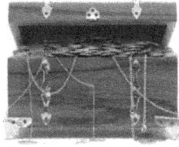

His Glory

His Glory (1)

"Glory to God in the highest, and on earth peace, good will toward men." (Luke 2:14)

His Glory (2)

"Ye that fear the LORD, praise him; all ye seed of Jacob, glorify him; and fear him, all ye seed of Israel." (Psalms 22:23)

His Glory (3)

"Therefore the strong people glorify thee, the city of the terrible nations shall fear thee." (Isaiah 25:3)

Discussion Questions

1. What observations are made in Daniel 7:9-14?
2. What observations are made in Acts 12:21-23?
3. What are we commanded to do in Romans 15:5-7?
4. Explain 2 Corinthians 3:7-14.
5. What is conveyed in Psalms 86:9-12?

Fill in the Blanks

1. "All nations whom thou hast made shall come and____ before thee, O Lord; and shall____ thy name."
2. "Saying with a loud voice, Worthy is the____ that was slain to receive____ , and____ , and____ , and____ , and____ , and____ , and____ ."
3. "That ye would walk worthy of____ , who hath called you unto his____ and____ ."
4. "Not unto us, O Lord, not unto us, but unto thy name give____ , for thy____ , and for thy truth's sake."
5. "So that we ourselves____ in you in the____ of God."

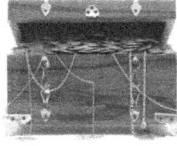

His Glory

G od must be hallowed; He must be treated with reverence and fear. He is worthy of our devotion, for He is our God. All glory, praise, and honor go rightfully to Him. It is He who has created us for Himself, and not we for ourselves.

His Glory (1)

Old Testament – Daniel 7:13-14 Leviticus 10:1-3, Deuteronomy 28:58-59 Exodus 15:11, Malachi 2:1-2 Psalms 115:1, 111:1-3, 96:1-8, 50:14-15, 23, 1 Chronicles 16:24-29, Isaiah 6:1-3, 43:5-7, 46:12-13, 60:21, 62:1-3

New Testament – Luke 2:8-20, John 1:14, 13:26-32, 14:13, 17:1-10, 24 Revelation 5:11-13

His Glory (2)

Old Testament – Leviticus 9:5-6, 22-24, Exodus 24:15-18, 40:34-38, 1 Kings 8:10-11, Haggai 1:7-8, 2:7-9, Isaiah 44:23, 55:5, 60:7-13, Psalms 22:23, 29:1-9, 66:1-5, 72:18-19, 86:9-12, 1 Chronicles 29:11

New Testament – Matthew 5:16, Galatians 1:24, 1 Corinthians 10:31, 6:19-20 Romans 11:36, 16:27

His Glory (3)

Old Testament – Daniel 5:22-23, Job 36:24-26, 37:14, 22, 40:9-14 Jeremiah 13:16-17, 9:23-24, 2:5-11, Isaiah 22:20-25, 42:8, 12, 49:1-3, Hosea 9:11-12, 1 Samuel 4:21-22 Proverbs 25:27

New Testament – Romans 1:20-23, 8:30, Acts 12:21-23, Luke 17:17-18, 2 Thessalonians 1:4-10, 2:14, 1 Thessalonians 2:12, 1 Peter 4:11-14, 5:8-10, Revelation 4:11, 7:11-12.

His Glory (4)

Old Testament – Ezekiel 1:24-28, 3:22-23 28:20-22, 39:13, 21, 43:1-7 Isaiah 2:2-5, 10-19, 4:2, 11:10, 26:13-15, 35:1-2, 44:22-23, 59:19-21, Zechariah 2:5, Psalms 145:5-12, 138:4-5, 104:31, 45:3-7

New Testament – Hebrews 1:1-3, 3:3-6 Romans 5:1-2, 8:17, 9:23, 15:5-7, 17 Ephesians 1:5-17, 3:14-21, 5:25-27 Titus 2:11-13

His Glory (5)

Old Testament – Jeremiah 17:12, 14:21, Isaiah 25:3, 28:5, 33:20-21, Psalms 102:13-16, 105:3, 8:3-5

New Testament – John 7:18, 8:50, 1 Thessalonians 2:19-20, 1 Corinthians 1:26-31, 3:19-21, Galatians 6:13-14, 2 Corinthians 3:7-18, 4:14-17, Jude 1:24-25, Colossians 1:27, Revelation 1:6, 21:9-11, 23-26

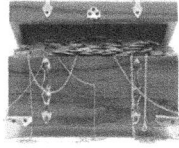

The Love Factor

The Love Factor (1)

"And because iniquity shall abound, the love of many shall wax cold." (Matthew 24:12)

The Love Factor (2)

"Though I speak with the tongues of men and angels, and have not charity, I am become as sounding brass, or a tinkling cymbal. And though I have the gift of prophecy, and understand all mysteries, and all knowledge; and though I have all faith, so that I could remove mountains and have not charity, I am nothing. And though I bestow all my goods to feed the poor, and though I give my body to be burned, and have not charity, it profiteth me nothing." (1 Corinthians 13:1-3)

The Love Factor (3)

"He hath shewed thee, O man, what is good, and what doth the LORD require of thee, but to do justly, and to love mercy, and to walk humbly with thy God?" (Micah 6:8)

Discussion Questions

1. Explain 1 Corinthians 8:3.
2. What requirements are given by God in Micah 6:8?
3. What did Jesus convey in John 13:34?

4. What happens if we do not love our brother?

5. What does it mean to walk in love according to Ephesians 5:2?

Fill in the Blanks

1. "Thou shalt____ the Lord thy God with all thy____, and with all thy____, and with all thy____."

2. "Let brotherly____ continue."

3. "O love the____, all ye his____: for the Lord preserveth the____, and ____ rewardeth the proud doer."

4. "Beloved, let us____ one another: for love is of____; and____ ____ that loveth is born of God, and____ God."

5. "He that____ not knoweth not God; for God is____."

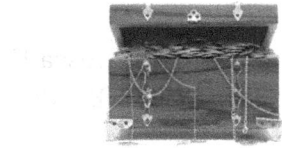

The Love Factor

C hristianity is a unique religion. The love of God is first and fore-most; secondly, there must be love for one's fellow man. Love is the guiding force to those who belong to Christ. It is love that constrains us. It is love that compels us. We are known by the love we have for one another and the love we have for our God.

The Love Factor (1)

Old Testament – Deuteronomy 7:7-8, 6:5, Exodus 20:6, Joshua 22:5, Nehemiah 13:26, 1 Kings 3:3, Psalms 5:11, 145:20, 69:35-36, 63:3, Isaiah 43:4, 63:7-9

New Testament – Matthew 22:36-40, 1 Chronicles 8:3, John 21:15-17, 15:9-16, 14:21-24, 8:42, 5:42, Romans 8:28, 37-40

The Love Factor (2)

Old Testament – Hosea 6:4-6, Zechariah 7:8-12, Micah 6:8, Isaiah 38:17, Psalms 31:23, 11:7, 33:5, 116:1, 122:6, 37:28, Deuteronomy 30:15-16, 28:47-48, Nehemiah 9:33-35, Numbers 14:8

New Testament – John 3:16, Romans 13:8-10, 1 Corinthians 13:1-8, 1 John 4:7-21, 5:2-3, 3:9-24

The Love Factor (3)

Old Testament – Song of Solomon 8:6-7, Hosea 11:1, 4, Jeremiah 31:3, 12:2, Job 19:19, Psalms 109:4-5 Isaiah 29:13, Ezekiel 33:31, 1 Samuel 13:14, Deuteronomy 13:3-4, 33:3

New Testament – Matthew 24:12, John 3:19, 2 Corinthians 12:15, 11:7-11, 1 Thessalonians 2:8, John 13:34, 1 John 2:5, Hebrews 13:1, 1 Corinthians 16:14

The Love Factor (4)

Old Testament – Ecclesiastes 9:1, 6, Zephaniah 3:17, Psalms 91:14, 37:28 Judges 5:31, Proverbs 8:17, 3:12, Psalms 119:132, 146:8

New Testament – Hebrews 1:9, 2 Corinthians 13:11, 2 Timothy 2:22, 1 Peter 1:22, 2:17, Ephesians 4:2, 6:23-24, 1 Thessalonians 4:9, Jude 1:21, Galatians 5:13, 22-23, 1 Corinthians 16:22

The Love Factor (5)

Old Testament – 1 Kings 10:8-9, 2 Chronicles 2:11, Malachi 1:2, Jeremiah 2:32-33, 9:24, Isaiah 49:14-16, Proverbs 22:11, 16:13, Psalms 119:47-48, 113, 163

New Testament – Titus 3:15, 1 John 2:15-17, 2 Timothy 4:10, 3:1-4, Matthew 6:24, 16:23, John 12:25, Romans 12:9-10

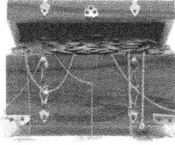

The Lie

The Lie (1)

"Now the serpent was more subtil than any beast of the field which the LORD God had made. And he said unto the woman, Yea, hath God said, Ye shall not eat of every tree of the garden? And the woman said unto the serpent, We may eat of the fruit of the trees of the garden: But of the fruit of the tree which is in the midst of the garden, God hath said, Ye shall not eat of it, neither shall ye touch it, lest ye die. And the serpent said unto the woman, Ye shall not surely die." (Genesis 3:1-4)

The Lie (2)

"Ye are of your father the devil, and the lusts of your father ye will do. He was a murderer from the beginning, and abode not in the truth, because there is no truth in him. When he speaketh a lie, he speaketh of his own: for he is a liar, and the father of it." (John 8:44)

The Lie (3)

"But the fearful, and unbelieving, and the abominable, and murders, and whoremongers, and sorcerers, and idolaters, and all liars, shall have their part in the lake which burneth with fire and brimstone: which is the second death." (Revelation 21:8)

Discussion Questions

1. What transpires in Revelation 21:8?
2. Discuss the deception found in Genesis 3:1-4 and its ramifications.
3. Discuss 2 Thessalonians 2:8-12.
4. Discuss Jeremiah 5:24-31.
5. What are we instructed to do in Colossians 3:9?228

Fill in the Blanks

1. "He that saith, I know him, and keepeth not his____ , is a____ , and the truth is not__ ___ ."
2. "If we say that we have____ with him, and walk in darkness, we___ , and do not the___ ."
3. "The proud have forged a___ against me: but I will keep thy____ with my__ ___ ."
4. "For we have made___ our refuge, and under falsehood have we__ ___ ."
5. "Who changed the truth of God into a___ , and worshipped and served the____ more than the Creator, who is blessed for ever."

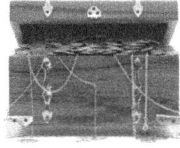

The Lie

*T*o speak untruths, to utter falsehoods, to practice deceit and treachery is to lie. Lying stands in stark contrast to the divine nature of God. No lie is of the truth (I John 2:21); the Devil is the Father of Lies. All liars will have their part in the lake of fire. Therefore, it behooves us to always speak the truth in love, to stand for the truth, and to abide in the truth.

The Lie (1)

Old Testament – Genesis 3:1-4, Psalms 120:2-3, 101:5, 7, 55:19-23, 52:1-7, 5:6, Isaiah 28:15, 17, 44:20, Jeremiah 5:26-31, 9:3-6, 20:6, 23:14, 16, 25-32, 36, Proverbs 21:6, 19:5, 6:16-19

New Testament – 2 Corinthians 11:3, 13-15, John 8:44, 2 Thessalonians 2:8-12, Revelation 21:8

The Lie (2)

Old Testament – Hosea 7:13-16, 10:1-4, 13, 11:12, 12:1-2, 7, 14:9, Ezekiel 33:31, 24:12, 13:8, 19, Psalms 78:36-37, 63:11, 62:3-4, 9, 58:1-5, 31:18

New Testament – Matthew 23:13-15, 24-30, Romans 3:3-4, Ephesians 4:25, 29, James 3:14-16, 1 John 2:4, 21

The Lie (3)

Old Testament – Isaiah 59:3-4, 12-15, 57:10-11, 32:6-7, Proverbs 14:5, 25, 13:5, 12:17-22, Jeremiah 7:8-11, 42:20-22, Job 15:31, 35, Micah 6:12, Psalms 144:7-8, 119:69, 163, Leviticus 19:11, Amos 2:4

New Testament – Romans 1:25, 2 Peter 2:3, 2 Timothy 3:13, 1 Timothy 4:1-3

The Lie (4)

Old Testament – Daniel 11:27, 1 Kings 22:20-25, Jeremiah 14:13-14, Micah 2:11, Zechariah 5:1-4, Judges 16:13-15, Proverbs 30:20, 26:23-28, 23:15-16, 23, 17:4, 7, 11:9, 18, Job 13:5, Zephaniah 3:13

New Testament – Romans 16:18, Acts 5:3, 6:10-13, 1 Timothy 1:9-11, Revelation 22:11, 15

The Lie (5)

Old Testament – Nahum 3:1, Habakkuk 2:1-10, 18-19, Isaiah 3:8, 9:15, 16:6, Jeremiah 48:29-31, 42, 6:28, Proverbs 10:18, 19:22, 25:18, 30:6, Psalms 40:4, 34:13, 31:13, 18, 109:1-3

New Testament – Matthew 5:11, Colossians 3:9, 1 Peter 3:10, 1 John 1:8-10, 2:4, 22, 4:20

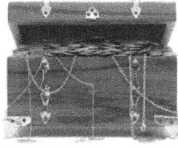

Our Labor

Our Labor (1)

"Who gave himself for us, that he might redeem us from all iniquity, and purify unto himself a peculiar people, zealous of good works." (Titus 2:14)

Our Labor (2)

"For God is not unrighteous to forget your work and labour of love, which ye have shewed toward his name, in that ye have ministered to the saints, and do minister." (Hebrews 6:10)

Our Labor (3)

"And to her was granted that she should be arrayed in fine linen, clean and white: for the fine linen is the righteousness of saints." (Revelation 19:8)

Discussion Questions

1. Explain Ecclesiastes 1:3, 13-14.
2. Explain 1 Corinthians 15:58.
3. What did the wise man, Solomon, convey in Ecclesiastes 5:15-20?
4. What will transpire when Jesus returns according to Matthew 25:31-46?
5. Explain Titus 3:8.

Fill in the Blanks

1. "He that laboureth___ for___ ; for his____ craveth it of him."
2. "For God shall bring every____ into____ , with every____ thing, whether it be____ , or whether it be____ ."
3. "For ye remember, brethren, our____ and travail: for____ night and day, because we would not be____ unto any of you, we____ unto you the____ of the God."
4. "Let him that stole steal no more: but rather let him____ , working with his hands the thing which is good, that he may have to give to him that____ ."
5. "Whereunto I also____ , striving according to his____, which___ in me____ ."

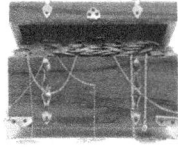

Our Labor

*I*n these passages of Scripture, examination is made of our labor and that for which we are striving. There is a great need to prioritize and make discernment concerning that which is temporal and that which is eternal.

Our Labor (1)

Old Testament – Genesis 3:19, Ecclesiastes 1:3, 13-14, 2:24, 5:3, 9:10, Proverbs 10:4, 16, 11:18, 12:11, 14, 24, 14:4, 23, 28:19 Nehemiah 6:3-4, 5:16, Psalms 128:1-2, 111:2-8

New Testament – John 4:34-38, 6:27-29, 9:4, Romans 2:4-10, 6:23, Titus 3:4-8, 2:14

Our Labor (2)

Old Testament – Exodus 36:1-2, 39:42-43 Deuteronomy 5:13, 28:8, 15, Haggai 1:6-11, 2:17 Job 36:8-12 Ecclesiastes 6:7 Proverbs 23:4-5, 13:11, 3:9-10, Psalms 104:23-24, 90:17

New Testament – Hebrews 6:10-12, 13:20-21, Romans 4:1-8, Titus 3:5 James 2:14-24, Luke 17:7-10

Our Labor (3)

Old Testament – Ecclesiastes 5:12, 15-20, 8:14-17, 12:14, 1 Samuel 14:45, Deuteronomy 24:14-15, Jeremiah 22:13, Job 9:29

New Testament – John 17:4, 14:12, Matthew 20:1-16, 9:37-38, 2 Corinthians 6:1, 1 Corinthians 9:1, 15:58, Galatians 4:19, Philippians 2:12-13, Ephesians 2:10, Titus 1:16, 2 Thessalonians 3:7-12

Our Labor (4)

Old Testament – 2 Chronicles 15:7, Nehemiah 4:15-23, Isaiah 66:18, 65:23, Psalms 127:1, Proverbs 13:13-31, 21:25, 13:4, 6:6-11

New Testament – Acts 9:36, 1 Timothy 6:18-19, Titus 3:14, Colossians 3:23-24, Ephesians 4:28, Galatians 6:9-10, James 1:27, 1 Corinthians 15:10, Revelation 2:2-3, 19:8, 14:13

Our Labor (5)

Old Testament – Job 7:1-2, 14:6, Ecclesiastes 2:17-23, 3:9-17, 22, 11:6, 2 Chronicles 31:21, 1 Kings 12:4-16, Proverbs 16:3, 26, 22:29, 24:27-34, 27:23, Isaiah 49:4, 55:2, 62:8-9

New Testament – Romans 12:6-13, James 5:4-8, 1 Thessalonians 2:9, Colossians 1:29, Ephesians 3:20, Matthew 25:31-46

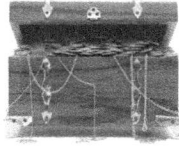

Tried by Fire

Tried by Fire (1)

"Every man's work shall be made manifest: for the day shall declare it, because it shall be revealed by fire; and the fire shall try every man's work of what sort it is." (1 Corinthians 3:13)

Tried by Fire (1)

"I counsel thee to buy of me gold tried in the fire, that thou mayest be rich; and white raiment, that thou mayest be clothed, and that the shame of thy nakedness do not appear; and anoint thine eyes with eyesalve, that thou mayest see." (Revelation 3:18)

Tried by Fire (3)

"The fining pot is for silver, and the furnace for gold: but the LORD trieth the hearts." (Proverbs 17:3)

Discussion Questions

1. Explain Daniel 11:35.
2. Can the trials we face bring the best out of us, as we exhibit the mettle necessary to meet those challenges?
3. Can trials also reveal any deficiencies we may have?
4. Explain Luke 22:31-34.
5. What lessons can we learn from the trials of Job?

Fill in the Blanks

1. "My___ I hold fast, and will not let it go: my___ shall not reproach me so___ as I___ ."

2. "The fining pot is for___ , and the furnace for___: but the Lord___ the___ ."

3. "Search me, O God, and know my___ ; try me, and know my___ : And see if there be any___ way in me, and___ me in the way___ ."

4. "Fear none of those things which thou shalt___ : behold, the devil shall cast some of you into___ , that ye may be___ ; and ye shall have___ ten___ : be thou___ unto___ , and I will give thee a___ of___ ."

5. "Confirming the___ of the disciples, and exhorting them to continue in the___ , and that we must through much___ enter into the___ of God."

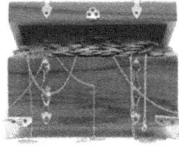

Tried by Fire

"Behold, I have refined thee, but not with silver; I have chosen thee in the furnace of affliction" (Isaiah 48:10).

*D*uring the refining process of gold and silver, the dross and impurities surface under the intense heat and are skimmed or removed. This process leaves a pure, clear, and shining product. And so it is with those refined in God's refining process.

"Now no chastening for the present seemeth to be joyous, but grievous: nevertheless afterward it yieldeth the peaceable fruit of righteousness unto them which are exercised thereby" (Hebrews 12:11).

Tried by Fire (1)

Old Testament – Daniel 11:33-35, 12:10, Isaiah 1:22-31, 4:3-4, 43:1-2, 48:10-11, Psalms 119:67, 71, 75, 139:23-24, Job 19:7-21, 23:10-12, 27:3-6, Proverbs 17:3

New Testament – 1 Peter 1:5-9, 4:12-13, 1 Corinthians 3:12-15, Revelation 3:18-19

Tried by Fire (2)

Old Testament – Malachi 3:3, Proverbs 25:4, Isaiah 30:20-22, 27-30, 26:11, Lamentations 1:13-18, Jeremiah 6:26-30, 9:6-7, 17:10, Psalms 119:50, 119, 66:10-12, 51:7-8, Ezekiel 22:18-22, 24:10-14

New Testament – Luke 3:16-17, 2 Corinthians 7:1, James 5:3, 2 Timothy 2:20-21

Tried by Fire (3)

Old Testament – Zechariah 13:9, Isaiah 66:15-17, 64:2, 54:16, 50:10-11, Proverbs 27:21-22, Job 33:19-30, Psalms 106:18, 89:46-47, 80:14-19, 79:5-9, 60:1-4, Jeremiah 5:3, 12-14

New Testament – Matthew 13:40, Hebrews 10:26-31, Jude 20-23, Luke 12:49, Mark 9:49

Tried by Fire (4)

Old Testament – Daniel 7:9-10, Deuteronomy 4:23-24, Exodus 20:20, Nehemiah 1:2-6, Job 13:15, 20:22-26, 23:14-16, Ezekiel 21:13-17, 5:1-4, Jeremiah 4:4, 12:3-4, Psalms 104:35, 59:12-13, 11:4-6

New Testament – Hebrews 12:11, 25-29, 2 Thessalonians 1:4-12, Revelation 2:10, 1 John 3:3

Tried by Fire (5)

Old Testament – Deuteronomy 9:3, 32:20, 22, Malachi 4:1-3, 3:16-17, Isaiah 29:6, 33:10-16, 42:25, 47:12-15, Jeremiah 10:24-25, 21:12-14, Psalms 97:3-6, 58:9-11, 50:3-4, 21:8-9

New Testament – Matthew 7:19, 13:47-50, Hebrews 6:7-8, Acts 14:22, Revelation 7:14

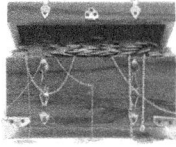

The Soul

The Soul (1)

"In your patience possess ye your souls." (Luke 21:19)

The Soul (2)

"Thus saith the LORD, Stand ye in the ways, and see, and ask for the old paths, where is the good way, and walk therein, and ye shall find rest for your souls. But they said, We will not walk therein." (Jeremiah 6:16)

The Soul (3)

"The soul of the wicked desireth evil: his neighbor findeth no favour in his eyes." (Proverbs 21:10)

Discussion Questions

1. Discuss Matthew 10:28.
2. According to Matthew 16:24, can the soul be lost?
3. When did man become a living soul?
4. Can the soul be made sorrowful?
5. Explain John 12:27.

Fill in the Blanks

1. "Which hope we have as an anchor of the____ ."

2. "My___ melteth for___ : strengthen thou me according unto thy___ ."

3. "Seeing ye have____ your____ in obeying the truth through the Spirit unto unfeigned love of the brethren."

4. "He restoreth my____ : he leadeth me in the path of righteousness for His name's sake."

5. "But we are not of them who draw back unto perdition; but of them that believe to the___ of the____ ."

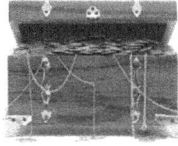

The Soul

*T*he Greek word *psuche* is translated "soul" in English. It is defined as "the seat of one's affections and will." It is a person's unique, distinct, and individual personality. God breathed into man, and man became a living soul.

The Soul (1)

Old Testament – Genesis 2:7, Psalms 139:13-14, 131:2, 119:28, 129, 175, 107:9, 88:3, 25:1-2, Ezekiel 18:4, 20-23, Proverbs 1:10-19, 6:32, 8:33-36, 11:25, 30, Jeremiah 38:16, Isaiah 57:16

New Testament – Luke 1:46-47, Matthew 10:28, James 1:21, 5:20, 2 Peter 2:7-9

The Soul (2) Old Testament – Deuteronomy 6:5, 10:12, 11:18, 13:3, Lamentations 3:25, 58, Isaiah 61:10, Psalms 35:1-3, 42:1-6, 11, 49:5-9, 84:1-2, 94:17-19, Genesis 34:3, 1 Samuel 18:1, Song of Solomon 6:12, Micah 7:1

New Testament – Matthew 22:36-38, 16:26, 11:28-29, 1 Peter 2:25, 1 Peter 4:19

The Soul (3)

Old Testament – Leviticus 16:29, Psalms 35:7-12, 43:5, 69:10, 18, Isaiah 58:3-8, Job 19:2-4, 16:1-5, 7:7-15, Jeremiah 6:16, 13:17, Judges 16:16, Genesis 35:18, 49:6, Proverbs 8:36, 10:3, 16:17

New Testament – Luke 12:19-21, 21:19, Hebrews 4:12, 10:39, 1 Thessalonians 5:23

The Soul (4)

Old Testament – Proverbs 25:25, 27:7, Psalms 63:1-8, 66:16, 72:12-13, 86:4, 97:10, 103:1-5, 22, 119:20, 25, 81, 167, 130:5-6, 143:3-12 Genesis 27:25, 31, Isaiah 26:9, 55:2-3, Jeremiah 31:12, 4:18-19

New Testament – 1 Peter 1:22, 2:11, 3 John 2:1

The Soul (5)

Old Testament – Isaiah 53:6-12, 54:7-14, Job 30:15-25, 3:20-26, Lamentations 3:17-21, Psalms 142:4-7, 62:1, 57:1-6, 34:1-2, 22, 23:3-6, 22:8-27, 6:3-10, Micah 6:7-8

New Testament – John 12:27-28, Matthew 26:36-39, 12:18-21, Acts 2:27, 31, Hebrews 6:19

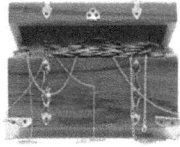

The King's Business

The King's Business (1)

"Go ye therefore, and teach all nations, baptizing them in the name of the Father, and of the Son, and of the Holy Ghost: Teaching them to observe all things whatsoever I have commanded you: and, lo, I am with you always, even unto the end of the world. Amen." (Matthew 28:19-20)

The King's Business (2)

"The former treatise have I made, O Theophilus, of all that Jesus began both to do and teach, Until the day in which he was taken up, after that he through the Holy Ghost had given commandments unto the apostles whom he had chosen:" (Acts 1:1-2)

The King's Business (3)

"And David said unto Ahimelech, And is there not here under thine handspear or sword? For I have neither brought my sword nor my weapons with me, because the king's business required haste." (1 Samuel 21:8)

Discussion Questions

1. In 1 Samuel 21:1-2, 8, what was the king's business, and how was it to be performed?
2. Jesus is King. What instructions did He give in Matthew 28:18-20?

3. What command is given in Mark 16:15-16?
4. Explain John 4:34.
5. Explain Luke 1:76.

Fill in the Blanks

1. "And David said unto____ , And is there not here under thine hand____ or____ ? for I have neither brought my____ nor my____ with me because the____ ____ required haste."
2. "And he said unto them, How is it that ye sought me? wist ye not that I____ be____ my father's____ ?"
3. "But if it be of God, ye cannot____ it."
4. "Not everyone that____ unto me, Lord, Lord, shall enter into the kingdom of____ ; but he that doeth the____ of my Father which is in heaven."
5. "Go ye therefore, and____ ____ ____ , baptizing them in the name of the____ and of___ the and of the____ ____ ."

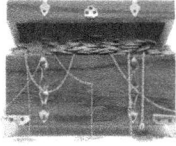

The King's Business

*T*here is an urgency to do God's business among those who belong to the Lord. God's desire is that all men be saved and render obedience to His Son, Jesus Christ. We are to embrace this good news and spread the gospel throughout all the world. We are commanded to teach and to make disciples of all nations. Let the redeemed of the Lord be about the King's business.

The King's Business (1)

Old Testament – 1 Samuel 21:1-2, 8, Jeremiah 1:4-12, 20:7-18, Amos 7:11-17, Jonah 1:8-17, 2:7-10, 3:1-10, Habakkuk 2:2-3, 2 Chronicles 20:5-6, Isaiah 6:4-11, 14:27, 33:13, 43:13

New Testament – Matthew 28:18-20, 10:11-20, Mark 16:15-16, Acts 1:1-2, Revelation 14:6-7.

The King's Business (2)

Old Testament – Psalms 147:15, 119:60, 104:4, 89:34, 68:11, 47:2-8, 33:9-18, Isaiah 51:4-5, 16, 52:7, 55:10-11, Numbers 23:19-21, 26, 2 Chronicles 35:21

New Testament – Luke 2:49, 18:28-30, 19:30-38, John 9:4, Acts 26:15-26, Acts 20:18-24, 1 Thessalonians 2:4

The King's Business (3)

Old Testament – Daniel 8:27, Proverbs 21:1, Ezra 6:22, Nehemiah 2:18, 20, 6:16, Isaiah 26:12, Psalms 74:12, 64:9, 1 Kings 13:1-24, 20:35-43, Jeremiah 48:10, Proverbs 30:6, 1 Samuel 15:1-3, 8-11, 22-23

New Testament – Acts 5:38-39, Philippians 2:13, 1 Corinthians 16:10. John 4:34, Matthew 7:21

The King's Business (4)

Old Testament – Genesis 49:9-10, Zechariah 14:9, 10:5-8, 12, 9:9, Hosea 11:10-12, Exodus 15:3, Psalms 44:4-5, 60:12, 110:3, Micah 5:7-9, Isaiah 31:4, 42:13, Proverbs 25:5, 20:8, Ezekiel 3:8-12

New Testament – Ephesians 6:10-20, 2 Corinthians 10:3-6, Revelation 6:2, 19:11-16, 2 Timothy 2:3-4

The King's Business (5)

Old Testament – 1 Samuel 8:11, 2 Samuel 15:1, 1 Kings 1:5, Malachi 3:1, 4:5, 1 Chronicles 26:30, 32, 2 Chronicles 30:12, Ezekiel 37:22, 24, Isaiah 9:6-7, Psalms 2:6-12, 40:8-10, 103:19-22, 119:4, Jeremiah 7:23

New Testament – Luke 1:76, John 10:16, Acts 5:30-32, 11:20-21, Hebrews 13:20-21

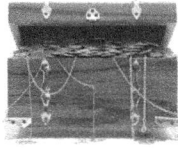

Haters

Haters (1)

"Hatred stirreth upstrifes: but love covereth all sins." (Proverbs 10:12)

Haters (2)

"If the world hate you, ye know that it hated me before it hated you." (John 15:18)

Haters (3)

"The world cannot hate you; but me it hateth, because I testify of it, that the works thereof are evil." (John 7:7)

Discussion Questions

1. What observations were made concerning Cain in 1 John 3:11-15?
2. What observations are made in Proverbs 26:24-28?
3. Do haters have eternal life according to 1 John 3:15?
4. Explain 1 Corinthians 6:9.
5. What is conveyed in Matthew 5:38-45?

Fill in the Blanks

1. "If the world____ you, ye know that it____ me before it____ you."
2. "For every one that doeth____ ____ the light, neither cometh to the light, lest his____ should be reproved."
3. "___ stirreth up strifes; but____ covereth all sins."
4. "Am I therefore become your____ , because I tell you the____ ?"
5. "Be not____ of evil, but overcome with____ ."

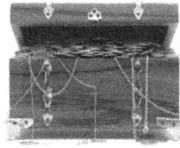

Haters

In the lives of some, a current of dislike, disdain, and discontent for others prevails. They utter words of discouragement, harsh words of contempt and dismay. When the heart becomes filled with hatred, it mars the character of the individual and thwarts their efforts to be like Christ, who is characterized by love, care, concern, and mercy for others.

Haters (1)

Old Testament – Genesis 4:3-8, 27:39-41, 37:3-4, 8, 50:20, Leviticus 19:17, 1 Samuel 18:5-9, 24:9-20, Deuteronomy 32:35, Proverbs 10:12, 11:17, 23, 26:24-28, 29:10, 27

New Testament – Luke 1:70-71, John 15:18, Mark 13:9-13, 1 John 3:11-15, Titus 3:3-7, Ephesians 2:1-3

Haters (2)

Old Testament – 1 Kings 18:17, 21:29-23, 22:7-8, Jeremiah 11:18-20, 18:18-20, 23, 20:7-11, Amos 5:10, 15, 7:10-17, 2 Chronicles 24:20-22, 36:15-16, Proverbs 9:7-8, 15:12, 31-32, Psalms 34:21

New Testament – John 7:7, 3:20, Galatians 4:16, Mark 3:1-6, 12:9-17

Haters (3)

Old Testament – Deuteronomy 19:11-13, Job 31:28-30, Proverbs 24:17-18, 30:21-23, Isaiah 66:5, Psalms 139:20-22, 81:15, 69:4-9, 68:1, 21, 97:10, Micah 7:8-10, Deuteronomy 28:7, Isaiah 54:17

New Testament – Romans 1:30-32, 11:28, 32, John 15:23-24, 16:2, Luke 16:22-23

Haters (4)

Old Testament – Proverbs 1:29-33, 6:16-19, 8:13, 16:7, Zechariah 8:17, Isaiah 26:10, Micah 7:5-6, Psalms 55:12-14, 20-23, Lamentations 3:59-65, Psalms 109:3-5, 59:1-13, 35:4-26, 25:19

New Testament – Matthew 5:38-45, 7:6, Romans 12:14, 17-21, 13:8-10, 1 Peter 3:9, 17

Haters (5)

Old Testament – 2 Samuel 13:14-15, 22, Isaiah 57:20-21, Proverbs 4:16-17, 2 Chronicles 19:2, Job 8:20, 22, 16:9-10, 30:8-12, Psalms 5:4-5, 10, 6:8-10, 7:11-16, 36:1-4, 10-12, 38:19-20, 56:1-9

New Testament – 1 Corinthians 6:9, Mark 9:42, 13:13, Matthew 13:24-30

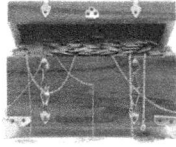

Miracles, Signs, and Wonders

Miracles, Signs, and Wonders (1)

"An they went forth, and preached every where, the Lord working with them, and confirming the word with signs following. Amen." (Mark 16:20)

Miracles, Signs, and Wonders (2)

"God also bearing them witness, both with signs and wonders, and with divers miracles, and gifts of the Holy Ghost, according to his own will?" (Hebrews 2:4)

Miracles, Signs, and Wonders (3)

"Charity never faileth: bur whether there be prophecies, they shall fail; whether there be tongues, they shall cease; whether there be knowledge, it shall vanish away." (1 Corinthians 13:8)

Discussion Questions

1. Discuss 1 Corinthians 13:8.
2. What was wrong with the miracles, signs, and wonders of 2 Thessalonians 2:7-12?
3. Explain Deuteronomy 13:1-5.
4. What transpired in Exodus 7:9-22? Does God display His awesome power the same way today? If not, why?

5. Explain Revelation 18:13-14.

Fill in the Blanks

1. "For there shall arise_____ _____ , and____ ___ , and shall shew___ ____ and____ ; in so much that, if it were possible, they shall____ the very elect."
2. "If there arise among you a prophet, or a dreamer of dreams, and giveth thee a___ or a wonder. . . ."
3. "We know that thou art a teacher come from___ : for no man can do these____ that thou doest, ____ God be with him."
4. "For the saith____ unto Pharaoh, Even for this same____ have I raised thee up, that I might shew my____ in thee, and that my name might be throughout all the____ ."
5. "Charity never faileth: but whether there be___ , they shall____ ; whether there be____ , they shall____ ; whether there be____ , it shall vanish away."

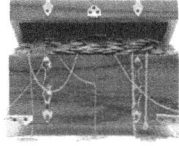

Miracles, Signs, and Wonders

*M*iracles prove to be a topic of intrigue. We have listed passages not only where miracles were performed, but also where the reason for their existence is revealed—to confirm the Word, to recognize Divine authority, to attest to the awesomeness and mighty power of God. Yet once their purpose was fulfilled, there was cessation, and the natural order continued.

Miracles, Signs, and Wonders (1)

Old Testament – Exodus 7:9-22, 8:5-24, 9:8-16, 28, 10:19-24, 12:29-31, 14:13-31, Nehemiah 9:9-10, Psalms 106:4-12, 136:10-16, Jeremiah 32:20-23

New Testament – Romans 9:17-18, John 3:2, 1 Corinthians 12:7-11, 31, 13:8-13, Matthew 7:22-23

Miracles, Signs, and Wonders (2)

Old Testament – Daniel 6:26-27, 5:24-30, 4:2-3, 2 Kings 2:1-25, 4:38-44, 5:10-27, 13:21, 2 Chronicles 18:18-34, Numbers 14:11, Psalms 78:20-22, 32

New Testament – John 2:11, 4:48, 6:2, 12:37, 20:25-31, Matthew 11:20-24, 12:38-39

Miracles, Signs, and Wonders (3)

Old Testament – Judges 6:11-22, 36-40, 7:2-22, 15:18-20, Joshua 6:1-5, 27, 10:7-14, 2 Kings 20:8-11, Isaiah 7:10-16, 1 Kings 17:17-24

New Testament – John 11:38-44, Hebrews 2:3-4, Mark 16:17-20, Acts 2:43, 3:6-7, 4:13-16, 30, 5:12, 8:5-18.

Miracles, Signs, and Wonders (4)

Old Testament – 1 Samuel 28:5-19, Deuteronomy 18:9-14, 13:1-5, Isaiah 2:5-6, 8:19-20, Jeremiah 23:25-32, 27:9-10, 44:28-29, Micah 3:5-7, Zechariah 13:1-5, 10:2, Psalms 74:9

New Testament – John 10:41-42, Acts 13:6-11, 19:13-16, 2 Thessalonians 2:7-12

Miracles, Signs, and Wonders (5)

Old Testament – Exodus 3:1-5, Deuteronomy 4:32-37, 7:17-21, Numbers 11:1-3, 16:1-4, 28-35, 20:7-13, 21:4-9, 22:21-35, 1 Kings 13:1-6, 2 Kings 2:11-14, 19-25

New Testament – Matthew 24:24, 1 Timothy 4:1-2, 1 Corinthians 1:22-23 Revelation 13:13-14, 19:20

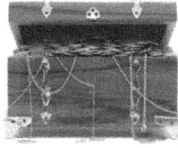

God's Judgements

God's Judgements (1)

"Although thou sayest thou shalt not see him, yet judgment is before him; therefore trust thou him." (Job 35:14)

God's Judgment (2)

"But we are sure that the judgment of God is according to truth against them which commit such things." (Romans 2:2)

God's Judgment (3)

"His ways are grievous; thy judgments are far above far above out of his sight: as for all his enemies, he puffeth at them." (Psalms 10:5)

Discussion Questions

1. What observations are made in Leviticus 26:14-42?
2. Explain 1 Peter 2:23?
3. What judgments are given in 1 Corinthians 11:29-32?
4. What warning is given in Hebrews 6:4-8?
5. Discuss Psalms 147:18-20.

Fill in the Blanks

1. "For we know him that hath said, ____ belongeth unto me,
   I will____ , saith the Lord. And again, The____ shall____
   his people."
2. "For he shall have____ without mercy, that hath shewed
   no____ ; and mercy rejoiceth against____ ."
3. "He hath not dealt so with any nation: and as for his____ , they
   have not known them."
4. "His ways are always____ ; thy____ are far above out of
   his____ ."
5. "But we are____ that the____ of God is according to____ against
   them which____ such things."

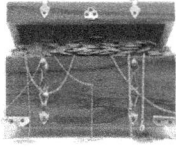

God's Judgements

A determination is made, a verdict is rendered, a just recompense is given—by definition, this is the meaning of judgment.

> "My flesh trembleth for fear of thee; and I am afraid of thy judgments" (Psalms 119:120).

The judgments dispensed by our God are a very thought-provoking topic.

God's Judgments (1)

Old Testament – Leviticus 26:14-42, Deuteronomy 32:41, Ecclesiastes 8:4-6, Psalms 9:16-20, 36:6, 72:1-2, Job 37:23-24, 36:8-18, 35:14, Isaiah 14:22-27, 26:8-9, 28:24-26, 30:18, Jeremiah 8:7, 25:13

New Testament – 1 Peter 2:23, Romans 1:26-32, 2:1-5, 11:33

God's Judgments (2)

Old Testament – Deuteronomy 1:17, Proverbs 19:29, Jeremiah 1:14-17, 2:34-35, 4:1-2, 11-26, 9:21-24, 18:7-11, 26:13, Ezekiel 5:15, 9:1-11, 14:13-21, Hosea 6:5, 12:6, 1 Chronicles 16:12-14

New Testament – Hebrews 2:1-3, 10:26-31, Galatians 5:10, 1 Corinthians 11:29-32

God's Judgments (3)

Old Testament – Psalms 147:18-20, 119:13, 20, 75, 102, 175, 94:1-15, 58:10-11, 11:2-6, 10:4-5, 13, 7:11-16, Ezekiel 35:2-11, 38:19-23, 39:21-22, Joel 3:9-17, Zephaniah 1:9-18

New Testament – Luke 17:1-2, Hebrews 13:4, 6:4-8

God's Judgment (4)

Old Testament – Exodus 6:6, Exodus 12:12, 1 Chronicles 21:1, 10-15, Jonah 1:2, 3:1-10, Amos 3:6-15, 4:1-12, Joel 2:12-18, Jeremiah 19:15, 40:3, Obadiah 1:10-16, 21, Ezekiel 16:38, 58-63, 18:4-9

New Testament – 1 Corinthians 10:1-11, James 5:9, 12, 2 Peter 2:4-9, Revelation 2:19-24

God's Judgment (5)

Old Testament – Judges 1:4-7, Ecclesiastes 3:14-17, 11:9, 12:13-14, 2 Samuel 12:8-12, Psalms 143:2, 105:4-7, 89:30-34, 76:6-12, 19:9-11, 1:1-6, Lamentations 3:37-39

New Testament – 1 Thessalonians 4:3-8, Matthew 23:32-33, Hebrews 3:7-11, 1 Timothy 3:6, James 3:1, 2:13

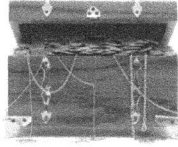

Righteousness

Righteousness (1)

"And they were both righteous before God, walking in all the commandments and ordinances of the Lord blameless." (Luke 1:6)

Righteousness (2)

"And if the righteous scarcely be saved, where shall the ungodly and the sinner appear?" (1 Peter 4:18)

Righteousness (3)

"But of him are ye in Christ Jesus, who of God is made unto us wisdom, and righteousness, and sanctification, and redemption:" (1 Corinthians 1:30)

Discussion Questions

1. Explain Romans 3:10-12, 21-26.
2. Explain Isaiah 59:16-17.
3. What does it mean to establish your own righteousness?
4. What is Paul saying in Philippians 3:10?
5. Explain Romans 8:1-4.

Fill in the Blanks

1. "But of him are ye in____ ____, who of God is____ unto us____, and___, and___, and___."
2. "For they being ignorant of___ ____, and going about to establish their___ ____, have not____ themselves unto the____ of God."
3. "Abraham believed God, and it was counted unto him for____."
4. "I do not frustrate the grace of God: for if righteousness come by the___, then Christ is dead in___."
5. "For he hath made him to be____ for us, who knew no___; that we might be made the____ of____ in him."

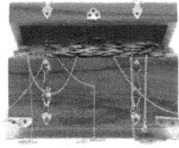

Righteousness

/n the simplest manner of speaking, righteousness means "to be right with God; to be faultless, innocent, or not guilty before God." Righteousness is imputed to those who have obeyed the gospel and that now abide in Christ. Christ, through his death on the cross, has become the atoning sacrifice for the sins of the entire world. We are righteous in God's sight because of what Christ has done on our behalf.

Righteousness (1)

Old Testament – Genesis 15:4-6, 18:23-33, Proverbs 11:5-8, 12:28, 14:34, 15:9, Job 9:2, 20, 10:14-15, 15:14-16, Psalms 143:1-2, 34:13-21, 32:1-2, Isaiah 61:10

New Testament – Romans 3:10-12, 21-26, 4:1-8, 23-24, 1 Corinthians 1:30, 2 Corinthians 5:21

Righteousness (2)

Old Testament – Deuteronomy 6:24-25, 24:10-13, 1 Samuel 26:23, 2 Samuel 22:21-25, Isaiah 3:10, 32:17, 59:16-17, Psalms 146:8, 132:9, 119:172, 106:30-31, Job 25:4-6, 29:24

New Testament – Romans 6:13, 2 Timothy 3:16, Ephesians 4:22-24, 6:14, Revelation 19:8

Righteousness (3)

Old Testament – Hosea 14:9, 10:12, 2:19-20, Psalms 85:10-13, 33:5, 40:9-10, 89:14-16, 11:3-7, Job 27:5-6, 17:8-9, 35:6-8, Ezekiel 18:20-24, Isaiah 64:5-6

New Testament – Romans 10:1-4, 5:17-21, 1:16-18, Galatians 2:21, Philippians 3:6-9

Righteousness (4)

Old Testament – Daniel 9:24-25, Jeremiah 22:1-4, 15-16, 23:5-6, Zechariah 2:1-2, Amos 7:7-8, 2 Kings 21:13, Isaiah 28:16-17, 1:25-27, 5:16, 16:5, 26:2, 42:6, Psalms 94:15, 99:4

New Testament – Matthew 5:6, 10, 20, Romans 8:1-4, Titus 2:11-12, 1 John 1:9, 3:7

Righteousness (5)

Old Testament – Deuteronomy 33:19, Ezekiel 14:13-20, 1 Kings 3:6, Daniel 12:3, Psalms 15:1-2, 37:25, 45:7, 65:5, 71:15-16, 103:17-18, 132:9, Malachi 4:1-2, Isaiah 11:1-5, 46:12-13, 51:4-8

New Testament – Hebrews 1:8-9, Matthew 6:33, 1 Peter 4:18, 2 Peter 3:10-13

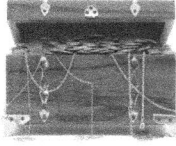

Roots of Bitterness

Roots of Bitterness (1)

"Follow peace with all men, and holiness, without which no man shall see the Lord: Looking diligently lest any man fail of the grace of God; lest any root of bitterness springing up trouble you, and thereby many be defiled;" (Hebrews 12:14-15)

Roots of Bitterness (2)

"The heart knows his own bitterness; and a stranger doth not intermeddle with his joy." (Proverbs 14:10)

Roots of Bitterness (3)

"Let all bitterness, wrath, and anger, and clamour, and evil speaking, be put away from you, with all malice." (Ephesians 4:31)

Discussion Questions

1. Explain Deuteronomy 29:18.
2. To whom does all vengeance and recompense belong?
3. Does anger and bitterness affect us spiritually? Explain.
4. Explain John 13:34-35.
5. What did the apostle Paul say about the Christians with the attributes found in 2 Corinthians 12:20-21?

Fill in the Blanks

1. "Looking diligently lest any man____ of the____ of God; lest any____ of____ springing up trouble you, and thereby many be____ ."
2. "But if ye____ and____ one another, take heed that ye be not____ one of another."
3. "Be ye angry, and____ ____ : let not the sun go down upon your ____ ."
4. "For this is the____ that ye heard from the____ , that we should____ one another."
5. "And it came to pass . . . king David dancing and playing: and she____ him in her____ ."

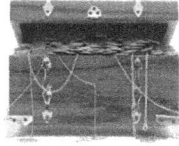

Roots of Bitterness

The expression "root of bitterness" typifies those whose hearts are inclined to vent angry and bitter words against those whom they harbor disdain, disgust, and perhaps unforgiveness toward. The heart becomes darkened, and the soul becomes defiled when we allow seeds and roots of bitterness to abide within our minds.

Roots of Bitterness (1)

Old Testament – Deuteronomy 29:18, 32:35, Leviticus 19:17-18, Genesis 4:1-8, 27:38-45, 49:5-7, Job 21:23-25, Proverbs 14:10, 22:8, 24-25, 26:21-26

New Testament – Hebrews 12:14-17, Galatians 5:15, 19-21, 26, Matthew 5:21-24, 1 John 3:10-15, Romans 1:29-32

Roots of Bitterness (2)

Old Testament – Ecclesiastes 7:8-9, Psalms 64:2-9, 37:8-9, 4:4-5, Proverbs 6:32-35, 12:14, 14:16-17, 29, 16:32, 17:14, 19:11, 19, 20:3, 22

New Testament – Luke 17:1-4, Ephesians 4:26-32, Romans 3:14-15, James 1:19-21, 2 Timothy 4:14

Roots of Bitterness (3)

Old Testament – Genesis 50:15-21, Job 7:11-21, 42:10, Ruth 1:19-22, 4:12-17, 1 Chronicles 15:29, 2 Samuel 6:20-23, 25:2-3, 36-38

New Testament – Mark 11:25-26, 1 Peter 3:8-9, 17, Acts 15:36-41, Romans 12:19-21

Roots of Bitterness (4)

Old Testament – Esther 3:5-6, 5:7-14, 7:3-10, 1 Samuel 24:11-19, Psalms 25:19-20, 5:5 Isaiah 58:4, Proverbs 16:19, 27-29, 25:28, 27:4

New Testament – Matthew 5:38-48, Luke 9:51-56, 1 Peter 2:19-23, James 4:1-6, 10-12, Jude 1:14-21

Roots of Bitterness (5)

Old Testament – Exodus 32:17-22, Numbers 20:7-13, Judges 15:1-8, 1 Kings 21:1-21, Proverbs 10:12, 18, 11:9-13, 17-29, 12:1-4, 15:1-4, 12:18-23, 15:1-4, 29:8-11, 22

New Testament – John 13:34-35, Titus 3:1-7, 1 John 2:9-11, 2 Corinthians 12:20-21

Turn

Turn (1)

"And many of the children of Israel shall he turn to the Lord their God." (Luke 1:16)

Turn (2)

"Turn ye at my reproof: behold, I will pour out my spirit unto you, I will make known my words unto you." (Proverbs 1:23)

Turn (3)

"O ye sons of men, how long will ye turn my glory into shame? How long will ye love vanity, and seek after leasing? Selah. (Psalms 4:2)

Discussion Questions

1. What observations are made in Psalms 119:10, 21, 118?
2. Discuss Luke 1:16-17.
3. What instruction was given to Joshua in Joshua 1:7?
4. Explain 1 Timothy 5:13, 15.
5. Discuss Romans 11:26.

Fill in the Blanks

1. "And the hand of the Lord was with____ : and a great number____ , and unto____ the Lord."
2. "And the____ shall come to____ , and unto them that____ from transgression in Jacob, saith the Lord."
3. "For some are already____ aside after Satan."
4. "All we like sheep have gone _____; we have____ every one to his own____ ; and the Lord hath laid on him the____ of us all."
5. "Having a form of godliness, but____ the power thereof: from such____ a way."

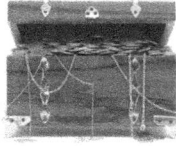

Turn

"Turn to me and be saved, all you ends of the earth; for I am God; there is no other" (Isaiah 45: 22, NIV).

*W*e must pivot our lives from that which is self-willed, worldly minded, and contrary to God's will to that which is in accordance to God or that meets God's approval. God is our Creator; it is He who has made us, and not we ourselves. It is in Him that we find hope, joy, purpose, peace, love, direction, completion, and even the salvation of our souls.

Turn (1)

Old Testament – Deuteronomy 5:31-32, 7:2-4, 11:16, 28, 13:5, 1 Kings 11:1-4, 9, 8:33-36, Nehemiah 1:7-9, Joel 2:12-13, Jonah 3:8-10, Lamentations 3:40, Psalms 40:4, 119:10, 21, 118, Hosea 5:3-4, 7:8, 16

New Testament – Luke 1:16-17, Acts 3:26, Acts 9:34-35, Acts 11:21, Acts 13:6-10.

Turn (2)

Old Testament – Proverbs 1:22-23, 32-33, 4:14-16, 26-27, 9:1-4, Psalms 4:2, 12:9-12, Haggai 2:17, Zechariah 1:3-4, 9:12, 10:8-9, Isaiah 59:20, 31:6, 30:21, 2 Chronicles 7:14, 19-20, 12:12, 15:3-4

New Testament – Acts 14:15, 15:19, 19:26, 1 Thessalonians 1:9.

Turn (3)

Old Testament – 2 Kings 23:25, 22:2, Joshua 1:7, 23:6, 24:20, Judges 2:16-17, Numbers 14:43, Job 22:23, 31:7-8, 34:26-27, Psalms 125:4-5, Isaiah 30:9-11, 44:20, 53:6

New Testament – Galatians 1:6-9, 4:9-11, Jude 1:4, 2 Peter 1:1-3, 6 1 Timothy 5:13, 15, Titus 1:10-14

Turn (4)

Old Testament – Jeremiah 2:19-21, 34-35, 3:14, 22, 4:22, 27-28, 5:25, 11:6-10, 14:7-8, 18:8, 11, Ezekiel 13:20-22, 33:10-11, Psalms 146:9, 129:4-5, 119:37, 39, 59, 79

New Testament – Hebrews 12:12-13, 25, 2 Timothy 4:1-4, 3:1-5, 1:13-15

Turn (5)

Old Testament – Deuteronomy 4:30, 17:18-20, 23:3-5, 30:7-10, 17-18, 31:18, 29, Daniel 9:9-13, 1 Samuel 12:20-21, Lamentations 5:21, Psalms 90:3, 85:4, 80:3, 78:38, 22:27, 9:3, 17, 7:11-13

New Testament – Acts 17:6-9, 19:26, 26:18-20, Romans 11:26, 2 Corinthians 3:12-16

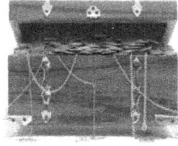

Parenting 101

Parenting 101 (1)

"For I know him, that he will command his children and his household after him, and they shall keep the way of the LORD, to do justice, and judgment, that the LORD may bring upon Abraham that which he hath spoken of him." (Genesis 18:19)

Parenting 101 (2)

"When I call to remembrance the unfeigned faith that is in thee, which dwelt first in thy grandmother Lois, and thy mother Eunice; and I am persuaded that in thee also." (2 Timothy 1:5)

Parenting 101 (3)

"Honor thy father and thy mother: that thy days may be long upon the land which the LORD thy God giveth thee." (Exodus 20:12)

Discussion Questions

1. As parents, how should we train our children?
2. Parents have the responsibility to teach their children to know the Lord. In what ways?
3. Explain 1 Corinthians 7:14.
4. Explain Proverbs 17:6.
5. What is the purpose of chastening a child?

Fill in the Blanks

1. "And that from a____ thou hast known the____ ____ , which are able to make thee____ unto ____through faith which is in____ ____ ."

2. "But Jesus said, Suffer____ ____ , and forbid them not, to come unto____ : for of such is the____ of heaven."

3. "Fathers, provoke____ your____ to____ , lest they be____ ."

4. "Take____ that ye____ not one of these____ ____ ; for I say unto you, That in____ their____ do always behold the face of my____ which is in____ ."

5. "And said, Verily I say unto you, ____ ye be____ , and become as a____ ____ , ye shall enter into the____ of____ ."

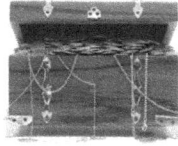

Parenting 101

*P*arenting is an awesome responsibility. It involves protection, support, and provision for the physical, emotional, social, intellectual, and spiritual development of a child from infancy to adulthood. Parenting has to be done God's way if we are to find success as parents.

Parenting 101 (1)

Old Testament – Genesis 18:17-19, 17:9, Deuteronomy 4:9-10, 6:6-7, 11:18-23, Psalms 127:3-5, 103:17, 102:28, Proverbs 1:8-16, 2:1-5, 3:1-4, 11-12, 4:1-6, 20-27, 23:26

New Testament – Matthew 19:13-15, 18:1-6, 10, 2 Timothy 1:5, 3:15

Parenting 101 (2)

Old Testament – Exodus 20:12, 21:15, 22:22, Leviticus 19:3, Deuteronomy 21:18-21, Malachi 1:6, 2:15-16, Psalms 78:2-8, Judges 2:10, 2 Kings 2:23-24, Ezekiel 18:1-20, Proverbs 30:17, 7:1-5, 27, 6:20-23

New Testament – 1 Corinthians 7:14, 2 Timothy 2:22, Ephesians 6:1-3, , Hebrews 12:9-11, Colossians 3:20-21

Parenting 101 (3)

Old Testament – Deuteronomy 31:11-13, 24:16, 23:7-8, 14:1-2, 12:28, Isaiah 54:13, 1 Samuel 8:1-5, 2:12-17, 22-25, Ezekiel 14:15-20, Proverbs 5:1-2, 6:1-5, 10:1, 13:1, 22, 24

New Testament – Matthew 15:3-6, 1 Timothy 4:12, 1 Peter 5:5, 1:14-15, Ephesians 5:1

Parenting 101 (4)

Old Testament – Exodus 12:26-27, 13:8-9, 14, Joshua 4:5-8, Joel 1:2-3, Isaiah 38:19, Psalms 44:1-3, 71:18, 145:4, Proverbs 31:1-3, 30:11-16, 29:15, 17, 21, 28:24, 27:11, 23:13-16, 19-25

New Testament – 2 Corinthians 12:14, 1 John 2:12-14, 1 Thessalonians 2:7-8

Parenting 101 (5)

Old Testament – Judges 13:8, 1 Samuel 1:8-17, 27-28, 1 Kings 3:7-9, Jeremiah 1:4-7, Ecclesiastes 12:1, 11:10, 4:15-16, Job 1:1-5, Job 29:16, 31:16-18, 21-22, Psalms 27:10, 119:9, 131:2, 144:11-15, Proverbs 19:26-27

New Testament – Luke 8:19-21, 16:27-31, Matthew 21:28-31, 1 Timothy 3:4-5, 5:8

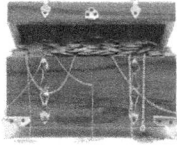

Wholeheartedly

Wholeheartedly (1)

"For the eyes of the LORD run to and fro throughout the whole earth, to show himself strong in the behalf of them whose heart is perfect toward him. Herein thou hast done foolishly: therefore from henceforth thou shalt have wars." (2 Chronicles 16:9)

Wholeheartedly (2)

"I will praise thee, O LORD, with my whole heart; I will shew forth all thy marvelous works." (Psalms 9:1)

Wholeheartedly (3)

"...I have found David the son of Jesse, a man after mine own heart, which shall fulfil all my will." (Acts 13:22)

Discussion Questions

1. Explain 2 Chronicles 16:9.
2. What observations are made in 1 Samuel 13:6-14?
3. In John 4:23, what type of individual was God looking for?
4. Why was David chosen by God?
5. Explain Ezra 7:10.

Fill in the Blanks

1. "Save Caleb the son of____ the_____, and Joshua the son of Nun: for they have_____ followed the Lord."
2. "And thou, Solomon my son, know thou the God of thy father, and serve him with a____ _____ and with a____ ____ ."
3. "Blessed are they that keep his testimonies, and that____ ____ with the____ ____ ."
4. "Wherefore I was_____ with that_____ , and said, They do_____ err in their_____ ; and they have not known my ways."
5. "So likewise, whosoever he be of you that_____ not all that he hath, he_____ be my_____ ."

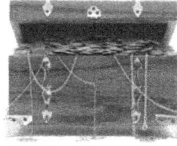

Wholeheartedly

*I*n Psalms 119:58, the Psalmist writes, "I intreated thy favour with my whole heart; be merciful unto me according to thy word." There are many passages of scripture that express this same sentiment. God desires from those who worship him that they do so with wholehearted devotion, sincerity and loyalty."

Wholdheartedly (1)

Old Testament – Joshua 14:6-13, 22:4-5, Numbers 14:1-10, 22-24, Deuteronomy 1:34-36, 10:10-12, 11:13-21, 13:1-3, 1 Samuel 12;20, 24, Joel 2:11-12, Psalms 9:1, 86:12, 103:1, 111:1-2, 138:1-2

New Testament – Luke 10:25-28, 14:33, Acts 8:29-39, 1 Timothy 4:13-15, John 4:23

Wholeheartedly (2)

Old Testament – Exodus 35:5, 21, 29, 36:1-2, Deuteronomy 4:24-29, 5:29, 30:1-3, 6-10, Numbers 32:6-12, Jeremiah 3:6-10, 14-15, 24:7, 29:13, 2 Kings 23:1-3, 25, 2 Chronicles 15:1-2, 12-15, 34:1-2, 27-31, Psalms 12:1-2, 69:9, 108:1, 112:1, 7-8,

New Testament – James 1:8, 4:8, Matthew 6:24, 22:37-38, Colossians 3:22-24, Hebrews 3:10

Wholeheartedly (3)

Old Testament – Deuteronomy:5-6, 8:1-2, 9:4-6, 26:16-19, 2 Chronicles 16:9, 1 Chronicles 28:9, 1 Samuel 16:7, 13:6-14, 7:3-4 Psalms 78:34-37, Hosea 7:2, 13-14, 10;1-2, Jeremiah 17:9-10, Proverbs 3:5-6, 23:26

New Testament – Mark 12:29-30, Matthew 15:8, 5:8, 2 Timothy 2:22, 1 Timothy 1:5

Wholeheartedly (4)

Old Testament – Ecclesiastes 9:10, Proverbs 22:29, 12:24, 27, 10;4, 1 Chronicles 29:1-3, 9, 2 Chronicles 17:3-6, 31:20-21, 1 Kings 2:1-4, 3:3, 6, 8:23, 44-49, 9:1-5, 11:4, 14:7-10, 15:9-14, Psalms 119:1-2, 10, 34-36, 58, 69-70, 145

New Testament – Acts 13:22, 11:19-23, Romans 12:11, Hebrews 10:22-24, Titus 2:13-15

Wholeheartedly (5)

Old Testament – Nehemiah 9:7-8, Isaiah 26:9, Proverbs 21:1-2, 4;23, Psalms 24:3-4, 27:8, 40:8-10, 51:10, 16-17, 57;7, 141:4, Jeremiah 20:7-12, 31:31-33, 32:39-41, Ezekiel 11:19-21, Ezra 7:9-10, 2 Chronicles 20:30-33

New Testament – 1 Thessalonians 2:3-4, 2 Thessalonians 3:4-5, 1 Peter 3:15, 1 John 3:18-21

Everlasting

Everlasting (1)

"And I saw another angel fly in the midst of heaven, having the everlasting gospel to preach unto them that dwell on the earth, and to every nation, and kindred, and tongue, and people, (Revelation 14:6)

Everlasting (2)

"Now the God of peace, that brought again from the dead our Lord Jesus, that great shepherd of the sheep, through the blood of the everlasting covenant," (Hebrews 3:20)

Everlasting (3)

"Thy righteousness is an everlasting righteousness, and thy law is the truth." (Psalms 119:142)

Discussions Questions

1. Explain Daniel 7:13-14, 27.
2. Discuss John 12:50.
3. What observations are made in Isaiah 9:6-7?
4. Discuss John 3:14-16, 36.
5. Discuss Revelations 14:6-7

Fill in the Blanks

1. "Verily, verily, I say unto you, He that _____my word, and believeth on him that sent me, hath_____ life, and shall not come into_____ ; but is passed from_____ unto_____ ."
2. "The Lord hath appeared of old unto me, saying, Yea, I have_____ thee with an_____ _____ : therefore with_____ have I drawn thee."
3. "And many of them that_____ in the dust of the earth shall awake, some to_____ _____ , and some to_____ shame and contempt."
4. "And I saw another angel fly in the midst of_____ , having the_____ _____ to preach unto them that dwell on the_____ , and to every nation, and_____ , and_____ , and_____ ."
5. "According to the_____ purpose which He purposed in _____ _____ our Lord."

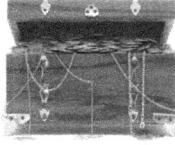

Everlasting

"Before the mountains were brought forth, or ever thou hadst formed the earth and the world, even from everlasting to everlasting, thou art God" (Psalms 90:2).

*T*he mind, as it contemplates God, cannot fathom the vastness and the magnitude of time. Perhaps Job expressed it best in Job 36:26, "Behold, God is great, and we know him not, neither can the number of his years be searched out."

Everlasting (1)

Old Testament – Daniel 4:3, 34, Daniel 7:13-14, 27, Daniel 9:22-24, Daniel 12:1-2, Isaiah 9:6-7, Isaiah 26:4, Isaiah 33:14-16, Isaiah 55:1-3, Isaiah 56:5, Isaiah 57:15, Psalm 24:7-10, Psalm 103:15-18

New Testament – John 3:14-16, 36, John 4:14, John 5:24, John 6:27, 40, 47, John 12:50, Acts 13:46, Romans 6:22

Everlasting (2)

Old Testament – Deuteronomy 33:27, 2 Samuel 23:5, 1 Chronicles 16:15-17, Isaiah 61:8, Jeremiah 10:10, Jeremiah 31:1-3, Jeremiah 32:37-40, Jeremiah 50:5, Psalms 105:7-10, Psalms 11:9, Psalms 119:142, 144

New Testament – John 5:11-13, 20, 2 Timothy 1:9-10, Revelation 14:6-7

Everlasting (3)

Old Testament – Genesis 21:33, Habakkuk 1:12, Habakkuk 3:6, Lamentations 5:19, Isaiah 40:6-8, Psalms 139:23-24, Psalms 119:89, Psalms 102:24-27, Psalms 100:5, Psalms 93:2, Hosea 2:19-20, Proverbs 10:25

New Testament – Romans 1:20, Romans 2:6-8, Romans 16:25-26, 1 Peter 1:23-25, Hebrews 13:8, Jude 1:21

Everlasting (4)

Old Testament – Genesis 9:16, Genesis 17:7, Isaiah 24:5, Isaiah 40:26-28, Isaiah 45:15-17, Isaiah 51:11, Isaiah 54:8, Isaiah 55:13, Isaiah 56:5, Isaiah 60:17-21, Isaiah 61:7-8, Isaiah 63:12-16, Micah 5:2-4, Psalms 89:22-29

New Testament – John 20:30-31, John 17:2-3, John 10:28, John 6:51-54, 68, John 5:39, Titus 3:6-7

Everlasting (5)

Old Testament – Proverbs 8:20-23, Proverbs 12:28, Ezekiel 16:58-60, Ezekiel 37:26-28, Psalms 9:6-7, Psalms 16:11, Psalms 37:18, Psalms 48:14, Psalms 106:48, Psalms 112:5-6

New Testament – 2 Thessalonians 1:7-9, 2 Thessalonians 2:15-16, 1 Timothy 6:9, Ephesians 3:20, 21, 2 Corinthians 4:17-18

God With Me

God With Me (1)

"What shall we say to these things? If God be for us, who can be against us? (Romans 8:31)

God With Me (2)

"When thou passest through the waters, I will be with thee; and through the rivers, they shall not overflow thee: when thou walkest through the fire, thou shalt not be burned; neither shall the flame kindle upon thee." (Isaiah 43:2)

God With Me (3)

"Yea, though I walk through the valley of the shadow of death, I will fear no evil; for thou art with me; thy rod and thy staff they comfort me." (Psalms 23:4)

Discussion Questions

1. What was Moses' request in Exodus 33:13-17?
2. Discuss Psalms 23:4.
3. What assurance did God give Joshua in Joshua 1:5, 9, 17?
4. Discuss Romans 8:31.
5. What observations are made in Zechariah 2:5-13?

Fill in the Blanks

1. "And, lo, I am with you_____, even unto the_____ of the_____."
2. "Take_____ together, and it shall come to_____; speak the word, and it shall not_____: for God is_____ _____."
3. "And he called the name of the place Massah, and Meribah, because of the_____ of the children of Israel, and because they_____ the Lord, saying, is the Lord among us, or not?"
4. "Ye are of God, little children, and have overcome them: because_____ is he that is in you, than he that is in the_____."
5. "And the night following the Lord_____ by_____, and said, Be of good_____, Paul."

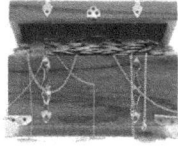

God With Me

*H*ow precious it is to have God with us as we journey through this barren land called life, with all its perils, difficulties, struggles, challenges, adversities, and complexities. If God be with us, the victory is assured.

God With Me (1)

Old Testament – Genesis 21:22-24, 26:3, 24, 28, 28:15, 20-22, 39:2-3, 21-23, Deuteronomy 20:1-4, 31:5-8, Exodus 33:14-17, 1 Chronicles 17:8, 2 Chronicles 1:1, Isaiah 8:10, 41:8-14, Proverbs 21:30, Psalms 23:4

New Testament – Romans 8:31, Hebrews 13:5, Matthew 28:19-20, 1 Corinthians 14:25, Revelation 3:9

God With Me (2)

Old Testament – Joshua 1:5, 9, 17, 2:8-11, 3:7, 10:42, Numbers 14:9, Leviticus 26:27-28, 1 Samuel 5:19, 2 Kings 18:1-7, Isaiah 42:13, 43:2-5, Jeremiah 20:11, 15:20, 1:19, 2 Chronicles 13:12, Psalms 44:5-8, 46:5-11

New Testament – John 14:23, 15:5, Colossians 1:27-29, Acts 5:38-39

God With Me (3)

Old Testament – Numbers 23:21, Ezekiel 34:28-30, 48:35, 1 Chronicles 22:11, 18, 2 Chronicles 20:12-17, Zechariah 2:5-13, 8:23, 10:5, Isaiah 12:6, 45:2-3, 14, Exodus 17:7, Jeremiah 14:8-9, 42:11, 46:28, Zephaniah 3:5, 15-17

New Testament – 1 Corinthians 3:16-17, 2 Corinthians 6:16, 1 John 4:4, 12-16

God With Me (4)

Old Testament – Deuteronomy 1:30-33, 2:7, 3:22, Leviticus 26:3-12, Numbers 14:14, Exodus 3:11-12, 14:14, 19, Judges 6:12-16, Haggai 1:12-13, 2:4, 2 Kings 6:8-18, 18:1-7, Isaiah 31:4-5, Psalms 34:7, 54:1-4, 118:6

New Testament – Matthew 1:23, Luke 1:37, Philippians 2:13, Ephesians 3:20, Revelation 21:3

God With Me (5)

Old Testament – Deuteronomy 23:14, Exodus 29:45-46, Ezekiel 37:26-28, Joel 2:26-27, 3:16-17, Hosea 11:9-11, Isaiah 40:27, 50:6-9, Jeremiah 23:23-24, 1:8, 2 Chronicles 32:7-8, 14:7-12, Psalms 56:9, 91:13-16, 109:26-31

New Testament – Acts 23:11, 27:23, 2 Timothy 4:17

www.ingramcontent.com/pod-product-compliance
Lightning Source LLC
Chambersburg PA
CBHW060301030426
42336CB00011B/898

9 7 8 1 7 3 7 5 2 8 5 1 7